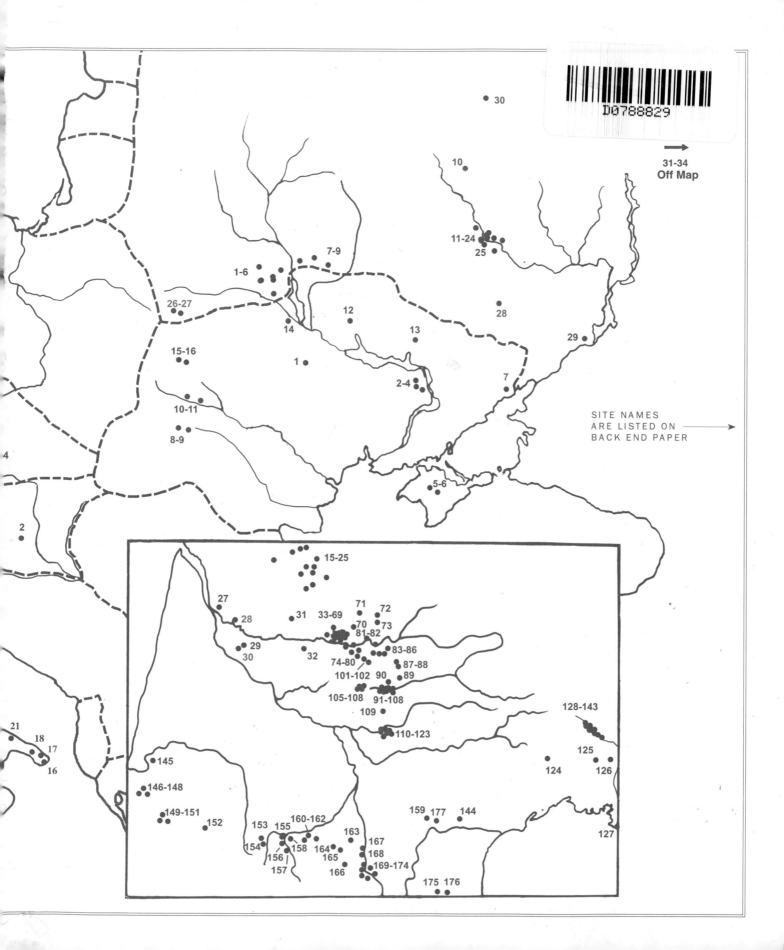

31-34
Off Map

SITE NAMES
ARE LISTED ON
BACK END PAPER

The Nature of Paleolithic Art

The Nature of Paleolithic Art

R. Dale Guthrie

THE UNIVERSITY OF CHICAGO PRESS

CHICAGO AND LONDON

R. Dale Guthrie is professor emeritus of zoology at the University of Alaska, Fairbanks. He is the author of *Frozen Fauna of the Mammoth Steppe: The Story of Blue Babe,* also published by the University of Chicago Press.

The University of Chicago Press, Chicago 60637
The University of Chicago Press, Ltd., London
© 2005 by The University of Chicago
All rights reserved. Published 2005
Printed in the United States of America
14 13 12 11 10 09 08 07 06 05   5 4 3 2 1

ISBN (cloth): 0-226-31126-0

Library of Congress Cataloging-in-Publication Data

Guthrie, R. Dale (Russell Dale), 1936–
    The nature of Paleolithic art / R. Dale Guthrie
      p.   cm.
    Includes bibliographical references and index.
    ISBN 0-226-31126-0 (cloth : alk. paper)
     1. Paleolithic period.   2. Art, Prehistoric.   3. Cave paintings.
   4. Antiquities, Prehistoric.   I. Title.
    GN772G87   2005
    930.1′2—dc22
                                2004014399

♾ The paper used in this publication meets the minimum requirements of the American National Standard for Information Sciences—Permanence of Paper for Printed Library Materials, ANSI Z39.48-1992.

*B*ooks like this are often dedicated to family, academic colleagues, or special teachers. And I too appreciate the uncountable contributions from those near me and from my colleagues, past and present, around the world. But, as you will see, this study has led me through some surprising paths and, in that process, to a renewed appreciation of my childhood.

So I dedicate this book to my boyhood hero, mentor, and maternal uncle, the late Glen Looper, who was, in my mind and perhaps in reality, the best fisherman and hunter in Pike and Calhoun Counties. In a young boy's careless way, I took his friendship as so normal I never thought to show my thanks. Though too late, I want to acknowledge my deep gratitude. He showed me how to skin a catfish, dig the guts out of sunfish by running my thumbnail under the spine, and make drowning sets for muskrats, how to wait patiently and move silently when squirrel-hunting in the dew of early morning woods.

He showed me a love of wild things and, most of all, encouraged my obsessive wondering about the why of everything. In the eyes of some neighbors he may have been an unsuccessful idler who drank too much, too often, but every boy deserves such a gentle giant and attentive presence.

Also, I dedicate this book to my boyhood buddies: Billy Lee Scranton, Don Capps, Junior Looper, Richard Dyer, and Gary Draper. Across the Mississippi from Hannibal, we grew up slow and easy in a rural feralness far from highways and curfews: naked afternoons in Spring Creek swimming holes, crawdads cooked in tin cans, cave exploring, lying in deep shady glades fantasizing about girls, stealing watermelons, building forts and rafts, hand-fishing, and following coon dogs on frosty nights. As much as my academic background, this study leans heavily on experiences with my uncle and these boyhood friends. Our earthy explorations were part of a venerable tradition.

Contents

Drawn from Life

Who were these peoples and what was the context of their art? What were those times like, across the 30,000 years we call the Eurasian late Paleolithic? Is it possible to resolve questions such as why people went into caves to do their art? The biases of preservation are profound, and we must be aware of how they affect our collection of art from this period. This is our groundwork chapter. | **1**

Paleolithic Artists as Naturalists

These artists were witnesses to a world very different from our own; what did they see? The images they made say something not only about the surroundings of those times but also about the preoccupations of the artists. They were immersed in the subject of large mammals, but why? They saw and drew things that paleontologists could never have reconstructed, for example, pin-striped horses and polka-dotted reindeer. Close attention to such observations helps us explore what may have been on their minds. | **51**

Tracking Down the Pleistocene Artists: The Unemphasized Role of Children

Were most Paleolithic people artists or was art making done by only a select few? Are there forensic clues as to which sex and which age-groups figured predominantly as the makers of preserved Paleolithic art? Few books on Paleolithic art mention children, but we know that children made up more than half of the Eurasian Paleolithic population, and there is good reason to believe that they were learning to use the art-making materials of the adult world. Is there any evidence of art making by Paleolithic children? There is, and children are going to be much more important in this "adult-interest" book than you might ever imagine. | **113**

Testosterone Events and Paleolithic Imagery

Biases in the fossil record are often the result of fundamental biological differences. Was that the case with preserved Paleolithic art? How could inherent differences between the sexes and among different age-groups influence art making? We'll consider this in terms of hand forensics, subject choice, art media, art location, and art preservation. It is quite an amazing story. | **151**

Preface

Reassembling the Bones

The greatest enterprise of the mind has always been and always will be the attempted linkage of the sciences and humanities.

E. O. Wilson, *Consilience*

The term "Paleolithic art" has fuzzy edges, but I use it to refer to art made during the late Pleistocene, from 10,000 to 40,000 years ago. Thousands of pieces of this typically representational art exhibit a striking integrity of style and subject matter. The character of this integrity and the origins of this art, as well as its changes with the end of the Pleistocene, are among humanity's most fascinating subjects. Let me begin by telling you how I got into all of this.

In 1979 I was invited to a symposium in Sigriswil, Switzerland, that included many scholars working in Paleolithic art. H.-G. Bandi, a Swiss archaeologist, was the organizer of the meeting. Bandi and I had met several years earlier when his work brought him to Alaska. He invited me to the conference as a naturalist, an artist, and paleobiologist familiar with Pleistocene animals represented in Paleolithic art. He had the vision that there was a potential access to Pleistocene natural history in these drawings if we but could bring it into focus (Bandi et al. 1984). I agreed and enthusiastically accepted Bandi's invitation. My previous research had focused on northern Pleistocene mammals—the mammoth, horse, and bison species featured in Paleolithic art—and I had already begun work-

ing with Paleolithic art in the way Bandi envisioned. So I prepared an illustrated talk outlining several new themes in Paleolithic natural history. But the meeting was taut with an unaccountable underlying tension and at its close I left quite puzzled.

I have come to understand the differences among us at that Sigriswil meeting pertained less to the detailed questions we discussed than aspects of our respective orientations and assumptions. In that meeting hall, with the bright spring alpine panorama of melting snow out the window, we sat on opposite sides of a dividing aisle as in C. P. Snow's *Two Cultures* (1959): those interested in the symbolic significance and spiritual motivations behind the art and those looking into the art for clues to life in the past. It was my first experience with this kind of dichotomy in scholarship.

Until then, I had looked at Paleolithic art both to appreciate the colorful renditions and to find useful and interesting details about Pleistocene animal anatomy. But the experience of that conference set me on a new course of trying to place Paleolithic art in a larger dimension of natural history and of linking artistic behavior to our evolutionary past. This book addresses common ground

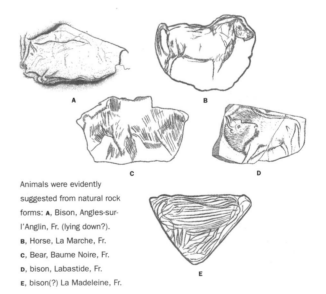

Animals were evidently suggested from natural rock forms: **A**, Bison, Angles-sur-l'Anglin, Fr. (lying down?). **B**, Horse, La Marche, Fr. **C**, Bear, Baume Noire, Fr. **D**, bison, Labastide, Fr. **E**, bison(?) La Madeleine, Fr.

shared by the humanities, social sciences, and natural sciences—attempting to step across Snow's aisle and try to fit all these interests together in a consilient manner. So it is an idea book, obviously not the normal, colorful, coffee-table sort but a new kind of investigation of Paleolithic art that develops insights into the natural history of art making and the nature of creativity—using our human nature to understand this old art and using this old art to understand human nature. I have tried to present all of this accessibly and artfully, because these ideas should be interesting to most people.

Over the last two decades, I have been able to examine most of the thousands of images that make up our collection of late Paleolithic art. Contrary to popular literature, many Paleolithic works do not seem to bear any obvious imprint of ritual and magic but, rather, express more casual and earthy themes. The majority were done quickly and are contingent and undisciplined, with overlapping, incomplete, and often askew imagery. I found details in which I was originally interested coalescing into unanticipated patterns. There are many unskilled Paleolithic drawings that are rarely reproduced in art books. Forensic work with fossil handprints of the artists greatly changed the way I looked at this art: I found that all ages and both sexes were making art, not just senior male shamans. Throughout all of this, my interests in the evolutionary and behavioral patterns of woolly large mammals turned into a study of Paleolithic artists and the evolution of their art.

For me, to recognize that so many of the preserved Paleolithic images were done casually, by both sexes and all age-groups, more often than not by youngsters, who even left their tracks under renditions of wounded bulls and swollen vulvas, in no way makes Paleolithic sites less hallowed. The possibility that adolescent giggles and snickers may have echoed in dark cave passages as often as the rhythm of a shaman's chant demeans neither artists nor art. Instead, it opens the possibility for us to conceive, with familiar warmth and greater immediacy, the entire range of preserved Paleolithic art. Indeed, as I will argue,

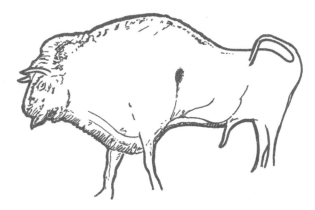

Engraving of fairly young bison bull from Altxerri Cave, Sp., pictured with weight on right front foot. Details are informative. Many images of large mammals include a bleeding thoracic wound. This bison appears to be a mortally wounded animal, tail up in mild alarm and pain, erection showing his ligamentous penis, specific to artiodactyls. The enlarged dorsal neck mane is characteristic of Pleistocene bison from southern Europe. This is a fine work by an experienced observer and artist.

our collection of this art is to a great extent a distorted sample. Preservational contexts, I propose, sometimes favored the art making of people whose technical art skills were not yet polished. I hope to make such neglected and underplayed aspects of Paleolithic art better known and appreciated.

My main conclusion is that preserved Paleolithic art, unlike most "tribal art," is a graphic expression whose articulation we can largely comprehend, and that the perspective of natural history offers an essential dimension to that appreciation; it is the "code-breaker." Paleolithic artist-hunters were keen students of natural history—they had to be. Their art is not an obtusely symbolic language but something very deep and very dear. Across a span of 30,000 years and despite the many different cultures that likely existed in western Eurasia during the late Paleolithic, their art displays a striking unity and is readily distinguishable from later, post-Pleistocene tribal art.

I began with Paleolithic art hoping to use it as a window into the Pleistocene, then came to realize that it is both a window and a mirror. And it is peculiarly distorted as both. It lets us see some things and obscures others, with distortions that are to some degree identifiable. Looking at Paleolithic art as a mirror sometimes lets us glimpse ourselves in the reflected fears, play, delights, and preoccupations that are drawn there. And this mirror, tens of thousand of years old, also reflects our animal-involved past. After all, watching other large mammals is one of the oldest intellectual, as well as aesthetic, human endeavors. We can see that the makers of these images were addicted animal watchers.

I depend a great deal in this book on our animal being, the animalness we share with other large mammals, and in developing my lines of thought about human universals, I will rely on the common evolutionary past that we share with Paleolithic peoples. Tastes in art to a degree do disclose character, both individually and for the groups to which we belong. And because this is so, we can pick among archaeological remnants to reconstruct imagination as well as artifact. There is much variety and a good measure of contingency in this old art, but out of it we can develop a little order, some principles, and more than a few insights.

The story I have to tell is not simple, and I hope you will bear with me, because my lines of evidence, like characters in a Russian novel, do weave among one another: evolution gets entangled with the natural history of hunting, love, nurture, the erotic, graffiti, creativity, youth, sexual differences, science, myth, and mystery. We'll meet all these influences as the story unfolds.

Note on the Illustrations

My line drawings are intended to convey a particular sort of information about Paleolithic works of art done in quite a range of materials and sizes; it is the best way I could find to show their unifying integrity. I am aware that this extraction and my rather flat renderings exclude much that is rich and satisfying about Paleolithic art, but I am after something different in this book and want to draw your attention away from the artistic ensemble in order to focus on aspects of natural history.

In many instances my line drawings are not too terribly distant from the mode of the Paleolithic original because so much of preserved Paleolithic art is itself in the form of lines: streaks of paint, crayon marks, grooves scratched on cave walls, and engravings on stone, bone, antler, and ivory, often employing the edge of a sharp stone. Authors and publishers of Paleolithic art books usually have chosen to showcase the most eye-catching paintings, inadvertently conveying the impression that Paleolithic art consists mainly of such work. Indeed, many observers experience the resplendent paintings and sculptures as quite superior to or more advanced than the engraved work, but the core process of visualization is similar in all, and the wealth of content in these less publicized engravings should not be missed or even de-emphasized.

I have spent much time over the years looking at original Paleolithic images, and many of my illustrations are

Pleistocene bison. One advantage of an ink sketch in these comparisons is that the images from a variety of different media are made more directly comparable. **A**, Sungir, Rus. **B** and **M**, Font de Gaume, Fr. **C**, Trois Frères, Fr. **D**, Altxerri, Sp. **E**, Trois Frères, Fr. **F**, Le Portel, Fr. **G**, Rouffignac, Fr. **H** and **R**, Altamira, Sp. **I**, Marsoulas, Fr. **J** and **N**, La Mouthe, Fr. **K–L** and **Q**, Isturitz, Fr. **O**, Montespan, Fr. **P**, Niaux, Fr.

drawn from these observations, but most were sketched from photos, my own and those of others. Occasionally, I have redrawn published illustrations. I was often able to locate several photos or drawings by different people of each Paleolithic piece that I used—so that I was not relying on a single lighting angle or one person's interpreta-

The people who drew these images from memory were experienced observers. The reindeer on the left is a prime bull in the late stages of rut. His omental and rump fat depots are depleted, giving him a concave abdomen and an angular rump. But he has not gone much beyond rut because his antlers are not shed (early November). The prime bull on the right is a fat pre-rut animal (September). Mature bulls use up most of their fat throughout the month of rut, during which they seldom eat. A, Kesslerloch, Switz. B, Laugerie-Basse, Fr. Note how the gaits (walking patterns) of both reindeer are depicted correctly.

tion. In quite a different process, I have occasionally tried to interpret an incomplete or rudimentary Paleolithic im-

age. These interpretations are clearly specified as such and are teamed with a line drawing of the original image. Redrawing these thousands of images from Paleolithic art has helped me notice innumerable details I would otherwise have missed. Drawing has a way of doing that, and I recommend it to students of Paleolithic art.

Of course, these line drawings do not replace the experience of seeing the originals—and it is possible to see most of them. Dozens of Paleolithic art caves are open to the public, and the original engraved mobiliary (portable) art is displayed in many national and regional museums.

The following abbreviations are used in the captions to the illustrations: Aus. (Austria), Austrl. (Australia), Belg. (Belgium), Czech. (Czechoslovakia), Fr. (France), Ger. (Germany), Hung. (Hungary), It. (Italy), Neth. (Netherlands), Pol. (Poland), R.S.A. (Republic of South Africa), Rus. (Russia), Sp. (Spain), Switz. (Switzerland), U.S.A. (United States of America).

1

Drawn from Life

Every few years news of the discovery of a new cave resplendent with Paleolithic paintings gets splashed across the front pages. Full-color images get double-page spreads in magazines and papers. While the stunning images in the new cave are always different from any discovered before, as we look more closely similarities to other Paleolithic art abound—similar subjects in that familiar figurative style. We are awed that here again among the scratches and splatters of "quick studies" are pictures of such vitality—mainly beautiful images of large mammals, made by people living tens of thousands of years ago.

And there is that same unsettling mystery about it. No one has credibly accounted for the subjects the artists repeatedly chose, nor their presence in caves, nor even enlightened us much about the lives of those artists. There have been many proposals employing hunting or other primitive magic, sexual symbols, initiation rites, shaman dreams, and more, but they seem pallid next to the array of Paleolithic artwork.

Whatever else it is, Paleolithic art is one of the true wonders of our world—thousands of art images preserved from the distant Ice Age. Yet, strangely, except for the most gorgeous images, which are reproduced over and over in glossy photo books, the multitude of Paleolithic images remain rather unfamiliar to most anthropologists, even to many art prehistorians, let alone the well-read public. The reasons for this at first appear opaque, but I suspect that's because we just don't know what to make of them, particularly of the many Paleolithic images that are not so artistically persuasive—what were these images about? Is there some underlying code we don't know? And why should we single out these late Paleolithic peoples of western Eurasia as special?

The answer to the last question is straightforward. This growing collection is the earliest unquestionable representational art we can document from the archaeological record. Art prior to 40,000 years ago exists, but it is more enigmatic, controversial, and rare at best.

Also, it is probably the fact of its preservation that makes Eurasian Paleolithic art so special. Fossilization seems to work that way. The pre-Neolithic "Ice Man," the frozen mummy from the Alps, was likely no important person in his region at the time, but he was preserved and found, while none of his neighbors were. The subject of books and television specials, he now lies in an environment-controlled showcase in a museum. And though his contemporaries remain anonymous, researching him and reconstructing his life allow us to better imagine his friends and relatives. Preservation is the key that unlocks more than what is at hand. The archaeological sites of some Paleolithic groups are immensely rich in visual art, while sites of other groups appear devoid of such artwork. We know that although art making is universal among our species, some cultures make visual art only in ephemeral, unpreservable media. So there are numerous aspects that seem fortuitous.

Fortunately, we do have preserved traces of the art of some cultures from this early time, even though this Eurasian record is a very fragmentary and undoubtedly a

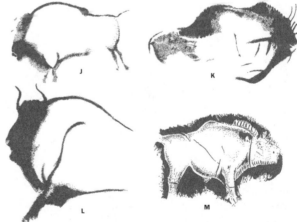

Wild cattle and bison were common in Pleistocene Europe and are among the most frequent images in Paleolithic art. Bison prefer cool, windy, open landscapes, and cattle more protected, wooded parklands. Images of cattle: **A**, Font de Gaume, Fr. **B**, Altamira, Sp. **C**, Levanzo, It. **D**, La Loja, Sp. **E**, Pileta, Sp. **F**, Castillo, Sp. **G**, Parpalló, Sp. **H**, Lascaux, Fr. **I**, Le Trou de Chaleux, Belg. Bison: **J**, Moulin, Fr. **K**, Marsoulas, Fr. **L**, Chauvet, Fr. **M**, Tuc d'Audoubert, Fr.

Bird sitting on the rump of a large mammal, from Altxerri, Sp. The artist first saw a natural form that suggested the image (*upper left*), then elaborated it with engravings (*upper right*). In the box is a reconstruction of how several species of birds perch on plains bison to look for skin parasites and insects, a common scene on the steppes and steppe margins.

Corvids land on bison backs in late winter to gather shed wool for their nests; note how the raven on the left has gathered a large bundle of underfur. This illustration was redrawn from a photo and resembles the ancient Pleistocene drawing from Altxerri.

The small Greek bronze from the eighth century B.C. illustrates how the image of a bird on another animal's back was considered interesting and worthy of depiction by another culture in a very different time and context.

biased sample. They were likely no more intelligent or even more "arty" than groups elsewhere; it is just that the preservation of their visual art provides us with a unique access to them. That is what makes them special. Despite its incompleteness, this huge sample of images presents forensic evidence from which we can perhaps reconstruct quite a bit about their lives. But this is not an easy task. First, the interpretation of the forensic evidence requires a complex interdisciplinary mix, with implications so intertangled and wide-ranging that it is not easy to know where to start or what questions to ask. Second, our study of these matters impinges on a plethora of presumptions about human nature, sex, religion, aesthetics, and philosophy.

These are good reasons why tensions sometimes arise concerning interpretations of our deep past—many of the key ideas about our personal lives rest on presuppositions that lie rooted in this fog of time. The vast majority of our species' experience lies beyond the reach of the historical record. Questions regarding child rearing, cultural versus genetic determinism, ecological issues, romantic and sexual relations, the origin of morals, intelligence, and tastes, spirituality, and even the meaning of individual life are colored by our vision of the early chapters of the human story. That is why we will ask, again and again, what our

"baseline," or baselines, may have been. Who were humans before all the stuff of crops, villages, churches, dogs, property, houses, and wars? Were Paleolithic folks who lived on the banks of true wilderness fundamentally the same people as we are today? Were there some, albeit diverse, native conditions to human life in the Paleolithic before societies went their even more diverse ways? As one of the Pleistocene large mammals, did humans have a characteristic niche?

What were the differing roles of men and women? What did kids do? Was life in the late Paleolithic a matriarchal order or a rule by demonic males? Was it deeply spiritual or earthy-empirical, creative or doltish, leisurely or brutally demanding, full of bonded love or rapine wantonness, and were their personal relations tender or cruel? Was there a characteristic kind of family life, a common group size, repeated patterns in child development, limits to kinds of group conflict, or certain types of supernatural worship? What was the evolutionary context in which we flourished for most of our species' existence, our ur-roots? Examining such questions can help us to better understand our present—at least that is my thesis.

Excavated chipped flints, a rare jawbone, and black hearths are rather closemouthed about such questions, but if we add two more elements, archaeological data can begin to come alive. The two things I seek to combine in this book are, first, the perspective of ourselves as evolved organisms, who, like every other organism, possess a core adaptive nature and an array of propensities through which learning is modulated, and, second, the forensic evidence incorporated in the thousands of Paleolithic art pieces. Although art inherently involves aesthetics, I shall primarily be examining Paleolithic images for clues quite aside from their aesthetic significance, digging into the underlying human context behind the art making. Paleolithic art provides the special occasion that dramatizes how art and our natural history are ultimately interwoven.

Natural History and Art

Step back with me to a quieter time. Imagine wooded gullies, grassy ridges, and distant plains, marked with a twisted yarn of game trails, birds silhouetted against a blue sky—a landscape where, at any moment, we might see the dark mass of woolly mammoths break the rise. Large mammals figured prominently in the lives of Eurasian Paleolithic peoples. Their landscape was populated but not domesticated. And their art, at least the sample that has been found, is obsessed with mammoths, steppe bison, horses, reindeer, ibex, red deer, lions, rhinos, aurochs, bears, and other large mammals. Those real scenes from the Ice Age are long gone, but their vestiges in the art remain to enliven our imagination.

Adjusting to the near dark, I search along the cave wall. I am working in the Paleolithic art caves of the French Périgord, and as the guide's torch flashes across the wall, the lines of an animal begin to appear: it is a mammoth! Mammoths were here in the French Ozarks and someone living here drew them fresh from memory. The reality of this double appearance floods over me—mammoths and people who knew them. For many years I have worked with mammoth bones and occasionally with bits of frozen soft tissue including their dark auburn hair. I am accus-

Quick and rudimentary renditions of mammoths from a variety of times and places. **A** and **M**, Réseau-de-Font-Serene, Fr. **B**, Le Figuier, Fr. **C** and **L**, Pair-non-Pair, Fr. **D**, Laugerie-Haute, Fr. **E**, Les Combarelles, Fr. **F**, Chauvet, Fr. **G**, Los Casares, Sp. **H**, **I**, and **K**, Dolni Věstonice, Czech. **J**, Mal'ta, Rus.

tomed to lifting mammoth bones from mudbanks and museum shelves; they have a familiar heft. I've also drawn and sculpted mammoths, but this Paleolithic image was not created secondhand. It was made by someone familiar with the flesh, the odor, and the rumble of mammoths.

Something else on the wall catches my eye: a fringe of hatch-marks, short parallel grooves made by the claws of cave bears. Such patterns are found in a number of art caves, and we can imagine how they too were made: a giant bear awakening after a long winter's hibernation deep in the dark cave (their hibernacula beds are still present in some caves) roams throughout the cave testing the walls in desperation because it has forgotten the way out. These hatch-marks made on top of the art represent a panic "trimline," bear stories mixed into human ones. Cave bear claw marks mar the ocher outlines of cave bears in Chauvet Cave—my own failing memory connected with this distant cave bear's failure.

Such elements make the setting for the story of Paleolithic art fascinating and enduring. For at least 30,000 years our ancestors lived with, hunted, and depicted the animals whose images fill these pages. During much of the Pleistocene a vast arid steppe stretched from England clear across Eurasia and into Alaska. This steppe had a rich diversity of large herbivorous mammals and a full complement of predators. As a professional paleobiologist I happen to specialize in these creatures: this Mammoth Steppe is my area of specialty and these are my animals. My other interests—in art, hunting, archaeology, and ethology—are also relevant to the study of this old art.

Most Paleolithic art scholars have come from backgrounds in art history, social anthropology, or religion, and their work has tended to be preoccupied with assaying Paleolithic images for symbolic meaning or ritualistic patterns. Their published works contain fascinating insights and stimulating ideas but rather scant interest in or information about the way animals look and act. Few researchers have been interested in or informed about details of hunting, which almost certainly was a key pre-occupation of late Paleolithic Eurasian people. And Paleolithic images have not been seriously mined for information about behavioral and anatomical features of species portrayed in the art.

Most books about Paleolithic art convey the persistent sense that the really important questions to ask are connected with uncovering or detecting the meaning of images. This reflects, I believe, rather widely held assumptions that our fragments of Paleolithic art were part of a symbolic code or elements of mystic rituals. And, as such, the traditional approach has been to search for clues to the symbolism and ritual meaning hidden in the images. This is not my aim. Indeed, I conclude that neither Paleolithic images nor accompanying contextual data support most of the above assumptions. Instead, the art seems more focused on complicated earth-bound subjects, diverse everyday interests and wonders.

Paleolithic art, as well as being a cultural treasure, is an immensely valuable archive for natural history, and so it is rather curious that this pool of biological data has, until recently, attracted so few natural historians in Europe. I suspect this may have been because "artistic creations" were considered outside the turf of biologists—art involves humans and their artifacts, which fall into the category of anthropology. Additionally, many regions of Europe are so densely rich in fossils and artifacts that studies there of history and prehistory have traditionally been highly partitioned. But, more important, these areas of European science remain, for the most part, very hierarchical and territorial. Thus, one specializes not only by subject but also by epoch and even by region: in Mid-Pleistocene bison of the Ukraine or Neanderthals of the Middle Rhine region or cave art of the Upper Lot Valley. The other side of this specialization is the stunning excellence one finds in focused European scholarship.

For better or worse, the natural history of Paleolithic art is my entry point, and at least at this starting juncture the challenges are not unlike those of a researcher working with pollen, varves, isotopes, frozen mummies, or behav-

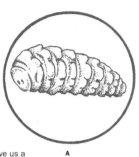

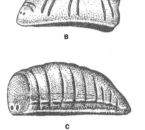

Much of the vocal and visual drama in the Paleolithic camp was from the birds overhead. Spending summers around limestone outcrops means living beneath the constant aerobatics and social gabble of swallows. Cliff swallows nest in limestone bluffs and feed on flying insects over streams in the valleys. My illustration is in the box at left. To the right are swallows portrayed in Paleolithic art at Laugerie-Basse, Fr. According to Eastman (1986) there are two other images of swallows at Raymonden, Fr.

There are thousands of images that can give us a more rounded view of Paleolithic people and their times, images that are not customarily shown in coffee-table volumes. Take, for example, these little wormlike creatures from Paleolithic art. Eskimo from northern Alaska delight in eating the large spring maggots, or larvae (**A**, circled), of the reindeer warble fly, *Oedemagena tarandi.* I suspect Eurasian people did the same in the Paleolithic. This is one of the few insects eaten by northern people. When reindeer are killed, the hide is skinned back and the warbles are exposed on the underside. They are fat and salty, a spring treat; I have tried them several times. During this time of year many people in the villages have sore throats from the raspers on the maggots' sides. **B** and **C** appear to represent warble fly larvae. **B**, Carved from a sesamoid bone, Laugerie-Haute, Fr. **C**, Carved from stone, Klein Scheur, Ger.

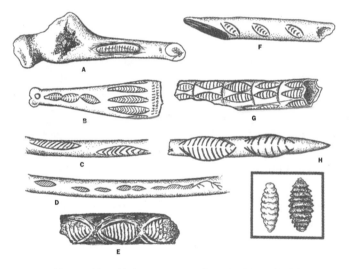

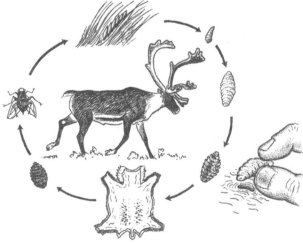

▲ Other possible warble fly larvae forms in Paleolithic art: **A–B**, Laugerie-Basse, Fr. **C**, Petersfels, Ger. **D**, El Valle, Sp. **E**, Lourdes, Fr. **F**, Gourdan, Fr. **G**, Le Placard, Fr. **H**, Villars, Fr. *Box:* White larva and dark pupa of warble fly. Seasonal treats become something to look forward to all year long.

▶ The cycle of the warble fly begins with eggs laid on the reindeer's back hair in autumn; the larvae burrow into the skin and by spring are large white larvae in the dermas. In early summer they mature to pupae and on into adults, which emerge and fly away. This leaves the reindeer's skin permanently scarred with burl swirls along either side of the spine—a pattern often sought after in leather.

ioral forensics. Working with art images is not without problems, but pollen, bison bones, and stable isotopes are not problem free either. In a moment I will describe my working approach, but first I would like to sketch a brief historical outline of the study of Paleolithic art.

Meaning and Purpose: The Historic Interpretations of Paleolithic Art

In the late 1800s, when Paleolithic art was first becoming accepted as genuine and people were acknowledging just how old it was, it was assumed that this art was done simply as *art pour l'art,* that is, done for its own sake. Richard (1993) refers to this as the *"art ludique"* phase. Many assumed the small, carved, figurative objects to be from simple people without abstract thought. For a long time this stood in the way of accepting the more splendid cave wall art, such as found in Altamira, as authentic. But in the early 1900s, cave art began to be accepted as legitimately Paleolithic, and theories shifted toward some religious or mystical explanation, with a tendency to interpret each image as a god, demon, totem, or ancestral spirit; Richard terms this the *"art magique"* phase. New ways to assess these old artifacts came into fashion.

ENTER THE ANTHROPOLOGIST

At the turn of the century, academic prehistorians developed their ideas about the function of fossil art by using the analogy of extant subsistence cultures. It was a logical assumption. Art among these modern groups of hunters, gatherers, and fishermen was often immersed in myth and magic, and the anthropologist's investigative approach was a major achievement. Researchers like Franz Boas ventured out of their own cultural standards and reported the beliefs of other people. They recognized that the art of living illiterate tribal peoples carried deep symbolic meaning and could not be easily deciphered by an outsider. This was true, for example, of the extravagant art from the Northwest Coast of North America and carvings from Polynesia and West Africa. In the late 1800s excavations of late Paleolithic burials with grave goods and deliberately

Paleolithic art contains the work of many inexperienced artists. Throughout this book I'll show you quite a few works by artists who are developing their drawing facility. Such works are usually bypassed in popular books on this subject. And they are not easily integrated into most theories explaining Paleolithic art. **A–C** and **E**, La Marche, Fr. **D**, Kronach, Ger.

spread ocher provided solid support to the idea that these earlier people also had a spiritual side.

By midcentury, two theories matured, both describing all Paleolithic art as mystical symbolism. Breuil (1952) proposed that such art was used as sympathetic magic to give hunters skill and luck. Leroi-Gourhan (1964) and Laming-Emperaire (1962) proposed that the art consisted of mystical images to enhance fertility or sexual fecundity. These theories were a reasonable response to prevalent motifs of Paleolithic art. Large mammals, many shown speared, are common in the art, and their bones are also found as food refuse in the Paleolithic middens. In addition, images of rotund nude women, vulvae, and men with erections are found at many sites.

Anthropological insights helped encourage the idea that all prehistoric art was created by illiterate peoples communicating mystical beliefs: sympathetic magic of hunting and fertility, totems, demons, gods, and the dream world. Academic studies of prehistoric art became preoccupied with symbolic interpretation — assuming every image also had an inner mystical meaning. I think Paleolithic art has suffered from this approach. There is evidence contradicting this magico-religious focus, and these images certainly do not reflect some primitive stage in art evolution. It has also become clear that modern trib-

alists are not particularly appropriate analogs to Paleolithic cultures and peoples.

Most historical groups, including such archetypal Paleolithic analogs as Eskimo, Bushman, and Australian Aboriginals, had, by the time of their discovery by anthropologists, already undergone cultural and economic transitions analogous to Paleolithic-Mesolithic shifts in Europe. Large-mammal hunting in particular changed because of a wider variety of technologies, plant/animal domestication, and often a more diverse subsistence base in a post–Ice Age environment. There is ample evidence that these transitions affected tribal approaches to the natural world and art. Later I will show that there is something contextually special about the economies and technologies of late Paleolithic peoples that is reflected in their outlook — the outlook we see in their art.

ENTER THE SHAMAN: THE MAGICO-RELIGIOUS PARADIGM OF PALEOLITHIC ART

Mystified by the power to create, it is no wonder that man should imagine the artist to be godlike. In the West, belief in a Creator-God was a way of confessing that the power to make the new was beyond human explanation.

Daniel J. Boorstin, *The Creators*

By painting, the Medicine Men made public their experience of the cosmos and man's place in it.

J. D. Lewis-Williams, *Believing and Seeing*

The "meaning and purpose" currently favored by many Paleolithic art scholars seems to be that most of the art was done by shamans for mystical reasons, involving some shamanic magical rites or trance visions. This view has been championed enthusiastically by Clottes and Lewis-Williams (1996). Other authors assume some form of underlying ritual magic (e.g., Marshack 1972; Gimbutas 1982; Abramova 1995).

Organized religion is a potent force, and religious stories shape our collective perceptions. For many people just a generation or two ago the universe was divided into these categories: inanimate objects, germs, plants, critters, living souls, nonliving souls (in the form of either heavenly angels or fallen angels), and God. A 1991 Gallup poll in the United States reported that 79% of the people believed creationism should be taught in the schools, and that 41% believed that humans and dinosaurs lived simultaneously. This legacy tends to isolate us from both prehistory and natural history and greatly affects how we see Paleolithic art.

Prehistoric art studies developed at a time when the church still played an important role in scholarship and education. Most Paleolithic art sites happen to occur in traditional Catholic countries in southern Europe: south-ern Germany, Italy, Portugal, Spain, and France. That religious context has had some effect on the direction of research and interpretation. The intellectual revolution spawned from newly developing ecological and evolutionary insights first swept through northern Europe and North America and has only recently influenced scholarly thinking elsewhere.

The early tone for Paleolithic archaeology and art studies was set by its first scholars, several of whom were members of the clergy, such as Abbé Glory, Abbé Breuil, Abbé Landesque, Abbé Bayol, Abbé Bouyssonie, Abbé Cau-Durban, and Abbé Lemozi in France and Abbo Sierra and Abbo Carballo in Spain. These men did enthusiastic and, for their times, outstanding work. Nevertheless, they approached their subject as part of a continuum of religious art — and with a sense of historic "progression," which was then so dominant. Each cave and rock shelter was investigated under the assumption that, like newly discovered remains of a Neolithic tabernacle, they mainly represented sacred sanctuaries full of symbolic meaning, awaiting scholarly illumination. It is easy to empathize with these assumptions. The unlit chambers deep within the earth, quiet except for dripping water and the sputtering of the explorer's lamp, felt like sacred places.

The magico-religious paradigm in Paleolithic art is well entrenched. It is so pervasive in art research that it is often uncritically evoked for any prehistoric art. There are many

Most theories attempting to account for the meaning and purposes of Paleolithic art seldom mention these minor images. For example, images of birds are scattered among the images of large mammals. Generally, the portrayals are of species of birds that today would be considered "game species," that is, species with substantial meat, waterfowl particularly. **A** and **C**, Gargas, Fr. **B** and **S**, La Bastide, Fr. **D**, Gabillou, Fr. **E**, Mal'ta, Rus. **F**, **I**, and **L**, Gönnersdorf, Ger. **G**, Escabasses, Fr. **H**, Montespan, Fr. **J** and **N**, Gourdan, Fr. **K**, Lourdes, Fr. **M**, Teyjat, Fr. **O**, Enlène, Fr. **P**, Lascaux, Fr. **Q**, Roc de Sers, Fr. **R**, Grotte du Loupe, Fr. **T**, La Vache, Fr. **U**, Belvis, Sp. **V–X**, Pergouset, Fr. **Y**, Morin, Fr. **Z**, Bruniquel, Fr.

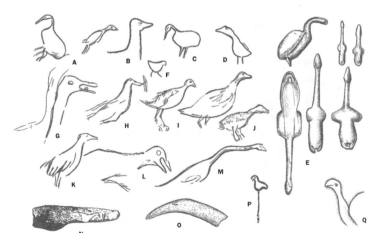

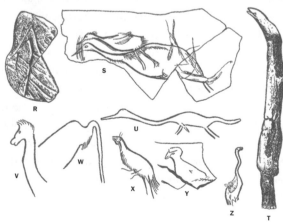

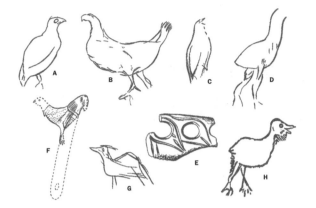

Grouse and related species of birds also occur in Paleolithic art; these are also among the meaty game species. **A**, Isturitz, Fr. **B** and **D**, Gönnersdorf, Ger. **C**, Laugerie-Basse, Fr. **E**, La Madeleine, Fr. **F**, Mas d'Azil, Fr. **G**, Marsoulas, Fr. **H**, Puy de Lacan, Fr.

examples. In her investigation of the use of images of a local bird, the roadrunner, by the 2000-year-old Ilama culture in the American Southwest, Cardale de Schrimpff concluded: "The mere presence of roadrunner tracks in prehistoric art was strongly indicative that the roadrunner and/or its tracks had religious significance in the prehistoric southwest" (1989, 86). Similarly, Marshack commented about wear polish on a small horse carving: "The amount of time required to wear down the mammoth ivory, if the horse were handled periodically in ritual, may have been a number of years" (1985, 95). I don't mean to be critical of the substance of these comments; roadrunner tracks and ivory horses may indeed have had some ritualistic religious significance. I only use these quotations to show the unquestioned way in which numerous researchers assume that the magico-religious paradigm is the most appropriate.

This dogma contends that when art first arose among early peoples, it was such a mysterious process that it was incorporated totally into the religious part of human behavior. There is absolutely no evidence whatsoever for this assumption. In fact, art seems to have a much deeper and more important role in human behavior, which I will return to later.

In its extreme expression not only has this magico-religious paradigm resulted in a derailment of rock art research, but at its worst it has presented early peoples in a distorted light as superstitious dolts totally preoccupied with mystical concerns. Yet the evidence from Paleolithic art tells a quite different story; it portrays people in close touch with the details of a complex earth. Religious images probably do occur, but they are part of a larger mosaic of experience.

The magico-religious approach has generated confusion and error about the function of Paleolithic art, which seems to increase with time (Macintosh 1977; Clottes 1989). Paleolithic mythograms (images that are regarded and used as containing mythic meaning, like a Star of David or those of Northwest Coast Indian totems) have not emerged. Attempts to associate some kind of symbolism with the dominant animals, bison and horses, have not been very credible (Ucko and Rosenfeld 1967). Parts of the fragmented whole of Paleolithic art have been used to champion a variety of special-case interpretations.

A wide range of experiences is revealed in Paleolithic art, and to insist on a flat-footed literalness would simply be to exchange one error for another. It is not that the many rock art researchers who see art as magic and mystical are totally wrong; it is rather that they have taken good observations on mystical components of Paleolithic art (and most prehistoric art, for that matter) and extended them universally to the entire art. I aim, not to deny the existence of these supernatural themes, but only to lift their tyranny. The mystical preoccupation has been so removed from the organic, the specific, that now it is quite adrift—wafting on the breezes of argument and speculation. It is a distortion to portray Paleolithic peoples as so mystically preoccupied and all their art as mystical symbols.

Potent interests support the magico-religious paradigm. For one segment of the public, the present sophisticated religions require some sort of primitive ancestral animism. For another segment, fossil art is the cradle of sacred religious symbols that testify to the elegant nobility of our lost innocence. To suggest otherwise can create

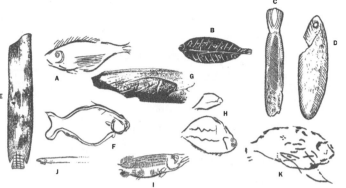

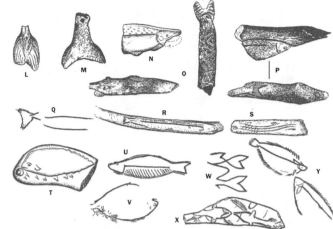

Even more so than bird images, images of fish are scattered among the large mammals that so dominate Paleolithic art. Fish are seldom mentioned among the different theories that try to account for Paleolithic art. As with the birds, most images are of fish species that are meaty and good for eating. Along the coast there are even images of marine species. **A** and **Y**, Altxerri, Sp. **B**, Lespugue, Fr. **C**, El Pendo, Sp. **D**, **R**, and **U**, Isturitz, Fr. **E**, **H**, **J**, **O–P**, and **V**, Mas d'Azil, Fr. **F** and **K**, La Pileta, Sp. **G**, **Q**, and **X**, Laugerie-Basse, Fr. **I** and **L–N**, Gourdan, Fr. **S**, Placard, Fr. **T**, Caldas, Sp. **W**, Raymonden, Fr.

a sense of grievous loss. For others, it is a flagrant error to look at people as creatures who have evolved—as animals among many others, forged by natural selection—through the same processes that produced chickadees, dung beetles, and dandelions.

However, the limitations of the "magico-religious paradigm" have caused researchers such as Conkey (1980) to treat the art pieces simply as artifacts, as if they were, say, stone tools, using art distribution and density to indicate such things as aggregation centers. Gamble (1982) has done something similar by using related art images and styles as a means of illustrating social network systems over broad areas. Impatience with an absolutist magico-religious focus does not stop here. Jochim (1987), Bandi (1984), Halverson (1987), Noiret (1990), Lorblanchet (1991), González Morales (1991), Dubourg (1994), Altuna (1996), and many others are looking at other nonmystical dimensions of Paleolithic art. And some, such as Balbín-Behrmann and Alcolea-González (1999), even question whether any of the art can be explained by invoking religious motives.

The shadow of this entrenched magico-religious paradigm and its frequent uncritical use often cloud open and frank discussion of alternative approaches and ideas about ancient art (e.g., see discussions following Halverson 1987).

The Comparative Approach

What can be said about this fossil art for which we have no cultural context? We can never interview an individual Paleolithic artist nor fully enter that culture. Our only guides are enduring human traits, the result of a common organic heritage.

But, you may object, plasticity and adaptability are enduring human characters too. Can we really presume to say anything about fundamental human traits? Are there really any such guides? Haven't we learned to suspect anything termed a universal? And for good reason.

My response is that behind our different histories there is a common evolutionary pilgrimage. Our humanness arises from and exists in an earthly context, and we share with Paleolithic peoples many evolutionary constraints, strengths, and propensities. We can track a tentative route between the late Pleistocene and the present, despite yawning differences, because evolution is our lodestar. Our shared evolutionary past makes for a common relief

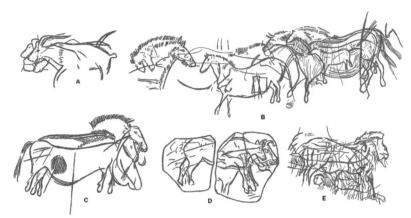

Rather scribbly works by inexperienced Paleolithic drawers who did a lot of redrawing: **A**, Ibex, Espélugues, Fr. **B–C**, Horses, Lascaux, Fr. **D**, Wild cattle or aurochs, Limeuil, Fr. **E**, A mix of images from Les Combarelles, Fr. Horses in **B** and **C** are speared; the one in **C** is penetrated by a spear in the gut and bleeding profusely (this portrays a botched killing job, as a spear-hunter must hit the thorax for a clean kill).

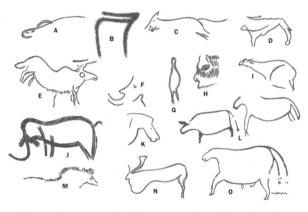

Large mammals done by inexperienced artists. One can only roughly identify the species in some cases. A large segment of Paleolithic art looks like this. **A**, **C**, and **N**, Lascaux, Fr. **B**, Merveilles, Fr. **D**, Los Casares, Sp. **E**, Labastide, Fr. **F**, Abri Fongal, Fr. **G**, Cosquer, Fr. **H**, Aguas, Sp. **I**, El Castillo, Sp. **J**, La Baume Latrone, Fr. **K**, La Calévie, Fr. **L** and **O**, Shishkino, Rus. (early Holocene). **M**, Oxocelhaya-Hariztoya, Sp.

in our behavioral topography; we share behavioral propensities, learning some things with downhill ease and others with tremendous uphill effort. Under our quilt of cultures, similar genes influence our learning and guide our diverse experiences. We do not always conform to these inner slants and tilts, but we feel their tugs at our very core.

There is a human nature (Bjorklund and Pellegrini 2002), and the main contours of that nature emerged in the Pleistocene. I'll make the case that this nature, which we still exhibit, formed as a result of adaptations to a fundamental human ecological niche, that Paleolithic people experienced their lives and earth similarly enough to the way you and I do that we can make numerous assumptions about their behavior based on cross-cultural studies of modern peoples and careful consideration of the evolutionary themes of our behavior as a human animal. These patterns are discernible. Indeed, Paleolithic art and artifacts compose much of the evidence for them.

It is difficult to comprehend being a warrior ant or a brooding raven, but sit at any human's campfire and you are with your own. With time, you can understand the essence of their pain, worries, aspirations, joys, tastes, and pleasures, no matter how exotic their culture. We are the same animal. The business of social anthropologists is to ferret out cultural differences, the more bizarre the better, but these various notes play over the chordal structure of human similarities.

Despite the counter-tugs of hormones, dreams, and personal and cultural histories, we each have the ability to reason objectively. It is this shared rational ability that is the main tie to other humans past and present—this ability to imagine a reality outside our subjective selves. The thesis I develop here is that the special human ecological

◄ Horses are one of the most common animals in Paleolithic art. These images are about average in technical execution—just barely identifiable as horses: **A**, Altamira, Sp. **B**, Font de Gaume, Fr. **C**, Vacheresse, Fr. **D**, Pair-non-Pair, Fr. **E**, Mazouco, Portugal. **F**, Mayenne Sciences, Fr. **G**, La Madeleine, Fr. **H** and **K**, Isturitz, Fr. **I**, Gourdan, Fr. **J**, Parpalló, Sp. **L**, Las Chimeneas, Sp.

niche demanded this close approximation between the outer reality and our inner perception and interpretation of that reality. Whether it is in mending and repair, proper rearing of children, making and interpreting images, we are all connected in this innate domestic science of reason and art of imagination so central to being human. Be assured that the Paleolithic artists found their order in this same way. We can see that in the art.

Elementary renditions of large mammals by Paleolithic artists, likely made by inexperienced drawers: **A**, La Madeleine, Fr. **B**, Baume Latrone, Fr. **C**, **H**, and **J–L**, Parpalló, Sp. **D**, Cosquer, Fr. **E–F** and **I**, Altamira, Sp. **G**, Ojo Guareña, Sp. **M**, Sudrie, Fr. **N**, Ardales, Sp. **O**, Oreille d'Enfer, Fr.

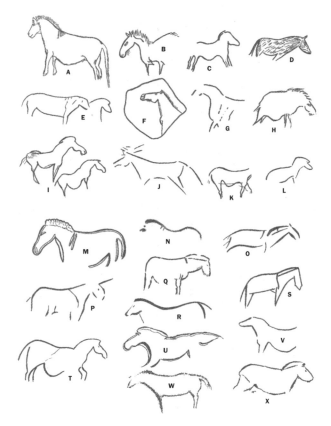

Another sampler of horse images done by people with elementary facility. This level is common in preserved Paleolithic art. **A**, Rouffignac, Fr. **B**, Gargas, Fr. **C**, Labattut, Fr. **D**, Tito Bustillo, Sp. **E**, **L**, and **R**, Altamira, Sp. **F**, Villepin, Fr. **G**, Mayenne Sciences, Fr. **H**, Gabillou, Fr. **I**, Ardales, Sp. **J**, Parpalló, Sp. **K**, Della Mura, It. **M**, Chauvet, Fr. **N**, Escabasses, Fr. **O**, El Pendo, Sp. **P**, Calévie, Sp. **Q**, Las Monedas, Sp. **S**, Lumentxa, Sp. **T**, Croze à Gontran, Fr. **U**, Niaux, Fr. **V**, Prado del Navarro, Sp. **W**, Marcenac, Fr. **X**, Sotarriza, Sp.

FINDING ORDER IN PREHISTORY

In addition to Paleolithic art, I will also draw on sources like human burials, animal remains, tools, and other archaeological materials. We will also take a careful look at the many biases in preservation, or *taphonomy,* as these are so crucial in understanding the art. We will also use a forensic approach to identify the ages and sexes of some Paleolithic artists. These findings help tighten the fit into the most coherent comparative contexts.

The approach used here is similar to what a natural historian such as Alexander (1979) would call the "comparative technique." It assumes that, underlying the buzz of apparent randomness, there is some order and reason in the tangle of unique forms and events that can be traced to both physical processes and life's ordering processes resulting from evolution. All this is best deciphered through a web of comparisons. This investigatory process has an eye for emergent pattern but is more a state of mind. Concrete comparisons catalyze the jump to a flash of insight, which in turn prompts connections we can test as falsifiable interpretations.

The comparative approach is one of the few doorways into the complex web of living things and their historical causalities (Gittelman 1989). But causality in animate

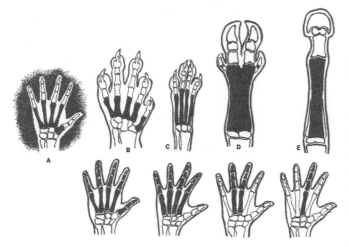

Evolution provides the basic order from which to understand much of biology. As a simple example in anatomy we can use the comparative approach to see the basic five-digit early mammal hand evolving into different hand and foot patterns. Metacarpal bones are shown in color in the upper figures; below are the schematics. We are old-fashioned in this evolutionary regard, having kept all of our original five digits (**A**). Wolverines and weasels (**B**) also retain five functional digits, but fleet carnivores, like cheetahs and wolves (**C**), reduce or lose the first digit (thumb and big toe), leaving them with a track of only four toes. Animals like bison reduce their "fingers" to cloven hooves (**D**) or, among horses, even to one digit (**E**).

meadows and forests can rarely be crystallized into "laws of nature." What is available are insights into connecting links of relationships. In evolutionary ideas, life's enormous diversity and complexity are not often clarified by middle-school science experiments. Understanding is often not simple, and order floats up on a plethora of integrated details and elucidating exceptions.

Through these comparative techniques we can analyze behavior as well as anatomy (Tooby and Cosmides 1992). But comparative anatomy of fossils is our benchmark. It allows us to see how, through evolution, the front gill arch of a filter-feeding fish was incorporated as a jaw, and tiny enamel-plated scales folded into the mouth as teeth. Step-by-step we see how the fishes' second gill slit became an ear duct covered by a tympanic drum in amphibians, which was then further modified into the middle ear of mammals. By comparing animals in the fossil record we can see how lobed fins became legs, how a five-digit reptile hand became a bat wing, and so on throughout mammalian hard anatomy. Hard tissues tend to leave a fossil record. Soft tissues of muscle and glands, however, seldom fossilize. Comparative anatomy of soft tissue has to use both embryology and extant species. But the logic of the anatomical study of patterns is equally rigorous in tracing the change from reptilian eggshell glands to mammalian uterus, from abdominal sweat glands to milk glands, from fish air-gulping pockets to lungs, from gill arteries to aortic arches, from epidermal scales to hair and feathers, and so on.

Comparative behavioral investigations proceed similarly. We can trace aspects of behaviors in hard tissues, and we can observe the diverse behaviors of living organisms—for example, the degree and forms of sociality, behaviors in rearing young, mate fidelity, and sexual differences. This is possible because the core behaviors of a given organism have a modest heritability; they occur within a pattern of inclinations and constraints. It is this adaptive pattern which allows us, through comparisons, to trace the functional history. We can reconstruct with a fair degree of reliability the fighting behavior of Pleistocene bison by noting horn structure and by comparing the behavior of modern-day "hookers," with sharp horn tips, with "clashers," with thick frontal bones (Guthrie 1990) or the protrusion of their orbits beyond what must have been thick hair padding between the eyes (Guthrie 1966). Other fossil evidence, such as canine tooth size, can be combined with behavioral biology to show how, in some lines of early horses, territorial behavior was abandoned in favor of mobile harems (Guthrie 2001b).

Like comparative anatomy, comparative ethology has this dimension of depth through evolutionary time (Krebs and Davies 1992). And comparative ethology embrace aspects of human behavior as well. Studies of other primates allow us to imagine how kissing evolved from prechewing food for infants and how romantic love-bonding with mates was genetically borrowed and built upon already extant bonds between parent and offspring. These bonds have evolved. They have essential genetic dimensions. And these genetic dimensions are subject to selection pressure and remodeling.

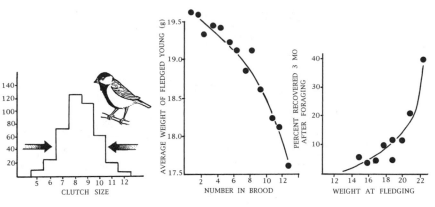

Balanced Selection. Evolution, remember, usually involves trade-offs. There is a constant evolutionary tension between spreading reproductive resources over many children or focusing on a quality few. We can see this in most animals. Here it is pictured in an English great tit (related to the American chickadee). Clutch size is significantly heritable, so natural selection favors the largest clutch that can bring most of its young to maturity. However, the larger the brood, the smaller the individual body size (the more mouths to feed), and the smaller the body size, the higher the mortality. So a balance is struck in a selective optimum in a given environment. This kind of balanced selection is found in most characters of most species. Evolution pictured this way is a dynamic force. After Perrins 1965.

DETECTIVE WORK: PALEOLITHIC ART AND EVOLUTION

. . . from so simple a beginning endless forms most beautiful and most wonderful have been and are being evolved.

Charles Darwin, last words in *On the Origin of Species by Means of Natural Selection*

Piecing together the evidence for an evolutionary adaptation using the comparative technique has a lot in common with detective work. There is no ultimate truth; rather, it is a matter of finding the most logically consistent story which fits the facts so well that there is no reasonable doubt. But to locate the soundest story from among a competing array, we must recognize some guidelines. The soundness of an adaptive scenario for a given character is strongest if:

► this character is too improbably complex a feature to be the outcome of sheer accident;

► there is evidence that variations in that character have a heritable component within populations;

► this character can be credibly imagined to positively affect net reproductive success;

► this character may be maintained in the population despite significant biological costs (that is, there are counterbalancing selection pressures);

► there is a logical pattern in the differences in this character between populations in different environmental contexts;

► we respect arguments of analogy (that is, this character can be placed in a pattern of similar adaptive characters in other species); and

► the character is adaptively explicable at different levels of organization: genes, physiology, anatomy, and behavior (that is, it is broadly consilient).

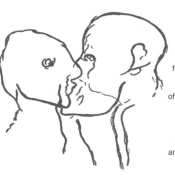

While most behavior is developmentally flexible, there are usually underlying predispositions or inclinations. The comparative approach, familiar from anatomy, can also be used to study the origins of behavior. For example, kissing evolved among apes mouth-feeding young and became a metaphor of family attachment and dependence. Couple kissing from La Marche, Fr.

These criteria help us evaluate alternative explanations. Let's attempt an evolutionary detective's case—one drawn in Paleolithic art. Paleolithic artists portrayed large antlers on adult bull reindeer and small antlers on cow reindeer. In no other deer species do females have antlers. Did the artists invent a cow with antlers, or was this a portrait of the way cow reindeer really looked? Actually, even if reindeer had become extinct, we could have tested this by looking at the fossils, because antlers preserve well in the fossil record. From fossils and living animals we know that the artists were drawing the literal truth. Reindeer cows are antlered now and were 30,000 years ago.

What is the story? We can go on to ask whether the antlers of reindeer cows are adaptive for some function or were simply a chance product or epiphenomenon. Why are reindeer cows different from cows of other deer? Does an antlerless cow fare as well as one with antlers? Do cow antlers aid in survival?

Thinking of anatomy in "survival" terms instead of "reproductive genic fitness" led early scientists to account for mammoth tusks as snow-shovel survival aids. They failed to consider the tusk's important social functions, and, of course, reproductive fitness is greatly influenced by one's social life. Similarly, early researchers envisioned reindeer antlers also functioning as survival aids in the form of snow shovels or temperature regulators. Fortunately, reindeer did not become extinct, and here are some pieces of information we can use from field studies:

Paleolithic drawing of an autumn cow reindeer, from La Marche, Fr., showing simple small antlers. Note the brow tine is missing, with only the forward-pointing bez tines present. This pattern is characteristic of cows.

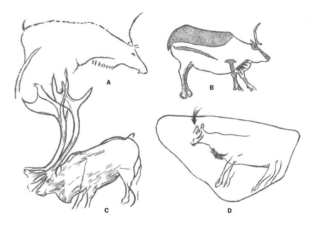

Paleolithic drawings of cow and bull reindeer showing antler differences. **A**, Cow, Las Monedas, Sp. **B**, Cow, Trois Frères, Fr. **C–D**, Bulls, La Marche, Fr. (note arrow, the velvet antler bud, in **D**).

► Reindeer do not use antlers to move snow; rather, they use them almost totally for social aggression and defense (Shea 1979).
► Reindeer are very social, especially in winter; animals in groups are more successful in avoiding predation than solitary migrants (Pruitt 1960a, 1960b).
► Bulls shed their antlers shortly after autumn rut, but cows keep theirs all winter, shedding them around calving time in early spring (Lent 1964).
► Bull antlers are heavily built and quite rugged. They are used in violent male-to-male rutting-season battles.

Cow antlers are thinly constructed and light in weight, are insufficient to survive rugged antler-to-antler fighting, and do not have the defensive forward-pointing brow tines (Pruitt 1966).
► Reindeer seldom try to fight off predators; rather, they try to outrun them (Espmark 1964; Shea 1979).
► There is a significant heritability to antler presence-absence, size, and shape: roughly 50% of a deer population's within-sex antler variations are traceable to genetic causes (Williams and Harmel 1984; Williams,

Kreuger, and Harmel 1994; see also reviews in Brown 1983; Goss 1983; Bubenik and Bubenik 1990).

► Antlers contribute enormous advantages in fighting (Shea 1979).

► Because male reindeer remain antlerless all winter, they are socially subordinate to the antlered cows (Lent 1964).

► The main winter food of reindeer is lichen buried beneath snow (Pruitt 1960b).

► Cows expend a great deal of energy digging large snow craters (using their broad forefeet, not antlers) to feed themselves and their calves; possession and successful defense of a large crater determine volume and quality of winter diet (Pruitt 1960b; Shea 1979).

► In deep and crusted snow conditions, there is aggressive competition for already excavated snow craters, and bulls and cows without antlers fare poorly in such situations (Espmark 1964; Shea 1979).

► In areas where snow is shallow, a high percentage of cows do not have antlers or have very small antlers (as in Newfoundland or the Altai).

From extensive fieldwork (Pruitt 1960a; Espmark 1964; Lent 1964; Shea 1979; and many others) naturalists have concluded that these small but sharp cow antlers make for an effective weapon in social squabbles with antlerless bulls or competing cows, providing great social benefits in crater defense all winter. Antlers directly affect a cow's reproductive fitness because her calf of the prior summer has better winter forage in its mother's well-defended feeding crater, and also because such a dominant antlered cow will be in better physical condition to nurse her newborn calf during the following spring.

The massive antlers of bulls would be even more effective in crater defense; however, male antlers are quite heavy and form an expensive post-rut millstone, as the animal must lower and raise its head with every mouthful (winter forage is survival food of low quality). It is apparently more economical for reindeer bulls to shed their antlers immediately after rut and dig their own craters, liv-

One can see adaptations to open country by comparing modern migratory and more sedentary populations of reindeer. Sedentary groups are shorter legged and put on large quantities of fat, whereas long-distance migrators are long legged and put on only modest amounts of fat (Klein, Melgaard, and Fancy 1987). Reindeer in Paleolithic art have more sedentary contours, suggesting that their migratory patterns were not many hundreds of kilometers but of shorter range.

ing away from the now more dominant antlered cows all winter. There are some costs for cows to grow antlers, but compared to bull antlers these small antlers of cows are economical to grow and to carry.

In summary, when snow is deep, antlerless cows are at quite a competitive disadvantage. Wildlife biologists have looked in a similar way at such traits as leg length, horn size, gut anatomy, gait physiology, and much else. Such analyses take place in a community of critical scholars. In this way, with check and countercheck, it is possible to construct a reasonable story about adaptation of things like reindeer cow antlers.

Humans don't have antlers, but much of our anatomy, physiology, and behavior is subject to comparable analysis. There will always be issues where we haggle over which is the soundest and best story. Often it is hard to obtain the full complement of firm answers to the above criteria for building a plausible adaptive scenario. We may confront irresolvable questions, but the relative soundness of the technique remains, as do the satisfactions and insights gained in the process along the way.

Most people and many scholars still view information about other animals as an anecdotal aside that is irrelevant to our understanding of human nature. Other animals are seen as quite separate from humans and their culture. But that is surely mistaken: we are part of the same menagerie under the sun, and this is the only home we have.

View from north pole. Although the glacial ice and frozen seas covered parts of landmasses during the last full Glacial, many regions, such as Alaska and northern Asia, were as large or larger than during Interglacial times such as the present. *Top*, Glacial. *Bottom*, the present. Continents are black, sea is stippled, ice is white.

Instead of searching for a system of cultural symbolism from the Paleolithic, I'll turn to the more knowable, using our fundamental evolutionary kinship. We can be confident of many similarities because of the immense weight of organic history. But the late Pleistocene was a very different time. The people who made the art we are about to study lived on the borderlands of a vast steppe that stretched across Eurasia. Their skies were different from those today, the landscape had a different look, and the air had a different feel and smell. All this figures importantly in their art.

The Ecology of Paleolithic Art:
The Mammoth Steppe

Several hundred million years ago the large landmass of Gondwanaland, centered on the earth's South Pole, began to break up. The continental mass we call the Indian Plate began to inch northward. About 60 million years ago it reached Southeast Asia and began to burrow into the underbelly of that continent. This slow-motion collision ultimately led to the buckling and rise of the Himalayas. During the last 2.5 million years, the Himalaya Range reached so high it began to block the atmospheric circulation of moisture from the south. This blockage of the Asian monsoonal flow produced an enormous band of aridity that still extends like a belt across Eurasia.

Not so long ago ecologists imagined Pleistocene Eurasia as a sort of tundra, because they assumed global cooling simply shifted plant and animal zones southward. We now know that this huge region, which I call the Mammoth Steppe, was a cold and arid steppe-like habitat, with no good modern analogs. The climate was too cold, windy, and dry for most trees, but arid- and cold-adapted forbs and grasses could thrive. During glacial episodes, as aridity intensified, the Mammoth Steppe spread northward as well as east and west, making most of unglaciated Eurasia an arid grassland, characterized by wind, low rainfall, and cloudless skies that were brilliant in the summer and blue frigid in winter (Guthrie 1990, 2001b).

Some Pleistocene large mammals adapted to the steppe's blessings and curses. Cold winds and lack of trees kept human colonization at bay. Woolly mammoths, woolly rhinos, woolly horses, steppe bison, saiga antelope, reindeer, and others roamed these immense plains unharassed by humans except at the southern border. Life was not predator free: wolves, lions, cheetahs, hyenas, and bears were also adapted to these steppe conditions. This community of cold-adapted steppe animals extended from Europe across Siberia, the Russian Far East, and the exposed Bering Land Bridge into Alaska and the Yukon Territory. After years of working with fossils of Ice Age mammals in Alaska, it is always remarkable for me to see the same species painted on cave walls in southwestern Europe. There in France, twelve time zones away, are all my old friends.

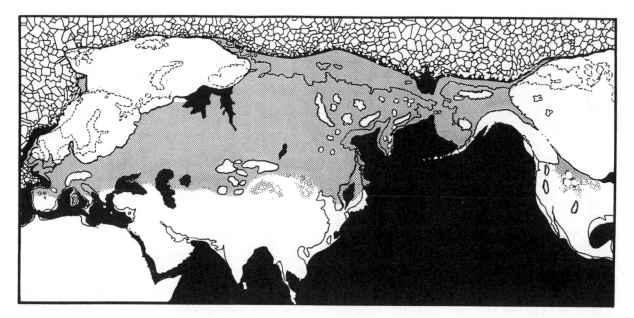

The Mammoth Steppe (*shaded area*) contained the large mammals we know well from Paleolithic art. It was the largest steppe that ever existed on earth. Clear in summer but unbearably cold in winter, it was habitable by many species of large plains mammals but, judging from the few archaeological sites, was rather hostile to a certain African colonizer, humans. South of the Mammoth Steppe continents are unglaciated.

It is curious that we have no vegetation analog today for this huge Pleistocene Mammoth Steppe—though a few isolated Siberian relict patches are close. Most grasslands today are in warmer climates, but the Pleistocene steppe was often underlain with permafrost, permanently frozen ground. Clear summer days would have allowed soils to thaw and encouraged grasses to reach deep with their roots, but in winter the wind would have stripped away the insulating snow, allowing much of the heat to escape. Today, the Gulf Stream keeps Europe and parts of northern Asia bathed in cloud for much of the winter and summer. The Gulf Stream, which now brings some of Florida's warmth to Europe, was diverted south during the Pleistocene, striking along coastal Africa. Cloudless skies allowed the summer sun to rake the land with fertility, but in winter clear skies work the other way. All winter during the Pleistocene the dark night sky radiated the earth's heat out toward distant twinkling stars and into eternity.

The animals portrayed in Paleolithic art were cold-hardy. Most wildlife species at home in Europe today could not have lived on these harsh steppes. Few fossils of wild boar, cattle (aurochs), moose (elk, as they are known in Europe), or roe deer have been recovered from those stretches. These animals require woodland food or cover and could have coped with neither the low sward of the steppe nor the race of unfettered cold wind without the break of trees.

Pollen cores indicate a late Pleistocene tree-barren steppe (e.g., Woillard 1978). But farther to the south, nearer the Mediterranean, the relatively milder weather allowed sparse riverine woodlands and copses to exist. During the last Glacial in that region, the percentage

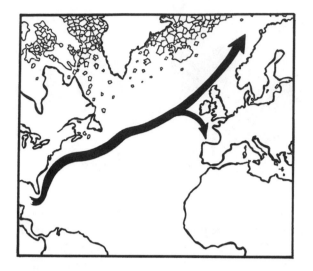

Europe is warmer than its latitude might suggest today because of the Atlantic current flowing past Havana and traveling to Murmansk (*left*). During the last glaciation, the Atlantic current dipped and ran down the coast of West Africa (*right*). Europe cooled and the steppes extended from the east to England, where small saiga antelope and horses kicked up dust as their herds moved across the treeless steppic landscape.

of fossil tree pollen is low, mostly pine. However, areas like the Dordogne River valley were a refuge for the now wide-ranging tree species of scrub oak, alder, hazel, and birch (Donner 1975). I am giving you the simple, broadbrush version here—there were many chronological and regional variations in climate and vegetation between 40,000 and 10,000 years ago (the time of Paleolithic art) across Eurasia (Van Andel and Tzedakis 1996; Stuiver and Grootes 2000), with varying faunas (reviewed by Rigaud 2000), but this steppe was the dominant theme. Peaks and troughs in radiocarbon dates of archaeological sites suggest irregularities in human densities, but basically the Mammoth Steppe was sparsely and intermittently occupied by humans (Pettitt 2000).

The Mammoth Steppe had species in different compositions and different distributions through time and space (Delpech 1975). Altuna (1979) has shown that, despite the faunal list being similar at different archaeological

sites, the proportions vary considerably from region to region, as one might expect. Reindeer bones are the most common in the Dordogne, horses and large bovines in the Gironde, and red deer and ibex in Cantabria. Camps near rocky sites often exhibit a predominance of ibex, an animal adapted to rocky landscapes.

The mix of Mammoth Steppe faunas astonishes our Holocene-tuned sense of biogeography. This is especially so along its southwestern border, where most of the Paleolithic art is found. Cattle are found alongside bison, hyena with reindeer, leopard with arctic fox. Kowalski (1967) stressed this late Pleistocene pattern in Europe of finding in the same site species that today live in quite distinct habitats. Poplin (1979) also pointed out that in France there seems to be a peculiar mixing of biotopes in the fossil record, in which steppe species occur with tundra species. Chaline (1979) has shown the same pattern with small mammals: mammals that are now considered arctic species (lemmings [*Lemmus* and *Dictostonyx*] and tundra voles [*Microtus oeconomus*]) are found with those that are now considered part of the eastern steppes (steppe voles [*Lagurus lagurus*] and ground squirrels [*Citellus superciliosus*]). Even the mollusks show this peculiar mixture of cold-adapted and arid-adapted species (Puisségur 1979), and so do the beetles (Coope 1977).

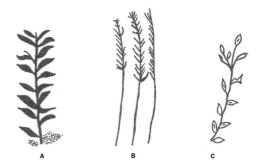

Compared to mammals, very few plants are pictured in preserved Paleolithic art, despite the wonderful potential of form and pattern presented by flower, fruit, leaf, and limb, so popular throughout the rest of human history. Although rare in the art, plants must have played a large part in people's lives, both indirectly and directly. There are no forest scenes, and only scattered trees are portrayed—this must have reflected the reality of living on the edge of the Mammoth Steppe. **A**, Parpalló, Sp. **B**, Montgaudier, Fr. **C**, Trilobite, Fr.

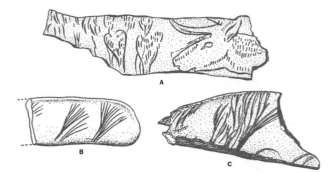

We know from the pollen record that there were thin stands of trees along the southwestern border of the Mammoth Steppe, particularly in southern France. These were probably borders along streams and clumps along the shaded north sides of mountains, where evaporation was not so great. **A**, Trees or shrubs(?), Murat, Fr. **B–C**, Massat, Fr.

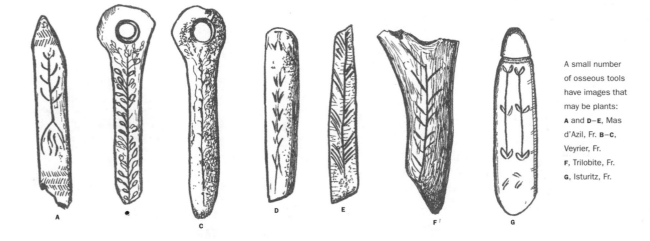

A small number of osseous tools have images that may be plants: **A** and **D–E**, Mas d'Azil, Fr. **B–C**, Veyrier, Fr. **F**, Trilobite, Fr. **G**, Isturitz, Fr.

It is not always easy to determine where and when certain species occurred. González Echegaray (1974) proposed that animal associations in various art caves could be taken as accurate reflections of real faunal assemblages of that period, from which we can gain ecological insights. That does not always seem to be true in detail, but it is true in the general sense that the same core species seem to recur. It is the relative proportions that are often skewed, both because of varying habitats and perhaps because of the bias introduced by the artists' exaggeration of the importance of the heroic species. In general, the various mixes of species portrayed in local Paleolithic art are simi-

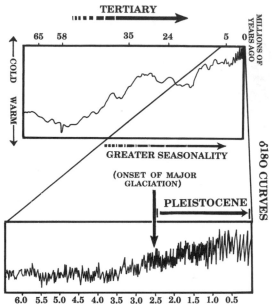

Nomadic plains animals are constructed for efficient long-distance travel. Unlike their forest relatives, their forequarters are large and they have an efficient canter. Many animals in Paleolithic art share this dorsal line, with high shoulders and low rumps. **A**, Red deer. **B**, Reindeer. **C**, Woolly rhino. **D**, Steppe bison. **E**, Musk oxen. **F**, Brown and cave bears. **G**, Woolly mammoth. **H**, Giant deer (shelk).

The Pleistocene was a time of greatly increased climatic variability. Oxygen isotopes are a rough proxy of these changes. On top is a large-scale view of the last 65 million years. On the bottom is a more magnified view of the last few million years, the Pleistocene. (After Partridge, Wood, and deMenocal 1995 and Schackleton 1995.) Note the increasing variability starting around 2.5 million years ago. When the earth's climate was steady, it favored steady creatures. The erratic Pleistocene climate sometimes made it hard for these species, but the more facultative and flexibly opportunistic creatures apparently flourished.

lar to those that paleontological excavations show existed in the wild.

The climate of the late Pleistocene, the Paleolithic art era, was unstable. We can see that from the cores from the Greenland Ice Cap. The climate was often wrenched around and was not as predictable as today. It was a more variable time on almost every scale: centuries, decades, and seasons. In an indirect way it was that instability which ultimately resulted in such diverse, mismatched biota—reindeer mixed with antelope, and musk oxen with leopard (Guthrie and van Kolfschoten 2000). Of course, this global-wide unpredictability helped make us who we are, sharp opportunists able to figure out how to change. It was a time that favored wit and logic, wise decisions embedded in empirical experience—dangerous and exciting times.

Paleolithic Art: What, Where, When, and How Much?

NEANDERTHAL NONDRAWERS

The Mammoth Steppe waxed and waned with the dozen or so Glacial cycles of the Pleistocene. During the warmer and wetter Interglacials, the steppes shrank, and much of Eurasia was forested as it is today (be reminded that we are now in an Interglacial). It is a complex story but the notion of oscillation is essentially valid. Especially during the last few warm, wet Interglacial cycles, much of Eurasia was littered with strange human-like tracks.

Hominids have been in Europe for at least over half a million years. The species that preceded humans by 200,000 years left especially broad, thick-toed tracks. These were prints of stocky Neanderthals, *Homo neanderthalensis*. (The first skeleton, or "type specimen," was found in 1856 inside Feldhofer Cave in the Neander Valley of the Düssel River, a Rhine tributary in Germany; "valley" in old German was spelled *thal*. Interestingly, Neander was the surname of a local poet.) Bones and artifacts of Neanderthals are most abundant during Interglacial times. Neanderthals were similar in many ways to humans, but they were long headed, heavy browed, much more robust, and more thickset. Their brain size was large, larger than that of most people today. This large brain was the main reason some anthropologists once insisted on including Neanderthals in *Homo sapiens.*

But Neanderthals were not humans, though light from their fires dotted the night landscape, as probably did echoes of their laughter, and indeed they often chose the identical campsites later human invaders were to select. Despite many similarities to us, no Neanderthal art has been found comparable to late Paleolithic human art. Neanderthals made little use of bone, ivory, or antler—especially in the form of sophisticated worked tools. However, an aesthetic sense is apparent in Neanderthal stone tools. Many were selected from beautiful stones, and several that incorporated natural fossils as part of the pieces have been found. The fuzzy margins of Neanderthal art are controversial; see Hayden 1993, D'Errico and Villa 1997, and Hawcroft and Dennell 2000 for discussions on this topic. The absence (or virtual absence) of a representational artistic tradition may not necessarily mean that Neanderthals were incapable of making such images, but across several hundred thousand years we have little evidence of that kind of art. Neanderthals' facultative skills are revealed in their ability to cope with northern Eurasian winters, to use fire, and apparently to make warm clothes and

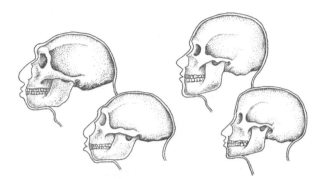

Two species of late Pleistocene European hominids showing general skull differences. Male and female Neanderthals on the left and humans on the right.

hunt wary and dangerous big game. Their work with stone tools indicates refined manual skills, suggesting that they spent considerable time at trial-and-error learning and in passing on handicrafts. The dating of the disappearance of the Neanderthals is controversial, but it is clear that their demise was not abrupt but varied across different regions of Europe between 35,000 and 28,000 years ago. Neanderthals persisted in some regions, overlapping with humans for 5000–10,000 years (Mellars 1996).

THE ARRIVAL OF HUMANS IN EUROPE

Around 40,000 years ago, anatomically modern people, *Homo sapiens,* swept into Europe and central Asia. Their arrival date is a little blurry and is further complicated by the fact that this time period lies just at the outer edge of the radiocarbon-dating range. It has become clear that these first humans arrived abruptly from the southeast and did not evolve in Europe from the thickset, heavy-browed Neanderthals (Bischoff et al. 1989; Cabrera, Valdes, and Bischoff 1989). The tools of these humans differed dramatically from Neanderthal tools in many ways, but especially in the newcomers' reliance on osseous materials (bone, ivory, and antler) to make a variety of well-designed and well-finished tools.

Unlike the rugged-boned, thick-muscled Neanderthals, the new people were relatively tall and lanky and comparatively thin boned. The type specimens were excavated from the floor of a rock shelter in the French Périgord named Cro-Magnon, after the old Périgordian *crô,* meaning "shelter" or "cave," and *magnon,* meaning "large" (as in a 1.5-liter magnum of wine). So these first European humans are called Cro-Magnon. Their artifact styles are referred to as Aurignacian, after another "type" site, near the village of Aurignac. Names in that area of France often have an *ac* ending, as in some familiar local namesakes: Cognac, Cadillac, and Cyrano de Bergerac. The suffix is short for *accum,* as in the necessary accumulation of years of a Gallo-Roman soldier's duty. After his long military stint, he was given title to a plot of land on which to build a farm, registered in his name. Some of these grew into hamlets, referred to with *ac* tacked on to the end, as in Guthrieac. Actually, my ancestors—the Guths, or Goths —were the enemy on the other side of the Rhine.

CRO-MAGNON ARTISTS

Objects of ornamentation such as beads, engravings, pendants, and ocher decorations are associated with these early Cro-Magnon. These objects were often made with a precision and an execution of form similar to work done by people today using those same media and technologies. In fact, it is difficult to justify a vision of historical progression in artistic competency or appreciation since those times 35,000 years ago and beyond, though styles and technologies of art have undergone many changes. One does not have to be patronizing to enjoy Aurignacian art—it includes images that are powerful for any time.

It is a little puzzling, though, why there are not more dated cases of cave incursions before, say, 32,000 years ago, when we know people had been in Europe for thousands of years prior to this. Could the reason be bears? Cave bear fossils are abundant during the warming epi-sode between about 60,000 and 30,000 years ago, but after that they decline markedly, so that they are quite rare after 25,000 years ago. Cave bears were enormous and would have been a fearsome menace lurking in the depths of caves, where they hibernated for six or so months of the year. For whatever reason, art of the first colonists is poorly represented in the deep-cave record.

Subsequent human remains are anatomically indistinguishable from these early, Aurignacian Cro-Magnon except in minor details. The subdivisions of later Paleolithic technologies in Europe and parts of eastern Asia are referred to as Gravettian, Solutrian, and Magdalenian, all based on stone artifact patterns, not on anatomical differences.

Most Paleolithic art has been found in Europe and eastern Asia, and there is a decidedly European bias to our conceptions of late Pleistocene peoples. Europe is a continental "peninsula" connected to Asia and Africa. Most hominid biological evolution occurred outside this peninsula, so questions about this region often focus on the "where and when" of arrivals.

WHERE IS PALEOLITHIC ART AND HOW MUCH IS THERE?

Our heritage of Paleolithic art is quite rich. Around 200 caves with art and about the same number of open-air sites that contain Paleolithic artworks have been discovered, and more are found every year. The number of carved and engraved antler, ivory, bone, soft-stone, and clay art objects is untabulated but runs into many thousands. The findspots span Eurasia from Spain to northeastern Russia. A few artworks from southern Africa, Australia, and India seem to be Pleistocene in age as well. It is certain that the number and geographic distribution will continue to expand with future finds. Nevertheless, our thousands of Paleolithic images constitute only a very fragmentary record.

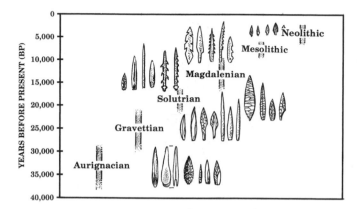

Principal Technological Zones for the Late Paleolithic in Western and Central Europe. Artifacts help date archaeological sites, but few items are preserved in the record. Stone and bone projectile points are the most durable and are one of the standards for assessing and identifying human cultures during the late Pleistocene. How they change (or do not change) with actual cultural changes, such as immigration, etc., is of course not always clear, and a change in artifacts does not always indicate a social change.

WHAT PROPORTION OF PALEOLITHIC PEOPLE WERE ARTISTS?

Not only is carving man's work, but it is something that every man of King and Diomede islands does. The majority of the carvers are real artists, creating lovely figurines and engraving ivory with imagination and talent. Almost the entire adult population, then, is made up of artists, in contrast to those cultures in which the role of artist is highly specialized as it was among the Kwakiutl of the Northwest Coast or, for that matter, in contemporary Europe and America.

Dorthy Jean Ray, *Artists of Tundra and Sea*

If you imagine that the Paleolithic art in caves was used in mystical rites, then you might believe that the art is the sporadic output of a small number of "gifted" shamans (Conkey 1983). In contrast, Sieveking (1979) envisioned many artists involved in Paleolithic art. Actually, there are data, mostly now in museum cabinets, that can help us determine the proportion of Paleolithic peoples who made visual art.

At least for men, it might be possible to answer the question by looking at individual weapons of violence, for example, spear-throwers (atlatls) and *bâtons,* also called point-straighteners or shaft-straighteners (I discuss these

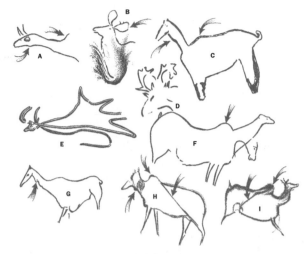

Some of the animals pictured in Paleolithic art became extinct at the end of the Pleistocene. These are Paleolithic images of giant deer, the shelk (genus *Megaloceros*). Most of these images are very amateurish, yet they still contain enough details to roughly identify this now-extinct species. The shelk had a large shoulder hump topped with a dark hackle tuft. Old bulls carried enormous palmate antlers. Some images also show a hyoid "Adams apple," as occurs in fallow deer today. This throat bulge seems to have been aligned at the point where the throat patch met the enlarged mane. A diagonal stripe apparently ran from the hump back toward the hock. **A**, Montgaudier, Fr. **B** and **H–I**, Chauvet, Fr. **C**, Lascaux, Fr. (Both **B** and **C** are young males.) **D**, Belcayre, Fr. **E**, Pech-Merle, Fr. (mature male). **F–G**, Roucadour, Fr.

tools in chapter 5). Cross-cultural comparisons show that among hundreds of groups that used point-straighteners and spear-throwers, these implements were used only by men and boys. Every man needed these critical tools. And ethnographic studies of small hunting bands also indicate that each man made his own weapons. We have no reason to think a Paleolithic band would have been different in this regard.

Each Paleolithic man and woman probably made most of his or her own tools, particularly those on which survival depended. If tools were broken when far afield, each user must have had the ability to replace them, because concentrating critical skills in a few hands would have left the whole group vulnerable.

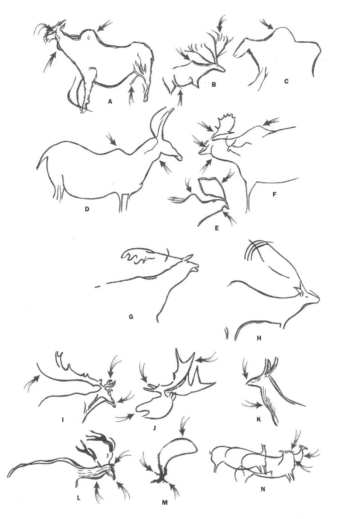

Additional images of shelk: **A**, Pair-non-Pair, Fr. **B–C** and **E**, Cosquer, Fr. **D**, Gargas, Fr. **F** and **M–N**, Cougnac, Fr. **G**, Buxú, Sp. **H**, La Hoz, Sp. **I**, Roucadour, Fr. **J**, Addaura, It. **K**, Altxerri, Sp. **L**, Abri Labattut, Fr.

son to think that taphonomic processes would favor decorated, rather than undecorated, weapons? Since most of the weapons we find are in fact broken and apparently discarded pieces, I will assume equal preservation. We also know that we can expect only a few of the millions of spear-throwers or point-straighteners to be preserved. These dynamics are reflected in archaeological sites. In fact, only a little over two hundred of these tools have been found and recorded.

So what do we find? What is the result of this test? Indeed, well over 90% of preserved Paleolithic spear-throwers and point-straighteners are decorated with engravings or carvings (Leroi-Gourhan 1964; Noiret 1990). Early ones are decorated as much as later ones. Clearly, this challenges the idea that only a few males made art. Rather, it suggests that most people matured as capable art makers. That agrees, for example, with what we know about Eskimos at the time of European contact. Each woman designed and sewed elegant and artistically conceived clothing for herself and her family. Each man normally made and decorated his own weapons. The decoration was not considered an afterthought but was an inherent part of the toolmaking. Although there was variation in artistic achievement, competent artistry was presumed to be an integral part of adult visual-kinesthetic skills.

UNITY IN DIVERSITY: PALEOLITHIC ART AS A PRODUCT OF MANY CULTURES

All these observations confirm the sense of unity in Paleolithic art. Distinctions exist, certainly, but they are more due to local peculiarities . . . than to a development with the passing of thousands of years, and even less to a progress in techniques and concepts.

Jean Clottes, in Roebroeks et al., *Hunters of the Golden Age*

Because most men hunted, they would likely have had a number of tools over a lifetime. Finding the fraction of decorated versus undecorated tools could help us answer the question posed by the title of this section. This is, of course, assuming no preservation biases. Is there any rea-

The fact that late Paleolithic art spans almost 30,000 years, and in Eurasia alone is found throughout many millions of square kilometers, no doubt means it was made by a succession of cultures. And remember, it is quite likely that the art making goes much farther back in time. Thus,

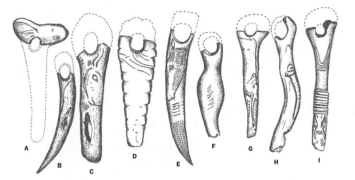

Along with osseous points, perforated *bâtons* (point-straighteners) are one of the more common decorated tools found in Pleistocene sites. Breakage patterns reveal how they were used. Breakage seems to almost always occur from stresses parallel with the shaft; snapping off the distal ends forms C-shaped fragments. Evidently, these tools occur in sites because they were broken and discarded. **A** and **G**, Laugerie-Basse, Fr. **B**, Massat, Fr. **C**, Enlène, Fr. **D**, Vogelherd, Ger. **E**–**F**, El Pendo, Sp. **H**, Arudy, Fr. **I**, Gourdan, Fr. **J**, My illustration of the likely cause of breakage.

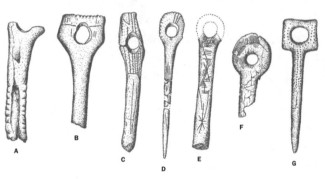

Although in this book I focus on the figurative images, there are some nonfigurative markings that are unique. One can see this tendency toward abstraction especially in the east, and it is also particularly apparent in late Glacial times, as I will discuss later. The following are all from Russia except **E**: **A**, Afontov Gora II. **B**, Kokorevo II. **C**, Eliseevici II. **D**, Kostenki IV. **E**, Mezhirich, Ukraine. **F**, Kostenki II. **G**, Sungir.

Paleolithic art does not represent a cultural unit, a homogeneous group of people. Its subjects and styles certainly are diverse, and the reasons for its execution were probably just as diverse. How then can we refer to it as a unit, and if so, what holds it together to allow us to talk about it as "Paleolithic art"?

One has only to handle the earliest sculptures from the shallow caves of southern Germany, squeeze through the entrance to the tight, gray-black, drippy cave of Chauvet, or walk through the great powder-dry halls of Rouffignac with its yellow flint nodules dappling the white lime walls to be humbled and surprised by the peculiar unity of Paleolithic art. The patterning of its subject matter begins to emerge: the predominance of large mammals forms the main theme, many bleeding and wounded; there are recurring fat women and isolated vulva triangles; and there are sprinklings of ocher handprints. Most of all, the artists' approaches have a literal tangibility to them. Is it possible to find some order and sense here? Who were these people and how did they live? How and where was all this art preserved?

SOUTHERN EUROPE AND ITS WEALTH OF PRESERVED PALEOLITHIC ART

Holding a distribution map of the world's known Paleolithic art at arm's length, we can see that the pattern of sites is not evenly distributed. Though hundreds of art pieces come from eastern Europe and Asia, most of the points on our map cluster in southern Europe. Southwestern Europe in particular was a special place during the last Glacial. Some authors have seen it as a human refuge (Jochim 1987) from the harshness of the treeless steppe farther north. While many large mammals apparently found the northern steppes quite habitable, human artifacts are not common. Humans needed the windbreaks and sheltered warmth of hills and trees and took refuge in the broken limestone hills of southern Europe.

A sampler of horse images, again, rendered with varying degrees of art experience (remember, although all of these are from the late Paleolithic, many were done thousands of years apart by folks of different cultures, regions, and languages): **A**, Parpalló, Sp. **B**, Kapovaia, Rus. **C**, Isturitz, Fr. **D** and **G**, Altamira, Sp. **E**, Saint-André-d'Allas, Fr. **F**, Rouffignac, Fr. **H**, Cosquer, Fr. **I**, La Mouthe, Fr. **J**, El Castillo, Sp. **K**, Bédeilhac, Fr. **L**, Experiment by A. Roussot.

Ibex done by drawers of varying ability: **A**, **J**, and **L**, Cosquer, Fr. **B** and **H–I**, Parpalló, Sp. **C** and **M**, Altamira, Sp. **D**, Bayol, Fr. **E**, Ardales, Sp. **F**, Nancy, Sp. **G** and **K**, La Vache, Fr. **N**, Hornos de la Peña, Sp.

From archaeological sites we can judge that humans were rare across northern Eurasia during full Glacial times (Otte 1990; Schneider 1990; Soffer and Gamble 1990). In fact, even much of central Europe was unoccupied (Hahn 1976; Kowalski and Kowalski 1979). Straus (1990) suggested this could have been due to the lack of large-mammal resources. But the rarity of humans may have

been due more directly to the windy, severely cold weather and its ramifications (Otte 1990; Powers 1990). Today, cloudless stable high-pressure systems drive winter temperatures down below −50°C every year in Siberia. And we know from the geological evidence that winter temperatures in Pleistocene northern Europe were more like those of Siberia than like those of northern Europe today. Facing such temperatures with only Pleistocene technologies would have made for tough tenting.

Farther south, people were sheltered from the full brunt of the cold, snow cover was low, and there were high levels of solar radiation in summer. These mixed rangelands consisted of diverse plant mosaics of grasslands, tundra, and beads of riparian woodlands and thickets. It was a physically diverse landscape, with mountains, uplands, flat tablelands, deeply dissected valleys, and broad lowland plains, all of which combined to provide diverse mixes of large-mammal resources (Mellars 1985).

The south was not exactly a paradise; winters were still cold, temperatures falling well below frost at night, with vestiges of frozen ground remaining through the summer. Cold fronts came roaring down from the continental ice to the north, making the skin blankets feel good and turning the crackling sparks of pine boughs into fine music. Even in southern Europe, there may have been very few people at the Glacial peak; for example, skeletons of Solutrians, the cultures who lived during the Glacial peak, are almost unknown (Straus 1990). Likewise, the small number of Solutrian sites suggests a brief occupation by only a few people (Rigaud and Simek 1990). Even with warm clothes, it apparently was a harsh time for a hairless equatorial primate afoot in the far north.

Not only was this refuge in southern Europe fortunate for Paleolithic people, but it was also fortunate for archaeologists. Underfoot were massive limestone deposits, intercalated with cave mouths and vast, overhung, south-facing ledges suitable for good campsites. These were protected from wind, rain, snow, and sleet. The alkaline environment of their terra rosa (red ocher) floors combined with the presence of some windblown silt favored preservation. The sites that are preserved seem to suggest an almost continuous occupation with stratigraphic complexity—real archaeological wealth (Rigaud and Simek 1990).

Many regions across Eurasia have Paleolithic art. The finds from some areas, such as Spanish Cantabria, the northern valleys of the Pyrenees, and the plains of the Ukraine, are remarkable, but no region quite competes with the Périgord, a small *département* in southwestern France. White (1985) described it well in pointing out that it is a "privileged" location, largely immune to the full direct effects of glaciation and changing sea levels. And although in this book I talk about Paleolithic art from many other places, our knowledge of these times would be rather impoverished if it were not for the wealth of art from this particular region. Whatever taphonomic quirk of fate favored this region in the Pleistocene, we must certainly be thankful for it.

Art Forms and Media

BURINS: CUTTING EDGE OF LATE PALEOLITHIC TECHNOLOGY

Osseous tools are a major marker of the first occurrence of *Homo sapiens* in the late Paleolithic. Neanderthals had utilized osseous materials but mainly with a flaking technique, similar to that used on flint. These new humans scraped, ground, and polished osseous tools into shape. Burins, specially shaped stone tools for bone working, appear with these osseous tools. This osseous technology accompanies a breakthrough in hunting technology.

Antler blanks for osseous points were removed from the hard cortex of reindeer antlers by using burins as "milling" tools. These rough blanks could then be scraped into slender, sharp points, called "sagaies." Attached to wooden shafts they made light spears or darts that could travel at high velocities and for comparatively long dis-

Paleolithic Artifacts as Refuse Although osseous materials do not preserve as well as stone, much material in archaeological sites is osseous, including camp refuse such as broken or discarded tools and art objects. Earlier interpretations treated these broken forms as though all had been intentionally and systematically desecrated, leaving nothing intact for posterity, until the archaeologists Capitan and Bouyssonie (1924) pointed out that what we find at campsites is the result of a refuse bias. As long as something is useful it seldom finds its way into the hearth or dirt. It is only the learning mistakes and worn-out or broken pieces that are tossed away, and it is this debitage that is most likely to be preserved. This principle is well understood by most students of archaeology today, but this has not always been the case. Another common phenomenon is that engraved plaquettes, stones, and bone tools are often used for other than their original purpose (Clottes 1989): as flagstones on floors or hearths or as chopping blocks, cutting boards, lamps, and so on. In the same way, flint tools often undergo several roles before being exhausted and discarded. So while the cave walls may be as people left them upon completion of the drawing (and often even they seem to have been redrawn and modified in later visits), the portable art found in sunlit camps is mostly refuse.

tances (especially when propelled with a spear-thrower, or atlatl). The patience, skill, and technology developed in osseous point manufacture were directly transferable to osseous sculpting and limestone carving. *Homo sapiens* brought this ability to contour bone when they arrived in Europe and eastern Asia around 40,000 years ago.

Osseous materials have unique properties. Bone, antler, and ivory are composites of rocklike apatite crystals of calcium phosphate in a matrix of organic collagen fibers. The result of this combination is a material harder and more durable than wood and yet lighter and less subject to breakage than stone. You can imagine this material being

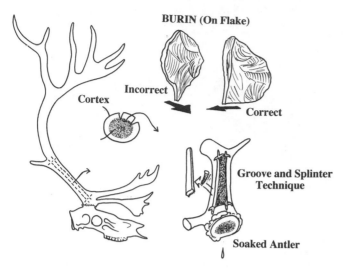

The burin was used to work osseous materials, particularly in splintering antlers for remodeling as a projectile point.

something like fiberglass, another composite, in which the combination of a brittle resin and resilient glass fibers yields new qualities. Working with osseous materials is easy once you know the techniques, such as soaking them in water for a day prior to working, and have the right burins and scrapers (e.g., Guthrie 1983). The best osseous materials of all seem to be reindeer antler and mammoth ivory—at least these are the materials of late Paleolithic choice, judging from their abundance in archaeological sites.

Scraping can be precisely controlled, unlike the percussion blows needed for stone working. This technique could also have been applied to wood, and undoubtedly was, but the advantage osseous materials have over wood is that they effectively have no grain, being a comparatively homogeneous medium. The implications for art making are obvious.

SIMPLE ART MATERIALS

What are the media of Paleolithic art? There are many ways to make images, and carving ivory or antler is among the most laborious. The most common visual-art materi-als and perhaps the first art media are probably soft, vertical loess banks, soft mud or sand, or even *montmilch,* a soft slurry of calcite that sometimes coats wet limestone surfaces. These soft sediments can be inscribed with a finger or stick. Often in caves one finds squiggles in the slick mud, representing fingertip "spaghetti" marks (as in children's finger painting today) or simple finger swipes. In fact, we have evidence of all these techniques preserved from Paleolithic art, and of course in various forms they are still used today.

Clay can also be molded into three-dimensional images. Such sculptures in fired and unfired clay have been preserved from Paleolithic times.

One of the easiest methods of making marks was to use charcoal sticks, common in every hearth. When these charred ends are dragged across white limestone, a striking jet-black line is laid down. Usually, charcoal marks are not very durable, but inside caves they stand a chance of being preserved and indeed are a common form of Paleolithic art.

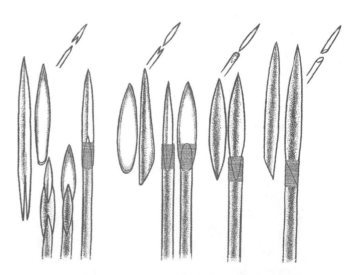

Antler, bone, and ivory were favorite materials for projectile points in the late Paleolithic. These points vary in form through time and over space; some of that variation is pictured here.

Fingertips were dipped in pigment and trailed along walls, leaving designs such as that shown here from Niaux, Fr. In other caves fingertips were drawn through *montmilch* (soft slurry of calcite on walls) or sheets of mud coating vertical surfaces. Such techniques were not used for technically challenging works but, as we know from our finger-painting days, are a lot of fun. Cave researchers refer to these as "macaronis" or "spaghetti tracks."

ENGRAVED STONE, BONE, ANTLER, AND IVORY

Another technique for making art is engraving: dragging a sharp stone across a hard substance such as stone, bone, antler, or ivory. Much more Paleolithic art of this type is preserved than any other class of images. Paleolithic bas-reliefs have also been found in caves. Sharp stones had been a part of human prehistory for millions of years, and they were always handy, so all it took was using them on dense materials. Engravings will play a central role in this book.

PIGMENTS: TECHNICOLOR
IN THE LATE PALEOLITHIC

The southern fringes of the Mammoth Steppe—where most Paleolithic art caves occur—are regions rich in deposits of earth pigments: yellow-orange-red iron oxides, called "ocher"; blue-black manganese oxide; and occasional deposits of white kaolin clay. Before synthetic pigments were made, red ochers from these regions were exported in large quantities to paint American barns barn-red. Because earth pigments are mineral oxides, they are not subject to microbial decomposition. They occur in consolidated formations a little less dense than chalk. But unlike chalk or charcoal, ocher is much more tenacious and does not wash off easily. Results are quick and colorful and not as ephemeral as lines in sand or mud. By mixing these pigments with water, saliva, blood, or other binders, one can paint refined lines, create graded shading, or even spray paint.

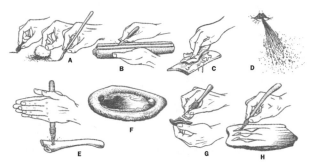

Paleolithic art and artifacts let us reconstruct some of the artists' tools, which were used in varying combinations: **A**, Direct application of pigment from crayon, puff applicator, or brush. **B**, Carving burin. **C**, Polishing with grit. **D**, Spitting chewed minerals. **E**, Borers-drills. **F**, Ground and mixed pigment in palette. **G**, Scraper. **H**, Graver. There were probably many more.

Much of the ocher on cave walls was applied by chewing and spitting; a fine, dry spray works best, producing a fine stipple. Sharp edges can be made by using the edge of the hand to prevent the spray from reaching the surface. Sometimes the palm was smeared with ocher and patted on the wall. Interiors of images were often filled in with the spit-spray technique, but this does not mean that the animal was literally spotted. The animal on the left is from Chauvet; the bison in the center is from Marsoulas, both in France. On the right I show an analogous example of this "stippling" of an ostrich image on stone, but in this case made with a hammer by a Bushman sometime in the late Holocene at Reit Pan, R.S.A.

Judging from the variety of mineral oxides on the walls of caves like Lascaux, people knew where they could find earth pigments. The deepest black came from manganese dioxide. Blue-black-gray manganese is common around limestone. It is one of the major elements that transforms limestone diagenetically into dolomite. Manganese is laid down in thin beds of dark seams in many limestone deposits. As the limestone leaches away, the manganese oxide remains as dark deposits.

Couraud and Laming-Emperaire (1984) experimented with a variety of liquid binders for mineral pigments and found that oils did not adhere well to moist cave walls; rather, water was the best binder. Ballet et al. (1979) found that calcium phosphate from bone was also used both for mixing into other pigments and for white. The calcium phosphate had to be from campfires because it had to be heated to 1000°C before it could be used. Kaolin clay and the calcite scrapings from bone were sometimes used for white (Couraud and Laming-Emperaire 1979) or perhaps to mix with other pigments to change their color. Because we purchase our art pigments today, making paints seems complicated, but making simple paints is not an elaborate process.

The organic pigments of roots, berries, bark, and so on were probably also used by Paleolithic peoples, but we do not have many materials that may have been organically dyed, such as leather clothing. What is critical to understand is that the subjects and style of images in these different media have great integrity (Airvaux 2001).

Fortunately, minute fractions of charcoal pigment or fat binder from the art on cave walls are datable by modern radiocarbon techniques (for reviews: Clottes 1997a; Watchman 1997; Davidson 1997). The dates we get generally occur in narrow clusters. Some clusters from different paintings in the same cave mark a single entry or a few entries over a short time. In other words, the radiocarbon dates do not suggest marks made by hundreds of visits to these caves. This fact will figure importantly in our later discussion.

▲▼▲

In sum, the materials and methods of preserved Paleolithic art are diverse, including three-dimensional sculptures in clay (some of it fired); portable carved figures in materials such as ivory; stone bas-reliefs; engraved line drawings; drawings using charcoal sticks, pastels from ocher crayons, or mixed paints; and jewelry and other body adornments. We can be certain, however, that this preserved art is in fact an incomplete subset of Paleolithic media, which likely included furs, leathers, lace, braiding, weaving, cosmetics, fiber and wood utensils, and more—but those pages have been torn out by the ravages of time.

The Geology of Art Preservation

DEATH IN THE AGE OF DINOSAURS
GAVE LIFE TO ICE AGE ART

Much of the preservation of Paleolithic art is connected with the ancient geology of Europe. Thick limestone deposits that formed in the Cretaceous (about 80 million years ago) lie across the continent in row after irregular row. This concentration of limestone created a rich Pleistocene substrate for soils, vegetation, and the large mammals that were to become the essence of the art, and it also played an important role in archaeological preservation.

The story behind this is rather incredible. The African Plate, sliding northward at a fast paramecium's pace from Gondwanaland, collided with the European Plate. Africa has been rooting into Europe ever since. This caused the crust of Europe to buckle in a series of irregular mountain ranges. At the same time the mid-Atlantic rift opened and separated Europe from North America. The sea, 300 meters higher than that of today, swept in and flooded Europe. The new ocean flowed into the valleys, creating a lattice of tropical fjordlike seas, with colorful pterodactyls wheeling overhead. Over time, dead marine organisms sinking to the bottom created deep limestone deposits.

Around 30 million years ago, as a result of other global changes, the sea level dropped, draining the shallow valleys of Europe and exposing the limestone. Rivers gradually incised and downcut these thick valley deposits. Flowing groundwater leached great spongelike cave systems

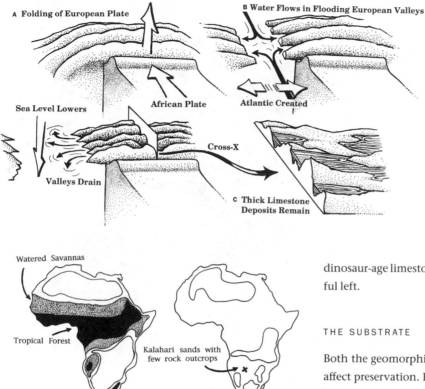

A. Folding of European Plate

B Water Flows in Flooding European Valleys

Sea Level Lowers

African Plate

Atlantic Created

Valleys Drain

Cross-X

C Thick Limestone
Deposits Remain

The African Plate grinding into the European Plate (**A**) has resulted in the east-west mountain belts. As Europe separated from the American Plate, the newly formed Atlantic Ocean flowed into the European valleys (**B**). The warm sea fingers formed deep limestone deposits. With later uplift this limestone was exposed in irregular arcs across Europe (**C**). This limestone was critical in the formation of caves and the alkaline soil conditions that allowed a high degree of preservation of Paleolithic archaeological materials (**D**).

Watered Savannas

Tropical Forest

Kalahari sands with few rock outcrops

Overall Vegetation Patterns

Rock Art Distribution

Not only did substrate and climate influence Paleolithic art, but they also influenced the distribution of later rock art. *Left,* the African closed-canopy tropical forests (black) and woodlands (stipple) have little rock art. *Right,* rock art centers are mainly found under more arid conditions, circled. But aridity alone is insufficient; you can't have preserved rock art without the right kinds of rocks. The places in the Kalahari Desert without much rock art are sandy areas. There is a climatic-ecological-substrate bias to where prehistoric rock art occurs.

dinosaur-age limestone, there would be only a small handful left.

THE SUBSTRATE

Both the geomorphic nature of the bedrock and latitude affect preservation. Bednarik (1986, 1995) has noted that known Eurasian centers of Paleolithic art are in areas where optimum geomorphic preservation of cave art was possible. Geomorphic factors often seem to have as much explanatory power as cultural differences as to where ancient art is found. For example, around 20,000 years ago, during the last Glacial peak, many caves located down in the steep-walled valleys, such as Niaux and others in the Pyrenees, were overridden by ice and back-flushed with runoff water, removing earlier cave art and artifacts if they did in fact exist. Also, the increased frost spalling (exfoliation) of stone was a major destructive agent in regions far removed from actual glaciation.

Stream banks, convenient to freshwater, are a good place in which to make camp, and one might expect to find Paleolithic art sites along waterways. But floods and redeposition forces tend to destroy most streamside sites. Likewise, it is difficult to know where to search for sites

beneath the surface. On the river bluffs the softer beds eroded more quickly, creating cliff overhangs that were later to be Paleolithic camps—waterproof, warm parabolas facing the winter sun.

The thick limestone was critical in preservation. If we subtracted from all Paleolithic art those specimens that, in some way or other, were preserved as a result of this

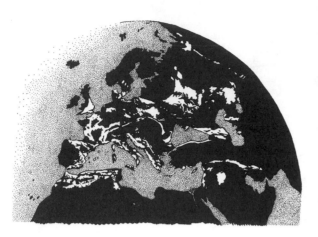

Limestone deposits are portrayed in light bands.

across broad plains. In limestone karst country this search is easier. One looks in the mouths of caves and in large, overhung shelters, which the French call *abri.* In the Périgord there are as many as twenty such ancient sites in a stretch of 10 kilometers of river bluff. Where art is preserved and where it is findable are to a great extent geological problems, and we should take care not to equate art preservation with art production.

CAVES

Paleontologists know that limestone caves are special preservational environments and prime fossil sites. Sometimes caverns are opened to the ground surface above by a collapsed cave ceiling or by deep-probing tree roots, which create vertical pipes that may eventually expand into natural pit traps. The bottoms of such holes are littered with the carcasses of unlucky animals. Other kinds of caves have accessible openings in the sides of hills. Some carnivores like to use such caves seasonally as dens and regularly bring back carcass parts for pups or cubs, creating a bone litter. Pleistocene lions and hyenas seldom used caves, but our terms "cave lions" and "cave hyenas" reflect the earlier misunderstanding that these animals were cave dwelling. The Latin word for "cave," *spelaeus,* became part of the specie's technical name for

No Such Thing as Cavemen There is no evidence that Pleistocene people commonly lived in caves—no evidence at all of an ancient troglodyte race. Most camps that have been preserved were tucked back under rock abris. Although some of these abris are really the mouths of deep caves, there is little evidence that people routinely used or even ventured into the depths and no evidence that they lived back there. For example, in the French cave of La Vache, situated in a valley high in the Pyrenees, people used a side chamber that had a crack of daylight reflected back into it, a shelter away from mountain weather. But there is no evidence of living floors situated well back beyond sun-lit parts of Pleistocene caves. We can take this rarity of deep-cave artifacts literally because caves preserve things so well that evidence is likely to have been saved. We must assume that Paleolithic people lived mainly in open-air camps, but these rarely preserve well.

Some of the misunderstanding about "cavemen" is a nomenclature problem. The meaning of the word "cave" in English includes a shallow pocket or cavity in stone, what the French would refer to as an *abri.* The word *cave* in French means "cellar," a cool place under the house (where you keep the wine and apples). *Grotte* is their word for "cave," and it implies a more elaborate tunnel or cavern with chambers.

these lions, bears, and hyenas. A similar bias is reflected in the term "cavemen."

Caves are a good place for bones to be preserved because caves are usually in limestone, an alkaline environment of mainly calcium carbonate ($CaCO_3$) ultimately derived from shells and skeletons of marine invertebrates. These are different in composition from vertebrate bones, whose chief mineral is calcium phosphate ($CaPO_4$). Calcium carbonate dissolves in a weaker acid solution than calcium phosphate, so the cave floor dissolves before the mammal bones. The interesting reason behind this difference in bone composition is probably that the increased muscle activity of very early vertebrates produced more

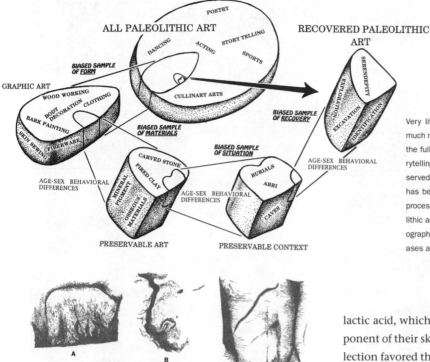

ALL PALEOLITHIC ART

RECOVERED PALEOLITHIC ART

POETRY
DANCING ACTING STORY TELLING
SPORTS
CULLINARY ARTS

BIASED SAMPLE OF FORM

GRAPHIC ART
WOOD WORKING
BODY DECORATION CLOTHING
BARK PAINTING
SKIN SEWING FIBERWARE

BIASED SAMPLE OF MATERIALS

BIASED SAMPLE OF RECOVERY

SERENDIPITY
COLLYBIOLVKE
EXCAVATION
IDENTIFICATION

BIASED SAMPLE OF SITUATION

CARVED STONE
MINERAL PIGMENT FIRED CLAY
OSSEOUS MATERIALS

AGE-SEX BEHAVIORAL DIFFERENCES

AGE-SEX BEHAVIORAL DIFFERENCES

BURIALS
ABRI
CAVES

AGE-SEX BEHAVIORAL DIFFERENCES

PRESERVABLE ART

PRESERVABLE CONTEXT

Very little of the past is preserved. Paleolithic art included much more than what we know of it today. We need to imagine the full array of Paleolithic art—dancing, music, clothing, storytelling, and so on—hardly any traces of which were preserved. And of the art that was preserved, it is likely that little has been discovered. That is why understanding taphonomic processes is crucial for interpreting and appreciating Paleolithic art. We must be alert to the preservational biases of geography, materials, subjects, and time periods, and even biases as to the age and sex of the artists.

One is struck by the number of Paleolithic images in caves that were obviously suggested by natural rock forms. A, Bear, Tibiran, Fr. B, Bison, Mas d'Azil, Fr. C, Mammoth, Pech-Merle, Fr. D, Horse, Rouffignac, Fr. E, Bison, Mas d'Azil, Fr. F, Rhino, Iain, Sp. G, Mammoth, Trois Frères, Fr.

Paleolithic images, particularly from deep in cave interiors, often are unfinished or have multiple overlapping lines. They tend to lack detail and generally aren't very well done. These are all from one Spanish cave, Altxerri; although in this cave there are other works that are quite well done.

lactic acid, which tended to dissolve the carbonate component of their skeletons. So, among early vertebrates, selection favored those with a higher fraction of phosphate than carbonate in their skeletons.

Art inside caves was simply much more likely to be preserved than art outside. Thus, the term "cave art" is analogous to "cavemen" or "cave lions"—which more accurately describe the taphonomic bias of preservation in caves than an actual life history. I suspect that had early researchers of cave art better understood this, they would not have sought elaborate scenarios to explain why Paleolithic peoples placed their art back in these remote spots. It is as if early paleontologists had attempted to explain bone concentrations in caves by suggesting that before cave bears died they made a mysterious migration into caves, like the myth of elephant graveyards. We can safely say that cave art is a small sliver of the Paleolithic art that existed and was preserved only because of its protected location.

For most people, wild uncharted caves are rather scary and potentially dangerous. It is true that because of this risk spelunkers find caves exciting. But archaeological evidence suggests that most early peoples steered clear of caves (I call this Sieveking's Law). One can understand such apprehension even today, when there are no hibernating cave bears . . . or goblins.

Sieveking's Law:
Paleolithic People Hardly Used Deep Caves

"Deep caves show rapid decoration and few signs of use. Here there are few footprints, no rubbish or hearths" (Sieveking 1986, 66). If we were to take all of our evidence about where Paleolithic people spent their time and round those data to the first approximation, we would say that no Paleolithic people went back into deep caves. The rare exceptions, the few individuals who did explore cave depths and create preservable art there, were a minuscule fraction of the millions of late Paleolithic people. According to Ann Sieveking, "We know virtually nothing about the use of deep caves, except that use hardly appears to have been made of them at all" (1979, 102). Preservation is generally so good in caves that even visits by 1% of the Pleistocene people every year would have resulted in considerable lampblack (soot from the burning of carbonaceous materials) deposits over all the ceilings and walls, but such blackening is not found. Regular use would have left worn trails and a variety of litter remnants, but these are also extremely rare (Sieveking 1979, 1991).

Yet some scholars continue to propose that cave art was the result of regular vision quests (Pfeiffer 1982; Lewis-Williams 1997, 2002). Such regular custom, however, simply does not agree with the actual cave evidence. It is much more coherent to assume that taphonomic processes preserve almost no art outside caves and to consider art found within caves must represent the raveling-thread edge of the far more extensive fabric of Paleolithic art that existed outside cave environments. From the evidence that cave visits were rare and from rough population esti-

Even in regions where Paleolithic art is concentrated, few caves have art. Of the caves that do have art, some have very little. Ground plans of seven typical caves (all in Spain) show the limited art locations: A, Cobrantes; B, Patatal; C, Cualventí; D, Sotarriza; E, Giboso; F, Juyo; G, Meaza. There are many caves like these in Europe.

mates, we can say that only one Paleolithic person in more than a thousand ever saw the inside of deep caves or made preservable art there. The image of a shaman taking the initiates into deep caves for secret rites, generation after generation, is bogus. Any further accounting of cave art must be reconciled with Sieveking's Law.

Also supporting Sieveking's Law is the fact that in most caves much, if not all, of the art shows only the styles of one or a few individuals, likely made either during one entry or possibly several entries (Sahly 1963; Lorblanchet 1980, 2001; Pales and St.-Péreuse 1981; Apellaniz 1984; Bahn and Vertut 1988). Individual artists inherently draw with a particular signature, an individual feel, and one can discern this at many Paleolithic localities. Early researchers interpreted this to mean that a few great artists did the work while the crowd stood back in awe. But we simply have no evidence of such a crowd, be they onlookers or artists, in the deep Paleolithic caves.

One spring I was crawling back into a tight cave in the Tolovana Limestone that arcs across Minto Flats near my home in Fairbanks, Alaska, exploring for old sites. I was unarmed, assuming all the hibernating bears had emerged a month earlier, only to flick the beam of my flashlight onto a large pile of shiny black fur curled up sound asleep 3 meters away. I backed out slowly and quietly, glad this bear was not a light sleeper. While we can crawl into a cave with some degree of assurance that our battery torch will stay lit, in the Pleistocene a burning twig or bit of fat had a limited life span and was easily extinguished in a mishap. Still, wild caves do have a magnetic attraction to

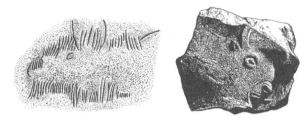

Technically more demanding and time-consuming works are seldom located in deep caves. They are usually found in shelters or sunlit parts of caves. The bison to the left was found deep in Gargas Cave, while the one on the right was more or less in direct sunlight in Angles-sur-l'Anglin, both in Fr.

some people, and why that should be is an interesting question.

A cave environment is also preservationally unique in that moisture and temperature are fairly constant, with only slight seasonal or annual changes. Paleolithic art occurs in caves where the temperature never drops below freezing. This moderation of temperature is critical because it is the expansion of water during freezing that ultimately causes stone to shatter and exfoliate. Art can also be lost, even in deep caves, from calcite formation. The slow movement of limy water can leave a transparent film of redeposited calcite over a Paleolithic image, sometimes even thickly enough to completely obscure the artwork.

There are few scavengers and few decomposers in caves. And there are no physical forces like abrasive stream tumbling or glacial erosion. Without light, all systems of nutrient cycling are constrained. And, remember, ultraviolet light is a quiet but powerful degrading force outside caves, tearing apart most chemicals by its daily bombardment. There are few extremes in caves, except darkness. That is why caves can retain such sharp imprints made by people tens of thousands of years ago—their fingerprints and footprints, traces of their torches and crayons, and artistic reflections of their mental images. The record of certain behavior is there too: for example, the vandalism of breaking off beautiful stalactite spires and of smearing over colorful art. Even hints of romance remain, as in the male and female handprints placed side by side. Caves are extraordinary places.

Not all Paleolithic art is found deep in caves. It also occurs in abri shelters and in open-air sites—for example, as engravings and carvings on osseous weapons, as fired-clay figurines, and images engraved on slate plaquettes. Clottes (1997b) calculated that, in France, late Paleolithic sites around the sun-lit cave mouths and abris have almost as much preserved art as the deep caves, 42.5% for the former and 57.5% for the latter. Though similar in many ways, the preservation of art outside caves has its own set of biases; that art too is not a random slice of all Paleolithic art.

ART IN THE LIGHT AND IN THE DARK

Clottes (1997b) comments that virtually all Paleolithic art preserved outside caves occurs at campsites, mostly as fragmented trash. This art was made in the midst of camp life—only an arm's length away from mothers nursing, guys flint knapping, and kids playing. It was not art made for and confined to a sacred site. Nothing suggests that the images from these campsites were specifically consecrated or sanctified. Likewise, the hundreds of engraved stone plaquettes were in fact preserved because they were incorporated as flagstones in the camp floor or just discarded in the dirt at the sites where they occur (Andernach, Gönnersdorf, Lortet, La Marche, Gourdan, Isturitz, Limeuil, Enval, Enlène, Mas d'Azil, and others). Hundreds of engraved bone fragments are found in thick camp-floor deposits just inside the cave entrances of sites such as La Vache and Mas d'Azil. Several of these abri sites have furnished spectacular contributions to Paleolithic art studies; those from La Marche are especially noteworthy (Pales 1976; Pales and St.-Péreuse 1969, 1976, 1981, 1989), and those from Gönnersdorf are also spectacular (Bosinski 1981). The latter two sites will figure prominently throughout this book.

Though the art in deep caves and that preserved in sun-lit areas is very similar in subject matter (for example, the same species of large mammals and images of naked women), we can note a few differences (Clottes 1997a). Images from deeper caves often show animals with arrows

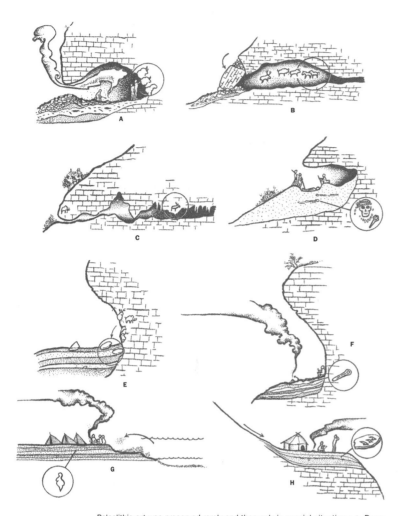

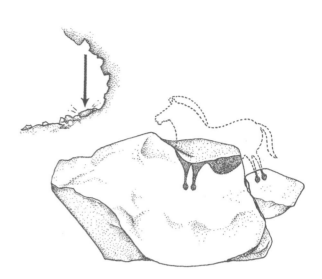

Sometimes the painted rocks outside caves preserve by falling facedown into the right kind of sediments. This piece fell from Abri Blanchard, Fr., preserving only part of the legs and abdomen of what seems to be a wild horse, judging by the monodactyl hoof. This and similar finds are evidence that exposed limestone surfaces everywhere, not just in caves, were painted and engraved.

Paleolithic art was preserved rarely and then only in special situations: **A**, Deep shelters that fill with sediment. **B**, Shallow caves where rockfalls have closed the entrances. **C**, Deep in caves beyond where the freeze-thaw cycle has effect. **D**, Burials in a mildly alkaline sediment. **E**, Rock carvings that break off, drop facedown, and become buried. **F**, Preservable materials dropped into shelter sediments. **G**, Preservable materials left where they were covered by alkaline overbank alluvium. **H**, Durable materials covered by downslope sediment movement.

sticking in them and blood coming from wounds or mouths and nostrils, while the portrayal of arrow hits is rare on the deep-relief engravings outside the caves. Laming-Emperaire (1962) has pointed out that well-drawn human faces are found mainly in sun-lit situations. Our most famous and finest Paleolithic wall art was made in the sun-lit cave entrances or under abris, for example,

in the wide walkways into Lascaux and Altamira. These differences may have little symbolic significance. It could be that they are simply the outcome of circumstances, deep-cave art being done more quickly by younger people with wilder, graffiti-prone imaginations. In contrast, most deeply incised reliefs outside caves were probably done by more mature and more experienced artists.

Over the millennia, as limestone around a cave entrance or abri erodes, it leaves earlier camp deposits out in front of the retreating, cliff-collapse debris. Occasionally, rocks spall off in large chunks, known as *éboulis*. When these are large enough and lucky enough to be well preserved, it is possible to piece together the rock wall surfaces of a much earlier period. Angles-sur-l'Anglin in France is a spectacular example. Images carved in high relief spalled off in large blocks and fell face-first into sediments that eventually covered and preserved them. The deep-relief carvings are badly weathered, but the large images are discernible. In a few instances ocher-colored stone fragments fallen from walls or ceilings have been

The Special Preservation of Lascaux

The main hall of Lascaux is spectacularly beautiful with its large-scale images of multicolored animals. While Lascaux is a deep cave now, in the late Paleolithic the "mouth" of Lascaux Cave was huge and sloped downward and inward at a shallower angle. The dense array of art was just inside, with sun reflecting back into the main chamber, the Hall of Bulls (Leroi-Gourhan 1982b). Most of the images in this part of Lascaux were made by very accomplished artists. One image, however, may have been made by a much less experienced artist. The animal portrayed has been called an Asiatic chiru, *Pantholops hodgsoni*. I'll discuss this enigmatic image in the next chapter.

The lower walls of this part of Lascaux had too rough a surface for artwork, so poles were dragged in as scaffolding to reach the brilliant white and smooth surface of the upper walls and ceiling (imprints of these remained at the time of discovery in 1940). The wide entrance hall at Lascaux made other passages more accessible. Farther back in the cave, where lamps were used, one finds hundreds of engravings.

The lack of smoke stains on the ceiling, lack of deep refuse, and other clues indicate that, even with its large mouth, the cave was used for only a short time by a limited number of people (Sieveking 1986). The sediments at the cave entrance contain normal camp litter of food scraps and bone projectile points, rough limestone lamps (130 of them), rock palettes, mineral pigments, and many flint scriber tools (Leroi-Gourhan et al. 1979).

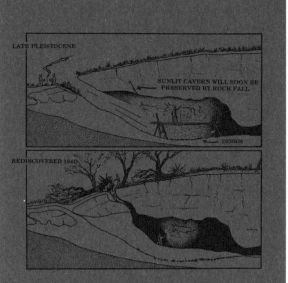

The geology of Lascaux Cave in the Périgord, Fr. A rockfall in the late Pleistocene opened up the cave, and for a short time it was used by Paleolithic people. Another rockfall closed the cave until 1940, when a tree fell in a storm and uncovered another entrance. The intensive use of the Hall of Bulls seems to be best explained by postulating that it was a sunlit chamber near the late Pleistocene entrance. The second rockfall sealed the cave, and the lack of temperature fluctuations preserved the once-sunlit wall art near the ground surface that otherwise would have been destroyed by frost-plucking of rock.

Actually, the open "mouth" may have been available only during a brief window about 17,000 years ago. Then the overhanging stone entrance collapsed (Leroi-Gourhan et al. 1979), sealing the cave and preserving the artwork. After some 17,000 years, an up-rooted tree tore loose a chunk of covering soil, and in 1940, Lascaux was discovered by adventuring teen-age boys.

found buried in abri sediments. All this is evidence that these were not secret sites or sights.

CAVE TAPHONOMY AND THE ORIGINS OF THE MAGICO-RELIGIOUS PARADIGM

Note the apparent paradox of using secrecy and darkness to impart information. If the objective was teaching, doing it out in the open where all could attend and share would seem to make more sense.

John E. Pfeiffer, *The Creative Explosion*

The discovery of so much Paleolithic art back in deep caves contributed to interpretations of magic or religious function. If indeed all the rock art was located back in these inhospitable, virtually inaccessible recesses, one could only conclude that the artists must have had a special reason to make this considerable effort just to draw and that cave art was deliberately hidden. But such conclusions can be drawn only by ignoring three features: (1) wall paintings made in cave environments are more

Paleolithic works by artists still figuring out visual imagery: **A–B**, Gargas, Fr. **C** and **E**, Pech-Merle, Fr. **D**, Gönnersdorf, Ger. **F**, Laraux, Fr. **G–H**, La Baume Latrone, Fr.

likely to survive than such art exposed to the elements, (2) there is strong evidence that all the deep caves were barely used, and (3) many abri and open-air sites contain abundant Paleolithic art—despite their greater vulnerability to the elements.

Failing to understand these points unavoidably leads one to imagine ideas such as shamans making seasonal ceremonial trips into cave recesses for ritual purposes. That misunderstanding makes *purpose* mandatory, giving credence to the magico-religious paradigm. Simultaneously, this mistake excludes more casual, everyday motivations from consideration.

The statement that all cave art could not have been casual art because "they would have carried out their artistic works in places where they could at least see their results" (Ucko and Rosenfeld 1967, 166) begs the question, for they indeed must have done most of their drawing and painting out in the light. Making art in caves was the exception. In fact, there is an easy test of the proposition that the very existence of images in places where they cannot easily be seen indicates some religious quest. If that were so, later cave explorers in both historic and modern times would not have made marks where they cannot easily be seen. Yet we know that historic and modern cave explorers have left behind too much casual litter and have scribbled drawings and their names and initials over Pleis-

tocene images on the walls—the practice is one of the very forces that has threatened the conservation of Paleolithic cave art!

OPEN-AIR SITES

The fantastic German Magdalenian open-air sites of Gönnersdorf and Andernach lie on either side of the Rhine at a narrow constriction as the river drains from the Neuweid Basin. They contain many slabs of slate (from nearby outcrops), along with a rich assortment of tools and the bones of thousands of birds and mammals. The sites are on side slopes of the Rhine terrace, located well above the present river. They appear to have been buried, and thus preserved, by the downslope wash of sediments. The sites were further preserved by a thick bed of pumice-tephra from a nearby volcano that erupted at the very end of the Pleistocene.

During the Gönnersdorf excavation, a researcher noticed that many slate slabs (plaquettes) were incised with images of people and other animals—in a manner similar to images found in Magdalenian sites in France, Italy, and Spain. Careful examination showed that many other slabs at the sites also contained engravings. These slates were evidently discarded and inadvertently buried during the camp's occupation or soon afterward. Engraved stone plaquettes have been found in large numbers at a handful of Pleistocene sites, for example, in round numbers, 1500 at La Marche, 1100 at Enlène, 1000 at Labastide, 6000 at Parpalló, and hundreds at Gönnersdorf (Bosinski 1981; Davidson 1986). Hundreds of small fired-clay figurines of women and large mammals (mainly carnivores) from campsites in Moravia also underline the fact that people worked in a variety of media in open-air camps (Soffer 1987).

RUPESTRAL ART

Up until a few years ago, it was assumed that no Paleolithic art survived on exposed stone faces in the open. This kind of art is referred to as "rupestral art." However, in Val

Comonica, a valley on the south face of the Italian Alps, thousands of images drawn or hammered into a very dense stone were found whose dates span much of the Holocene and probably reach back to the latest Pleistocene (moose are portrayed, which are not found in post–Pleistocene sediments). From this evidence one might expect to find Pleistocene rupestral works at other European sites. In fact, many drawings in Paleolithic style and, perhaps, of Paleolithic species (e.g., the extinct shelk, *Megaloceros*) exist at open-air sites, such as Siega Verde and Mazouco (Balbín-Behrmann, Alcolea-González, and Santonja Gómez 1996), Coa Valley (Zilhão 1996), and Domingo García. These sites are located in arid regions of Spain and Portugal where preservation is high. Dating rupestral art is always problematic, but these images seem to be late Paleolithic in age. Fortunately, the images are incised into very hard stone. Stone type is highly relevant, as susceptibility to erosion and exfoliation depends on the nature of the rock. Also, these images occur in an area of Iberia that has unusually equable weather, with low rainfall and no extremely cold weather.

Biological Biases in Preservation

Of the gigatrillions of creatures that have lived, only a scant few have left a trace. The carcasses of land animals are usually dismembered by scavengers and soon weather to basic molecular components. If not covered quickly, even hard bones will begin to flake apart and disappear in a matter of years, leaving no sign of that individual's existence. Most fossils are not formed directly from a part of the animal itself but secondarily record traces of its actions: tracks, beaver gnawings, burrows, reefs, eggshells, casts, regurgitated pellets, feces (coprolites), gizzard stones, and so on. Paleolithic art can be thought of as such a "trace fossil."

SPECIES DISTORTIONS IN TAPHONOMY

Taphonomic processes often erase the remains of entire groups of animals. Chimpanzees occupy tropical wood-lands, which have acid soils that leach away bone minerals, and not unexpectedly there are no fossils at all of chimp bones, anywhere. Bird bones, adapted for lightness in flight, are so fragile that most are either eaten by predators or are destroyed by physical-chemical forces. As a result, fossils of bird bones are rare. Some birds, however, leave a remarkable trail. Alaskan grouse and ptarmigan swallow pebbles for their muscular gizzards, where the stones are used to grind plant parts for digestion in the stomach. Screen-washing of Alaskan Pleistocene silts has produced virtually no bird bones, but this does not mean that birds were rare, because tens of thousands of these highly polished little pebbles, called gastroliths, turn up in our screens.

Normally, the larger and more dense a bone, the more likely it will become a fossil. Imagine the difference between mammoth bones and squirrel and rabbit bones. Because I have found roughly a thousand mammoth bones for each rabbit bone does not mean that mammoths and rabbits occurred at that ratio in the Pleistocene.

AGE DISTORTIONS IN TAPHONOMY

The fossil record is notoriously biased when it comes to age. Young mammals are virtually always underrepresented. Bones of the young are thin and fragile, easy for carnivores or scavengers to bite through or swallow. Delectable brains and marrow mean few bones of young animals are left entire. Contemporary field biologists seldom find remains at a fresh kill where young reindeer or even young elephants were consumed. The plate is licked clean. But sometimes youth is overrepresented, as in the case of cave bear young, which die during hibernation in caves at a higher frequency than other age classes and are easily preserved in the unusual cave environment. There are a few examples outside caves of differential favoring of young animals as fossils. Shed antlers of young deer are disproportionately common compared to shed antlers of older deer. I will come back to this particular point in a couple of chapters because the phenomenon underlying

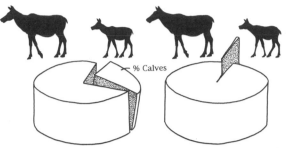

ACTUAL LIVING POPULATION   PALEOLITHIC ART POPULATION

Young animals are pictured in Paleolithic art, but they are not as proportionally numerous in the art record as in real life. Animals in their first year (calves and gangly yearlings) constitute over 25% of the total population; in Paleolithic art the young are pictured less than 1% of the time. Why were Paleolithic artists so predisposed to draw adult large mammals? I think it is because male hunters gain status by which prey they stalk and kill. Bringing home an adult horse has a profoundly different social impact than bringing in a newborn foal. Even though occasionally much of the bag may have actually been young animals, art is not about statistics.

the distorted number of shed antlers of young deer in the fossil record is, curiously enough, relevant to some biased preservation in Paleolithic art.

SEX DISTORTIONS IN TAPHONOMY

Male and female fossils are rarely preserved equally. For example, most skulls of steppe bison, *Bison priscus,* found in Alaskan Pleistocene deposits are from male bison (Guthrie 1990). Skulls of bison cows are rather rare; the ratio is roughly 10:1. This ratio is about the same in Pleistocene sand deposits along the Rhine in Germany (Guthrie and von Koenigswald 1997). Pleistocene bison bulls did not outnumber cows even by a ratio of 2:1; rather, this particular preservational bias is attributable to "bullheadedness." As an adaptation to violent head-to-head clashing, bison males have very rugged skulls and horn cores. After death, that ruggedness renders the skulls of large bulls particularly resistant to physical breakup and disintegration. Carnivores rarely even attempt to gnaw through such heavy bone, as this requires considerable energy and

The Bias of the Few   The ratio of 10 bull bison fossil skulls to 1 cow skull should not lead us to imagine that, for example, 50% of male bison skulls were preserved in contrast to only 5% of the female skulls. In fact, we know that virtually none of either sex were preserved. A better estimation would be that 99.995% of the bulls were not preserved, compared with 99.9995% of the cows. On a pie chart, the difference between these two percentages is barely perceptible. The forces working against preservation are so pervasive and overwhelming that any bias that favors preservation, however slight, is emphatically reflected in the fossil record.

The dynamics of these taphonomic processes warrant our interest because it is highly likely that our collection of Paleolithic art has been distorted on a comparable scale. When so little of something is preserved, very slight preservation differentials often lead to distortions in the final sample. Indeed, much evidence supports that expectation. We will review reasons why the art of the different sexes and age classes is unlikely to have been preserved symmetrically. But it is essential to remember that, say, 99.99995% percent of the art was not preserved. Some art was preserved and a fraction of that has been recovered. What we have is not Paleolithic art but a very taphonomically curated, thus heavily distorted, *sample* of Paleolithic art. The dynamics of that distortion will be part of our story.

time and risks damage to irreplaceable gnawing teeth. Bison cows, while horned, do not fight like bulls, and the skulls of cow bison are more lightly constructed and tend to break into smaller, less durable pieces. This explains the 10:1 ratio of bison bull skulls to cow skulls in the fossil record.

The sex ratio of Pleistocene Alaskan Dall sheep skulls, *Ovis dalli,* is even more distorted. While fossil ram skulls are common, fossil ewe skulls are virtually unheard of. Pleistocene saiga antelope skulls are a most extreme case;

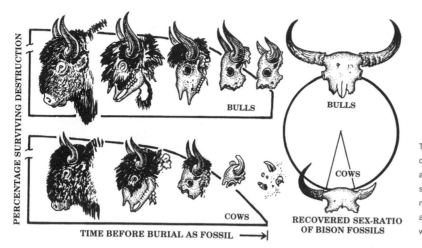

PERCENTAGE SURVIVING DESTRUCTION

BULLS

BULLS

COWS

COWS

TIME BEFORE BURIAL AS FOSSIL ⟶

RECOVERED SEX-RATIO
OF BISON FOSSILS

Though it is not easy to show the scale of relative percentages of destruction, this illustration helps reiterate differences in preservation between female bison skulls and the more robust skulls of bulls. The ratio of male to female skulls preserved in the fossil record is about 10:1. Ruggedness has a profound influence on what becomes preserved as a fossil.

not a single fossil female saiga skull has been recorded in all of northern Asia and Beringia (Guthrie, Sher, and Harington 2001). Again, we do not take this literally as indicating no female saigas in the Pleistocene. I am recounting these instances of taphonomic bias because I think taphonomic processes have grossly distorted our record of Paleolithic art. Preservation of Paleolithic art also seems highly sexually asymmetric. The forces of destruction are neutral, but the resistance they meet is not uniform between the sexes.

EFFECTS OF BEHAVIOR ON TAPHONOMY

Taphonomic distortions are not simply a matter of physical anatomy. Animal behavior can also result in great biases in the fossil record. The millions of small rodents found in deposits in cave-mouth sediments (usually mixed with Paleolithic debris) were mostly derived from owl pellets, indigestible remains that owls regurgitate while back home at the daytime cave-mouth roost. Since these were nocturnal owls, their prey seldom included rodent species that were active only in the daytime, so the resultant sample is not at all representative of the entire wild-rodent community.

Behavior can also influence preservation ratios within species. Gold-mining activities around Fairbanks, Alaska,

uncovered hundreds of Pleistocene horse remains as miners washed away entire valleys of frozen silt to reach underlying gold-bearing gravels. Curiously, very few of these Pleistocene horse fossils are colts, fillies, mares, or stallions in their prime. (Horse skulls can be sexed by the large, sharp male canines and can be aged by incisor wear.) Instead, the horse skulls uncovered by the miners are almost all juvenile males and old stallions. Why?

Horse skulls are not as robust as those of wild bison or sheep, and male and female skulls differ little except for the canines. Lack of robustness may explain why the skulls of the youngest colts are rare but accounts for little else. It is a long story (Guthrie 2001b), but eventually I concluded that the bias in this sample related to the various uses of the landscape. The broken terrain in the mining district gave Pleistocene predators good cover and thus was a relatively dangerous area—one that socially dominant stallions with harems would have avoided (just as zebra harems and their stallions avoid similar terrain today). Alaskan stallions with harems of mares and young to protect most likely kept to open flats, where predators were more visible. More risk-tolerant bachelor bands were free to take advantage of the more diverse vegetation but riskier life in the hills. And they occasionally died there. The silty gullies in the hills were highly depositional "preserving" habitat. All this contributed to the distortion in the fossil record. And even if stallions and their mares became fossilized, they are hardly likely to be unearthed because mining does not occur in the flats along the Tanana River.

▲▼▲

I give these examples because an appreciation of the force of taphonomy is going to be important in this book and accounts for many of the subjects of preserved Paleolithic art, how they were done, the main character of their unity, the high incidence of rudimentary works, and much more.

Cave Art's Unity

The preserved Paleolithic art has a remarkable integrity, yet part of that integrity is its elasticity and freedom. Its character is readily distinguished from later prehistoric rock art and from historic tribal art. This unity is a puzzle and will be an important theme in "breaking the code"— helping us understand the order in Paleolithic art and its underlying connections with the lives of the artists and their surroundings. I will return to this theme again and again, but for now it is relevant to set the stage with some introductory expectations.

TAPHONOMIC CONTRIBUTIONS TO THE UNITY

The kinds of age and sex distortions we see in Paleolithic art explain some of the unity of the art. The fragmented evidence suggests that some art contained themes of power for adolescent hunters-to-be. It is logical for this age and sex to be preoccupied with large mammals. Hunter-gatherer studies tell us that successful hunting of large mammals would have been the social currency for male status, marriage, health, and much more. This age distortion also may account for why there are so many simple handprints and graffitiesque vulvas, erections, and voluptuous nudes in cave art. Taphonomic distortions also help explain why so many other images from these people's lives are missing from the art. The following chapters are about these effects and the basic evolutionary biology that underlies the differing age and sex predispositions.

One of the most important observations is that the art throughout this time period was mostly *representational*. That is, one can decipher an image because it relates to something identifiably concrete. There is a consistent at-

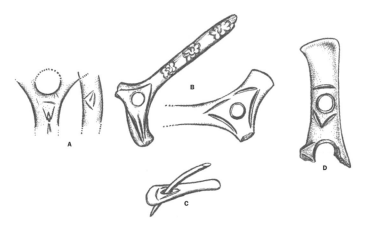

Nude females and genitals are other repeated themes in Paleolithic art. Does this pattern indicate fertility magic or a mystical clan emblem, or does it have a more universal aesthetic appeal? I will address these issues later. **A**, La Madeleine, Fr. **B–C**, Rochereil, Fr. **D**, Mas d'Azil, Fr. Lower sketch shows how a straightener was used as a lever.

tempt to portray each animal more or less as it was seen, rendering telling details of head, hoof, tail, antler, hock, rump, and so on. Of course, there is some stylization—all art is an abstraction—but the art keeps referring to actual animals rather than a preset, formulaic mythogram or memorized crutch. For example, image after image of bison tails, though diverse, converge on an informative picture of what bison tails were like in the Pleistocene. Nevertheless, among these representational attempts are abstractions of female genitalia and body forms, negative and positive handprints, rows of dots, parallel slashes like finger dabs (as well as real finger marks), crosshatches, and similar marks without direct reference to representational images.

It is true that the art is not literal: Paleolithic art is far from being photographic portraiture. Selective exaggeration and deletion, like caricature, emphasize special features to which artists attach a particular focus. Some early researchers of Paleolithic art, like Abbé Breuil, understood this well, because they were artists themselves (Breuil 1969). Breuil recognized that to draw, an artist must project onto the rock an inner vision of the animal, and that inner image of the animal must be learned by experiencing the look-draw-look-draw process.

Every process of artistic representation must reduce the tremendous complexity of the actual world to a simpler identity. Any artist has to use conventions in selecting a subject from the limitless raw information, say, of a bison in its different seasons, positions, movements, lighting, and context. Clottes (1989) saw that much more detail is used in Paleolithic art than is required for a symbolic mythogram, and he argued that the elements of a mythogram do not necessitate the reproduction of nuances of fur patterns, nor did the artists need to add such details to demand admiration for their drawing skills. These seem superfluous as an elaboration of a symbol. Clottes concluded that the competence and creative enjoyment of the artist may have been significant factors. But few other authors have shared Clottes's interpretation.

Many images in Paleolithic art that deviate from recognizable representations usually also have marks of only rudimentary artistic skill. This free and loose feature also adds some coherency to the art. The possibility that a portion of Paleolithic art was made by beginning drawers is frequently overlooked, yet it is critical to any analysis of the art. Did all Paleolithic artists spring into full artistic competency and power without passing through a long period of unskillfulness? I stress the opposite point: namely, that there is no reason to think that only artistically mature adult art was preserved. Paleolithic demographics of more young than adults, as I will discuss later, would almost certainly lead to the opposite bias. And, given that likelihood, we should not view all the Paleolithic artworks with an uninformed literalness—as though each and every one is the work of a successful artist with skills of uncompromised power and maturity.

Later I will present evidence that those who went back into caves were not a random sample from all Paleolithic people and that the art made there was a tiny fraction of the art done outside deep caves. But the vagaries of preservation outside cave environments have filtered our art collection even more dramatically. Only certain types of things stood an even chance of becoming artifacts. Robust osseous materials, used for violent high-energy tools, pre-

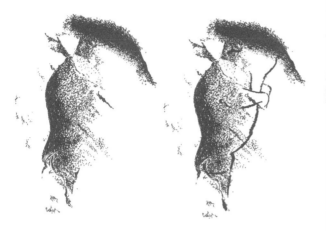

Somebody walking through a deep cave was reminded of a bison dorsal line (despite its being upright instead of matching the real-life horizontal back) by a shadow created by the irregular limestone surface. Only a few red lines were needed to bring out its bison-ness. Niaux, Fr.

Babies, Butterflies, and Buttercups: The Main Subjects of Paleolithic Art?   Imagine for a moment that babies, butterflies, and flowers were the most common recurring motifs in Paleolithic art. The range of all possible subjects was, after all, enormous. What if, from tens of thousands of years and millions of square kilometers, we had found mainly images of rotund, smiling babies and a variety of colorful flower species and brightly patterned insects, repeated again and again—not only drawn in cave mud with fingers but modeled in clay, carved in stone and ivory, painted in caves, and scratched on bone fragments, tools, and plaquettes? Say, also, that there was a background scatter in many caves of hedgehog, songbird, and mouse images, but babies were a common theme in almost every site.

Merely playing with that notion highlights the extremely narrow range of subjects that were actually chosen, over and over again. Additionally, the art styles could have been more diverse: rectangular formats, sweeping ovoids, intricate knotted curves, a busy dither of lines. Despite its remarkable freedom, the naturalistic styles of Paleolithic art fall within a rather narrow range compared to all those available. In short, Paleolithic art exhibits amazing unity. And this unity has been reinforced with each new discovery of Paleolithic art, no matter how distant in time and place. For example, the images from the French caves of Cosquer and Chauvet, where some images date as early as 30,000 years ago, greatly resemble those of Altamira and Le Portel in Spain, where similar art was made almost 15,000 years later.

serve with much greater frequency than skin, horn, wood, and fiber. Such preservational biases have been constant forces and have contributed to the unity of the art, primarily by eliminating entire categories of materials from our collection.

UNITY OF IMAGE SELECTION

One recurring feature of Paleolithic art, whether in carvings, paintings, engravings, or modeled clay, is the realistic representation of large mammals. Paleolithic Eurasians were apparently both devoted to and dependent upon large terrestrial mammals. And despite frequent deficiencies in individual drawing development, they chose to depict these artistically difficult subjects. Large mammals were the mainstay of their diet, their tools, their entertainment, their fears, their celebrations, their movements, and their lives and deaths.

Bison, horses, mammoths, rhinos, chamois, lions, reindeer, ibex, red deer, musk oxen, seals, saigas, wolves, bears, and other large-mammal species usually appear without much background or context and almost universally in side view. For a hunter this is the best view. Quite a few people are depicted, but they are mostly women. And, unlike the men, women are drawn or sculpted naked and usually rotund. I will argue presently that for human males this is often the best view.

The proportions of different species represented in the art does not correspond to the proportions repre-

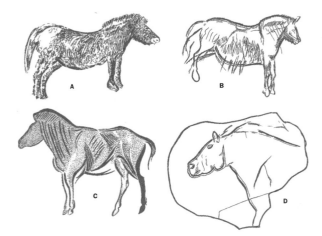

Horses were a favorite subject for Paleolithic artists. Here are four from different places and times, exhibiting different skill levels and different styles and media. All are done by technically rather competent drawers. **A**, Niaux, Fr. **B**, Trois Frères, Fr. **C**, Bédeilhac, Fr. **D**, Limeuil, Fr.

Carnivores are not as common as their ungulate prey in most Paleolithic art sites, but there are sufficient images to work out their identities and often the details of their appearance. Above is a particularly scribbly image of a lion from Aldène, Fr. Despite its technical shortcomings, a bold side-stripe is very clear in this image—such a side-stripe is not seen in living lions. Is this a case of artistic license or accurate observation? I'll try to use the art to answer such questions. Below is a work showing a leopard, from Chauvet, Fr., certainly not a native European animal today. From a comparison of modern felids, we can take these spots literally, unlike the bison spots shown earlier.

Carnivores were of course less numerous in life than herbivores, and in most regions they were more rarely depicted by Paleolithic artists—but they do exist as subjects in modest numbers. There are some sites where fired-clay images of carnivores are more common than images of herbivores. The most frequent large carnivores, both in the preserved art and in paleontological sites, are bears and lions, undoubtedly the two most threatening species. But wolves, wolverines, foxes, seals, weasels or ferrets, owls, and other predators were also portrayed on occasion. A few carnivore species are rare; for example, one hyena and one leopard, at most, are depicted in the art. So far, there is no cheetah, though we know from the fossil record that these animals were present at the time. Not only mammals are represented; we find a large assortment of fish images (particularly salmonids and other large edible fish), quite a few birds (especially the large-breasted game birds), maybe one amphibian, a small number of reptiles, and even an insect or two. At a few localities people are drawn rather frequently, while at others images of humans are rare or absent.

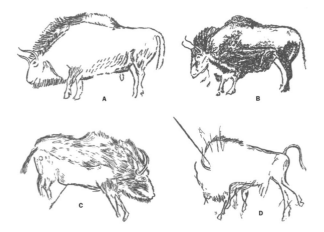

Bison are second only to horses in their abundance in Paleolithic art. These were done by artists who had acquired, or were starting to acquire, technical competency. **A**, Niaux, Fr. **B**, Santimamiñe, Sp. **C**, Fontanet, Fr. (gut shot). **D**, Trois Frères, Fr.

sented in the diet (bones in the middens). The food scraps are mainly reindeer bones, while horses, bison, and mammoths dominate in the art. Ibex and red deer are common in both middens and art. Chamois and saigas are rare both in art and in the middens.

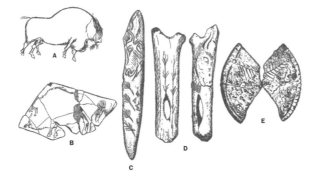

Several drawings in Paleolithic art might be interpreted as bison eating grass. **A**, Candamo, Sp. **B**, Labastide, Fr. (bison graze by twisting their tongues around grass tufts to gather them into their mouths). **c**, La Vache, Fr. **D**, Point-straightener with bison on one side and grass on the other, Enlène, Fr. **E**, Pendant with rushes or grass(?), Mas d'Azil, Fr.

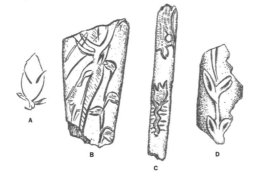

Despite the dominance of its usual subjects, Paleolithic art has some diverse surprises. There are even a small number of images in Paleolithic art that might be forbs. **A**, Bud(?), Montgaudier, Fr. **B**, Bird heads or buds, Fontarnaud à Lugasson, Fr. **c**, Flower, Laugerie-Basse, Fr. **D**, Leaves or catkins from Le Placard, Fr.

Grass: The Foundation for Paleolithic Art and Artists

In ending this chapter, let me take the art's unity full circle, back to the people's main environment, the Mammoth Steppe. Art does not occur in a vacuum. The late British wildlife artist Hubert Peppar suggested I name this book *Grass and Paleolithic Art*. Our ties to grasslands go back to our earliest African origins. A few million years ago we left other apes in the forests and moved into developing scrublands and grassy savannas. African aridity had promoted the grass, which in turn supplied nutritional

opportunities to which many large mammals adaptively responded. In this more open environment a wealth of diurnal, large, grazing mammals lived, exposed for all to see. When humans first entered Eurasia prior to 40,000 years ago, they came to a northern grassland. Across Eurasia, grass and grasslike plants that grew in quite open environments were essential dietary staples of the large herbivores pictured in Paleolithic art. Horses, bison, woolly rhinos, woolly mammoths, red deer, reindeer, and saiga antelope are all grazing animals, not typically woodland species. Paleolithic art is not about woodlands. Most woodland mammals have a secretive nocturnal bent, but there is no place for daytime seclusion or cover in open grasslands. There, large mammals were in plain sight and part of an artist's visual world.

The ecological strategies of woody plants and grasses are quite different. Woody plants have most of their tissue above ground. The advantage of this is to gain canopy height and breadth by additive growth each year in order to dominate competitors in the struggle for light. But woody plants can pay a steep price for leaving vulnerable tissue above ground year-round. This tissue is always at risk of being eaten or damaged by processes of wind, fire, lightning, abrasion, blights, and so forth. Exposed tissues are subject to desiccation and chronic abuse, like a turtle without its shell. The evolutionary outcome of that has been for woody plants to devote much of their resources to chemical or physical defenses, to effectively grow shells in the form of thorns, thick bark, thick cuticles, tannins, resins, terpenes, and so on.

In contrast, grasses keep most of their living tissue protected below ground. Grasses compete for moisture and nutrients beneath the soil in the root zone. With the main body of their tissue below ground, grasses can risk the occasional grazer or fire, as this is only a minor loss. Grasses abandon their aboveground tissue every autumn anyway and regenerate it anew every spring. As early as midsummer, grasses begin to remove resources from aboveground tissues and translocate them for winter storage

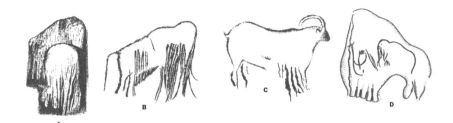

below ground. The winter sward of grasses is dead fibrous tissue, of only modest to poor nutrient quality. This dry fiber is, however, digestible and high in energy, and unlike woody plant tissue it does not have to be defended against grazing, so it is low in toxic chemical defenses. Grass seeds and natural hay made good fodder for the large mammals pictured in Paleolithic art. Grass supported the grazers, and the grazers supported the people.

As I said earlier, the late Paleolithic was a time of considerable climatic instability on a scale unknown today. The grassland probably owed its ability to outcompete trees to this climatic instability. As the climate experienced irregular swings throughout the late Paleolithic, the proportions of large grazing species shifted back and forth, but the overall character of the fauna seems to have remained. Judging from archaeological evidence, the late Paleolithic people of Europe were prairie-edge people, who, tied to firewood and windbreaks, lived among the wooded fingers reaching out into the plains. They must have been familiar with wide vistas, known the wind and big skies of open landscapes, and been experts in the behaviors of large mammals.

The Art of a Large-Mammal-Hunting Lifeway

Hunting behavior is a central, unifying feature of Paleolithic art. I will discuss this at length in chapter 5. I propose that there is something about the connection between large-mammal hunting and the human psyche that is unique, because this behavior involves interacting with beings similar to one's own. One is trying to find, stalk,

spear, feel its surprise, fright, and death, smell its mammal warmth, dismember, prepare, and take into one's body a species rather like one's own. After all, we are not soybeans, witchetty grubs, mongongo nuts, salmon, or beaver, but another large mammal.

Our visceral kinship with large mammals is still evident. It makes for being a vegetarian. It is relatively easy to drum up support for efforts to "save the mustangs, elephants, rhinos, seals, tigers, wolves, gorillas, or whales." It is much more difficult to marshal public enthusiasm for preservation of some distant spinifex mice or numbats, which are arguably more rare and threatened. Also, size is something we inherently relate to in animals. Thousands will enlist to save the alligator or Komodo dragon, but passionate care for the rare Iowa Pleistocene snail has to be nursed with knowledge and reflection. As biologist Jonathan Kingdon noted: "There is a school of ecologists that, making the best of the world as they find it, assert that rats can be just as interesting as elephants. This may be true, yet the human animal within the naturalist still finds himself gripped by an excited interest in those animals that are bigger than himself" (1979, 6). Though Paleolithic people were intimately involved with many lifeforms, the preserved portion of their art overwhelmingly

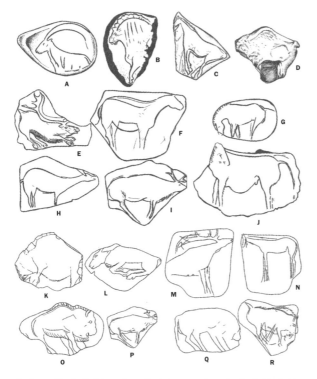

depicts large mammals. These Paleolithic people had to know large mammals well, almost as extensions of themselves—the visual brain centers of Paleolithic people were stuffed with those images. That is lesson number 1 from Paleolithic art.

🌀

In a great knot, the ribbon of life flowed from the grass to the woolly grazers, to the sizzling meat at camp, recombining in gray brain and tanned hand that produced the art—then, double-looping, drew the grass that fed the bison and drew the bison, from whose molecules the artist was. Strewn camp refuse from bison dinners, burials blanketed in ocher-red bison skins, both turned back to grass, twisting again and again into millions of bison, loop-the-loop back into millions of artists, millions of new artworks—source and outcome biting tails in intricate tapestry.

The "recognition" principle applies not only to cave walls and antler bulges but to stones as well. **A**, La Mouthe, Fr. **B**, Tagliente, It. **C**, Laugerie-Basse, Fr. **D**, Tuc d'Audoubert, Fr. **E**, La Marche, Fr. **F** and **H**, Parpalló, Sp. **G**, **J**, **M**–**P**, and **R**, Montastruc, Fr. **I**, Bruniquel, Fr. **K**, La Madeleine, Fr. **L** and **Q**, Isturitz, Fr.

Paleolithic Artists
as Naturalists

Since dawn, hidden by broken ground, we watched the small herd slowly working our way. Peeking through the lace of grass, we could see their twitch of skin and swipe of tail and hear their soft whinnies. Beautiful to watch, they fed slowly, colts frolicking together. The scarred stallion tested one of his barren mares, touching her tail with a wrinkled lip. Tan summer pelts reflected a polished sheen, unlike the ocher shag of winter. A mare up front, probably the first wife, with very striped legs like her colt, moved closer to us, but breezes began to skitter and grasses bent toward the harem. Held my breath, hugged the ground. Come just a few more steps, please a few more steps. The first wife snorted and all stood at attention, tails lifted, heads up, nostrils flaring at our scent. They were still a futile spear's reach away. I felt her alarm inside me as she bolted, the harem exploding in a cloud of early summer dust. Beautiful! Beautifully close, quenched mind but empty hand. . . .

Pleistocene Animal Watching

Paleolithic art offers us a glimpse of the earth as these artists felt it. And it tells a story of people intimately involved with their natural surroundings. To plumb this relationship let's turn to ethology, the study of animal behaviors in their natural setting. I will use the vocabulary of ethology. We will focus for a bit on licks, lip curls, kicks, tongue flicks, raised tails, gaits, social anatomy, and more, because such ethological grounding will help us appreciate in more detail what the Paleolithic artists observed and why they chose to portray certain images. An ethological background will give us a common base from which to assess their images.

As I have already stressed, artists do not choose images and motifs at random. And at least in our collection of Paleolithic art that was preserved, we can see that the artists focused again and again on a particular range of large-mammal images. This intensity of animal observation reflects a kind of obsession that is apparent in the subjects selected and the manner of presentation.

Curiously, most Paleo-art scholars don't directly address the wealth of ethological and anatomical detail in Paleolithic art. Many books fail to mention this subject, and even in popular syntheses of Paleolithic art one can find statements like the following: "We have already seen that little reliable zoological or ethological information can be extracted from the Paleolithic images" (Bahn and Vertut 1988, 183). Yet in that same book Bahn is actually very insightful about naturalistic details in the art.

Preserved Paleolithic art has the earmarks of work by naturalist-hunters and would-be hunters. These images are both evidence for and an avidly motivated study of animal life, and the art requires a comparable curiosity and intensity from us. Details add up and they can lead to sur-

Three wild horses in summer coat from Ekain, Sp., show details about late Pleistocene coat pattern variations. As an aside (there are a lot of asides in Paleolithic art), note that two are speared in the exact spot a spear thrower would hope to hit, heart shots low in the ribcage, just behind the foreleg bone and muscle.

How reliable, how literal, are the details in Paleolithic drawings? The markings on living species offer some guidance. Living lions, like the one drawn on the left, have light-colored muzzles but have dark spots at the base of each whisker cluster. Paleolithic artist(s) at Chauvet, Fr., carefully drew these dark spots (three lions on the right). To try to determine what markings we can trust to be literal, not artistic license or mistakes, we must lean on a knowledge of natural history.

prising changes in our understanding. Attention to ethological and anatomical details will keep us on track in reading the art and help us as we assess animal behavior, human behavior, and the behavior of making art. I will begin this chapter by discussing Paleolithic artists as natural-

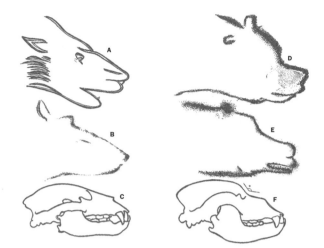

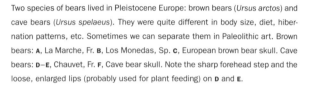

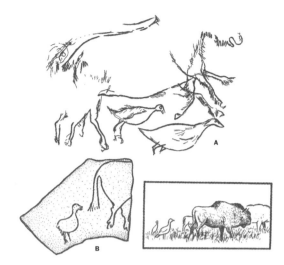

Two species of bears lived in Pleistocene Europe: brown bears (*Ursus arctos*) and cave bears (*Ursus spelaeus*). They were quite different in body size, diet, hibernation patterns, etc. Sometimes we can separate them in Paleolithic art. Brown bears: **A**, La Marche, Fr. **B**, Los Monedas, Sp. **C**, European brown bear skull. Cave bears: **D–E**, Chauvet, Fr. **F**, Cave bear skull. Note the sharp forehead step and the loose, enlarged lips (probably used for plant feeding) on **D** and **E**.

While Pleistocene artists drew many ordinary things, they did not portray everything but focused on a segment of life. Here they caught some details of animal interactions—birds following horses and bison. Letting the herd flush grasshoppers and other small animals is a common feeding strategy for grassland birds. **A**, Gönnersdorf, Ger. **B**, Puy de Lacan, Fr. *Box:* Reconstruction of such a Paleolithic scene.

ists; later in this chapter I will reverse that emphasis and discuss the behavior of Paleolithic naturalists as artists.

Paleolithic Large-Mammal Ethology

Hunters of large mammals spend most of their time walking, waiting, watching—and thinking. Hours, days, occasionally even weeks may pass in finding, then watching a herd, hoping it will move into a vulnerable position. Food and more than food are involved. Certainly, large mammals were appreciated with taste, as their bones are campsite staples in Paleolithic refuse. Paleolithic art shows the grittiness of reality but also the sensitivity of sophisticated animal watchers, hunters, trackers, and admirers. In the art we see that they observed how different animals fed, drank, nursed, knelt, slept, rested, defecated, fought, moved, groomed, courted, copulated, and retched to death on lung blood. The biological content of the drawings gives us a new comprehension of late Paleolithic in-

tellect. These hunter-artists of Eurasia documented mammalian behaviors that were not studied and illustrated so well again until the twentieth century, when natural historians refined observations of animal behavior in the wild into the evolutionary discipline of ethology.

Remember that natural selection is not simply about survival. Differential reproduction is what drives evolutionary changes, and social life figures importantly into how early, how often, and how successfully one reproduces. The outer appearance of large mammals can be understood as social dress. Imagine that, rather like medieval lords and ladies of rank, animals are dressed in bold stripes, spots, manes, beards, humps, eye rings, and contrastingly colored muzzles and white foot spats as part of their social presentation. Many animals also carry dramatic weapons, openly exposed. There are differences between the sexes and these change with age. Animals wear their badges of sex and approximate status—always ready for important social occasions—but in some species certain elements of fancy regalia are discarded during less

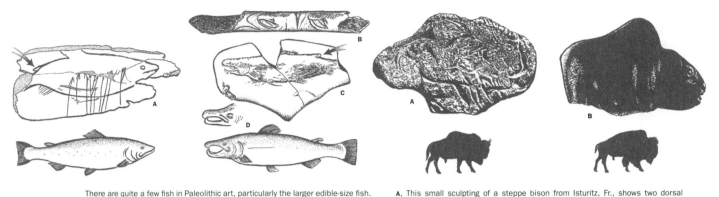

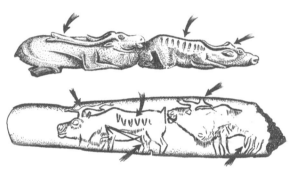

There are quite a few fish in Paleolithic art, particularly the larger edible-size fish. Salmonids are common, especially Atlantic salmon (*Salmo salar*). One can see the small posterior fleshy fin (*arrow*) along the back, characteristic of salmonids. Sufficient details are often provided to sex the fish. **A**, Speared female still gravid with roe, Labastide, Fr. Hook-jawed males: **B**, Roc de Courbet, Fr. **C**, Trois Frères, Fr. **D**, La Vache, Fr. Female salmon choose males with whom to mate, and males fight other males for the privilege; that is what the large hooked jaw and saber teeth on males are about. Drawn from memory, these show the artists were experienced observers.

A, This small sculpting of a steppe bison from Isturitz, Fr., shows two dorsal manes, one on the neck and one behind the thoracic spines, leaving a saddle in between. **B**, On the little bison sculpture from Alberta, Canada, done by a Plains Indian, the summit of the hump is in the forward part of the thorax. Both carvings accurately portray the body contours of, respectively, European Pleistocene bison and, more recently, American plains bison. See Guthrie 1990 for a discussion of the biology underlying these two different contours.

This figure of a reindeer from La Marche, Fr. is in the process of either getting up or lying down. Artiodactyls (deer, bison, etc.) get up and down in a different fore-aft leg sequence than perissodactyls (horses, etc.) do. Reindeer go down first on their fore legs, then hind legs. They get up first with the hind legs, then fore legs. Horses are the opposite. The drawer got it right.

These two pieces are loaded with information about Pleistocene reindeer. In both cases the bull is sniffing the female's genitals—a behavior that tests for estrous condition and readiness for copulation. Male antlers are much larger than those of the females. Females appear to be spotted and males are not. The upper piece is from Bruniquel and the lower from La Vache, both in Fr. The La Vache piece shows a male with an erection and hindquarters bunched ready to mount this estrous female. The La Vache female is shown with spears in its throat and in the base of the neck—possibly added well after the original work was made, an addition that would appeal to hunter-artists. These details are all useful and fascinating if you know how to read them.

socially pressing parts of the year. Thus, anatomy and social behavior are intimately tied together. For example, if we learn that the sexes in a given species are adorned very differently and have very different body sizes, this has profound bearing on understanding the social life of that spe-

cies. Dramatic sexual differences in appearance are associated with social behavior in predictable ways.

Thus, animal anatomy illustrated in Paleolithic art can actually help us understand the behavior of now extinct species. Details of appearance, like fullness of mane, leg

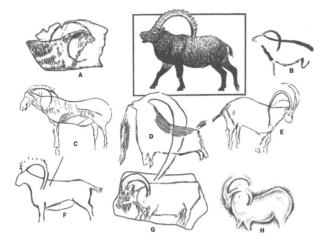

Paleolithic art is loaded with interesting details about Pleistocene animals. For example, alpine male ibex today have horns that are relatively straight, only slightly arcing. However, many ibex in Paleolithic art are portrayed with very arcing horns that even bend downward on either side of the body. Was this real or not? It is possible that this tight curve was a common variant, as extant related species in nearby northern Africa and western Asia do have this kind of curve. **A**, Derava, Rus. **B**, Ussat, Fr. **C**, Veyrier, Fr. **D**, Saint-Martin, Fr. (note the blood spewing out of the mouth/nose, characteristic of a lung hit). **E**, Trois Frères, Fr. **F**, Niaux, Fr. (note a hit high in the lungs). **G**, La Marche, Fr. **H**, Abri Pataud, Fr. *Box:* Reconstructed Pleistocene arcing-horn variant.

decoration, and rump patches, can provide significant information about how animals fought and which gestures were used in status display (Guthrie 2000). Take, for example, the images of steppe bison in Paleolithic art. These bison do not have such thick pads of hair on their faces as do living American bison. We know that such padding in American bison is part of an adaptation to violent, head-to-head clashing. Depictions of Eurasian bison in Paleolithic art and other sources of anatomical information, like the pattern of horn damage to skulls (Guthrie and von Koenigswald 1997), can be combined to reconstruct behavior and appearance in life. These suggest that European bull steppe bison probably lived more intimately with their competitors and did much more preliminary displaying of their social station and weaponry (Guthrie 1990) than, say, American bison. The latter live in large impersonal herds and tend to resort readily to head-to-head violent clashes. Volumes of information are available in the detailed notes of animal appearance and behavior made by Paleolithic artists.

The detailed information recorded in some pieces of Paleolithic art is truly fabulous. The art makes it quite clear, for instance, that shelk (giant deer, *Megaloceros*), woolly rhinos, woolly mammoths, steppe bison, reindeer, cave bears, and northern lions did not look like their nearest living analogs. Again, such well-documented differences in appearance enable us to say something of the species' respective social behaviors: for example, pride size in lions, mating structure of shelk, and fighting positions and techniques and sexual segregation among bison.

IS PALEOLITHIC ART A RELIABLE SOURCE FOR RECONSTRUCTING NATURAL HISTORY?

Can we rely on Paleolithic art to help us reconstruct natural history? Can we really go from a shoulder hump drawn on a cave wall to a firm knowledge of anything? This does sound rather speculative. Perhaps that anatomical feature is simply artistic fantasy? The argument has been made that fossil art is unreliable because of the human element, that art is irreparably tainted by weaknesses of human memory and the wiles of human imagination. This position further implies that Paleolithic art can tell us little about the nature of the artists themselves, because these were superstitious people who were preoccupied with magic and religion, recording symbols, not images of nature. Let me propose otherwise. Paleolithic art contains a great deal of information about the community of animals among which these people lived. It clearly shows that the artists were keen observers of nature. There is one caveat: we must approach these works with a knowledge of natural history and remain judicious about what we take as literal. Fortunately, there are some obvious tests available to us in this endeavor.

First, most species in Paleolithic art did not become extinct. Thus, we can compare the portrayals in Paleolithic art of horses, red deer, ibex, reindeer, and chamois to the appearance of their living analogs for fidelity. Certain de-

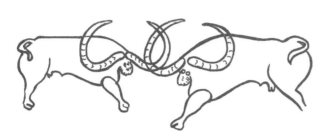

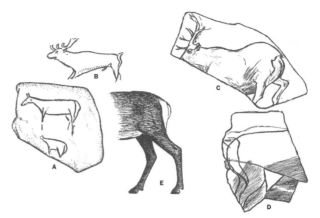

The last giant buffalo, *Pelorovis antiquus,* was distributed over most of Africa in the Pleistocene but died out in the north as late as 2000 years ago. Two bulls are drawn fighting at El Richa, North Africa. If we did not know about the fossils, these old drawings would be enigmatic.

There are a number of ways that we can evaluate what is to be taken literally and what is not. For example, we can see details in these images of red deer that we know to be correct from extant species. **A**, Schweizersbild, Ger. **B**, Lortet, Fr. **C**, La Mouthe, Fr. **D**, La Marche, Fr. **E**, My drawing of extant red deer.

Unlike African elephants, woolly mammoths were specialized grazers and as a part of that adaptation had a "handlike" trunk tip. Frozen mummies from the permafrost corroborate the specialized trunk tip we see in Paleolithic art (the evolutionary origin of the trunk tip was the old nose tip). **A**, Les Combarelles, Fr. **B**, Pech-Merle, Fr. **C–F**, Rouffignac, Fr. **G**, Gönnersdorf, Ger. **H**, Arcy-sur-Cure, Fr. **I**, La Baume Latrone, Fr. **J**, Chauvet, Fr. **K–N**, La Marche, Fr.

tails in Paleolithic art, such as preorbital glands, lip spots, pygal stripes, neck manes, and details of antler structure of Pleistocene large mammals, can be compared with those of living animals.

Second, in the case of species that are now extinct, we often have bones, skulls, horns, antlers, tusks, and even some soft-tissue parts from mummies of animals found frozen in northern permafrost to assist us in evaluating the reliability of certain details of Paleolithic art. I have worked with many of these frozen mummies in Alaska and Siberia. When I discuss mammoths and other extinct species from Paleolithic art in detail, I will use data from both living analogs and preserved fossils.

Third, we can examine the art of more recent hunter-gatherers. Some Holocene groups—certain Australian

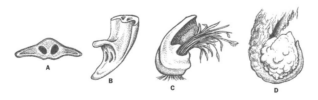

Illustration of a woolly mammoth trunk tip from frozen mummies showing (**A**) cross section, (**B**) the hand shape, and (**C**) how this hand grasp might have worked as a grass gatherer and (**D**) as a snow scoop during winter when water wasn't available.

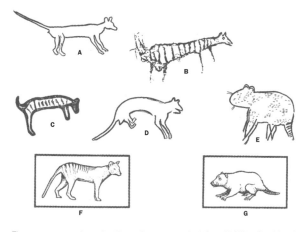

There are some unique situations where we can test the reliability of prehistoric art by comparing old drawings with living species. For example, the dingo's introduction into Australia about 4000 years ago resulted in the extinction of the thylacine (marsupial) "wolf" or "tiger" (*Thylacinus cynocephalus*) and the marsupial devil (*Sarcophilus harrisii*). But we still have old Australian drawings of them prior to their extinction. Fortunately, dingoes did not become feral in Tasmania, an offshore island, so marsupial wolves and the Tasmanian devil made it to modern times. **A** and **D–E**, Arnhem Land. **B**, Mount Pilot. **C**, Pilbara. Drawn from photos: **F**, Tasmanian wolf. **G**, Tasmanian devil.

A, Someone walking by a large white sheet of stalactite at Cougnac, Fr., imagined it to be the lower margin of a deer's neck and was struck by the similarity to a mature bull shelk, *Megaloceros*. That person filled in the details, even adding a cow in the background. This elegant piece allows us to see the dark mane on the shoulder hump and two dark lines radiating from the hump. One strikes backward to the hock, and the other forms the rear limit of the large neck mane. Below the throat patch we can see a dark contrasting delimitation at the start of the neck mane. There is also a dark pygal stripe that borders the male's rump patch. An isolated shed antler is drawn above the male's shoulder but may have nothing to do with the other part of the drawing. These antlers would have made wonderful natural platters. Other Paleolithic drawings of shelks illustrate aspects of these same markings. **B**, My reconstruction of a bull shelk using Paleolithic art as a guide.

Aboriginals, African Bushman, and native New Zealanders—also drew species that they hunted. Indeed, their art also suggests that even if we had no other information on the appearance of quaggas, moas, thylacine marsupial wolves, marsupial devils, royal albatrosses, and other species, we could gather important information from their images in prehistoric art. Again, it is absolutely essential to work from a sufficient array of images and a grounding in natural history to best appraise what can and cannot be taken literally in the art.

SPECIES RECOGNITION:
EMBLEMS OF SPECIES IDENTITY

How is it that we recognize one distant animal to be a bear and another as a moose, or tell an elk from a reindeer? We use overall shape or contours—particular mane shapes, splashes of white, and uniquely shaped antler patterns—as well as manner of movement and other behaviors. And that is how Paleolithic artists learned to portray species. In

fact, Paleolithic artists normally provided enough species-specific detail that we can distinguish such look-alikes as hemiones (an asslike equid) and horses, saiga antelope and chamois, salmonid fishes and nonsalmonids, or shelk and red deer. Why were these animals so dramatically different in appearance? What is the biological story behind this diversity in body forms?

Let's start with hoofed animals. One has to step out of our visual gestalt, developed through literally years of nurture and parental care, to realize that most other animals need an immediate ability to recognize members of their own species. For many animals it is necessary that their own identity (REINDEER, REINDEER!) be imprinted very quickly. They don't have, nor can they developmentally afford, years of parental dependence. We take our species identity for granted, but many other animals do not have such a slow upbringing in which to learn the complexities of species recognition. When a foal is up and running after its first few hours, how does it know which mare to follow? And a new fawn hidden away in the swale must be able to recognize when its mother is approaching and not

Species evolution is shaped not only by physical environment and social behavior within a species but also by other species. Individuals need to know who they themselves are, and are not. Most species use smell and calls, but in addition each has a visual insignia that allows clear identification for purposes of social cohesion, sexual attraction and mating, and status battles and competition. The main species on the Eurasian Mammoth Steppe are portrayed here in "thumbnail sketches." Their pelage and weaponry patterns form their insignias. *Top row:* Steppe bison, aurochs, horse, shelk, woolly mammoth, red deer, reindeer, and human. *Bottom row:* Woolly rhino, musk ox, chamois, ibex, saiga, brown bear, cave bear, lion, spotted hyena, and wolf.

follow any four-footed or two-footed species that wanders by. Likewise, a bull must be able to challenge bulls of his own species for sexual privileges. A female must not allow a member of another species to court her.

Ethologists have found that in many species this recognition process is incredibly rapid and keyed to a few salient characteristics. Rather like a stylized flash card or cutout billboard, if these key elements are there in the right form, the animal "clicks in" visually as, for example, a reindeer. These elements can sometimes be shockingly excerpted by biologists or hunters as a disguise and still be plausible and convincing.

Fascinatingly, these species-specific ornamentations, as well as social scents, calls, and so on, are the most evolutionary labile traits. They can change rather rapidly. Proof of this is that closely related species and even subspecies often exhibit dramatic differences in coloration or horn patterns. In fact, some of these subspecific differences are shown in Paleolithic art, but more on that later.

Lorenz (1966) referred to species-specific visual insignias as the *poster-board effect*. He pointed out that they are most elaborated in conditions of high species diversity. His example was drawn from small-sized fish species using the same coral reef. Anything that causes an individual to regularly spend time and energies inappropriately directed toward members of another species usually detracts from its evolutionary fitness and is selected against. So there is a "centrifugal selection" to separate species that live together, and apparently the more complex the community, the greater the repulsing forces. One can see this clearly in a field guide to birds.

All this means that anatomical features of species identity were both available and naturally emblematic (almost like flags or the stylized roundels, stars, rising suns, and crosses on war planes) as a ready focus for Ice Age artists intent on capturing an animal's marks of identity. But Paleolithic artists went beyond species-specific emblems and also drew details of animals' age and sex.

INSIGNIAS OF SEX, AGE, RANK, AND CLASS

Species recognition alone is insufficient. Animals also need to know if another of their kind is the same or opposite sex, older or younger, stronger or weaker, in estrus or not. They get this information from class-specific biological insignias on individuals of their own species. And we can see from Paleolithic art that the artists usually understood the ethological significance of such insignias of rank, sex, and age as well.

As visually oriented primates, we are comparatively insensitive to the respective smells of large mammals, but

Many of the grazing mammals portrayed in Paleolithic art have their heads down, apparently eating; that is, most of the animals are portrayed doing normal, natural things. **A–B**, Reindeer, Limeuil, Fr. **C**, Red deer, Prado, Sp. **D**, Reindeer, Labastide, Fr. **E**, Mammoth, Pindal, Sp. **F**, Mammoth, Gönnersdorf, Ger. **G**, Bison, Bédeilhac, Fr. **H**, Horse, Labastide, Fr. **I**, Horse, Angles-sur-l'Anglin, Fr. **J**, Horse, Lascaux, Fr. **K**, Horse, Marie, Fr. **L**, Horse, Minateda, Sp. **M**, Rhino, Gönnersdorf, Ger. **N**, Rhino, Rouffignac, Fr.

Images of horses and reindeer drawn in apparent feeding positions: **A–G**, La Marche, Fr. **H–I**, Angles-sur-l'Anglin, Fr. My reconstruction in box.

we are highly sensitive to their visual uniforms. As a result, we completely miss much of the world of mammalian communication. We are simply uninformed about many identifying odors. But since the abilities of our Paleolithic ancestors were similarly restricted, we are able to read the same books, so to speak, and their art preserves appearances long after a particular animal's odor and calls dispersed on Ice Age breezes.

EVERYDAY BEHAVIOR

Watching animals for many hours, one collects images of the most common behaviors: resting, eating, cud chewing, and grooming. Watching large herbivores, especially, one mainly sees them eating, because that is how they spend at least half the hours of their day. Indeed, we find that animals in Paleolithic art are sometimes portrayed in grazing postures. Horses, for example, are normally midsward grazers, but when, on occasion, they have to feed on very short, new growth or already grazed pastures, they must stretch their necks downward in a characteristic posture. This behavior was also noticed by Paleolithic artists.

When not eating, most large mammals spend much of the day bedded down. Ruminants, like reindeer and bison, will normally feed for an hour or so and then lie down for an hour while they regurgitate and chew their cud. Paleolithic peoples would often have seen large mammals in such prone positions, and indeed, there are numerous Paleolithic images of animals lying down. Yet this is a challenging posture to draw, and I'll come back to that in a few pages.

Grooming is not just for looks. Most mammals are subject to a variety of ectoparasites, or skin pests, including flies, ticks, fleas, and mosquitoes. And lacking hands with which to scratch pests off or wave them away, a quadruped must stand and suffer or try somehow to dislodge them. In a herd of reindeer pestered by biting insects one sees continual stamping, tail twitching, and head swinging to gain

Animals in Paleolithic art are shown in various postures, one of which is simply looking to the rear or reaching around and grooming the flank. **A**, Red deer, Lortet, Fr. **B**, Bison, La Madeleine, Fr. **C**, Red deer, Murat, Fr. **D**, Ibex, Mas d'Azil, Fr. **E**, Red deer, Laugerie-Basse, Fr. **F**, Horse and ibex, Pair-non-Pair, Fr. **G**, Red deer, Covalanas, Sp. **H**, Reindeer, Laugerie-Basse, Fr.

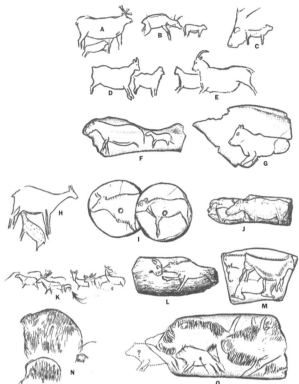

Even though most mammals portrayed in Paleolithic art are adults, there are a few young animals. **A–C**, Reindeer, La Madeleine, Fr. (females shed antlers within a week of calving so these are perhaps very young calves). **D**, Ibex, Angles-sur-l'Anglin, Fr. **E**, Ibex, Rouffignac, Fr. **F**, Horses, Mas d'Azil, Fr. **G**, Reindeer, Mas d'Azil, Fr. **H**, Red deer, Parpalló, Sp. (hind nursing a spotted fawn). **I**, Bison, Mas d'Azil, Fr. **J**, Aurochs, Mas d'Azil, Fr. **K**, Red deer, Limeuil, Fr. **L**, Bison, Brassempouy, Fr. **M**, Ibex, Montastruc, Fr. **N**, Mammoth, Gönnersdorf, Ger. (cow, calf, and juvenile?). **O**, Bison (note speared calf), La Morin, Fr.

momentary respite. For ungulates, the mouth is the main organ for keeping skin parasite levels down. Ungulates have raspy projections on their tongues that can be used to comb hairs clean of crawling parasites, parasite eggs, and dirt. Lower incisor teeth are also used to scrape and comb the skin.

There are some portrayals of grooming in Paleolithic art. The most famous one, a broken spear-thrower or simply a carving, found at the site of La Madeleine in France, shows a young bison licking its flank. A red deer hind from Abri Murat, France, and stags from Lortet and Laugerie-Basse, France, have their heads turned backward in a similar grooming fashion. This grooming posture is sometimes difficult to distinguish in the art from images of animals simply looking to the rear.

Calves and colts at play would have been a common sight, at least during the summer months. In a herd of animals, it is common to see one frolicking youngster chasing another or pestering an adult. A bison calf incised on a piece of bone from Brassempouy looks to be playing. Images of young animals are present in Paleolithic art but uncommon, especially in contrast to the actual numbers of young animals in wild populations. Paleolithic images of yearling animals, judging from their size and degree of antler development, are likewise scarce.

Although in life, behaviors of resting, sleeping, eating, grooming, copulating, and playing are the most common by something like 95 to 5, images of these daily behaviors do not predominate in Paleolithic art. Such quiet behaviors are portrayed but they are not numerically dominant. Apparently they did not register with the Paleolithic artists as the most memorable or most remarkable. Many more animals are portrayed in tails-up alertness, in threat or status displays; and there are more notes of drama and blood splatter than we would find in a balanced record of

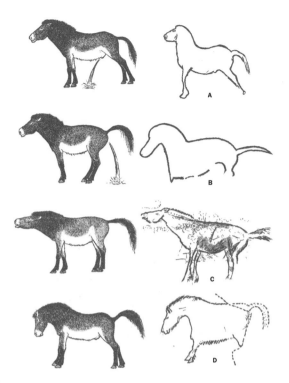

While there are few actual "scenes" in Paleolithic art, large mammals are sometimes portrayed in groups. Interestingly, these group scenes are of animals that are social today, so we can take this portrayal as literal. **A**, Horses, Lascaux. **B**, Horses, Isturitz. **C**, Horses, Chaffaud. **D**, Chamois, Gourdan, **E**, Rhinos, Chauvet. **F**, Bison, Chauvet. (All from Fr.) We can assume Paleolithic people saw such herds. While modern elephants and plains bison often occur in herds, mammoths and steppe bison are seldom, if ever, portrayed in herds (the string of bison at Chauvet, Fr., is one exception). This distinction from the modern may be just happenstance or may indicate that bison did not form as large herds as they do today.

A raised-tail posture is used not only for urination-defecation but for some social situations. To the left are my reconstructions of various tail-up postures among horses today; to the right, comparable images from Paleolithic art. **A**, Male urination posture, Fontalès, Fr. b, Female urination posture, Gargas, Fr. **c**, Threat vocalization posture, Trois Frères, Fr. **D**, Arched-neck, raised-tail threat position, Gönnersdorf, Ger.

daily life. A distinct taste for excitement is one of the biases of Paleolithic art.

Social Displays of Pleistocene Animals

We have images of large Pleistocene mammals fighting and displaying because these behaviors have been captured in Paleolithic art. We are not the only species concerned with status and social image. Social station is so important among large mammals that one does not observe any group of animals for long without seeing status displays. Status is the main coin of evolutionary social currency because it so influences access to the good things in life that are limited and are not created equal: the choicest feeding locations, the safest and most comfortable bedding spots, the best food, and, especially, sexual access to the strongest, healthiest, and cleverest mates. Frequent direct combat, however, is not in anyone's interest. So outright fighting is usually avoided by signals of status and status recognition. To keep one's station, an animal must continually signal and reply to status signals of neighbors. Social state is fluid: it changes with body condition, age, confidence level, reproductive state, injury, health, and so on.

Ethologists use the term *agonistic displays* to describe these exchanges regarding social status. Agonistic displays include everything from a subtle glance to diverse threats, all-out fights, submission, and flight. Paleolithic artists keenly observed and recorded agonistic displays. Welté (1986) has noted that many associations of large mammals shown in Paleolithic art are agonistic. While most agonistic displays are not in themselves violent, there is an implied threat of violence behind them. If neither of the belligerents can negotiate a settlement, there will be a fight—and we know from damaged skulls, broomed horns, and splintered antlers and tusks that there were dusty, blood-splattered, Ice Age fights of behemoth pitted against behemoth.

Threat displays are portrayed in Paleolithic art, as are images of intraspecific combat, including pairs of fighting bison, ibex, rhinos, and mammoths. The bison and ibex images illustrate fighting positions one could photograph today, detail for detail, from their living relatives. But several drawings and carvings of fighting mammoths portray postures that are quite different from those we know to be typical of the mammoth's living analog, the elephant. Were the artists wrong? Or did mammoths actually fight differently from elephants?

A comparison of (**A**) woolly mammoths and (**B**) African elephants showing (**C**) how elephants are adapted to reach upward, browsing from the canopy. African elephants feed principally on tree leaves and bark during the dry season and can reach high into the canopy. Woolly mammoths, however, were adaptive grazers and could not lift their heads above the horizontal. **D**, Arcy-sur-Cure, Fr., a study from life of what must have been the maximum upward rotation of the skull—reconstructed at right (**E**). The Pleistocene image was made on a naturally suggestive contour of a cave wall.

FIGHTING POSTURES OF WOOLLY MAMMOTHS

Elephants and mammoths are members of the same order, Proboscidia, but they are, in fact, not too closely related and are built quite differently. Unlike modern elephants, which do considerable browsing on trees, woolly mammoths were mainly open-ground grazers preoccupied with grass. The more vertically oriented mammoth head allowed them to feed closer to the ground with less energy expenditure. That this difference in feeding posture and head arrangement on the body would also affect the respective fighting positions of elephants and mammoths is entirely plausible. It is a true case of a behavioral pattern recorded in art and rediscovered millennia later. I think

Paleolithic images do correctly illustrate positioning in mammoth fights. We can imagine the vertically placed mammoth head used with force in a frontal-frontal shoving match, with the tusks curving around the opponent. The first to try to turn and run away is subjected to the sharp tusks of its opponent, as we see among some other species (Guthrie 1990). We have mammoth ribs in the University of Alaska Museum collections showing how sharp tusk tips created such injuries behind the shoulder.

BULL NECKS

Necks of most hoofed animals have become important in threat displays because the necks lift, swing, and thrust weaponry of antlers or horns. Like a man flexing his thick arm, shoulder, and biceps, neck size indicates strength and suggests the potency of horn/antler power. Neck muscle tissues of male deer have special testosterone receptors that respond to increased testosterone prior to and during

A, This fine portrait at La Marche, Fr., of two young mammoths sparring or perhaps actually fighting clearly shows heads held vertically in an eye-to-eye position that is not characteristic of modern elephants but apparently was used by woolly mammoths in serious pushing contests. B, Another image of the behavior from over 15,000 years earlier at Chauvet, Fr.

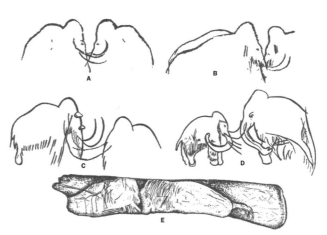

There are several other Paleolithic art scenes of mammoths in frontal-to-frontal positions. Mammoths would have both sparred and had serious bouts using this position. The tusks of adult bulls would have enclosed the opponent's shoulders and any attempt to turn away or disengage would have risked injury from one of the opponent's tusks. Head-to-head: A–C, Rouffignac, Fr. D, Les Combarelles, Fr. E, Laugerie-Haute, Fr. (note this latter one seems to portray a serious fight between two mature bulls).

rut, creating neck muscles that bulge like those of an athlete on steroids—indeed, the mature bull's distended neck during mating season is the product of natural steroids.

But evolution is tricky. If strength can be assessed from neck size, and a large neck can encourage an opponent to back down without fighting, this sets up an opportunity for a sort of deception. Manes and wattles are just such a deception, just as beards and muttonchops are among biters. Ungulate exaggeration of neck contour creates a fake neck of sorts. Just as jackets with padded shoulders visually enlarge a human's physique in a critical spot, manes are real power dressing. Evolution does occasionally favor cheating—or at least good lies.

Several species use a display of lowering the head to emphasize the height of the shoulder crest and/or the raising of the shoulder hackles. This emphasizes the height of the animal, and size is an important cue in assessing an opponent's age, strength, and power. In Paleolithic art, bears, woolly rhinos, bison, and even horses are sometimes shown in head-down threat displays, just as these species threaten today. Bears, African rhinos, cattle, and bison use these same gestures toward people today, and we can assume that Paleolithic artists were occasionally the recipients of such threatening displays.

NECK LINES

Neck contours are often a good clue to species identity in Paleolithic art. The necks of horses, ibex, woolly rhinos, bison, and aurochs bulls typically have a convex arc to the upper line, whereas all cervids (red deer, reindeer, and shelks), aurochs cows, mammoths, chamois, asses, and saigas most typically have a concave upper margin. The anatomical reasons behind this relate to different feeding and fighting postures. Long-limbed grazers normally have long necks that allow them to reach grasses near the soil surface: red deer and shelks, for example. Shrub-tree browsers, like moose, generally have shorter necks. Be-

Vestigial Fangs and Fossil Black Lip Spots

Early mammals fought with their teeth, and many mammalian threats still center on baring one's canines. In its most extreme form, this canine display consists of raising the snout high, retracting the lips, and exposing white fangs against lip spots colored black for eye-catching contrast. Often a white throat patch adds further emphasis.

However, as some herbivores increased in size (to house an enlarged gut—a compost pit for slow-digesting fibrous forage), this bigger body size meant that more damage could be caused by swinging the head in a powerful blow to the opponent than by biting—enter horns and antlers (Geist 1966). Remarkably, even as many of these newly horned species abandoned teeth and bite fights, they retained the old behavior of canine threat display. This is true despite the fact that the teeth they were displaying were small, vestigial, or even entirely lost.

Behavior is often more evolutionarily conservative than anatomy. Red deer, for example, still use a wrinkled upper-lip gesture that reveals quite useless, blunt canines. They have retained a black lip spot, which once showed off the much larger and more effective fighting canines. Once a social-signal behavior is established, it,

A lot of detail is inserted into Paleolithic drawings. The preorbital gland (used in social signaling) of red deer was sometimes illustrated, as were muzzle hairs and even the black lip spot. **A.** Mas d'Azil, Fr. **B.** Trois Frères, Fr. **c.** Fontarnaud á Lugasson, Fr. **D.** La Vache, Fr. **E.** Torre, Sp. **F.** Teyjat, Fr.

curiously, can become almost independent of its origin. At this point the given behavioral pattern can take on a new meaning, even a new use. We know that Paleolithic hunters noticed this spot in red deer because it is portrayed in a few Paleolithic drawings.

Of course, behaviors can and do disappear. Reindeer and moose have lost the upper canine, the black lip spot, and all associated behaviors of baring upper canines. All primates except humans fight by biting, and they threaten by revealing canines in a snarl. We have largely stopped biting and instead use hand-held weapons, but we retain the canine-exposure display in an angry snarl.

cause of the massive weight of the skull and tusks, mammoths had very short necks, and their seven cervical vertebrae were flattened together like stacked saucers. Male bison, sheep, ibex, and musk oxen fight by clashing head on, often after a running charge. A long, flexible neck would obviously be a disadvantage among these species.

TAIL-UP DISPLAYS

Many of the animals portrayed in Paleolithic art have their tails up. The adrenergic response to seeing a potential predator often causes animals to lift their tails and urinate or defecate at this first hint of alarm. One can easily imagine that most large mammals would have come to recognize Paleolithic hunters as serious predators and would have shown alarm at every meeting. We observe this today, even in some areas closed to hunting. It has been presumed that this physiological alarm response has a selective value, because it reduces body weight, and the loss of even a little ballast can make the difference between escape and death. (Jockeys and their saddles are not weighed for nothing. In steeplechase racing, for example, a one-pound handicap weight on the saddle is estimated to be equivalent to one horse length at the finish.)

Among social species, when a herd member becomes alert, looks in the distance, and raises its tail, other herd members recognize this as a signal of alarm. Seeing the tails of other individuals go up elicits riveted attention,

A head-down posture does not necessarily mean an animal is eating. Many ungulates hold the head down and arch the neck to signal a high-level threat. **A**, **C**, **E**–**F**, and **J**, Bison, Trois Frères, Fr. **B**, Bison, Gargas, Fr. **D**, Horse, Gönnersdorf, Ger. **G**, Bison, La Marche, Fr. **H**, Horse, Parpalló, Sp. **I**, Brown bear, Limeuil, Fr.

Males of most large-mammal species portrayed in Paleolithic art, except chamois, are known to fight in a head-to-head position. **A**, Bison, Trois Frères, Fr. **B**, Ibex, Roc de Sers, Fr. **C**, Bison, Pekarna, Czech. **D**, Woolly rhino, Chauvet, Fr. **E**, Bison, La Madeleine, Fr. **F**, Bison, Font de Gaume, Fr.

Thick neck ruffs on woolly rhinos. Woolly rhinos had horns that were not at all like those of living rhinos. A number have been preserved in the permanently frozen ground of Siberia and the Far East. The large "nasal" horn was long and flattened laterally, more fragile than the nasal horns of living rhino species. Annual growth rings in these horns indicate that some animals lived more than thirty years. Its lower edge was flattened, actually beveled from sweeping along the ground, probably in threat rather than in foraging. Since the nasal horn lengthens with age, I suspect it was mainly an organ of status display. The conical "frontal" horn was short and stout—the main weapon used against the opponent's face, as shown by healed conical craters in woolly rhino skulls. The five drawings of rhino heads are all from Gönnersdorf, Ger., and show some of the details of these two horns.

not wild panic (panic is expensive and is reserved, pending further evidence). Pruitt (1960a) described an offshoot of this tail-raised alarm in reindeer. In certain moments of alarm, reindeer assume an exaggerated spread-leg urination posture, which seems to be a related signal with even more dramatic emphasis.

The tail-up behavior may also be similarly triggered by adrenaline in intense social confrontations with one's own kind and thus can become a signal of social dominance—social glands associated with the anus are flaunted—demonstrating that an individual is confident or flushed with adrenaline and ready for combat, if need be. Dog owners are familiar with such tail-up displays. When ungulates display to each other in serious agonistic bouts, the tails are usually carried high, as a similar social metaphor. Subordinate animals assume an opposite pose—lowering the tail out of sight between the hind legs.

Dramatic incidents in which animals strut with mild alarm or are riddled with spears and wheezing blood are common in Paleolithic art. This fact is significant and I'll return to this theme later, as it affords an important forensic clue to help us answer several questions, but for now

Bull-Necked Fighters Pictured in the Art

A Spanish fighting bull can lift both horse and rider off the ground with the force of its head and neck. This incredible power comes from the thick muscles along the top of the neck, which give bulls their dramatic convex neck curve. Among cattle, the neck muscle complex is the most sexually dimorphic of the entire body. The reason for this is that bulls fight one another with much more violence than do cows. More is at stake. Dominance in cows decides such things as who gets to lie in the best spot; among bulls, it determines who gets to breed and who does not. In evolutionary currency, breeding is more crucial than comfortable bedding. Bulls try to dig their horns into an opponent (or predator) and then drive them further in with a violent head lift. What interests us here is that this powerful muscle affects the lateral profile of bulls. It sometimes helps us to separate their images from those of other species in the art, and almost always to distinguish images of bulls from cows. Instead of having an upward-bulging, muscle-bound neck, cows have a thinner, concave, "ewe-neck" conformation. When a bull locks horns head-to-head and twists and pushes, it sometimes gouges the opponent's neck. The necks of bulls are covered with an "armor plate" of thick, dense hide, which is often used in rattlesnake country for boot tops.

In a fight, the neck muscles are a bull's main asset. We can see their importance in bullfighting, for it is almost impossible for a matador to kill a bull with-

Bull aurochs have large neck muscles that give the dorsal line a thick bulge, unlike cows of that species. This specialized hump allows males to strike a potent upward blow with their sharp horns. A, Romito, It. B, Parpalló, Sp. C, Cosquer, Fr. D, Mas d'Azil, Fr. E, Cross sections of bull and cow necks. Bottom two drawings illustrate neck musculature and underlying skeleton.

out first weakening the attachment, or "origin," of the neck muscles at the shoulder crest. This is what the picadors and banderilleros are all about. A bullfighter seldom gets a side view of the bull, and normally there are no targets vulnerable to a hemorrhage-causing weapon from the front. The bullfight, however, is orchestrated to first numb and weaken the powerful neck so that the weakened bull lowers his head as he charges, allowing the unprotected area between the shoulder blades to be exposed to a well-guided sword. Paleolithic art records the powerful neck muscles of wild bulls, and certain images of wounded bulls express very eloquently just how dangerous wild bulls could be.

let's continue with our inventory of animal behaviors depicted in Paleolithic art by turning to images of animal courtship.

Ice Age Sex: Animal Courtship in Paleolithic Art

Paleolithic animal watchers could have seen sexual behavior throughout the year: horses mated in June, mammoths in July, bison in August, red deer in September, reindeer in October, woolly rhinos in November, ibex in December, and wolves, lions, and most other carnivores in late winter. How can we know this? Well, each of these groups has a different length of gestation. Among large herbivores birth has been evolutionarily coordinated to coincide with first spring green-up, when food is at peak quality. This scheduling is particularly crucial in northern climates, where young animals must make the most of brief summers. A birth in late July often spells disaster, and

This may seem like a very esoteric point to some, but for a naturalist or a sculptor of Ice Age animals it is noteworthy. Elephants lift their tails, like many other mammals, during times of excitement, but their vertebral anatomy limits them to sticking the tail out horizontally at best. Woolly mammoths, on the other hand, could apparently raise theirs. A–C, Chauvet, Fr. D, Madeleine, Fr. E, African elephant lifted tail. F, Reconstructed mammoth raised tail.

a birth too early, say, in February, means severe cold for a newborn and a mother too stressed to easily produce adequate milk when she has only the last bits of dead, dry, winter-range vegetation to eat. Nursing females require an additional 50% of energy and nutrients. Only spring flush guarantees that.

The complex demands of embryonic development cause gestation lengths to be very conservative. That is, evolutionary change in gestation periods seems to have occurred at very slow rates. Thus, we can reliably calculate approximate gestation lengths in Pleistocene species based on known gestation periods of living relatives.

Paleolithic artists observed and recorded many courtship gestures, and I would like to discuss the biology of some of these. Again, we see the Paleolithic artists' interest in particular behaviors of actual animals—this horse, that mammoth, a bison cow, and so on—rather than adherence to a preset, codified animal design. Paleolithic ethologists noticed that, for stags and bulls, successful court-

Smelling the urogenital area for important sexual and status information: A, Aurochs, Font de Gaume, Fr. B, Aurochs, Levanzo, It. C, Bison, Santi-mamiñe, Sp. D, Lions, La Vache, Fr. E, Horses, La Vache, Fr. F, Reindeer, La Vache, Fr. G, Reindeer, Madeleine, Fr. (seems to be two males). H, Reindeer, Chaffaud, Fr. (note pygal rump patch outline and black lip spot). I, Reindeer, Laugerie-Basse, Fr.

Some social gestures of naso-naso contact have evolved from facial grooming, from smelling face glands, from regurgitation of food in canids, and from mouth-mouth transmission of gut flora in herbivores. A, Reindeer, Font de Gaume, Fr. B, Reindeer, Trois Frères, Fr. C, Bison, Le Portel, Fr. D, Bison, Gargas, Fr. E, Horses, Mas d'Azil, Fr. F, Wolves, La Vache, Fr. G, Horses, Les Combarelles, Fr. H, Horses, Gourdan, Fr.

It is not bizarre to have copulation scenes portrayed in premodern art. Copulation scenes of other large mammals occur in a variety of Holocene art: **A**, X-ray moose, Norway. **B**, Vaal Rehbok, Kuuffel's Shelter, R.S.A. **c**, Moose, Tomsk, Lake Baikal, Rus.

ship required social and physical stature. Females are, and must be, picky about their partners. And young bulls, no matter how cute their auburn locks, normally wait until they can successfully challenge older and stronger males. Among senior males a set of signals communicates assumed status, according to size, experience, age, and confidence. Social displays are employed to convince as many opponents as possible of the displayer's dominance, without resorting to a fight. Adult fights are a serious business, costly in energy and risking grave damage. So bulls and stags assess their rivals carefully, often in an elaborate ritual of parade and posturing.

Assume that the stag we're watching has achieved a dominant stature. His next hurdle is to attract females. He scatters his sexy odors to the winds or bugles loudly to draw females in, using the same smells and bugle that served as a male-male challenge. Sex and aggression often intertwine. It behooves a female to carefully pick a dominant male, for some of this bull's status success has a genetic component and will be passed on to her daughters as well as her sons. Indeed, females' ability to recognize and pick a winner has been selectively honed.

LOW STRETCH

Once a dominant male has found an interested female and presented his bona fides of rank, she must be approached. But what can a big buck do to keep a cow from running away when he wants to test her for estrous smells? Normally, his bellicose presence means trouble,

and she is somewhat anxious and ready to move away when he approaches. There are special behaviors that signal "no offense" to such estrous cows, who would otherwise get away from a belligerent male. The first signal, one used by a number of species, is a tongue flick. In many species this is combined with a "low stretch," performed with outstretched neck, lowered head, and raised snout. When calves want to nurse, this is how they approach their mothers. And so, like a calf, the big bull now lowers his head toward the female's groin, twists his head and neck as if to reach her udder, then tongue flicks and bleats like a calf: "I need milk." The courted cow apparently recognizes the bull's metaphor of nonaggressiveness and pauses.

The next question concerns the cow's sexual readiness—has she ovulated and is she receptive to copulation? A receptive cow will usually respond to a bull's low-neck-stretch approach by staying still for a moment, then urinating (urination accompanies tension, and having such a big lug so close is a tense time). The bull smells this fresh urine to check for distinctive estrous odors. He can sense even minuscule amounts of a special pheromone in her urine (which our prosimian ancestors once had, but in the course of our evolution was lost). To smell this odor a special behavior called "flehmen" or "lip curl" is used, which opens the vomeronasal organ, located just under the upper lip.

We humans are no exception to this mammalian pattern of mimicking youth in adult courtship. Virtually all the "sweet nibbles, kisses, and coos" of human courtship are metaphors derived from mother and baby beginnings.

A few images in Paleolithic art appear to be horse copulation scenes: **A**, Forêt, Fr. **B**, La Chaire à Calvin, Fr. **C**, Laugerie-Haute, Fr. (reversed for comparison). *Box:* Reconstruction of horse copulation from photo.

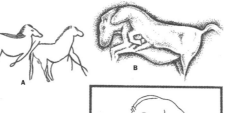

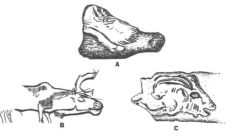

There are postures of outstretched heads in Paleolithic art that might be interpreted as low stretches. **A**, Bison, Mas d'Azil, Fr. **B**, Reindeer, Morin, Fr. **C**, Ibex, Chaffaud, Fr. Modern bison seldom use the low stretch but do stretch their heads outward during flehmen.

A, Drawing of bison from Puy de Lacan, Fr., that may show a flehmen posture.
B, Reconstruction of bison posture and upper-lip curl.

Small bone fragment from Massat, Fr. It shows a cow reindeer urinating for a bull. Bulls test for estrus by using their vomeronasal organ. They may place their muzzles directly in the urine stream or inhale the steam rising from the fresh puddle. Cows in or nearing estrus spread their legs and urinate like this for sexually aggressive males. If the signifying urine hormones are absent, further aggression is deterred. Tens of thousands of years ago, some observant animal watcher's eye caught this behavior and understood its significance or at least found it a worthy artistic subject. The portrayal is truly amazing—it could easily be used for an illustration in a university textbook on animal behavior. Below is my drawing of that important communication episode, which still occurs today.

When used by adults, these gestures assumed meanings beyond their original ones as they evolved into courtship gestures. This emancipation process is so thoroughgoing that we can be incredulous at the idea that lovers' kisses evolved from a mother's mouth-to-mouth feeding of her baby with well-chewed food, blunting the sharp nutritional transition from breast milk to coarse adult food. Yet intermediate lip-smacking patterns along that evolutionary route are clearly seen in a number of other primates (Anthoney 1968). Such comparative observations underscore the plausibility of the evolutionary origins outlined here. Evolutionary expansions and extensions of gestures from one context to another are not limited to courtship settings, however.

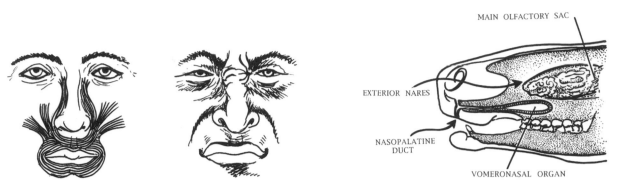

The vomeronasal organ is reduced in human evolution, still playing an important role in our unconscious recognition of social scents (Watson 2001), and we have kept the innate flehmen gesture, which we use for strange odors, especially those from inherently dangerous bowel smells, blowfly by-products, or even plant toxins. The complex muscle that wrinkles our nose is called the *levator labii superioris*.

A reindeer's vomeronasal organ. When the upper lip is raised in flehmen, the nasopalatine duct opens, allowing the animal to smell estrous pheromones. This duct is separate from the main olfactory sac. Apparently, it is a remnant of an ancient olfactory system from early vertebrates. Many mammals retain this sensory system, but it has been lost among primates.

LOW STRETCH IN A NEW CONTEXT

The metaphoric meaning of gestures, such as kisses and low stretches, hinges on context. There are many other cases in which a given gesture is used in a different context and undergoes changes in meaning. Ethologists describe this as *emancipation*. The low-stretch gesture between calf and cow that later was "borrowed" by the bull to approach the cow was emancipated. In some species the low-stretch gesture is used in still further contexts.

For example, we can look at the ways a ram puts a subordinate herd mate in his place without using serious animosity. One common behavioral metaphor involves treating the subordinate like a female. Among wild sheep and ibex, females have a much lower social position than males, so a dominant ram uses a parody of courtship display to metaphorically signal that the recipient is being treated as a mere female, a subordinate. A dominant ram using a low stretch toward a subordinate adult ram is expressing social dominance, not sexuality. The dominant ram may even mount the subordinate briefly. The subordinate ram then signals his acceptance of subordination by acting like a ewe, arching its back downward in lordosis position, the ewe's posture in copulation. Again, this is about status, not homosexuality or sexual aggression.

Male mammals often use gestures of sexual display in their agonistic interactions (this, of course, is what under-

lies guys giving other guys "the finger"). Such gestures are employed in their emancipated capacity to articulate dominance. It can seem ironic when one observes a magnificent bull or ram approach a much smaller subordinate with a low stretch, the gesture used by young to their mothers. But the meaning of the gesture in this context is totally different. Many low stretches seen by Paleolithic artists, and portrayed in their art, were undoubtedly those used in male-male interactions, where, emancipated from seasonal courtship, they were employed on a daily basis.

FOSSIL LAUFEINSCHLAUG?

Behavioral signals also can evolve as an abbreviated distillation of a more full-blown original. A bull pawing the ground and a carnivore curling its lips in a snarl are schematic "intention movements" of a charge and a bite, respectively. Another, first recorded and described by German ethologists, is formally known as "laufeinschlaug." During rut, males of many types of deer and bovids constantly test females to see if they are ready for copulation and will stand still. Instead of a direct mount, males of many species swing their forelegs toward the female. This light nudge or kick is done with a stiff foreleg. If the female does not move off, she is signaling that she is ready for copulation. As with the low stretch, sometimes a domi-

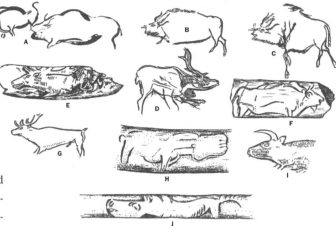

A low stretch of a modern male ibex toward a female.

nant male flaunts his stature with a laufeinschlaug aimed at a subordinate male. This is another example of a seasonal courtship gesture used year-round in agonistic display. This gesture may be the one portrayed on a Pleistocene engraving of Spanish ibex found at Bolinkoba. Laufeinschlaugs, used in both contexts, would have been familiar to Paleolithic ibex hunters.

Some of the outstretched heads in Paleolithic art are clearly a low stretch, while others are more uncertain. **A**, Bison, Le Portel, Fr. (a nice courtship head twist, low-stretch portrayal). **B**, Bison, **C**, Bison, and **D**, Reindeer, Trois Frères, Fr. **E**, Red deer, La Madeleine, Fr. **F**, Bison, Rochereil, Fr. **G**, Red deer, Lortet, Fr. **H**, Horse, Morin, Fr. **I**, Aurochs, Rochereil, Fr. **J**, Horse, Mas d'Azil, Fr.

FOSSIL BUGLES

In many places on earth the autumn season is announced by the rough bugles of stags in rut. Below my house, in Goldstream Valley, morning mists of fall are often penetrated by powerful, sharp exhalations of bull moose: UNGNhhha! A dominant animal declares its presence with striking appearance and short, loud calls. The ribs heave as its ventilation carries across the landscape. Mammal calls are usually simple, like a startling bark or bugle.

Unlike birds, mammals are quite odoriferous, and when simple sounds are added to strong complex smells and imposing appearance, these can set an opponent off

balance and shake his confidence. One shows dominance with threat before engaging in actual combat. Serious threat gestures are usually evolved metaphors from fighting. Threat gestures quote elements of aggressive intent, such as the stylized first movement of a charge: elevating body contours, staring, baring fangs, tilting horns to point in the direction of an opponent, scraping or stomping hooves, and mimicking the sounds of the rush toward an opponent. Gestures of submission, deference, or recognition of threat usually take forms opposite to those of threat: averting the gaze, turning away, keeping quiet, or lowering body contours.

Images of a bison mounting another. **A**, Drawn from memory in the Pleistocene, Altamira, Sp. **B**, Drawn from Dale Lott's photo of recent American plains bison. The Pleistocene version looks like homosexuality but probably is not. Dominant male ungulates often mount or try to mount subordinates as a show of social superiority, a signal that the one being mounted has the lowly stature of a female in those species.

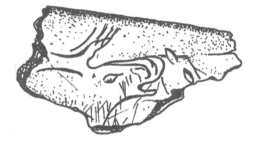

An engraved scene of two male ibex. One interpretation is that the rear male has one of its legs raised toward the rear of the animal in the front. This is a characteristic laufeinschlaug posture, in this case to signify dominance. Bolinkoba, Sp.

A red deer flehmen or bugle (note cow in background), Polesini, It.

Sounds do not fossilize—yet, they almost do: the bugling pictured in Paleolithic art activates our imagination so that we can envision the bull's sides heaving as he exhales the eerie whine-and-roar that spreads across the valley. The deep bugle the artist heard has long died away, but the picture captures some of it in the breathless stretch of a stag reaching for full resonance.

Size and Environmental Context

The underlying reason for the relationship between body size, social weaponry, and environmental context is that evolutionary pressures are continuously active in every population. A character like body size is a floating compromise between social pressures and the availability of abundant and nutritious food to eat. That is why body size and the size of social organs (tusks, antlers, or horns) are often good indicators of habitat quality. Individuals have a genetically delineated range of growth potential, and in-

Red deer stags have a bugle that is both a threat and an advertisement of the presence of a dominant stag (hunters, of course, understand the ethology and mimic the call to lure a challenging stag close enough for a shot). **A**, Red deer, Fontalès, Fr. **B**, Probably red deer, Brassempouy, Fr. We may assume that these little squiggly marks are the bugle sounds. **C**, Pair-non-Pair, Fr. **D**, Montastruc, Fr.

An open mouth and raised head are characteristic of vocalizing animals. Possible vocalizations: **A**, Red deer, Labastide, Fr. **B**, Red deer, Fuente del Cabrerizo, Sp. **C**, Red deer, Les Hoteaux, Fr. **D**, Red deer, Solana de las Covachas, Sp. **E**, Bison, Altamira, Sp. **F**, Bison, Fontanet, Fr. **G**, Red deer, Morin, Fr. **H**, Reindeer, Limeuil, Fr. **I**, Aurochs, Castillo, Sp.

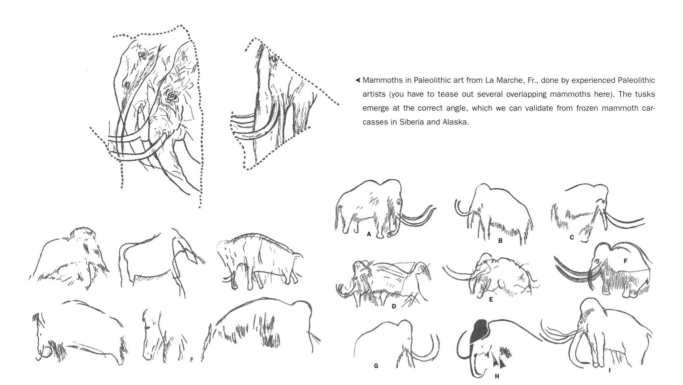

◄ Mammoths in Paleolithic art from La Marche, Fr., done by experienced Paleolithic artists (you have to tease out several overlapping mammoths here). The tusks emerge at the correct angle, which we can validate from frozen mammoth carcasses in Siberia and Alaska.

Judging from their bones, Pleistocene mammoths were quite variable in size both within and between populations. These illustrations of mammoths just prior to their extinction at the end of the Pleistocene are all from Gönnersdorf, Ger.

These Pleistocene mammoths are carrying very large tusks, as some bulls undoubtedly did in life: **A–B** and **G**, Rouffignac, Fr. **C**, Bernifal, Fr. **D**, La Madeleine, Fr. **E** and **I**, Les Combarelles, Fr. **F**, Font de Gaume, Fr. **H**, Chauvet, Fr.

dividual development within that spectrum relates to available resources.

But average body size among different populations is not just a matter of developmental potential. The larger *genetic* variants (e.g., huge savanna elephants) of most species are found on the best ranges; the genetically smaller variants occur on poor ranges (e.g., dwarf elephants on islands and in dense rain forests). Virtually every species conforms to this kind of genetically governed pattern. Thus, it appears that among ungulates, all else being equal, an environment that consistently provides maximal food quality selects for individuals with high genetic potentials for large size, and poor range inevitably selects for individuals with conservative growth strategies (Guthrie 1984a). This phenomenon is even more exaggerated in

social organs. For example, populations of elephants with a long history of poor range conditions can even become genetically tuskless. Wildlife management research is rich in this subject, because it relates so closely to the details of "trophy" management.

Thus, we see that the size and the flamboyance of social weaponry for any given species allow us to conclude something about the forage that was available (Guthrie 1984a). Images in Paleolithic art record such changes in animal evolution and development. Mammoth images found at Gönnersdorf, a very late Paleolithic site, have quite small tusks. This feature is corroborated by the small size of mammoth tusks excavated from sediments at the site, and the greatly reduced tusk size supports the controversial idea that declines in forage quality and/or quantity caused a significant reduction in mammoth "quality" in the Rhine Valley prior to their extinction.

Seasonal Changes in Appearance

Reindeer undergo marked seasonal changes in appearance. They are most rounded with fat after a summer of ample food, exhibiting a round rump and sagging belly in early fall. Fall is also the time of full antler development. Recall from the first chapter that mature male reindeer drop their antlers soon after the October rut and do not begin to grow them until the following spring, whereas cows retain antlers through most of the winter. Paleolithic artists observed these details, which let us deduce the season of the year represented. Perhaps these were the times of year during which the animals were usually seen or were most memorable to the artists.

Dominant reindeer bulls so greatly reduce their food intake during the October rut that they lose their omental fat and their abdomens become almost concave. A few such reindeer are pictured in Paleolithic art. There are even some portrayed with antlers in the velvet, the summer velour, a live skin that covers the growing antlers all summer. Most reindeer are portrayed in autumn pelage and with rounded body contours of peak late-summer/ early-fall condition. Paleolithic people were energy limited (fat is the most concentrated dietary source of energy), and fat fall reindeer would have been highly prized (Spiess 1979).

Pelage patterns can also be indicators of season. This is particularly true of horses, whose winter pelage is quite shaggy. Winter leg hair is long and "feathers" around the hoof. Abdominal hair provides an irregular contour instead of the clean lines of summer animals. But one of the most marked seasonal differences, and one most apparent in Paleolithic art, is hair on the mandible area of the head. In a cold climate it is so extreme as to give the appearance of a beard. Horses have two different pelage coats per year

Reindeer go through color changes not only throughout their lifetime but even during one year. **A**, Young animal with dark brown to rufous body color and black muzzle. **B**, Mature animal in autumn pelage. **C**, Mature animal in summer pelage (tints and colors vary from region to region).

A, Caribou just prior to full rut, with peak fat and freshly shed antler velvet. **B**, Post-rut appearance: irregular, worn mane, scar of shed antlers, angular rump with little fat, and no abdominal fat, making for a concave abdomen. **C**, Reindeer, La Colombière, Fr. (note concave abdomen of empty rumen, shed antlers, and bony hip). **D**, Reindeer, Fontalès, Fr. (note freshly shed antler).

(most bovids and reindeer have only one); the summer coat is distinctly short and of a different color (a light yellow gold). Paleolithic artists recorded horses in summer and winter pelage, taking notice of seasonal differences. All the horses portrayed in Chauvet Cave in the far south of France are shown in winter pelage, but the beard length is quite short, suggesting warmer winters in that region.

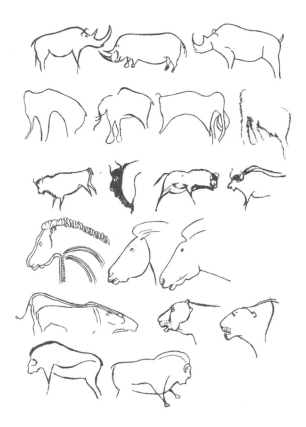

The images from Chauvet Cave are similar in many ways to those from other caves, but there are some differences. The site is located near the Mediterranean life zone, which today is dominated by small-leaf evergreen oaks. The art in Chauvet has been dated to 27,000–32,000 years or so ago. What is unusual is that the mammals are not "woolly." This is true even though some, like horses, are portrayed in their winter coats. Animals such as musk oxen, rhinos, and mammoths that typically have long tresses of guard hairs all year round are all drawn rather short-haired. This consistent pattern across several species suggests a real phenomenon: that animals in the lower Rhône, the southernmost area of their ranges, were less woolly, at least during that time bracket. *Far left:* All from Chauvet. *Left, top to bottom:* rhino, Font de Gaume; mammoth, Rouffignac; bison and horse, Niaux; lion, Les Combarelles; musk oxen, La Colombière. All from France.

Most of the horse images from Gönnersdorf, Ger., appear to be of horses in winter pelage. Analysis of the other artifacts at the site also shows mainly winter occupation. One can see that horses at this latitude became quite long-haired during winter.

Seasonal coat variations in horses: **A**, Gabillou, Fr (winter). **B**, La Pasiega, Sp. (summer). **C**, Le Portel, Fr. (summer). **D**, Ekain, Sp. (summer). **E**, Covalanas, Sp. (winter). **F**, Rouffignac, Fr. (winter). **G**, Lascaux, Fr. (summer). **H**, Lourdes, Fr. (summer).

Biogeographic Variations

Large mammals of the Mammoth Steppe were adapted to a very cold and windy climate. The density and length of pelage and the reduced size of ears and tails of Siberian and Alaskan frozen mummies of woolly mammoths, woolly rhinos, bison, and others all indicate very severe winter climates. Mammalian portraits from the southwestern European cave art centers of the Périgord and Cantabria, however, consistently show a more complex picture. Along this southwestern border of the Mammoth Steppe, the art depicts cold-tolerant features such as long pelage and reduced ears and tail that are somewhat less extreme than cold adaptations of fossil bison and woolly mammoths found farther north (Guthrie 1990). In the case of bison this difference is dramatic. Other biogeographic variations in Paleolithic art images are more difficult to explain than simple adaptations to cold.

Individuals of any species vary both within and between areas. The range or degree of this variation can be from almost imperceptible to quite remarkable. While some variation may simply be random, natural selection is a universal force, and most of the obvious variations among mammals have significant heritability. Certainly, the effects upon reproduction of these physical and behavioral variations are not random.

Underlying pressures for biogeographic variations are such things as climate, terrain, population density, and diet. Today, roe and red deer, for example, are much larger bodied and antlered in northeastern Europe than in Spain and Portugal. One explanation for this biogeographic size gradient is that plants mature rapidly and more or less at the same time in warm climates. This means that young vegetation, which has the highest levels of nutrients, is actually available for a shorter time in Spain than in Sweden (Guthrie 1984a). This may seem paradoxical at first, but the levels particularly of protein and other critical growth nutrients are highest in immature plants. Although there may be several fewer months in which green forage is available at high latitudes, if animals in those regions can find six to eight weeks' worth of high-protein young plants, they can grow larger than southern counterparts who may have only three weeks of such high-nutrient foraging. Protein and other critical growth nutrients are key here—not simply caloric energy.

But it is not just size that is involved. Extant roe deer and red deer also exhibit pelage differences along this same geographic gradient. Is it possible to use animal imagery in Paleolithic art to investigate whether gradients like this also occurred in the Pleistocene? And if so, can we make some sense out of them? I would answer yes to that first question. For some species we do have Paleolithic images from enough localities that we can say with a fair degree of confidence that this is how a species tended to look in one area compared to animals in another region. Generally, the biogeographic variations I detect in late Pleisto-

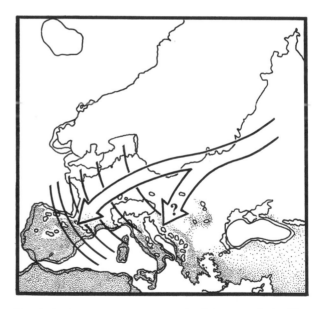

The animals of northeastern Europe during the late Pleistocene and today differ from those of the southwestern part. There is a gradient along this axis. Because of the scarcity of Paleolithic art in southeastern Europe, changes in that direction are uncertain.

cene images sweep in an arc from northeast to southwest (i.e., to southern France, Spain, and Portugal). We lack a complete array of sites and a continuous record through time to work out these patterns in detail, but the scattered evidence that is available suggests such a trend.

I was previously familiar with the gradient in body, antler, and horn size among both extant and late Pleistocene species along this axis. I was surprised, however, to find such consistent Pleistocene gradients in pelage, as depicted in the art, and am still at somewhat of a loss to account for them. I will offer a working hypothesis but would like to note that portrayals in Paleolithic art also suggest more variation in appearance *within* populations than we see today. We know that some northern populations of large mammals are today often highly variable. For example, brown bears range in size from 100 to 600 kilograms and vary in color, with morphs of cinnamon, golden, and black being common. One also finds black, tan, gray, and white wolves in the same population. There are cross (dark back and shoulder stripes), silver-black, and red phases among northern red foxes, and white and blue phases among arctic foxes. Charcoal and white forms of wild Dall sheep occur within certain populations. We also know from extensive samples of northern mammoth fossils that unusually large and unusually small adults occurred within the same populations. Perhaps the more variable northern climates, particularly those in Pleistocene times, promoted broader intrapopulational variation.

COLORFUL BISON

Spanish Pleistocene bison were apparently spectacular, more colorful and more highly patterned than living European bison. Paleolithic Cantabrian images portray bison with reddish bay pelage and black legs, manes, and tails. Horse breeders would call this pelage pattern "bay" or "black points." In many Paleolithic images from Spain both bison bulls and cows are shown with black legs, faces, necks, posterior thorax humps, flanks, and lower abdomens. Pleistocene art records these colorfully patterned bison in Spain and around the Pyrenees into southern France. But farther northward, bison images include variants that are less striking and closer to the gray-brown monochromatic pelage of living eastern European wisents.

Does this variability in Paleolithic images record the actual past appearances of bison? The fact that such imagery is widespread and occurs over many thousands of years lends support to its reliability. Also, vestiges of these Pleistocene variants do occur in living European wisents (a few individuals show distinctly darker facial hair). So I suspect Iberian bison really did sport this dramatic high-contrast pelage and that somewhat less colorful bison were the most common variants in more northern populations.

STRIPED HORSES

Przewalski's horse, the nearly extinct wild Mongolian horse that is now found only in zoos, is the closest living descendant of late Pleistocene horses. These animals undergo dramatic seasonal changes in coat color. In summer the body is a golden buffy tan, while in winter it is a reddish ocher, and some variants are apparently grayish. Przewalski's horses have black points (i.e., legs, mane, and tail) and white eye rings and muzzles in all seasons (Bannikov 1959).

Horse images in Eurasian Paleolithic art show pelages remarkably similar to those of present-day Przewalski's horses—except for one thing. In Paleolithic art, horses are often portrayed with stripes—neck stripes, shoulder stripes, face stripes, and upper-leg stripes—in various patterns and combinations. What are we to make of these? Is this merely artistic license? I don't think so. Supporting evidence that Pleistocene horses actually had such stripes comes from several sources. First, we occasionally see striping in some Przewalski individuals and among mod-

According to Paleolithic art, bison populations to the southwest were more colorful and contrastingly marked.

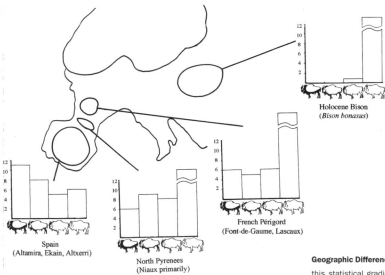

Holocene Bison
(*Bison bonasus*)

French Périgord
(Font-de-Gaume, Lascaux)

Spain
(Altamira, Ekain, Altxerri)

North Pyrenees
(Niaux primarily)

Geographic Differences in Coat Patterns of Bison in Paleolithic Art One can see this statistical gradient in bison coats by comparing samples from the Iberian Peninsula, France, and Holocene bison from western Europe.

ern domestic horse breeds. These unusual variants are "throwbacks" from the past, atavistic genetic patterns remaining among today's domestic horses. Darwin (1859) illustrated just such a case in his *Origin of Species:* a local hack with leg and shoulder stripes and dorsal line. Striping is apparently an old genetic pattern among equids. Mare zebra and jack donkey hybrids, called "zebdonks" (Smithers 1983), produce a similar striping. And feral "mustangs" in the American West occasionally exhibit a genetic reversion to a more wild pelage, which cowboys call "zebra dun." This resembles the Przewalski pattern, and like Przewalski's horses, these mustang variants often have vestigial leg stripes and a shoulder stripe or two. Other domestics are known to revert to a wild appearance. For example, domestic goldfish often revert to the brownish color of wild fish when they become feral (the origins of North American carp).

Second, the markings of modern Burchell's zebra give further credence to the geographic variations of equid striping that we see in Paleolithic art. If we travel south through Africa, starting in Kenya we will see zebra that are striped over their entire bodies. Traveling in a zigzag gradient passing through Namibia, Botswana, and Zululand, we will see that zebra leg striping disappears first and then the striping on rumps becomes tangled. On toward the Cape of Good Hope, the Burchell's zebra subspecies called quagga (actually, this was the Cape Dutch word for all zebra) had only neck stripes. The last quaggas were shot in the late 1800s, but quagga skins are still preserved in several museums. The variability of striping within southern zebra herds is quite marked, with high intrapopulational variation, so I am comfortable with the variations of horse striping pictured in Paleolithic art. The more intriguing issue for me is the pattern of variability. The variability in striping among Burchell's zebra seems to be a clinal pattern of increasing stripe loss toward the south. In these zebra, I would say that stripe patterns were original pelage patterns and that the stripeless patterns are derived. Among the late Pleistocene northern horses, I would argue the reverse, that striping is a return to an ancestral early Pleistocene pattern. But why?

WHY ZEBRA (AND PLEISTOCENE HORSES) ARE STRIPED

The answer to that question is not trivial for our interests here. Recognizing the forces that drove pelage variations among Pleistocene horses will help us better appreciate the nature of European Pleistocene ecology. Simultaneously, this effort can help us assess the reliability of Paleolithic artists as reporters on their surroundings.

There have been three prominent (and dozens of less prominent) theories as to why zebra have stripes: (1) Black-and-white patches act as thermoregulatory devices, alternately flushing capillaries under the black stripes during cold weather to increase heat absorption and under the white stripes during warm weather to radiate extra heat. Alas, this idea lacks any supporting physiological evidence, as stripes are not capillary-plumbed hot and cold. (2) The second theory holds that although the stripes may be eye-catching when viewed close up, they blur into tan at a distance on the shimmering plain. But zebra have to be far away for black and white to create this blend. Why not just be tan like horses in the first place? (3) A third theory, the dither factor theory, is that a field of moving stripes confuses a carnivore's ability to stay focused on any one individual animal. However, if striping is effective in this regard why did other equid groups, like kiangs, kulans, donkeys, and horses, lose their stripes? These stripeless species also occur in herds (sometimes very large herds) that suffer predation pressures very similar to those of zebras. One could also propose that the first animal that tended toward bold contrasting stripes would call attention to itself and hence be selected against. Criticisms of these theories abound and none of these three have gained common acceptance. Let me propose a new idea which I think fits observed variations in zebra pelage, accounts for the nonstriping in nonzebra equids, more closely links striping to

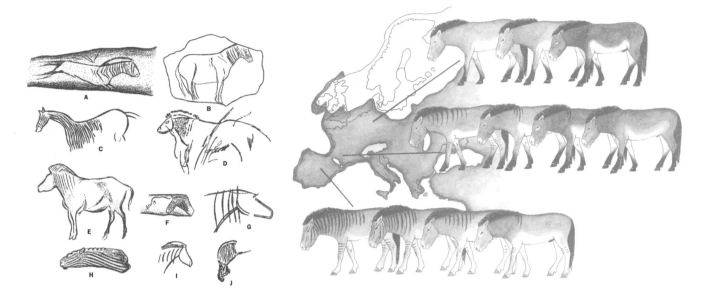

Some Paleolithic engravings and carvings show striped horses. Many more are portrayed elsewhere in this book. **A**, Lortet, Fr. **B**, La Marche, Fr. **C**, Gouy, Fr. **D**, Trois Frères, Fr. **E**, Bédeilhac, Fr. **F**, Arudy, Fr. **G**, Altxerri, Sp. **H**, Dolni Věstonice, Czech. **I**, Bize, Fr. **J**, Candamo, Sp. Some of these stripes may be fortuitous marks but their recurrence is indicative of actual pelage patterns.

Late Pleistocene horses showed considerable striping in southwestern Europe, less so to the north. Striping seems to be highly variable in each population, however.

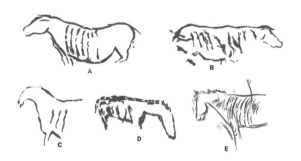

Striping on the trunk is particularly common among Pleistocene horses in the southernmost areas: **A–D**, Nerja, Sp. **E**, Cosquer, Fr. These sites are both on what would have been the southernmost European coast.

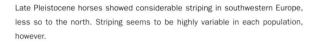

A, Horse from Abri Labattut, Fr., showing neck stripes. The neck stripes on horses may have had their evolutionary origin in the visual lines created by the bulge of shoulder muscles, as in **B**. When dark hair tips separate from the underlying lighter base, it creates what breeders call a "smutty" appearance: as the hair arcs around a sharp angle it appears as a darker line on the dun background. Once this was enhanced by the evolutionary addition of pigment as a real dark line, this pelage marking was further exaggerated by repetition. Repetition is common in the evolution of body markings.

specific habitats, and best explains the gradients discernible among horse images in Paleolithic art.

I'll start with the reverse question: why are the nonzebra equids stripeless? Looking at nonzebra equids we see that northern caballoid horses are dun, desert asses are a soft gray, and hemionids are a buff tan. Subspecies of these are of different colors that usually match the winter or dry-season background color value of the local habitat. Let us also note that all of these nonstriped species show strong countershading; that is, they have dark upper bodies and

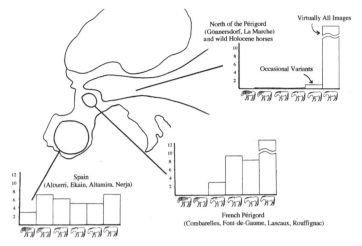

Geographic Differences in Coat Patterns of Horses in Paleolithic Art The frequency of striping is higher in the south.

light underbellies. Such countershading is considered adaptively cryptic patterning and is a trait shared by most antelope, goats, sheep, deer, and, indeed, most large mammals that live in more open plains or mountainous or desert extremes.

Is there anything unique about the habitats in which the striped equids (zebra) reside, or in which they did reside prior to recent alterations by human pastoralism and fire? I propose the common key is savanna vegetation, particularly scrub savanna. Most savannas are not the open grasslands sparsely dotted with acacias that we know from television specials on Kenya and Tanzania. Most savannas are thick with small trees a few meters tall, almost equally spaced like a close polka-dot pattern. The trees' drip-lines do not overlap, but their wide-reaching, deep root systems abut one another. They are not competing for canopy light but for soil moisture. The shallow-rooted grass sward (which makes up the fabric color) and the scrub trees (the polka dots) form an unusual double system, with little direct competition between them, because grasses use direct rainy-season moisture and woody plants draw from deeper soil reserves. Circumstantial evidence suggests that this kind of scrub savanna was the ur-vegetation of much of the late Tertiary, at least in North and South America, much of Eurasia, and Africa. I am not saying plant or animal species were the same, just that plant communities shared this scrub savanna character.

So then, what would have constituted a cryptic coat pattern for a medium- to large-sized mammal in such a scrub? Antelope offer some idea. Blue wildebeest (*Cannochaetes*), nyala and kudu (*Tragelaphus*), eland (the Dutch word for "moose"; *Taurotragus*), and bongo (*Boocerus*) all live in various versions of scrub vegetation and all have some vertical body stripes. Vertical stripes such as these do not totally camouflage an animal, but they do break up the body outline just as spotting does among forest deer and piglets and large woodland cats like leopards and jaguars. This spotted pelage mimics the sun-dappled light filtering down from high-canopied forest or dense stands of floodplain trees. The key is to realize that sunlight in scrub vegetation appears as vertical bands rather than dapples. Fingers of vertical bars of light and dark form the foreground, and bands of light and dark comb the midground and, in less extreme values, continue even into the haze of the background. This is true both in full sun and in moonlit night.

The quagga, that now-extinct Burchell's subspecies, provides a beautiful clue about stripes and habitat. A quagga looked like a zebra that had had its stripes rubbed off from back to front, with only a few stripes remaining on the neck. Was savanna scrub missing from quagga habitat? In fact, it was. The quagga range was relatively arid. The offshore flow of air that for the last million years has kept the Namib a desert also affects much of western South Africa, producing the Karroo and Kalahari and the plateau grasslands south of the Rand. Though there are some scattered scrubby trees and small shrubs, this is naturally open country. These sparsely vegetated plains interfinger northward into uplands as well. But as one moves farther north through Zimbabwe into Malawi, the scrub thickens and zebra are striped head to toe. When the

Where Did Striping among Horses Originally Come From? Among equids, striping is apparently an ancient evolutionary pattern. Wild North African asses (*Equus asinus*) and Asiatic hemionids (*Equus hemionus*) have leg, back, and shoulder stripes. I suspect stripes first arose as a cryptic (camouflaging) pattern involved in hiding young (as spots do for deer fawns). This probably occurred early in horse evolution, before horselike animals became so disposed to living away from woodlands. Woodland deer and antelope are hiders; that is, they hide their young during the day (technically, the young hide themselves). Young of most hiders have coats with patterns that make them less visible to predators. But today the young of horses are followers; they do not sequester themselves away for the day but precociously keep up with their mothers, starting only a few hours after birth. We know from the fossil record that early horses were more woodland or scrubland creatures, unlike equids today. There is no living analog to these forest-dwelling horses of the dis-

High-contrast cryptic markings in the young of forest species: *left*, deer; *right*, tapir. This suggests that equid striping arose first in the young and only later in the adults.

tant past; however, we can see beautiful black-and-white striping among the young of living tropical-forest-adapted tapirs (a distant perissodactyl relative of horses and their kin). This circumstantial evidence suggests that early forest equids were hiders and their foals were camouflaged by a contrasting stripe pattern. I would further suggest that this cryptic neonatal pelage pattern later became characteristic of adult equids, as in "zebra" pelage, when they moved into a different habitat.

Afrikaners moved northward from the Cape, quaggas occupied the highveld grassland, a habitat they shared with white rhinos, blesboks, and black wildebeest—other species that lacked vertical stripes.

The quagga was originally a striped equid that originated in the scrub savanna and later expanded its distribution into a more open landscape. Of course, the southern half of Africa was even more open during the arid times of the last glaciation (Vrba 1995). In this more open region these equids reduced their stripes, and quaggas became a cryptic buff-brown color with strong coun-

tershading. One might hypothesize that although zebra undoubtedly used plains, pans, and meadows in the core part of their distribution, where stripes might not always have been ideal, the dominance of the surrounding scrublands would have kept selection from tending toward stripe loss.

Now, let's return to our partially striped horses in Paleolithic art. Though these look much like quaggas, I think the artists recorded an opposite evolutionary history. Pleistocene caballoid horses had their main center of distribution in the treeless northern steppes, and from there

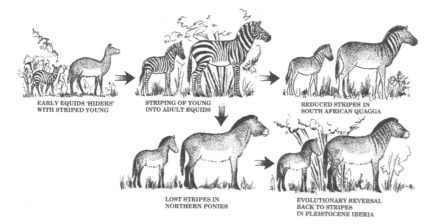

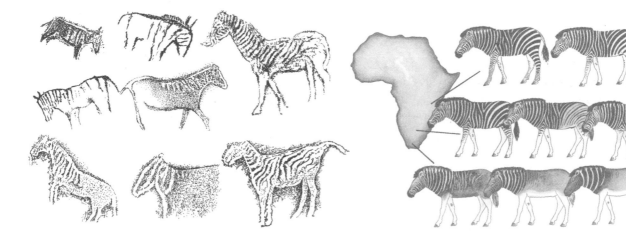

Quagga images in prehistoric Bushman art, all from R.S.A.

Striping in Burchell's zebra in southern Africa. Quaggas are the southernmost.

EARLY EQUIDS 'HIDERS'
WITH STRIPED YOUNG

STRIPING OF YOUNG
INTO ADULT EQUIDS

REDUCED STRIPES IN
SOUTH AFRICAN QUAGGA

LOST STRIPES IN
NORTHERN PONIES

EVOLUTIONARY REVERSAL
BACK TO STRIPES
IN PLEISTOCENE IBERIA

The young of early "hider" equids were striped, and this was later brought, evolutionarily, into the adults. Subsequently, it was partially reduced among quaggas, the southernmost variant of Burchell's zebra. Stripes were almost completely lost among northern horses, but during the late Pleistocene the horse populations in southwestern Europe began to regain the stripes.

horses moved into southern Europe, where amid scattered trees and scrublands their ancient striping pattern was apparently revived. Fossil evidence suggests that Spain and some other parts of southern Europe were a heterogeneous mix of woodlands, scrublands, parklands, and grassy uplands during peak Glacials and perhaps some In-

terstadials (temporary retreats of the ice) as well. During the Pleistocene, mammoths, saigas, and woolly rhinos, the typical obligate grazers of the Mammoth Steppe, only reached as far south as northern Spain. In contrast, bison and horses were found all the way to Gibraltar. Other evidence shows that bison and horses are not so narrowly specialized as other mammals and are more eclectic in their ecological tolerances. Remember that bison and horses were two of the species that survived the end of the Pleistocene, despite the dramatic vegetational changes brought about by the Holocene climate.

Late Pleistocene vegetation in Iberia was probably closer to that of African scrub savanna. In fact, from southern Spain one can see Africa spreading to the south from horizon to horizon. The slatted light of such a scrub environment may have been the context in which the older striped pelage was revived. The Pleistocene artists may have been reporting the facts when they gave their horses stripes, and this may also be why Paleolithic artists put spots on their reindeer images.

REINDEER SPOTS

Were Pleistocene reindeer spotted? Hubert Pepper, a British artist from a small village in Wales, was the first to recognize that this spotting corresponded to real spots in some living reindeer (Pruitt and Pepper 1986). Pruitt, a biologist, called these "Pepper's patches." Again, as with the stripes portrayed in some Pleistocene horse images, the Paleolithic artists' spotted reindeer are made more plausible by variants found among modern populations of reindeer that have a similar row of spots along the sides of the body (Flerov 1952).

Such rows of spots also occur in the pelage of fawns of virtually all deer species during their early "hiding-out" period. Presumably, this spotting serves as camouflage for a lying fawn hiding alone most of the day. And both fallow deer and axis deer retain this spotting pattern into adult pelage. It is likely that spotting arose evolutionarily in young deer and then, also for evolutionary reasons, was maintained into adulthood (as I also hypothesize for striping in adult equids).

Reindeer are an exception to the predominantly parkland focus of the deer radiation. Reindeer are well adapted to life in the treeless far north and have probably occupied this habitat for nearly a million years (Guthrie and Matthews 1971). Reindeer have abandoned the classic deer pattern of hiding young, and instead, reindeer calves follow their mothers soon after birth. Reindeer calves are vulnerable for only a day or so, then they run as fast as their

Spotting among Pleistocene adult cow reindeer is more frequent in Paleolithic art from the south. Although some bulls are shown spotted in the art, this could be a mistake.

mothers. Among living reindeer it is usual for the young to be a dark rust color (sometimes almost black) and without spots. Large herds of wild reindeer move to expansive calving grounds where predator density is low, and the hundreds, even thousands, of cows give birth over a short period. This decreases net mortality by swamping carnivores with more opportunity to take the vulnerable young than they can realize in just a few days.

Early in their evolution, reindeer herds were probably smaller and occupied woodland habitats and probably sought thickets for calving in the ancient deer pattern. This woodland context is the reason spotting has been maintained in woodland deer, and I propose that the reindeer spotting portrayed in Paleolithic art was a revival of an abandoned, much older, pelage pattern favored by the less open habitats during the late Pleistocene in southern Europe and maybe across much of Asia as well.

The frequency of reindeer portrayed with spots in Paleolithic art seems to increase from Germany southward toward the Iberian Peninsula. Virtually all the reindeer pictured at Altxerri Cave in northern Spain, are spotted; over half those pictured in Trois Frères, in the French Pyrenees, are spotted. Much farther north, the Paleolithic sites of La Marche in France and Gönnersdorf in Germany show no spotted reindeer, and of course among today's

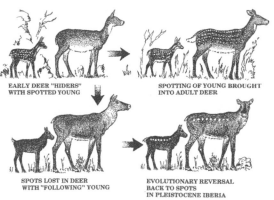

Spotted reindeer in Paleolithic art: **A**, Altxerri, Sp. **B**, La Mouthe, Fr. **C** and **G**, Limeuil, Fr. **D**, **F**, **H**, Trois Frères, Fr. **E**, Forêt, Fr. **I**, Morin, Fr.

Early deer were woodland-adapted "hiders," sequestering their young during the day. From modern analogs we can reconstruct the young of these ancient deer as spotted, a cryptic, concealing pattern. From living deer we can see that spotting was brought into the adult coat. But among open-ground animals it was lost from the young. According to Paleolithic art, there seems to have been an evolutionary reversal among late Pleistocene reindeer in southern Europe.

European reindeer in Scandinavia very few are spotted. I suspect this evidence reflects an actual north-south Pleistocene gradient. Whitehead (1972) observed that while southern subspecies of living spotted deer, *Cervus nipon,* are brightly spotted, the northern subspecies have barely visible spots. The gradient of spotting among Pleistocene reindeer as one goes toward the south is similar to the gradient of pelage change shown for horse and bison images.

In Asian reindeer populations today in which some spotting is found, a row of spots occurs among the young (most common in the natal coat) and occasionally in adult cows, but never, to my knowledge, among adult bulls. What are we to make of the spots shown on several male reindeer portrayed in Paleolithic art? I don't know, but the absence of spots among adult bulls today makes me think that the few occasions where this occurred in Paleolithic art may simply have been mistakes.

RED DEER

One can see from fossils that red deer, *Cervus elaphus,* from the time of the last full Glacial (18,000 years ago) were quite large, larger than most living European red deer, in body

and antlers. There were few red deer in the far north during this period, so it is difficult to determine what, if any, geographic variations may have existed. Both fossils and Paleolithic art representations suggest that red deer today in Spain and Portugal are particularly small and have simple antlers compared to their Pleistocene ancestors. Extant red deer exhibit an increasing size gradient northward, which culminates in the huge marals of the Altai Mountains in central Asia. Antlers of European Pleistocene stags show a different pattern from those of today. Currently, antlers of most European stags terminate in a "crown" of tines; fossil antlers and many images in Paleolithic art show a preponderance of a more open tine pattern like those of the Altai maral and American wapiti. The reasons for these differences are unclear, but the multiple-tined crown is a more defensive structure, whereas the long, sharp tines of larger deer seem to be a more offensive, high-risk weapon. One might guess that the latter would be selected for when rut is short (short summers focus rut in northern climates) and more lethal—a sweepstake all-or-nothing strategy. This general phenomenon seems to pertain to the social weaponry of many northern large mammals.

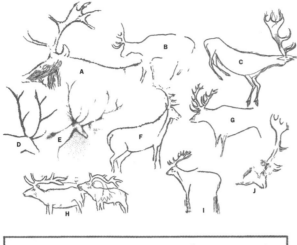

Throughout their range red deer subspecies differ as to whether their antlers terminate in crowns or in long, sharp tines (some populations have both variants). There seem to have been fewer crowns in the European Paleolithic than today: A, Altxerri, Sp. B, Levanzo, It. C, Lascaux, Fr. D, Las Chimenas, Sp. E, Tête-du-Lion, Fr. F, Niaux, Fr. G, Minateda, Sp. H, La Madeleine, Fr. I, Trois Frères, Fr. J, Ekain, Sp. Crown and dirk morphs below (my drawings). Some have proposed that crowns are more for defense and long tines are more for offense.

IBEX

Judging from fossil evidence, the living alpine ibex, *Capra ibex,* is a limited geographic remnant of the ibex that extended over much of Europe during the last full Glacial. Alpine ibex are rather monochromatic; males are especially drab, almost a solid dark brown. The living Spanish ibex, *Capra pyrenaica,* on the other hand, has smaller horns but is much more colorfully and contrastingly marked. The pelage of Spanish ibex is more similar to the "goat pattern" which is widespread among other members of the genus across Asia: dark legs, trimmed with light spots and stripes, black shoulder stripe and dorsal line, along with black side stripe. The horns of Spanish ibex are

flatter than those of alpine ibex, with a goatlike twist that accompanies the posterior arc. Females of alpine ibex and Spanish ibex are more similarly marked than are males.

Paleolithic images of European ibex look very similar to the two extant ibex species except for one notable exception. Some images in Paleolithic art show ibex with a much tighter arc to their horns than occurs in European ibex today (Alvarez 1990). However, such tightly arced horns are present among other ibex species that exist in Asia and Africa (Schaller 1977). Pleistocene ibex had quite large horns for their body size, as indeed Siberian ibex do today, reflecting a phenomenon discussed in regard to red deer—more resources allocated to weaponry mass in the north.

CHAMOIS

Like ibex, these little bovids were much more widespread throughout Europe during the late Paleolithic. The chamois *Rupicapra rupicapra* of the Alps is the least colorfully and less boldly marked of all the chamois subspecies. Its coat color is a monochromatic dark brown to black in males and soft brown in females. Subspecies in the Pyrenees and in Italy are more striking. This continues the pattern of more dramatic southern variants that we have noted in other extant species. Is there any pattern like this in chamois images in Paleolithic art? Paleolithic images of chamois are not abundant, but they do reflect differing regional appearances characteristic of modern chamois subspecies.

LIONS

The relationship between the present African-Asian lion *Panthera leo* and the cave lion of the Eurasian Paleolithic is not totally clear. Whether they are linked at the subspecific or specific level, they do seem to be related (Kurtén 1985). Lion images in Paleolithic art do have some key differences in appearance. I illustrated some differences

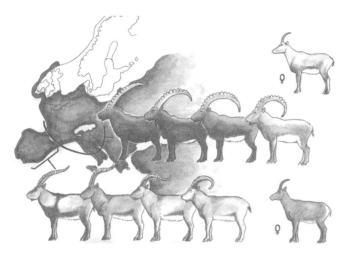

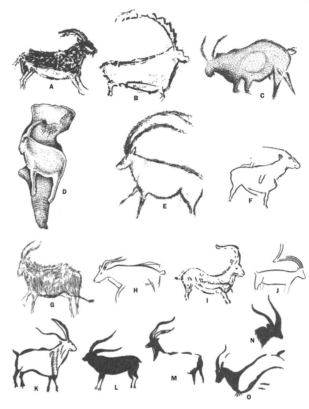

Pleistocene ibex variations as suggested by Paleolithic art and modern populations. Local variants are presented as a gradient from left to right. Females of all populations are usually monotone in medium hues.

▶ Ibex images from Europe: **A–F**, Continental Europe, **G–N**, Iberian Peninsula. **A–B**, Niaux, Fr. **C**, Cosquer, Fr. **D**, Mas d'Azil, Fr. **E**, Chauvet, Fr. **F**, La Mouthe, Fr. **G**, El Castillo, Sp. **H**, Espélugues, Fr. **I**, La Pileta, Sp. **J**, Pasiega, Sp. **K**, Minateda, Sp. **L**, Coto del Ramat, Sp. **M**, Peña del Escrita, Sp. **N**, Coto del Puntal, Sp. **O**, Charo del Agua Amarga, Sp.

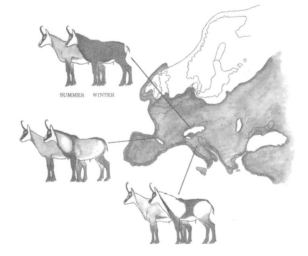

Chamois also exhibit more contrastingly marked coat patterns to the south. My images here are from living populations, but we can see these same markings in Paleolithic art.

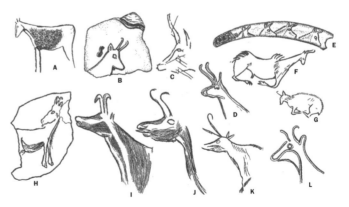

Chamois in Paleolithic art showing different coat patterns: **A**, Altxerri, Sp. **B** and **E**, Gourdan, Fr. **C**, Fornols-Haut, Fr. **D**, Ker de Massat, Fr. **F**, Montastruc, Fr. **G**, Laugerie-Basse, Fr. **H**, Mas d'Azil, Fr. **I–J**, Peña de Candamo, Sp. **K**, El Castillo, Sp. **L**, Las Chimeneas, Sp.

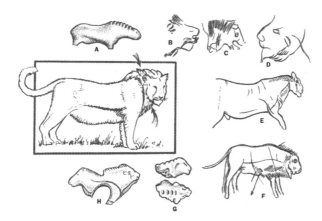

Lions are found as Pleistocene fossils all across the north, and of course lions appear in Paleolithic art. What did these cold-adapted lions look like? They appear not to have had the African-Asian lion's neck ruff but had manes limited to a dorsal and ventral crest. *Box:* My reconstruction of a male Pleistocene lion in winter pelage. **A**, Vogelherd, Ger. **B**, Trois Frères, Fr. **C**, La Clotilde, Sp. **D–F**, Les Combarelles, Fr. **G**, Dolni Věstonice, Czech. **H**, La Vache, Fr.

Paleolithic art of European lions shows a dark side-stripe line between the upper-body color and the lower light countershading. The line may have been a simple artistic delimitation; however, modern lions do not have a sharp value transition at this point. Many mammals do have a dark side-stripe located at this juncture and so may have European Pleistocene lions. *Box:* Reconstructed female in summer coat. **A**, Lascaux, Fr. **B**, Trois Frères, Fr. **C**, Chauvet, Fr. **D**, Labouiche, Fr. **E**, Aldène, Fr. **F**, Gabillou, Fr.

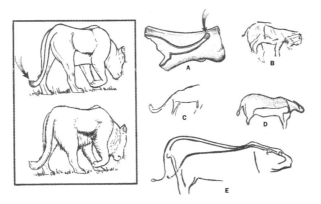

Paleolithic images of lions show a large tail tuft similar to that of extant African and Asian lions, but the color and size of this tuft may have changed with the season. *Box:* Reconstruction of summer coat (*top*) and winter coat (*bottom*). **A**, Laugerie-Basse, Fr. **B**, Labouiche, Fr. **C**, Gönnersdorf, Ger. **D–E**, Chauvet, Fr.

Some of the drawings of Pleistocene lions show a distinct dark posterior vertical line where the neck hits the shoulder. This may only have signified a shoulder contour, but it seems to be more. *Box:* Reconstructed female in winter coat. **A**, Lascaux, Fr. **B**, Pech-Merle, Fr. **C–F**, Chauvet, Fr. **G**, Los Casares, Sp.

Missing Lion Manes at Chauvet   Today, male lions typically have large manes, and females are maneless; however, the manes of male lions pictured in Paleolithic art are short. These short manes may have been the result of less emphasis on male competition because of the small size of prides (Guthrie 1990). I contend that pride size in the Pleistocene was smaller than that of today because of low mammalian prey density on the cold Mammoth Steppe. However, the selection dynamics of mane size may be more complicated. Manes are social organs, and the small manes in Paleolithic art may indicate a social system completely different from the one seen in African lions today. The striking climatic seasonality in Pleistocene Europe would have dictated the timing of reproduction, and Pleistocene lions, like wolves today, would have had to have their young in spring. That meant that, given lions' 110-day gestation, estrus would have occurred during a short peak in midwinter.

Today, African males stay with the pride year-round, as females can come into estrus any time of the year. The continual presence of a large and, at times, crazily aggressive male helps the pride defend their kills from other species and their territory from other lions. However, males are costly and belligerent, often driving females (who have done the hunting/killing) and their cubs off the fresh kills. Small pride size and a fixed mating season might shift the balance of advantages and disadvantages of having a male around full-time—making the male's year-round presence too burdensome for the females. If so, small prides in the Eurasian Pleistocene would have regularly been female, with males hunting singly or with one or two other cooperating males.

Though a male's mane gets him more social status as a threatening display organ and pads the neck against opponents' violent bites, this "moving haystack" is not conducive to cryptic stealth. Lions must stalk to within a short distance of their prey before the chase begins, because they can run at full speed for only a short distance. Large manes thus become a handicap for males hunting on their own. Perhaps Pleistocene art does accurately reflect the minimalist manes of lions living out on the short-sward Mammoth Steppe—and the complete absence of manes in the case of the images from Chauvet Cave in southern France. As discussed elsewhere in this book, Chauvet Cave seems to be a contrary place/time with regard to the gradient in portrayals (and perhaps in life) of pelage patterns of several species of large mammals.

earlier in this chapter. The ears of lions in Paleolithic images are significantly smaller than the ears of living lions, indicating a cold adaptation. Also, the manes of lions in Paleolithic art are more like those of young African lion males today, that is, a row of tufted hairs along the dorsal and ventral parts of the neck. This is rather like the "maneless" males common in the Tsavo Flats in East Africa or the small-maned lions occasionally found in the Kalahari. Compared to wolves, say, many lions are portrayed in Paleolithic art. I suspect this abundance of lion images reflects Paleolithic artists' attentive lion watching and concern. Surely, lions were the subject of many exciting stories. While visiting a graduate student in the field in 1985, my family and I were tenting (unarmed) near a borehole at Savuti in Botswana. One night around midnight a large lion pride came into our camp and bedded down just outside, up against the tent wall. I lay there in the dark listening to the deep breathing of a sleeping lion, just inches away through the tent. Myself, I was quite awake. Like grizzlies in Alaska, lions add a unique spice to life, probably one quite familiar to Paleolithic people.

WHAT CAN WE MAKE OF THESE GEOGRAPHIC GRADIENTS AMONG LARGE-MAMMAL SPECIES IN PALEOLITHIC ART?

I think these gradients point to greater habitat, climatic, and hence mammalian diversity on the southern fringes of the Mammoth Steppe. The presence of arid scrub and woodlands would have favored selection for genetic vestiges, producing markings adapted to a phylogenetic past in open woodlands and scrub savannas. What existed in southern Europe during the late Pleistocene was perhaps more reminiscent of the kinds of communities and the kinds of climates from which northern-adapted steppic species had once arisen in the late Tertiary.

In sorting out causes for such trends during the last Glacial maximum, it is important to remember, first, that most of the dominant large mammals of the Mammoth Steppe (caballoid horses, reindeer, woolly mammoths, and steppe bison, in particular) were adapted to cold and open country. And second, Pleistocene habitats, both the steppic and the more diverse southern fringes, have no simple analog in today's vegetation.

Finally, we need to be aware that these biogeographic gradients were likely not static. After all, the late Pleistocene was a turbulent time—with dramatic changes in climate, major expansions and contractions in the distribution of individual species, strange community associations of floras and faunas, and large-scale extinctions. In comparison, the 10,000 years since the Pleistocene have been climatologically dull.

Although in some continental localities like the Russian Plain, humans lived rather far north (West 1997), they mainly stayed in the scrubby woodlands of the south or their riparian fingers reaching northward. So we have an incomplete record of the full geographic spectrum of species in Paleolithic art, limited not only to the animals to which humans paid attention but also to those living in the regions where humans could live. This restricts the geographic comparisons we can make, but the glimpses we get through the preserved art are sufficient to charge the imagination.

IMAGES OF PEOPLE IN PALEOLITHIC ART

One cannot leave the train of examples of this north-south gradient of large mammals without calling attention to the size and pelage of another mammal: humans.

Airvaux and Pradel (Airvaux 2001) teased out facial images from Marche, Fr. These slate drawing stones apparently were used over and over, leaving superimposed figures. Emerging from this stone is a Pleistocene bald guy, which I show here along with a comparable image from an ancient Greek bust of Socrates, now on display at the Vatican Museum.

Evolution has affected the appearance of human races as it relates to geography. Though there has been much large-scale movement of peoples in post-Pleistocene times, there still, despite much admixture, seems to be an irregular but significant gradient in body size (and in skin and hair color) from the Mediterranean to Scandinavia (Cavalli-Sforza, Menozzi, and Piazza 1994).

According to archaeological evidence, people remained marginal to the Mammoth Steppe, so we don't have a large northern range of Pleistocene comparisons, as with bison and reindeer. It is difficult to deduce things like Pleistocene skin color gradients from the images of people in the art. In fact, the blue eyes, freckles, blond and red hair, and transparent-white skin of northern Europe may have been a post-Pleistocene phenomenon. But it is also possible that blond hair and blue eyes characterized Pleistocene people from southern Europe. The northernmost part of Europe was mostly uninhabited at the peak of the last Glacial, 18,000 years ago (Otte 1990; Schneider 1990) and was colonized by southern and eastern European peoples about 13,000 years ago. Paleolithic art in the Franco-Cantabrian region is not much help in resolving the issue of individual human variation, but it does show basic features that resemble those of modern Europeans. Hair is shown mostly straight, sometimes wavy, and occasionally curly. While there are some longish noses, individual vari-

This figurine of a naked female, nicknamed "Fanny," is from Stratzling-Galgenberg, Aus. It was cut from a sheet of serpentine. Human forms in Paleolithic art will be treated in later chapters. Although this is one of the oldest of the European "Venus" figurines, apparently older than 32,000 years ago, it is among the most dynamic, with bent leg and raised arm.

Assuming the guise of an effective predator or of the game you hunt is a common impulse among hunters worldwide. Recent Eskimo groups employed labrets (lip inserts), gores (white insets in parkas), and tattoos to convey a walrus tusk effect.

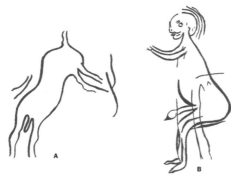

The drawings of people, especially those of males, in Paleolithic art are poorly done: **A**, Pergouset, Fr. **B**, Saint-Cirq, Fr.

ability is the recurrent theme. Human skeletons preserved from late Paleolithic Europe are certainly large in stature and of a Caucasoid build and skull shape.

Paleolithic Naturalists as Artists

I have given only a few samples of how Paleolithic art can give us a glimpse of how people saw their surroundings. The lip curls, striped horses, and the like are not just trivial asides but are critical for grounding us in how these people experienced their natural surroundings, and I will build on this theme throughout the rest of the book. This approach focuses on Paleolithic imagery as the work of artist-naturalists with the emphasis on artists as naturalists. Now, I want to twist that around and look at these images for what they might reveal about the Paleolithic naturalists as artists.

Imagine spending many hours of your life lying concealed in a bit of cover along a windy ridge, watching a woolly herd grazing below. You watch and doze, and look again, comment to a companion: "Did you see that? What was she doing, that mare? Is she the leader? Oh, yes, she must be. Notice how she looks different from the others." Year after year, lifetime after lifetime, lore of animals accumulated. Animals were the Pleistocene libraries, newspapers, comics and videos, classrooms, shop floors, soccer matches, and churches. One mastered reindeer and horses the way a surgeon or diamond cutter learns a craft. When hunters closed their eyes, we know that they could see muscle and tendon in their proper positions and articulations. Yet such an inner vision was no instant gift but was accumulated and honed by observation and experience, and the spoor of that learning is visible in Paleolithic art.

INEXPERIENCED DRAWERS AMONG
THE PALEOLITHIC ARTISTS

In the pages that follow I will be talking about making images of animals—the process of learning to make images and the particular sorts of problems that arise in drawing large mammals. It is necessary to do this because Paleolithic art is not a collection of masterworks. Certainly, Paleolithic art includes images that are fluid, are totally persuasive, and are aptly called masterpieces. But our collection of Paleolithic art also has images that are not artis-

Living Inside the Animals You Are Drawing

Bushman informants have repeatedly emphasized that the best hunters imaginatively become the animal they are hunting; they thus are better able to think like it does (Silberbauer 1981; Liebenberg 1990a). It is "being that animal; what did I do or what will I do?" This may sound strange to nonhunters, but most hunters immediately relate to this point, as do field ethologists (Valerius Geist, pers. comm.). This is also familiar to experienced wildlife artists. Such imaginative work has both behavioral and anatomical dimensions. Large-mammal anatomy is close enough to our own that once you have worked out the evolutionary analogies, you can imaginatively inhabit an animal, getting a bodily sense of their being, as a way of visualizing their movements.

This absorption that immerses a hunter in the desired animal makes large-mammal hunting different from many other kinds of hunting and from foraging. It is a highly effective strategy because humans are similar enough to other large mammals that, when such imaginative focus is combined with enough experience, a hunter almost anticipates what the animal will do next. This is a learned skill, honed by thousands of hours of observation. One cannot just step into another organism at will. Searching for, tracking, and stalking large mammals are fraught with consid-

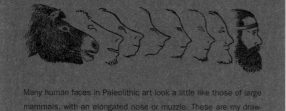

Many human faces in Paleolithic art look a little like those of large mammals, with an elongated nose or muzzle. These are my drawings to illustrate the character or flavor of this gradient.

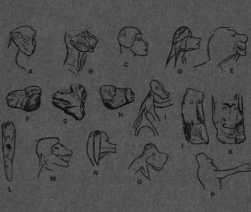

This long-muzzle imagery is recurrent in Paleolithic art. Some may be inadvertent, made by inexperienced drawers, but remember, large mammals were the focus of these hunters' lives—that is one of the central messages of this book. A, Trois Frères, Fr. B–D and N, La Marche, Fr. E, Enlène, Fr. F–H, Kostenki, Rus. I, Los Casares, Sp. J–K, Altamira, Sp. L, La Garenne, Fr. M, Massat, Fr. O, Torre, Sp. P, La Colombière, Fr.

erable indecision and complexity. One needs every edge, and while modern hunters can identify with the idea of completely focused immersion in another animal, this must have been even more effective for a Paleolithic professional.

This deep involvement with other large mammals informs and animates Paleolithic art. Maybe it also explains the remarkable frequency with which prehistoric and historic hunters have drawn people who have partly become the hunted. One can see this theme in various cultures, especially in pictures of the human face. People are often given muzzles. While some of these man-beasts may represent specific images from myths or visions, I do not think it is always necessary to presume that magic or trance is implied. In drawing oneself, or others, the artist is drawing "sense-of-self," not simple photographic images. And one must walk around being more than a little bit bison if one is a true bison hunter.

ticaly proficient. Nevertheless, even these images are usually quite informative about how carefully Paleolithic artists looked at animals. And some of these individual works exhibit technical mistakes completely parallel to those made by inexpert animal artists today.

In stating this so baldly I do not, in any way, intend to dethrone Paleolithic art. Quite the reverse. I suggest you set aside ideas you may have held about the brilliance of Paleolithic artists just long enough to examine some of the less publicized images made by artists with different

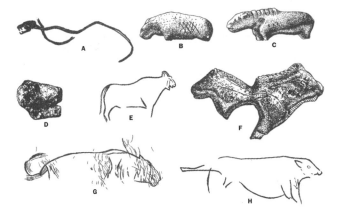

I have presented Paleolithic works showing different levels of ability and experience. Here are some more examples of that gradient of technical competence in lion portrayals: **A**, La Baume Latrone, Fr. **B–C**, Vogelherd, Ger. **D**, Kostenki, Rus. **E**, Los Casares, Sp. **F**, La Vache, Fr. **G**, Aldène, Fr. **H**, Gabillou, Fr.

degrees of skill and experience. I will argue that our collection of Paleolithic art serves as a wonderful document of individual drawing-skill development among people tens of thousands of years ago. Its images record moments in learning to see, which are always individual. I think some subjects in Paleolithic art have been misidentified because recent scholars assumed all Paleolithic artists were completely competent; that is, these scholars mistakenly assumed every artist was able to draw exactly what he wanted to draw. But this conjecture misunderstands the drawing process. And I suspect this error was frequently compounded, if not produced, by assumptions that specially gifted shamans were the only artists.

PERSPECTIVES: TENSIONS BETWEEN KNOWING AND SEEING

Let's say that you have seen hundreds, maybe even thousands, of bison. Now you sit down to draw one. Where do you begin? Like virtually all large mammals, bison are complex and challenging forms to draw. Examine the problem of drawing an animal from an artist's viewpoint. You can't draw the whole bison at once. In fact, you can only see one side of it, one-half of the animal at one time. The images in our collection show that Paleolithic artists

evidently preferred side views. I think a prime reason for this is that side views show a hunter's ideal target, and such views contain a wealth of artistically diagnostic information. But whether side or front, top or bottom, we can see only half an animal well. We know a bull has four legs and two horns—but how do we represent that? We could use some artistic license and push the legs around where all four can be seen and twist the head a little so that both horns show . . . but what about the eyes?

The Halibut Effect: Pleistocene Four-Eyed Horses? Though it may seem trivial, one thing that happens in representational drawing is navigating the differences between what you *see* and what you *know* to be there. For example, from a side view only one eye is visible, yet we know that animals have two eyes and that eyes are very important. One solution to this quandary is to draw a head from the side but two eyes as well. My daughter calls these "Snoopy eyes" after the childlike presentation of the beagle in Schulz's cartoon *Peanuts*.

If you were to draw, for example, a side view of a horse with two eyes this way, someone "reading" your image very literally might say you have drawn a four-eyed horse. Certain marine flatfish (halibut, sole, turbot, etc.) have an adaptive behavior of pushing themselves into the bottom sediments for concealment. The fish does this while lying flat on one side, but the "bottom" eye of these fish has evolutionarily "migrated" onto their "topside." When Paleolithic artists draw two eyes on one side, I will call this—whether it is deliberate choice, artistic convention, or learner's mistake—the "halibut effect." This technique is related to the x-ray view of art rendition that I will discuss in the next chapter.

The halibut effect can involve most paired organs—horns, ears, and legs—because these paired characteristics are such a central part of an animal's identity. One other solution is to bring both horns or eyes into the drawing perspective by simply twisting the head to a three-quarters view. Some Paleolithic artists did just this, but most artists took the shortcut and twisted the horns around and left

This artist's solution to the complex problem of depicting both forelegs of an aurochs was to use a twisted perspective. Lascaux, Fr.

Much later, one can see similar shoulder solutions using a twisted perspective. **A**, Wild cattle on Gundestrup cauldron, early Iron Age, Denmark. **B**, Egyptian painting. **c**, Libyan rock art showing milk cow. **D**, Eland from Atrallingskop, R.S.A.

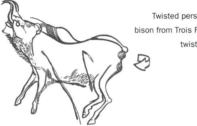

Twisted perspective of a speared cow bison from Trois Frères, Fr. Anus and vulva twisted around toward viewer.

the head in a straight side view. We can find a gradient of head and horn perspectives in Paleolithic images, but the profile, or side view, predominates.

Most Paleolithic images do not employ more complex perspectives. I think this is largely explained by the difficulties involved. There are a few examples where something other than a side view was attempted both for parts and for entire bodies. Little wonder Paleolithic artists avoided more difficult perspectives; their complex subjects were demanding enough!

These matters may sound elementary, but the briefest experimental foray into drawing should reveal the quite substantive challenges we are discussing. There are many dimensions to the drawing process, including important neurophysiological aspects.

Among Paleolithic images we find many skewed horns, halibut-eyed horses, and animals with legs dangling hither and yon. These are not unique to the Paleolithic; we find them in rock art from a variety of prehistoric cultures, as well as in contemporary work of children. Later, such features became stylized and incorporated into codified

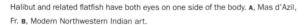

Halibut and related flatfish have both eyes on one side of the body. **A**, Mas d'Azil, Fr. **B**, Modern Northwestern Indian art.

Twisted perspective also occurs in representations of eyes, ears, and noses. **A**, Lion, Gabillou, Fr. **B**, Lions, Chauvet, Fr. **c**, Horse, Niaux, Fr.

Four-eyed animals, the "halibut effect" in Paleolithic art: **A**, Aurochs, Pair-non-Pair, Fr. **B**, Bison, Gabillou, Fr. **C**, Musk ox, Lascaux, Fr. **D** and **F**, Horses, Lascaux, Fr. **E**, Horse, Trois Frères, Fr. **G**, Reindeer(?), Limeuil, Fr. **H**, Reindeer, Saint-Eulalie, Fr. **I**, human, Saint-Cirq, Fr. **J**, Horses, Marsoulas, Fr. **K**, Giant deer (shelk), Belcayre, Fr.

Artists from many prehistoric Holocene cultures employed this twisted-eye perspective. **A–D** and **G**, Saharan rock art. **A**, Sheep. **B**, Wild ass. **C**, Black rhino. **D**, Elephants and lion. **E**, Lion and ungulate, Helanshan, China. **F**, Bear(?), North American Woodland Indian. **G**, Extinct giant horned buffalo, *Pelorovis*. **H**, Dingo, Barralumma, Austrl. **I**, Kangaroo, Queensland, Austrl.

symbolic art forms. But culturally defined forms or preset motifs are not a characteristic part of Paleolithic art. Let's review a sampling of features with which Paleolithic artists struggled.

Getting the Tusks Right: The Pleistocene Double Helix   Want to try drawing a difficult subject? Try mammoth tusks. Mammoth tusks grew continuously throughout the life of the animal, but they did not grow straight. A mammoth tusk describes a wide arcing spiral; it is in fact a segment of a helix. Drawing the mammoth tusk helix is even more demanding because it is a gaining helix, one that widens as it grows. The tusks make this gaining helix in opposite (left, clockwise; right, counterclockwise) directions.

When fossil skulls and tusks were unearthed, no one knew exactly how to mount them because skulls and tusks were usually found disconnected or the tusks were loose and had rotated in their sockets. Cuvier, the great French naturalist of the late eighteenth century, logically argued that the tips must point upward and outward like giant horns do, because tusks could have been of little use to the mammoth if the tips met inward. However, when more complete specimens were finally discovered, Cuvier turned out to be wrong. He had the tusks switched left-and-right. The tusks on old bulls did arc toward one another, their tips sometimes coming together in the midline—admittedly a counterintuitive position. Even with this anatomical puzzle solved, many modern renditions of mammoth tusks still miss the mark of accuracy. The renowned wildlife sculptor, painter, and fossil reconstructionist Charles Knight flubbed it in one of his earlier drawings of mammoths, and so did the excellent artist Abbé Henri Breuil, one of the fathers of Paleolithic art study. The helical arcs are simply very hard to represent accurately in two dimensions. The evolution of mammoth tusks is unusual, as the tusk is not an enlarged canine but an upper

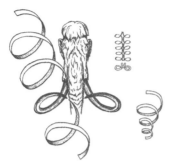

Mammoth tusks, or second upper incisors, grow in spirals in opposite directions; they are actually "gaining" helices, opening up the circles they describe as the tusks age. They are very difficult to draw.

Let's see how Paleolithic artists drew these opposite gaining helices of mammoth tusks. The evidence confirms it was tough. Some tried it, more inexperienced artists just took a shortcut, and some truly botched it. **A**, Rouffignac, Fr. (the best gets an A+). **B**, Pech-Merle, Fr. **C**, La Mouthe, Fr. **D**, Chauvet, Fr. (not bad). **E**, Gargas, Fr. **F** and **J**, La Baume Latrone (some of the most exotic solutions). **G–H**, Colombier, Fr. **K**, Bernifal, Fr.

Woolly mammoths drawn in the twentieth century by (**A**) American wildlife artist Charles Knight and (**B**) Henri Breuil, one of the most famous Paleolithic art specialists (and an excellent artist in his own right). Compare these two with (**C**) a woolly mammoth reconstructed using actual fossil material, from a sculpture in Jardin des Plantes, Paris.

To Me, I²

Hint of yellow smooth,
not wood, you caught my eye,
deep program to alert my wandering
mind, intruding on my dreams.
Double take, back-paddle the canoe.
Caught you, slipping out of
your dirt bank frozen tomb,
creamy spiral blanketed in mud.
Yes, I know you, old timer.

Your emblem, spiral monolith,
fitting marker for your grave.
Precious ivory to the trade,
coffee-marbled scrimshaw.
Only a tool to you, a prod
to get your way, to lift and jab.
To me, I², second upper incisor,
small nibbler grown into
megatooth, runaway evolution.

So let me tie you under thwart
and gunnel, and take you home.
Resurrected, or as close as one can get.
Make your distant time my own.
I mean you no irreverence.
I, too, face soon the frozen tomb,
and perhaps in far millennia, will,
like you, slip that grave, to be shelved
in thermoregulated museum range.

second incisor. These greatly enlarged second incisors, the I^2 teeth, were mammoth social regalia and social weapons.

Antlers and Horns of a Dilemma The complex three-dimensional forms of horns and antlers are right up there with mammoth tusks as a representational challenge. Bison and wild cattle horns also describe the curve of a helix that widens as the animals grow older. As with mammoth tusks, most Paleolithic artists solved the problem by mak-

Like mammoth tusks, bison horns are also complex helices, as are those of aurochs, ibex, and chamois.

Two-dimensional illustrations of complexly three-dimensional horns are indeed difficult. These are from Paleolithic art. **A**, Saiga or chamois, Gargas, Fr. (one would better appreciate this drawing if you suspected that it was done by a child). **B**, Bison, Trois Frères, Fr. **C**, Bison, Gargas, Fr. **D**, Bison, Lascaux, Fr. **E**, Aurochs, Chauvet, Fr. **F**, Chamois, Candamo, Sp. **G**, Bison, Laugerie-Basse, Fr. **H**, Bison, Font de Gaume, Fr. (quite good). **I**, Ibex, Limeuil, Fr. **J**, Bison, Font de Gaume, Fr. (dynamic solution—one of the best). **K**, Aurochs, Chauvet, Fr. **L**, Ibex, Nerja, Sp. **M**, ibex, Niaux, Fr. (great posterior view). **N**, Bison, Trois Frères, Fr. **O**, Aurochs, Chauvet, Fr.

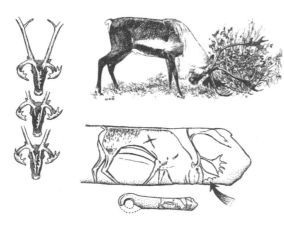

There are many ways to draw antlers and we can see them in Paleolithic art: **A, E, G**, Red deer, Lascaux, Fr. (note spear and blood). **B**, Red deer, Del Niño, Sp. **C**, Reindeer, Trois Frères, Fr. (note spears). **D**, Reindeer, Gourdan, Fr. **F**, Reindeer, Laugerie-Basse, Fr. **H**, Red deer, Calapará, Sp. **I**, Reindeer, Chauvet, Fr.

ing two parallel S-shaped lines, though we can see that Paleolithic artists sometimes struggled for more precise representation.

Antlers are even more difficult to draw, especially reindeer antlers, which are very asymmetrical. Most bull reindeer have only one brow tine; sometimes it is the left and sometimes the right. Fewer than 10% of living reindeer have "double shovels," or two palmate brow tines, and this is true of Pleistocene fossils in Europe as well.

SCENE COMPOSITION AND PERSPECTIVE: CHALLENGE OF A SECOND ORDER

Relatively few images in Paleolithic art represent a scenic assemblage of figures. Again, this may simply reflect the more complex compositional and representational challenges. Art history books reveal conventions later art-

◄ Almost unique among mammals, reindeer have a forward-projecting brow tine flattened like a shovel. It was portrayed well in Paleolithic art in a specimen from Thayngen, Switz. It was once thought, incorrectly, to have been used as a snow shovel. Pruitt (1966) proposed that it was to protect the eyes while bush-thrashing (drawing by William Berry). Here I suggest that it was a defensive structure used in fighting. It can be asymmetrically exaggerated on either the left antler or the right or is sometimes symmetrical on both sides. When the brow shovel is on both sides, it is known to hunters as the "double shovel."

Holocene solutions to tough perspective problems using twisted and inverted images to show three dimensions: **A** and **E**, Kimberly, R.S.A. (the people are not leaping over the eland). **B**, Yinshan, Mongolia. **C–D** and **F**, Narsinghgarh, India. **G**, Mongolia. **H** and **L**, Val Camonica, It. **I**, Isaagen, Sahara. **J**, Orange Free State, R.S.A. **K**, Kivik, Sweden.

ists have used for coping with these problems. Nevertheless, we can see that some Paleolithic artists did engage in these challenges. Clottes (2000) refers to Aurignacian artists, 32,000 years ago, expressing complex perspectives in meticulous realistic detail, full-face orientation, and exquisite animation. That is, we cannot see different stages in artistic development from simple to complex throughout the span of late Paleolithic art. I illustrate a number of "scene" drawings from Paleolithic art throughout this book.

Normally one draws subjects as if one were standing on the same plane, but the problem with this is how to show parts farther away than others or animals standing behind others. Depth of field is a second-order elaboration of the halibut effect. One solution has been to show figures from a top view, which may result in an image that looks as if people surrounding a bull, for example, were jumping over the bull in some ceremonial rite. Such a perspective is employed in images from a number of cultures, both prehistoric and modern: for example, Bushman and Saharan art. Some prehistorians, perhaps inexperienced in drawing, have tended to give rather mystical interpretations of scenes composed in this way. The images I illustrate here show the solutions Paleolithic artists achieved. These include solutions that contemporary artists, struggling with similar representational challenges, would term technical mistakes.

In one prehistoric clock-face perspective of a hunting scene, men and dogs appear to be flying around a wild bull. The image comes from a seal on the inside of the famous Gundestrup cauldron (see above, p. 94), from the

What we see when watching a moving animal is actually a staccato series of fixed images; every twenty-fifth of a second an image is erased and replaced by new one. Although we actually see static images, which our brain compiles into the process of movement, we cannot "stop action" on leg movements of running animals, like these reindeer on the left, drawn from a photo. We experience more of what is shown on the right, a blur of legs.

Danish Iron Age. The metalsmith who made this exquisite silver cauldron had the same problems anyone faces when attempting to represent images in perspective. Note that the artist twisted the bull's right shoulder, on the far side of the body, around so you can see it. His solution to problems of perspective was similar to that employed in another image of a bull, this one in Lascaux Cave.

As with the first-order choices and difficulties posed in representing individual animals or people, we need to be cognizant of the challenges of presenting complex scenes in perspective, because, if we are not, it is that much easier to misinterpret certain elements of Paleolithic art. Drawing problems in image construction are as important for us to appreciate as the details of the natural history the images portray.

ART IN MOTION: PERCEIVING AND RENDERING PROCESS

The aim of every artist is to arrest motion, which is life, by artificial means and hold it fixed so that 100 years later when a stranger looks at it, it moves again since it is life.

William Faulkner, *Lion in the Garden*

Quadruped Legs: Where Are the Elbow, Knee, and Ankle? While I've stressed that Paleolithic images are the marks of experienced observers of animals and can indeed teach us much about the Mammoth Steppe faunas, there are also aspects of some images that are technically unreliable and there are anatomical points that are not intentionally "drawn wrong" but inadvertently came out that way. Images of legs are a good example. In fleet ungulates, the hock on the hind leg is actually homologous to our heel. When this is understood—when the relative lengthening of the ungulate's lower leg bones (our foot bones) is sensed clearly—one can see and draw ungulate legs without making it look as if the hind legs bend opposite to ours. But this matter is not transparently obvious, and such leg confusions are frequently found in art, even

among people who have looked at a lot of animals. Instances occur in Bushman and Paleolithic art.

Human legs move rather simply, hinging from the hip, knee, and ankle, with broad arcs of flexibility. Our knee hinges backward, with a stop keeping it from hinging forward. Our arms hinge in a similar but reversed way; that is, the elbow joint hinges forward, and the stop keeps it from hinging backward. This is an ancient quadruped pattern dating back to amphibians in our past, their fleshy paddles evolving into limbs as they came onto land. Their fossil limbs show us exactly how this happened and when.

After mastering a stick figure, the next step is to create images with muscle-mass dimension. Drawers at this developmental level tend to portray animal legs that look something like table legs. The next challenge is to show life, to animate the animal by moving or lifting its legs. Difficulties abound. It is quite an accomplishment to show one leg off the ground and weight shifted to the other foot; it is even more difficult to suggest movement.

Gaits and How Legs Move Developing an acute sense of how limbs move and representing that movement in two dimensions are among the more difficult aspects of drawing animals. I think there is a neurophysiological reason why this step is so difficult, in addition to its artistic complexity. What we see when watching a moving animal is actually a staccato series of fixed images; each immediately erased by the subsequent one. That is, we actually see static images, which our brain compiles into the process of

Man-Beast Sorcerers or Leg Mistakes?

Some Paleolithic images identified as part man and part beast may simply be artistic bloopers. This is not to say that all such hybrid-appearing images are. Some may indeed be religious or mythical creatures. Others appear to be hunting disguises—but more on that in a later chapter. I just want to point out that it is easy and common to get the hinge pattern of quadruped legs mixed up with the human pattern and that doing this can easily turn what was meant to be

Some of the enigmatic "anthropomorph" forms can be explained otherwise than as transformed shamans. **A.** Here is an example from Gabillou, Fr. The artist seems simply to have drawn the hind-limb joint of a bison incorrectly. **B.** Reconstruction with changed bone proportions (tibia filled in).

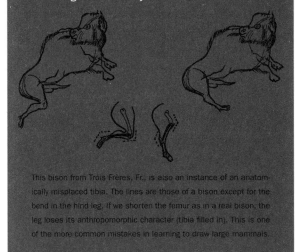

This bison from Trois Frères, Fr., is also an instance of an anatomically misplaced tibia. The lines are those of a bison except for the bend in the hind leg. If we shorten the femur as in a real bison, the leg loses its anthropomorphic character (tibia filled in). This is one of the more common mistakes in learning to draw large mammals.

a picture of a bison into a man-beast. I think the peculiar image of a bison bull from Les Trois Frères is an example of such a mix-up. This bison has been identified as a sorcerer because it is a combination of man and beast. Yet every feature in the image represents a bison except the hind leg. That leg is bent the wrong way for a bison. The knee (femoral-tibial joint) is too low for a bison and is depicted more like that of a human. The feet are bison feet and even the genitals are

movement, like the frames of a movie, only we are unable to "stop action." We are not able to isolate a momentary position within a moving series. It is much easier to recall or construct a mental image of someone standing still than it is to imagine that person in motion.

Our ability to perceive movement is like a digital device with rather limited capacity. Every twentieth of a second or so a photosensitive cell in your eye transmits (or does not transmit) an impulse as to whether it is being stimulated by light—a true digital system. We can see individual blinks of a light that is flashing fifteen times per second, but a light blinking at a little over twenty flashes per second begins to appear as a steady light. Of course, cinema and television work, in just this way, by supplying an illusion of movement at a frequency just beyond our ability to isolate individual images. The ability to freeze the leg action of a running horse is well beyond our capac-

ity, and the detailed action of a horse's trot was not "seen" with precision until about a hundred years ago. Leland Stanford, after whom Stanford University in California was named, wagered with another man as to whether a trotting horse had a moment when all its feet were off the ground. To settle the bet they enlisted the services of a local photographer, Eadweard Muybridge, who solved this problem by taking a series of stop-action photos. Muybridge found that horses do have a brief moment of floating. Stanford won. Muybridge was so intrigued by the process that he went on to specialize in such stop-action photographic sequences, making over 10,000 photos and changing the way artists envision and portray locomotion. It has been said that you can tell the day when the American painter-sculptors Charles Russell and Frederic Remington first saw Muybridge's 1887 book by the effects on their art.

A. Bison, Gabillou, Fr., showing a mistake similar to the one in the last illustration. Note that if the hock and elbow are pulled up as in a real bull, no other trait is human-like. **B.** Reconstruction (tibia filled in).

of a pointed, ligamentous, bovid type unlike the clubby, hydrostatic ones of stallions and men. Baffier (1984) has also questioned the identification of this bison from Les Trois Frères as some kind of sorcerer.

Two other ambiguous bison-men are found at Gabillou. In one case not only are the hind legs bent wrong, but human feet are included and the animal is bipedal. What makes me suspect this is a drawing error rather than a deliberately executed image of a

"sorcerer man-beast" is that the legs are attached to a different line separate from the bison's, and within the near thigh one can see two legs that are bison-like. These appear as if someone corrected his own or someone else's drawing. The forefeet of this same piece, though bison, also show some indecisiveness. Both images of bison are made by artists not clear about bison anatomy. There are analogous images in other prehistoric art—for example, the eland from Snowhill, in South Africa, which is traditionally called an anthropomorph.

Of course, artists had successfully suggested animals in motion long before Muybridge—you only have to look at Lascaux for a start. This has been done in individually inventive ways as well as via such artistic conventions as the "flying gallop." Again, I am not saying these things are not artistically successful but only threading my way between the paired issues of anatomical action and challenges of representation.

While Paleolithic artists usually represented leg anatomy with accuracy, they often had more difficulty representing quadruped leg movement. It is all too easy to appreciate the trouble this poses even though we have photographs and slow-motion films to aid our representational efforts. We go through life seeing thousands of different animals walk, trot, or gallop, and yet few of us can describe in simple terms how the quadruped legs move during each gait. And fewer still could draw how the legs

move in relation to each other during these gaits. Many famous artists, including contemporary animal artists, occasionally put the legs in the wrong places, unintentionally. Knowing the anatomical mechanics does not ensure the ability to make an accurate or persuasive image of that motion.

Drawing a horse with the legs in the wrong places for a particular gait may not look so bad, but it is analogous to drawing a person walking, or especially running or jumping, with his arms and legs swinging in same-side synchrony. We are sensitive to the latter, because we have a kinesthetic knowledge of the way we move. That is why we see such a representation as an error and feel it as wrong. Most of us lack that kinesthetic sense or an informed imagined substitute for, say, reindeer.

Paleolithic artists rarely pictured animals at top speed, but when they did, they generally represented a gallop by

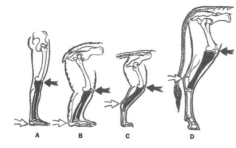

Common ancestry means the bones of mammalian limbs are homologous in origin. However, in function, the basic pattern has been adapted to different kinds of locomotion. Humans (A) and bears (B) retain a primitive walk, with heels flat. Dogs (C) walk on the digits. Efficient quadrupeds like bison and cattle (D) have undergone a shortening of the upper limb and an elongation of the lower part. This pulls the "knee" up so close to the body it can hardly be seen. The calcaneum, or "heel," becomes the cattle's hock. They walk on tiptoe (fingernails become hooves). For comparison, solid arrows point to kneecaps, or patellas, and hollow arrows to heels/hocks, the lever arm of the calcaneum. Their equivalents are something an artist of animals has to sort out.

Illustrated limb angles clarify these homologous structures. Human and reindeer limbs do bend the same way: they just appear to bend as opposite hinges because people get the homologous joints mixed up.

showing the front legs together and extended forward and the hind legs together and extended backward. Such a gait does not actually occur, but this was the most common way artists represented the gallop for literally tens of thousands of years. And I doubt that even people who rode and watched horses every day of their lives found it strange before the advent of photographically articulated images of the positions of galloping. The "flying gallop" is an effective way of expressing all-out full speed and we all readily understand it visually. To portray running people, most prehistoric artists used a two-legged version of a flying gallop, but this is a literally incorrect portrayal of any running movement except the *grand jeté* of ballet.

There are three basic quadruped gaits: the walk, trot, and gallop (a slow form of gallop, but with three beats, is called a canter). A fourth gait, called the pace or rack, is

the basic gait used by camel and giraffe groups, as well as by saiga antelope and hemiones. There are advantages and disadvantages to each of these gaits—depending on speed, terrain, and the physiology and anatomy of the particular animal using them.

The walk is uniquely efficient energetically, but it is not very fast. The trot and canter retain some of the efficiency of the walk but are faster, while the gallop is fast but energetically costly. Pacing animals swing both legs on one side of the body, then move the legs on the other side. The advantage of the pace over the trot is that the stride length can be longer, because the fore foot doesn't get in the way of the hind foot, since hind and fore legs move in unison.

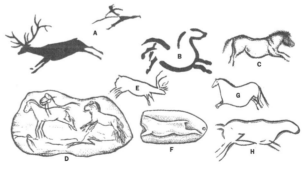

The most common pre-Muybridge solution for drawing running animals was the "flying gallop," with legs widely extended. This never happens in any running gait. But it is a dramatic visual effect and conveys the feeling of a gallop. A, Both people and red deer in a flying gallop, Mas D'en Josep, Sp. (Holocene). Paleolithic examples: B, Horse, Altamira, Sp. C, Horse, Font de Gaume, Fr. D, Horses, Limeuil, Fr. E, Reindeer, Gabillou, Fr. F, Red deer(?), Saint-Marcel, Fr. G, Horse, Lascaux, Fr. H, Horse(?), Soucy, Fr.

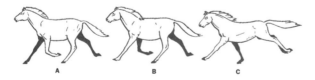

A horse frozen midstride in three different gaits: A, trot; B, pace; C, gallop. Much of this was not really understood by artists until Eadweard Muybridge took stop-action photos of horses in 1887.

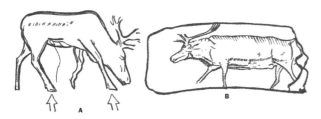

Two Paleolithic representations of reindeer. But reindeer legs never move like this. The artists have inadvertently drawn a pace, in which the left fore and left hind leg move in the same direction at the same time. Reindeer never pace. But the drawers can be easily forgiven because it is tough to work this out. **A**, Limeuil, Fr. **B**, Kesslerloch, Switz.

Two different attempts to make the animals appear to be running—not a bad job even if technically incorrect: **A**, Red deer, Calapatá, Sp. **B**, Horses, La Madeleine, Fr.

But this unison movement makes pacing a more unstable gait, usable only on rather flat ground, and it requires special anatomical compensations such as one sees in the strange build of a camel.

Some reindeer in Paleolithic images look a bit odd because they are shown walking in a pace, which reindeer never do. Camels and saigas are natural pacers and sometimes even horses and canids move like this, but never reindeer. Often the hind and front pairs of legs are drawn independently of one another as a beginning drawer might do. In other drawings the weight is not placed where it should be; a real animal assuming this position would fall flat. But there are some drawings where one can almost feel the weight settle into the limbs properly.

The Arc of Rump   Each species has its own subtly different gait preferences, which are adaptations to different parts of the landscape and kinds of favored escape terrain: horses are sprinters; bison, reindeer, and saigas are high-endurance, long-distance migrators; ibex and chamois are climbers of steep slopes; and so on. These adaptations affect species anatomy—for example, how the muscles attach to the upper parts of the bony girdles and leg bones. Thus, rump contours vary from one ungulate species to another. Eland, cattle, and reindeer, for example, have horizontal rump lines that end abruptly in a tail as the rump falls at right angles. Horse and mammoth rumps are rounded, with the root of the tail at modest height, while

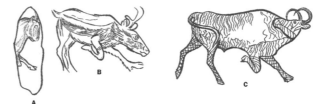

While these limb positions do not occur in life, as pictured images they convey dynamic movement. **A**, Ibex, Montastruc, Fr. (reversed for comparison). **B**, Reindeer, Trois Frères, Fr. Compare this to **C**, a Neolithic wild aurochs bull from Tassili, Sahara.

Top, two dynamic horse images from Lascaux, Fr. *Bottom,* my drawings of a trot and a rearing horse.

There are other images of animals in motion in Paleolithic art: **A**, Aurochs, Teyjat, Fr. **B**, Horse, Le Portel, Fr. **C**, Bison, Trois Frères, Fr. **D**, Horse, Font de Gaume, Fr.

the rounded rumps of red deer, African buffalo, and hartebeest have the tail root quite low. Since the head is one of the most diagnostic parts of ungulates, many artists master differences in head shape and just depict a "generalized rump" for any species they draw. In some Paleolithic

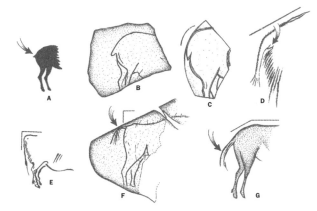

The shape of the rump is a product of muscle attachment mechanics. Not only did the more experienced artists get the animals' heads right, but the careful observers got the arcs of the rumps right as well. Red deer rumps: **A**, Calapatá, Sp. **B**, Polesini, It. **C**, Isturitz, Fr. We can identify a mammoth's rump by the anal flap: **D**, Rouffignac, Fr. Cattle have sharp-angled rumps: **E**, Mas d'Azil, Fr.; as do bison: **F**, Roc-la-Tour, Fr. Horse tails are rooted low: **G**, Ekain, Sp.

Bull resting with correct leg position. From one of Leonardo da Vinci's notebooks.

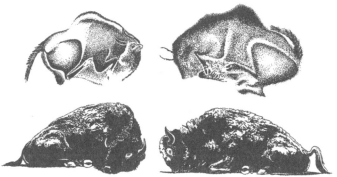

Two bison images from Altamira, Sp. (*top*). One can see from their placement next to my drawings of modern bison (*bottom*) that they are meant to be portrayed as lying down.

works, however, rump curves and angles are precisely represented. This sort of incisiveness is won by repeated observation and practice.

Lying Down in Paleolithic Art Quadruped legs can be difficult to depict, even when one is making an image of an animal that is lying down. Ruminants, which include most cloven-hoofed animals, cannot lie fully horizontal on their sides for any length of time because their rumens are like compost tanks. Ruminants coarsely chew food, which is then swallowed and processed in the rumen, the first of their four stomachs, by microorganisms that break down cellulose. During this rumen preprocessing, the larger plant particles float to the top and are regurgitated and rechewed as cud while smaller particles continue on to the next stomach chamber. This process is upset when a ruminant lies on its side because the microbial digesting processes also produce volumes of rumen methane that must be expelled by burping. That is why deer and bovids lie with their chests and heads more or less upright. Normally, they will lie on one hip and twist their torsos

so the sternum of the brisket is centered over the forequarters. Ungulates smaller than rhinos and proboscidians maneuver into this position by folding one ham under themselves.

This lying-on-a-thigh and upright-brisket posture has the advantage in a cold climate of keeping the thin-skinned and sparsely haired lower abdomen off the wet or cold ground. The flank of the leg is well insulated with thick skin and coarse hair as is the sternal pad. The latter also has a thick deposit of connective tissue and fat. This "sleeping pad" lets ungulates lie on ice or snow and still not lose much heat. Horses and zebras lie down this way as well, but since these equids are not ruminants, they can also flop down on their sides for hours. Elephants and rhinos are also not ruminants and additionally have a quite different leg structure. They lie down more like bears or lions do, often with legs splayed akimbo.

Bedded Upside Down on the Ceiling of Altamira

The cluster of bison on the cave ceiling at Altamira, near the northern coast of Spain, is one of the most spectacular assemblages of Paleolithic art. However, because it contains bison in such odd positions it has been an enigma. While bison from virtually all other localities are drawn rather conventionally, that is, standing broadside, several bison at Altamira are depicted prone, legs pulled beneath them and heads arced downward or twisted around to face the rear. Over the century since they were found, the Altamira bison have been given all kinds of special interpretations and symbolic meanings. It has also been suggested that these images are portraying bison rolling in a rutting pit (bison bulls do anoint themselves with their urine by rolling in their urine puddles in freshly dug ground). The problem of interpreting these forms arises partly because most of them are drawn so well and thus are subject to more speculation about meaning than is art of lesser quality.

I think that much of the enigma is derived from how these images are viewed, or how they are commonly photographed. They are situated upside down on a low ceiling, and when photographed from below, they do look strange in the resulting two-dimensional pictures. But when viewed in person or photographed

from the side (there are very few published photos taken at an oblique angle because of technical depth-of-field problems in this situation), one can see that the central bison in this group (those with folded legs) were actually painted over natural bumps in the cave ceiling and clearly do look like bison lying down. Bandi and Maringer (1955) and others have, in fact, noted that the natural bumps on the ceiling suggest a bedded herd of bison even without the painting. Yet the dominance of this opportunistic, contingent element of the artistic representations has been largely ignored by mainstream art historians. I will revisit this aspect of cave art in the next chapter and find its place in the bigger story.

A bison group from Altamira, Sp. Note the four animals lying down. These four animals are drawn over large projecting bumps in the ceiling—another case of elaborating a natural form.

Why would someone draw bison lying down? I think this is just a natural part of the way most Paleolithic images were made—the magnificence and inherent grandeur of the animals were sufficient. We see this same subject choice in Holocene Bushman art: A, springbok bedded down, Warden District, R.S.A. Animals simply lying down are likewise present in Holocene Saharan rock art from later times: B, gazelles, Tassili, North Africa. Note how the demanding choice of subjects almost got the best of the artist's abilities.

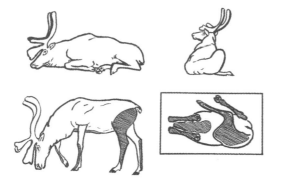

Most quadruped species lie down by placing the thigh of one hind leg on the ground to protect the thin-walled abdomen by using the thick skin and tough hair as padding. (*Box:* View from underneath.) One has to get very close to lying animals to see how this works (dark areas are the portions that touch the ground).

Pleistocene drawings of animals bedded down: **A** and **E**, Reindeer, Trois Frères, Fr. **B**, Chamois, Laugerie-Basse, Fr. **c**, Ibex, Bédeilhac, Fr. **D**, Red deer, La Griega, Sp. **F**, Chamois, Montastruc, Fr. **G**, Ibex, Hornos de la Peña, Sp. **H**, Reindeer(?), La Madeleine, Fr. **I**, Unidentified, Chabot, Fr. **J**, Red deer, Parpalló, Sp. **K**, Reindeer, Isturitz, Fr. **L**, Bison, Castillo, Sp. **M**, Crôt-du-Charnier, Fr.

Looking at Paleolithic images of animals lying down, we can see that most of the artists did not represent the actual ways that animals fold their legs or twist their hips. Indeed, even when seen up close this is not easy to sort out, nor is it easy to draw from memory. Some Paleolithic artists solved this problem by simply drawing legs bent under, correct anatomically as legs bend but not in the exact way ungulates bend them when they lie down. I doubt that Paleolithic hunters were often close enough to bedded animals for extensive study; they were likely preoccupied with other concerns. Remember, animals knew these hunter-artists as mortal enemies. A hunter approaching a bedded herd would be creeping along on the ground and at best would see only the back of the animal being stalked.

ARTISTIC LICENSE OR LITERAL LINE

What follows are a few examples of Paleolithic art interpretations where there is an apparent disparity between what might have been meant and what was actually rendered, showing how one cannot take an image literally outside its artistic context. Most of the problems between artistic intent and result were undoubtedly inadvertent on the part of the artists, and most are traceable to inexperi-

ence and probably to novices. The reasons for this statement will become apparent in the next chapter.

Lascaux Licorn: Mistaken Identity? One of the famous large painted images at Lascaux is that of a strange creature known as the "fabulous beast" or "Licorn." It is a four-legged animal with a long rectangular muzzle, with thick lips and two straight parallel horns, longer than those of any European mammal. Bate (1950) once proposed that the Licorn was an Asiatic chiru, *Pantholops hodgsoni,* but I consider this highly unlikely because no late Pleistocene European fossils of chirus have been found.

I think the best clue to the Licorn's identity is found right in Lascaux, just across the passageway. There, on a nearby wall, is a beautifully rendered polychrome image of an aurochs bull, *Bos taurus,* one of the wild cattle of Paleolithic Europe. This aurochs and the other aurochs painted at Lascaux were finely drawn or painted on the cave walls. The Licorn image was made quite differently. It was made by spitting ocher, a cruder technique, chosen perhaps because the wall at that point is covered by bumps

"Mystery bull" from Lascaux on left and my drawing on right showing that the mystery is primarily the peculiar long straight horns. Had the artist not drawn such long horns, the identification would be clearly a bull aurochs. It is primarily the horns that are the problem. The neck hump characteristic of bull aurochs is clearly apparent.

A, Why does the mystery bull have a short tail if it is an aurochs bull? Aurochs have long tufted tails. **B**, Yet only a few meters away in Lascaux one can see a short tail on another aurochs (reversed for comparison). Actually 2% of the bison in Wood Buffalo Park, Northwest Territories, Canada, have stub tails, and I have seen about this same frequency among wild zebra. Presumably this results from unsuccessful attacks by predators.

of rough calcite, which make it difficult to apply paint smoothly in any way other than spraying.

As the Licorn image has prompted so many explanations, I would like to take a moment to add my own to the collection. I think the evidence points to the Licorn's being the effort of an inexperienced artist, trying to imitate the marvelous image of the bull on the opposite wall. The Licorn's horns, for example, do not convey the complex three-dimensionality of the aurochs on the opposite wall. As I said, many beginning artists do not try for complex horn twists but use a straight line. We can see such artistic shorthand in other Pleistocene aurochs images (e.g., Gönnersdorf) and in cattle drawings from other prehistoric peoples, for example, in rupestral art from the Sahara. The strange bulbous muzzle is another feature that I think is most plausibly explained as a rather unsuccessful effort to make an image of an aurochs muzzle, but the spray of ocher produced a much larger nose than proportion demanded. Cattle snouts are not pointed like those of deer and are indeed rather thick, and there are some large

Compare the head of the Lascaux mystery bull (**A**) with another bull (**B**), just across the cave's passageway, which is reversed for comparison. The mystery bull has features that point to its being an aurochs. The angle of horns from the head is forward. Only wild cattle have such horns: in most other species, the horns rise vertically (*left to right*: **C**, aurochs, male and female; **D**, bison, saiga, ibex, chamois, chiru). The mystery bull has a large posterior neck hump, which occurs only in wild male cattle. Some other prehistoric drawings give wild cattle unusually long horns. **E**, Kazakhstan, Central Asia. **F**, Libya, North Africa. **G**, Parpalló, Sp. **I**, Levanzo, Sp. The large lips on the mystery bull are due to the "broad-brush" sprayed-pigment technique used in constructing this image; some other bulls in prehistoric art are also given larger-than-life lips: **H**, Gönnersdorf, Ger.

Facial Lines or Bridle Leather? In a line drawing, a line can demark the edge between what artists refer to as positive and negative space (the outline of the subject against its background). Lines are also employed to indicate changes of color or major contour changes within the outline. Apparently, the edge receptors in our visual processes are able to interpret lines within outside contours, such as those used to indicate a change in hair color from brown to white or the slight shadow difference from a rounded to a flatter curve, as well as those used to demarcate a figure against its background.

Paleolithic line drawings of horses' heads often include a line delineating a color change from the white muzzle to the brown head. I emphasize this because the large number of horse images in Paleolithic art allows us to conclude that Paleolithic horses were almost identical in appearance to living Przewalski's horses. Such a pattern is today observed in the winter pelage of Przewalski's horses.

Also, Paleolithic artists often used lines to characterize the sharp break in contour of the masseter muscle as it angles down to the mandible from its lengthy horizontal origin just below the eye. Just forward from the heavy masseter, folds of labial muscles controlling the lip also create lines converging toward the angle of the mouth. These contours and the horses' beards were often represented by simple lines.

Bahn (1980) has interpreted these lines literally and suggested that they represent bridles or halters, leading him to conclude that Paleolithic people used

The markings on horse heads in Paleolithic art have been referred to as bridles or halters, leading some researchers to propose that horses were controlled/domesticated? very early. One can see in the anatomy of modern horses (*above*) that a line occurs naturally (1) at the insertion of the horse's exaggerated masseter muscles on the zygoma. Also, the labial muscles back from the lips run parallel to the skull, making fold lines (2) that look like a strap. I suspect that lines drawn just over and behind the muzzle (3) in fact portray the pelage change from white to dun. Thick jaw hair creates an apparent chin strap (4). A, La Marche, Fr. B–C, Mas d'Azil, Fr. D, Arudy, Fr. E, La Loja, Sp. F and H, Rouffignac, Fr. G, Castillo, Sp. I–J, Angles-surl'Anglin, Fr.

and controlled horses. As one can see from the drawings, it is easy to arrive at such a conclusion, and this again demonstrates why contextual information is so critical. If there was any other evidence of domestication of Paleolithic horses, this reading of the drawings might be plausible, but our other evidence argues for a very late date for horse domestication. Thus, it seems most likely that the interior lines in Paleolithic images of horses' heads were only indicating details of facial contour, color, shadow, and texture.

snouts in other Paleolithic drawings of cattle. The Licorn has a short tail but so does one of the well-done bulls in the same hall.

I am not the first to suggest this interpretation. Apellaniz (1984) arrived at this conclusion in the course of his examination of individual artistic techniques in Lascaux. Apellaniz also noted that the pigments used for the Licorn differ from those used for the other aurochs bulls at Lascaux. Finally, I do not think the row of spots running along the Licorn's back are illustrating a Pleistocene aurochs variant. We know that a number of paintings from other times and places use spots to "fill in" body color and texture. The famous horses of Pech-Merle are a ready example. Neither these nor the Licorn should be construed literally as recording actual spotted cattle and horses.

Quirky Lines in Nature and Art There are numerous instances of Paleolithic animal images in which body parts,

It is not easy to know what to take literally in Paleolithic art. These rhino images from one of the oldest Paleolithic art caves, Chauvet, Fr., have what appears to be a broad dark belt. The question is whether this is reality or artistic license. It would be easy to dismiss it as simply artistic whimsy if it were not for the presence of several genes among mammals that result in similar contrastingly colored belt patterns. There is thus a good possibility that this pattern was characteristic of that subspecies of Eurasian rhinos 30,000 years ago (the general date of these particular drawings in Chauvet).

Contrastingly colored belting is found in many mammalian species, both wild and domestic varieties, indicating a widespread genetic variant for this pattern. Here are but a few examples: **A**, Malayan tapir, *Tapirus indicus*. **B**, Belted domestic Hampshire hog. **c**, Holstein domestic milk cows. **D**, Taltuza, *Macrogeomys underwoodi*. **E**, Harp or saddleback seal, *Pagophilus groenlandicus*. **F**, Dutch banded guinea pig. **G**, Panda, *Ailuropoda melanoleuca*. **H**, Saddleback domestic rabbit. **I**, Racoon dog, *Nyctereutes procyonoides*.

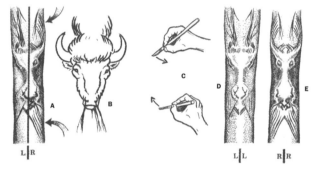

Some of the asymmetries in Paleolithic art may simply be due to the way one's hand works. A small carving of a bison on a bone cylinder (**A**) from Mittere Klause, Ger., might be reconstructed (**B**) as a bison bleeding from its nostrils and mouth. The biomechanics of the hand (**c**) means it can work in some directions better than others. If we split the image in half and fold over the mirror image to make two symmetrical animals (**D** and **E**), it dramatizes how the sides unintentionally differ.

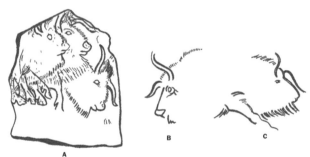

Occasionally horns, antlers, and tusks become disfigured, as commonly seen among modern bison populations. Horns are especially sensitive to this, and one sees such pathological specimens in Paleolithic art. Some Pleistocene images of deformed horns were probably literal, the deformation caused by violent head clashing during the early formative stages of the horns. **A**, Puy de Lacan, Fr. **B**, Mas d'Azil, Fr. **c**, Niaux, Fr.

particularly antlers or horns, are warped to make the imagery better fit the shape of the stone or bone fragment on which it was made. Artistic license is obvious in most such cases. There are a few images, however, in which distortion is more ambiguous. These images may be accurate reports of naturally occurring pathology or oddity. Deformities do happen and familiarity with them can be useful in reading such images.

Sometimes antlers or horns are deformed during growth due to an accident. We have a Pleistocene steppe bison skull in the University of Alaska Museum that corresponds almost exactly to the bent-horn form seen in Puy de Lacan and Mas d'Azil bison. Such deformed horns are occasionally seen among herds of American bison or African antelope, for example. Both antlers and horns are vulnerable to distortions if injured early in the course of their development. Injury can cause growth to occur at unusual angles. Where trophy records are kept, they occupy a separate class, referred to as "atypicals." Because horns or antlers may not impact an individual's speed, eating, or other physical activities, the anomalous structure may not affect survival. Reproductive success is another matter; deformities may not be so neutral when it comes to social status. This is probably why outstandingly odd antler and horn shapes are not frequent variants in populations but occur only as occasional individual pathologies.

ARTIST'S INTENT AND ATTEMPT: BULLS OR BOARS?

What more savant distribution of accents, both from constructional and decorative view-points, could one desire than that of the boar? With what exact aesthetic skill the calcanea are accentuated! How the fleshy line of the abdomen is left as a finely traced, but, this time, unaccented curve! With what address are the accents placed along the tremendous rhythm of the spine, and how they remind one of the deft handling of some great Chinese master of the brush! No, it is difficult indeed to relegate such work to the naive realms of primitivism. . . . Drawn upon a rock wall, the Altamira boar seems, even to modern me, if you will, the splendid perspective science of the Sistine Chapel.

V. Blake, *The Art and Craft of Drawing*

At the periphery of the Altamira bison grouping, there are two figures that are usually identified as wild boars; they indeed look like wild boars. Reproductions of these Altamira figures are—like so much cave art—strongly influenced by lighting, photographic angle, and cropping. Many reproductions emphasize cracks in the stone that make one image appear even more to have a pig's snout. But these two figures owe much of their purportedly piggish identity to Abbé Breuil. In a famous illustration, Brueil rendered these figures unambiguously as pigs. And many folks since have sought to see the originals as pigs. Yet these are clearly, albeit poorly drawn, images of bison. The complex lines of a bison's head and neck are not easy to do, and in these two renditions the Paleolithic artist skewed the bison head so that the muzzle looks forward rather than down, giving the face a more piggish look. The small S-shaped horns on the head of one of these piglike

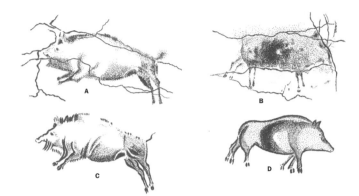

Paleolithic art studies have been plagued by a number of misidentifications that have affected the ideas behind the art. For example, Breuil drew two of the bison in the "herd" at Altamira, Sp., as wild pigs (**c** and **D** below). This mistake is understandable given (1) the poor quality of the lighting he worked under, (2) the poor preservation of the art, (3) the fact that the original two bison are, technically, poorly drawn (drawn with piglike heads, very different from the other bison), and (4) natural cracks give the bison piglike snouts. *Top,* from photos in Leroi-Gourhan 1965. *Bottom,* from Breuil's drawings (1952).

bison and the traces of its long woolly bison tail are harder to see, and these subtle features are not emphasized in reproductions. Breuil simply "overdrew" on that occasion, and honest scholar that he was, I believe if he were around today he would say, "Oh yes, my old drawing should be altered to read better as bison."

These two piglike bison have other bison insignias. The Paleolithic artist gave them a bison's black neck and posterior-hump manes, and the red abdomen of a nearby bison and that of one of the piglike bison share exactly the same pattern. The two piglike bison are apparently later additions (they are at the periphery of the panel) by a more inexperienced artist(s). An art instructor would have given them a few pointers and some encouragement to keep up the practice and pay closer attention next time they saw a bison. Paleolithic images were not always the work of geniuses. These two bison images are analogous to the Licorn aurochs from Lascaux, and they illustrate the point I would like you to consider, namely, that preserved Paleolithic art captures the whole gamut of artistic ability.

These images highlight a recurring problem for traditional approaches to Paleolithic art, which assume that all

Many people still argue that these pig-headed bison at Altamira are images of wild pigs. I offer a sample of rather poorly done bison from other Paleolithic art sites and times to show how this pig-headed contour does occur elsewhere in this old art—a mistake easily made. **A–D** and **H**, Trois Frères, Fr. (**D** and **H** reversed for comparison). **E**, Roc de Sers, Fr. **F–G**, Isturitz, Fr. (**F** reversed for comparison).

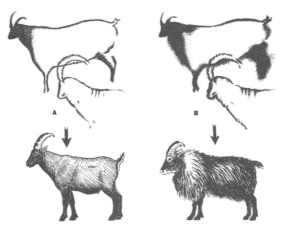

There are rare occasions where photography of Paleolithic images has distorted species. The two overlapping ibex (**A**) from Cougnac, Fr., are such a case. **B**, Interpretations of a photographically overexposed image of these ibex mistakenly identified the upper image as that of an Asiatic tahr, *Hemitragus jemlaicus*. See Kurtén 1968.

artistic forms and lines were intentional—the work of gifted shaman artists for whom there was never a gap between intent and the resulting content. Researchers subscribing to this model can only conclude that if the Altamira images look like pig-bison they were meant to be pig-bison. But, in fact, there are other cases where bison are misdrawn in a very similar way, like wild pigs, and yet clearly are intended to be representations of bison. Freeman et al. (1987) came to this same conclusion.

THE MIX OF KEEN OBSERVATION AND CASUAL IRREGULARITIES IN PALEOLITHIC ART

Keen observation and technical irregularities are not mutually exclusive. If we think of them as skill-related characteristics, observational power and artistic ability often strengthen and become more unified with use over time. The path to such mastery is littered with art making, strewn with art that is likely to have the casual irregularity we so often find in our Paleolithic collection. Indeed, some Paleolithic art researchers have begun to acknowl-

edge this in a more recent turnabout from an all-out search for symbolism in the art. There has even been limited discussion of technical deficiencies in Paleolithic art. For example, Pales and St.-Péreuse (1981) have recognized many anatomical errors, inaccuracies that a more experienced artist would not likely have made. Clottes (1989) has commented that some clumsy lines exist, in which heavy-handedness and the lack of artistic experience are striking. In an analysis of Paleolithic art in the Pyrenees, Clottes, Garner, and Maury (1994) concluded that mainly large bulls were drawn, and these include many anatomical mistakes. Clottes and colleagues (2003) also proposed that Magdalenians did not make stereotyped images of bison but represented individual details of age, sex, posture, and so on, "as they perceived things, and not as a symbolic depiction."

Early in this century, before the magico-religious paradigm was thoroughly entrenched, two other researchers, Luquet (1910) and Deonna (1914), innocently pointed out the many confusions, slipups, and ragged incompleteness in Paleolithic art. However, instead of drawing the

Paleolithic images usually wrap around irregular bone and stone surfaces, and an image's contours often depend on the viewer's perspective. Here are two views of the same rhino in Chauvet, Fr., from slightly different vantage points. (After Clottes 2003.)

A little striped Pleistocene horse drawn in Ekain Cave, Sp. The real model lived up against the hills near the exposed plains now covered by the Bay of Biscay, which stretched across to the French plains of Aquitaine.

obvious conclusion that such mistakes were made by people who were still developing their drawing skills, they unfortunately proposed that the cause was the innate clumsiness of Paleolithic adults, who lacked the mental capacity to master the required demands of the complex subject matter. Even for a short time the renowned Paleolithic art specialist Leroi-Gourhan broke ranks with the "genius-art" crowd and acknowledged the varying quality and general disarray in Paleolithic art, but he quickly countered this admission with the idea that the artists actively pursued ambiguity (Leroi-Gourhan 1965).

Most researchers still overemphasize the technical quality of Paleolithic drawings. And this assessment is generally accepted. I suspect this is largely because the model of an ancient artistic potency fits so well with the notion of contemporary artistic genius, with its emphasis on a different order of perception, divorced from ordinary life and experience. Yet this is exactly the opposite of what most professional artists tell us and show us. Henry Moore's workroom was scattered with the smooth, irregular flint nodules he found in his pasture, and these swells and connected masses are everywhere in his art. Even Duchamp's urinal was an attempt to help us regain possession of our own independent and individual visual sense of the world around us. But that adult vision of the

world around us does not arrive fully formed from nowhere.

Amid these many images of behavioral details "drawn from life," a fuzzy picture is beginning to emerge. Part of that is a sense of something missing, particularly in the subjects addressed. This and other factors provide an impression that the preserved Paleolithic art we have discovered may not represent the broad range of art done by all ages and sexes. I think this will become a key element in understanding the integrity of Paleolithic art, in breaking its code, if we can but follow the right trail of evidence.

⊚

. . . after the herd of horses bolted, we relaxed, our talk turning to girls. Yet, lying in the noon grass with closed eyes, I was still focused on the mare, her memory still warm in my sight: I am her, nervous tail raised and black nostrils flaring. I think I could draw her now, let myself flow out from my eyes into my hand and see her re-form on the stone. Had the bold stallion led, we would have had him, but his first wife with foal is too alert and keen. Still, they were almost in spear's reach, their beauty, black-striped trim and sheen of summer coat in the year's first hot sun. Fine luxury to behold the caper and gambol of new foals—a matchless sight after the long winter.

Tracking Down
the Pleistocene Artists

The Unemphasized Role of Children

CAVE SHADOWS

Deep in caves from the Old Stone Age
There is a faintest touch that lingers
In filmy prints, of phantom fingers.
El Castillo shadows aren't black but white,
And left hands multiply more than right.
Who once owned such ancient hands—
—sinestral sorceresses or brigands?
Lefties meeting in caves clandestine?
Grizzled old guys or just some teen?
It begs to be solved, was it hes or shes?
Forensically, can we compute these?
Digitizing old digits, a mystery for to tell,
Making Pech-Merle magic with Excel?

On Sony monitor, Bernifal makes a dot.
I squint at each metric scatterplot
Trying to find the whole Lot—when
Pixels, in the screen's cave, come alive.
People, disquieting inky dark, arrive.
Illuminating virgin black with yellow,
Flickers sputter from burning tallow.
Terra rosa squishes under barefoot gait—
Merry spitters, not worshipers we venerate?
Breaking stalactites, disfiguring walls,
A discord of yells and bravado calls,
Giggles, nudges, even errant meanness of
Cosquer vandals, despoiling cleanness.

Ocher dry-spewed makes new tracks
Fine-spray spitted onto hand-backs.
Hands laid to Chauvet's cool white
Like photo imprints leave a negative light.

Stamped here and there at whim
In flocks and apart, now growing dim.
At Bayol hands were smeared in clay
Quick grabbed from underfoot that day.
Mostly left hands, guided by the right
Already busy minding the light,
So the left was chosen to foul with crud,
Sticky with boy-spit, ocher, and mud.

Brief smears, prints done in passing,
Not meant to keep and yet were lasting.
Spittle fleet with no care lent—
Gargas lugs silhouetted by fingers bent,
Like old amputees, toughened by scar,
Make-believe fantasies of male valor,
Badges of pubescence these likely are.
Just so, kids find happy ways to play
With whatever comes along their day,

Soon discontent when stilled by wonder,
If they linger in the cave to ponder.
Young hands must make some mark
These yet remain—still—in the dark.

But not all old art was done so rude
As novices stenciled these fingers crude.
Someone more practiced deftly traced
A tufted fetlock and fine mare's face
With skills steadied leisurely, out in sun.
And to what end? Art's usual one—
With leave, that special tickle of delight.
We see—and know—these marks alright,
Fun, now accounted by today's reason
Fossils of a developing imagination,
Hints of a young brain's configuration.
Recognize—and reach—gently thus,
Our hand to theirs, in humanness.

Caught Red-Handed: Forensic Evidence as to the Artists' Identity

There must be a certain percent of meaningless scribble, limited ability, or simply crude attempts by children or beginners, and so we should not assume that everything had complex symbolic meaning.

P. Bahn and J. Vertut, *Journey through the Ice Age*

We are unlikely to ever know just why any particular Paleolithic artwork was made or to be assured of a work's ultimate meaning. Fragmentary evidence can, however, help us discern certain patterns and allow us to make some general observations. As we have noted, an alertness to taphonomic biases in preservation is essential, for fossils are rarely ready-made indicators of a past average or norm. They are, however, what we have to go on, so what then does our collection of preserved art suggest? Does it represent the art making of select senior shamans, or do we have a collection of work done mainly by women? Or maybe our collection is biased toward children's works, or perhaps most unlikely of all, it is a balanced sample fully representative of male and female, young and old alike.

There are indeed some major preservational biases, particularly regarding art made by certain ages and sexes. In the next chapter I will analyze evidence suggesting that Pleistocene men and women tended to specialize in many pursuits of daily life. These patterns would have influenced both materials and subject matter of art-making choices. And some of this we can discern forensically in the art.

I'll start this forensic work with a look at Paleolithic handprints and footprints. Most of these handprints were made contemporaneously with, and often occur among, more familiar representational Paleolithic images and were made with the same pigments. All of the hand- and footprints used in this forensic study were preserved in European cave or shelter (abri) settings. They provide one of

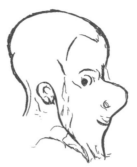

Boys in the band. Plaquette engraving, drawn from life in the Paleolithic. Note facial fuzz. Excavated from La Marche, Fr.

La Marche, Fr.

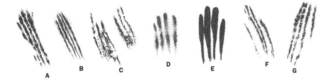

Pleistocene finger smears from a variety of caves in France: **A**, Gargas, **B–C** and **G**, Pech-Merle, **D**, La Baume Latrone, **E**, Le Portel, **F**, Cougnac.

the best sets of forensic clues we could hope for. But let me jump ahead and confirm what you've likely guessed. Yes, a significant segment of these Paleolithic handprints and tracks were made by young people. Furthermore, additional evidence allows one to conclude that youngsters were responsible for much more of preserved Paleolithic art than scholars have assumed.

I certainly did not expect to reach these conclusions when I began my study. But having lived with this outcome of the forensic data and having to come to terms with the logically associated consequences, I now find that this evidence does align well with patterns we find in the execution, location, and individual subject choice in Paleolithic art. I must emphasize, I am *not* concluding from these data that all Paleolithic art is children's art, only that works by young people constitute both a disproportionate and a largely unrecognized fraction of preserved Paleolithic art.

The Lost Children of Paleolithic Archaeology

. . . what we really discover is our own childhood, we discover ourselves, because we observe the same essential aspirations in the depths of our souls.
Teilhard de Chardin, standing before Altamira (*El fenómeno humano*)

Few archaeology texts so much as mention artifacts made by children (for discussion, see Dawe 1997; Derevenski 2000; Lillehammer 2000). Likewise, I have not seen a significant treatment of children's art making in books about Paleolithic art. These are notable oversights, and curious. Perhaps this is due in part to our present experience, our customs which tend to mutually isolate children and adults. But such separations would not have been the case in Paleolithic times.

Both direct archaeological evidence and indirect ethnographic comparisons show that children were far more important demographically in the Paleolithic, and we can surmise that children were an omnipresent part of most aspects of everyday life. We must presume that Paleolithic children played with and made art, including works in preservable materials, at a very early age. Furthermore, this occurred not in the confines of a schoolroom but in the very places we identify as archaeological sites. In short, children's artifacts and art should be a significant presence in the archaeological record. Indeed, much of what follows in this book revolves around this matter.

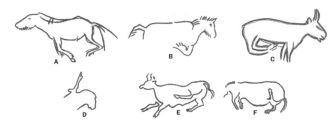

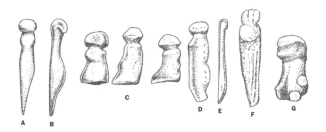

Even though there are many images in Paleolithic art that are characteristic of beginning drawers, few scholars have ever mentioned the possibility that children have played any role in these old drawings. **A**, La Paloma, Sp. **B–C**, Laugerie-Basse, Fr. **D**, Teyjat, Fr. **E**, and **F**, Lascaux, Fr.

Little Pleistocene-aged sculptures that were made by modifying a natural bone with stone tools into human-like images that tweak the imagination: **A**, Brassempouy, Fr. **B**, Enval, Fr. **C**, Predmosti, Czech. **D**, Vogelherd, Ger. **E**, Pavlov, Czech. **F**, Gargano, It. **G**, Avdeevo, Rus.

How could we have so neglected the role of children in prehistory, human evolution, and archaeology?

Svensson (1993) has stressed one possible cause that I have just mentioned. Children tend to be a hidden part of modern life, not central to most people's daily experience. While some soccer moms and family-active dads, among others, might disagree, it is certainly true for most adults, and especially for many scholars. Professionalism tends not to tolerate the casual presence of kids, who are increasingly growing up in age-stratified day-care centers, schools, clubs, and sports and entertainment arenas. With regard to parenting experience, in America the level of formal education is negatively correlated with number of children. Among people with advanced degrees the birthrate has dropped to around half of what is required for demographic replacement. Americans with advanced academic degrees, including anthropologists, tend to have no or few children and begin having them later in life (Bachu 1993). European figures are even more extreme.

While the above is true, I tend to think our modern academic opacity to children's worlds in prehistory is even more profound than can be explained by a simple dearth of adult-child interactions. I suspect that the older magico-religious paradigm has played a hand, mesmerizing attention toward what it deems serious and significant—and weighting children very lightly. In the old dichotomy of sacred and profane, children simply weigh in as lightweights compared to the many other, more officially important or spiritual concerns of adults. Education of kids may warrant general attention, but rarely (unless

In the late 1800s Edward Nelson's expedition collected these little dolls from young Eskimo girls in northeastern Alaska. There is erotica in Eskimo art, but as one must admit, no trace of it is found here in these little dolls.

you are the parent) do their playthings. In later chapters I'll argue that the adaptations of our early ecological niche primarily targeted changes in childhood, changes necessitating a longer, much more elaborate route to reproductive age, and that this new and expanded childhood indeed became an evolutionary driver of our human nature. Art making of children as well as adults has been and still is a central player in that story.

While we might easily misconceive childhood as a mere preface or warm-up to the real life of adulthood, Paleolithic people would have been less likely to do so. For starters, those populations were dominated by people under age twenty. In the Paleolithic setting of small intimate bands, children were around all the time, involved in nearly every aspect of life, always participating and observing. Confined to the tent or shelter during inclement weather, they were packed in close, always demanding stories and games. Parents and the other adults in the group had to be teachers, coaches, guides, entertainers,

The possibility that much of Paleolithic art could have been done by young people has been disparaged, because the most beautiful and accomplished Paleolithic images are, naturally enough, the best known. Just to emphasize how well many children can draw, I submit this unprompted picture of a dancer by my youngest daughter when she was eleven. This is typical of her unschooled, self-motivated ability in those years. By fifteen years of age my children were able to draw at levels comparable to many of the preserved Paleolithic images. While my kids may have been atypical among their peers, they were far from extraordinary.

Three late Pleistocene images from Addaura, It., that try to solve the problem of how to portray legs. Note how the horse at the top has the "elbow" joint far too low on the leg. But at least the artist tried. The cattle shown below were more stick-legged.

counselors, doctors, toy manufacturers, clothes designers and makers, and much more. And, every night, kids were not down the hall in their own rooms but rooting under the covers with you or sleeping an arm's length away.

I'll discuss this child-centric view of human evolution at some length in chapter 4, arguing that the evolution of "quality-plus children" was essential in creating adults capable of the myriad intellectual and personal demands of the emerging human niche. Specifically, I'll argue that these novel adult capacities arose not just from attentive education but are programmed to develop via a lot of play. Play was an essential focus of that adaptive solution.

Young people's art is an important thread in that story and must be addressed in any study of Paleolithic art. While I didn't start this study with the thought of focusing on Paleolithic youth, it elbowed aside many of my preconceived directions and took over. Let's start now by looking at some of the data that forced me to rethink my entire view of Paleolithic art and, indeed, human nature.

Top, an enigmatic engraving on bone from La Riera, Sp. It looks like a fantasy animal, but I would argue that, like much of Paleolithic art, it is simply a rudimentary attempt at a conventional subject, in this case a running horse made by a novice. *Bottom,* my reconstruction of what the drawer seems to have had in mind. This flying gallop is not a gait seen in nature, but it takes very little movement of the left foreleg to make it into a legitimate gallop.

Caught Red-Handed in the Paleolithic

Paleolithic handprints are found in about thirty well-known European Paleolithic art caves. These include hundreds of prints made as ocher, manganese, or clay negatives and a few positive prints made with pigments or mud applied to hands that were then placed on the cave surfaces. In addition to these deliberately made handprints, several hand impressions have been found that were made when Paleolithic people inadvertently leaned or balanced by pressing their hands into soft cave substrates. The question is whether it is possible to identify the handprints by age and sex.

SEXING AND AGING ICE AGE HANDS

A number of scholars have studied these old handprints in Paleolithic art (Sollas 1914; Leroi-Gourhan 1967; Verbrugge 1969; Sahly 1969; Pradel 1975; Groenen 1987; to name but a few). Though all the above researchers agreed that there are age- and sex-specific hand patterns, it proved exceptionally difficult to identify the sex or age of the individuals who left these particular prints. Why has identification been so intractable? Studies of modern peoples have shown marked sex and age differences in hand dimensions (Snyder et al. 1977).

Perhaps the most important obstacle in the earlier studies was that most of them were done prior to the desktop computer and photocopy machine. These tools

How Were Negative Handprints Made?

How the images of these Paleolithic handprints were produced remained a controversial puzzle for decades (e.g., Cartailhac 1906; Regnault 1873; Capitan 1911; Weissen-Szumlanska 1937). Casteret (1934) was the first to propose that they were made from liquefied pigment sprayed on with the mouth. During the 1960s and 1970s several researchers presumed that spraying pigments onto cave walls probably required some sort of device like a blowpipe or hollow tube (e.g., Nougier 1966). But Pradel (1975) and Barrière (1976) championed direct blowing with the mouth as the main process. This controversy is well reviewed by Groenen (1987). Both Groenen (1987) and Lorblanchet (1991) have argued that complicated paraphernalia are not necessary. Rather, all that is needed is to nibble off a bit of common oxide pigment or charcoal and to spit a fine spray on the wall. It requires a little practice, mainly the knack of spitting tiny amounts in little high-pressure sput-sput-sput fine jets. At its best, this results in a smoothly graded spray, like a modern airbrush. Of course, many images were made hastily with cruder, spit-splatter-spray glops of pigment chunks here and there.

While many hand images are well made (they are the ones usually reproduced in coffee-table art books), most are rather rudimentary and incomplete. Some are hardly recognizable, with one or two jets of ocher leaving a faint negative of two fingers without terminal ends. That is why different scholars provide different lists of caves with handprints or have had widely varying estimates of total handprint numbers for the same cave—it depends on what level of smear one counts as a hand.

I encourage you to try this method of hand stenciling at home. Use red powdered cake coloring, not ocher, as the latter is inordinately difficult to clean off your face. The best result is had by keeping the mouth about 20 centimeters away from the hand and background. It takes only a minute per hand. The most rudimentary Paleolithic ones may have been done in a matter of seconds.

---

proved invaluable in my study. The standards of age-sex identification of handprints here, however, are not the same as those used to try cases in courts of law, as in DNA fingerprinting. I have sought only more general statistical standards of assurance, where 95% confidence levels were quite acceptable.

I used a few published photos or outlines of the Paleolithic hands showing size scale. Though images of many others were published, few of these were shown with scale. However, I was able to visit the majority of the caves possessing hand images and, with the kind help of colleagues and generous local authorities (some wonderful stories here), to take photos with scale or to measure scale from already-published photos of hands. While most government agencies and private owners were cooperative, I was not able to gain access to some caves or to obtain photos with scale. This meant I would have a somewhat incomplete collection to analyze. Additionally, I chose to exclude many hand images that were questionable or had marginally usable data. Some were definitely handprints but showed little more than smears or blurs or were made over extremely irregular surfaces. Presently, I have 201 usable hand images in my Paleolithic sample, the bulk of the known handprints that contain measurable data. I do still hope to obtain data for some of the few dozen remaining images, but they are not included in the work that follows.

SAMPLING PROBLEMS?

In addition to the most obvious matters of incomplete and fuzzy-edged prints, there are other points to be aware of before one simply starts measuring. It has been proposed that some of these Pleistocene handprints are from the same individuals; that is, that certain individuals made multiple prints either during the same visit or during numerous cave entries over their lifetimes. I deleted samples where side-by-side multiples of identical hands seemed obvious, but in general, I hope to have minimized

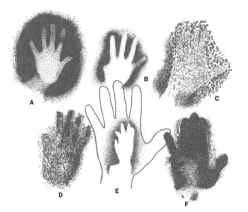

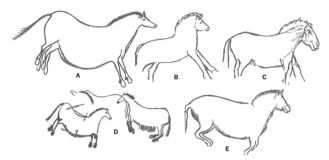

There are many attempts at rendering movement among the Paleolithic images. Usually, these are very rudimentary. **A**, Lascaux, Fr. **B**, Teyjat, Fr. **c**, Les Combarelles, Fr. **D**, Lascaux, Fr. **E**, Trois Frères, Fr.

One can see at first glance that many of the handprints in Paleolithic art seem smaller than modern hand dimensions. For example, here are six handprints from different sites compared with an outline of a medium-sized hand of a living person, mine. **A**, Fuente del Salin, Sp. **B**, Maltravieso, Sp. **c–D**, Altamira, Sp. The hand image (**E**) from Gargas, Fr., is enclosed in the outline of my hand (note that it is the image of a hand of a very small child along with its sleeve). **F**, Bayol, Fr. It does not take a statistical analysis to see that many handprints in caves are those of children.

these potential biases by relying on the large sample of usable images taken from a number of different caves.

Statisticians prefer to work with homogeneous samples from populations constrained by known parameters. Paleolithic prints coming from a wide variety of local habitats, different cultures, and such varying times (tens of thousands of years apart) are not a statistician's dream. But since I seek a more general picture from western Eurasia throughout the whole of the late Paleolithic, the diversity of this collection has obvious advantages. The scatter of our sample should buffer situational extremes in demographics, diet, and health. In short, we can hope that the handprint sample broadly reflects an ancestral Caucasoid stock, subjected to a variety of local dietary regimens, at different times, and is generally representative of the Paleolithic people who went back into caves (where a large segment of preserved art is derived).

ARE MODERN ANALOGS A VALID COMPARISON?

I had hoped to find a ready-made thorough statistical study with diagnostic sex and age metrics of modern hands that I could use for comparisons with my Paleo-

lithic hand images. I found dozens of metric analyses of modern hand variations, but alas none of these studies focused on the data I required which would allow me to identify unknowns.

Therefore, a baseline collection of handprints, from different ages and sexes, was required for this study. But is it reasonable to use a sample of present-day hands in a quantitative comparison with handprints of people living tens of thousands of years ago? With prudence, yes. Obviously, hand (or foot) shape and size depend on many variables, not simply age and sex. At least in Europe, hand size does not seem to have undergone significant evolutionary change since the Pleistocene. It is true that people in different parts of the world exhibit subtle differences in hand size and shape and that this seems to have some genetic basis. For example, the hands of Australian Aboriginals are more gracile for their body size than are those of Europeans (Kirk 1986). Northern Mongoloids have rather shorter appendages, including hands and feet, for their height than do, say, Nilotics (Roberts 1978; Harrison et al. 1988). A literature review, however, of metric dimensions from a variety of different racial groups from all over the world found only minor between-group differences in size and shape of hands and feet, except for the groups with extremely large or small body sizes (NASA 1978).

Nutrition, particularly prior to maturation, is a well-known component of human size variation. The level of nutrients (and to some extent sheer number of calories) during development can significantly reduce body size or push size to its fullest genetic potential. Informative anec-dotal evidence of shifts in glove and shoe sizes is found when generations make great changes from one nutri-tional level to another.

Physical use may also influence the shape and size of hands. But there is no suggestion that Paleolithic people used their hands in repetitious and heavily forceful work continuing in rather set patterns over a lifetime of long workweeks, such as digging, using picks, axes, and adzes, rowing, or handling ship's rigging, as have laborers in more recent history. It is unlikely that Paleolithic people used their hands in such chronically repetitive ways. One corroboration of the idea that some distinctive Paleolithic usage did not greatly modify hand size and shape is that the largest handprints in the old art are quantitatively indistinguishable from the largest hands in modern samples.

Given the similar body and hand sizes of late Paleo-lithic Eurasians to modern people (Sahly 1969; Frayer 1980), and surmising from the abundant midden refuse of large mammals, fish, and other animals (Delporte 1990; Mellars 1998), it is reasonable to imagine that these people were living on a nutrient-rich diet, sufficient to produce growth near its potential genetic maximum.

Of course, other factors can affect body size, including parasite load, disease, and chronic stress. But modern analogs tend to support theoretical views that late Pa-leolithic peoples would have been well adapted to the emotional stress levels under which they evolved. Paleo-lithic lifeways seem to have necessitated camp relocation, which undoubtedly worked in favor of keeping parasite loads low. And small population numbers would have curbed the spread of contagious diseases. Finally, regular intergroup warfare and its attendant stresses and disrup-tion of resources seem unlikely; I will present evidence for this in a later chapter. Most of the above forces, if present, would have decreased Paleolithic hand size and robustic-ity, which would in turn lead us to underestimate male-ness—that is, to predict fewer males. As we shall see, this does not seem to be the case.

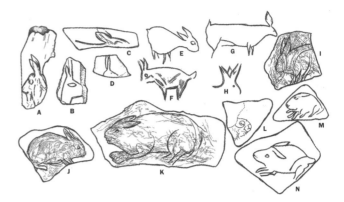

In the Paleolithic, hares and rabbits were not necessarily considered the cuddly creatures we today associate with children's toys or traditions but were often im-portant wild-game supplements to the diet, as middens of some sites show. Not only do their bones salt the sites, but their images are sprinkled throughout the art, not common but widespread. Paleolithic art theorists who invoke shamanism or hunting magic have never referred to the role of hares and rabbits in Paleolithic art. **A–D**, Polesini, It. **E**, Gabillou, Fr. **F**, Altxerri, Sp. **G**, Trois Frères, Fr. **H**, Laugerie-Basse, Fr. **I–N**, La Marche, Fr.

Still, given that some component of hand size is heri-table, won't we encounter certain problems comparing Paleolithic hand size with that of modern peoples? Whose hands are we to choose—Norwegian, Basque, Mediter-ranean? We know that throughout history some genes were flowing into Europe from Asia and North Africa, but generally European genetic mixing was mostly internal to Europe (Cavalli-Sforza, Menozzi, and Piazza 1994; Torroni et al. 1998). In other words, a present-day population of mixed Caucasoid background on a high-nutrient diet is probably as representative of late Pleistocene genetic stocks as we can hope for.

THE BASELINE SAMPLE: DESCENDANTS
OF PALEOLITHIC EUROPEANS LIVING
IN THE NORTH ON HIGH-PROTEIN DIETS

What baseline sample to use? After some thought, I chose to obtain my sample from individuals living in my home-town of Fairbanks, Alaska. Fairbanks is a long way from Eurasian Paleolithic art caves, but one could also argue that it is an outstanding choice, in that the population is mainly a heterogeneous genetic mix of west European stock. Individuals of obvious African or Asian descent were sorted from my final sample, though interestingly, statistical runs revealed no quantitatively detectable differences. Even more important, Fairbanksans have a diet high in nutrients (150–300 grams of protein per day), as is illustrated in their large stature. Many Alaskans eat a lot of wild game, including moose, caribou, sheep, mountain goats, bear, waterfowl, and wild salmon. Such ample dietary protein is not necessarily standard in many modern Eurasian diets. Thus, the thoroughly stirred European genetic kinship and high level of nutrition made my Fairbanks sample a good modern baseline.

From this baseline sample, I collected photocopy images of left handprints of each sex equally distributed from age five to adults. The sample totaled just under 700 individuals. For convenience I used classes from the borough school system, kindergarten through grade 12 (ages five through nineteen). I considered nineteen-year-olds as adults, because growth epiphyses in hand bones fuse prior to that age. I presumed that my youngest age-group —the kindergartners—would be younger than any Paleolithic children who would have ventured into caves. This assumption was later shown to be mistaken, as there are several handprints in the Paleolithic collection that I can now identify as younger than five. Students were chosen at random in the hallways between classes, until a sample of twenty-five was reached for each sex and age.

WHAT SHALL WE MEASURE?

It became rather easy to make rough age assessments and to recognize males and females from the photocopies, but when I tried to analyze just how I was making those decisions, it was like the difficulty of verbalizing how one distinguishes male and female faces. As difficult as it is to select a key distinguishing face measurement, the difficulty is even greater for hands. The main clue to age seemed to be hand size, particularly hand length. For sex, I caught myself looking at three main features: palm width, thumb

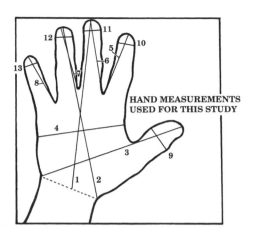

Hand measurements used in this study. These were chosen because they were the most available, repeatable, and clear measurements from Paleolithic hand images.

width, and fingertip widths. In the end I chose to take thirteen measurements, a mix of lengths and widths, as shown in the figure. Obviously, there would be much covariance among these, but many Paleolithic hand images are incomplete, and thus redundancy would be an asset.

The classic study of American body dimensions by age and sex was done by Snyder et al. (1977). Their study did include some finger widths and lengths, thumb widths, palm widths, and hand lengths, taken from life with calipers. I saw in their sample a phenomenon I was later to find in my own study; namely, size divergence between the sexes started at eight to nine years old and increased with age so that by eighteen to nineteen some hand measurements between males and females had virtually no overlap. This sexual divergence was true for all width measurements (at the 95% level of confidence) but not for the various hand length measurements. Their sample was spotty for some age classes and only provided ranges, means, and standard deviations. I needed multivariate regressions for the higher resolution identifications I hoped to make, but their study provided important preliminary guidance.

I enlisted the aid of a professional statistician at the University of Alaska to help me combine forward stepwise

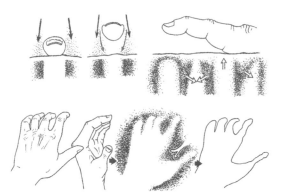

Some Paleolithic images of hands were not usable. The poorest ones were made by just one or a few spurts of pigment. Many were incomplete; even so, they still contained a few measurable dimensions. These three are from Gargas, Fr., with my reconstructions of the parts of the hand they describe.

Usually the prints of the hands are rather clear, but sometimes spray creeps into the silhouette. From experiments using my own hands I can say that this happens when parts of the hand do not make complete contact with the wall surface. Most of the time such images are not usable for my study. This phenomenon is also responsible for the false appearance of deformed hands; see lower print (from Gargas, Fr.) and how it can be explained by insufficient hand contact.

multiple discriminate analysis, forward stepwise multiple regression, logistic regression, factor analysis, and other statistical techniques (those interested in further details should see appendixes 1 and 2) to isolate quantitative specifics of age and sex. Strong overall patterns did emerge from the Fairbanks sample, illustrating that hand outlines can be used to closely approximate class identities of age and sex.

PALEOLITHIC HANDPRINTS AREN'T PHOTOCOPIES

As mentioned, I had to exclude from my Paleolithic sample some images that did not allow clear measurement. In several cases spray had undercut the edge, as happens when a hand is held somewhat away from the wall and when a hand is moved halfway through the process. I will show later how some Paleolithic handprints were intentionally distorted. Nevertheless, I found the edited sample of Paleolithic prints clearer than one might imagine, and I was able to take at least several good measurements from most images.

Fortunately, statistical methods make it possible to check some aspects of the accuracy of these measurements. One simply does a number of regressions of one measurement on another and compares these to similar ratios and regressions from my known (age and sex) baseline data. The fuzz of plotted points, an indicator of inconsistency, is greater in the plots of Paleolithic hand images, but the regressions are not wildly off. (The fossil bivariate average correlation coefficient was 0.6, compared to a baseline average of 0.5.) It is my impression that the higher correlation among measurements on the Paleolithic hands can be attributed mostly to the variations in underlying rock substrate rather than edge quality from the spit-spray technique. In sum, the fossil material appears quite usable for a metrical analysis, as long as the measurements can be relatively well approximated.

The most troublesome factor, as I proceeded with measurements of the Paleolithic sample, was the rarity of complete Paleolithic handprints. When one is trying to make thirteen measurements from each image, incompleteness means that one is sometimes left with many blanks in the worksheet. Often fossil prints have only five or six measurable dimensions, and there were a few with only one or two possibilities. Fortunately, this proved less of a handicap than anticipated, as the covariance among both width and length measurements is quite high. That is, say, a width and length of the index-finger image are almost as good predictors of age and sex as all the measurements from that hand. So a direct bivariate calibration of one measurement (say, thumb width) will involve a slightly different set of individual hands than any other measurement (say, little-finger width).

ON HAND LENGTH AND WIDTH, AGE AND SEX

Factor analysis delimited the first axis (Factor 1), which accounts for the largest fraction of variation. Factor loading on this first axis was highest among the *length* measurements. Judging by my bivariate plots, these length variations corresponded to *individual age.*

The second axis, the next most important component of the variation (Factor 2), was related to *sex.* In most biological characters, the first and second factors account for the bulk of the total variation observed in any given population. The heaviest loading for the variations of Factor 2 was found among the *width* measurements. The correlation matrix illustrated that width measurements have a high correlation with other width measurements, and we see the same phenomenon among length measurements.

This quantitative pattern in which length is most closely related to age while width is most closely related to sex makes intuitive biological sense as well. In both sexes, bones generally grow most dramatically along their linear axis. Also, males generally have broader and meatier hands, because muscle and tendon robusticity is related to testosterone levels. Judging from boys' large growth spurt in hand width measurements at puberty (and the cessation of growth among young women at this time), the tissue of the hand seems to be more steroid sensitive than some other tissues (Snyder et al. 1977).

THE IDENTITY OF THE PEOPLE WHO MADE
THE HANDPRINTS: STATISTICAL RESULTS

First, the statistical analyses tell us that the majority of the Paleolithic artists who left these handprint stencils in

**Paleolithic Art Caves and Abris
That Contain Handprints**

Abri du Poisson, France*
Abri Labattut, France*
Altamira, Spain*
Arcy-sur-Cure, France
Baume Latrone, France*
Bédeilhac, France*
Bernifal, France*
Chauvet, France
Cosquer, France*
El Castillo, Spain*
Erberua, France*
Font de Gaume, France
Gargas, France*
Grotte du Bison, France
La Fuente del Salin, Spain*
La Fuente del Trucho, Spain*
La Garma, Spain
Le Bayol, France*
Les Combarelles, France
Les Fieux, France*
Les Merveilles, France*
Les Trois Frères, France
Maltravieso, Spain*
Moulin-de-Laguenay, France*
Paglicci, Italy
Pech-Merle, France*
Roucadour, France*
Roc-de-Vézac, France*
Tibran, France*
Tito Bustillo, Spain
Asterisks show my sample localities.

caves were young people. But they also show a great diversity of ages. As noted by other researchers, some prints were made by very young children (younger even than those in my baseline sample). Two hand images are so small that the toddler/baby had to have been carried back into the cave. These occur in Gargas Cave in southern

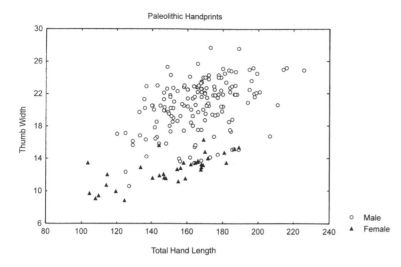

Thumb width plotted against total hand length Multivariate analysis of these Paleolithic hand measurements is impossible to portray graphically when many variables are used, but for a simple visualization I can show some of the differences with a bivariate plot of thumb width (highly correlated with sex) and length (strongly age related). The program had identified sex using more variables from my baseline data.

France, which is unusual in having passageways that are easy to traverse and an easy entrance which remained open during much of the past. That is shown by the protohistoric, Gallo-Roman, and medieval graffiti carved in the cave wall (Barrière 1976). But this is not typical for Paleolithic caves; there are few deep caves one would try to visit with a babe-in-arms.

Handprints of adolescents are the most numerous among the Paleolithic sample. An additional 20% of the hands are within the preadolescent size and shape ranges. From various statistical tests we can conclude that, while most ages seem to be represented in the sample, it was mainly adolescents who were involved. On numerous plots, the number of prints rises with age, peaking in adolescence, then decreases toward adult sizes. From a modern perspective, one might say that a Paleolithic police officer in charge of cave vandalism could predict that the individuals frequenting caves were mostly adolescents.

The second important observation is that the vast majority of these individuals were males. From the total sample of 201 Paleolithic hands, discriminate analysis classi-

fied 162 as male and the other 39 as either female or young male. That analysis used the measurements of thumb width, index-finger width, and index-finger length for the program (statistical techniques for accommodating the missing data by logistic regression are treated in appendix 1). This is consistent with the results of other tests used to age and sex the sample. For example, the cluster of cohorts from the Fairbanks baseline sample that presented the most parsimonious fit with the Paleolithic hand images using only aggregate-age samples (not splitting age-groups) for all the width measurements consisted of a block of age classes of males from eleven through seventeen. This, of course, does not mean that some of the hands did not belong to adult males, females, or very young children. It is not easy to separate the 20% of preadolescent hands according to sex using conventional statistical techniques. But by using the assumption that the sex ratio of the pre-twelve-year-olds visiting caves would be roughly similar to that found among post-twelve-year-olds, one can hypothesize that most of these preadolescents were boys.

The most parsimonious fit for the polygon plots (both in mean and in shape pattern) generated for each width measurement plotted against abundance (see appendix 2) also indicated a predominance of adolescent males.

HANDPRINTS IN MUD

Paleolithic caves were not always a clean canvas of white limestone. Many caves were quite damp and even muddy. Occasionally, Paleolithic people exploring caves touched up against the soft cave walls, and some of those impressions have survived. Many of these inadvertent handprints (and some footprints) are known to be Paleolithic in age because cave entrances were closed by naturally occurring landscape changes at the end of the Pleistocene (e.g., Pech-Merle). Openings were regained only in modern times. Furthermore, the fact that most of these mud prints are geologically infused with calcite means they are not recent. It is possible to set an upper geological age limit

Positives and Negatives, Lefts and Rights

The Paleolithic handprints I used for my study seem to be a representative sample. Among these, 78% of the prints were negatives of left hands. Only 17% were negatives of right hands, and 5% were positives of right hands. (Similar percentages are found in prehistoric handprints in many other cultures: Bushman, Aboriginal, Mayan, etc.) There have been a number of references to this phenomenon of left-print dominance over the years, some implying an underlying mystical reason. But I think the more recent consensus is that the most naturally dexterous hand would have been used to hold the lamp and/or spray materials. About 90% of most populations are right-handed (Coren 1993). There are very few positive handprints in my sample (which is the general case for Paleolithic handprints), and for these positive prints the ratio of L:R is reversed (1:4) from that found for the negative prints. The most parsimonious explanation is that one usually grabs for mud or pigment with the most dexterous hand.

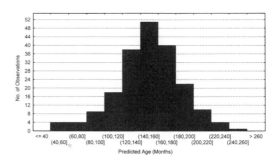

A bar graph of the multivariate results of Paleolithic handprints, showing an enormouis spread of ages, with a median and mean around twelve years of age and with most of the individuals falling between ten and sixteen. Note there is no lopsided, one-tailed, Poisson-shaped curve with a skew to the right as would occur if a large fraction of adult (humans have a determinate growth pattern) handprints had been present in the caves.

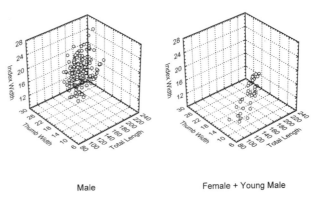

Predicted Sex of Paleolithic Handprints

Male   Female + Young Male

When three Paleolithic measurements are used, the points show a scatter of all ages and both sexes, but a skew toward young males. The female scatter may include some young males, for reasons I develop in Appendix 2.

as well. Neanderthal tracks and handprints are distinguishable from those of humans.

At Massat Cave in France, Barrière (1997) measured fifteen impressions in mud made by human fingers during the late Paleolithic. These holes range in width from 14 to 16 millimeters. From my baseline data I can say that these are clearly from person(s) younger than eleven or twelve. In the main chamber of Niaux Cave, France, small fingerprints, where a projection was touched, are from children (Garcia and Duday 1993). In Montespan, France, the image of a horse drawn by fingers in the mud and punctured with finger holes is associated with children's tracks and fingerprints (Garcia and Duday 1983).

At Fontanet Cave in France, imprints were left when Paleolithic visitors leaned against muddy walls. There, two clear handprints were identified as belonging to children of different ages (Clottes 1985). In that same cave, an adolescent visitor (age appraised by foot and finger measurements; Duday and Garcia 1983) squatted and punched out

The usual dimensions of the artwork seem to fall into two modes or classes produced simply by the two conveniences of human scale illustrated here.

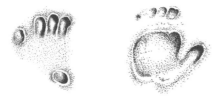

Two hand-tracks from Paleolithic kids who leaned against a muddy cave floor in Fontanet, Fr. From the size, these were identified as children's hands.

a heart shape in mud with his finger. I have measured hand marks in the mud in the Paleolithic art cave of Bayol in the lower Rhône drainage and these are adolescent in size. The French cave of Tuc d'Audoubert, renowned for its mud-clay sculptures of two bison, also contains hand- and foot-prints of young people (Bégouën 1925).

Again, these hand and finger markings point to cave visitors who were primarily of adolescent age and younger. The age variation is similar to that of the ocher handprints. From this comparison of the individuals intentionally making the painted handprints with those making the inadvertent and intentional impressions in mud, we can draw an important conclusion. Namely, it would be unreasonable to argue that it was mostly Paleolithic adults who went back into caves and that the few children to do so were the ones who made ocher handprints. Rather, most Paleolithic cave visitors seem to have been young people.

ARE THE HANDPRINTS REPRESENTATIVE OF PALEOLITHIC CAVE ARTISTS?

Could it be that a very large fraction of cave art was actually made by young people, and predominantly by adolescent boys? The evidence is circumstantial, yet a strong association seems to exist. First, we have the evidence that very very few Paleolithic people explored the dark caves. Second, we find a predominance of young boys making handprints in many of the same caves where we find other images made using very similar materials and techniques. Of course, we do not need to assume that everyone who drew in caves made handprints, nor that everyone who

made handprints made other cave art as well. What we have are data that make it reasonable to consider that there may have been a significant overlap. Handprints and images of horses, bison, and other animals are often in the same parts of the cave, and rendered with precisely the same pigment mix (Lorblanchet 1991). If these associations were the only evidence we had to suggest this hypothesis, it is still enough evidence to warrant serious consideration. However, as I hope to show, other forensic evidence points to the same conclusion.

OBSERVATIONS FROM OTHER PALEOLITHIC HAND STUDIES

. . . at Gargas and elsewhere the imprints are those of a small hand, such as might have belonged to the Grimaldi Race.

W. J. Sollas, "Crô Magnon Man"

The suggestion that adolescents made the majority of Paleolithic handprints may seem heretical. But this possibility is not a new idea. Virtually all twentieth-century scholars of Paleolithic hand images and imprints have arrived at similar conclusions. This may surprise you, as the hand studies have not been widely disseminated. Most are found in specialized regional European journals or remain as unpublished graduate theses. They are not easily accessible, especially in the United States. Even many European scholars of Paleolithic art are not acquainted with their existence.

Paleolithic hand images at Gargas, in France, have been studied repeatedly. In addition to its many Paleolithic wall engravings, at Gargas there are more than 100 moderately clear handprints. In one of the earliest printed reviews of handprints in Gargas, Cartailhac (1906) remarked that most of the hands were quite small. Likewise, Casteret (1934) argued adamantly that although some of the handprints were of medium size, most were very small hands, smaller than those of the average person today. Casteret observed that since Paleolithic skeletons are not appreciably smaller in size, the small handprints might well be those of women or children. In his study of the hands, Leroi-Gourhan (1967) also concluded that the small hands at Gargas were likely prints of adolescents or children.

In quite another view, Sollas (1914), observing the smallness of these hands but assuming they were imprints of adult hands, proposed that they confirmed the existence of a distinct and smaller race of small-handed Aurignacians.

Sahly's (1969) unpublished doctoral thesis, from Toulouse University, is one of the largest and most exhaustive studies of Paleolithic handprints. He clearly showed that fossil bones do not exhibit a division into two races of late Paleolithic people, one quite large and one quite small, as proposed by Sollas. Therefore, he concluded that we must explain the abundance of smaller hand negatives as a matter of age, not racial identity, and he proposed they were made by adolescents. Verbrugge (1969) likewise observed that most of the Paleolithic hand images were small, and so did Pradel (1975). More recently, Groenen's (1987) work, published as a thesis from the Free University in

Brussels, came to the same conclusion. He found a considerable range of dimensional variants, but children, and adolescents in particular, were most common. He identified only a few hands of adult size, probably made by men and women. His plates 41 and 48, which are scatter diagrams using measurements of palm width, wrist width, and thumb length from images at Gargas, show a clear predominance of male hands, using as a baseline his modern sample from Belgium.

I propose we consider this evidence of hand images to be a significant clue to the people who explored caves in the Paleolithic, and I will use this information as an important starting point in my effort to make sense out of preserved Paleolithic art.

Paleolithic Footprints

Fossil hominid footprints go back a long time in prehistory. Australopithicines left their tracks in the ash fall in

early Paleolithic times in northern Kenya (Behrensmeyer and Laporte 1981). Sometimes the footprints of late Paleolithic peoples survived in the soft-clay deposits on cave floors, which were later hardened by lime water seeping through the clay. More rarely, Paleolithic footprints have been found that were not hardened but simply remained undisturbed on cave floors for millennia. Most of these latter prints were destroyed by twentieth-century cave explorers, but in some of the most recently discovered Paleolithic art caves, these have been saved, thanks to the new approaches of sophisticated French conservators.

The preserved Paleolithic footprints are virtually all made by bare feet (there is one possible exception) and range from quite small to adult size. Of course, such fossil tracks may yield considerable information about Pleistocene cave explorers. Remarkably, one set of tracks in the Italian cave Grotte de la Sorcière (Tana della Basura) has been described as that of a Neanderthal (Pales 1954), but that is now questioned. There is even a term for the academic study of tracks, *ichnology,* or in this case paleoichnology. Fortunately, foot dimensions of modern peoples have been studied in detail. See White 1982 for biometrics and literature review.

Footprints are present in the Paleolithic art caves of Niaux, Fontanet, Pech-Merle, Erberua, Aldène, Montespan, Tuc d'Audoubert, Réseau Clastres, and Chauvet. In the early part of this century, Bégouën and Vallois (1927) and Vallois (1962) deduced from the size of such footprints that most late Paleolithic visitors to Aldène, Pech-Merle, Montespan, and Tuc d'Audoubert were children. They concluded that at Tuc d'Audoubert, five or six children between eleven and fifteen years old went under a low ceiling, having to crouch, which resulted in their heels digging into the floor.

At Niaux two individuals left tracks, and judging from size they were between nine and twelve years of age (Pales 1976; Clottes 1985). At Pech-Merle footprints seem to be from either one individual or perhaps two very similarly sized individuals of about fifteen to sixteen years of age

A series of late Pleistocene human tracks have been discovered in cave passages at Réseau Clastres near Niaux Cave, Fr. These tracks have been forensically identified as those of young people.

(Duday and Garcia 1985). At Montespan tracks are clearly from two individuals about eleven and six years old. There is one Pleistocene cave in Spain, Ojo Guareña, that has a number of footprints, all of which appear to be those of children as well (M. Garcia, pers. comm.).

Another cave floor that received careful protection upon discovery is in a portion of Fontanet Cave, in the Ariège region of southern France. Luc Wahl discovered a new passage there containing paintings and footprints and immediately notified French authorities. Again, these footprints were identified as being those of children. In the same cave, at one slick passage, there are several places where hands were placed on the walls for balance, and again biometrics identifies these as being made by children.

In another passage at Réseau Clastres, one lying beyond a lake that had to be drained before modern access could be gained, hundreds of footprints were found. A radiocarbon date of 10,000 years ago suggests that the last exploration in this cave was in the latest Pleistocene. Though the tracks were certainly old, it is unclear whether they really corresponded to the radiocarbon date. Among these many tracks, those of children were by far the most numerous. It is also interesting that fossil tracks found in a post-Pleistocene (Chalcolithic) French cave, called Fois-

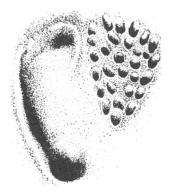

A Paleolithic young person walking barefoot on the soft muddy floor of Fontanet Cave, Fr., apparently squatted and with a finger made a stippled triangle. As I will show later, triangles are a familiar subject for Paleolithic cave goers.

sac, are also mainly from children (Garcia, Cours, and Duday 1987).

Chauvet, in the Rhône drainage of France, is one of the most famous recently discovered art caves; in addition to its paintings, it has handprints and footprints. These were dated to around 26,000 years ago. Garcia (2003) identified the footprints as being made by a preadolescent boy around eight years old. This agrees with the size and shape of some of the handprints also discovered in that cave.

Three young boys, from the family Bégouën, who discovered and explored the deep passages of Tuc d'Audoubert early this century, found in that cave handprints and footprints made by similarly aged Paleolithic children. Count Bégouën, the father of the Tuc d'Audoubert discoverers, wrote about the Paleolithic travelers in the cave, imagining a sort of Paleolithic initiation ceremony: "since the heelmarks clearly follow five different paths, there is every right to think that this march was directed and ordered, indicating a sort of ritual dance. The fact that the heels are those of young men between thirteen and fourteen years at the time of puberty, and that five sausages of clay in a phallic shape were dropped in a corner, awakens the idea of initiation ceremonies so frequent among primitive peoples" (Bégouën 1925, cited in Hadingham 1979, 181).

It is a great image, but the tracks of the adult initiation "director" are missing here, just as they are in most other dark cavern floors. What we do find are kids' footprints, and these are rare. We have simply no evidence whatsoever of regular use of these caves for ceremony. As I mentioned in the first chapter, there are no well-worn Paleolithic footpaths or trampled floors leading back into the deep caves, not even in those that have been explored carefully for such possibilities. We find no thick coatings of carbon soot on the cave ceilings such as one might expect from regular torch or lamp use. (Today, cave chambers routinely frequented with burning carbide lamps or candles soon become darkened.) There are few Paleolithic possessions found lying about. This evidence of light use supports other evidence (e.g., radiocarbon dates of the art) that in most caves the art was made by very few people on very few trips.

Pales and his colleagues Garcia and Duday have thoroughly studied the various fossil human foot imprints from Paleolithic caves and have compared them with foot sizes from living European populations. They concluded that all, or virtually all (there is one that is in the adult size range), of the foot tracks in Paleolithic art caves are those of children (Pales 1976; Duday and Garcia 1983, 1985). Duday and Garcia, reviewing all the foot imprint data, came to the same conclusion as earlier workers: "On conçoit aisément que les résultats doivent etre assortis d'une large marge d'incertitude, mais il est désormais bien établi que la plupart des empreintes préhistoriques se rapportent à des *enfants*" (1990, 64, italics mine).

We can find many examples of children leaving tracks in off-the-beaten-path places from more recent cultural settings. Surveys of old Roman tiles have found tracks of free-ranging livestock, presumably made when the wet clay tiles were drying in the sun. On those same tiles there are imprints made by people. As you might guess, these footprints are those of children. Handprints of male adolescents are a common feature in modern graffiti, and youngsters' prints are often squished into wet concrete

Tracks—The Neglected Spoor

Knowledge never learned in school,
For, eschewing books and tasks,
Nature answers all he asks,
Hand in hand with her he walks,
Face to face with her he talks,
Part and parcel of her joy,—
Blessings on the barefoot boy!

John Greenleaf Whittier, "Barefoot Boy"

Why don't we hear much about studies of the forensics of tracks in Paleolithic art caves in English publications? Most of these tracks have been known for a long time: Niaux in 1906 by Breuil and Cartailhac; Tuc d'Audoubert in 1912 by Bégouën; Montespan in 1923 by Casteret; Pech-Merle in 1923 by David and Lemozi; Aldène in 1948 by Cathala; and, a little more recently, Ojo Guareña in 1971; Réseau Clastres, another portion of Niaux, in 1971; and Fontanet in 1972.

Garcia and Duday (e.g., 1993) have repeatedly emphasized that most of the tracks are those of children, particularly boys. Clottes (1985) noted that as the large art caves were frequented by children, it was unlikely that these chambers were "sanctuaries reserved for sorcerers." Clottes also drew attention to the fact that the wide variation in size, and hence age, of these children's tracks made it doubtful that they were there as part of a puberty rite or passage-to-adulthood ceremony.

Why have these tracks not been highlighted more as forensic evidence? I suspect the answer is because they were discounted as being clearly made by kids. The idea of mere boys authoring Paleolithic artworks does not fit our old magico-religious paradigm. And patriotic pride wasn't eager to embrace art that some might call adolescent graffiti.

left to set by masons. Most telling of all, perhaps, is the fact that so many Paleolithic art caves and their art were first discovered in modern times by young boys.

Further Evidence as to the Artists' Identity

The physical evidence discussed above seems to reveal a consistent bias as to who went back into caves in the Paleolithic. I will develop that point more in the next chapter, where we look at analogous evidence of today's spelunkers. Additional indications of the identity of the artists responsible for Paleolithic art are presented in the next four chapters. This evidence involves sex-specific tools and their decoration, the kind of subjects and "scenes" portrayed, the difference in quality and quantity of male and female images, and the way different parts of the human body are exaggerated or selectively de-emphasized. However, for now I wish to present some other testimony not in those chapters. The first has to do with the handprints already discussed.

MISSING FINGERS IN ART: RITUAL, DISEASE, FROSTBITE, OR KIDS PLAYING?

Many hand images in the French Gargas-Tibran cave complex and Cosquer and in Maltravieso Cave in Spain appear to have missing fingers or other malformations. These "disfigured" hands have fueled discussions for the last 100 years. Groenen (1987) has provided a review of this debate. The central issue, of course, is that virtually all apparent mutilations are also replicable by simply contorting fingers in the stenciled hand (as one does in shadow art). But many people still insist that these represent real ritual amputations.

More recent speculation on possible causes of these disfigured hands has focused on Raynaud's disease, in which capillaries fail to respond normally by flushing with warm blood when hands or feet get cold. I find

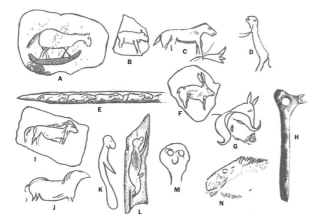

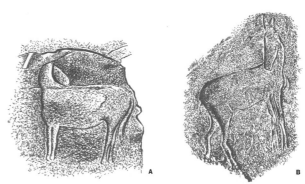

A hodgepodge of images that do not normally make it into popular Paleolithic art books: **A**, Lourdes, Fr. **B–C**, **F**, and **I**, Limeuil, Fr. **D**, Candamo, Sp. **E**, Abri Morin, Fr. **G** and **L**, Lascaux, Fr. **H**, Espalungue à Arudy, Fr. **J**, Le Portel, Fr. **K**, Los Casares, Sp. **M**, Marsoulas, Fr. **N**, Gourdan, Fr.

In the preceding illustration I do not wish to imply that all Paleolithic art bears the rudimentary stamp of children's art. There are many examples of art by accomplished drawers: **A**, Angles-sur-l'Anglin, Fr. **B**, Levanzo, It.

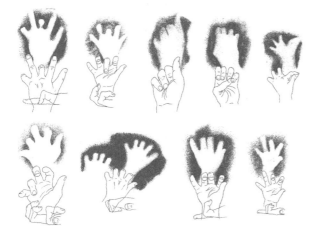

It seems likely that the missing finger segments as portrayed in Paleolithic art are just the result of bent fingers. Of course, there may be some exceptions that do represent actual missing digits. All handprints shown here are from Gargas, Fr. My reconstructions are the line drawings.

In some of the Paleolithic hand images one can see the actual bent fingers portrayed by the ocher spray. All examples shown are from Gargas, Fr. My reconstructions are the line drawings.

this explanation unconvincing, because Raynaud's disease is seldom expressed in young men (Larson 1996), and the hands with the "missing fingers" are mainly those of young males. Individuals who experience extreme winter temperatures, like cross-country dog-mushers, winter mountain climbers, and so on, do sometimes suffer frozen tissue. Yet, in Alaska, certainly among the coldest well-populated places on earth, complete loss of individual fingers due to freezing is rare. I have never seen one case. Nor have I seen any in my travels in northern Siberia. This is despite the fact that many residents in both places have had multiple experiences of frostbite.

These Paleolithic images will, no doubt, continue to puzzle and prompt speculation. Having played with making spatter stencils of my own hands, I find the ease with which one can replicate the "maimed-hand look" has left me very convinced that all, or virtually all, were done in fun, especially when we recall that these are largely young

A few of the Paleolithic hand images are quite enigmatic, as in the above case from Gargas, Fr., appearing as a dinosaur track or that of some deformed troglodyte hermit. But these oddities can usually be accounted for by conscious manipulation of the hand being sprayed. See my interpretation below this image.

This Paleolithic hand from Bayol, Fr., looks like a polydactyl print, with six fingers and two thumbs. But two right-hand muddy prints, by the same person, are obviously superimposed, the second one with fingers and thumb shifted in position while the palm remains in the same place.

people's hands and appreciate the quick, almost careless, casualness with which they were made. This phenomenon of altering the hand stencil patterns by finger contortion is also well documented from a number of other cultures. I would like now to take another branch in this line of reasoning and ask you to revisit the subject of taphonomy, as taphonomic biases are going to be critical in appreciating the products of children in the archaeological record, particularly our collection of Paleolithic art.

THE "YOUNG MOOSE ANTLER EFFECT" AND PALEOLITHIC ART

We saw in the first chapter how significantly taphonomic processes can distort the fossil record. In some cases entire age classes and even sexes are not preserved as fossils; for example, young animals are particularly underrepresented in the fossil record. But this bias is reversed when we look at fossil shed antlers. This reversal has prompted speculation that fossil deer must have had smaller antlers than their living descendants.

Curiously enough, the shed antlers that dominate our museum fossil collections are mainly antlers of young animals. Wouldn't you imagine that the massive, rugged, palmed antlers of adult moose would preserve better and

A Pleistocene-aged, ocher-sprayed, polydactyl hand image from Pech-Merle, Fr. In this case the left hand was sprayed on its right half, and then probably flipped with its back against the wall and the left half sprayed. This makes the usual and supernumerary little finger look as long as the index finger; indeed, it is the imprint of the index and ring finger.

hence be more common than the much smaller antlers of young moose? But that doesn't seem to be the case.

Why would that be? Moose shed, or "drop," their antlers annually. This normally occurs soon after autumn rut, and then they grow new ones the following summer. Antlers of every individual get to be larger and larger each year until the individual is six or seven or so years old. Unlike reindeer, cow moose do not grow antlers (with rare excep-

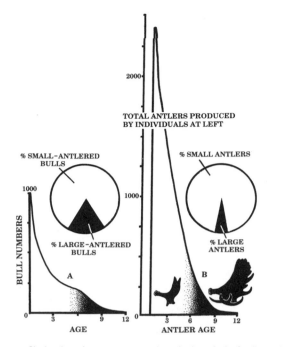

Shed antlers of young moose greatly predominate in the fossil record over antlers of older bulls. Why? If we examine a typical age structure for moose at any given time slice (**A**), one can see that it is not until about age six that bulls begin to produce large antlers, but fewer than 20% of the bulls live until age six, as seen in the pie diagram. This explains some of the distortion. But the main distortion comes from the fact that these older bulls of course have already shed at least four pairs of smaller antlers, as seen in **B**. The living bull moose (in time slice **A**) produced an accumulation of antlers shown in **B**. This cumulative-antler phenomenon skews the fossil numbers toward younger ages.

tions). Shed antlers must become covered by sediment to be incorporated into the fossil record, but there is nothing obvious about that process that would greatly favor the physical preservation of small antlers over the gigantic ones of larger bulls. What force then might explain the bias of smaller antlers in our collections?

The answer lies in the fact that during the first six years of its six- to eight-year life span, a bull moose is growing and shedding smallish antlers. The largest antlers are produced only after age six. But few bulls live beyond the year in which they reach full breeding dominance, because depletion of fat reserves and violent fights of full rut participation make it unlikely a bull will survive the following winter. Thus, the solution to this puzzle is simple. If we

imagine each bull's contribution to the pool of shed antlers as a row of six to eight antlers, most of the antlers in this row will be small or modest in size. Few will be large. The smaller ones predominate in our hypothetical antler row, just as smaller antlers are most numerous in the fossil record. Additionally, many bulls die before reaching six years of age and these animals contribute only small shed antlers to the record. It is a major taphonomic bias, accumulating into a real distortion over time.

This "young moose antler effect" is also at play in other taphonomic contexts, among them, Paleolithic art. Part of this is due to brief Paleolithic life expectancies, around fifteen years. (Those demographics are discussed in chapter 5.) This means that, in the Paleolithic, most of one's life was spent as a child. Today, the years of childhood and adolescence are perhaps only a fourth of the average life expectancy of seventy-five years. We quite rightly think of spending three-quarters of our lives as adults as normal, but that was not the case in the Pleistocene.

The very different Paleolithic family profile means that, at any one time, fully two-thirds of the people were in their twenties or younger. If we assume for a moment that all individuals generated "art-ifacts" at the same rate, well over half of Paleolithic art would be produced by people under twenty, *for any one year.* Now even that becomes greatly exaggerated when we consider the cumulative effect of art generated over *millennia,* because of the "moose antler effect." That is, the art of young people available to be fossilized (like shed moose antlers) becomes several times greater than that produced by adults. Remember, all Paleolithic adults may have produced children's art when they were young, whereas all children may not have lived to produce adult art. Even if there were no other biases favoring youthful production of art (an assumption we know to be incorrect because learning demands a higher level of intense participation), we must expect that the artistic equivalent of "small moose antlers" will be, by far, the most numerous in the human Paleolithic record. The evidence supports that expectation.

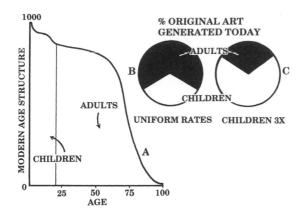

Just as the accumulated effect of producing a set of antlers each year creates a collection in which small antlers are disproportionate to the age structure of the moose population, a similar process works for things like human drawings. From the survivorship curve for modern humans one can see that today in developed countries people typically spend only a small part of life younger than eighteen— around a fourth of it. But if we preserved all the drawings, much more than one-fourth of them would be from children under eighteen, as all people older than eighteen had to have made drawings as children. If all ages produced drawings at equal rates, more than one-third of the art produced would be by children. But children produce more visual art than adults; I'll estimate, say, three times as much. With these assumptions, two-thirds of all original drawings today should be by children. I think that is an underestimate.

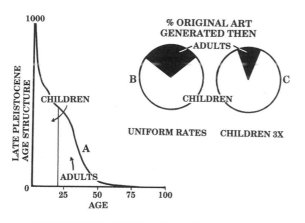

The late Pleistocene survivorship curve was different from that of today. On average, people spent more than half of their lives under the age of eighteen. If all ages produced drawings at the same rate, under-eighteen drawings would have made up two-thirds of the total. If children produced three times more drawings than adults, then the overwhelming majority would have been produced by people under eighteen. This is a taphonomic bias we have to keep in mind when looking at Paleolithic art. Theoretically, most of the drawings could have been produced by people in the first half of life—under eighteen.

IMPROVISATION AND SERENDIPITY IN PALEOLITHIC ART

If it occurred to man to create his own images, it's because he discovered them all around him, almost formed, already within his grasp. He saw them in a bone, in the irregular surfaces of cavern walls, in a piece of wood. One form might suggest a woman, another a bison.

Pablo Picasso (quoted in Brassaï, *Picasso and Company*)

Picasso grasped a principle of perception that forms another unifying aspect of Paleolithic art. In cave after cave one is struck by the way Paleolithic artists made use of existing contours on the limestone walls or ceilings. A touch of pigment to make a horn here, a mane and nostril there, or incising ears and an eye on a suggestive contour—time and again Paleolithic artists developed natural irregularities into striking images. There seems to have been a widespread propensity to transform, consolidate, or enhance some suggestive natural feature.

Similarly, in the sculpting of such mobiliary art as spear-throwers and point-straighteners, the shapes of the available pieces of antler obviously influenced the choice of image carved, including the species and its posture and attributes. Sculptors today often say each piece of material "requires acknowledgment and dialog." Engravings on plaquettes and other stones often fit the piece; that

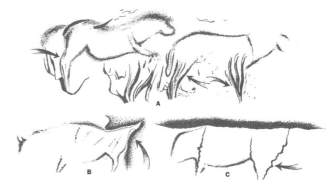

A, Stalactites in Font de Gaume, Fr., reminded these artists of horse rumps, legs, and tails. **B**, The projecting rock form looked like a raised bison tail. **c**, The cracks reminded someone of a ham and leg shape. **B** and **c** from Altxerri, Sp.

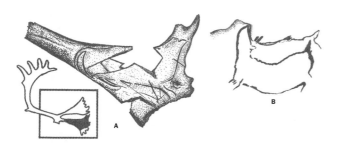

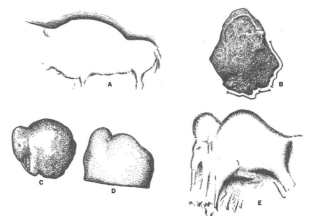

A, The projecting tine of a reindeer brow tine from Laugerie-Basse, Fr., reminded someone of a bull bison with upturned head (shot in the throat). **B**, To the artist, the cave contours in Le Portel, Fr., suggested a deer with upturned tail and head.

One can see what Paleolithic artists had on their minds by what they improvised from natural shapes on cave walls and stones. Here are a few examples: **A**, Ekain, Sp. (a bison's back was imagined from the stone irregularity). **B**, Angles-sur-l'Anglin, Fr. (note three faces, one pointing downward and two to the right). **C**, Avdeevo and, **D**, Kostenki, Rus. (mammoth-like stones and bones made more so by carving). **E**, Bernifal, Fr. (cave wall irregularities that looked like mammoth underparts—improved upon by filling in the upper contours).

is, the relation of image to surface and edges seems very deliberate.

This theme of responsive perception, of an interactive, artistic play with a naturally occurring form, is quite distinct in Paleolithic art. Once we recognize the extent of this improvisation we can see it is possible that (1) people did not necessarily go into caves with the intent to make a particular image or motif, as would have been likely with art making for cultic purposes or other very codified symbolic imaging. The perception of aesthetic opportunities and artistic pleasure may have been much more casual and spontaneous. Also, (2) since the natural relief is transformed where it is found, this throws into question the idea that images of particular animal species were carefully placed at different locations in caves for worship or to represent symbolic relationships.

A PALEOLITHIC RORSCHACH TEST

Playful use of natural irregularities is found again and again in different caves. It is not that smoother walls lacking suggestive contours are avoided, but rather that the serendipitous use of something "given" is a repeated theme. Again, this spontaneity is consistent with qualities we've noted in much of Paleolithic art: irregular image overlap, unfinished forms, and often quick execution.

I think such spontaneity may be forensically informative. The well-known Rorschach test employs the fact that

our brains are most likely to recognize—and even to superimpose onto inconclusive and ambiguous new forms—images with which we are already quite familiar. More precisely, we tend to recognize, to conceive as it were, images of subjects with which we are most preoccupied. It is more than a metaphor to say that we have an available archive of images that are the most readily used cerebral avenues of our imaginations and/or experience.

As you can see from the many images in this book, Paleolithic spelunkers were not preoccupied with frogs, beetles, babies, mice, hedgehogs, elaborate coiffures, and ornate robes but predominantly recognized limestone bulges as parts of large mammals, game birds, large fish, naked women, a scatter of ugly faces, and erections and vulvae. Later I will present evidence that these are not foremost on everybody's minds but are especially indicative of one sex and one age-group in a Paleolithic large-mammal hunting society. Who? Well, you know that already by now.

The interesting point is that Paleolithic artists using naturally suggestive formations developed these into explicit identities—bison backs, horse necks, breasts of nude

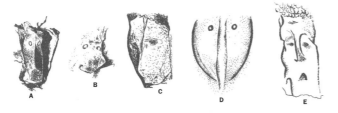

Well-drawn faces do not typically appear back in deep caves; rather, human images in deep caves have a graffitiesque character. The best explanation for this seems to hinge on the age and sex of the artists frequenting these places. A free spontaneity seems particularly apparent where these Paleolithic cave visitors have seen a simple large mammal or human face in the natural irregularities of the stone wall and enhanced it with a little ocher. **A–C**, Altamira, Sp. **D**, Deux Avens, Fr. **E**, Cueva de Hoz, Sp.

It is a commonly understood principle that what one sees as suggestive forms among random lines depends, to a great extent, on the subjects that are already on one's mind. Paleolithic art based on suggestive lines usually depicts large mammals. I can show only a few in this book, but enough to present the case. Natural cave wall contours, on the left, were modified to emphasize bison-like lines, on the right, even though the upper bison image is in a position that bison cannot take. Le Portel, Fr.

women, etc.—that do not differ notably from the subjects "made from scratch" on the smooth cave walls or flat antler surfaces.

How our brains go about "seeing faces in the clouds" is an interesting process (Guthrie 1993). Probably as a result of our extreme sociality, we humans evolved a very keen ability to analyze and identify visual form, particularly faces and body shapes. For example, we can scan a large crowd of people and pick out the face of a friend in a millisecond. For a long developmental period, children, much more than adults (Piaget 1964), are prone to pick out a face among clouds, wall cracks, or rock outcrops, and not just faces; they find many common objects in their visual vocabulary, especially animals.

Another class of Paleolithic "developed imagery" goes beyond the kinds of naturally evocative forms that are obvious to most observers, such as an inverted V-shaped rock that suggests a horse neck and head. This class consists of forms developed from simple cave features such as a small round nodule or dimple. Rorschach insights are especially poignant in cases such as these. How can an artist incorporate a small, round irregularity in the middle of his or her canvas? In the Paleolithic case the answer is clear. It became a woman's nipple or the eye of a horse. In other words, they used these little irregularities to portray the same subjects they created from suggestive natural cave wall curves and the same subjects they depicted on clean white walls or smooth ivory surfaces. This lack of differ-

ence supports the forensic principle that people see what is already handy in their imaginations—perhaps what is of foremost importance to them. This book is about making sense out of the forces that must have been behind those image choices—the patterns and subjects of Paleolithic art.

NOVICE KNAPPERS AND DRAWERS?

How do you separate the work of a novice drawer from that of an experienced artist? The short answer is—it is not always possible. Certainly though, we can look at art with that question in mind, just as we do with other human actions and skills. Flint knapping was practiced by Paleolithic peoples, and while shaping flints is not the same as drawing, aspects of the learning process are similar.

Researchers can sometimes identify contemporary knappers by the unique characteristics of an individual's inadvertent "signature." Using that background, archaeologists can occasionally trace the work of individual knappers in the debris of a prehistoric site. Most of the variation in knapping patterns, however, arises not from individual signatures but from differences in skill. In learning to knap, people experience a learning curve, from novice to mastery and excellence.

Complex skills are acquired only with much practice, and though individuals may progress through this arc of

Another aspect of seeing images in natural forms is making images out of rather neutral, *nonsuggestive* forms. Here are horses from Les Combarelles, Fr., all scratched into the cave wall around small nodules or pocks in the wall, some for eyes, others for nostrils, and in some images both.

In Pergouset Cave, Fr., small irregularities prompted a beginning drawer to engrave heads of large mammals into the wall using these natural lumps as eyes.

Many images were engraved around otherwise nonsuggestive cave wall forms (such as a small round lump). This is a collage of images from just one cave, Les Combarelles, Fr., that shows mainly large mammals, nude women in suggestive poses (more on this posture in chapter 6), faces, and fish. These are almost identical to the subject choices found in the rest of preserved Paleolithic art.

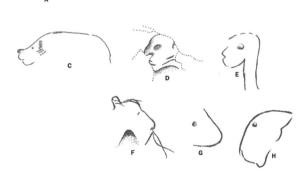

A, Fish, Massat, Fr. **B–H**, Fish, bear (drawn from suggested "nose" contour), people, lions, and other forms, Les Combarelles, Fr. All of these images were engraved around natural nodules.

apprenticeship at different rates, learning generally correlates well with individual age, especially with respect to common adult skills practiced in subsistence cultures. Some experienced modern flint knappers can examine a stone tool and assess the skill level of the individual who made it (see Grimm 2000 for a review). Moreover, these master knappers can make such assessments using only waste flakes. Often, the waste flakes are all that remain in archaeological sites, but this debris may be refitted to approximate the original core and thus to reconstruct the pattern and sequence of knapping, a process referred to as *chaine opératoire* (Leroi-Gourhan 1965), the operational chain of manufacture. The forensic criteria researchers use (e.g., Dawe 1997; Grimm 2000) to identify the work of a novice can be summarized as follows:

➤ Errors are often made in the initial visual conception. This misconception occurs before the first blow is made

Sometimes people not only improvised on natural contours but even improvised on different images they saw in other people's drawings. Someone saw a woolly mammoth in the woolly rhino drawing at La Mouthe, Fr., or vice versa (note the protruding spear with blood spewing). **A**, Possible original drawing, with exploded mammoth, **B**, and rhino, **C**.

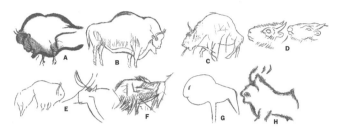

As with flint knapping, it is possible to determine the experience of the artists by their products. Upper images are from more experienced artists; lower ones are more likely to have been done by less experienced artists. **A**–**B**, Font de Gaume, Fr. **C**, Abzac, Fr. **D** and **G**, La Madeleine, Fr. **E**, Les Combarelles, Fr. **F**, Lascaux, Fr. **H**, Grotte Richard, Fr. **I**, La Souquette, Fr.

and results variously in inappropriate size, shape, proportion, and control.

▶ Subsequent failures to conceptualize solutions to problems encountered once the work is under way become apparent in poorly conceived changes in knapping direction.

▶ The goal may be practice rather than a finished piece, as indicated by leaving the finished piece at the knap site.

▶ Core preparation and maintenance are absent or rudimentary.

▶ The core materials (and perhaps the knapping tools) are not of high quality or are inappropriate for the intended product.

▶ The artist often worked peripherally to the central camp and even in areas distant from traditional work sites.

▶ Finished products deviate considerably from sizes and shapes normally produced by master knappers.

▶ Cores are often abandoned prematurely.

▶ Tentativeness of blow intention shows in hinge, rather than clean, feather fractures, while at the same time there are often strong bulbs of percussion showing excessive force.

Drawers can often be identified by characteristics of their work, probably more so than knappers. That is ultimately how art experts recognize forgeries. We sometimes refer to these individually distinctive qualities as the artist's "hand" or "signature." Despite this uniqueness, most variation among drawings is related to developmental skills, which are highly correlated with an individual's age. I was challenged by Dawe's and Grimm's characterizations of novice knapping skills to articulate a comparable list that could be used to characterize novice drawing skills:

▶ Errors are often made in the initial visual conception. These result in difficulties in size, shape, proportion, and control.

▶ There is an inability to conceptualize solutions to visual problems encountered in the work or its design.

▶ Images are often done on scraps or fragments of material and are clearly not intended as finished works. Often the images are discarded soon after execution. Thus, the goal seems not so much the production of a finished piece but practice.

▶ Images often are made without proper preparation of a surface, even superimposed or overlapping older drawings.

▶ Materials and techniques are often simple, with, for example, very little investment in complex paint preparation or preliminary sketches.

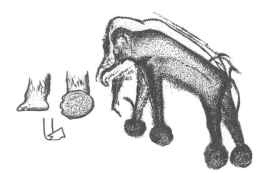

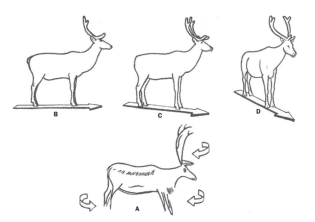

In some Paleolithic animal images the feet are twisted around to show the bottom surfaces of the hooves. Some researchers explain these peculiarities as drawings of dead animals lying on their sides with soles visible. However, I find a more credible explanation in the hunter-artist's association of a specific track pattern with an animal. Thus, it is logical to include foot information with a drawing. This is akin to the perspective problems in drawing antlers and eyes—drawing what one knows rather than what one can actually see from a single perspective. Mammoth, Chauvet, Fr.

A, Different aspects of a perspective solution show up in this little Paleolithic drawing of a reindeer bull from Ekain, Sp., that are typical in Paleolithic art. The twisted-antler and foreleg perspective at first appears as an attempt to fore-shorten—to draw the whole animal in a view other than 90° to the observer (**B–D**). But, remember from the last chapter, it is an attempt by an experienced artist to cope with the half-animal problem, a form of the "halibut eye" solution.

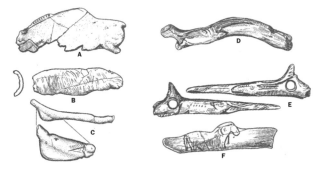

Sometimes the shape of a bone suggested an art image, and in other cases the image had to be greatly modified to fit the shape. **A**, Bison, Isturitz. Fr. **B**, Lion Laugerie-Haute, Fr. **C**, Horse from horse hyoid bone, Isturitz, Fr. **D**, Ibex, Arudy, Fr. **E**, Reindeer, Laugerie-Haute, Fr. **F**, Horse, Morin, Fr.

► Materials and techniques are often used that are not well suited to the substrate, theme, or size of the image.

► Drawings sometimes are done in unusual places, often well away from camp and even in places not only difficult to access but unlikely to be revisited.

► Final work deviates from forms used by more masterful drawers.

► Images are often abandoned prematurely, while very incompletely done.

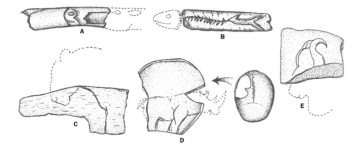

Most art, even on bone, was not preserved. It is thus not surprising that so many individual artifacts are incomplete. Even as such they contain picture-puzzle pieces of information. **A**, This small fragment from Belvis, Fr., shows a horse muzzle, from which one can see that the area of white on the noses of French Pleistocene horses was very similar to that on wild horses today. **B**, This fragment from Espalungue à Arudy, Fr., is a double metaphor for refuse because it is a piece of refuse that portrays refuse—the remnants of a consumed fish carcass. **C**, The muzzle from Mas d'Azil, Fr., looks like that of a lion. **D**, This image from Isturitz, Fr., was engraved on the inside of a human skull and appears to be a rhino. **E**, This fragment from Grotte Richard, Fr., shows part of a bison.

► Tentativeness is apparent in overdrawing and changing of lines, and at the same time many novices' drawings have a crude and rudimentary aspect characteristic of a "heavy hand."

PALEOLITHIC GRAFFITI?

Another fact of this "novice signature" is that it contributes to the feel of unity of Paleolithic art, from what I can only call its graffitiesque quality. I will address this aspect later in the book as well but would like to point out that art in caves does not occur in such well-organized layouts as commonly printed in books. Instead, images are scattered irregularly from the entrances of caves to the darkest recesses; they are often wedged in between other images or natural barriers, are superimposed, or are done at skewed angles, on their sides, or in quite different media; they are made by a variety of artists and generally without indication of a ground surface or encompassing scene; that is, they are unrelated to adjacent pieces. Thousands of quickly executed images found outside caves on slate or on bone often have the same tone or are even more haphazard, with a palm swipe erasing one form and allowing another to be made on top of the original—fish are mixed with red deer, copulation scenes are superimposed over bison. The art is frequently quite disordered in its presentation. If most kinds of Paleolithic art images were mysteriously painted overnight on museum walls, it would be called coarse vandalism and removed immediately.

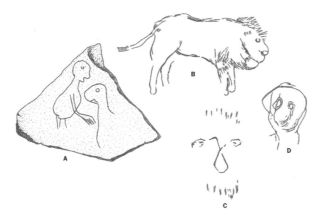

Some clearly rudimentary Paleolithic art: **A**, People, Enlène, Fr. **B**, Lion, Les Combarelles, Fr. **c**, Face, Gabillou, Fr. **D**, Face (using some natural rock contours), Les Combarelles, Fr.

This is why I use the term "graffiti." Graffiti, like Paleolithic art, are a little wild and disorganized. In fact, the word *graffiti* (*graffito,* singular) is the word used in Italy today for Paleolithic rock engravings. This Italian word can be translated as "little image" or "little scratch"—a quick image done without the trappings of formal sanction. Perhaps modern graffiti, in part, evince an atavistic impulse to draw in public places with abandon. But modern graffiti also convey a violation of somebody else's property and space, private or the state's. Not merely unsanctioned, urban graffiti resist the desires of the community, are unwanted, and are suppressed. Paleolithic art contains none of these overtones. There are some marks of pleasure in today's graffiti—their creators are apparently having fun—but the frequent sense of anger, ugliness, and pique communicated by modern graffiti does not emanate from Paleolithic works.

I think the term "graffiti" does include the larger phenomenon evidenced throughout history, an inclination to make some visual mark—to leave a personal scratched or painted trace behind in private spots. This is particularly true in caves but also under concrete bridges or in underpasses, train yards, subways, culverts, and of course toilet booths. Such graffiti are found on Egyptian, Greek, and Roman buildings and monuments and among the ruins of Asia. What is most central for our interests, however, is that these thoughtless scrawls were not done by all ages and both sexes in proportion to their numbers. Today, frequented caves that are unprotected are certainly littered with such marks. Acknowledging the widespread historical and contemporary experience of this tendency, let us think about the often asked question "Why did Paleolithic peoples go down into caves to make their marks?" in a new light. It is not just Paleolithic folks but rather a widespread phenomenon. It endangers the security and conservation of much Paleolithic cave art today. All art caves have to be closed to the unescorted public for this reason. Every conservator knows that if you let people wander unchaperoned down in caves, especially young people, they will mark all over the walls.

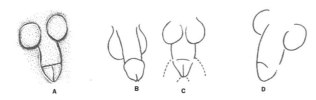

A, One of the numerous Pleistocene images of genitals, from Cosquer, Fr., compared to, **D**, a modern one from the elevator wall in the Museé de l'Homme, Paris (spring 1995). My images **B** and **C** are different sexual versions of the potential double entendre of the penis from Cosquer.

This scene of a copulating couple (with onlookers?) is poorly done, likely by an inexperienced drawer, as are virtually all the copulation scenes in Paleolithic art. This is not much different from graffiti done by young boys in toilet stalls today. From Los Casares, Sp. **A**, Original. **B**, Exploded view.

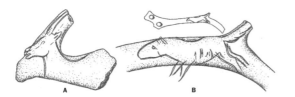

What do reindeer antler tines remind you of? Antler tine art from the Paleolithic: **A**, Ibex, Laugerie-Basse, Fr. **B**, horse, La Madeleine, Fr.

Please do not mistake my point. I am not saying that Paleolithic art is exactly like modern graffiti. The people who used charcoal sticks and red ocher to produce the bison murals seem to have worked out of enthusiastic respect for both the hunted and the hunters. But at the same time they drew in ways that were often free, careless, casual, alive, gritty, and occasionally erotic. And there is abundant evidence that they did not abstain from modifying, marking over, or scratching out previous art.

Graffiti and bullet holes on a rusty "no trespassing" sign on the gate to the Solutré Archaeological Site in 1980, translated basically as "excavators stink," with accompanying graphics. Isolated penises are one of the common forms of graffiti used by young males throughout the world.

PALEOLITHIC CHILDREN'S ART
FOUND OUTSIDE CAVES

Forensics of human traces in Paleolithic caves highlights the role of youngsters. In fact, there are taphonomic biases which may exaggerate the abundance of children's art outside caves as well. One of these forces, the "moose antler effect," especially applies here. Consider evidence from decorated hunting weapons: points, spear-throwers, point-straighteners, and so on. Competence with such weapons is achieved by thousands upon thousands of practice throws. My custom recurve wooden bow came with the maker's promise that "this bow is guaranteed for 100,000 shots or 1 year, whichever comes first." The implications of that made me gulp; it was properly assumed I would shoot it tens of thousands of times in the first year to master its particular character.

Indeed, we know Paleolithic life demanded such levels of expertise. One had to start early to develop superlative proficiency, and we do find suggestive traces of this in the archaeological record. There are many smaller-than-normal weapons (short-shanked spear-throwers and shaft-straighteners) and simple disposable projectile

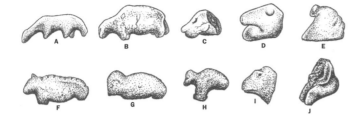

Children's art? In eastern Europe and western Asia there are many of these simply done, golf-ball-sized figures. Many are made from fired clay (loess usually), but some are carved from soft stone or osseous materials. **A–C**, Dolni Věstonice, Czech. **D–E**, Kostenki I, Rus. **F–J**, Pavlov, Czech.

A small, fragmented ivory sculpture of a rudimentary horse(?) from Avdeevo, Rus. The many almost-decomposed art pieces in the record allow one to imagine the innumerable artworks that have not preserved.

points (such as small bone points) among our collections of Paleolithic artifacts, and these may in fact be childhood weapons—toys, by any other name. Is there any reason to think that Paleolithic children would not also have been playing with art making?

The Paleolithic site of Dolni Věstonice, in the Czech Republic, contained over 700 golf-ball-sized hearth-fired clay images, the majority portraying lions, bears, mammoths, and woolly rhinos, with a few wolverines. Other figures were images of commonly hunted large mammals, like bison and horses. There were also voluptuous nude women. (Does this list sound familiar by now?) An additional 10,000 fragments of such images were found at that site and at several other sites in Moravia. Some scholars have assumed that these were adult art and have proposed that they were broken intentionally (Soffer 1987) as part of a sacred rite of destruction or ritual closing (Vandiver et al. 1990). But one could also imagine that the figures were products that saw hard use by youngsters. All of these clay images exhibit rather quick and unrefined modeling, and many show intense use wear. At Avdeevo, Kostenki, Tolbaga, Ust'-Kova, Buret', Mal'ta, and other sites in Russia, similar images of people and Pleistocene animals, only a few centimeters in length, were carved or modeled in diverse media in a rudimentary manner (Abramova 1995).

Foley (1962) observed that miniatures of this size and character are highly indicative of children's toys in early historic times. Several plausible, nonmystical ideas can account for the many broken fragments occurring at the above-mentioned Paleolithic sites. We can assume with certainty that Paleolithic children's lives were dominated by play, as play is a truly human universal (Brown 1991). Svensson (1993) emphasized that playthings of children—toys and toy fragments—are the items most often broken and/or left as debris at or near campsites. Most other, more useful items are usually transported away. Lillehammer's (1989) work with Norwegian Mesolithic sites showed this pattern, and he proposed that children's toys were common in most campsite debris.

In the case of Paleolithic fired-clay images, we know that most were not carefully made, and for many it is hard to discern exactly what they are meant to portray. It is reasonable to assume that these very rudimentary figures were not carefully dried or carefully fired. Solid clay pieces that are bigger than golf-ball size are indeed difficult to dry and fire successfully. Solid, ungrogged clay figures have to be carefully dried and slowly heated to bisque, or "brick," temperatures; otherwise, the enclosed moisture turns into steam and the figures crack apart or even explode. Modern potters and clay sculptors still contend with this problem; one must use patience, first in slow air-drying, then in bringing kiln temperature up slowly to dry out the remaining deep moisture bonded to the clay particles— even so, explosions and breakage are common. The Paleolithic objects in particular are easily broken because they were made, not from pure clay, but from local loess (mainly silt-sized particles).

Breakage during firing and the fragility of these low-fired (500°C) clay toys can account for the high percentage of broken clay art in the Pleistocene. The artificial problem

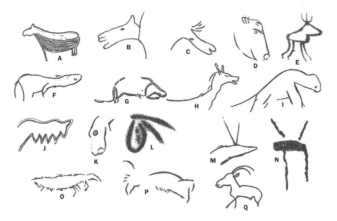

These are some more quick studies of a variety of large mammals by people in the early stages of drawing development. Use your own guess as to species. **A**, Laugerie-Haute, Fr. **B**, Abri Cellier, Fr. **C**, Rouffignac, Fr. **D**, Mas d'Azil, Fr. **E**, Carriot, Fr. **F** and **H–I**, Les Combarelles, Fr. **G**, Bernous, Fr. **J**, La Clotilde, Fr. **K**, Aguas, Sp. **L**, Chauvet, Fr. **M**, Parpalló, Sp. **N**, Grotte des Eglises, Fr. **O**, Villars, Fr. **P**, Cosquer, Fr. **Q**, Tossal de La Roca, Sp.

in accounting for the high percentage of breakage only occurs if they are seen as being made and carefully kept by adults. Were these clay figurines made by children as toys? Well, certainly that is as likely a possibility as assuming they were made by adults for a sacred purpose.

In most open-air archaeological sites rudimentary pieces are found lying among others that are unarguably the sophisticated work of adults. And, of course, some art could have been made by adults for young children. Objects made by and for children are a whole class of art in many cultures. The burials of two youths at Sungir in Russia contain small, delicate, stylized bison and horse carvings, as well as small ivory spears and point-straighteners.

The variability and inconsistent quality of many Paleolithic artifacts may be most simply explained by allowing youngsters into our vision of the past. The taphonomic processes that curate our collections of Paleolithic objects and art are hardly respectful of seniority, artistic quality, or maturity.

DEVELOPING ARTISTS

We now appreciate that young children tend to proceed along certain pathways in their drawing development that relate to age, practice, and aptitude (Grötzinger 1970). Kellog (1955, 1970) worked with over a million drawings made by children between the ages of two and eight, from fourteen countries. She traced clear developmental patterns in these drawings and formalized them into a series of stages. These stages are not definitive for every child but describe a general pattern.

Within each of these stages, children's drawings explore forms that Kellog found repeated in all her cultural groups. It is important to understand that these stages occur rather spontaneously. The forms drawn are usually not copied from or influenced by direct models in surrounding art (Hickle and Hickle 1984). It seems that the forms children draw are directed not so much by learning progression but by different stages in brain development. Hickle and Hickle (1984) argue that there is a fundamental biological basis for visual art development. The Kellog (1955) and Gardner (1980) approach to art development through a succession of fixed schemas has been challenged by some researchers, who would, in essence, give these stages more fuzzy edges.

Morris (1962) and Rensch (1965) were able to show that chimps enjoy scribbling on white paper and that the chimps made circles and crosses, two of the recurrent motifs that Kellog found to be universal in early stages of children's art. A chimp studied by Kohts (1935) even made a circle face with limbs. However, chimps seem to have cerebral limitations regarding potential drawing skills.

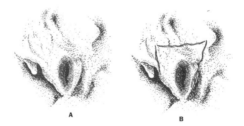

Tens of thousands of years ago, some person, seeing this little palm-sized opening, **A**, in the cave wall in lamplight, took a sharp stone and quickly enclosed it in a simple triangle, **B**, and had a ready-made image. Pergouset, Fr.

Kellog (1970) has pointed to prehistoric motifs that are similar to those in the children's drawings she studied. Such motifs are found in rock art sites all over the world. Several authors have suggested parallels between the art of children and the art of "primitive" people. I propose a simpler explanation: much "childlike" ancient art is probably children's art. All mature Paleolithic artists made thousands of artworks on their way to acquiring proficiency, and the artifacts of the early stages of their development—like antlers of young moose—were potential subjects for fossilization. This is not to say that all Paleolithic people eventually became master artists.

In summary then, we should expect to find traces of young people's arc of development scattered among the artifactual remains. Whether they were learning to make a particular style of stone point or to engrave an image on bone, it is likely that a ten-year-old's competency, as well as choice of imagery, might well differ from those of an eighteen-year-old. I think we can often see a rudimentary character in the art suggestive of the earlier stages of learning to draw. Indeed, the rudimentary and repetitious pattern discernible is itself a part of the essence of Paleolithic art.

It is worth noting that Edwards (1979) and other researchers find *repetition* to be a salient characteristic of young, even adolescent, drawers. Children draw and redraw subjects of keenest interest, whether those are dragster after dragster, horse after horse, or fancy dress after fancy dress. It is a stage that may frustrate art teachers and disturb parents. Finding what Paleolithic folks had on their minds, and accounting for that, will be our challenge in this book.

REPRESENTATION IN PALEOLITHIC ART

The representational character of Paleolithic art does not mean that we can be flat-footedly literal in our approach to it as viewers. What one sees and what one knows, and this interaction, are always at play in both art making and

A few lines of a lion seen from behind. Grotte Montagnola di San Rosalia, It. A simple but sophisticated presentation from someone experienced at drawing.

art viewing. Also, we have to be careful not to presume that a drawing, just by virtue of being a drawing, successfully reflects the maker's intent. The outcome of a drawing is rarely just as imagined. There are gaps in execution and various excursions, developments, and even mishaps along the road of creation in any piece. Sometimes non-drawers don't realize this and tend to take each work literally as being exactly what the artist had in mind at the outset. I suspect much of this is due to the predominance in our lives of photographic images and polished professional art. We should not interpret Paleolithic images too simplistically. For example, the giant penises that occur throughout Paleolithic art are unlikely a credible basis from which to argue that there has been a Holocene dwarfing of penises, nor can we imagine Paleolithic women were always nude.

We can only hope to be as informed and sensitive in our approach to representation as possible. One step toward that goal is a more active awareness of the participation of children and adolescents when we consider Paleolithic life, artifacts, and art. If we presume that a collection of drawings, for example, was made only by fluently accomplished adult artists, most of us will tend to look at these works differently than if we know drawings of youngsters are included as well.

We must recognize that the Paleolithic art we have is not uniformly great art. All of it is precious, yes, but artistically superb, no. Much is clearly the stuff of beginners by any measure. And works of beginners seem to predominate in some locations.

It may also be that Paleolithic youngsters had much greater artistic capacities than we would be inclined to

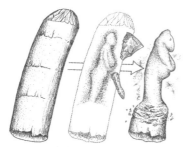

People who don't draw or sculpt should be reminded that the image one might imagine inside a mammoth tusk to be carved is never exactly what one ends up with. Sometimes, for an experienced sculptor, the final form will be even better than the imagined, but especially for a beginner, it probably will not. Here is one of the least publicized "Venuses," from Avdeevo, Rus.

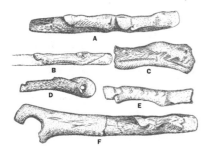

An observant artist with butchering experience would have a chance to examine animal legs in detail numerous times. So they were sometimes carved as a separate entity: **A**, **C–D**, and **F**, Mas d'Azil, Fr. **B**, Cueto de la Mina, Sp. **E**, La Madeleine, Fr.

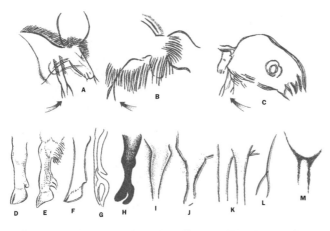

There are many legs shown in Paleolithic art. These are all bison legs. **A–B**, Cosquer, Fr. **C**, Massat, Fr. The lower row shows a spectrum of drawings from highly detailed on the left to rudimentary on the right: **D–F**, Mas d'Azil, Fr. **G**, Gargas, Fr. **H**, Lascaux, Fr. **I**, La Grèze, Fr. **J**, La Mouthe, Fr. **K**, Pair-non-Pair, Fr. **L**, Cosquer, Fr., **M**, Altxerri, Sp.

We can see that the people who made these forelegs were very familiar with artiodactyl anatomy and were experienced artists. The one to the left is a little gracile for a bison, maybe a giant deer (shelk), *Megaloceros*. The large dewclaws are emphasized, and one can almost feel the phalanges in the swell where they engage the metacarpal. The one on the right is clearly a bison; the ventral mane gives it away. Both are from Mas d'Azil Fr.

imagine based on our own youth. For all its hardships, Paleolithic life seems to have been a time of more balanced use of the brain. For example, one had to implicitly know a lot of calculus, probability, and statistics, but these were learned inductively by weight and feel, not formulae. Everything in its current state would have had importance in relation to other things, with complex implications for one's next move or lack thereof. Paleolithic cognition may have involved a tighter linkage between imagination and reason. And perhaps, as part of that, drawing was more mainstream, in expression and outlook, more readily at the heart of Paleolithic experience, than it is in our more complexly divided lives. Is it possible that in some late Paleolithic groups everyone could and did draw, much as today most people can write? Perhaps so.

Another side to this matter of the artists always playing with what they know and what they observe in their drawings is highlighted by x-ray drawings, which mix outer and inner anatomical elements in a single view. These occur in many cultures. For example, x-ray views are especially common among Australian Aboriginal motifs. Occasional x-ray views are also seen in the prehistoric art of Malaysia, as well as in India and Baja California.

Learning to draw today differs little from 30,000 years ago. New materials and technology supply only a few shortcuts to a developing art maker. The complex experiences of a youngster's playful efforts—or an adult's continuing ones—are individually gained, and because this is

Tension between Seeing and Knowing: X-ray Images   In order to understand the motivations of an x-ray drawing, you have to imagine the whole artist as two persons, a susceptible drawer and a naive onlooker who keeps asking, "Yes, that is an antelope in side view but do not antelope have two eyes?" You can see this same process going on in elementary school when children warp perspectives to see all the essential parts or draw transparent boats or planes with people inside them, x-ray view. Drawing the animal's insides is acknowledging the reality that there is more there than the outsides, but it is more a logical statement than a perceptual one. It is a characteristic commonly encountered when learning to draw (Gardner 1982).

Tindale (1928) pointed out that Australian x-ray paintings prominently and conspicuously feature the backbone and often the liver and fat depots. He associated this with the fact that Aboriginals were always in a chronic "fat hunger," and kidney fat is particularly sweet and oily (and often the only source of fat avail-

able from lean desert mammals). Some Australian Aboriginals once used a special bag for storing kidney fat (Taçon 1987). In no art do x-ray images seem to have become a rigid style, but they are always a possible method of representation (Taçon 1987).

In several Paleolithic large-mammal images, a curious zigzag pattern appears about where the backbone should be. It is not certain that this is meant to represent a vertebral column, but the pattern does recall x-ray art.

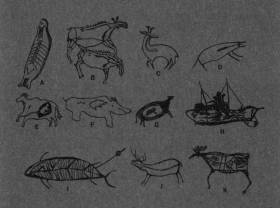

X-ray views from post-Paleolithic cultures throughout the world: A. Western Alaska, Eskimo. B and K, Norway, Neolithic. C, New Mexico. D, Canadian Indian. E, Central India. F, Libya. G, Malaysia. H, Australia. I–J, Baja, California.

A number of animals in Paleolithic art are drawn with rough zigzags where the backbone should be; these might be interpreted as x-ray views, so common in much of prehistoric art throughout the world. A, Reconstruction. B–F and I, Trois Frères, Fr. G, Les Eyzies, Fr. H, Limeuil, Fr. J–K, Roc-la-Tour, Fr.

Inside views are common in rock art. In more recent Australian art, x-ray views are a tradition. The vertebrae are quite often present. Here are a few examples from various sites in Australia.

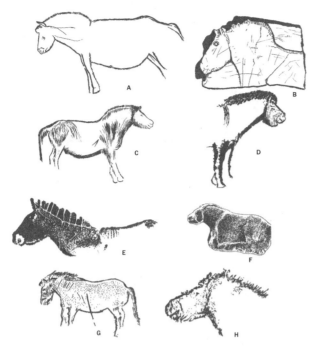

These Paleolithic horse images reiterate the idea that a portion of Paleolithic art was made by experienced artists. Again, I do not want to convey the idea that all preserved Paleolithic art was a product of young people. **A**, **C**, **D**, **H**, Niaux, Fr. **B**, Laugerie-Basse, Fr. **E**, Cosquer, Fr. **F**, Druthy, Fr. **G**, Tibran, Fr.

true we feel strong connections to the makers of these Paleolithic works despite gulfs of time and cultural change. We have that shared experience of having gone through the same complex processes of learning, each of us in a slightly different way from the other, but not very different. Though these old images are from art makers long dead, we can almost know them through their art objects, feel the same processes operating in their minds, for those are not just marks made by hands but marks of consciousness, marks of developing brain synapses and circuitry in no large way different from our own.

A Summary of the Evidence That Paleolithic Art Is an Age-Biased Sample

I am about to change subjects, from age to sex, starting in the next chapter. Before I do so let me provide a quick re-

view of the patterns of taphonomic bias we found among Paleolithic artifacts. These patterns suggest the large role of children's art in our collections of preserved Paleolithic art.

➤ Throughout much of prehistory, well over half of the people died before attaining full adult status, and people were old by forty. *Most of Paleolithic life was spent under twenty.*

➤ The *biometrics of hand- and footprints* shows that it was predominantly Paleolithic young people who ventured back in deep caves and left their marks.

➤ Contrary to one's notion from colorful art books about Paleolithic art, *many images are rudimentary,* done quickly, casually, often overlapping, and efforts were often discarded on the camp floors, consistent with having been made in a playful manner.

➤ A disproportionate adolescent presence in the caves would explain some of the *graffitiesque character* of a portion of the art, such as the imitation of mutilated fingers.

➤ Spontaneous employment of *suggestive natural contours within caves* is evidence that people did not enter caves intending to make a specific image. A

The bias of art publication is shown here in the form of a rarely shown, not-so-elegant "Venus" from the famous Willendorf site, Austria. The fame of the other lady is from her textbook presence, but this one, like so many rudimentary images, gets little popular coverage. This bias has allowed the idea to persist that all Paleolithic art was made by adults.

Youth is an important feature of Paleolithic artists, but it is an uncommon feature of their subjects. For example, images of young mammoths are few. Gönnersdorf, Ger.

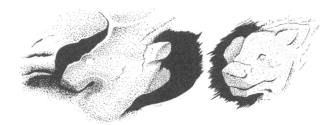

Two forms from the large cave of Mas d'Azil, Fr., that may have suggested large-mammal heads have been doctored up to look more like those subjects.

similar contingency occurs outside caves, prompted by irregularities on stone plaquettes and bone or antler fragments.

▸ Because of the way our brains develop, children are more likely than adults to recognize familiar images in the forms of other materials in their surroundings — *"pictures in the clouds."* This phenomenon extends to natural contours of cave walls and other Paleolithic art media.

▸ The Rorschach kinds of logic used to incorporate *concretions or other irregularities* (which did not self-evidently suggest the images they were used to make) on cave walls or other media also indicates a more casual approach, a preadult artist.

▸ Because the same limited choice of subjects occurs in three different contexts (suggestive contours, enigmatic holes or bumps, and smooth surfaces), one can say that much of preserved art was created by the *same group of people,* the same age and sex bias. The narrow range of subject matter highlights the intensity of *preoccupation of the artists with these subjects.*

▸ In a related way, the fossil record is inherently biased further toward artifacts produced by the young because the aggregate time spent as a youth is not expressed by an instantaneous age-structure slice. *This phenomenon especially distorts the overall age-specific proportions of artifacts generated* — the same way the fossil record is distorted in favor of young moose antlers.

▸ *Repetition is critical in learning.* The time and attempts dedicated to development of skills (e.g., flint knapping, sports, drawing) are significantly greater during the early, vertical part of the learning curve than during the later, horizontal part. That is, the most prolific stages in performing a skill are often in the early stages of developing proficiency.

▸ *Characteristics of the art itself often indicate a novice at work.* One can compare the acquisition of skills in things like knapping and see the analogy.

The Handwriting on the Wall: Testosterone Titer and Paleolithic Art

I want to introduce the next chapter by saying that a little "reductionism" helps pin some of these biases to a common source. The chemical regulators that consistently produce dimensional differences in hands and feet along observable patterns according to age and sex can ultimately be traced to growth hormones and anabolic steroids. One hormone especially — testosterone — will play an important role in subsequent chapters.

In a way, the biometric study of shape variations in hands is almost a titer assay for individual differences in testosterone during development. But testosterone affects more than hand dimensions; it also affects what one does with those hands — one's thoughts and one's actions. Ste-

This cow bison from Trois Frères, Fr., is one of the most dynamic images in Paleolithic art, one of my favorites: a speared animal, bolting at full speed, spewing lung blood.

roids have evolved to both affect and effect passions—and, as such, are deeply entwined in art-making choices. Our own existence is proof that many Paleolithic boys living in small hunting bands matured into men who were courageous and empathetic and capable of group cooperation, fidelity to mate and friends, and involvement with their children. While all those civilizing behaviors were to take on great meaning in their adult lives, it is likely that what occupied the minds of teens were other, more passion charged traits. These traits were also being tailored by evolution: competitive excellence in the search-and-kill part of hunting and the ability to acquire the best mate (and perhaps foggy fantasies of premarital and extramarital affairs while they were at it). I think these, or their appropriate cultural equivalents, are important animating forces for adolescent boys in most societies. For such ado-

lescents, testosterone is active in both the obsession with excellence and an aroused preoccupation with different kinds of love, including the coarsest sex, the latter in mind more often than in action. Throughout the next four chapters we will examine aspects of youthful testosterone as we build a more complete understanding of our collection of Paleolithic art.

᭰

Finger trace made in dust,
ROOound circle in mud,
Nearly a face—add
Big nose, stiff hair,
Dotted eyes, slit mouth,
Stick body, dangling legs,
Echoing over and again,
And thus we learn to draw.

Graduating. An engraved line,
Darts flying, striking home,
Deftly empowered vision,
Acumen expressing intuition,
Wounded stallion looking back.
Stiff mane and lifted tail,
Again and again, that echo.
And thus we learn to draw.

4

Testosterone Events and Paleolithic Imagery

A different view of the adolescent, less perplexing to adults and more nearly true, is to see him moving toward a peak of discovery and sensitivity that he may never again experience. The extremes are his measuring of the range of life. The enormity of what is possible to be is opened like a landscape before his eyes, inseparable from what it is possible to feel and believe. Adolescence . . . is an evolutionary adaptation that developed during centuries of high human maturity in small, hunter-gatherer groups. All its characteristics have an internal logic and purpose. Paul Shepard, *Tender Carnivore*

Paleolithic Art and the Evolution of Human Nature

The pattern is not subtle. On your first trip into a Paleolithic art cave, scan across the images on the dim walls. Visit any museum with exhibits of Paleolithic art or pick through museum drawers containing the broken refuse of engraved art, and there it is, that skew

Left, Geissenklösterle, Ger. *Right,* Barfaluy 2, Fr. Who among Paleolithic people chose to make such art images and why? Is there some universal human behavior that can help us make some sense out of these patterns?

toward hunted, large, edible game and dangerous beasts for the most part and to a lesser degree nude, curvaceous women. This book attempts to account for that skew by looking at the universals of human nature from an evolutionary perspective. But to do that we have to back up and see ourselves in a different light from that of our everyday experience. The story is about sexual differences and ultimately about "quality children," that is, those who meet new, higher standards. As you saw in the last chapter, children play an important part in this book, as indeed they seemed to have played an unusually large role in Paleolithic art. Ultimately, many Paleolithic artifacts, including those incorporating art, relate to the tools of parenting.

I have already introduced the thesis that preserved art is a biased sample of the wide array of all Paleolithic art and that this bias involves a major skew in the age and sex of the artists. In this chapter we will investigate why there was a limited range of age and sex classes who had risk-taking inclinations, the social sanction, and free time, including free time to go back into caves, where much of Paleolithic art is preserved—and then we will try to account for this. Also, I will identify the sex that made sharp stone tools and was mainly responsible for using them on the hard substances of antler, bone, and stone—the main archaeological materials preserved outside caves. These biases brought us very different kinds of images and subjects compared to what we would have if all art had been preserved for us to discover, study, and account for.

Beneath the cultural differences we see today among different sexes and ages are deep adaptive processes, im-

portant parts of whose evolutionary history we are just beginning to understand. The popular "men are from Mars, women are from Venus" observations from contemporary experience are insufficient to provide the depth we need to start to comprehend the magnitude and complexity of those forces—forces that underlie the recurring patterns of Paleolithic art.

Sex, Parenting, and Human Evolution

Once upon a time sex did not exist. For hundreds of millions of years the fossil record shows no seeds dappling puddles or young animals murmuring in their dens. The earth was rich with life, but this life reproduced by tiny single cells squeezing apart into identical twins. After eons had passed, fossils, hardly more than smears on rocks, show that some early single cells changed into multicellular organisms which could then let some cells specialize, forming tissues and organs. The cells remained members of the same genome but were not exactly clones; they specialized as movers, defenders, healers, smellers, respirers, eaters, and digesters. And, likewise, these new multicellular organisms left the job of reproduction to a few specialist cells.

The first multicellular organisms were probably hermaphrodites. Each hermaphrodite mixed its paired chromosomes into reproductive cells of two types: an egg cell filled with nutrient and energy stores to jump-start the new organism and a mobile and wiggly sperm cell, traveling light, carrying the other half of the genetic material, whose role it was to find the egg once they were all released together into the body cavity or the warm water of the outside world. When these egg and sperm cells recombined, the genetic "cards" of the single parent's chromosome pairs were effectively reshuffled. Its children were no longer identical genetic clones.

It is easy to see the selective advantage of this innovative hermaphrodite shuffle. The self-fertilized egg af-

Bison attacking man from Villars, Fr., and my rendition of the Paleolithic scene below. This experience, or rather the aesthetics around the idea of it, would have been one of the major testosterone themes. Both biological evidence and scenes from Paleolithic art suggest that Paleolithic steppe bison were more aggressive and dangerous than modern bison (Guthrie 1990).

Nurture. *Top,* this little drawing on stone from Parpalló, Sp., shows a cow reindeer smelling the rear of a calf. There is a biological story behind this. Cow reindeer are strongly bonded to their young but cannot easily tell their own calves by sight and must smell them. During the first few hours after birth, a cow imprints on those odors unique to her calf. Reindeer travel in big herds and young can easily become separated from their mothers, especially during stream crossings. I have seen many mix-ups, cows bawling everywhere for their young, smelling each new calf and rejecting it until they find their own. Adoption is costly and evolution keeps lean books. *Bottom,* my version of the Paleolithic scene; this behavior is a common spring sight in reindeer country.

forded vastly more genetic variants among offspring than simple cloning. Evolution is not about monotonous genetic strategies, because circumstances for life are rarely constant. Things are always changing: climates, predator tactics, parasite virility, disease resistance, and so on. Genetic variation means each generation includes a range of individuals, each responding somewhat differently, and the more the genetic variation, the faster the selection response. Sexual reproduction means each player is not putting all its coins on one numbered color in the roulette wheel of future fitness. Of course, there are many constraints on this idea, but here I'll stick to outlines.

Independently, and in many evolutionary lines, hermaphrodites started trading with other individuals—sperm for eggs and eggs for sperm. Again, because of this shuffling, much more genetic variation developed.

Early hermaphrodites did not stop here. Most evolved two distinct, specialized morphs, a Yin and a Yang. One morph produced only eggs and the other produced only sperm. Bimodal sex was born. Why not three or four morphs? Though evolution is a little sloppy, it is basically a minimalist, and two forms worked just fine. Male and female life forms became wildly successful. Each sex took on different ecological roles, different body forms, and bent their behaviors to benefit those bipolar specialties. There are several theories on the evolution of sex, but all insist on the potency of creating and constantly mixing genetic variation. Evolution loves sex.

Is that why you and I exist in morphs of men and women? Is that the root of the sexual emotions and behaviors we experience—to flirt, fall in love, become jealous, neck in the back seat, get married, have in-law problems, commit adultery, go through aching divorces, worry about crow's-feet and liver spots, compete at our jobs—all driven simply by the need to re-sort and shuffle variation in the gene pool? Though incredibly bizarre, any answer has to begin, yes, certainly, the demands of sexual reproduction permeate our being.

Those early bimodal animals had many fertilized eggs; the losses were high for little packages of eggs and sperm tossed to the tides. Some animals took a different tack and hid their eggs under cover or packaged them in leathery envelopes or shells. This extra attention to quality cut the losses but also meant fewer eggs could be laid. It was the first step toward parental care. It was not necessarily a better solution, but it allowed some species to compete with those that were stressing quantity.

LOST SHELL GLANDS, MODIFIED SWEAT GLANDS, AND SINGLE MOMS

The mammalian enterprise was a basically new way of parenting. About 90 million years ago a group of reptiles abandoned the eggshell and instead retained the developing egg inside the mother. Our mammalian uterus evolved from an ancestral reptile shell gland. This new strategy had many direct benefits: there was no longer a need to guard the clutch from the growing numbers of nest robbers and cuckoo egg-switchers or to contend with a limited supply of good nest sites. There were many side effects of this tactic — long-term evolutionary repercussions that still affect mammals. Because the developing young was inside for so long, male participation was reduced. Male birds can take a turn hatching the clutch of eggs, but male mammals cannot.

Mammalian gestation periods are now much longer than bird incubation times. This reflects the chicken and egg dynamics of gestation and incubation. Development time inside the shelled egg is limited by the supply of nutrients inside the egg. In utero development means a slow but continuous, almost indefinite, supply of nutrients. But after the long mammalian gestation, the father may or may not still be around. A skin gland complex on the abdomen of early female mammals provided nutritious sweet sweat for the newborn. Male mammals do not have functional breasts (actually, there is one species of fruit bat from Southeast Asia that we know little about but from which a few lactating males have been captured). This milky sweat for the mammalian baby meant that the adult female could specialize in eating things the infant could never manage. A sequence of adaptations reverberated through all evolving mammals and resulted in a pattern of a very limited paternal role in direct care and nurture of offspring. There are exceptions, but generally, the male's role in the reproductive process terminates after ejaculation. Stags take off. A more telling fact is that there is not a single mammalian species in which the rearing of the young is left completely to males; males of many different species of fish, amphibians, reptiles, and birds do this, but male mammals do not.

Primates continued this traditional mammalian pattern of leaving the main responsibility of nursing, nurture, transport, and care, in addition to bearing the young, to the female. But the male role began to shift in some primate groups, particularly among those that structured themselves in wide-ranging mobile troops based on genetic kinship. The primate troop became a mixed band of all ages and both sexes in which dominant males took on the role of defenders and protected members of the group, including offspring, from dangerous predators and from violence within and outside the group. The consorting of males with females was mainly linked to estrous condition. Males competed among themselves for the right to copulate with all estrous females. As a result, there is marked sexual dimorphism: males are generally twice the weight of females. Among our nearest primate relatives (gorilla, chimp, and orang), males do not significantly contribute to direct care or provisioning of the young (Mitchell 1979). These ape species are basically herbivores, eating food that comes in small packages, and every adult is as good as any other in this crumb-feeding, so males could be of little help in nurturance anyway. But

Even among our nearest ape relatives, chimpanzees, parental care is mainly a daily attendance by the mother. Males may protect young from carnivores or marauding neighbor males but otherwise do no caretaking. It was an important change for hominid males to form close bonds with females and help with the caretaking of young.

One of the most dangerous animals in the Pleistocene neighborhood was probably the bear. People had no weapon to guarantee instant death. **A**, Abri Sud de la Baume Noir, Fr. **B** and **G**, Les Espélugues, Fr. **C**, La Madeleine, Fr. **D**, Les Eyzies, Fr. **E**, Gourdan, Fr. **F**, Arudy, Fr. h and **M**, Isturitz, Fr. **I**, La Vache, Fr. **J–K** and **N–Q**, La Marche, Fr. **L**, Dolní Věstonice, Czech. **R**, Lascaux, Fr. **S**, Santimamiñe, Sp. **T**, Massat, Fr. **U**, Ekain, Sp.

there are some informative exceptions in which males do become caretaker fathers. Such active fathering occurs only among primate species with strong monogamous bonds.

For male parenting behavior to evolve in humans, wolves, or pigeons, it had to have a heritable component. We can see this in familiar species where the genetic portion is greatly reduced or almost lost—for example, in a comparison of domestic dogs, feral dogs, dingoes, and wolves. Wolves are active caretaking fathers, bringing

A, A testosterone event: a man being attacked by a bear's paws; pike or spear behind them. Mas d'Azil, Fr. **B**, My reconstruction.

food to their young and recognizing them as special individuals. Domesticated dog species have lost this behavior, even those that have gone feral. Australian semiwild dogs, dingoes, on the other hand, are not as far along in the spectrum of changes wrought by domestication and so still retain the wolf pattern of good fathering (Masson 1999).

There are a lot of asides in primate evolution, and the above discussion outlines just the mainstream pattern. In general, female primates provide most of the direct care and nurture for the young, while as protectors, male primates contribute to the band's safety and security. Our older primate background would have been a version of this model. But then things changed.

LONG-TERM CONSORTING IN THE SAVANNA SUN

At least by 100,000 years ago, and probably much earlier (Lovejoy 1981), members of our genus began to take a novel evolutionary turn when individual males and females began to bond. These more lasting relationships were unlike the ephemeral unions within a group of chimps. Long-term bonding expanded opportunities in the open savannas. A primate troop living among a complex savanna community of large mammals required more flexibility—an unprecedented level of facultative opportunism. Not only was the savanna environment demanding for a large-bodied primate, but the violent climatic vicissitudes of the Pleistocene (see discussions in Vrba 1995) meant frequent adjustments and readjustments.

Out on the savanna, at least one line of hominids evolved into a special niche, and that niche was especially demanding on cognitive facility, communication, social skills, and much else. This adaptation began to evolve around quality parenting to produce a new standard of offspring. A child had to be raised who was capable of meeting changing cognitive demands. And despite the paucity of archaeological details, we know the outcome—it was hugely successful.

The new adaptations within the genus *Homo* involved a longer period of youthful dependency, a longer potential life span, and the necessity of a higher survival rate for offspring. The most striking shift was an extremely prolonged adolescence/childhood (Bogin 1999). This ex-

tended the time to learn from peers and from parents and slowed entry into full adult responsibility. No other animal is as subject to the same degree of strictures in child rearing as humans. The task required not only much more maternal nurturing but also a father, who in addition to defending the group could focus care on selected young, hopefully his own. To increase the likelihood of paternity, he needed to consort with specific female(s) who would afford him a monopoly on copulatory privileges. It was the premium recompense the female could offer to a male who would join her as a parent—more on this in the next chapter.

A new sort of parenting was required to successfully bring the incredibly dependent human infant through so many years of childhood. The archaeological record shows a reduction in sexual dimorphism, which suggests that male and female roles became less dichotomous, and it is thus likely that some parental duties were shared, or at least divided. But a blurring of roles was not biologically completed; sameness seems not to have been adaptively ideal. The best interest of the offspring called for a bimodal specialization in active parenting roles for men and women.

Modern ethnographic analogs suggest that the economic role of *Homo* males focused on obtaining protein and essential fats, particularly for their most direct kin. Thus, hunting was added to the male role of providing protection from predators, bullies, or enemies. *Homo* males vastly expanded their protein provisioning, or at least the violent part of it, through hunting and killing large mammals and/or competing for their carcasses. In a landscape occupied by large carnivores competing for human food and by large prey which sometimes fought back and by potential human competitors, those men willing to take some risks were often favored: as sons, potential sons-in-law, husbands, and hunting partners—but most of all as fathers. The primate legacy of long gestation and nursing periods was emphasized further by the extraordinarily dependent offspring. Females expanded

The Paleolithic Band   The structure of late Paleolithic bands seems to have changed very little over tens of thousands of years. Late Pleistocene groups were undoubtedly family based—uncles, aunts, and so on—and probably no larger than twenty-five to forty people. We deduce that size from modern analogs, from the size of archaeologically preserved Paleolithic camps, and from theoretical minimum numbers for basic operation and survival. Pleistocene village sites have never been found, just small encampments.

The small bands probably were part of a larger "neighborhood" identity that met together on occasion, and thus members of the constituent bands were likely to have been well acquainted. The size of that more encompassing group was probably no more than 150–200 people (see discussion in Dunbar 1995). Mobility had to be a persistent theme of life. Pleistocene sites show rather transient occupation, and small hunting bands would have been most successful if they moved seasonally and did not remain too long in one camp location. Every bit of information we have suggests that Pleistocene life was occasionally very demanding, and certainly shaped by unpredictable elements. Life could have been sustained only by cultivated skills, keen attention to events, and a perceptive interpretation of them. There could have been little room for repeated mistakes or gross ideological misconceptions.

Be sure to include children in your mental portrait of the Paleolithic experience. Today, children tend to be relegated to special corners of life, excluded from most workplaces and unwelcome or restricted in other settings. But children and juveniles would have been a dominant and ever-present part of late Paleolithic life. Camp would seldom have been without the schoolyard discord of yells and yelps, kids tearing around in rough play, getting into everything, needing minor injuries to be mended and questions to be answered. After all, remember the young made up the majority of the band.

their core specialty of nurture and food gathering to include food preparation, sanitary and health ministrations, transport, garment making, education, and care of dependent young.

While defense of mother and young remained important, it appears that early human males developed a new role in caring for and educating children, particularly their own: they taught their sons to become providers of animal tissue. All parent-offspring relations were changed tremendously by this new upgrading of tutorial education. The bar was raised. But juvenile-juvenile relations may have been changed most of all. Juvenile competition could be less intense because it was less necessary for survival. Imagine how it changed a child's life to have, in ad-

Paleolithic Demography   Paleolithic Art

Why so few babies in Paleolithic art? Stable hunting societies have something close to a ratio of 17:3, women to babies. I am aware of only one possible image of a baby, from Gönnersdorf, Ger., and perhaps a few young children from La Marche, Fr.

Compared to Holocene Bushman art, Paleolithic scenes of women doing their own work, life with children, and women's belongings are rare. **A**, Two Bushman women wood-gathering with child, Cathkin, R.S.A. **B**, Bushman women's decorated collecting bags, Giant's Castle, R.S.A.

There are a few exceptions to the predominant nudity in Paleolithic art. This person with an anorak-like garment is portrayed in Gabillou, Fr. The figure was developed by utilizing naturally suggestive calcite bumps on the cave wall.

Recent Eskimo anorak-style winter parka, from northern Alaska. Most art objects did not preserve in the Paleolithic. Take clothing, for example. There are, however, many preserved Paleolithic needles, and we know that the late Paleolithic climate in Eurasia would have made good, well-fitting clothing essential. Millions upon millions of garments were made during the Paleolithic, yet not a single garment is preserved. Until recently, Eskimo women made many parkas during an average lifetime. During the late Paleolithic of Europe, individuals must have had to have many clothes throughout their lives.

dition to a mother, an experienced and well-armed virile male guardian taking care of one's genes as he would his own. Juvenile play could then expand into the staging ground for developing cooperative, intelligent adults. Remember the small groups of young people who made the Paleolithic handprints and tracks found in the caves? Evolving social and family ties were a critical part of our human emergence.

DUAL PARENTING, SHARING, AND SPECIALIZING

The emergence of a male parenting role is a striking human innovation, and this must also have greatly affected the female's contribution. Although a woman's time would still have been irregularly and unpredictably marked by nursing and care of baby, toddler, or small child

(and often more than one of the above), she was relieved somewhat from age-old worries regarding protein and security. As a result she could further develop new skills which made children more clever and knowledgeable and camp more livable, healthy, warm, and efficient. These would have included locating and gathering more complex food and medicinal sources. We know from historic analogs that the hunting/defense effectiveness of males is critically dependent on effective garments, quality survival gear, and well-preserved, transportable, and nutritious food.

Because they leave so little record, the importance of garments and food preparation is often underplayed in archaeological studies. But one must remember that the very existence of people in the cold winters of the Eurasian Paleolithic was made possible by well-designed, well-constructed, and well-maintained garments. These garments were, of course, intimately tied to food, since they were derived from hunted game, and the warmth and comfort they afforded were critical in obtaining more food, which in turn was the foundation for . . . everything.

Thus, after children were dragged out onto the African savanna and ever since, they have required two kinds of parenting or, perhaps more correctly, parenting across a broad spectrum of needs that was difficult to span by one person, because needs were so bipolar. I emphasize children to elucidate this sexual polarity because it is the core of our evolutionary differences as potential or real parents. Evolution revolves around reproduction, and reproduction around having and then raising quality children to adulthood. Evolutionary biology is built on evidence of that premise. Reproduction is not the shorthand answer. It is the whole book. All else is annotations, footnotes, and appendices. But there are indeed some interesting footnotes, and this chapter is about one of those as it relates to Paleolithic art.

Occasional risk taking is in the couple's interest, but so is being risk averse in the attentiveness of child rearing. Morris (1997) captured the evolutionary essence of our bi-

Fitness and the Single-Parent Stretch

There are two main arms in raising quality kids. Both have deep evolutionary histories. One embraces proximate nurture and attention and includes wanting and needing children, child bonding, maintaining a network of friends for information and aid, and providing direct quality care for children's emotional and physical needs. The other, while bonded to the child, involves the less proximate aspects of protecting and provisioning by securing quality resources, providing healthy and comfortable campsites (or their equivalent), developing enough status to protect the family from the harmful edges of social competition, and generally providing the physical foundations for well-being and safety. No human culture is without this sexual specialization in child-rearing roles (Brown 1991).

Every single parent can testify to the tensions of embodying these two roles on a daily basis. These tensions exist because maintaining either end of the spectrum at premium levels has, since early savanna days, been a full-time occupation. And since both affect the quality (and fitness) of the child as a future reproductive adult, they are high on the evolutionary docket. In hunting societies, children with only one parent have significantly lower chances of living or doing well (Hill and Kaplan 1988). Loss of a parent has less extreme consequences among tribal pastoralists than among hunter-gatherers (Borgerhoff Mulder 1988b). But even among village pastoralists with large extended families, the loss of a father has dire consequences, although much less severe than the loss of a mother.

Even today, with considerable social and financial support, Canadian and American children living with only one parent are statistically more likely to be abused than children in two-parent homes (Daly and Wilson 1983, 1997). In fact, children of single parents are, statistically, less likely to do well across a broad front of categories than children living in two-parent households. Modern circumstances, especially, allow individual men and women to step into any part of the parenting spectrum. What has not changed, however, are children's needs, and raising kids remains a stretch for one parent. Today, technological and cultural changes mean couples can trade off and mix parenting roles and enjoy those reciprocal pleasures, while the bipolar requirements remain. And our most intelligent, liberal, and liberating responses to these aspects of life must surely begin by acknowledging their evolutionary past and continuing presence in our lives.

modal parenting specializations with the statement that this paired role of mother/father is an adaptively efficient way of *safely* rearing one's offspring and of *unsafely* inventing the future at the same time. The reproductive advantage of this complementary combination in humans seems to have been the crucial force for interdependent pair-bonding because it provided the best environment for the lengthy enterprise of raising an open-ended, opportunistic, good-at-fooling-around, free-spirited, able-to-love/bond, smart-cookie human kid.

The patterns of these parental specializations were (and are) not merely produced by immediate circumstances but also shared by natural selection and have thus developed into innate tendencies for differences in temperament, kinds of satisfactions, risk-taking behavior, and perhaps aesthetic taste. I am about to propose that some of these differences are visible in Paleolithic art.

SHELTERED FOOLING AROUND

When we imagine our human ancestors on the African savannas, we should remember that they lived among some of the most dangerous mammals in the world. Yet given their conservative life strategy, in which it took almost two decades to bring each child to full social maturity, they could simply not afford a high mortality. Humans had to be the most ferocious mammal out there. Without speed, tough armor, protective cover, or escape terrain,

Is Nurturance Heritable? Different species vary considerably in how much care they devote to their young, implying genetic differences. Also, individual people vary in their attachment to young and ability to nurture. But does this variation in human nurturance have a significant heritability, some genetic legacy from the Pleistocene, or is it only cultural? In their study of 573 twin pairs, Rushton et al. (1986) found a moderately high genetic component, a heritability of 0.6 (i.e., 60% of the variation between individuals can be explained by genetic inheritance). Not only is this important in understanding human evolution, but it is also interesting to wonder if genetic changes may have occurred along with the shift from Paleolithic patterns to Holocene tribal patterns.

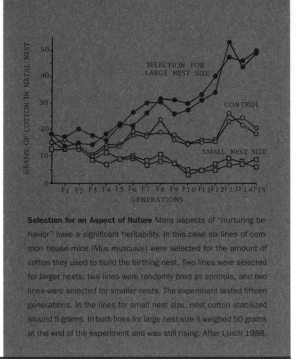

Selection for an Aspect of Nuture Many aspects of "nurturing behavior" have a significant heritability. In this case six lines of common house mice (*Mus musculus*) were selected for the amount of cotton they used to build the birthing nest. Two lines were selected for larger nests, two lines were randomly bred as controls, and two lines were selected for smaller nests. The experiment lasted fifteen generations. In the lines for small nest size, nest cotton stabilized around 5 grams. In both lines for large nest size it weighed 50 grams at the end of the experiment and was still rising. After Lynch 1988.

they had to be armed sufficiently to guarantee mortal wounds, if not immediate death, to any desperately hungry lion or other predator. Pikes and spears were longer and faster than any sabertooth's canines or oryx's horns, and there were many of them. As a group, people had to be formidable. Those pikes and spears were men's weapons, and providing for and protecting the young constituted their job description.

I won't dwell on the familiar and wide-ranging contributions of mothers to offspring development. These are generally both direct and pervasive. Instead, I would like to discuss a particular male contribution to parenting that is not so obvious and yet its role was especially significant in the Pleistocene. Babies and children need a specially modified environment buffered from the full force of competition, want, and harm. That environment was secured by adult males engaging in risky, sometimes violent behavior. Strong male bodies, weapons of violence, and risk-accepting behavior were a requisite to face the challenging and often hostile forces that loomed over the human horizon and roared in the night. Children of the most ferocious species on the landscape needed a start in life as carefree as a Pleistocene existence could allow.

Development of children, male and female alike, with excellent cognitive skills and a creative outlook required more than sunshine and a good diet. It required long years of experiences that are best nourished with interesting leisure activities, relatively free from immediate worry and fear. Human development required much fooling around, pretending, playing, and making mistakes in a context where they did not have serious consequences. And it required exploring, both metaphorically and actually. Of course, a few of those Paleolithic explorations into caves figure importantly in our story.

In later chapters I will propose that diverse forms of play are not an epiphenomenon of behavior but clearly involve part of our specifically human development in a very specialized ecological niche that required considerable opportunistic flexibility. We see this in comparative evidence of play in other species — only cognitively facultative animals play; the more opportunistic they are, the more play figures into their development. Dedicated play behavior is like an installation program for undedicated facultative software; in fact, there are specific kinds of play for different brands of flexible behavior. I will propose that art is one of those kinds of human play, the software in-

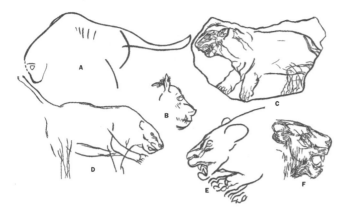

Not so long ago, where the Paris suburbs now lie and around what is now Fairbanks, Alaska, one could hear the roar of distant lions on a quiet snowy winter night. **A**, Rouffignac. **B**, Roc-la-Tour. **C–F**, La Marche. All in Fr.

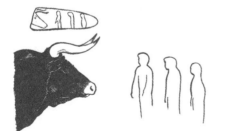

Top, man being attacked by a large bovine-like creature, from Roc de Sers, Fr. Probably this is a musk ox, but it may be a bison. The scene rendered here isn't first-rate, but the essence comes through. On unusual occasions, musk oxen can be dangerous to humans, and they are well armed with upward-sweeping, sharp horns. *Bottom,* my rendition of scene.

There is no question that life in the Pleistocene among large dangerous mammals carried some risk. This elementary scene of an aurochs head and three people on a bone sliver, from Bruniquel, Fr., was made by someone with elementary drawing skills. *Below,* my interpretation.

stallation for its own special brand of human behavior. And those installations take hold best during a protracted and protected childhood with room for lots of cognitive and physical exploration.

THE SPECIAL TOOLS OF MEN'S PARENTING

This chapter is about the biological forces that underlie males' developing and fulfilling their sex-specific role as parents because we need that information to study Paleolithic images. Men who occupied the fathering role in the late Pleistocene required special tools for defense and protein provisioning. We don't know a lot about the complete range of Paleolithic tools because taphonomic processes have surely edited our collections, but some tools did preserve in the archaeological record and other tools are pictured in Paleolithic art. In a moment we'll discuss the editing performed by taphonomic processes and my premise that many complex Paleolithic tools that happened to preserve are weapons of virility and violence: hunting tools, like spears with hard, sharp points and atlatls with which to throw spears, or tools to construct and maintain such weapons. Paleolithic men engraved hundreds of different representational images on their hunting tools, and these images give us insight into a part of their lives and

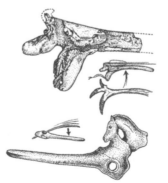

Spear-throwers and shaft- or point-straighteners—men's tools of large-mammal hunting—are scattered among Paleolithic art sites. Generally, they are decorated with images of large mammals. Both from Mas d'Azil, Fr. Images with small pointer arrows show how these were probably used.

Pleistocene images of two people from Addaura, It. How divergent were the sex-specific job descriptions in the Paleolithic?

Surely there is little argument over what this scene is about. Some large mammals are quite dangerous when wounded; apparently Pleistocene bison fell into this category. Above, from Lascaux, Fr., is a gut-shot bison, with intestines bulging out the spear hole (not an uncommon experience for hunters to witness, as abdominal contents are under pressure). The hunter is chased down, spear-thrower lying on the ground. Today and in the Pleistocene, corvids (ravens and jays in particular) learn to follow hunters around, as it is an easy way to get scrap tissue from butchered carcasses. This is not the kind of scene young women normally draw—why is that? My rendition below.

interests. Preserved tools will feature importantly in our discussions about their art.

On Fletchers and Knappers:
Sexual Specializations

In their classic study of 185 different ethnographic histories, Murdock and Provost (1973) found that most chores (they mapped fifty different technical activities) vary from culture to culture as to whether they are exclusively male, mostly male, shared between the sexes, mostly female, or exclusively female. Murdock and Provost, however, did find a special range of activities that were performed only by men in all ethnographically studied cultures. These strictly male activities included

hunting large land fauna,
working in stone,
working in bone,
trapping,
hunting large aquatic fauna.

These activities can be described as being generally risky, physically forceful, and sometimes violent. Killing large mammals is associated with certain tools, such as harpoons, spears, spear-throwers, bows, knives, and projectile points, and with making weapons with which to do the killing part of hunting. Murdock and Provost record that users and makers of these tools are the same sex: "Our

data indicate a general tendency for the sex that uses a product to be the same as the sex that produces it" (1973, 220). This study showed minimal overall pattern differentiation from region to region and within regions, and in no cases were the above tasks assigned to females. Butchering of large animals, while not universally restricted to males, was overwhelmingly a male activity (as was the knapping of butchering knives). Cooking and preparation of vegetable food, on the other hand, were overwhelmingly female tasks. Among hunting bands, tanning fur and sewing tents, blankets, and clothing were almost exclusively women's activities. Daly and Wilson (1983) and Brown (1991), using expanded ethnographic samples, found much the same pattern.

In a factor analysis of the data, Murdock and Provost (1973) found that male "strength advantage" and ability

If the thought of being attacked by a large bison was a key testosterone theme, an encounter with a large carnivore must have been the very ultimate testosterone event. An attack by a cave bear or lion was probably the preeminently exciting experience—something that would have been told over and over, discussed in vivid detail, dreamt about, and sometimes made into art. Bear attack, Péchialet, Fr. My rendition below.

to produce brief bursts of excessive energy accounted for the highest percentage of the variance. However, among nine activities normally done by women, a definite "feminine advantage" was delineated. On that subject they quote Brown (1970, 1074):

The degree to which women participate in subsistence activities depends upon the compatibility of the latter with simultaneous child-care responsibilities. Women are most likely to make a substantial contribution when subsistence activities have the following characteristics: the participant is not obliged to be far from home; the tasks are relatively monotonous and do not require rapt concentration; and the work is not dangerous, can be performed in spite of interruptions, and is easily resumed once interrupted.

To this Murdock and Provost also added to women's specialties "the kinds of tasks requiring almost daily atten-

tion" (1973, 211). (For a discussion, see more recent work by Watson and Kennedy 1991; Conkey 1991; Gero 1991.)

Often chores are dichotomous between males and females. In a cross-cultural study Costin concludes, "In ethnographic comparisons there is a remarkably consistent ideal of keeping men's and women's labor distinct" (1996, 123). Ethnographic exceptions to this dichotomous pattern in the traditional activities of men and women are quite interesting. For example, Gero's (1991) exception to men's always working the lithics was among Andaman Islanders. Andaman women smashed imported bottle glass and used the sharp shards to shave and tattoo. General principles are often highlighted by such telling exceptions.

In prehistoric Bushman art and in Australian Aboriginal art, women and only women are shown with digging sticks. In the rock art of these same traditions men are portrayed hunting large mammals and fighting. Dichotomous patterns in women's and men's activities observed in art images are also reported in ethnographic studies as characteristic of actual practice. I will present evidence in the next two chapters that a parallel pattern can be found in Paleolithic art and artifacts and that this most probably reflects a similar dichotomy in Eurasian Paleolithic hunting cultures.

I do not want to underemphasize the cultural diversity humans construct from our innate predispositions. These have been thoroughly publicized and are a central feature of social anthropology. What has been missing from contemporary intellectual tradition until very recently is a broad airing of the continuity within this diversity, the human universals. A grasp of natural history and its role in these matters, which underlie those universals, allows unique access to Paleolithic life and art. Thus, I think it is worthwhile to review the biological history and regulation of our morphs of maleness and femaleness. Let's first give our discussion a bit of context.

POLITICS, SEX, AND PALEOLITHIC ART SINCE THE 1960S: THE CONFLATION OF EQUALITY AND SAMENESS

Nowhere do I suggest that I have found any material which disproves the existence of sex differences. . . . This study [*Male and Female*] was not concerned with whether there are or are not actual and universal differences between the sexes, either quantitative or qualitative.

Margaret Mead's comments regarding her book *Male and Female*
(in S. Goldberg, "The Erosion of the Social Sciences")

We live in the wake of major social changes which began in the late 1960s in America and which ultimately included much of the Western world. These changes originated in the determination of a newly maturing generation to challenge widespread attitudes of racial, ethnic, and sexual categorization and bias. With time, this movement included challenges to then-current sexual mores, organized religion, technoscientific approaches, medical and business authority, and more.

It can be difficult to remember or imagine the atmosphere prior to those times because the subsequent changes have so thoroughly modified our sensibilities. As it happened, however, the wholly warranted need for change often became conflated with particular solutions.

Some of these solutions were quite simplistic and allowed room for little more than slogan-based discussion. For example, popular hard-left views sought a reconstitution of society in terms of social, economic, and political equality, but the conception of equality was often merely sameness or symmetry. In that era, cultural determinism had an obvious appeal. Studying biological differences was on the outs, because, if there were differences, there shouldn't be.

I had colleagues in the biological and arctic health institutes at the University of Alaska, where I worked in the late 1960s, who were studying racial and sexual differences in cold tolerance and such metabolic and dietary differences as sugar and alcohol metabolism among northern peoples. Frostbite susceptibility of soldiers of different racial backgrounds was of particular practical interest. However, the politics of the time quietly shut these and related projects down.

We now appreciate the need for research into biological patterns of differences between groups. Today, physiological studies would be considered misleading or, at least, inadequate if they examined disease resistance, physiological function, growth timing, aging processes, and much else in only one sex from one population, for example, white European males. Nevertheless, we still drag our feet when it comes to examining human behavioral differences that may not be accounted for by experience alone.

There indeed is reason for caution, because purported differences in race and sex have been misused, but counter-distortions are not the way out of this corner. In terms of male-female differences, the evidence is clear that we have evolved, and our evolution has not been sexually undifferentiated.

Human male-female differences are often subtle and stochastic and are apparent mostly in matters of taste and proclivity. Paradoxically, these sexual divergences relate to parenting. I have proposed that there is a fundamental biological reason for that. The first step in parenting is to have children. There are deep biological forces designed by natural selection to facilitate this first step. One involves the adaptive male-female differences in erotic attraction and mate preference; that is, we have different ways of assaying mate value. The second step is to raise highly adaptable and capable children, and that involves all the things we have been discussing: our heritage from Pleistocene roles involving violence and nurture.

SEXUAL ROLES IN PALEOLITHIC ART

As humans moved north into Eurasia from southern latitudes, they became more involved with hunting (Klein 1999), women as well as men. We know from ethnographic studies of subsistence groups in warm climates that women gather substantial quantities of food from wild plants. In fact, many prehistoric art sites from Africa and Australia show women with tools (digging sticks) for gathering plant foods. Paleolithic art lacks such images. We know that the late Pleistocene climate marginalized the gathering of plant foods in Eurasia. Ethnographic parallels suggest women's specializations would have shifted to address the challenges of living in the north, which were substantial, given our organismal tropical adaptations. These specializations include clothing technologies, food processing, cooking, fiber and sinew making, leather and fur tanning, tarp and tent making, and so forth. Such roles are normally taken by women in the north (Murdock and Provost 1973; Daly and Wilson 1983; Brown 1991). Yet images of women engaged in such activities, with the possibility of a rare exception, do not occur in Paleolithic art. As we have seen before, our collection of this art simply fails to depict huge sectors of life that we know must have existed.

Conversely, Paleolithic art sometimes shows males with hunting weapons such as spears or spear-throwers. Men are shown in hunting scenes and being attacked by wounded game or dangerous carnivores. I do not think this is evidence that Paleolithic women were never attacked by bears or that women never took up hunting

There are many household and children scenes in later Holocene Bushman art. This is a hut with weighted digging sticks, women's tools, stuck handily in the ground outside the opening. A pattern of these kinds of themes would suggest that they were done by people for whom these subjects were among their most important interests and experiences. There are no such scenes in Paleolithic art. *Left,* Mhlswazine, R.S.A. *Right,* Ndhloveni Mountain, R.S.A.

tools in special situations. What we probably have here is (1) a notable taphonomic bias, due to media and location, in the preservation of artworks, combined with (2) a dramatic difference in sex roles and hence the kinds of images made by each sex. Men's art often depicted the species of large mammals requiring high-risk hunting. This view is completely consistent with hundreds of cross-cultural studies in which the manufacture of certain classes of tools, particularly hunting weapons, is done by males. For functional reasons these tools are made of materials that are generally highly preservable (stone, bone, ivory, and antler).

As we have already seen among primates, the primary caregivers of young are more risk averse and longer lived (Allman 1999). Large-mammal hunting often involves serious risk and great strength and would have occasionally necessitated long-distance travel across rough terrain with long absences from camp. The needs of babies and young children are not compatible with this kind of activity. Ethnographic data support an almost universal pattern of women as the primary caregivers of young children.

I am aware of only three ethnographic cases in which women were traditionally engaged in the killing of wild large-mammal species. On Melville Island off northern Australia, women traditionally hunted kangaroos, while men hunted dangerous sea mammals and fished (Goodale 1971). Among the Agta, a Negrito group in a small region in northeastern Luzon, women regularly killed young

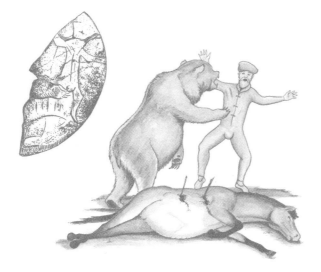

This broken bone disk from Mas d'Azil, Fr., shows a bear paw reaching toward a person with arms outstretched standing over a horse carcass. For large-mammal hunters there is always a tension over competition for carcasses. When I leave a large-mammal carcass in the Alaskan wild to go back for packing assistance, the chance of a bear being on the carcass when I return is significant. The new owner does not easily relinquish this prize. It is a true testosterone event.

There were probably times when lions were speared, again a very dangerous episode. Perhaps the confrontation was about who owned a carcass. Pergouset, Fr.

Killing large mammals is not without risk and thrills. Paleolithic art contains a number of these kinds of episodes. More often than not, one draws what is on one's mind. For some people in the Paleolithic this kind of subject seems to have been an obsession. Two speared horses: *left,* Mas d'Azil, Fr.; *right,* Montastruc, Fr.

wild piglets, using bows and dogs (Estioko-Griffin and Bion-Griffin 1981). And in some Andean societies, women hunted young guanacos (a kind of wild llama) with dogs and sticks, while men hunted adult guanacos. These exceptions serve to highlight specializations of men's and women's skills and activities among traditional hunters of large mammals. We find no society where women specialized in the most physically risky part of large-mammal killing while men tended to the myriad demands of children and camp life. Paleolithic images certainly address the testosterone side of this picture.

On How and "Y"

Let's turn briefly to the biology of maleness. The basic human ground plan for every individual is female. Special modifications are required to alter that. Among Mesozoic reptiles, temperature mainly determined maleness or femaleness of the developing embryo (the heat of a crocodile nest still determines sex). But with the coming of mammalian temperature regulation, this, of course, didn't work. Instead, in birds and mammals, independently, one of the chromosomes acquired this task.

In humans, that Mesozoic legacy means that an XY pairing produces maleness. The Y chromosome indirectly induces the development of the endocrine portion of the testes, which then produces androgenic hormones, including the large amounts of testosterone (T) or T-like steroids that circulate in blood and link to receptors of the developing cells to inform them that they are to do something different, to make maleness. Though it will be a decade and a half before they will produce live sperm, the testes begin their other function of hormonal production very early in development, between 8 and 24 weeks (Kemper 1990). In fact, this is the first of three peaks in T production. The second occurs from right after birth until about 5 months of age. The third, of course, is around puberty. Kimura (1999) provides a good summary of T production and its effects.

Lamp shadows of natural contours in Le Portel Cave, Fr., apparently reminded some Paleolithic person of upright erections.

There are two dimensions to T's effects on anatomy. One is *developmental and long term.* The levels of T in the growing fetus and child affect the brain's microstructure, the formation of endocrine glands, and other physiological developments. Overall male virility is a product of a sustained titer of T in the fetus, child, and adolescent. The second dimension of T is more *activational* and has *medium- and short-term* repercussions. Injecting T in an adult can change emotional state for a while. On the other hand, because of accumulated long-term developmental processes, cessation of T production in an adult man does not totally reverse virility. For example, genital anatomy or brain structure is little affected by changes in T production in adults.

There seem to be two parallel processes involved in converting the basic female developmental plan into a male one. In addition to the more obvious process of *masculinization,* there is *defeminization* (Kimura 1999). The first relates to the "add-ons," like beards and thick shoulders; the second involves inhibition of female traits, like breasts, a wide pelvis, and female fat depots.

DEVELOPMENTAL TESTOSTERONE

The presence of the hormone testosterone in living tissue is not sufficient to produce any change. Cells have receptors to enable them to respond to T, and genetic information to produce T receptors is encoded on the X chromosome. Females and males have basically similar T receptors. These receptors are not spread evenly throughout body tissue, but as one might expect, parts of the body that are more exaggerated in males have more T receptors: for example, neck and hand muscles, larynx tissue, hair follicles of torso, lower arms, and legs. Less obvious are the T receptors in parts of the brain. Synaptic connections, functional specificity of brain regions, degree of lateralization, and number of interconnections between hemispheres are influenced by T, as are the hypothalamus, hippocampus, and parts of the cerebral cortex—the very parts that become dimorphic in adult males and females (Allen and Gorski 1986; Kimura 1999). See Moir and Jessel 1991 for a very readable review of the effects of hormones on brain development.

Since women and men have very similar T receptors, we must look at actual levels of T concentrations to see how sexual differences are produced and maintained. To simplify a complex issue, I am using "T" here as shorthand not only for testosterone but for a complex of related androgenic compounds including dihydrotestosterone, dehydro-epiandrosterone sulfate, androstenedione, and other similar anabolic steroids. But the main androgenic steroid is testosterone.

Levels of T vary considerably from person to person both in the uterus and in postnatal development. Individual characters (hirsuteness, deepness of the voice, etc.) can be arrayed along a gradient among males from highly masculine to more effeminate; the same is true for females. Studies have shown that the heritability of variations along the gradient of masculinity-femininity within each sex is 0.85; that is, well over half of the variation along this masculinity-femininity axis can be explained by genetic components. But at the proximate level, the most obvious sexual characteristics are created by different levels of T during fetal and childhood development. As I said, our basic genetic blueprint is female (Moir and Jessel 1991; Becker, Breedlove, and Crews 1992), and the presence or absence of the Y chromosome mediates that basic plan. Most of the time, a baby is distinctly male or female. But this norm is not always the case, and the range of anatomical and behavioral variation reveals the delicacy of developmental processes (Moir and Jessel 1991).

For example, in clinical pseudohermaphrodism, high T in the uterine environment has a significant masculinizing effect on the child. Girls born to these mothers expend significantly higher energy during play, prefer boys for playmates, initiate more fighting, have fewer fantasies about motherhood, show much less interest in dolls, have a high aversion to infant care, prefer strictly functional to femininely styled clothing, and show no interest in jewelry, makeup, or hairstyling (Ehrhardt and Baker 1974; Reinisch, Ziemba-Davis, and Sanders 1991). Pregnant mothers given large amounts of the synthetic female hormone diethylstilbestrol produce very effeminate boys because the hormone blocks the T processes. Likewise, boys born with a congenital T deficiency consistently scored well within the female range on tests for sex-specific differences (Hier and Crowley 1982). There are hundreds of publications on the hormonal effects on sex differences in brain function and behavior (for reviews, see Moir and Jessel 1991; Kimura 1999). These discuss not only pathological extremes but also the normal range of variants.

Females also produce T, so the degree of biological male-female differences is a matter of T levels during and after childhood. An XX or X0 girl who is exposed to inordinately high T levels in the uterus appears and acts as a man, except she does not produce viable sperm. Similarly, a developing male fetus develops into a female if unmodified by large amounts of T. Girls who are X0 (Turner's syndrome) have underdeveloped or no ovaries and so have reduced T levels; these girls are characteristically superfeminine in behavior. Uterine T concentration (from a variety of different sources) is the main trigger determining the degree of masculinity or femininity among us all.

The usual range of T titers among adult women is between 20 and 80 nanograms per deciliter of blood (ng/dl); whereas among reproductively mature males it is between 385 and 1000 ng/dl. (Baldwin 1993). But T is still an important hormone affecting female development. Not only do women have T receptors in their cells, but female tissues are extremely sensitive to T (that is why female athletes can achieve dramatic effects by taking much smaller doses of anabolic steroids for muscle building than men).

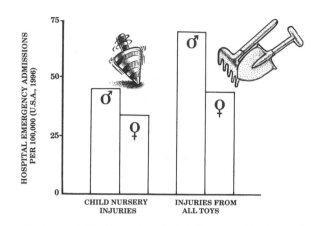

Attitudes toward risk taking are formed early in life, prompted developmentally by testosterone. Injury rates are sex specific well prior to adolescence. U.S. Consumer Product Safety Commission, National Injury Information Clearinghouse, 1996.

Female variations in temperament, personality, and body structure are due in part to variations in T production in ovaries and adrenals.

It is the different amount of T production in boys that is responsible for their developing male features (in prepubertal boys this amounts to 120–600 ng/dl). Adrenals, in both boys and girls, produce significant amounts of T before puberty. However, in the early teens the gonads take over most sexual hormone production. This is a major endocrine event, and ovaries begin to produce quantities of estriol, estrone, estradiol, and T, while testes mainly produce T. The details of organ sources and diversity of sex hormones are another complex story which must lie outside our review.

Boys play at being violent, courtesy of T. And it is a curious feature that the first adolescent stirrings of courtship behavior in males are often expressed in physical aggression: braid pulling, softly punching or hitting girls, and verbal accusations against girls, who may or may not recognize this attention as affection (Michael 1983). Many games that boys play tend to have a physically aggressive rough-and-tumble edge to them (Blurton-Jones

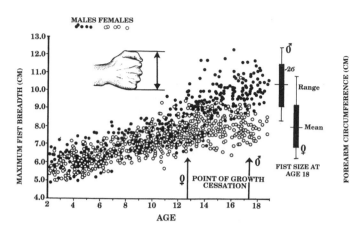

Fist breadth among adult humans is sexually dimorphic. The black bands at right are 2σ; that is, each spans 95% of the variation for that group. At about age thirteen the hand bones of females cease growing, whereas males of that age experience a growth spurt, induced by testosterone from enlarging testicles. Why this difference? Hands are the main human "tools," and our Pleistocene behavior included a specialization of sexual roles and functions. For males that involved violence, high-risk hunting, fistfights with other males (there is a strong cross-cultural taboo against using fists in male-female confrontations and in female-female fights), and the use of heavy weapons against hunted large mammals. Data from Snyder et al. 1977, a large U.S. sample.

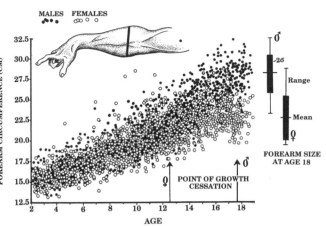

The complex muscles in the forearm control power grip, wrist strength, and fist ruggedness. As with hand size there is a significant sexual dimorphism in these muscles, mediated by testosterone. There is virtually no overlap at 2σ (the black bars span 95% of the variation) among adults (over eighteen years of age). If the hand is the main tool, it is these muscles that will determine how that tool can best be used. Data from Snyder et al. 1977, a large U.S. sample.

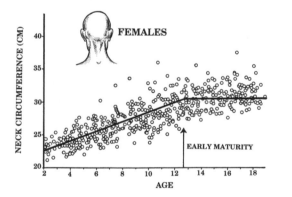

Neck muscles are also extremely sexually dimorphic. The size of the mastoid process, the insertion point of the sternomastoid muscle, is one of the most reliable forensic means to identify the sex of human skulls when no other data are available. Even among women who daily carry 50-kilogram loads on their heads, the neck muscles are smaller than those of men who do no work with their heads. Females, cross-culturally, do not normally have to suffer social violence to the head. It can be noted here that female cervical vertebrae and neck muscles reach their growth plateau at around thirteen years of age. Data from Snyder et al. 1977, a large U.S. sample.

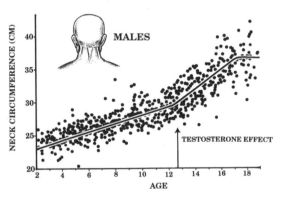

Unlike the growth curve for women's neck circumference, male necks do not stop growing at age thirteen, but instead the curve experiences a marked upward deflection as a product of greater postpuberty testosterone production. Muscle tissue in necks is especially sensitive to androgenic steroids. It has been proposed that these rugged neck muscles among males were selected for to add protection against cervical and skull damage during violent fighting activity. Necks are used here as a metaphor for many bodily features; remember, testosterone affects not only specified muscle tissue but also specified neural tissue. Data from Snyder et al. 1977, a large U.S. sample.

1967; Humphreys and Smith 1984). Such play develops skills that require physical strength and even violence.

Levels of T influence toy choice among children (Berenbaum and Hines 1989). The role of T in children's play preferences is highlighted in the play preferences of young girls with a genetic condition in which high levels of T are produced. These girls consistently prefer to play with boys' toys. Girls with congenital adrenal hyperplasia (producing large quantities of androgenic hormones) assume more body positions and movements characteristic of boys (Dittman 1992).

Sex hormones not only produce the divergence at puberty of secondary sexual features but also produce differences in weight gain and distribution; females tend to accumulate fat on their arms and legs while boys tend to increase their muscle mass. Boys also tend to have higher systolic blood pressure and a higher basal metabolism, more body hair, thicker vocal cords (affecting voice pitch), general bone ruggedness, coarser skin, more violent tendencies in agonistic behavior, and more sexual assertiveness (Overfield 1985). Testosterone makes the neck bulge and broadens the shoulder muscles. It still produces the old primate dimorphism in human canine size and shape (Scott 1991). Although the brain does not undergo a great growth spurt at adolescence, it does undergo considerable maturation and reorganization in mental processes at that time. One of these involves visual perception. Adolescents and preadolescents are less predisposed to draw abstract forms than adults; youths are more oriented toward concrete-empirical objects (Michael 1983).

Many social scientists have attributed features of adolescent behavior to upbringing only (Gagnon and Simon 1973; DeLamater 1981; Reed and Weinberg 1984; Tiefer 1987). Beach (1957) asserted that adolescent boys' preoccupation with sex and violence is due solely to cultural exposure, not hormones. But this is contradicted by research in humans and other mammals. In fact, in their multivariate analyses, Urdy and Billy (1987) found that the main explanatory statistical variable of human male adolescent behavior was hormonal state. The same was true for females (Urdy, Talbert, and Morris 1986). The role of surges of T in adolescent behavior is no longer a controversial issue among human endocrinologists.

It seems reasonable to suppose that in the Pleistocene context the direction of these T-mediated developmental patterns was adaptive. Men's and women's roles in the Pleistocene were quite distinct. Adolescence was a time when the differences between growing men and women were greatly amplified, as young people took major steps toward their respective adult roles.

ACTIVATIONAL TESTOSTERONE

In addition to its long-term masculinizing developmental effects, testosterone plays a central role in maintaining virility in adult males. Adult males are literally shaped by high T concentrations. Testosterone hardens bone and, combined with strenuous muscle use, produces large muscle mass and strength. Testosterone maintains body contours, models fat depots in shoulders and torso, directs coarse-hair distribution patterns, and so forth. It also affects male behavior.

We have experimental data on how male mammals behave in the absence of T; after castration, aggression in humans and other animals is reduced (Wingfield, Whaling, and Marler 1994). Higley et al. (1996) found a strong correlation between cerebrospinal fluid T/5-HIAA and aggression in domestic animals. The presence of high concentrations of T in the human bloodstream unquestionably affects what one thinks about, and what one thinks about affects what one is likely to draw. That is where the train of this discussion is heading.

There is a physiological side to every emotion. One *changes physiologically* in response to different events. Social behavior can change biology, and physiology can change social behavior. There is ample evidence that when social power is lost, the corticosteroid hormone cortisol is elevated and T decreased, whereas in situations of

We cannot say how surly or dangerous Pleistocene woolly rhinos were, but at least we can say that they were sprinkled among the art. **A**, La Colombière, Fr. **B** and **J**, Rouffignac, Fr. **C** and **K**, Font de Gaume, Fr. **D**, Three rhinos from a panel in Rouffignac, Fr. **E**, Saut-du-Perron, Fr. **F**, Trois Frères, Fr. **G** and **N**, Chauvet, Fr. **H** and **O**, Les Combarelles, Fr. **I** and **L**, Lascaux, Fr. **M**, La Mouthe, Fr. **P**, Les Ré-bieres, Fr. **Q**, Dolni Věstonice, Czech.

success or victory, the reverse occurs. Cortisol fights stress, while T activates or enhances both sexual confidence and status assurance (Wingfield, Whaling, and Marler 1994).

Research on this process is not simple because (as with blood sugar or blood pressure) it is difficult to determine a standard set point of T for an individual. The half-life of T in the bloodstream is short and secretion uneven. Among men, the degree and timing of T surges seem to vary with many factors, including age, social situation, time of day

(highest in morning), time of year (highest in spring), degree and kind of stress, and health. Testosterone surges have been shown to be particularly common during or at the end of events in which one has a striking success or otherwise increases one's status. But before we assume that this T surge simply accentuates confidence and sense of stature, we should note that research on winning and losing in random-chance gambling by McCaul, Gladue, and Joppa (1992) concluded that the euphoric mood itself produced a rise in T.

Bernstein, Gordon, and Rose (1974) have studied the reverse process and have shown that defeat results in major T reduction. They found that among experimental animals when losers were injected with T they did not rise in stature but they did fight more and had a higher frequency of wounds. Thus, Symons (1978) concluded that reduced T after defeat is probably an adaptation to avoid further fighting when success is improbable. It is telling that, in virtually all circumstances, male T production is more elevated when females are present (Bernstein, Gordon, and Rose 1974). This has been shown to be true among humans and is also characteristic of other primates.

Libido in both human males and females relates somewhat to T levels. At lower endogenous levels, supplementary T can be successful in treating sexual dysfunction in both women and men. Supplementing T in men affects libido and ejaculatory competence but not erectile initiation (for reviews, see Kemper 1990; Bagatell and Bremner 1996). Diminution of T due to hypogonadism is associated with decreased libido and sexual activity (Kemper 1990).

The effects of T levels in adults are not limited to libido. One striking effect of T is that moderately high levels enhance concentration, sometimes to the point of obsession. One can see how this link could have evolved. For example, the T levels of adult stags are quite elevated during rut. A bull moose of breeding stature, for example, becomes dulled to the possibility of predation, fails to eat regularly, and spends considerable energy in pursuit of a single theme. Yet this obsessive rut behavior can be adap-

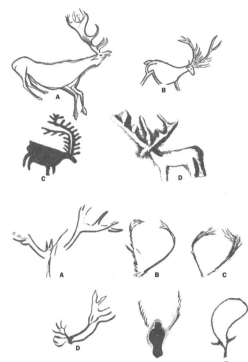

Most men today are more proud of killing a large buck than a doe. The complex reasons for this go way beyond the fact that bucks produce twice as much meat. It may have to do with bucks being less numerous and harder and more challenging to kill. In the Paleolithic one could add that, in addition to more meat, an autumn buck carried proportionally much more highly sought-after fat than a hind. All this adds stature to the hunter who kills a stag. Perhaps this is why hunters delight in the aesthetics of large complex antlers. A grand rack is emblematic of these emotions. Large antlers are a common sight in Paleolithic art: **A–B**, Lascaux, Fr. In later historic art: **c**, Utah rock art, U.S.A. **D**, Csépaje, Hungary.

Isolated antlers were occasionally rendered as an aesthetic subject in the Paleolithic: **A**, Bois du Cantet, Fr. **B–C**, Chuffin, Fr. **D**, Mas d'Azil, Fr. **E**, Niaux, Fr. (antlers added around a hole to highlight this silhouette cross section of a stag). **F**, Cougnac, Fr. (shed antler of shelk).

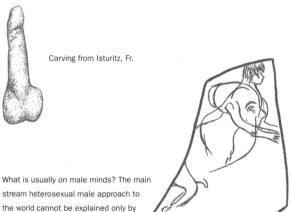

Carving from Isturitz, Fr.

What is usually on male minds? The main stream heterosexual male approach to the world cannot be explained only by culture but has its inherent predispositions, just like lions—but not so extreme. Most males, especially young males, have some aspect of sex and competition on their minds much of the time, in different versions. Though the overlap of these two images at La Marche, Fr., is probably more fortuitous than intentional, it makes a good metaphor for one male preoccupation.

tive, especially given the short estrous periods of northern large mammals. Increased concentration for tasks is positively related to T levels among human males, as is persistence of effort. Increased persistence and attention and focus are highly correlated with serum T levels in males (Andrew 1978). A number of studies have tied physical energy (as monitored by such things as red blood cell production) to T levels (e.g., Strand 1983).

Among mammalian species in which males contribute directly to the care of young, there is a reduction in T production at the specific time when young are most dependent. The readiness for violent engagement associated with elevated T is apparently at odds with patient and attentive care of young. The main rise of T secretion in humans occurs at seventeen to nineteen years of age (Strand 1983). This was apparently prior to fatherhood in the Pleistocene. I suspect that at age seventeen Pleistocene young men were proving themselves for their later roles as husbands and parents by high-risk behavior as defenders of the family and band and as hunters of large mammals, as we see today among Bushman (Silberbauer 1980).

Testosterone and Physical Aggression

Most general categories of behavior have both environmental and genetic components. Even though we may not understand it in detail, we are very familiar with the idea that the environment can affect behavior, both from a century of research and from common experience. But the genetic component and its interaction with development are less well understood. The genetic component of behavior is very visible in domestic strains or breeds. Fighting cocks do not behave the same as Buff Orphingtons, nor do Spanish fighting bulls bear much resemblance to Herefords, nor pit bull terriers to beagles. Further, in many species, males and females exhibit different behaviors. A rooster, for example, makes a different sort of pet than a hen, a mature boar hog behaves in different ways than a sow, and keeping a billy goat poses different problems than keeping a nanny.

Symons (1978) contended that although females of many simian primate species may exhibit more aggressive episodes than males, male aggression tends to be more violent and deadly. Symons also worked with sexual asymmetries in play fighting among young rhesus monkeys and found their behavior consistent with that of other Old World simians: males play fought, play chased, and initiated play fights 2.5 to 3.5 times more frequently than females. Male play fighting was much rougher, faster, and more vigorous than female play fighting. Males fled from play fighting less and refused play fighting less. Male play fighting ended in real fights more frequently than female play fighting did.

Is there a genetic component to aggressive behavior? In fact, several mammalian species have been changed in that direction by artificial selection. Researchers at the Institute of Genetics in Novosibirisk have produced over thirty generations of fur-farm foxes that were selected for either aggressiveness (one strain) or gentleness (the other strain). I had the chance to see these and approached the individual pens of the aggressive ones, which either cowered or attacked, while individuals of the gentle strain wagged their tails and greeted visitors like contented puppies. Researchers have found that in the gentle, doglike, tame fox strain the amount of the neurotransmitter serotonin had been greatly increased (Popova et al. 1991).

But could primates respond to such selection for personality differences? Stephan Suomi, of the National Institute for Child Health and Human Development, and J. D. Higley, of the National Institute on Alcohol Abuse and Alcoholism, have successfully produced three genetic

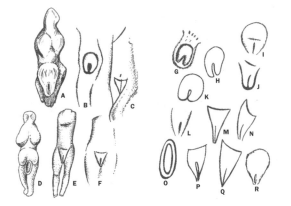

The idea that there are disembodied images of vulvae in Paleolithic art has been criticized by a number of authors. For example, Bahn and Vertut (1988, 163–164) propose that groups of these images appear more like horse hoofprints or bird footprints. The problem with this latter idea is that when these images are found in isolation (as shown on the right), they are identical in every way to how they are drawn, carved, or engraved on images of women at the point in the front where both legs meet (as per the images on the left). **A**, Grimaldi, It. **B** and **G**, Tito Bustillo, Sp. **C**, La Madeleine, Fr. **D**, Montpazier, Fr. **E**, Laugerie-Basse, Fr. **F**, Angles-sur-l'Anglin, Fr. **H**, Abri Poisson, Fr. **I**, Tuc d'Audoubert, Fr. **J**, Le Portel, Fr. **K**, Laussel, Fr. **L**, Commarque, Fr. **M**, Rochereil, Fr. **N**, Micolón, Sp. **O**, Saint Marcel, Fr. **P**, Pergouset, Fr. **Q**, Ölknitz, Ger. **R**, Abri Blanchard, Fr.

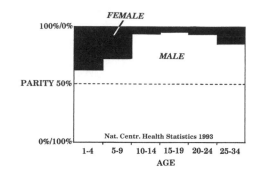

Deaths Due to Firearms among American Youth Young males are much more prone to be victims of violence than are females, for example, violence and accidents involving firearms. These differences are greatest around the ages of fifteen to nineteen, when testosterone is at its peak.

strains of rhesus monkeys that are individually inhibited, uninhibited, or aggressive (Gallagher 1994). We have not conducted such an experiment using humans, of course, but it is possible to assess heritable variation in aggression.

There are several human studies on comparisons of monozygotic and dizygotic twins with regard to T titer. Meikle et al. (1987) found a heritability averaging around 50% (0.50) for blood T plasma content. Loehlin and Nichols (1976) and Matthews et al. (1981), using large numbers of twins, found heritability estimates for aggression ranging from 0.20 to 0.72. More recently, Bouchard et al. (1990), using monozygotic twins reared apart from birth, found aggression to be heritable at 0.46.

TESTOSTERONE AND ABUSE OF SEX AND POWER

The male proneness toward physical risks is sometimes taken to deleterious extremes in aggressive actions beyond typical male behavior. There is a strongly disproportionate male bias to such extreme behaviors as violent

crime, unruliness in competitive violent sports, sadism-masochism, and military atrocity. Take rape, for instance. Brown (1991), in his study of the ethnographic literature, found that rape was present in every society. Rape also occurs in many mammalian groups—among younger male orangutans forcible sex is the norm. See Wrangham and Peterson 1996 for a broad discussion of rape and sexual aggression in primate groups and the selection forces that reward such aggression.

We know that between young men and women there is a considerable statistical difference in the intensity and character of sexual desire. Statistical reporting of sexual behaviors such as sexual abuse, rape, prostitute purchases, and seductions are always heavy on the male side. I believe most men understand this difference in terms of lust. And its extremes make this starkly clear. We must agree that virtually no women molest children on busses, make obscene phone calls, display their genitals to passersby, or set fire to a building in order to have orgasm (Hudson and Jacot 1991). I think the high incidence of male-male rape in many prisons (Wooden and Parker 1982; Donaldson 1993), where this kind of violence is not directed at females, shows the lust-driven edge behind rape and its emergence in undisciplined criminal behavior.

But why should the male libido be evolutionarily set at such a "close to the red-line" point that they would scrawl

Arousal, Memory, Subject Interest, and Art

Memory fidelity is intimately related to high-arousal episodes (Gold 1987). Ethologists have observed the association of arousal level and memory for a long time. Lorenz (1952) discussed the difficulty in getting corvids to talk, a training process that usually requires the repetition of words thousands of times. However, a bird can learn a complete sentence during one moment of keen arousal. Lorenz told the story of one of his own pet hooded crows, named Hansel. One time when Hansel returned from an absence, he had a freshly mangled toe and a new phrase: the Low German equivalent of "Got 'im in t'bloomin' trap! Got 'im in t'bloomin' trap!"

Paleolithic artists' choices of what parts of people to portray were apparently not random. For example, there is no consistent pattern of feet being portrayed in site after Paleolithic site, but there are frequent images of vulvae and midsections of naked women. What is the most coherent explanation we can logically attach to those choices of subject? All items portrayed are from Chauvet, Fr.

A. This little sketch on a rock from the Paleolithic site of Gourdan, Fr., is very elemental and scrawly, but its intent is still clear. Somebody is being attacked from behind by a creature with a big mouth.
B. My reconstruction of the drawing's most likely intent.

In art as well, interest, recall, and focus are much better in those areas that provide high arousal, both for the things we draw and the art we like to view. I suggest that this is partially why so many "T events"—noble species, erotic images, blood-dripping wounded game, dangerous beasts, and such—are drawn in Paleolithic art. These subjects are wondrously exciting for some people, and modern analogs provide clear clues as to what group of people that would most likely be.

all these vulvae and fat nude women in every art medium? This set point may have produced little rape in the Paleolithic context, but it leaves us with too much in today's more anonymous societies. Such male appetites were apparently selected for because, overall, a high set point increased net reproductive impact. Supporting evidence for this is that women in their fecund years (twelve to forty-four) are the most likely targets for rape (Thornhill and Thornhill 1983).

Ethologists who were outspoken in the 1960s about this violent thread of male behavior received heated criticism, but thirty years later, additional physiological work and tens of thousands of hours in ethological field studies have basically underscored the persistent presence of this thread of primate violence (Wrangham and Peterson 1996).

So this is the potential dark side of males' high libido. But its expression and origin are important to bring to light, because watered down they better illuminate their normal expressions in the benign forms of big penises and vulvae engraved on the Paleolithic cave walls. Sexual libidos and their repercussions are not trivial forces in human psychology. They are not something ephemerally cooked up on a whim today, but their well-integrated forms are a natural part of mainstream human development modeled in the Pleistocene. We can reconstruct all this without the Pleistocene evidence, but it helps to see it writ large in stone 30,000 years ago.

A LITTLE CRAZY CAN BE ADAPTIVE

Clearly, testosterone is sometimes associated with behaviors that border on craziness, but that T edge has distinct selective advantages in certain contexts. When a lioness is outnumbered more than three-to-one by spotted hyenas,

Heritability Estimates   The degree of heritability was one of the criteria I listed in the first chapter as an important element in evaluating evolutionary adaptations. Heritability is a simple statistic for a complex phenomenon. It partitions the additive variation of a continuously varying trait (i.e., a trait that is not an either-or kind of trait such as one that is either dominant or recessive) into its different components. It is widely used in livestock breeding (tenderloin length) and horticulture (grapefruit sweetness).

Heritability estimates are expressed as fractions of 1.0, where 0.0 means no variation is attributable to genetic origins, and 1.0 means all of it is. Heritability can be estimated by breeding manipulations (response to artificial selection) or by correlation coefficients and regression plots of individuals with known genetic relationships. One of the best ways to estimate heritability among humans is to compare identical (monozygotic) twins adopted and reared apart with fraternal (dizygotic) twins also adopted and reared apart. This neutralizes many problems, such as maternal effects (shared uterus). Presumably, any variation between identical twins is environmental. In contrast, since dizygotic twins share, on average, half the same genes, the genetic component of variations found between these fraternal twins should be half that of identical twins.

Remember, heritability statistics do not measure what part of an *individual's potential* is genetic and what is environmental; rather, it partitions the actual variation of a given *population* sample. And it is a population-specific value. If all individuals in the sample experience a very similar environment, the environmental component will be reduced, which will, in turn, reduce the overall variability (e.g., all individuals eating the same food, participating in the same health care program, going to the same school with the same teachers). However, such a reduction in the environmental portion will create an *increase* in the genetic fraction—and thus will increase the heritability estimate. Likewise, if a very genetically homogeneous group (Icelanders, say) were all to emigrate to diverse places and be exposed to quite variable environments, this would *decrease* the genetic component of the heritability estimate.

A heritability estimate of 0.5 for a given population segment does not mean that half of any *individual's* character (height, femininity, or IQ score) is due to his or her genes and half to the environment. Yet it does imply some probabilistic relationship for that particular individual. Thus, an IQ heritability of 0.4 indicates that the extremes of high- and poor-quality parenting/schooling can radically affect the test performance of most individuals.

---

she abandons her kill; the situation has become too dangerous. By backing off she does the right thing for her long-term interests. Territorial male lions don't behave that way. Sue Cooper (1991) showed that hyenas know not to challenge a male lion protecting the pride's kill, because his behavior is usually very different from that of a female lion in the same predicament. A male lion attached to a pride responds to the presence of a group of hyenas with anger and high aggression. The male lion's behavior may be more than a little crazy and his actions are certainly dangerous to himself as well as the hyenas. But, on average, males are the master of a lion pride for only two years. And that changes the evolutionary risk/reward calculation. Though there is one book, so to speak, for lion evolution, detailed records are kept independently for female and male behaviors. Lion females tolerate the male's presence even though he often chases a female from a kill she has just made until he has had a chance to feed. Females both benefit and suffer from the male's aggressive behaviors.

Human aspects of T-related virility can be distinctly double-sided as well. Potential heroism and potential criminality share a T twang. And these are the strictly individual faces of this force, which among humans

Couple copulating? From La Marche, Fr.

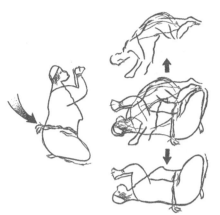

Perhaps one has to be in a certain frame of mind to see the markings on these immature teeth of horses as pubic triangles, but that is indeed what they seem to be, examples of the few cases of pubic hair seen in Paleolithic art. I'll suggest reasons for this rarity of pubic hair in chapter 6. *Left,* La Marche, Fr. *Right,* Goudry, Fr.

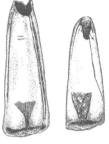

A picture of what seems to be a couple copulating, engraved on a piece of stone from La Marche, Fr. In most books the woman is pictured as sitting with arms raised (as on the left). On the right is an expanded version of two people teased apart from the engravings. Note that the only clothing is a belt and bracelets.

can be emphasized by cultural dimensions. The willing readiness—even appetite—for violence characteristic of T virility is a power, an evolutionarily developed potential. Its appetites have been fed by a quite mixed array of cultural innovations. We can grasp this by recollecting such institutions as gladiator arenas, bullrings, or sporting spear-hunts for boars and bears. These and many other cultural forms were not established by women.

A couple coupling from La Marche, Fr. Note her simple belt and bracelet. This is about as much as one sees women wearing in Paleolithic art. Some scanty adornments are more sexy than pure nudity; see the present erotic-fashion industry for examples.

GLADIATORS, BROKEN SKATEBOARDS, AND CHERRY BOMBS

Case by case, the developmental products of testosterone add the nudge to get the risky zing—but also the potential injury. Most recreational endeavors that can be bent to higher risk, like swimming, biking, hiking, skateboarding, climbing, spelunking, and handling weapons, result in more casualties among young boys than any other sex-age class. For example, in the United States we traditionally celebrate July 4, Independence Day, with fireworks. In many states families still buy their own explosives and ignite them in the backyard. Every year thousands of Amer-

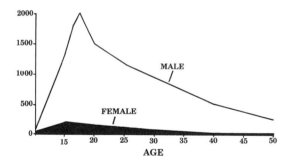

Violent Crime Index Arrests per 100,000 (U.S.A., 1992) The American FBI puts together a violent-crime index annually, based on arrest rates. These compilations show that females peak around sixteen years of age while males peak around seventeen to eighteen. Though scales and ratios vary somewhat due to a variety of cultural influences, this same pattern seems to predominate in all societies.

Testosterone activates a crazy edge of adaptive behavior in male lions. It is the male's role to defend pride territory against other lions and to defend his females from other carnivore competitors, like hyenas. Female lions do most of the hunting and tolerate breeding males as part of the pride because they serve these functions. Normally, a male's tenure is rather short-lived—the dominant male breeds for only a few years before he is sidelined by injuries or ousted by competitors. All this means that selection pressures keep pushing male lion behavior toward the extreme. The king cannot be overly cautious but has to be a little crazy. Sketch from photo.

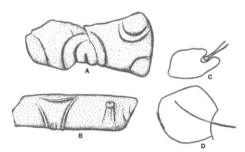

There are many images like these in Paleolithic art. I find the traditional idea, that these represent some kind of fertility magic, contrived. They seem to be simple, erotic, graffiti-like images. **A–B**, Castanet, Fr. **C–D**, Gönnersdorf, Ger. These are inappropriate illustrations for a professor to have on his desk when biology students come in for advising.

Scratched very crudely into the cave wall of Réseau Guy-Martin, Fr., are Pleistocene vulvae with a person bending and reaching toward them. All were seemingly prompted by one little triangular natural irregularity in the wall.

Testosterone and Baby Nurture   I don't want to overemphasize the bloody edges of this testosterone legacy. Most men love their kids and grandkids with a great passion and feel intimately attracted to the details of their rearing and development, but we know from the biological record that male nurture is fairly recent in our hominid line and is thus less evolutionarily polished. Unmarried females undergo iris dilation, an autonomic response to intense interest and attraction, when they see babies; unmarried males do not (Hess 1975). Married males, however, do have a dilation response, and iris dilation of fathers is close to that of mothers. In our phylogenetic line, women have been nurturing for some 200 million years; men for less than a million. Thus, one can understand that the cross-cultural pattern of paternal nurture is less genetically elaborated than that of good mothers and grandmothers. If this were not so, men would take more extensive pleasure in baby clothes and blankets. Studies of variations in human nurturance behavior have shown a significant heritability of 0.60 (Rushton 1997).

icans are injured and some are killed by these fireworks. Boys aged thirteen to fifteen are the ones mostly responsible for July 4 accidents, not only to themselves but to bystanders (*American Society of Ophthalmology Report* 1998). Thus, hospital admissions understate the prime group responsible. Every year, television and radio spots warn people of the obvious risks involved, but for young boys that adds to the draw—that is part of the reason they are doing it.

Such boys have a much higher incidence of accidents and criminal behavior than the population at large. Males are three times more likely to commit suicide than females. Young men were and are the gladiators; they are the high-risk category par excellence—as every parent who pays their teenage son's automobile insurance knows.

Biological aspects underlying our male-female differences as well as their cultural universality have received

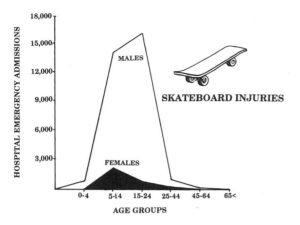

Skateboards are used predominantly by boys. It is a rather high risk sport, and the low number of female accidents reflects the higher participation by males not only in risk-taking stunts but in taking up skateboarding in the first place. U.S. Consumer Product Safety Commission, National Injury Information Clearinghouse, 1996.

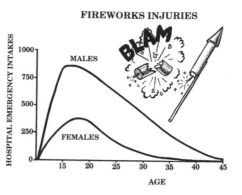

Fireworks Injuries Smoothed curves for male vs. female injuries from fireworks in the United States. U.S. Consumer Product Safety Commission, National Injury Information Clearinghouse, 1996.

much discussion (e.g., Broude and Greene 1976; Chodorow 1978; Adams 1983; Wright 1994; Clutton-Brock and Parker 1995; Wrangham and Peterson 1996; Morris 1997). I understand that individual, as well as thematic, exceptions are always part of any general patterns one attempts to delineate regarding human behavior, but many such patterns do exist, and I propose the following working list for our forensic study of Paleolithic art imagery. Higher male T levels are probably a significant aspect of the following list. Compared to women, men characteristically

➤ are more attracted to physical action via sports competition or other behaviors that have a violent edge, including fights, physical combat, war, and media action-adventure themes, both real and fantasized;

➤ are more attracted to physical risk and physical adventure;

➤ have a predilection to participate in hunting, particularly hunting involving the killing of large mammals;

➤ have a predilection for visual erotica utilizing the most emphatic visual cues, which can be both remarkably schematic and/or coarse;

➤ exhibit an aggressive and less discriminating pursuit of copulation opportunities;

➤ have a pronounced tendency to make objects into subjects and subjects into objects: "D#&%!! that nail!" or "Bob, check out the knockers on that chick";

➤ have more of a tendency to practice, as well as fantasize about, such sexual deviancies as bondage, sadomasochism, and clothing fetishes; and

➤ have a tendency toward obsession rather than balance.

While the variations in the whys and hows of art making are a matter of individual differences and characteristics, my point is that these choices in art making are not uni-sex or uni-age: focus, interest, pleasure, and aversion are tellingly reflected in the images people chose to draw. Testosterone has been the proximate agent of human sexual asymmetry in ecological specializations and social behavior. Being aware of the T patterns of influence in sexual comparisons within groups and cross-culturally can afford a unique understanding of the broad range of our lives, including violence, risk, nurture, fantasy, and erotic experiences.

The logic of my corroboratory evidence for the forensics of the first chapter begins with "forensic signatures" within representational Paleolithic art. The preserved images mainly portray subjects that, I would argue, were the focus of Paleolithic males' lives: hunting scenes and the hunted large mammals. Remember, for a Pleistocene

When you finally track down a speared animal, it is normally dead or expiring. But not always. A sublethal hit requires continued attempts at spearing from a considerable distance when the injured animal still manages to keep ahead. Inevitably, there are times when this chase is long and botched. But this can be exciting to young hunters and can even form a particular aesthetic. It is one that is seen in different forms and degrees in much of Paleolithic art and in other prehistoric art from around the world. It has to do with testosterone-driven behavior and is not about cosmic magic. From Candamo, Sp.

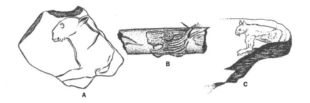

Lynx or similar predator images from Paleolithic art: a and **c**, La Madeleine, Fr. **B**, La Vache, Fr.

male, hunting prowess was intimately correlated with status and thus related to his opportunities for sex; whether, when, and whom he could marry; how many wives he could have; how much he was respected by in-laws, family, and friends; the health of his kids; care in old age; and when and how he died; as well as being limbic fun beyond imagination. This focus for a young Paleolithic guy encompassed desires and thrills now aimed at becoming a fighter pilot, football quarterback, cinema hero, rock star, star-warrior, and Olympic gold medalist. Likewise, the many Paleolithic images of nude women, exaggerated sex organs, and coarse graffitiesque human bodies allow insights into the erotic imagination of Paleolithic artists. What better phrase to capture some of these themes in preserved Paleolithic art than *testosterone events?* But I do not mean this to be reductionistic; on the contrary, we have to draw information from across a broad front to find some order, to make some logical sense out of this slice of human behavior.

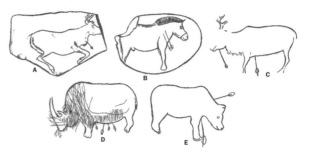

A collection of Paleolithic animal images showing them wounded with spears (note fletching): **A**, Reindeer, Montrastruc, Fr. **B–E**, Horse, reindeer, woolly rhino, and bear, Colombière, Fr. All of these animals are poorly hit. Spears sticking anywhere in a rhino may mean exciting trouble and, located in the shoulder or neck muscles of a bear, are sure to mean big trouble. Adult hunters would see such a neck wound as a kind of failure: lack of a solid hit can mean danger and the extra demands of tracking. However, we can say that for young guys it would have been exciting, as well as an occasion for putting hunting-tracking skills to the test. I even see a version of this in my young Lab retriever. A ptarmigan dropped as a clean kill is exciting for him to retrieve, but a running wounded bird quickly getting away is pure heart-thumping euphoria.

TESTOSTERONE IN WAR AND PLAY

"Now, we'll start this band of robbers and call it Tom Sawyer's Gang. Everybody that wants to join has got to take an oath, and write his name in blood." Everybody was willing. So Tom got out a sheet of paper that he had wrote the oath on, and read it. It swore every boy to stick to the band, and never tell any of the secrets; and if anybody done anything to any boy in the band, whichever boy was ordered to kill that person and his family must do it, and he mustn't sleep till he had killed them and hacked a cross on their breasts, which was the sign of the band. And nobody that didn't belong to the band could use the mark, and if he did he must be sued; and if he done it again he must be killed. And if anybody that belonged to the band told the secrets, he must have his throat cut, and have his carcass burnt up and the ashes scattered around, and his name blotted off the list with blood and never mentioned again by the gang, but have a curse put on it and be forgot forever. Everybody said it was a real beautiful oath, and asked Tom if he got it out of his own head. He said some of it, but the rest was out of pirate-books and robber-books, and every gang that was high-toned had it.

Mark Twain, *Adventures of Tom Sawyer*

In Paleolithic art, scenes of human-to-human violence are not as common as hunting scenes or erotic images. I have found only sixteen, isolated drawings that portray people (or seem to—most are very rudimentary) riddled with spears or darts—but no portrayals of fights between individuals or groups. It is possible that one or two of these images in fact may be misdrawings of large mammals that

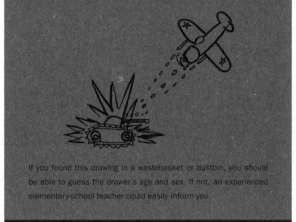

Scenes of predation by wolves on reindeer, red deer, and bison appear in Paleolithic art. These are solid testosterone events, not subjects normally chosen by women. **A**, Wolf and reindeer, Altxerri, Sp. **B**, Wolf (or fox?) and reindeer, Mas d'Azil, Fr. **C**, Wolf and reindeer, El Pendo, Sp. (wolf marked by my pointer arrow). **D**, Wolf and deer, Les Eyzies, Fr. **E**, Wolf and bison, Fontalès, Fr.

inadvertently look like humans, such is the quality of these art pieces. Unlike images in later Bushman, Australian, or Eskimo art featuring group warfare, human aggression in Paleolithic images is strictly of single individuals being speared. These Paleolithic images of human violence are significant, but so is the fact that there are so few of them and that they occur singly, as isolated pieces. We have, then, no clear record of Paleolithic warfare. In contrast, archaeological and artistic records of group warfare are common in later cultures.

Among Paleolithic graves we have not found the mass graves that often result from group fights or warfare, although there may have been instances of lethal individual fights, or murder (Binant 1991a; Otte 1995). Mass burials date only from the post-Paleolithic, and there they are common.

Is it possible that Paleolithic life had little warfare or lethal intergroup conflict? I will return to this question in a later chapter, because there is other evidence from Paleolithic art to bring to this question, but now it would be best to say that low densities in the late Paleolithic would have been far less likely to foster intergroup conflicts. Full-blown, organized war seems to have originated as a tribal phenomenon, with its own inherent character (McNeil 1976). While the elements and emotions of intergroup aggression must have been part of Paleolithic life, it seems probable that these did not often result in full-blown war in the Paleolithic. Smaller-scale fights of the Pleistocene that adjudicated disagreements not tractable to discussion probably lacked critical mass to become war. Fighting was probably not the norm, but the threat of physical violence supported the normal surface of group life and was ready to delimit unreasonable behavior.

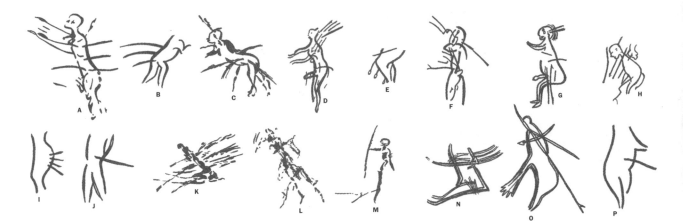

Unlike the scene below, Paleolithic art has no scenes of war or group violence. This is in remarkable contrast to tribal art, in which such scenes are common. There are, however, at least sixteen single Paleolithic images that might be speared humans, mortally wounded or corpses. **A** and **N**, Pech-Merle, Fr. **B–C**, Cougnac, Fr. **D**, Sous Grand Lac, Fr. **E**, Gourdan, Fr. **F**, Paglicci, It. **G**, Saint-Cirq, Fr. **H**, Bédeilhac, Fr. **I**, Cobrantes, Sp. **J**, Gabillou, Fr. **K**, Nerja, Sp. **L**, Grajas, Sp. **M**, Pileta, Sp. **O**, Cosquer, Fr. **P**, Patatal, Sp. Multiple wounds on many of these suggest an attack by more than one person. Is this fossilized hate? One can imagine a too belligerent, very uncooperative, or demagogic person finally getting it. There were no police, no courts, no jails. You had to get along or else. These are probably pictures of "or else." Since the person was probably someone you knew as a neighbor or even a relative, the killing would be a serious event.

Shields, throwing sticks, axes, spears—lots of valor, death, blood, and destruction. A Bushman's view, from later prehistoric art, of two Bantu groups fighting. Brakfontein Range, R.S.A. There is nothing like this in Paleolithic art.

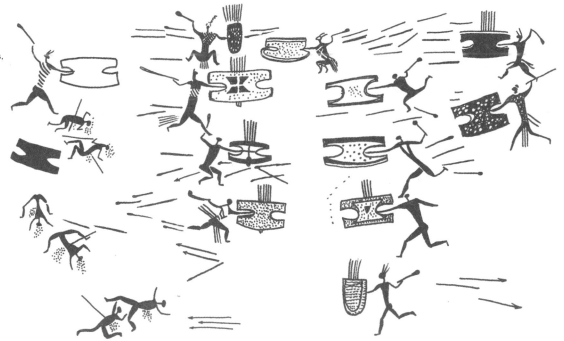

Mortal violence seems to be one of our hominoid legacies. Chimp groups occasionally raid the territories of other groups and participate in confrontations between groups, during which whole bands may be annihilated (Goodall 1992; Wrangham and Peterson 1996). Though gorilla mortality is not close to that of warfare, Fossey (1976) found that 25% of gorilla mortality is due to other gorillas, making even the highest human mortality by violence seem rather mild. Chimp mortality may not be too different (Wrangham and Peterson 1996).

In sum, Paleolithic art is remarkably lacking in group aggression and has only a few possible cases of human aggression toward other humans. Rather, T appears in Paleolithic art expressions of hunting performance and erotica, images of temperate life within the band.

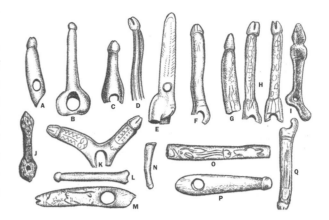

Shaft-straighteners made to look like penises. It is quite likely that the humor behind this also translates back to Paleolithic times, a case of visual double entendre, particularly appealing to a male bent of mind. **A**, El Pendo, Sp. **B**, Farincourt, Fr. **C**, **J**, and **Q**, Isturitz, Fr. **D** and **H**, Bruniquel, Fr. **E**, Le Placard, Fr. **F**, La Garenne, Fr. **G**, Cueto de la Mina, Sp. **I**, Saint Marcel, Fr. **K**, Erbe, Fr. **L**, Gorge d'Enfer, Fr. **M**, El Pendo, Sp. **N**, La Madeleine, Fr. **O**, Massat, Fr. **P**, Pavlov, Czech.

Women and Skin, Men and Bone

The carving of ivory is man's work. If a woman wanted to carve no one would stop her, but public opinion still keeps her at furs and away from the traditional carving of men. . . . In the Eskimo culture carving was as important as hunting, and today the two are reciprocal. Without walrus tusks there would be no ivory carving and without ivory carving there would be no purchase of guns, ammunition and the other imported gear the Eskimos now use. Hunting is still so important on these islands that not to be a hunter is almost synonymous with poverty. A carver said once, "He is poor; he doesn't go hunting and so he doesn't have clothes like we have—only white people's clothes."

Dorthy Jean Ray, *Artists of the Tundra and Sea*

Among Eskimos, men worked in ivory, bone, and stone because the hardness of these materials was an essential property of harpoons, bows, shields, armor, spearthrowers, and other tools central to the men's activities as hunters of large mammals. The two tasks of protection and of procuring large game were the males' specialty. And the men who worked in these durable materials also made artwork in those same materials and sometimes on the tools themselves. Women specialized in tailoring furs and sewing skins, and these materials were also their media for artwork. Under most conditions, the only tools or artwork that stand a chance of being preserved are objects of highly durable materials, and in older Eskimo archaeological sites, the finds are mostly remnants of men's tools and art. Taphonomic processes severely edit the full human spectrum of tools and artwork and inadvertently bias our archaeological collection toward the male end of the spectrum. This is the general pattern, and undoubtedly it occurred in the Paleolithic as well.

Most Paleolithic art in our taphonomically curated collection was made with sharp stones: engraved, carved, scratched, and chiseled. Again, ethnographic data (Murdock and Provost 1973) show that only males worked sharp stone for tools, and predominantly males used those tools.

INFORMATION FROM GRAVE GOODS

Grave goods have the potential for telling us something about that person in life. There are a lot of caveats, for one does have to recognize the possibility, among other possible scenarios, that mourners sometimes placed their own possessions in the burial as gifts. So, simply interpreting grave goods as the belongings of the deceased is too naive, but we can step back a bit and check for patterns in grave goods from the Eurasian late Paleolithic.

Even if the Eurasian population totaled only a few tens of thousands of people at any one time, the sum would still be many millions of people over the 30,000 years covered by the late Paleolithic. Considering that number, very few actual burials (not isolated skeletal remnants) have been discovered (Binant 1991b lists about ninety). Thus, one can conclude that most of the dead were either not buried, not preserved, or for some unknown reason never found. The former seems most likely. Burial seems to have been a rather rare and erratic phenomenon. There are regional time blocks of thousands of years with no identified burials found at all. Among those found there is often considerable age and/or sex bias. For example, most of the Gravettian (20,000–30,000 years ago) burials in Italy are males and include no children under age twelve (Mussi 1995). But despite the small and incomplete sample, when we take the aggregate collection of all late Paleolithic burials, both sexes and most ages are present in the sample.

What grave goods are found in these Paleolithic burials? Most burials are not accompanied by preservable materials. Just the skeleton or parts of the skeleton are present. Among those in which grave goods are found there are few differences between sexes and ages. For example, there are no outstanding differences in body decoration, which includes things like snail shells and the teeth of red deer and carnivores. These are found with several males, with females, and with children. Likewise, ocher was commonly scattered over bodies of adults and children of both sexes. And while art occurs in the graves, it also shows no major patterns. Data like these have logically prompted scholars to conclude that there are no clear sex and age patterns in late Paleolithic grave goods (Binant 1991a, 1991b) and, by implication, no sexual differences in behavior. However, I would submit that there are some sex-specific patterns in the tools associated with Paleolithic burials.

For example, batons, or point-straighteners (whose probable function I will discuss in chapter 5), seem to be male tools. Six late Paleolithic graves contain one or more straighteners, and the remains of all those individuals seem to be males. The sites are Arene Candide and Cavillon in Italy; Hoteaux in France; Cueva de Los Canes in Spain; and the double burial at Sungir in Russia. There is some controversy about the identity of one of the individuals in the double burial at Sungir. The older skeleton, aged twelve to thirteen, has been identified as a male, but the skeleton of the seven- to nine-year-old is so young that sexing is difficult. It was originally thought to be a young girl. However, other researchers contend that both are male (see May 1986; Rogacev in Bosinski 1990). It is noteworthy here that both skeletons in the Sungir burial were accompanied by a spear made from mammoth ivory; in addition, the excavators were able to reconstruct outlines of what must have been wooden spears. Part of the sex identification problem with the younger individual is that the child seems to have had a chronic disease; bent limb bones prompted Bader (1984) to conclude that the child had suffered from rickets. I should also note that the baton, or straightener, found with the adult male from Cavillon in Italy was at a depth of 6.40 meters, very near but not attached to the skeleton itself, which was at 6.55 meters (Mussi 1995).

Likewise, stone-knapping tools or objects thought to be used as such (Broglio 1995) are found mainly in graves of males. Finished projectile points of stone and osseous materials are also more likely to occur in male burials. Extremely long flint blades (ranging up to 250 millimeters) are likewise found mainly in male graves. Needles and awls are found predominantly in female graves. There are only a few exceptions to the above patterns (see reviews of data in May 1986; Binant 1991a, 1991b; Otte 1995).

Adolescence and the Yang of the "At-Risk" Age

I suspect that most adults, especially those reared in middle-class suburbs, cannot bring themselves to acknowledge the innate savagery of preadolescent boys. From the ages of nine to fourteen they are naturally predisposed to set up blockwide territories, run in gangs, and bully to gain acceptance, to swagger, to boast, to dare, and call back and forth to one another in loud and honking voices of emerging male adolescence.   E. O. Wilson, *Naturalist*

AN APPETITE FOR RISK

Who is most prone to risk taking? Comparative ethology tells us a lot about the variation in risk behavior between species and within species. The push and tug between more cautious behaviors and hazardous ventures relate to the prospective losses and gains. A bolting prey running just in front of a predator gambles with high-stake routes, risky moves, and physiological overextension, but a predator is rarely so desperate. The prey is risking the loss of life; the predator risks only the loss of dinner. A juvenile squirrel or lion assumes high risks when venturing out into unknown territory, but dominant seniors, be they lions or squirrels or most other mammals, resist dispersal from known territories. Dispersing juveniles have little to lose and much to gain; dominant seniors have little to gain and much to lose. Generally, low status makes risk more rewarding. And in general, males have more to gain from risk taking than females, particularly young males. Risk taking is an adaptive part of animal behavior and is a principal component in much of human behavior as well. As with most mammalian species, we know that young men, who are without much status, are the main risk takers. The situation of young women is quite different for important evolutionary reasons, and I'll discuss those dynamics later.

A young gangly bull moose is singularly unappealing to females, and he is disdained by older bulls (Bubenik 1998). It is the most powerless stage of life for moose. For most male mammals, including humans, there is a wide gap between physiological maturity and social maturity (this is not true for females). Across human cultures, a sixteen-year-old male has little power; he is untested and untried and has not entered the ranks of men with stature and reproductive claims.

As with other species, this window of human adolescence and youth is a time in which they can influence their status by more risky behaviors—gambling with risk. All youth stand to benefit from some risk, but this is particularly true for boys of lower social status. For millennia, Pleistocene boys' best bet for increasing their status involved physical risk in the high adventures of hunting and individual and group protection. The social stature of Pleistocene men was ultimately pegged to their hunting prowess and ability to provide protection from harm, including the possibility of violence from other males.

This T-charged period of indeterminate potential is probably prolonged for today's young men beyond its Pleistocene range. Today, most men do find interests and work that engage their powers in positive ways, but the challenges young men choose and the sorts of risks they take are not always positive. Statistics on risky, unsophisticated crime—vandalism, theft, drug abuse, assault, arson, burglary, robbery, disorderly conduct, joyriding, and speeding—show that the great majority of these perpetrators are young males. Policemen can tell you that the fresh paint thrown on broken classroom furniture was not splattered there by girls or by women or by mature men. The culprits' modus operandi identifies them as young males. This is a time in males' lives in which most fights occur, gangs form, most injuries happen, most graffiti is made, and the wildest erotica is designed. Yet most boys live good lives in which this risky behavior is integrated and domesticated.

The degree of male-female differences increases as we move toward more violent behaviors. Prisons for violent criminals contain disproportionately few women, and surely the developmental and activational role of T is a major factor. High-security prisons and capital punishment are basically institutions for males. If males committed violent crime at the same rate as women, our penal institutions could be totally transformed, perhaps abandoned and the problem dealt with on an out-patient basis. We cannot deny the everyday fact that if you find your car broken into and vandalized or your house robbed, the em-

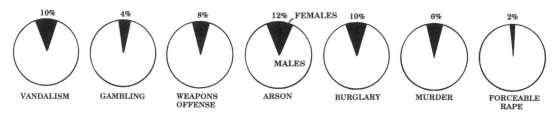

10%	4%	8%	12% FEMALES	10%	6%	2%
VANDALISM	GAMBLING	WEAPONS OFFENSE	MALES ARSON	BURGLARY	MURDER	FORCEABLE RAPE

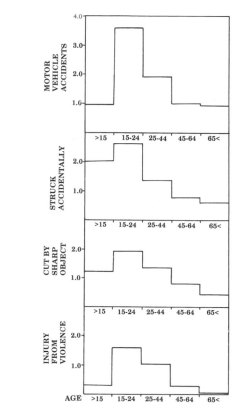

Hospital Emergency Visits (both sexes, in rate per 1000, U.S.A.). These graphs illustrate something that people the world over know about the age pattern of people who arrive at hospital emergency doors. National Center for Health Statistics, 1992 (*n* = 33,950).

Arrests of Persons under Eighteen Years of Age (percent female–male). Young males under age eighteen commit more violent crimes than females of the same age, as these plots dramatize. (Note that some of the female crime shown here is probably the result of having accompanied a high-risk-taking young male.) FBI crime statistics, 1993.

"Age, like gender, resists explanation because it is so robust a variable. None of the correlates of age, such as employment, peers, or family circumstances, explains crime as age itself. Age is robust not only across contemporary conditions but across time and geography, again like gender" (1985, 205).

Risk-taking behavior, such as enjoying dangerous sports, apparently has a high heritability (see *Nature,* Genetics Section, Jan. 15, 1996). In fact, a gene for extreme risk is located on the chromosomal block known as D4DR.

If one of the main benefits of high-risk male behavior is sexual access, usually in the form of marrying and marrying well, then one would predict that once married well, high-risk behavior would change considerably. That is in-

Another testosterone event. This engraving (*upper right*) is from Laugerie-Basse, Fr. A mortally wounded bull bison is shown with a man, one arm raised, lying on the ground in the background. Whether he is wounded or is getting ready to throw another spear is not clear. My reconstruction of the possible scene below.

pirical odds are overwhelmingly in favor of an adolescent or young man as the culprit.

In their text on causes of crime, Wilson and Herrenstein reviewed studies from all over the world. They showed that sex (male) and age (youth) were by far the best predictors. They commented on those predictors:

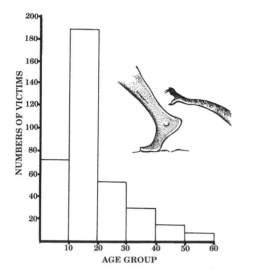

Annual Snake Bites in the Republic of South Africa Which sex and age is bitten most by snakes in South Africa? Statistics from Visser and Chapman 1979.

deed the conclusion of Dench (1994) in his book entitled *The Frog, the Prince, and the Problem of Men.* Risk taking is related to potential gain or loss. Once a man has gained a sought-after spouse, the balance has shifted, and he now has important evolutionary currency to lose. So risks must be more thoughtful and less wild. Indeed, this is the pattern that emerges in the modern occurrences of injuries and crime rates. Why do most men decrease their playing of team sports (or going back into caves) about the time they get married? Do sports have something to do with showcasing their value as mates with displays of their power and strength?

THE SPONTANEITY OF CAVE ART IMAGES: A JUVENILE TESTOSTERONE IMPRINT

Madeline soon ate and drank,
On her bed there was a crank,
And a crack on the ceiling had a habit
Of sometimes looking like a rabbit.   Bemelmans, *Madeline*

I mentioned the association of children and image spontaneity in the last chapter. Now we can take it further. Walks with my children have reminded me that they see the world differently than I do. My son, Owen, would often stop me and say something like "Dad, see that elephant." "Where?" "The cloud—it looks just like an elephant." I remember how as a child I used to lie in bed and see things like deer antlers and horses in the ceiling cracks. My youngest daughter, Mareca, when seeing her first fig leaf, remarked that it was just like a gecko hand. Adults lose this freshness through years of practice of having to see things in practical terms and as having consequences—clouds that may mean rain or ceiling cracks that should be repaired before spring.

The art they left tells us that some Paleolithic artists saw stags and bison bulls in limestone irregularities of cave walls. A row of stalactites became, for another artist, flowing mammoth tresses, sharp projections for another became bison beards, and bowed arches looked like deer necks. For many, natural formations were elaborated into identifiable animals by the addition of a few lines and a little color. I suspect that for most adult Magdalenians, cave walls were consistently damp and lumpy, and bison remained outside in the sunny meadows.

I proposed in the last chapter that this spontaneity itself is forensically informative. The technique of a Rorschach test may tell us not only what was on their minds but who those minds belonged to. We've seen that the Paleolithic cavers seem not to have been imagining frogs, beetles, babies, moles, hedgehogs, or beautiful necklines. Instead, they recognized stalactites and cracks as parts of large mammals, a scatter of ugly faces, erections, and vulvae. These subjects were likely not foremost on everybody's minds.

There is something here that transcends our own culture. The act of scrawling something in covered recesses or even out in the open, defacing natural surfaces, has a certain attraction. It may not always be vandalism, but it is a root behavior from which vandalism sometimes arises. The fact of its existence (its graffiti-like character) and the nature of its content suggest maleness, male adolescence. Bednarik (1994) also points out that the evidence suggests

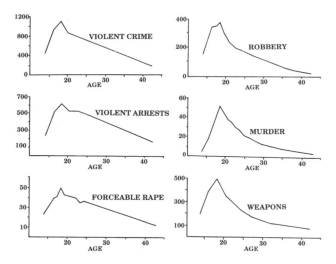

Arrests and at-Risk Ages (rates per 100,000). Criminal arrest records reveal that the most at-risk age is seventeen to eighteen. *FBI Report of USA Arrests,* 1994.

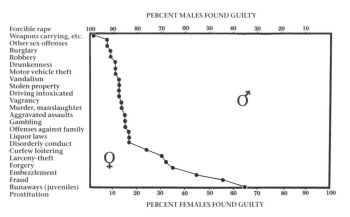

Relative percent of male vs. female types of crime. Female crime is very different from male crime. The central difference is degree of violence and risk of violence. U.S. Department of Justice, Bureau of Statistics, 1995.

that much of rock art was produced by juveniles. Scholars often remark on the abundant Paleolithic vandalism in Paleolithic art caves.

SAMOAN ADOLESCENT TESTINESS AND THE SEARCH FOR THE "NEGATIVE INSTANCE"

New York City, 1920s: Anthropologist Franz Boas had already resigned his post at Clark University following a heated argument with Clark's founder, G. Stanley Hall. Hall was of the opinion that adolescence was an innately intense period in one's life and that its agonies and ecstasies recapitulated some time of cultural stress in human evolution. As did many scholars of his time, Hall championed an extreme sort of genetic determinism. Boas left Clark for Columbia University, where he intended to pursue his own ideas about the nature-versus-nurture issue. Boas and his young graduate student Margaret Mead planned a research study on the island of American Samoa. On the eve of Mead's departure, Boas noted that in America "We find very often among ourselves during the period of adolescence a strong rebellious spirit that may be

expressed in sullenness or in sudden outbursts" (quoted in Freeman 1983, 63). Was this also true of adolescents in the purportedly idyllic South Sea island? Documentation of a "negative instance" would be hard evidence for Boas's theories of cultural determinism.

In 1925–26, Mead interviewed about twenty-five Samoan schoolgirls (the field season was cut short by a typhoon and other events), and unfortunately their answers were too equivocal to settle her thesis question. However, two unmarried young women her own age were happy to inform her of their many escapades with young boys. Years later, one of these women lived to testify that the stories they told Mead were just jokes; they had had no such free-love experiences (Freeman 1999). Margaret Mead returned home with what she thought was evidence, the negative evidence Boas had hoped for: adolescence in Samoa was free of the censure and tension seen in industrial societies. It thus seemed clear that the storm and stresses of American adolescence could be attributed totally to nurture, that is, to cultural factors. In *Coming of Age in Samoa,* Mead portrayed Samoan society as simple and casual—a society with ready solutions for conflicts and Samoan individuals with few deep feelings or strong passions. The minds of Polynesian adolescents were un-

conflicted and sex was free and easy. The book was hugely influential and Mead became a central figure in the new field of cultural anthropology. Mead's book was required reading for decades of anthropology students, including myself. Indeed, its philosophical impact on the spirit of the twentieth century was enormous.

Unknown to me, and perhaps even to my anthropology professors, there was some hushed discord surrounding Mead's book. Before she died, Mead admitted to the growing conflict in interpretations of Samoan society. And as Samoans themselves started going off to college and reading the book, they were incredulous of Mead's descriptions of their home life.

Researchers reexamining Samoan society found an enormously complex social system, with hierarchy relationships much more intricate than our own (Freeman 1983). In fact, it was an aggressive, warring society replete with violence and plagued by strife-rent male-female re-

lations and troubled adolescences. Researchers combed the police logs recorded while Mead was on the island and found that the incidence of rape was no different from that in the United States. They also found that a significant percentage of Mead's schoolgirl informants had histories of delinquency, but Mead missed this or at least failed to present a more complete picture. Nonetheless, seventy years later, students in some colleges are still uncritically reading *Coming of Age in Samoa* as received wisdom.

Why was there so much opposition to the idea that some behaviors might have a heritable component? I think it is because if one admits to some inherited behavioral component, then one must admit that a trait may have evolved. Cultural anthropology was in its origins antievolutionary. Boas argued that "human species were exempt from the laws of biology," and Alfred Kroeber contended that humans had surpassed the organic: "The su-

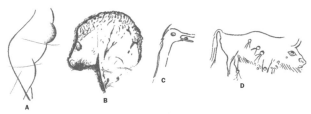

As we go through the text, I am sprinkling reminders that what people see in Rorschach inkblots or natural patterns can often yield important insights into the things foremost on their minds. If you have read this far, you won't be surprised at the results: **A**, Woman's breast, Les Combarelles, Fr. **B**, Horse's head, Bara-Bahau, Fr. **C**, Bird, Escabasses, Fr. **D**, Speared bison, Niaux, Fr. **E**, Giant deer, Montgaudier, Fr. **F**, Women in a stooped, lordosis position, Les Combarelles, Fr. **G**, Chamois, Massat, Fr. **H**, Mammoth, Rouffignac, Fr. **I**, Deer or ibex(?), Rouffignac, Fr. **J**, Snake, Rouffignac, Fr. **K**, Lion, Les Combarelles, Fr. (eye-stone put in by later cave visitor—which age and sex would you guess committed this bit of vandalism?). **L**, Bull aurochs, La Mouthe, Fr. **M–N**, Bison, Montespan, Fr.

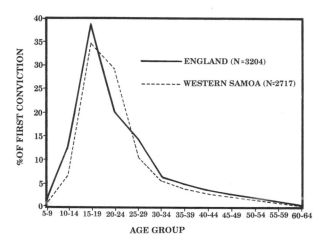

In her book *Coming of Age in Samoa* was Margaret Mead right that adolescents in the South Pacific did not experience any emotional, rebellious, at-risk spirit? Freeman (1983) compared crime in Samoa with that of England by age-group.

perorganic had originated in a sudden leap, or saltation, springing fully formed from the organic as did Pallas Athena from the brow of Zeus" (cited by Freeman 1983, 55). But they turned out to be wrong. We are, and always have been, immersed in the organic past.

GUY GLAND TRACKS IN THE ART

For boys growing up in a small hunting-band society, the highest aspiration is to be an excellent hunter. Among such enthusiasts, animals are watched and admired with a passion not easily translated to nonhunters. In Paleolithic times immense large mammals meant more than difficult-to-obtain food; they were a test of skill, bravery, will, and wits—and, most of all, they were dangerous. The Paleolithic woolly large mammals were the license to social stature, to manhood and marriage. In such a society, hunting must have been the main thing that could kill you, give you status, bring you the best of wives, and provide you with everyday respect. Women who chose not to select a good hunter for a husband were more likely to leave behind fewer of their genes. Millennia of matings bred into us a reverence for being good at one's work.

Hunting large mammals and defending yourself against large competing predators would be natural subjects to dominate your thoughts, especially just before you went to the front lines as an adult. Paleolithic large-mammal hunting was not for little boys.

Whatever their adolescent preoccupations—soldiering, hunting, sailing, monsters, trains, kites, cars—one consuming interest is shared by boys all over the world and during all times in the past and will be so long as boys shall exist: an ear-ringing, mind-buzzing preoccupation with hard-core sexual fantasy. Those physiologists who specialize in human sexuality tell us that this obsession peaks in the late teens for boys, somewhere around sixteen to nineteen. Yet most societies cannot accommodate or condone full reproductive access at this age.

It is illogical to suppose that adolescent boys would have been back in caves, in what must have been the ultimate in privacy for those times, charcoal crayon in hand, drawing any subject of their choice and never have drawn

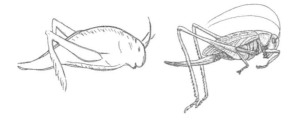

Despite all these patterns I have been mentioning, the actual details of Paleolithic art are very diverse. For example, a cricket was engraved on a broken bone fragment (*left*) from Enlène, Fr. The damp recesses around limestone bluffs would have been frequented by these insects, and their chirping would have been common during a black Paleolithic night. Dr. Judith Marshall from the British Museum identified the image as a "bush cricket," *Decticus verrucivorus* or *D. albifrons* (*right*). These, by the way, are edible.

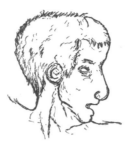

We know that large quantities of testosterone circulating in the blood affect how the body and brain develop, profoundly influencing thoughts, emotions, and aesthetics. There is every reason to believe this also happened many thousands of years ago in patterns not unlike those of today. Paleolithic boy from La Marche, Fr.

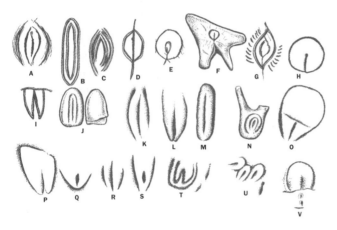

It is difficult to hold to more traditional paradigms in Paleolithic art when faced with all the bare vulvae: **A**, Arudy, Fr. **B**, Gourdan, Fr. **c**, Mas d'Azil, Fr. **D**, Isturitz, Fr. **E**, Maszyska, Pol. **F** and **K–M**, Laugerie-Basse, Fr. **G**, La Madeleine, Fr. **H**, Brno, Czech. **I**, Batusserie, Fr. **J**, Laussel, Fr. **N**, Pair-non-Pair, Fr. **o**, Tuc d'Audoubert, Fr. **P–S**, Commarque, Fr. **T**, Caville, Fr. **U**, Abri Cellier, Fr. **V**, La Ferrassie, Fr.

an erotic lady or her parts. In fact, Paleolithic art caves, rock etchings, bone and antler carvings, and stone and clay images portray erotic women or women's breasts, butts, and genitalia in addition to erect penises. This differs little from adolescent erotic art in any other society. While most renderings are rather crude, many forms are drawn with an exquisite deftness and a keen eye for detail. Preserved Paleolithic art includes numerous images of female genitals; sometimes these are repeated again and again in the same artwork. It is easy to imagine young Paleolithic guys enjoying some rowdy sex talk in their pri-

vate, lamp-lit caves. Most genitalia are drawn hairless, interestingly. I will come back to that later, as it may suggest the age of the drawer.

While initiation ceremonies involving the band's mature men and pubescent boys might be envisioned, I find such sexually explicit drawings strongly suggestive of less formalized coming-of-age behaviors. Among Bushman, for example, males have basically two kinds of relations with other males. Though complex, a ready key to this dichotomy is how freely they talk with each other about sex. One relationship, characteristic of youthful male cohorts, allows constant sexual banter, including sexual allusions and insults and jests about impotency, cuckoldry, and the like. Much as in our culture, sexual jokes often feature in the verbal exchanges of closely bonded males. In the other category of male Bushman relationship—strangers, fathers, grandfathers, in-laws, formal acquaintances, or seniors—sexual banter is seldom or never used (tensions of sexual bonding and inbreeding discourage this). This dichotomy may be nearly universal among males, but few ethnographers obtain such data. Certainly, sexual subjects are loaded with tension, and sex talk is not done openly in any society; that *is* one human universal (Brown 1991).

With regard to graffiti and Paleolithic art, certainly "The Guys"—youthful peers, the boys one grows up with—formed the nucleus of a group free to joke about erotica. These unchaperoned boys would likely have felt free to carve curvy ladies and vulvae and have had great

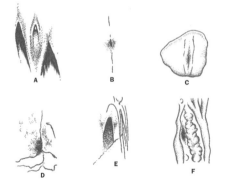

Stalactite enhancement with pinkish ocher to accent these little life-sized vulvae: **A**, Font de Gaume, Fr. **B** and **E**, Gargas, Fr. **C**, Laugerie-Basse, Fr. **D**, Niaux, Fr. **F**, Villars, Fr. Now who would pull a stunt like that?

More below-the-belt art from the Paleolithic. Limeuil, Fr.

A natural stalactite formation was enhanced to appear more like a naked woman. La Varende, Fr.

uninhibited fun at it. Mixed-generation adult males from the band would likely have inhibited such erotic fun.

CAVES ARE FUN

Encouraged by this success we began to go through the cave. . . . Our joy was indescribable. A band of savages doing a war dance could not have done better. Then we made a promise to say nothing to anyone about our discovery. . . . The next day, armed with our essential equipment, we set off at ten-minute intervals, taking different routes, like a band of Indians covering their tracks. When we arrived at our "treasure" we set about improving the entrance and then headed once more into the unknown. . . . Next we came to a vertical hole which we could not see the bottom of. There we paused.

Marcel Ravidat, one of the teenage discoverers of Lascaux,
quoted by M. Ruspoli, *The Cave of Lascaux*

Wild unexplored caves are fun, a particular exciting fun, somewhat like the fun of winter mountain ascents, sky-diving, and formula-one racing. This fun is quite unlike that found in croquet, backlot volleyball, or body surfing on gentle green sea swells. Caving fun is about risk and adventure—especially for young boys who are not encumbered by an excess of good judgment.

If you have not explored a cave, let me tell you that it is rarely a matter of strolling back into a spacious tunnel, as in most developed tourist caves. You often begin by squeezing through a hole with sandpaper-raw edges and are unable to light the blackness below, which may drop many meters. Caution on entering is advisable because the damp shade just inside is an excellent place to find poisonous snakes; where I grew up these were usually copperheads. Once in, you usually have to crawl, worming your way between a rough ceiling and mud below. Often you have to enlarge the hole to go further; twisting your head sideways helps. Straight drops of 10 meters or more are not unknown, and you should bring a knotted rope or little cable ladders. Few cavers have not been in some alarming situations. Cavers have lots of stories.

As in rock climbing, caving requires excellent physical condition and muscle power. In beyond any reflecting sunlight, a cave smells strange, probably due to fermenting bat guano. There is no way to maintain a sense of direction amid irregular openings along crazed joint lines. Even with good gear it takes courage and not a little craziness to enjoy such fooling around. Indeed, caving claims lives every year. Caving does not appeal to everybody; most people find plenty to interest them above ground. But recently, when out hunting, I found this rock opening with quite a draft, and I suspect it is that famous lost hiding place where . . . but, you wouldn't be young enough to still believe in that kind of stuff.

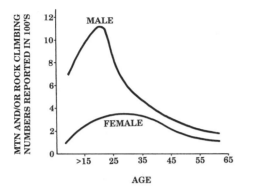

Climbing Injuries by Sex Hundreds of thousands of people every year are injured when climbing around on rocks. They are admitted to hospital emergency rooms and become reported to the National Injury Information Clearinghouse. Along with rock- and mountain-climbing hobbyists, anyone who is injured on rocky slopes in backyards or on picnics gets reported. As you might predict, males predominate, and it is by far young males, with a peak in the teen years. The graph shows smoothed-curve estimates for 1996.

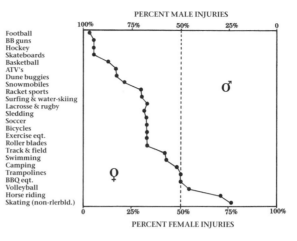

The relative male-female percentages of significant accidents vary consistently across several activities. This reflects not only accidents but the likelihood of each sex to participate in these activities. Generally, the higher the risk of an activity, the higher the proportion of males injured. U.S. Consumer Product Safety Commission, National Injury Information Clearinghouse, 1996.

MODERN DISCOVERERS OF THE ART CAVES: THE TROIS FRÈRES EFFECT

It is a telling fact that many Paleolithic art caves as well as Paleolithic images in known caves were discovered not by geologists or art historians but by local teenage boys. Les Trois Frères was discovered in 1914 when three young brothers climbed into a cave in the Pyrenees and found Paleolithic art. In 1895 neighborhood boys in the Vézère Valley climbed 100 meters into the cave of La Mouthe and discovered pictures on the walls and ceilings. In 1940 a group of teenagers from Montignac followed their dog into a curious hole and discovered the famous paintings of Lascaux. The artwork in Ekain, perhaps the best Paleolithic art in Spain, was discovered by teenage boys in 1969. Such discoveries by boys show a definite pattern. Pech-Merle was found by two sixteen-year-old boys. Font de Gaume art images were well known by the boys from Les Eyzies, as was the art in Niaux by Alliat boys (the oldest graffito there was marked 1684), but the antiquity of this art went unappreciated for years. La Baume Latrone and Bayol in Gard were also first discovered by young boys. Pech-Merle,

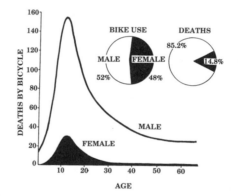

Although both sexes use bicycles about the same amount (52% male, 48% female), males predominate in the numbers of reported deaths resulting from accidents. Data smoothed after Rodgers et al. 1994. In this report to the U.S. Consumer Product Safety Commission, the researchers propose that this great disparity is due to males (especially young males) being much more prone to risk taking.

Gouy, Tuc d'Audoubert, and other caves with Paleolithic art were discovered by adolescent boys, exploring on a neighborhood scale. Similarly, fifteen-year-old Mohammed adh-Dhib and his young herd-boy buddies stumbled onto the Dead Sea Scrolls in 1947. Many boys of this age are predisposed to fool around in risky and adventure-

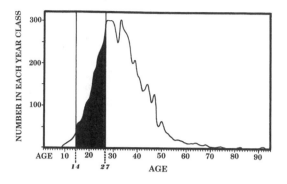

Numbers and Ages of Members in the French National Speleological Society
One can see that the mean is in the late twenties and has its steepest slope for new membership between ages fourteen and twenty-seven, then it plateaus and more people begin to quit than join. This is what an evolutionary perspective and everyday experience would have led us to expect. Data from 1994, Fédération Française Spélélogie, M. Bernard Jodelet, director.

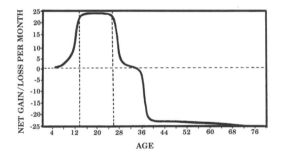

One can better see the caving interest between ages fourteen and twenty-seven by looking at the percentage dropping or joining for any given year. A smoothed curve from 1994, Fédération Française Spélélogie. Data from preceding illustration.

some places. To such boys the darkness and unknown aspects of caves are positively magnetic.

AGE AND SEX IN TODAY'S SPELEOLOGICAL SOCIETIES

Of course, we do not have a record of the discoverers of all caves in the past, but the membership of today's caving groups offers a clue. Who searches for and explores wild caves today? Cave-exploring clubs flourish in Europe and America, and as you might imagine, their members are predominantly male. The ratio ranges from 8 : 1 to 10 : 1. Of course, clubs charge membership dues and go about caving in an organized and disciplined way, which means many youngsters who like cave exploring do not belong to such clubs. I suspect only a fraction of the kids who fool around in caves are speleological club members, but as these individuals grow older and earn a little money, many do become interested in the journals and cave news bulletins and so they eventually become members. (Club membership data confirm this pattern.) Of course, some women do belong to these clubs, and one presumes they find spelunking fun and exciting.

However, it may not be accurate to take the proportions of male-female members in such clubs as indicative of inherent interest. The club atmosphere may put off some women (men, too, for that matter) who enjoy caving. Other women may be members largely because of the interest and enthusiasm of their husbands or boyfriends. From my knowledge of spelunkers and canvassing of colleagues abroad, this usually does not work the other way around: few men join simply because their wives are committed cavers. These biases mean we should not assume that membership data from speleological societies exactly reflect innate interests; however, there is clearly a disproportionate appeal for males, particularly young males.

CAVEMAN OR CAVEBOY?

We went to a clump of bushes, and Tom made everybody swear to keep the secret, and then showed them a hole in the hill, right in the thickest part of the bushes. Then we lit candles, and crawled on our hands and knees. We went about two hundred yards, and then the cave opened up. Tom poked about amongst the passages, and pretty soon ducked under a wall where you wouldn't 'a' noticed that there was a hole. We went along a narrow place and got into a kind of room, all damp and sweaty and cold, and there we stopped.
Mark Twain, *Adventures of Tom Sawyer*

In September 1940, while a nightmare of war descended on Europe, four teenagers from the town of Montignac in the Périgord carried on as boys do in more normal times (the local boys included some refugees from northern France as German forces occupied the north). Seeking adventures, they went out to look for the rumored underground passage to an old manor house and its purported treasures. First, they attempted to get some of the refugee girls to come along into the woods with them; that failed. Undaunted, they continued. That local estate, called Lascaux, was owned by the Rouchefoucaulds and had been planted in vineyards in the 1800s, but the phylloxera virus had killed most of the grapevines in Europe, so the rolling hills were planted in pines. Some years before 1940, one of the pines had fallen, uprooting a large mass of soil and exposing a karst pit in the limestone bedrock. This hole had been blocked off to keep livestock away (after a donkey had fallen into the small opening and died). The boys knew about this old hole or pit and decided to check it out. A dog named Robot, belonging to one of the boys, went into the hole and alerted the boys to the possibility that this could be the rumored secret passage. What would Tom Sawyer and his friends have done?

Exactly! They swore never to tell adults. The Montignac boys returned the next day with a homemade oil lamp, and a real adventure began. But word eventually leaked, and every boy in the region was soon crawling back into the cave. They then took the news to their teacher, who, first of all, did not believe them. But soon enough the adults took over. While caves may not be exciting for everyone, there is no doubt that there is a special relationship between boys and caves.

KIDS AND CAVES

I once was an adolescent cave explorer, growing up on the northern edge of the Ozark Plateau, a hilly limestone country remarkably similar to the Périgord. Had there been any Paleolithic art in our domain, our juvenile explorations would probably have found it. We knew no adults who explored caves, and contrary to our fantasies, young girls were never allowed to come along. Few archaeological digs occur in deep art caves, not only because they were uncomfortable places for prehistoric peoples to spend enough time to leave behind artifacts, but because deep caves are also uncomfortable for adult archaeologists (Hadingham 1979). The scale of adult exploration is both more realistic and more grand, to the horizon and beyond. Kids have enough time and constraints that they are the ones who comb the local neighborhood in detail, and Paleolithic kids had some time on their hands: they did not have the daily mind-numbing "weeding-the-mealie-and-watching-the-cattle" field chores of later tribalists.

We have seen that the statistical analysis of Paleolithic hand- and footprints in caves shows a mixed group of

Paleolithic kids? La Marche Fr. Exploration is an important kind of play behavior. And as we will see later, play is serious evolutionary business.

kids, not just teenagers. If adolescents boys are the group most likely to go back in caves, then why were even smaller footprints and the smaller hands scattered among the adolescent ones? Is the image of a T-driven band of Paleolithic teenagers wrong?

The Paleolithic cave club, as seen from my forensic study, was a diverse group; with several teenagers, a smaller child or two, and maybe an individual entering manhood. The plaquettes at La Marche supply a fascinating portrait of Paleolithic boys. There are several faces of single boys, two images of two boys, and four images in which four boys are portrayed together. Interestingly, this corresponds to the groups of Paleolithic tracks in caves, which record two, three, or four youths, and also to our theoretical estimates of children's groups based on a Paleolithic band size.

The explanation for the mixed-age group seems rather simple. Paleolithic encampments were unlikely to have produced half a dozen boys of the same age at any given time. Recent hunter-gatherer analogs and evidence from Paleolithic refuse piles suggest that *year-round* band size could not drop much below nor rise much higher than twenty-five to thirty-five individuals. Sizable groups of teenagers would not regularly occur until Neolithic changes led to larger populations and tribal densities.

If we presume that a Paleolithic band averaged thirty individuals, roughly half would be males. Among those fifteen (in a balanced population at maintenance level) there would have been, statistically, only three males in each decade up to age forty and, say, a total of three beyond age forty. Archaeological evidence suggests a comparatively short life expectancy past thirty-five to forty.

The fossil record of bear bones shows that during the period in which most Paleolithic cave art was done, around 13,000–25,000 years ago, cave bears were not common. However, in Chauvet, Fr., where the early art dates to around 28,000–30,000 years ago, there are not only skeletons of cave bears but clearly drawn images of them as well. I pointed out earlier that we can identify them by the forehead step and floppy lips. These enlarged lips were probably used to feed on vegetable matter. We know from their molar patterns and stable isotopes from bone samples that cave bears ate considerable vegetable matter—probably tubers, as do many brown bears today.

greater strain on their limited fat reserves. Young bears are less capable of building up winter fat than adults.

But why are there more remains from male bears? Curiously, this differential pattern is common among mammals (Kurtén 1964), and a dip in the mortality curve of male adolescents of many species is also widespread. While the reasons are complicated, most relate to testosterone; for example, males have a higher metabolic rate than females and there is that matter of risk-prone male behavior.

Each adult female bear can have a litter of one, two, or three cubs every three or four years, and female bears normally live into their late teens. Yet, on average, each sow bear in her lifetime raises only two cubs to adulthood. What happens to all the other cubs? Most die.

The imbalance of who dies and when, combined with hibernating back in caves, inadvertently resulted in a disproportionate number of bones from young male bears ending up in caves. Similarly, inadvertent taphonomic distortions of cave art occur because of a confluence of factors: among humans, drawing is most prolific at a young age, and boys are inclined to greater risk taking than adults and are attracted to the adventure of exploring caves.

Thus, there would have been, on average, three boys within the age scatter from seven to seventeen. Thus, our Paleolithic group might have had three boys, let's say, aged seventeen, fourteen, and eight and an occasional sister as well. In farm communities or small villages one notes similar groups of disparately aged children with the occasional smaller child tagging along. The youngest, frequently a younger brother or cousin, is a responsibility. Similar combos, from my youth, explored creeks and woodlands, built forts, fished, and made general mischief. And in many ways this kind of mixed-age group buffers lots of potential trouble. It is a rather tame combination compared to a larger gang of six or more fifteen- to seventeen-year-olds on the prowl. The older pack can create certifiable trouble because theirs is a more combustible mix of high-octane testosterone. Yet these are differences in degree rather than in kind, and I'll return to this and other band-tribal differences in a later chapter.

GRAFFITI AND TESTOSTERONE

There seems to be some link between youthful testosterone titers and graffiti. Modern graffiti are overwhelmingly made by young males (Kinsey et al. 1953) and range from angry expressions to snickers of private humor. Women seem to do much less graffiti making, and the graffiti that they do make tend to be more political (Able and Buckley 1977). The one female sex-humor inscription in Able and Buckley's study reads "A little coitus won't hoitus." Boys would call this "decaf graffiti." Females should not feel slighted: a disinclination to inscribe raunchy graffiti is not necessarily a deficiency.

Three graffiti-like drawings from Gabillou, Fr., showing a woman and two aurochs cows in "erotic" positions, with open vulvae. The latter aurochs is speared and something is coming out of the vulva.

Another example of below-the-belt art, from Enlène, Fr. One cannot unquestionably assume this was great art or a portrayal of some ceremonial dance.

There are Paleolithic versions of "brains on the sidewalk" boys' art: mortally wounded beasts with guts spilling out. Exciting stuff. Both lion and bison are from Lascaux, Fr.

The books about graffiti that I reviewed contained few pictures, yet the graphicness of male graffiti is widely acknowledged. Those books that did include pictures of graffiti avoided the rawest images of cartoon genitalia in action, which are among the commonest images in public toilets—these graphics are often more charged than literal photos. Even the drawings of Paleolithic art in this book are likely sufficient to keep some libraries from adding it to their holdings, and these images do render this work hard to take home to mom or to send to grandkids.

Books on graffiti discuss violence, homosexuality, racism, and other themes, but tough talk is easier to print than crudely erotic visual images, even somewhat humorous ones. The main themes of graffiti are tough talk and lots of coarse erotic images, both normally embedded in some humor. Of course, what is done in men's toilets is only a portion of modern graffiti, and modern graffiti are not the same as Paleolithic art. That said, it is worth observing that maybe a lot of youthful testosterone is splattered in both.

Inscribing one's name can be considered graffiti making. We find a patinated haze of signature graffiti in many caves today. Yet in caves in the American Midwest, Australia, central Asia, and southern Africa, as well as in many art caves in Europe, the majority of names are male: Clement Arthur 1894, Billy Lee Scranton 1945, and so on.

PLEISTOCENE VANDALISM

There seems to be a mark-making continuum from what we'd call beautiful prehistoric art toward graffiti, and this behavior trails off or curls back on itself in the form of vandalism. There is even evidence that Paleolithic explorers occasionally marked up cave art by earlier artists. A lot of images are redrawn, and many are overdrawn, as though ignoring what was there beforehand. Cosquer Cave supplies clear evidence of Pleistocene vandalism (Bednarik 1994). The entrance of Cosquer Cave was sealed about 10,500 years ago as the level of the Mediterranean rose. There is evidence from radiocarbon dates of at least two main episodes of cave entry at Cosquer, one clustering around 30,000 and the other some 20,000 years ago (Clottes, Courtin, and Valladas 1992). During the second episode, explorers did much damage to paintings that were already about 10,000 years old. Hand stencils were crisscrossed with deep incisions and stalactite points were broken—actions almost identical to cave vandalism today. By any definition, Cosquer Cave records Paleolithic vandalism. Sticking bones, bone fragments, and stones (perhaps sticks too—but of course they don't preserve) into cracks and into soft mud is common in Paleolithic art

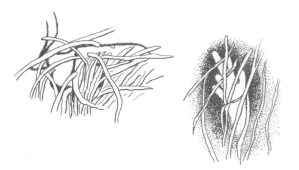

Vandalism even occurred in the Paleolithic. For example, there seems to have been only several major episodes, thousands of years apart, of Paleolithic visits to Cosquer Cave, Fr. Later visitors defaced some of the drawings of the former. *Left,* a reindeer that has been disfigured and almost destroyed, much like vandalism today. *Right,* a handprint that has been scratched out, in the same careless way.

caves (Clottes 2003). And ancient vandalism is not unique to Paleolithic art; similar damage and overmarkings have been found in early Egypt, ancient Rome, and Mayan ruins (Bednarik 1994).

The Taphonomy of Missing Chapters

If this book were about the evolution of human parenting, I would pair this testosterone chapter with one on the biology of nurture and the evolution of the mother-offspring bond. But there simply are very few images of such subjects in our Paleolithic collection. To some extent we can see around this taphonomic bias. Analogs from other hunter-gatherer cultures suggest what may be missing and help make the most of the Paleolithic evidence that we do have. But the first step is to recognize that our collection of Paleolithic art has been taphonomically distorted and simply does not reflect many aspects of Paleolithic life.

If sounds could crystallize, we could dissolve them back to Paleolithic songs and dances aplenty and hear the wealth of children's stories and learn about herbal tonics and unique ways of making and preserving delicacies. Such sounds were in the air for tens of millennia, accompanying diverse activities of tangible Paleolithic people. In addition to the nonmaterial arts we lack entire categories of material arts. Paleolithic peoples probably had decorated wooden camp tools: stools, scoops, sieves, combs, stirrers, and such. Weavings, coiffures, robes of intricate fur and leather patterns, and tailored clothes have not preserved, but hints in the images of Paleolithic art make it clear that they existed.

CLOTHING

By all rights there should be a chapter on clothing in a book about Paleolithic art. We know that Eurasian Paleolithic peoples had to have well-made clothing. It would have been crucial to their well-being and to their very survival, because without highly effective garments humans are not physiologically able to withstand daily life in such a climate as we know existed then. One can imagine that Paleolithic clothing was beautifully tanned and tailored and probably dyed, painted, or otherwise adorned. This is true of northern people's clothing today. Look, for ex-

Alas, we have little information on Paleolithic clothing. One raveling of evidence is connected with the handprints in sprayed ocher. Some include parts of the cloak or sleeve of a garment. Images are from Gargas, Fr. My drawing above illustrates the kind of garment that was captured inadvertently by the spray technique.

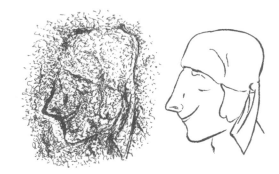

Image of person with head covering from Abri Bourdois, Fr. My line drawing on right.

Head coverings seen in images from Paleolithic art. All are from La Marche, Fr., except the bearded man, second from last at lower right, from Grotta di Vado, It.

ample, at the remarkably beautiful garments of traditional Eskimo groups.

Slender awls are found in the Aurignacian record and later; they were probably used to sew tailored Paleolithic garments of skin and fur. From about 26,000 years ago we find delicate bone needles (Klíma 1990) that would have made that job faster and easier, and these are so delicate that they could have been present even earlier and not preserved. Also, evidence of plant fiber weaving has been found on baked-clay impressions in Moravia (Adovasio et al. 1999; Soffer 2000).

A few Paleolithic hand stencils, made by blowing ocher onto cave walls, stand as a poignant metaphor for these lost dimensions of artistic activity. We have discussed the forensic aspect of those handprints, but some prints contain hints of something else. Several hand stencils from Gargas Cave seem to record a shadow made by the sleeve of a garment, corroborating our assumption that Paleolithic people were dressed in tailored clothes. In fact, one of the hands we can attribute to a woman has the rather fuzzy outline of what could be a draped garment.

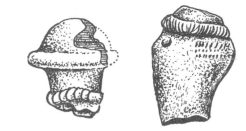

Two hatlike features on images of heads from Pavlov, Czech.

BODY ADORNMENT: JEWELRY AND ACCESSORIES

On some Paleolithic figurines and engravings of women one can make out various kinds of body adornment, in-

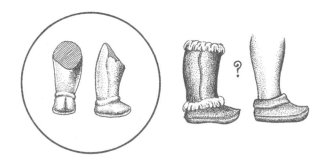

A lower-leg image from Kostenki, Rus. It is not clear if this is a boot or a shoe.

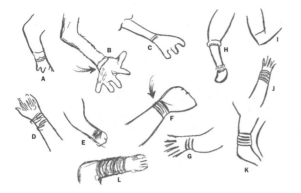

Bracelets portrayed in Paleolithic art. Bracelets have been around a long time. **A–G**, La Marche, Fr. **H**, Kostenki, Rus. **I**, Geldorp, Neth. **J–K**, Isturitz, Fr. **L**, Enlène, Fr.

cluding jewelry, scant clothing, and coiffure patterns. Sofer (1987) pointed out belts in some of the Russian female figurines, worn both above and below the breasts. Paleolithic burials of men and boys reveal a variety of bone and shell adornments, yet virtually no Paleolithic image depicts any adornment on males. Maybe this is not too significant, as virtually all of the males are drawn poorly, almost schematically.

Actual fragments of jewelry are both common and widespread, occurring in many late Paleolithic sites in Europe and Asia. Jewelry items are usually found in burial sites or in sites that were evidently used as home bases for extended periods. The preserved jewelry items are made mainly from animal teeth and other skeletal parts which resist destruction; jewelry materials include snail shells, mammoth ivory, antler, bone, and many canine teeth of fox, bear, lion, wolf, and wolverine. Of course, ornaments may have also been made from seeds, wood, fiber, feathers, keratin horn, claws, hooves, flowers, insect parts, braided leather, and hair or fur tufts (like tail tips), but these and any number of other less preservable materials have simply not survived. This is unfortunate, because most body ornaments were likely composed of such materials.

Why adorn the body? It seems to be both a form of play and a means of adjusting our physical appearance. The practical requirements of clothing are somewhat negotiable. Dress is an art form in which we all participate. Today, it is big business as well. Shops selling clothes are second only to food shops in volume of business. We know that how we dress and groom ourselves affects and relates to status, sexual attraction, and group allegiance, all rather fundamental biological attributes and potent players in our evolution (Morris 1976, 1987; Guthrie 1976). Unlike other animals we are not limited to evolutionarily arranged fur, feathers, or muscle and fat contours to present our image; we can crop, shave, wave, color, tattoo, puncture, scar, clad, pad, bind, and warp our image almost infinitely, limited only by one's creative style and the bounds of social acceptance. However we dress, or undress, we go out in costume into the theatrics of life.

Body decoration is part of the visual arts; and as White (1985, 1989) emphasized, adornment provides insights into human character. Persons of high status in many societies are often elaborately adorned in full color, and the reoccurrence of this phenomenon in so many different contexts over time speaks of something very basic. Just as adding a handsome carving increases the quality of a spear-thrower by adding aesthetic value to its strictly functional merits, personal adornment can also increase social stature. Rare and valuable items of adornment suggest the wearer's value. Well-being is rarely paired with a grossly unkempt appearance. Ornamentation draws attention to a person—it is more than a symbol of stature; it is both an act and a declaration of flamboyant confidence. The person is not hiding.

Paleolithic "accessories" were generally made from locally available materials, but rarity does seem to have been a sought-after feature. For example, perforated marine shells have been found in Paleolithic sites that are far from the sea. Symbolic impact was also important. Many of the perforated teeth used in Paleolithic jewelry are sharp canines from carnivores (White 1989), sometimes of quite common species. The glossy enamel and tapering shape do make a handsome piece, but canines are also the killing

Rhythm in Work and Art   Necklaces, bracelets, and amulets from the late Paleolithic are virtually all decorated with repeated abstract patterns. In contrast, 93% of the shaft-straighteners are decorated with representational imagery (Noiret 1990). I can offer a hypothesis of why that might be. It is possible that women were incorporating the motifs from soft-tissue media into preservable materials. For example, it is easier to make abstract patterns when weaving fibers, stitching, lacing, braiding hair, and plaiting leather. For example, we see comparable abstract or geometric patterns among the traditional artwork of Plains Indian and Eskimo women.

Perhaps the explanation goes even deeper than that. In such a hunting society men would most likely have performed the tasks that were done at irregular intervals but required peak performance, whereas women would have performed certain tasks daily (Murdock and Provost 1973). Among hunters and gatherers, men normally have the irregular, large-muscle demands, for example, sled pulling, fighting, and transporting meat, whereas women do the more repeated dexterous work, for example, collecting plant foods, preparing and tanning skins, making and repairing clothing, carrying children, and caring for babies (Brown 1970). It is possible that the different rhythms of work might carry over to other realms. One can make sewing more creative by using beautiful and intricate stitchwork. Weaving functional items can be made more interesting by varying the weave pattern and fiber colors. Thus, abstract patterns would have been a motif familiar for other visual artwork.

A number of Paleolithic pendants, buttons, and other accessories have deliberately notched edges or

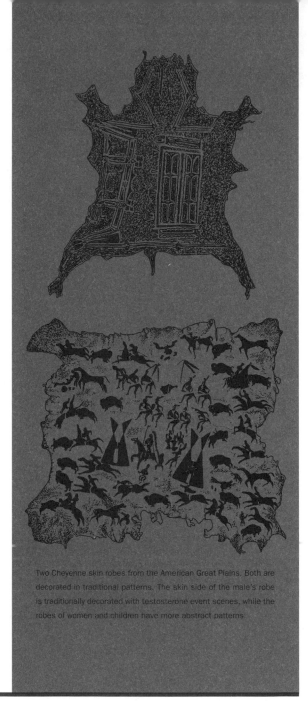

Two Cheyenne skin robes from the American Great Plains. Both are decorated in traditional patterns. The skin side of the male's robe is traditionally decorated with testosterone event scenes, while the robes of women and children have more abstract patterns.

teeth, and those who selected them for adornment must have been quite aware of this. Canines from stag red deer are also common, and even ungulate incisors. One site, Mladec in Czechoslovakia, contained mainly beaver incisor ornaments (Szombathy 1925).

One can imagine the taphonomic gulf between the jewelry worn and the infinitesimal amount that happened to be preserved. Over a lifetime of say thirty-five to forty years, a Paleolithic person probably had a number of pieces of jewelry. Some were lost, some perhaps broke while away

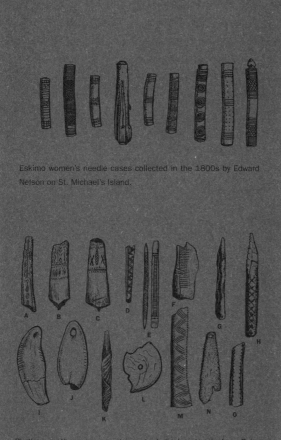

Eskimo women's needle cases collected in the 1800s by Edward Nelson on St. Michael's Island.

Rhythmic patterns preserved in osteological materials from Paleolithic art: A–C, Marsoulas, Fr. D, I–J, and M, Le Placard, Fr. E, Saint Marcel, Fr. F and H, Laugerie-Basse, Fr. G, Gourdan, Fr. K, Lortet, Fr. L and O, Mas d'Azil, Fr. N, La Madeleine, Fr.

engraved zigzag patterns. We enjoy such patterns today and can see that the Paleolithic eye was likewise engaged. Increased numbers of edges or lines, such as toothed edges, toggles, parallel grooves, crosshatching, or beads on a string, catch and hold the eye longer, as part of their physiological affect on the brain.

from camp, some were thrown away with camp debris, and perhaps a few were buried with the owner. At least that is the pattern shown in the archaeological record. In some Aurignacian sites the living floors are littered with bead and pendant ornaments (Hahn 1986), and yet beads and pendants do not seem to occur with burials in the earliest Aurignacian sites (White 1989). Later, ornaments are profusely represented in Gravettian burials. At Sungir, for example, a 22,000-year-old site near Moscow, the arrangement of the ornaments in a burial suggests that they probably were attached to the edges of the garments, giving us some sense of the nature of the garments. Since garments like these would have taken days to make, it seems unlikely that they were specially made for the burial.

Recent archaeological evidence from India reveals that late Paleolithic peoples there used ostrich eggshells to make perforated disks (ostriches lived in India and even reached China during the late Pleistocene). Perforated ostrich eggshell disks were found in at least forty-one sites in India. Paleolithic disks from India are remarkably similar to the ostrich shell ornaments still made by Bushman in Namibia and Botswana. European Paleolithic beads made from other materials seem to have been produced by similar techniques.

PALEOLITHIC COIFFURES

Paleolithic carvings of female figurines show what the hairstyles may have been like. The carved woman's head from Brassempouy, France, shows a checkerboard pattern, perhaps simulating braids or plaiting. Details are unclear; the hair does not look unkempt or straight. The hair on the Venuses of Willendorf, Austria, Gagarino, Italy, and number 24 from Mal'ta, Russia, also shows a similar crosshatch pattern, which might represent curly hair, though in a bowl shape. Short hairstyles are most common in the art. Fine hair texture is indicated by vertical engraved lines on a figurine from Kostenki I, Russia. The figurine from Lespugue, France, has long hair pointing down to the small of her back, and the bas-relief from Laussel, France, also shows long hair. Though these are very indirect ways of looking at Paleolithic hairstyles, they do suggest that hair was groomed and that, at least among women, hairstyling was a form of decorative art.

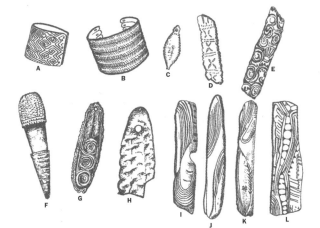

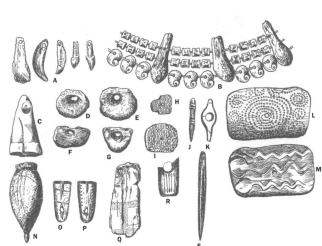

Decorated ornaments from Paleolithic art: **A–B**, Mezine, Ukraine. **C–E**, Eglises, Fr. **F** and **H**, Brassempouy, Fr. **G**, Saint Marcel, Fr. **I–K**, Isturitz, Fr. **L**, Laugerie-Basse, Fr.

Paleolithic jewelry: necklaces, pendants, buckles, disks, etc. **A**, La Marche, Fr. **B**, Barma Grande, It. **C**, Saint Germain-la-Rivière, Fr. **D–G** and **N–Q**, Kostenki, Rus. **H–M**, Mal'ta, Rus. **R**, Sagvardzhile, Rus. (Caucasus). **S**, Mgvimev, Rus. (Caucasus).

Paleolithic rhythmic decorative patterns on bone: **A**, Lalinde, Fr. **B**, Dolni Věstonice, Czech.

Hunting and Sex

Whether prehistorians accept or deny the magic or religious character of the designs, or their deliberate or fortuitous placing in different parts of subterranean systems, all authors find themselves very generally agreeing that the images in the caves were the framework for an ideology which is expressed in symbols associated with fertility and the hunt.

André Leroi-Gourhan, *The Dawn of European Art*

Il nous semble que c'est cette dualité femme-animal qui convient le mieux comme hypothèse explicative de la nature et de la morphologie des figurations paléolithiques.

Henri Delporte, "L'art mobilier et ses rapports avec la faune paléolithique"

Almost all of the images from the Kostenki culture are of either a woman or an animal, and quite often they are closely interchangeable.

Mariana Gvozdover, *Art of the Mammoth Hunters*

Is there a symbolic connection between the recurrent Paleolithic testosterone images of nude women and noble beasts, the *dualité femme-animal,* as Delporte so insightfully called it? These images frequently occur together at

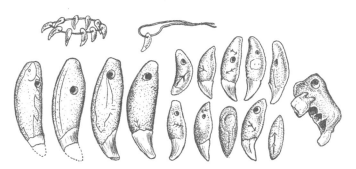

If a large carnivore threatens, attacks, or kills you, it will be using its canines. So in a way canine weapons are easy metaphors for human danger and power. They also have the beauty of a simple form combining ivory with a glint of shiny enamel. Lion (*smaller*) and bear (*larger*) canines from Duruthy, Fr., and on left a human mandible fragment from Enlène, Fr. All these teeth have perforations as if to be worn on thongs, as portrayed in the two images at top.

the same site, often on the same tool, plaquette, or rock wall. It is easy to speculate on a variety of symbolic connections. Absolon (1949) concluded from the repeated imagery of pornography (his term) and hunted game that early peoples had only two things on their minds: sex and hunger. I propose that in a roundabout way Absolon's conjecture and the duality seen by Leroi-Gourhan (1982b) and Delporte (1990) are correct. These two themes may be related in many functional ways, including their contri-

Dangling Snails and Canines: The Ornamental Click and Tick of Paleolithic Life   In the rich outdoor quietness of Paleolithic life, people shared a sound heard around the world until recently: the soft tick, crackle, and click of ornaments—mainly of ivory and shell—tapping against one another with body movement. These soft sounds accompanied the movements of playing children, mothers rocking babies, people dancing, and adults doing their work. Small bony pendants were sewn on caps or head-nets, on clothing around elbows, wrists, knees, and ankles, and along jacket edges and were made into necklaces and bracelets. The furs, skins, and fibers are long decomposed but perforated and sewn to them were, quite frequently, rows of snail shells and dangles of canines, some of which have been preserved. Several

Paleolithic necklace made from Tertiary fossil snails from the Paris Basin. Goyets, Fr.

species of these snails still frequent the rich earth around limestone cliffs. Osseous ornaments would have also created a striking visual effect: handsome white highlights against leather darkened from the smoke of many campfires and the touch of unbathed bodies.

Stylized decorated osseous materials. All from Mas d'Azil, Fr., except the one at lower right, which is from Mal'ta, Rus.

A single Paleolithic burial in Sungir, Rus., revealed considerable beadwork (over 1500 beads), apparently attached to the man's clothes. I have reconstructed, with considerable liberty, this beadwork—elaborate women's art that unfortunately was not preserved.

bution to "evolutionary fitness," but operationally, they are mostly separate.

Among some historical hunter-gatherer groups the themes of women and game have been culturally conflated. Parkington and Manhire (1997), relying mainly on data from Biesele's (1993) fieldwork, discuss this connection among Kalahari Bushman. The first menarche for young women and the first eland kill for young men mark the entrance into adulthood, their attainment of procreative powers. Biesele's (1993) book title captured this in three words, *Women Like Meat.* A young Bushman couple constantly use metaphors of fat cow eland in regard to her fecundity and of large male eland in regard to his sexual and hunting potency. For example, failure to recover an arrow-hit eland is a failed opportunity, and this image is used as a metaphor to refer to menstrual blood as a failed

Plaquette Engravings from La Marche

Russell (1989) has proposed that some of the stone engravings found around Paleolithic campsites were done by women. La Marche would be a good candidate for that. The La Marche engravings, scribed with a stone engraver on rough stone plaquettes, are remarkable for their information content. There are images depicting individual faces of men of different ages. Were these particular engravings made by a woman or women? Likewise, there are engravings of children's faces. These are generally outline drawings, but some show a subtlety of observation and execution of facial detail virtually absent in other Paleolithic images. I think it is fair to say that the makers of these portraits knew these particular faces and enjoyed looking at them. Yet most of these engravings were casually executed and incomplete. Further, there is repeated overdrawing. This reuse suggests that the engraved stones were not revered objects with a special place and status. The fact that they were found scattered about the site (as are drawings on flat stones at other sites) suggests that they were ephemeral sketches. Their creators may have delighted in making them, but when the artists were finished or were called away to other tasks, they simply dropped their creations to the ground—the pieces were not kept as permanent artworks.

I do not mean to imply that there is a lack at La Marche of sexual and heroic imagery such as I have been attributing to adolescent male themes. These are present. There are many engravings I would call testosterone images: copulation scenes (more here than in any other Paleolithic locality), naked fat ladies, erect penises, beautiful stags, mammoths fighting, and so forth. It is the sensibility of the portraiture that is distinct. The general predominance of people as subjects is unusual at La Marche (Pales and St.-Péreuse 1976b).

The more sensitively rendered La Marche portraits do not bear the stamp of juvenile art, either of boys or of girls. Young people of all existing cultures seem not to focus on realistic faces of older adults as subject matter for their drawings—even though parents or their substitutes are vital to a child's well-being. Perhaps the faces of key adults are simply part of the assumed "given" and children find other variables more arresting. It is certainly possible that the La Marche faces were made by men, but most men strongly prefer to draw women. So, unlike much other Paleolithic art, which is flecked with juvenile or adult testosterone, I suspect some of the La Marche engravings were done by adult women, but a mystery it will remain.

opportunity. Parkington and Manhire (1997) propose that this cultural connection of sex and hunting helps make more sense of the associations of eland and naked women in Bushman art. Among Bushman, nakedness in women is considered erotic—as genitals are normally covered in public. In many of the portrayals of women in their art, the genitals are not covered.

I see no evidence of such a direct symbolic conflation of sex and hunting in Paleolithic art, however. I propose instead that these themes simply reflect the most persistent interests of the male artists whose work predominates in our very skewed sample of Paleolithic art. Understanding the biologically intertwined role of these subjects in

the artists' lives helps us appreciate their frequent proximity, but I see no evidence that this recurrent proximity is more than fortuitous or that it had an explicitly symbolic significance. Paleolithic art does provide ample evidence that for some 30,000 years, erotic visual attraction to women and successful hunting were important themes for men. As it happens, these are apt subjects for representational art, and hence the subjects of the next two chapters. Many other related pleasures are not as well suited to visual rendition, such as holding a daughter on your lap while telling her stories. These latter, more complex pleasures mature later in life and are not part of a young man's fantasy.

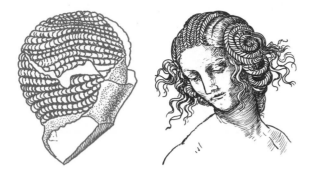

In many cultures head hair is a medium of art. *Left,* Kostenki, Rus. *Right,* sketch from one of Leonardo da Vinci's notebooks.

We do not have any fossil hairdos from Pleistocene mummies, but fortunately we do have Paleolithic images of coiffures: **A** and **DD**, Laussel, Fr. **B**, Buret, Rus. **C**, Entrefoces, Sp. **D–H**, **N–O**, and **AA**, Mal'ta, Rus. **I**, Bédeilhac, Fr. **J** and **X**, Dolni Věstonice, Czech. **K–L** and **Z**, La Marche, Fr. **M**, Murat, Fr. **P** and **V**, Grimaldi, It. **Q**, Willendorf, Aus. **R**, Pavlov, Czech. **S**, Isturitz, Fr. **T**, Nerja, Sp. **U**, Kostenki, Rus. **W**, Massat, Fr. **Y** and **BB**, Brassempouy, Fr. **CC**, Avdeevo, Rus.

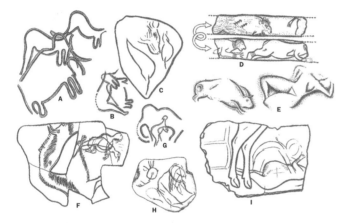

A mixed association of large mammals and sexual imagery: **A–B**, Mammoth and hanging breasts, Pech-Merle, Fr. **C**, Bison or wolf(?) and stylized nude women, Fontalès, Fr. **D**, Bison and nude women, Isturitz, Fr. **E**, Bison and naked lady, La Magdeleine, Fr. **F**, Bison and copulating couple, Enlène, Fr. **G**, Mammoth and naked lady, Pech-Merle, Fr. **H**, Mammoth and vulva, Tuc d'Audoubert, Fr. **I**, Ungulate hind legs and copulating couple, Laugerie-Basse, Fr.

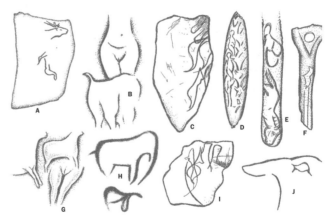

More associations of large mammals and sexual images: **A**, Reindeer and female bodies, Fontalès, Fr. **B**, Below-the-belt art and bison, Angles-sur-l'Anglin, Fr. **C**, Mammoth feet and female bodies, Gönnersdorf, Ger. **D**, Ibex and naked bodies, La Vache, Fr. **E**, Horse and lady with large naked breasts, La Madeleine, Fr. **F**, Horse and vulva, La Madeleine, Fr. **G**, Aurochs and below-the-belt art, Angles-sur-l'Anglin, Fr. **H**, Mammoth and woman with hanging breasts, Pech-Merle, Fr. **I**, Mammoth and naked women, Gönnersdorf, Ger. **J**, Ibex (the outer line) and naked woman (headless—stooping toward the left), Pech-Merle, Fr.

As we turn in the next two chapters to testosterone-filled Paleolithic images of nude women and isolated vulvae, of fighting mammoths, nose-bleeding horses, and gut-speared bulls, I hope you will not be put off or prejudge the people who made these images. Such visual expressions of hugely natural preoccupations were probably seen as images of beauty by their Paleolithic makers. Why not appreciate them as part of our strange and wonderful evolutionary story, which they both embody and illus-

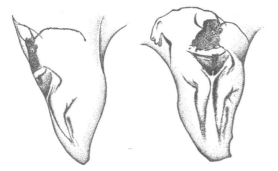

Drawn from life in the Paleolithic. La Marche, Fr.

Left, when this bison on a hanging rock was discovered in Chauvet Cave, it was logically referred to as the "Sorcerer." One can imagine a standing bison-man with a human leg. However, when it was studied from another angle (*right*), the leg turned out to be the left leg of a "below-the-belt" image of a nude woman. Images of large mammals so dominate cave art that when one draws a lone vulva or below-the-belt image of a woman on a wall where other art is being done, the nude, fortuitously, is likely to be near an image of a large mammal.

trate? Indeed, these images are part of a larger behavior cementing half of the family bond. Testosterone has been, for better and worse, a key component of bimodal parenting, and it has a central role in the bonds of love. For those Paleolithic youth and for boys today, most wild testosterone attractions mature and combine, if all goes well, into an adult virility, a unique male civility and gentleness, and an ability to bond to a new family, to hold and shelter one's mate on starlit nights, to help nurture, protect, and educate children and adolescents, and to share in the care of the sick and aged. It does not always work well, but fortunately it does regularly. Had it not, the male's half of the evolutionary human bond would have failed, and perhaps with it, much of the grace we know.

It was starlight, and very still. The mighty river lay like an ocean at rest. Tom listened a moment, but no sound disturbed the quiet. Then he gave a low, distinct whistle. It was answered from under the bluff. Tom whistled twice more; these signals were answered in the same way.

Then a guarded voice said:

"Who goes there?"

"Tom Sawyer, the Black Avenger of the Spanish Main. Name your names."

"Huck Finn the Red-Handed, and Joe Harper the Terror of the Seas."

Tom had furnished these titles from his favorite literature.

"Tis well. Give the countersign."

Two hoarse whispers delivered the same awful word simultaneously to the brooding night:

"BLOOD!"

Mark Twain, *Adventures of Tom Sawyer*

5

The Art of Hunting Large Mammals

When one is hunting, the air has another, more exquisite, feel as it glides over
the skin or enters the lungs . . . the hunter feels tied through the earth to the
animal he pursues, whether the animal is in view, hidden, or absent.

J. Ortega y Gasset, *Meditations on Hunting*

The Niche for Which We Were Fitted

Images of large mammals in a certain style constitute the chief unity of Paleolithic art. Large mammals
were central to the lives of Paleolithic artists and, I
would further propose, played an essential role in our
evolution.

It is easy for us to intuit the complex evolutionary
adaptations that so marvelously align large mammals,
like bowhead whales, Alaskan caribou, and Kruger
leopards, with their ecological niches, but it is less easy

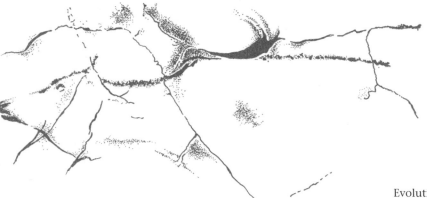

to view our own evolution in these terms. Of course, one reason for this discrepancy is that the story of our evolutionary adaptations is not so simply apparent in our present lives; that is also true of kiwis and penguins, as birds that no longer fly, and of Chihuahuas, who no longer roam the wilds in packs. Yet the prior evolutionary adaptations of kiwis, penguins, and Chihuahuas still resonate through their beings today. Perhaps, we retain traces of our evolution as well. As Williams (1992) noted, organisms are historical documents. My aim here is to imaginatively reconstruct the ancient connections, the evolutionary dynamics, that transformed a branch of forest apes into our human ancestors. I hope to enlist Paleolithic art as an informant in that process.

What was the evolutionary niche for which we were once fitted? What ecological and evolutionary adaptations exaggerated the characters that became so unique to the human animal? Convention has assumed that our defining adaptations were focused on creative versatility itself, on an ability to fill almost any niche. Today, we see that people can eat seaweed or sunflower seeds, fly to the moon or tunnel miles deep into the earth. But this modern bias masks older realities. Rather, I will emphasize another idea, that selection pressures responsible for humanness were precise and well defined—just as targeted and dramatic as those that shaped animal flight—and they permeated the evolutionary restructuring of every fiber of the human body plan and behavior.

Evolution is an oblique process and is not always easy to imagine or discuss, so we grasp for crutches and use suggestive metaphors. Just as chemists know molecules are not the toy lattice of colored balls they keep in their labs, and astronomers understand the visual metaphor of constellations, evolutionary biologists know there is no *adaptation* in the sense of an accommodating adjustment, no *fitness* in the sense of athletic aptness, and no *selection* in the sense that there is a judicial arbiter. Evolutionary biologists employ the retailored definitions of these terms in context because this convention allows us to talk about widely observed patterns, for example, reproductive success. But it remains understood that this simplified language is not to be taken literally.

Natural selection is sometimes unidirectional, but this process is not "strategic," not heading for some future goal. But our understanding is often aided when we smooth out complex realities into simpler metaphors. Thus, if we look at evolution in a retrospective, metaphoric way, we might visualize it as solving puzzles. How these puzzles were solved (and by which groups) leads to some of the most interesting stories in evolutionary biology. For example, in solving the puzzle of how to fly (only a few animal groups have ever succeeded in sailing high through the air for hours), each successful group used similar but unique solutions. Our own evolutionary puzzle was not flight, but it was something like flying—on that scale of difficulty. Of course, there have been many challenging evolutionary puzzles: how to feed on the vast volume of minute marine plankton or how to dive kilometers deep in the ocean, how to achieve anatomical miniaturization, elaborate chemical defenses, undetectable camouflage, and so on.

Human evolution resulted in an interconnected suite of traits, including extensive intellectual capacities, dependence on learned behavior, opportunistic versatility, capacity for complex language and communication, dexterous and versatile hands, material-manufacturing potential, and cooperative social abilities, all of which in degree distinguish us from other apes. These interlinked human traits were not the result of a few megamutations or an instantaneous gift from a deity; rather, they were evolutionary adaptations, acquired and refined over countless generations—the result of an adaptive occupation of a new and demanding ecological niche. To review human evolution, let me talk simply in terms of stages.

Something Like Flying

GLIDING OUT INTO THE SAVANNA

The setting for our story begins in Africa, around 7 million years ago. Prior to that time most of Africa was forested, but as seasonal aridity increased, low and midlatitude forests gave way to more open scrub savannas. Hominids, one of the main ape branches, expanded onto those savannas and thereby diverged from forest-adapted ancestors of living chimpanzees. It seems that the formerly successful forest adaptations of our Pliocene ape ancestors came up on the losing side because of long-term climatic changes that periodically reduced the extent of tropical forests and provided more open and drier habitats. These grassy scrub savannas apparently afforded new opportunities.

Early African hominids, of the genus *Australopithecus,* occupied these grassy scrub savannas, and as they began to prosper they diverged into several species scattered widely throughout the African savanna. Still, their success did not mean large numbers or high densities. Fossils of a few dozen individuals have been found in sediments dat-

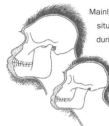

Mainly because fossils do not preserve well in woodland situations, the early story of the transition prior to and during the shift to savannas is not well documented in the record. What we do know is that there were several hominid groups living at this time. It is not clear from which of these our line arose. I portray one here, *Australopithecus africanus,* dated over 3 million years ago. Male and female.

ing across millions of years. From those bones we know that, by 5 million years ago, they walked upright and that their brains were larger, but not much larger, than those of forest apes.

Why did these hominids do well in a seasonally harsh and dry savanna? To a gardener used to the demands of watering, it may seem strange that seasonal aridity could be conducive to any sort of abundance, but steamy tropical forests actually have a low biomass of mammals compared with African savannas. Savannas undergo harsh seasonal aridity but are among the earth's richest landscapes in terms of both numbers of mammals and total mammalian biomass. Thus, we surmise that the emergence of more savanna landscapes created new evolutionary opportunities for many mammals. The puzzle was how to exploit them.

To understand this better, let's return to the perspective of our earlier tropical forest adaptation. Food for large mammals is rather limited in a tropical forest. Leafy vegetation, for example, is out of reach for most mammals; moreover, it is highly defended against herbivory. That is to say, much plant tissue is too coarse or too toxic for large mammals (except for the few mammals who specialize on fruit). Tropical forest plants have abundant energy supplies—heat and water—but nutrients are limited. The precious nutrients in their tissues must be well protected; as a consequence, they strategically have strong biochemical or biomechanical defenses against mammalian herbivores. There is competition in the plant world too, of course, so tropical forest trees have evolved to compete for sunlight by growing or climbing taller than their neighbors. The expensive construction of these woody towers with large leaf surfaces also tends to use up soil nutrients. Decomposition on the forest floor is rapid, and yet plant growth is such that tropical forest soils are so scarce in nutrients that the soil surface under the great trees and vines is almost bare, and root systems beneath the soil are shallow.

Seasonal aridity is the principal factor that makes a savanna. Out there, plant growth is more limited by moisture than by nutrients. Trees compete more for water beneath the deep soil surface, root versus root. This results in that polka-dot scatter of trees that I mentioned earlier, where leaves have little need to compete for sunlight. Between this loose scatter of trees the shallowly rooted forbs and grasses can thrive. So the savanna system is a two-piston arrangement of trees and grasses/forbs, with very little competition between the two. Seasonal aridity favors more open and low-growing vegetation, like grasses and shrubs. Savanna vegetation laid an entirely different banquet table for large mammalian herbivores. It was more accessible, more nutritious, and because it contained fewer toxins and less lignin it was more palatable, more tasty.

Is the vegetation what lured those chimplike ancestors of ours out onto the savanna? Many kinds of fruit trees do better out in the open; likewise, there were ample opportunities for other supplements, like seeds, tubers, and nuts. Because the tooth enamel of these early australopithecines is thicker than that of chimps, we can assume that these colonists had a tough and abrasive diet. We can also legitimately imagine that they took advantage of animal protein, at least as much as chimps do today, and probably much more, because savannas have much more animal biomass and it is more visible and accessible. In some chimp populations today, meat makes up 5% of their diet, and among some individuals it is 10% (Stanford 2001). Australopithecines were slightly larger than chimps. In general, their diet was more plentiful, diverse, and perhaps more seasonally specialized than that of chimps, with more animal tissue.

Chimps spend around 60% of their time on the ground, but knuckle walking is not as efficient as bipedal walking (Foley 1987). Life on the savanna meant larger home ranges and longer daily travel, and perhaps greater use of hands to manipulate food. Even though bipedal, the australopithecines retained many body structures that relate to climbing and their forest ancestry, indicating some ties to food sources in trees and perhaps tree climbing as one means of escaping large terrestrial predators.

Throughout these evolutionary discussions recall that feeding competition within and between primate groups (as well as with carnivore species) led to long-term divergence not only in food choices but in all the anatomical, physiological, and behavioral characters in a species' life history (Isbell and Young 1996). In other words, built-in forces drove hominid evolutionary change as they continued to exploit the savanna.

The story gets a little more complicated here, because there was another, later group, the robust australopithecines, which were larger in body size, were thicker in build, had prognathous but otherwise flat faces, and had especially large molars with quite thick enamel. Their brains were only slightly larger than those of the earliest australopithecines. It has been proposed that this megadontic ("big-toothed") anatomy was an adaptation to even coarser fibrous vegetable food, perhaps a product not of the trees but of the open ground—more tubers and seeds. Isotopic analysis of their bones has suggested that they made use of significant animal resources, but as with the early australopithecines we can assume that their diets did not consist of more than 10–20% meat (Foley 2001). It is possible that some of this was scavenged from larger animals, but more likely it was opportunistically taken from common smaller animal species. Out on the savanna these hominids were undoubtedly tool users, lived in stable but complex social groups, and likely did some sort of hunting in addition to their eclectic plant gathering.

But something began to change in the late Pliocene, prior to 2 million years ago. Fossils occur that resemble later species of the genus *Homo* more than they do the australopithecines. They are intermediate in many ways and anatomically quite variable. The teeth of *Homo habilus,* a species that dates to roughly 2 million years ago, are smaller than those of the australopithecines, and yet other traits such as brain size are slightly larger but remain relatively australopithecine in character. So, for now, the earliest origins of *Homo* remain blurred. The early ecological role is also unclear. There is a possibility of stone tool use: some of the animal bones found in middens seem to show clear cut marks. At present, all these images of early *Homo* are subject to controversy, but the tantalizing fragments allow one to suspect that the beginning of a new adaptive radiation was occurring (see Foley 2001 for a review).

FLIGHT ACROSS THE SAVANNA AND BEYOND

Just prior to 2 million years ago, the beginning of the Pleistocene, Africa experienced a sharp change toward even stronger seasonal aridity. Not long after this crease line in climate change, the direction of change in *Homo* became clearer, with the emergence of *Homo ergaster/Homo erectus* (they may have been African and Eurasian versions of the same species). Their cranial capacity (over 1000 cubic centimeters) lets us estimate their brain size as nearing the smaller end of the range of living humans. The postcranial skeleton also was much more like that of living humans than like that of the australopithecines. This species dispersed rapidly, their artifacts and archaeological sites are rather common, and we have enough fragments of information to begin reconstructing something of their way of life. Compared to australopithecines they had a more sophisticated capacity for bipedal locomotion, smaller pelvic basin (reduced gut size), broader rib cage (greater lung capacity), much larger brain size, indicating complex cognition and an extended juvenile period (Bonner 1988),

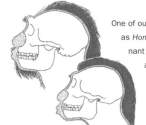

One of our distant relatives, the species referred to as *Homo erectus* and related forms, was a dominant force throughout the Old World for almost a million years. Male and female.

and larger body size (around 60 kilograms for males). Sexual dimorphism was still marked but was much less than among australopithecines. Growth chronology changed from that of chimps: slower maturation rates, an especially lengthened childhood, and a greater potential life expectancy, though none of these approach human patterns. The stone tools consist of thoughtfully flaked cores, known as Oldowan industries in Africa and as Acheulean ones in Eurasia. Most noteworthy is the presence of many large-mammal bones in their middens. They seem to have been hunters and meat eaters. Foley (1987, 2001) proposed that meat eating was an alternative to an increasingly more arid Pleistocene environment. What is the story behind this possibility?

THE WINGS OF A SOLUTION

As I said, forest trees compete for sunshine while grassland trees (and grasses) compete mostly for subsurface moisture (that is why acacia leaves can be so lacy thin). The great belowground biomass of roots in the savanna creates nutrient-rich soils at the same time that aboveground growth produces green lawns.

The elaborate storage system of the roots means that aboveground leafy tissue can be abandoned by the plants at the start of each dry season. This is why grasses do not waste expensive structures and chemicals to heavily defend their aboveground annual growth from fire or grazing. In short, this disposable sward is unlike forest plant growth and constitutes a unique ecological opportunity for herbivores. But all this is relative: the savanna vegeta-

Every species has a dietary specialization to which it is adapted. For example, the large grinding platform of horse teeth, like the teeth of many grazers, acts almost like a metate, a grain and seed grinder, allowing the animal to grind large quantities of grass, including the relatively poor quality dried grasses during winter. For horses, this adaptation requires not only a large tooth surface but also enormous, powerful jaw muscles and large surfaces on the mandible for insertion of these muscles. This gives the horse mandible its characteristic massive appearance. **A**, Fragment of carved horse skull from Mas d'Azil, Fr. **B**, Modern horse skull and metate.

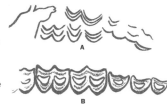

A, These wavy lines to the right of an ungulate portrayed at Ardales, Sp., may be patterns remembered from the complex enamel of a grazer's molar crowns. The lunate ridges reduce grass stems to fine, digestible particles and grind small, hard seeds. **B**, My drawing of bison cheek teeth, looking down from above.

tion is not totally undefended. From what we can reconstruct, grasses on the expanding African Pleistocene savannas were coarse, the trees and scrubby bushes were thorn studded and hard barked, and the forbs were ephemeral and their roots were deeply buried. However, it is clear from the fossil record that groups of herbivorous mammals did manage to prosper. Again we ask, how?

The first savanna specialists probably came from groups that already used forest clearings. Over time their game trails began to lace ever deeper across that open panorama. Three evolutionary radiations of large herbivorous mammals managed to claim part of the sweepstakes prize of foraging in the open. These were the proboscideans (the elephant group), the artiodactyls (antelope, bovines, pigs, deer, etc.), and the perissodactyls (mainly equids and rhinos). Members of these three groups would

become the dominant large mammals of Pleistocene Africa, Eurasia, and the Americas.

Ancestors of horses, bison, and mammoths independently solved the evolutionary puzzle of how to thrive on this new vegetative abundance. These herbivores circumvented their own enzymatic deficiencies by hosting decomposer microorganisms that were able to digest fibrous plant tissue. This allowed the large-mammal hosts to subsequently digest both the microorganisms and their byproducts. The incubation occurred in large composting chambers in the gut, which burbled and fizzed like brewery vats. They compensated for the low nutrition of dry grasses by consuming and composting massive quantities of vegetable tissue, which in turn required a large digestive tract, and hence a large body. The complex digestive physiology required to convert a coarse bit of gray shrub into a healthy eland is a little like trying to make cheese from chalk, the constituent plant and animal parts are so different.

Back to hominids. *Homo erectus* sites are found across Africa and in parts of Eurasia. We do know from the robustness of the bones that they were thickly muscled, which was undoubtedly associated with hard and rough activity. Each year brings more sites, and anthropologists continue to learn more about them. This evolutionary course is interesting, but we are still faced with the question of what adaptations underwrote the lifeway of these Pleistocene *Homo?* Was this the beginning of a human-like niche or something very different?

As more sites are found and we have more bone litter and more stone tools to analyze, it is becoming clear that these primitive *Homo* were well along in solving the puzzle of how to take advantage of many savanna possibilities in the sun-lit open, and that they did this, not as the large herbivores had, by eating the fiber-digesting microorganisms, but by eating the herbivores, who had digested the gut flora that had digested the cellulose of the plants adapted to living in the open. Once the evolution of this hominid sequence had gotten as far as the eating of large mammals, the dietary process of converting large mammals into us was comparatively simple and direct; it is "apples to apples" or, in this case, "meat to meat," because we are large mammals too.

Protein would have been the scarcest dietary component in the forest habitats, and I suspect it was the greater amounts of both plant and animal protein that first lured the australopithecines into the savanna. The prelude to *Homo* hunting may have started early (Bunn 1999), but we just don't know when large-mammal hunting commenced, although the evidence is solid that it intensified throughout the Pleistocene (Carbonell Roura 1999). The kinds of stone tools and their wear patterns, butchered bones in the middens, isotope chemistry, and patterns of molar wear show an increasing specialization toward meat (Keeley and Toth 1981; Foley 2001). Plants may have continued to supply a large proportion of dietary calories in Africa, but because protein and other nutrients are crucial to growth, to embryonic and childhood development, and to healthy immune systems and parasite resistance, meat was a bonanza. But collecting this mammalian bounty was not easy.

HOMINID WEAPONS: A REQUISITE ACCESS TO THE SAVANNA

I must digress for a moment and say that the first hominids may not have been hunters, but they were likely armed. Forest apes could not have adapted to life in the open without an effective defense. In the forests their

Person with spear, Les Combarelles, Fr. My reconstruction at right.

Box: Person facing bovine from Gabillou, Fr. Note line of dots coming from nose—more on those later in this chapter. My reconstruction at right.

safety lay in their sociality and their use of trees as refuges. Out on the savanna a total reliance on those strategies may not always have worked. Unlike the forests, the savannas of Africa harbored one of the earth's most complex communities of large mammalian carnivores (Walker 1984). No amount of shouting and limb shaking, baring small canines, or even rock throwing would have driven off a hungry large carnivore once it had learned that it could kill hominids with impunity. What level of defense did these hominids have? We can begin with a comparison: an almost lethal zebra kick or a thrust from the horn of a sable antelope or gemsbok is not enough to exempt these much more powerful species from predation. These antelope must resort to fleetness—but hominids were not fleet. Only adult elephants, hippos, and rhinos can stand and confront large predators. They do so by using their formidable mass—hominids had no such mass. These comparisons let us see that hominids had to have some defensive weapon at least as effective as the defensive advantage of pachyderms.

In fact, we can surmise that hominids had a weapon effective enough to virtually guarantee the death of most attacking predators, because, unlike zebra or antelope, hominids could simply not afford to be exposed to many lethal risks. Even the earliest hominids had a very conservative life history, and like elephants, they needed to live for thirty years simply to have the fifteen to twenty years necessary to raise young to maturity. This means that a hominid population could not have lost a significant fraction annually to predation. Evolution provided such little

Most of the common large mammals in Africa have sharp, projecting weapons: teeth, horns, fangs, or tusks. These extensions of the body are innately recognized as dangerous by every other mammal, just the way pikes or spears would have been recognized as formidable weapons by carnivore and herbivore alike.

Hunting large herbivores is not easy. Even in almost modern times many were looked upon with a great deal of respect. This later prehistoric elephant hunt with bows and spears is Bushman work from Zastron, R.S.A.

fangs that hominids had to construct their defensive weapons.

We can narrow down the list of such possible weapons. For example, thrown rocks cannot guarantee death from impact, so they can be eliminated. Ideally, a hominid weapon would be something a predator could easily interpret as a significant threat, so that every predator did not have to personally experience the weapon in attack to grasp its significance. An acacia thorn branch or a long sharpened pole qualifies in this regard. Predators readily see its ability to inflict harm as a new extension in a continuum of defensive long horns, antlers, tusks, fangs, and kicking legs of their age-old prey. Any lion could have understood the formidable nature of a hominid group bristling with sharp poles. Even Hannibal's elephants bolted when faced with lethal rows of Roman pikes.

Millions of years after our ancestors first explored the savanna with their sharp poles, late Paleolithic peoples still carried something similar as their principal weapon. A hand-held thrusting spear or pike is exceptionally effective, and many cultures still kept it in their armory long after thrown spears, atlatls, and even bows had been invented. Of course, once hominids had an effective defensive weapon, it was ready for offensive, as well as defensive, use. The adaptive leap of later hominids toward large-mammal hunting was a critical turn in the revolutionary track of our kind, and they already had inherited the beginnings of the right kind of weapon. But successful hunting of large mammals with a primitive pike or spear as the main killing weapon was not simple. In fact, it was close to impossible.

DOING THE IMPOSSIBLE—OR ALMOST IMPOSSIBLE

How did distinctly non-Olympian hominids circumvent the superior mass, powerful muscles, and dangerous defenses of the large herbivores? Herbivore species had sharp horns, antlers, or tusks, and many made use of powerful kicks, thick hides, speed, and strength, as well as fantastic olfaction, eyesight, and hearing. Most herbivores had large and complex brains to learn the tactics of new predators and outsmart old ones. That is why so few evolutionary lines of predators were ever successful in solving this puzzle. We can see that the few successful large-mammal land predators (cats, hyenas, and canids—and one strange line of primates) used fantastically honed abilities, among which was cooperative hunting. Though these carnivore species are large-mammal specialists, none are purists when it comes to an easy meal.

EVOLUTIONARY SPECIALIZATION AND THE CRITICAL ROLE OF SUPPLEMENTS

Archaeological evidence makes it clear that our distant ancestors managed to kill fleet and strong herbivores, as well

The Paleolithic economy was diverse, but the land did not brim with milk and honey. When fat times came, there were salmon and venison. Salmon and red deer stags were engraved in the round on a small bone, from Lortet, Fr. Below is an unrolled reconstruction (with hypothetical image in stippled area).

Red deer and what looks like a whale or fish. Arucou, Fr.

A Pleistocene fish story?
"I looked out across the riffles
and there was the largest salmon I had ever seen . . ." Arucou, Fr.

as ward off imposing predators. Tools were critical, but those folks needed much more. Remember for a moment an important principle in evolutionary ecology, that particular food resources underlie most ecological specializations. Pit vipers, for example, have infrared sensors which enable them to detect warm mice in the black of night. Mole rats thrive in underground communities solely sustained by roots. The acrobatic grace of swallows and swifts arises from and is sustained by the hum of airborne insects; mosquitoes are sustained in turn by the ability to tap into shallow vascular circulation. Can we speak of humans in terms of such an adaptive specialization? I think so. This is not to say that a specialist may not often make use of other resources. Diverse and episodic windfalls often remain very important: grazing specialists like horses often eat spring willow leaves and fallen fruit, and reindeer sometimes eat lemmings in summer. Still, we see how each species' adaptations revolve around its respective core specialty food. Large predators may hunt from a wonderful bounty of large herbivores, but this bounty is both demanding and unpredictable.

The archaeological record supports the idea that early humans were hunting specialists and took advantage of supplementary foods. Many Paleolithic sites, for example, contain skeletal elements of fish, small mammals, birds, and invertebrates in addition to abundant remains of large mammals. Ethnographic studies of Holocene hunting-dependent societies show a similar pattern. In historic times reindeer- and whale-hunting specialists are known to have utilized a variety of other resources (e.g., fish, sum-

mer greens, tubers, bird eggs, and small game). Nevertheless, opportunistic use of other potential food sources does not compromise their ecological and cultural focus as large-mammal-hunting specialists. Indeed, the cultural and intellectual versatility associated with large-mammal hunting apparently assists in exploring the potential of other, usually supplemental, foods.

The role of supplements seems to have been "part of the bargain" of our human specialization as large-mammal hunters, and it highlights the fact that putting together a lifeway that was able to successfully specialize in hunting large mammals was very difficult. Supplements are not always, or only, animal tissue. We have maintained a taste for plant carbohydrates and the requisite anatomy and physiology to process them (Hladik et al. 1993). But the Paleolithic theme seems to have been that one eats all the fruit and tubers one has to and all the meat one can get.

The Key to the Puzzle

If this scenario is correct, then our early hominid ancestors did not compete as herbivores among these burgeoning savanna faunas; rather, they transformed this increasingly diverse and dense herbivore community into their own food. And they did so via increased cleverness rather than by physical power. A creative consciousness was the key. Other predators relied more on power—using dangerous techniques of plunging one's face in among the powerful horns and hooves in a bite 'em, drag 'em down, and gobble 'em up fashion. Lions broke large-herbivore defenses by developing stealth, patience, rapid acceleration, power, and group attack. Wolves, hunting dogs, and spotted hyenas also used massed strength but developed an uncanny ability to recognize, from the slightest hints, the halt and lame in a mixed and moving herd and then exploit that individual's weakness in a grueling chase of endurance.

The development of sociality expanded the hunting success of all the social predators and allowed them to defend their kills against more solitary (sabertooths and brown hyenas) or small predator species (jackals, hunting dogs, etc.). Even so, most carnivores hunt mainly at night, when they can avoid overheating and when the prey's vision is at a disadvantage. Carnivores work every edge, challenged as they are by the acute senses and physical abilities of their prey species.

The strongest defense of large herbivores was not simply speed but their quick and profound acumen. Challenging herbivore intelligence, as much as herbivore physical superiority, shaped the evolution of our ancestors. It was hunting of such intelligent and capable prey that created such humans. Our complex and highly social intelligence was honed by this hunting specialization from its African origins at least 2 millions years ago in the early Paleolithic through to the late Paleolithic, when we engage its drama in fossil art. Those thousands of images from the late Paleolithic, and the manner in which they were portrayed, serve as dramatic posters for that long lineage of human ecology and evolution.

NEOCORTEX EXPANSION: A WIDE-ANGLE VIEW OF OBJECTIVE REALITY

Human-style hunting required a close correspondence between the events going on outside one's person and one's perception and modeling of that reality. What is real?

Bear from Lourdes, Fr., with a salmon in its mouth. The arrow points to the small posterior fin unique to salmonids. In general, bears are not fish-eating specialists, but during the right conditions they hunt fish, especially salmon with roe, as a supplement.

Was it the long period of education required for the complex modes of all the endeavors associated with hunting that selected for extended childhoods, enlarged brains, cognitive skills, flexible opportunism, complex interdependent social behavior, and many other features associated with our human nature? Rock engraving from La Marche, Fr.

Some species of female mosquitoes searching for warm blood are attracted to anything that emits butyric acid molecules and is 39°C. It is a simple and cheap adaptive device that works. But a warm, smelly mammal is more than those two elements. Through complex movements and planning, a wolf may try to spook a bedded deer toward a waiting member of its pack—and then demand part of the meat for this cooperative effort. For such complex relationships, neural processes evolved that afford a more differentiated approximation of surroundings. The "cinema" a mammal sees, smells, and hears is an immeasurably richer rendition of its environment than anything a mosquito is capable of. And these perceptions have to be inserted into a format that can be manipulated with an inner logic that operates similarly to the complex interactions going on outside. Along with this was the great human innovation of communicating complex thoughts in addition to simple emotions. All these—the recording of sensory information, its manipulation, and its communication—require a tremendous neural complexity.

Comparisons of brain sizes (Allman 1999) show that disproportionately large brains are characteristic of mammals, like primates, that rely on intricate social relationships (Dunbar 1998) and among species with opportunistic hunting strategies like those of carnivores (Ewer 1973). Brain size is largest where the two are combined, as in species that hunt large mammals opportunistically using considerable social cooperation and interdependence. These include humans, wolves, bottled-nosed dolphins, and killer whales; all of which have exceptionally large brains. In fact, the neocortex of a killer whale has much more complex folds (gyri-sulci) than that of a human. Killer whales are very opportunistic hunters that take an array of large prey using sophisticated cooperative efforts. These whales also depend greatly on play for their socio-physical education and practice. In a later chapter we will examine the links between our large neocortex and art making. The evidence is clear: complex social cooperation in the pursuit of complex prey species places high demands on attention to information gathering, intelligent analysis of that information, and its creative uses. Among primates, brain size is correlated with time spent as a juvenile (Bonner 1988), which is in turn related to exploration, learning, and play—themes that emerge again and again in the study of this old art.

Exploiting the full scope of this demanding niche required a reorganization of hominid life history, which included extending gestation, lengthening the childhood-juvenile period (Bogin 1999), postponing sexual and social maturity, and lengthening the potential life span. Anatomically, it required an increase in body weight at birth and an increase in brain size both at birth and in adulthood. We can see all these elements by comparing humans with other apes. The resultant decrease in reproductive potential (increase in time to reproductive maturity) because of these changes was partially compensated for by shortening the time from birth to weaning, from the ape's four to five years to our three. Dual parenting also facilitates a shortened potential birth interval, as the father can not only share in child care and education but help provide digestible, nutrient-concentrated meat. Meat, probably pre-chewed by the mother, may have al-

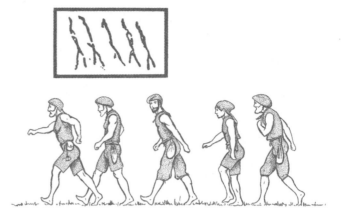

Women are attracted to risk-taking males, and their attraction ultimately forms the selective pressure that is responsible for maintaining a dimension of men's violent behavior. Male stick figures at La Vache, Fr. My enhancement below.

lowed earlier weaning in humans because meat is more nutritionally equivalent to milk than is the fruit of ape diets. Nevertheless, the very long human childhood meant that more than one offspring at a time needed care and high-quality food, not simply fruit, leaves, or cucumber sandwiches. The existence of a "family" of both parents and several young helped meet these new demands and had many advantages, including a longer and more intense period of potential learning.

SOCIAL HUNTERS: THE EVOLUTIONARY STAKE

Ethnographic work with northern hunting cultures (e.g., Rasmussen 1930; Carpenter 1973) makes it clear that hunting is not simply something men do. Paleolithic men, women, and children were probably all hunters of some kind and degree. Ethnographic parallels show that such large-mammal-hunting skills as gear manufacture, tanning, trapping, animal driving, and meat preparation have figured significantly in women's pride, power, and stature. Aspects of hunting likely influenced courtship appeal and choice of mate for both men and women. Hunting supplied the staples of life, including delicious and nutritious food, and was crucial for reproduction and happiness. None of this is evolutionarily neutral.

Traditional reconstructions of Paleolithic diets simply place large-mammal hunting on a list of dietary possibilities that include specializing on scavenging, digging tubers, picking fruit, harvesting grass seeds, and so forth. Today, oversaturated with plenty, readers may view meat and fat as neutral or low-priority items, well down the menu from a Caesar salad with dry Chablis. But envisioning month after month of a limited and unpredictable subsistence diet, combined with hard labor, long hikes with heavy loads, exposure to cold and wind, and periods of lactation and child dependence, brings the nutritional value of meat, viscera, and fat into clear focus.

I recall an anthropology lecturer talking about how, when hungry, a Paleolithic hunter could just go out and select the best-quality animal for dinner, as one might simply pick the ripest tomato, as though Paleolithic hunting was a matter of aiming a high-powered rifle at the choicest cow in the pasture. There was a complete failure to realize the astonishing difficulties of big-game hunting in the Paleolithic. Use of reconstructed Paleolithic weapons and experience with wilderness hunting reveal that those challenges were just short of impossible.

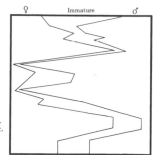

A FEW DIFFERENT PHASES OF HUNTING:
- Hunting play-education
- Search of game areas
- Preparation
- Organization of equipment
- Special equipt. construction
- Weapon manufacture
- Travel
- Spike camp set up
- Scouting search
- Stalk-tracking-killing
- Butchering
- Transport
- Food preservation and prep.
- Cooking and cooking equipt.
- Skin and sinew treatment etc.
- Social and religious rituals
- Ceremonies of distribution,
- Luck, sharing, thanksgiving

Large-mammal hunting involves diverse activities and skills. Here is my rough guess at the relative percentages of male-female Paleolithic participation in hunting (based on historical analogs and indirect evidence discussed in text). Everybody is involved to varying degrees with the different elements of hunting.

As shown in Paleolithic art, as well as by ethnographic data, primarily men engaged in the physically violent part of hunting. As I said in the last chapter, relative success or failure at hunting and killing large mammals must have hugely determined a man's sense of pride or disgrace, social stature, quality of friendships and connections, currency of courtship, access to women, success at extramarital affairs, prospects of a second wife, and ultimately the number of well-cared-for children—the guts and glands of male evolutionary fitness. In those days, there were no roles for corporate executives, salesmen, chimney sweeps, waiters, lieutenants, or grocery store managers. Small bands could afford scant specialization, and though individuals undoubtedly excelled at different skills, they were all members of the one and only union hall.

Hunting large mammals with simple weapons may well have exceeded the thrills of team sports, bungee jumping, or skydiving. It was the bullring without the cape . . . or ring. We have good evidence of these risks from work with native northern peoples (e.g., Laughlin 1968). The violent end of hunting large mammals likely played out in every boy's dreams; it determined the rhythms of a man's days and years, was a persistent preoccupation, and was the ticket to love, a sense of beauty, health, security and risk, and maybe death. Large mammals were more than symbols, shamanic forms, or stylized territorial markers. Paleolithic large mammals were the big game of life. Little wonder they are the core of preserved Paleolithic art.

THE RISE OF A HUMAN-LIKE ANIMAL

Sometime around 500,000 years ago (the exact dates are in a state of controversial flux at this time) hominids appeared that were close to being like ourselves in many ways, but they were clearly not us. Some major evolutionary changes had evidently taken place that are not clear in the archaeological record and may not even have been preservable. Again nomenclature is still fluid here, but definitely we can call those in Europe (and western Asia) after around 300,000 years ago Neanderthals. There is little in the archaeological sites that would suggest that

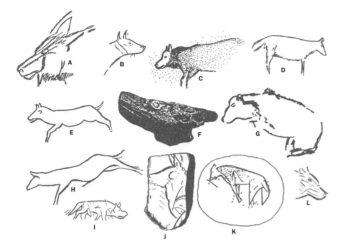

As I said in the first chapter, at least two species of hominids dominated the latter Pleistocene: Neanderthals and our own line. The archaeological evidence shows that both lines were heavily involved in hunting. Hair pattern in these early hominids is conjectural.

Wolves are social hunters of large mammals; they hunt cooperatively in family groups. It is only through this combined effort that they are able to pull down herbivores much larger than themselves. Wolves are not common in Paleolithic art, but like so many Pleistocene mammals they do occur. **A**, Les Combarelles, Fr. **B**, Gabillou, Fr. **C**, Font de Gaume, Fr. **D**, Gönnersdorf, Ger. **E**, Pileta, Sp. **F**, Laugerie-Basse, Fr. **G**, Trois Frères, Fr. **H**, Gourdan, Fr. **I**, Les Eyzies, Fr. **J**, Lortet, Fr. **K**, Polesini, It. **L**, Fontalès, Fr.

Neanderthals exploited large mammals in ways fundamentally different from those of later humans in the later Paleolithic, although their tools were different, their densities were low, and their geographic distribution was more restricted. The deep beds of butchered bones that make up their middens are evidence that Neanderthals were very effective hunters who brought their meat back to base camps, where they roasted it and perhaps shared it with others (Speth and Tchernov 2001). What was this preoccupation with hunting all about?

Animals That Kill as a Lifeway

Does a hunting lifeway that revolves around killing, preparing, and eating large mammals affect a people's perspective on life? Because Paleolithic art is such a clear expression of these hunters' regard for other large mammals with which they shared life, I want to reflect on their state of mind, from a modern perspective, by taking a short philosophic look at this matter of our own food. Nowadays, we generally find what we eat in supermarket aisles,

and procuring food is often largely a monetary experience. Only rarely do we wonder at the complex history of this individual fish, pear, or egg, as we heft our self-contained groceries home.

Life is never so self-contained, self-sufficient—it is an essential characteristic of living things to interact with their environment, and this is brought home with each breath. The "great system of lung and leaf," as the poet Nemerov expresses it, is one aspect of that interaction. The reciprocity of plant and animal respiration is something we have no hesitation in affirming—inhaling the breath of plants and they ours—even if we have not thought about it since first tracing out the flow of CO_2–O_2–CO_2–O_2 in elementary biology class. Plants use the carbon from our breath to grow, and that carbon ultimately becomes its tissue, our food, or the food of the animals that become our food—exchanging the C, getting it back—for a time. Interchange is not always so tidy though, and when we move to observe exchanges in fin and fur, feather and flesh, what we see can appear as a Boschian horror. As one of my mammalogy students said, in a period of deadly silence after a vivid classroom video featuring lions and hyenas competing for food in Botswana, "Why can't we all just get along?"

This not getting along began billions of years ago. It is easy to forget that our lives are sustained by the lives of others—by the deaths of others. We are inhabited, cohabited, with myriad floras and faunas—how many billions of individual organisms exist on our skin? We kill these co-

Wolverines are solitary hunters with large home ranges. They occasionally take large mammals, but it is not their specialty. A few images of wolverines occur in Paleolithic art: **A**, La Madeleine, Fr. **B**, Les Eyzies, Fr. **C**, La Marche, Fr. **D**, Enlène, Fr. **E**, Andernach, Ger. **F**, Lortet, Fr. **G**, Vielfras, Fr. **H**, Saulges, Fr.

Paleolithic butchering scene on a pendant (broken hole was on the far left) engraved on a thin piece of long bone, Raymonden, Fr. My reconstruction below. Note ribs and lower legs lying to the left. The bison has been "boned out" (by about seven people), leaving behind the heavy bones and head, taking mainly fat, viscera, and muscle. This is how I and many other hunters still operate in the Alaskan wilderness. When a kill is made near camp, one brings much of the carcass back, but a kill many kilometers away, involving lots of packing, means that time spent processing on-site pays off in lightening the load. For a hunter this is not a repugnant scene but a happy and an aesthetically appealing one.

inhabitants in untold numbers with the pleasure of every shower, but we are never truly pure.

As we drive through bucolic countryside we know that advertently and inadvertently death abounds. These pastoral fields are full of expropriation and extirpation: thousands of small mammals are plowed under with every tilling; concealed chicks are exposed by the mower bar; insects, arachnids, shrews, rodents, blights, nematodes, rusts, and weeds are killed by the millions to grow our bread. Agriculture is all about tilting organic processes to human needs, but the elemental organic interchange, the feeding of life on life, is clear in any sojourn in wild places as well. Newborn carabid beetles help feed newborn jays, who in turn give their lives to newborn martens and newborn eagles and are scavenged by newborn vultures and then by newborn carabids. Life feeds on life. Inescapably.

Between this realization and the next time hunger strikes, we might consider our situation as generation after generation has done. What response to all this feeding and killing is most fathomable? What response to this demand and gift of life? To resolve not to eat? Or to eat without pleasure? To deny pleasure just because there can be no utopia, where one is free to live without taking life, is to utterly mistake what we are offered. Despite the obfuscation of vacuum-wrapped groceries, we are no less subject to these interconnections than Paleolithic peoples. Let me review the deep roots of that story for you; otherwise, our picture of Paleolithic art will be out of focus.

PRECAMBRIAN HUNTING

From the first amino acid soup, the new phenomenon of life blossomed until the free-for-the-taking goodies were used up and the soup became water thin. Physical processes eventually return dead cells to constituent elements, but long ago some cells apparently short-circuited the physical processes of breakdown and surrounded dead cell bodies and actively disassembled and remade them into their own kind. Daughters of those single-celled organisms that first abandoned sunlight continue to thrive today by finding and decomposing the dead, and we are all their food tomorrow.

Next, perhaps, came the first animal parasites. These innovative cells did not wait for death as decomposers do but slipped through living cell membranes, injecting their life into a cell and going along for a free ride. Most of the DNA in our chromosomes and all of our important mitochondrial DNA, as well as plant chloroplasts, seem to be

Why was the Raymonden butchery scene portrayed in the art? We can see that the aesthetic of successful hunting is shared by later hunting cultures. Such butchering scenes are not gory imagery of gross violence but a harvest of excitement. **A**, Eskimo ivory pipestem, St. Lawrence Island, Alaska. **B**, Makumbe Cave, Zimbabwe. **C**, Tamrit, North Africa.

Weasels or ermine had to be common carnivores around the landscape where Paleolithic peoples lived, though they are rare in the art. Small mustelids are innate hunters and killers. Within hours after the young open their eyes in the nest, they are able to kill mice with an innately directed neck-bite. **A**, Ojo Guareña, Sp. **B**, Niaux, Fr. **C**, Gabillou, Fr.

descendants of such early parasites. Today we live in a world of many kinds of parasites; inhaled at every breath, they coat our skins and line our guts. In fact, they may even be a prime reason we have sex, mixing genes to become a moving target, to keep a genetic jump ahead of parasites' mutations toward ever greater virility in circumventing our defenses (see Ridley 1993 for a review). Then a new kind of cell arose.

This was a time when the first "hunters" came into being, somewhere around 3.5 billion years ago. These new single cells neither fed on the chemical soup, absorbed their energy from the sun, took the parasites' free ride, nor waited to decompose the dead. Instead, they surrounded the living cell, disabled it, killed it, digested it. Billions of years later, this way of life has been enormously elaborated. We are descendants of that branch, as are zebras, koalas, perch, and spiders. In fact, virtually all animals are, though a few have developed a taste for well-aged meat. We animals, herbivore as well as carnivore, take the fresh tissues of other lives to sustain our own. An herbivorous animal is no less a killer and is no more or less exempt from this feeding interchange just because the tissues it eats drip sap. Not all plants just passively use the sun—some plants are semicarnivorous. There is also some plant-plant predation. Seeing a wild Australian strangling fig silently squeezing the life out of a giant eucalyptus is a little like watching a python digesting an antelope in superslow motion. Most plants, of course, continued to turn to the sun. Yet plants, decomposers, and parasites are still our close relatives in cytoplasm and chromosomes; they and we appear as the present expressions of a continu-

ing life handed on from what appears to have been that single evolutionary source. We are all relatives, inextricably awash and feeding, one way or another, in the stream of life.

A PALEOLITHIC OVERVIEW OF DEATH AND LIFE?

Kindness toward animals demands a true sense of kinship. To be kindred does not mean we should treat animals as our babies. It means instead a sense of many connections and transformations—us into them, them into us, and them into each other from the beginning of time. To be kindred is to share consciously in the stream of life. P. Shepard, *Traces of an Omnivore*

Contemporary life has made it difficult to see our part in this stream. Our distance from the Paleolithic artists' relation to large mammals is doubled. First, in addition to our loss of the wilderness experience of taking our food, we are commercially far removed from our domestic sources. Most of us live without everyday farm experience. Second, we know other animals primarily as household pets. Pets are our social intimates, their lives almost as precious as those of family members. This is the origin, I suspect, of something in us today that does not want to kill other animals, especially those more similar to us. Our marvelous human empathetic ability evolved in concert with deep biological inhibitions against hurting fellow humans, and it is readily extended to domestic intimates. Pets bring much delight. Living with animal-others, we get to enjoy their beauty and are beguiled into a more careful observation of them as well as enjoying their company. The catch comes if we cannot step beyond this one mode of rela-

Otter and fish, Laugerie-Basse, Fr.

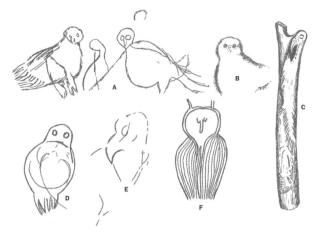

Raptors, beautiful animals to watch, play a role in the art of many societies and even show up in Paleolithic art. Eskimo in Alaska traditionally hunt owls as a fine delicacy, and the bones of many predatory birds are found in Paleolithic sites. **A** and **D**, Trois Frères, Fr. **B**, Le Portel, Fr. **C**, Chancelade, Fr. **E**, Fornois-Haut, Fr. **F**, Chauvet, Fr.

tion—when, for example, one can imagine other animals only as dependent and socially intimate. This is a particular hazard if we also downplay the contents of those grocery bags, or otherwise forget the lives it takes to feed us and our pets.

With wild animals, too, we share a position in that long history of the web of life and death. Some religions looking for ultimate meaning tend to underwrite the social lie that would set us far apart from other creation—"humans and animals." This is unfortunate, in that it discounts the utterly fierce costs of our lives and at the same time obscures the evolutionary-ecological dimension of who and what we are.

Not only does this social lie hide our dependence on the lives and deaths of others, but it disguises our mortality and that of those near us, robbing us of the opportunities to realize our immersion in the pattern of life and death. Smoked duck at the Chinese restaurant can become a menu item losing all reference to the individual duck it once was, particularly if it was an industrial farm product, not the two-year-old wild drake pintail shot at dawn on Minto flats. Illusions often obscure biological fundamentals, and nowadays few of us participate in domestic food production and even fewer in nondomestic hunting and gathering. So such participation tends to be viewed as anachronistic crudity or romanticized as the stuff of native people's privileged innocence.

Meanwhile, the social lie reigns happily while we are diverted from the key issues by debates about eating meat versus organic vegetables. Silvery fish in the creel almost keep the secret; the magnificent magenta moose quarters hanging in the beams of the garage as I write these lines do not. Like you, I get most of my food from grocery shelves, but I sometimes participate more directly in the life and death of wild large mammals, enough that it colors the way I think and feel about the costs of my existence and how I honor the lives these animals led and the nondomesticated landscape that allowed me to be a part of this flow of life. A very specific moose graces our table and tonight's table is part of that continuing gift. It is not a casual toast that we make to his life and death.

Paleolithic art is a testimony to the fact that our Pleistocene ancestors were neither cruel brutes nor noble savages. People of their times, individuals like ourselves, they did mainly what evolution had them do best. They must have found goodness, beauty, and happiness in that lifeway, along with excitement, difficulty, and danger—differing only in degree to what we feel today, for we are essentially the same creature, however different the context of our lives. But in that old life, daily experience would have repeatedly grounded issues about ethics and other animals. Along with the jubilance as they approached their reindeer, so weakened from the spear wound that it could not stand, fearfully widening the whites of its eyes toward their approach, some of them must have been poignantly touched.

Jubilation and poignant awareness of death can occur together, and we need to rekindle these emotions when

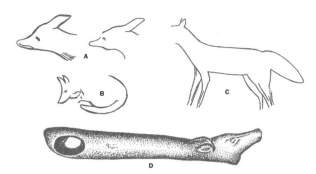

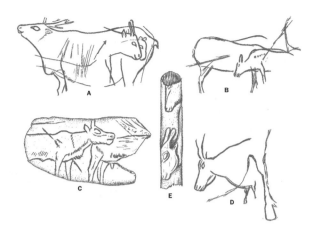

Foxes are mouse specialists but quite eclectic in their breadth of dietary supplements. Unlike wolves, foxes are solitary hunters. They are even rarer in Paleolithic art, despite their abundant bones in some archaeological sites (like Gönnersdorf). Foxes were probably taken for their soft and warm fur. Today arctic foxes occur in northern Scandinavia, but Europe in the late Pleistocene was much colder than today and the distribution of arctic foxes extended south to Spain. **A**, La Marche, Fr. **B**, Lourdes, Fr. **C**, Santimamiñe, Sp. **D**, Arudy, Fr.

Young animals are not common in Paleolithic art, but although an adult bull provides more meat, yearlings are the most tender eating and are easier to approach and kill. Several of these first-year, spiked-antlered reindeer are shown hit with spears. **A**, Montgaudier, Fr. **B**, Bigourdane, Fr. **C**, La Madeleine, Fr. **D**, Altamira, Sp. **E**, Laugerie-Basse, Fr.

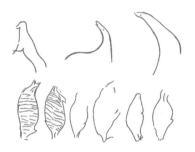

Seals from Nerja, Sp.

we think about our human past. Such a long-running play, such a long success, means the Paleolithic hunting lifeway had to be deep fun. Selective processes operate at many levels and the pleasure principle in evolution is quite real. Evolution has provided all animal hunters with that elixir to supplement the incentive of hunger for acquiring food. Cats do not kill mice just for a tasty morsel; they do it with exhilarating pleasure, and that pleasure is part of the definition of a feline; pleasure is part of their excellence as predators. If we miss this, if we set aside pleasure, disregard it as mere frivolity, call it an epiphenomenon, we'll overlook these evolutionary forces and will be unable to fully understand the hunters' art portrayed on cave walls so long ago, life and death by the light of a small yellow flame.

HUNTING IS MORE THAN A STRATEGY OF FOOD PROCUREMENT

I looked at him, big, long-legged, a smooth gray with the white stripes and the great, curling, sweeping horns, brown as nut meats, and ivory pointed, at the big ears and the lovely heavy-maned neck, the white chevron between his eyes and the white of his muzzle and I stooped over to touch him and to try to believe it. He was lying on his side where the bullet had gone in and there was not a mark on him and he smelled sweet and lovely like the breath of cattle and the odor of thyme after rain.　　　Hemingway, *Green Hills of Africa*

I remember participating in a zooarchaeology conference in London years ago in which a young Japanese researcher showed slides of an enormous archaeological mound of seashells and had calculated how many kilograms of protein dry weight had been obtained. When it came time for questions, someone in the audience stood up and commented that it was roughly equivalent to two adult red deer. One reason large mammals were so important in our past was that each one provided so much food.

Hawkes (1991) has argued that women in many subsistence groups provide more protein than men do—so on the basis of dietary demands, large-mammal hunting was superfluous. She proposed that because a hunter's large-mammal kills are shared, they have insufficient dietary force to underlie hunting as a potent male preoccupation, and she concluded that large-mammal hunting was a

Hunters are more successful when they have an innate thrill of hunting. The clear pleasure all carnivores take in hunting is an example of that predisposition. Although it is strange to think of lions chasing reindeer across the slopes of Montmartre and Denali, that was the norm for most of the last half a million years; the present is the exception.

Bone engraving of what could well be a Pleistocene hunting party of nine individuals walking along carrying their spears among scattered trees(?). A large bison is engraved in the foreground. Les Eyzies, Fr.

symbolic vehicle to exhibit strength, skill, and hence status—a form of showing off. A lot of this does ring true, as indeed successful hunting clearly has implications for status. But in most historic economies based on large-mammal hunting (bison, whales, walrus, caribou, etc.), women did not bring home the most protein. Certainly that must have been true for groups in the late Pleistocene of Europe, because gathering opportunities would have been quite limited much of the year. Many other demands of the large-mammal-hunting lifeway would have taken precedence (e.g., complex clothing making and maintenance, skin tanning). Few cultural analogs available to field anthropologists are representative of Eurasian (Palearctic) Pleistocene scales of large-mammal dependency, especially those in low latitudes.

Limiting hunting to symbols of social stature discounts its long history of providing nutrient bounty. I certainly agree that hunting is more than foraging; it has a transcendent excitement that goes beyond procurement. Hawkes's observations do appreciate the broader social reputation of hunting excellence. But instead of viewing men's preoccupation with storytelling about past hunts as just status displays in disguise, we should recognize that such storytelling also allows one to relive those experiences of exquisite pleasure and excitement, which burned the events so indelibly into the brain. Proximately, the search-and-kill parts of hunting are not driven by rational process alone.

Emotions are evolution's shortcut prompters that guide complex activities in general directions. Nutritional factors, status, and social symbolism were likely all involved in the selection for large-mammal-hunting behavior, but—like sex—most hunting is done for the love of it; it is not just a trip for groceries. Recall the quotation from Ortega y Gasset at the beginning of this chapter. Our hunting of large mammals takes on a special aspect because we are another large mammal. We are akin to them in multiple ways not true of a field of corn, school of fish, or harvest of acorns. When a seed or fish dies, it does not appear to die as we do, it is not born as we are, it does not sleep as we do, it does not care for its young as we do, and it does not scratch or bask in the sun as we do. With large mammals, we face the same scale of interaction with the land: finding the best routes and shelter from predators and bad weather, fulfilling needs for food and water, and reacting to disability, sensory perceptions, and so on. A lot of what we feel is what they feel. But those are only garnish on the ecstatic thrill of the chase and stalk, and I will return to that thread in a few pages, for it is a critical component of carnivore emotions.

Because we share ancestral roots, it is possible to use expressions like fear, lust, inquisitiveness, uneasiness, play, courtship, anger, nurture, jealousy, and mourning to accurately describe observed emotions or states in our fellow

Historic Eskimo use many hunting scenes in their art. It is part of their aesthetic. And it is particularly a male aesthetic, done by males on male tools.

I am illustrating samples of hunting art from a variety of prehistoric cultures, showing that the broad and deep aesthetic of the Paleolithic hunter-artist continues in later cultures. Killing scenes from late Neolithic Chukotka, Siberia. Reindeer are driven into lakes or rivers and killed from a kayak. Whales are taken from skin whaleboats.

large mammals. Many of our behaviors and emotions are from older parts of the brain dating back to the early roots of mammals and evolved before we and they diverged from a common stock. Aboriginal hunters and animal trainers have long recognized this, and we are just beginning to be able to account for these similarities scientifically (Wright 1994; Wrangham et al. 1994; Masson and McCarthy 1995). It is not foolish anthropocentrism. A lot of conceptual nonsense has been stirred up by the idea that emotions are exclusively human and therefore it is anthropocentric to detect emotional states in other animals. But the real challenge for an ethologist, animal trainer, hunter, pet owner, or anyone else is not that large mammals lack feelings, but that we may misidentify them or fail to recognize them at all, as indeed can sometimes happen even when we are dealing with other people.

As you become skilled in reading other animals, you may even detect emotions in tracks. As Leibenberg points out in his book on Bushman hunters, knowledge of animal behavior is essentially akin to the anthropomorphic (Leibenberg 1990a). Tracking is a highly cultivated ability that enables the hunter to imagine the other animal's emotions and behavior. Aboriginal hunters look upon the behavior of the animals they hunt as rational, based on how people behave but altered to fit circumstances faced by individuals of other species (Blurton-Jones and Konner 1976; Heinz and Lee 1978; Silberbauer 1981). And because spoor is always fragmentary, a tracker creates a template or story upon which he works to piece together what may have happened and what may be happening. How long would an animal lie watching its back-trail? Did herd members abandon that limping individual? Does the irregularity of a lion trail indicate it is hungry and hunting? Trackers must use as a base the template of behavior that is most familiar—one's own (from which others deviate in kind and degree). I emphasize tracking because it is easier to picture and discuss, but all kinds of hunting require similar attention and imagination: what it is the animals have done and will do. How would animals behave during a particular kind of weather, how might animals behave during a particular stalk? What camouflage is appropriate and sufficient? What is proper decoy decoration? When is a situation becoming dangerous? No recipe is totally adequate; every hunt is new and slightly different. To hunt is to be learning about hunting—past experience never totally replaces attention and thought. Each hunt is a practicum, and the hypotheses of past lessons are always subject to a new test. Hunting is profoundly empirical and imaginative.

Certainly, similar processes are brought into play in figuring out where grubs concentrate or what birds or fish or squirrels will do in given situations, and all that becomes part of one's skills as a hunter or gatherer. These challenges can be quite demanding and success quite satisfying, but hunting large mammals is not the same, because of our evolutionary kinship. That proximity both requires and promotes a lifetime of intimacy. What is crucial here is to see behind this old art and recognize hunting as more than just another chore. I hope moralistic inhibitions do not prevent you from imagining hunting talk around the campfire or keep you locked in a definition of hunting as yet another rationalized "optimum economic

Bushman art with images of killed animals: **A**, Speared elephant and buck, Mtoko, Zimbabwe. **B**, Bowman with dead cow kudu and dogs, Makwe Cave, Zimbabwe. **C**, Dead buck and vulture, Buffelsfontein, R.S.A. **D**, Spearman and dead elephant, Buffelsfontein, R.S.A. **E**, Dead buck and vultures, Abbotsann Dordrecht, R.S.A. Hunters often use vultures and ravens in the sky as a means of locating hit game, as the birds often find it first. These were undoubtedly interesting and exciting pictures for hunters in those different cultures.

Fore-end made from the dense lower part of the tree

About 2 m long

A representative spear from the early Paleolithic hundreds of thousands of years ago is rather javelin-like, heavy at the fore end and tapered at the rear. Replicas have been thrown about the same distance as modern regulation athletic javelins. Like the latter, the replicas fly fairly well without fletching. Animals struck by projectiles without cutting edges, like this, take a long time to die and hence require much tracking.

Rear tapered, javelin-style

strategy." Perhaps the spoor of Paleolithic art can help us find ways to enter into how Paleolithic people lived.

The Hunting Hypothesis: Evidence for Large-Mammal Hunting as the Driving Force in Human Evolution

The following sections present a summary of the evidence that large-mammal hunting underlies human evolutionary adaptations.

EVIDENCE FROM THE DIRT

No other explanation accounts so well for patterns observed in hominid artifacts as the idea of an increasing specialization on hunting large mammals. From these artifacts (see reviews in Keeley and Toth 1981; Walker 1984; Bunn and Kroll 1986; Gamble 1986; Mellars 1996; Vrba et al. 1995; Kimbel et al. 1996; Thieme and Veil 1997; Bunn 1999; Klein 1999; Foley 2001) we can say the following:

➤ *Stone tools* associated with thousands of Paleolithic archaeological sites are primarily tools for killing, butchering, and preparing large-mammal carcasses. We can surmise this from broken, butchered mammal bones and the tool shapes and worked edges. Evidence of

hunting specialization from archaeological sites is more than suggestive by at least 1.6 million years ago. By 300,000–500,000 years ago the evidence for hunting specialization is overwhelming, including kill-sites and camp middens with skewed age classes of game, butcher marks, hunting weapons, and so on.

➤ *Electron microscopy* reveals patterns of wear on the edges of many of these tools that could only be made by slicing animal tissues.

➤ *Cut marks on bones* from early archaeological sites show the use of stone tools.

➤ *Food remains* preserved in early, mid-, and late Paleolithic sites vary, but bones of large mammals stand out. If the preserved remains at each site are presented in terms of biomass of living animals, large mammals almost always predominate in comparison to the edible portions of invertebrates, fish, birds, and smaller mammals.

➤ Recently, remains of *sharpened wooden spears* have been found where unusual conditions allowed the preservation of wood. These uniquely preserved spears are associated with large-mammal butchering sites dating hundreds of thousands of years ago, before our own species, even before Neanderthals.

Ecological Significance of the First Worked Stones It may be faster to make a pointed digging stick or spear with a sharp-edged stone, but with a little more effort one can make an effective weapon from a naturally dried hardwood pole by sharpening the point by abrasion against a large boulder. This makes a crudely effective defensive or offensive weapon. But a sharpened wood point does not readily afford access to meat through a large mammal's skin. This requires a cutting edge like that of a broken edge of stone. Carnivores evolved special teeth, called *carnassials,* for this task, and without these specially shaped upper fourth premolars and lower first molars they could not scissor open the tough skins of their large prey. There is a lesson here. At least in part, this is why chimps confine their mammalian kills to baby antelope and monkeys. What would a chimp do if it managed to kill an adult zebra? It could poke out the eyes and chew the lips, tongue, and penis, like a scavenging bird, but chimp's teeth, like ours, cannot cut into the thick hide of larger animals; without a cutting tool it would be impossible to get to the delicious meat.

Those sharp stone edges from prior to 2.0 million years ago, and thereafter, could have been used for many things; nevertheless, they are evidence that hominids were capable of butchering large mammals. Eurasians who made the cave art, more than 2 million years later, were still using the sharp edges of broken stone to open the skin of bison, horses, reindeer, and other animals we know from the art. Stones and things made with stones were their main tools. Many of the images I illustrate in this book were engraved or carved with a sharp stone. This discovery/invention of how to make stone edges was critical in human evolution. Paleo*lithic* sites bear that noble name for good reason.

EVIDENCE FROM OUR NEAREST RELATIVES

No other explanation relates comparative evidence from other apes to human evolution as cogently as does this model of large-mammal hunting. From other primates (Ridley 1993; De Waal and Lanting 1997; Wrangham et al. 1994; Stanford 1999, 2001) we learn the following:

▸ Our nearest relatives, chimps, show *the beginnings of specialized hunting behavior,* very unlike gorillas and orangutans. Male chimps are the seek-and-kill specialists, and they do this cooperatively. The main exception observed was a single infertile female who hunted with the males (Stanford 2001). Chimps of both sexes have a great hunger for red meat, share it grudgingly, and do so mainly as part of temporary and long-term alliances.

▸ Chimps do not usually obtain a major part of their diets from red meat, but, significantly, no other food is *regularly shared among adults.* Meat sharing from hunted animals is thought to have been important in the early stages of human male-female interdependence, which developed into mate bonding. Without a larger amount of hunting, there is very little advantage for a female chimp to bond with a male or to provide sex to him alone; likewise, there is little advantage for a dominant male chimp to restrict his mating to one female.

▸ Among chimps the successful killers of game have *greater reproductive access to females,* as a result of meat sharing. In fact, Goodall (1986) observed that virtually all the females with whom males shared meat were in estrus.

▸ Among chimps one can see the *beginnings of weapon use.* Male chimps frequently use tree limbs and stones as offensive tools to threaten or hit other male chimps. They use these same tools defensively against potential predators. Other ape species also shake limbs (gorillas) or drop and throw broken limbs (orangutans) at opponents or predators. There is a sharp sexual dimorphism in incidence of throwing, favoring males (Goodall 1986).

▸ Some aspects of human *hunting-band structure* are present in chimps. Male chimps are philopatric (patrilocal), with all males remaining in the area in which they were born; whereas females generally emigrate to other com-

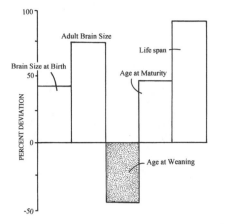

Comparison of Life History Features between Humans and Other Primates (corrected for body size). In general, when humans are compared to other primates, we have rather conservative life-history features, except for age at weaning. Humans wean their young disproportionately early. After Low 2000.

munities. Male groups patrol and defend the perimeter of their territory against other males. They bond as a team to confront males from other areas and to hunt red meat, but in no other situations do all the males actively cooperate as a team.

➤ The chimp ecological niche of broad-range foraging *demands a considerable cognitive capacity* for social interaction, memory to locate seasonal foods, etc., but requires minimal planning, toolmaking, imaginative creativity regarding group organization, future activities, etc.

EVIDENCE FROM THE ETHNOGRAPHIC RECORD

No other story better explains the life-history features seen among recent and late prehistoric hunter-gatherers and their interactions with wild environments than an evolutionary account of a large-mammal hunting lifeway. A comparative examination reveals the following:

➤ The majority of historic hunter-gatherers (and prehistoric ones for which we have a good archaeological record) *are preferentially attracted to a large-mammal hunting lifeway.*

➤ Historic hunter-gatherers who specialize in large mammals *divide chores between the sexes* and most are patrilo-

cal. Males form close search-and-kill groups, share meat resources, strive to excel at hunting yet take care not to brag about their skills, help in the raising and education of their own young, and are strongly bonded to one or a few wives and become violently jealous at the threat of cuckoldry. Those who are the most successful hunters receive considerable privileges. And in all these groups women's participation in the hunting lifeway is crucial to its success.

➤ The *greatest success in this hunting lifeway* requires outstanding skill, years of experience, foresight, dedication, stamina, good judgment, finesse, confidence, and wisdom.

➤ Success also requires *great intellectual ability.* Outstanding individuals command many facts and use complex reasoning.

➤ The members of historic hunter-gatherer bands *cooperate* to face the challenges of large-mammal hunting, engage in complex *sharing activities,* and raise skilled and well-educated offspring. They exhibit social sensitivities and skills of the first order (see reviews in Lee 1979; Ridley 1993, 1996; Stanford 1999; Stanford and Bunn 2001).

EVIDENCE FROM PHYSIOLOGY AND SOCIOBIOLOGY

No other model accounts for the collage of emergent traits we associate with universals of human nature so well as the "large-mammal hunting hypothesis" (for various aspects of this story, see reviews in Wright 1985; Brown 1991; Ridley 1993, 1996; Lee 1994; Aiello and Wheeler 1995; Wilson 1998; Masson 1999; Stanford 1999; Milton 1999; Stanford and Bunn 2001). The hunting of large mammals in a rationally opportunistic human style would have necessitated the following biologically expensive traits:

➤ Intellectual potential for *environmental interpretation and manipulation* (tool manufacture, cooperative game drives, etc.) and capacity for social interaction and organization.

A Bough Already Bent

Our forest ape background fortuitously set us up for human-style hunting with the following traits:

➤ An *opposable thumb and forefinger*, once important for grasping tree limbs, became important for the precise and powerful manipulation of tools. In fact, without that part of our arboreal background, there would likely have been no Paleolithic people and certainly no refined visual art.

➤ *Stereoscopic vision* of forward-facing eyes, originally useful for life in the three-dimensional tree habitat, proved crucial in precise tool manipulation (e.g., garment lacing and stone knapping) as well as in large-muscle activities (e.g., pike thrusting, spear throwing, and using digging sticks).

➤ A past of upright climbing and erect stance developed into *bipedal locomotion* out on the savanna and allowed hominids to more efficiently range far and wide. Bipedalism later freed the hands for toolmaking, hunting, defense, and transport of food back to camp. An upright stance also allowed hominids to carry altricial babies as well as children.

➤ The firm attachment of the *arm at a shoulder with 180 degrees of global motion*, which evolved from brachiating in trees, facilitated later spear-throwing abilities.

➤ A *creativity in finding protein* that we see among chimps led some hominids from killing young of large mammals into successfully killing adult mammals.

➤ Inquisitive behavior on the forest floor and elaborate traditions about annual timing of arboreal resources (e.g., the savvy extraction of rare protein sources) promoted *problem-solving skills* and served as a base for later refinements in intelligence and rational thinking.

➤ The *intense sociality of the chimp community* was greatly expanded and became the cooperative behavior of the more organized hominid band.

➤ *Elaborate nonverbal and verbal communication abilities* of forest apes were exploited among hominids and further enhanced with verbal language.

➤ *Separate sex roles* in ape society remained a platform for sexual specialization modified by many dynamics associated with the evolution of human-style hunting.

➤ The *lengthy development of young* and the closely associated reliance on complex learned behavior characteristic of forest apes were even further exaggerated among humans. The other side of the clever hominid hunter was a more elaborately dependent child, needing lengthy nurture and protection for years of learning.

➤ Not only a longer childhood and longer time until sexual-social maturity but especially an expanded, very *long potential life span*, inherited from our ape ancestors, made this new strategy possible.

By pointing out that we can see many rudiments of these traits among today's forest apes, I am in no way implying chimps or bonobos are an inferior, half-baked human. Their adaptations to forest life are exquisite. It would be just as silly to say that we are a second-rate chimp because our adaptations are now so ill suited to a forest niche.

➤ Long human development and *many years of intense education* from both parents and the extended family to fully develop the above abilities.

➤ Complex communication that allowed the *sharing of experiences and knowledge* gained over many years.

➤ A social structure based on *cooperation, interdependence, and mutualism, particularly with respect to critical nutrient resources*, especially meat of large mammals.

➤ A sociality predicated on *strong male-female love bonds*, in which the talents and assets of each partner can be

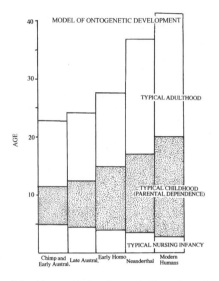

This engraving, on reindeer antler from Cueva de Valle, Sp., may picture a Pleistocene hunting party confronting a wounded deer hind. Note lines emanating from the nose and mouth.

A very elementary drawing of a group of masculine-like figures. Nowhere in all this old art are groups of fifteen or more male figures pictured together. This seems to be significant. El Castillo, Sp. *Below*, note similar, Holocene images from Larson Cave, Wisconsin, U.S.A.

interactively combined to create more than additive advantages.

➤ A strong *father-child love bond* built on the male's assurance of paternity from a loving wife, robust protection of the wife and child, and participation of the father in child rearing and education.

➤ *Risk-taking behavior,* especially among young males emerging into adulthood.

➤ Selfish ardor to thrive and to personally excel, balanced by the scale and context of band life, which thrived on a combination of *individual excellence and sharing.*

➤ *Patrilocal community structure* (which meant that most males of the band were rather closely related) to ameliorate testosterone-driven competitive behavior and allow teams of males to cooperate in hunting large mammals.

➤ Means of extended *cooperation and interchange among neighboring bands.*

➤ Sensory systems and brain modules structured to *perceive and reflect events* outside the person in a way that approximates external reality.

EVIDENCE FROM ECOLOGY

We have physical and circumstantial evidence (see reviews in Stanford 1999, 2001; Vrba et al. 1995; as well as discussions earlier in this chapter) that this large-mammal hunting specialization made great sense in the Paleolithic ecological context of carnivory:

Using chimps as the baseline and tooth eruption and body size of fossil hominids, one can compare timing of developmental shifts. The main trend is that the episode we might call childhood (time between infancy and full independence) increases disproportionately along an axis of greater conservative development. Modified from Bogin 1999.

➤ *Carnivores cooperate when the probability of success is thereby increased,* as in the hunting of larger, difficult, or dangerous game. They are much less likely to do so when smaller game can be taken without assistance (Sheel and Packer 1991). This is the pattern among chimp and human hunters as well (Alvard 2001).

➤ *Hominid expansion took advantage of savanna resources.* That is, the expansion and radiation of human ancestors out into the open habitats supposes that there were attractive resources and that these ancestors had the means to capitalize on those resources.

This is the only scene of a mother and baby in all the thousands of Paleolithic art pieces. And even this case has often been questioned; perhaps a backpack is pictured rather than a child. Gönnersdorf, Ger.

➤ Whatever hominids were doing out on the savanna, it involved weapons that could have *reliably provided a robust defense* against large social predators such as lions and hyenas. Because of our conservative life history (altricial infants, long childhood development, long time to reach sexual maturity), these weapons had to guarantee death to any predator.

➤ Such a defensive weapon may have had sufficient killing potential to also be exploited as an *offensive weapon,* used opportunistically to take game.

➤ With the rise of protohumans around 2 million years ago, there was a *major extinction of large African carnivores* (Walker 1984), such as large hyenas, dirk-toothed and saber-toothed cats, and so forth. These events may have been interrelated, but separating causes and effects is difficult.

➤ A complete nonspecialist was ecologically impossible. There was no universalist niche; one had to be *some kind of specialist.* The ecological record shows that each species must have its own distinctive strengths. One can be very eclectic and range far from one's niche focus, but we have no biological evidence of a truly nicheless species.

➤ An ecological niche had to allow *open access to an abundant and ubiquitous resource,* rich in nutrients and energy. The main underexploited resource was not nuts, tubers, grass seeds, fruit, leaves, herbs, grubs, dead animals, termites, or birds but hundreds of thousands of large mammals of every stripe, age, and sex, found in virtually every local habitat.

➤ *Handicaps had to be transformed into advantages.* For example, our ape ancestry left us with poor night vision. Most carnivores use their excellent, high-resolution, black-and-white vision to make their kills at night when prey is more vulnerable. While ape color vision is a handicap at night, one can skirt this limitation by hunting only during the day. Color vision provides better discriminating resolution for seeing prey during the day than does black and white (for such important things as following a blood trail). Daytime hunting also mitigated our handicap of poor blood-scenting ability, and instead we follow potential game or wounded individuals by tracking visually.

➤ Australopithecines show a primate pattern, similar to baboons, monkeys, gorillas, etc., of high geographic species diversity (baboons in Ethiopia are very different from those on the Cape). This is very unlike other widely dispersed, widely ranging groups of carnivore species (lions, hunting dogs, and hyenas). A lion in the African Cape is not much different from one in Arabia. Foley (2001) uses this "geographic-diversity" pattern to argue that *there was a major life-history change between the australopithecines and the later hominids, who show very little diversity over vast regions,* carnivore style.

These points summarize arguments for large-mammal hunting as fundamental to human ecological history; this is a hunting hypothesis, but not its 1960s–1970s version.

MISCONCEPTIONS OF THE 1960S "HUNTING HYPOTHESIS"

Discussions about human evolution in the 1960s and 1970s prominently featured the role of hunting. Ardrey (1966) coined the expression "Hunting Hypothesis" in a book of the same name. Some of the 1960–1970 work was remarkably insightful and has been an influential guide

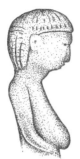

Paleolithic large-mammal hunter from Avdeevo, Rus., but probably not a Pleistocene killer of large mammals.

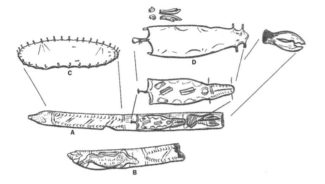

A and **B**, Two Paleolithic pieces of engraved bones from Abri Mège à Teyjat, Fr. These images have been interpreted as a number of things but they are clearly seals and seal skins (Sonneville-Bordes and Laurent 1983). There are two main ways of skinning animals. One is called flat-skinning, with a cut up the ventral abdomen. Eskimo stake out flat-skinned hides as shown here in **c**. The other kind of skinning is called case-skinning, where the main cut is between the feet and across on a line that crosses the base of the tail, allowing the skin to be peeled off forward, like a sock. Case-skins are turned wrong side out and dried with the hair inside, on a frame, as shown in **D**. Note fore-flippers and hind-flippers next to skin. Skinning is an important part of hunting, and a role often taken by women.

complemented by later work in archaeology, primate field studies, comparative ethology, and so on. However, this nascent version of the hunting hypothesis incorporated three substantial misconceptions:

1. First, it was preoccupied with a misleading focus on men's role in hunting. I have revisited this point numerous times because that mistake derailed a generation of scholars. Articles that appeared in the famous (or infamous) Lee and Devore (1968) volume *Man the Hunter,* summarizing that version of the hunting hypothesis, simply equated the whole of hunting with the portion I have

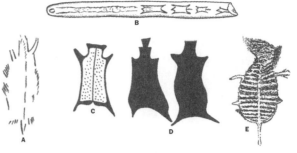

Flat-skins. Skins would have been a big part of Paleolithic life. Paleolithic northerners had to be connoisseurs of fine pelts, as they were crucial to winter survival. Pelts would have been admired and talked about—not only their beauty but the skinning, tanning, and sewing and the giving of them as gifts. There are very few pelts pictured in Paleolithic art: **A**, Mas d'Azil, Fr. We also see some skins in later prehistoric art: **B**, Kitluk Lake, Alaska, U.S.A. (fox pelts). **c**, Kushana, India. **D**, Mtoko, R.S.A. **E**, Warrenton, Kimberly RSA.

termed "seek-and-kill." Whatever this misconception says about our own culture in the 1960s, ethnographic analogs suggest that Paleolithic women would have been full participants in the hunting lifeway; they were hunters, just not the ones who regularly dispatched the large mammals. Leaving women out of the evolutionary model was like saying Eskimo or Plains Indian women had no role or achievement because it was men who killed the whales and bison. Paleolithic large-mammal hunting was an entire lifeway, and we will misunderstand it if we fail to grasp the whole enterprise or fail to imagine the interactive, yet generally distinct, patterns of women's and men's lives (Estioko-Griffin and Bion-Griffin 1981; Goodale 1971) and forget the central importance of children. Preserved Paleolithic art provides a larger window on the tools and interests of Paleolithic boys and men, especially on the most dramatic aspects of hunting; but again, Paleolithic art is an incomplete report. It does not portray the full breadth of Paleolithic hunting—for example, garment and shelter making, animal drives, small-game snaring, and the preparation of fur, leather, and food—nor does it touch on many other dimensions of their lives, such as child care and childhood play, gathering, and group life.

2. A second misconception concerned the evolution of the human nuclear family. Washburn and Lancaster

(1968) recognized that early human hunting groups both required and made possible a novel bond between women and men, but this mated-pair bond was quite misunderstood. They missed the utterly important role of the long human childhood and its demands. The mating bond was a direct prerequisite for the well-educated, quality-plus children so essential to the new human niche. Washburn and Lancaster were sidetracked into ideas about simple male-female sharing, provisioning, and anti-inbreeding incest taboos. Evolutionarily, the fact that human pair-bonding developed to the degree it did is clearly connected to the extraordinarily open-ended and lengthy developmental processes of human kids.

3. The third, and perhaps the most telling, misconception was the mixing of intraspecific aggression with interspecific predation. In short, hunting was confounded with social aggression. But predation and aggression are quite different animal behaviors. Indeed, they are controlled by quite separate limbic modules in the brain. We see no pattern of association between these two behaviors in other animals, and particularly not in other primates. Doves can be violently aggressive to other doves, and hawks can be gentle familial creatures with their own kind. Leaf-eating gorillas are sometimes violent murderers of their own species. Writers of the 1960s focused on the misconceived "killer ape" aspects of human evolution; for example, Cartmill in his literature review of the objections to the 1960s hunting hypothesis offers the following quotations from opponents: "the hunting hypothesis and its attendant misanthropy," "mentally unbalanced predator," and "*Homo sapiens* a psychopathic ape cutting a bloody swath across the face of sweet green nature" (1993, 13, 14, 26). Even Will Durant, a prolific synthesizer of philosophy and history during the 1960s, fell victim to this fashion of conflating a hunting lifeway with unsavory behaviors: "Throughout 97 percent of history, man lived by hunting and nomadic pasturage. During those 975,000 years his basic character was formed—too greedy acquisitiveness, violent pugnacity, and lawless sexuality" ([1970] 1991, 25).

Alaskan Eskimo ivory pipe from Saint Lawrence Island scrimshawed with images of weaponry being used for two quite different purposes: killing other humans and killing whales, two behaviors for which English has only one word. We connect the two in action, when behaviorally they are quite different. What they have in common indirectly relates to testosterone titer.

It was muddy thinking to conflate intraspecific and interspecific violence. Turnbull was a rare voice in the 1960s —the main dissenter at the now famous, or infamous, "Man the Hunter" conference: "I am bothered by this assumption that hunters are aggressive. . . . I am also not convinced that hunting is itself an aggressive activity. This is something that one must see in order to realize; the act of hunting is not carried out in an aggressive spirit" (1968).

Turnbull was clearly right; gentle people can be avid hunters. Ethnographic evidence bears that out. Not all cultures handle aggression and conflict in the same way, but this has nothing to do with how they get their food. A Bushman or Ituri hunter is no more or less socially aggressive than a Masai or Zulu pastoralist or a Highland New Guinea or Mohawk farmer. This confusion arises from nonhunters whose images of hunting are shaped by inaccurate and misleading sources.

In the past twenty years, more insightful and adequate models of the hunting hypothesis have been reintroduced and explored by scholars. See, for example, Shepard 1966, 1973; Tooby and DeVore 1987; Klein 1989, 1999; Adams 1990; Tiger 1992; Boyd and Silk 1996; Wright 1994; Morris 1994; Dunbar 1996; Bunn and Ezo 1993; Cartmill 1993; Aiello and Wheeler 1995; Hrdy 1999; Allman 1999; and Milton 1999. The discussions of this subject by Ridley (1996), Foley (2001), and Stanford (1999, 2001) are particularly noteworthy.

MINDFUL HUNTERS

The above conflation of hunting and social aggression likely is based on a combination of lack of experience and antihunting ideology. Certainly it is easy to confuse affect and effect. Let us look at the two ends separately. For a deer

The neck or throat is the best place for a carnivore to inflict mortal damage; in fact, it is almost the only place. **A**, In this little quick-study from Parpalló, Sp., a carnivore attempts to grab an ibex by the throat. **B**, I reconstruct this unclear carnivore as a hyena.

The Paleolithic attraction to images of humans hunting seems to have extended to images of other carnivorous animals. **A**, In this Paleolithic image from Niaux, Fr., a carnivore attacks a horse. **B**, My reconstruction depicts the very enigmatic carnivore as a wolf. Wolves would likely have been the most common large-mammal predator across the Mammoth Steppe, as indeed they still are in the north today.

hunter and a murderer the emotional experience during the killing is very different, but for the recipient the end is obviously the same. So whether a serial killer or white shark is stalking you makes little difference to you emotionally. In fact, prey often give *inappropriate socially submissive* calls when they are caught by a predator. Contrary to the dubbed-in nature films, lions don't growl aggressively as they stalk an impala, but the buck may bleat when it is caught. Imagine that a person might inappropriately weep or scream as a shark grabs hold from beneath the water. The emotion of fear triggers the submissive signals, but of course the shark does not know them; for her it is all just a successful hunt and tasty dinner, screaming or not. Goodall captured this ethological concept in the title of her book *Innocent Killers,* which is about predation. Humans have an inherently different ethical relationship with other animals than we do with our own species (Guthrie 1967).

Unexamined emotions may obscure our view of the past. So this deserves our attention and care. In animal watching it is easy to empathize with both prey and predator, taken individually. Pelicans are beautiful to watch as they plummet into the waves, and it is difficult to see clearly what they are doing. Often, however, we just don't want to see what is at the core of it all, don't want to accept this idea that life is built on someone else's life. At the other end, a terrified fish (fish have brain regions and hormones for terror) feels the pain of predation (fish have pain receptors as well). And there is something at the core

that is even more difficult to accept, that this natural taking of life is done as neither a chore nor a solemn occasion but is great fun. Pelicans do not fish in anger or aggression. All predatory species learn how to hunt and kill by playing, and that same spirit of play infuses their hunting activities as adults, with all the signs of added excitement and enthusiasm when it is the real thing.

A wolf employs its "weapon of violence"—its long canine teeth—for two quite different uses: to attack competitors and to kill deer. In these two different actions it is evident that a wolf experiences two quite distinct emotions, vividly portrayed by different physical signals and behaviors. Human hunters and soldiers certainly are likely to use a rifle with different purposes, motives, and emotions. You may protest that because the outcome is death, such distinctions are moot. I suggest quite the opposite and suspect that failure to recognize this difference clouds our view of life. It is important to understand that a hunting lifeway did not mark Paleolithic people as vulgar or vicious. Similarly, a Paleolithic weapon adorned with a bison head cannot be interpreted as an image of a hated enemy, even though bison were undoubtedly dangerous at times. Hunters respect and celebrate the splendor of their prey, and Paleolithic art is evidence that this cross-cultural pattern is ancient indeed. The images of prey in Paleolithic art are far from being aggressive portrayals of cruel violence and gore. Rather, it seems that they are generous images recalling components of a larger, and not simply pretty, beauty.

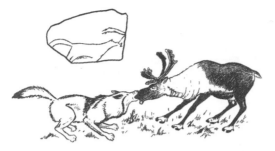

Wolves often grab the muzzle to get the blood flowing and weaken the prey or to hold the prey while other pack members pull the animal off its feet. I should emphasize that this behavior is not about aggression. Parpalló, Sp. My reconstruction below.

Predation scenes are common in prehistoric and historic art. Here a lion grabs the muzzle of a wild ram. Lions kill their prey mainly by suffocation, which explains this otherwise enigmatic hold. Scythian belt plaque from the late Holocene.

The evidence we do have about our past implies that our ancestral hominids became less violently aggressive during the rise of our hunting specialization. If anything, hunting made us the cooperative ape. The evolution of human-style hunting required a new level of cooperation and intimacy that far exceeded that of our ancestral apes. The absence of group warfare scenes in Paleolithic art is informative here. Virtually all the killing shown in Paleolithic art is about hunting, that is, a predation kind of killing (splendor), not aggression killing (hostility). Repetitive wound marks on a few images of bears and lions are rather like the "pincushion-appearing" speared human images in Paleolithic art in that they do suggest socially aggressive, violent, adversarial motives. This is understandable given the real threats lions and bears occasionally, but persistently, posed to Paleolithic people.

PALEOLITHIC ART FROM VEGETARIANS OR SCAVENGERS?

What might be some alternative viewpoints to the hunting hypothesis? What counterarguments are there, particularly for the late Paleolithic? Pollen evidence from across Pleistocene Eurasia (e.g., Woillard 1978) suggests that, for much of the late Paleolithic, a vegetarian diet was impossible. Historic ecological constraints on native peoples in northern regions are not precise analogs, but they can be informative about life in European cave art regions during Paleolithic times. Inland Eskimo, for example, did collect and store some tubers, willow leaves, mushrooms, and berries, but the caloric content of these was negligible. These plant foods tended to be condiments, alleviating the monotonous winter diet consisting mainly of fish, birds, and mammals. This virtual absence of carbohydrate foods among former Eskimo populations is dramatized by the fact that some individuals in these groups actually lack the enzyme sucrase, which is essential for proper breakdown and assimilation of the common sugar sucrose. Patterns of diabetes and nutrition-related diseases are also strongly suggestive of very limited short-chain carbohydrates in the Paleolithic diet.

Today, most plant species in the far north are well defended against herbivory, and that, not winter cold per se, is the main reason large-mammal density is often so low at high latitudes. Pollen and other evidence suggests that the cold steppes of Pleistocene Eurasia were similarly lacking in vegetable resources of staple quantities. Thus, we conclude that animal tissue constituted the crucial base of most Eurasian Paleolithic diets.

Eurasian late Paleolithic sites do show that people were highly eclectic in their utilization of animal tissue, but the quantities of meat obtained from invertebrates and fish were not great, and similarly, the small proportion of energy or nutrients accounted for by the sometimes large numbers of bird and small-mammal bones (Delporte 1990) suggests that people ultimately depended on large mammals, whose bones are often preserved in abundance. There may be exceptions on the extreme southernmost fringes, but across occupied Eurasia large mammals provided the basic food source.

If we conclude that large mammals were the dietary staple, there is still the question whether this is truly

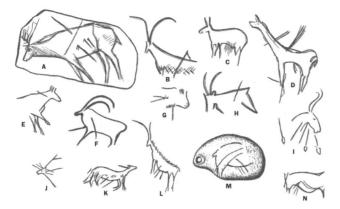

Paleolithic images of speared animals. The technical level of some is so poor it is not easy to make age, sex, or species identifications. **A**, Red deer, Isturitz, Fr. **B**, **F**, **H**, and **L**, Ibex, Cosquer, Fr. **C**, Red deer or ibex(?), Cosquer, Fr. **D**, Giant deer(?), Vigne-Brun à Villerest, Fr. **E**, Chamois, Haréguy, Fr. **G**, Reindeer, Roc-la-Tour, Fr. **I**, Ibex or chamois, Gabillou, Fr. **J**, Red deer, Altamira, Sp. **K** and **N**, Red deer, Parpalló, Sp. **M**, Artiodactyl, Laugerie-Basse, Fr.

Speared horse images from Spanish Holocene rock art: **A**, Cautos de la Visera. **B**, Bojadillas. **C**, Minateda. **D**–**E**, Raco de Nando. **F**, La Araña. Several are intentionally shown just wounded. Note the variety of places where the hits occur, including one in the hoof, some in the rump, and one in the head.

evidence of hunting or simply a record of supplemental large-mammal scavenging. Some authors have suggested that scavenging, particularly winter scavenging, was the major source of meat in the late Paleolithic (Gamble 1986, 1987). I have some insight into this matter from forty years of experience with wildlife in the far north and can see significant problems with this proposal.

First, few animals simply lie down and die. Debilitation is rarely so sudden. Old age, starvation, injury, and disease are usually processes that predators note, and as animals slow, from whatever cause, they are usually killed. Wolves, for example, are constantly testing herds to note the slightest sign of disability, because catching a caribou or killing a healthy bison or moose is quite difficult. Pleistocene Eurasia had not only wolf packs but also hyena clans and lion prides, and not only would these predators have culled ailing herbivores, but such large social predators also consume most usable material from any carcass in a short time. Wolverines, foxes, and especially diverse bird scavengers, like the corvid group (including ravens, crows, and magpies), were waiting on the perimeter to consume the leftover bits. These peripheral scavengers can make much greater use of the carcasses than their size might suggest, because they cache large quantities of food.

Edible leftovers are scarce on Alaska's predator kills today, and I suspect they were even more efficiently cleaned up in the Pleistocene. And remember, Pleistocene lions and hyenas were as large or even larger than their African counterparts today (Kurtén 1985; Klein and Scott 1991). Such formidable predators would not have casually relinquished their prey to human scavengers. Unsatiated carnivores usually defend kills well past their normal caution point. Grizzlies, for example, normally run from humans, but grizzlies on moose carcasses are very possessive, dangerous to approach, and responsible for human deaths nearly every year in Alaska nowadays.

Second, some authors have imagined that large mammals that do simply die in winter would immediately freeze and thus be conveniently preserved, but two things generally prevent this. Rumen and/or caecum-colon contents, particularly of large herbivores, tend to keep fermenting after death, and the pelt of northern animals is such a good insulator that even after death heat is retained in the body. This heat soon allows viscera and surrounding meat to decompose and become gangrenous; green ooze develops and spreads via the vascular system to other major muscle masses. Within days after death there is a steamy composting mass inside an unopened carcass (Guthrie 1990). I have seen bison, caribou, and moose carcasses lying in snow at extremely low temperatures that were still warm after several days of such fermenting. Despite very cold temperatures, an unopened mammoth, well insulated by a thick pelt, would have gone into an internal "meltdown," as African elephant carcasses do today. Rank, decomposing carcasses are neither palatable nor safe for humans. Aversion to anaerobic decay is part of

A prehistoric American Indian in Wisconsin, U.S.A., chose to make this image on the wall of Samuel's Cave. One can imagine the hunting traditions and aesthetic that linked this person to Paleolithic artists. Note the blood coming from the muzzle, raised tail, and defecation.

especially when food was in limited supply. Even if humans did scavenge this way, the available bones in any one area would have been quickly used up. Bone litter is simply never very dense. No historic group—Bushman, Australian Aboriginals, Athabascans, Eskimo, etc.—ever makes a routine effort to scrounge calories from found bones.

In short, waiting around for large mammals to die would simply not have worked as a means of getting energy and nutrients for an entire camp. Living in the cold climate of the Eurasian late Pleistocene, someone had to go out and make animals die, and the archaeological evidence is rich with tools made to do that very job. Projectile points are common in the record. And some of the main nonlithic tools are spear-throwers and spear shaft–straighteners. From modern analogs it is clear that these are the tools of people who hunted large mammals.

In summary, I find no other comprehensive model of our evolutionary specialization that has a more robust fit with current evidence or the explanatory power of this model of our Pleistocene genus developing as social hunters of large mammals.

our ancient ability to recognize a class of odors produced by anaerobic protein fermentation, which is often associated with dangerous toxins.

A third scavenging scenario, involving bones, has been proposed, but because of the low densities of most large mammals on the Mammoth Steppe, there would have been few bones to scavenge, and competing hyenas and wolves would surely have made thorough use of bones,

ANATOMICALLY MODERN HUMANS: FROM KNUCKLE WALKING TO SMOKING FASTBALLS

But this book is about humans, and an aspect of their uniqueness. The evolutionary rise of *Homo sapiens* related to innovation, which is the main trait that typifies our species. And it would seem that innovation had something to do with a new kind of hunting lifeway. The African archaeological record is not clear as to when our ancestors

An engraving in the round on a small bone from La Vache, Fr. I reconstruct this piece as a group of humans facing a bear, salmon, bison, and a mortally wounded horse—a Pleistocene hunter's cornucopia.

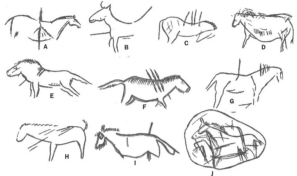

Speared wild horses in Paleolithic art: **A**, Pileta, Sp. **B**, Parpalló, Sp. **c**, Ermitta, Sp. **D**, Altamira, Sp. **E**, Limeuil, Fr. **F**, Gourdan, Fr. **G**, Calévie, Fr. **H**, Matutano, Sp. **I**, Bara-Bahau, Fr. **J**, Murat, Fr. Note that most are done rather poorly.

became clearly human, but skeletons in the Middle East and mitochondrial evidence suggest this must have occurred between 100,000 and 200,000 years ago. By at least 40,000–60,000 years ago members of our species had spread from Africa into Eurasia, even pushing northward to the outskirts of the Mammoth Steppe, where they overlapped with Neanderthal hunters. What selective forces drove the transition from protohuman to human? We don't know the details, but the trigger appears to have been an enhancement of pressures we have already noted. It is as if the bar had been raised from high-jump to pole-vault levels when it came to cognitive excellence, elaboration of language, new levels of group coordination-cooperation, and perhaps deeper intimacies, but most of all creativity. Midden records show that the large-mammal hunting niche became ever more flexible, including new supplemental game resources, and that lines of trade expanded far and wide. Preservable tools show dramatic changes, with more osseous materials and, dominating the fossil assemblages, light stone points. Not least of all, representational art appears in the archaeological record. What does this art show us about hunting?

IMAGES OF HUNTING IN PALEOLITHIC ART

Leroi-Gourhan (1965) estimated that about 15% of the large ungulates portrayed in Paleolithic art, especially horses and bison, are shown speared and bleeding. Images of wounded animals occur in cave engravings and paintings and on tools, stone plaquettes, and bone scraps, and they are found in different time horizons and different geographic locations. In other words, they scatter through virtually all of preserved Paleolithic art in virtually all media.

First, let's note that these images record informative details about the nature of mortal wounds made by Paleolithic weapons. A hemorrhaging weapon is most effective if it penetrates deeply into a large mammal's thorax (Guthrie 1983). Sharp bone points and flaked stone edges kill by hemorrhaging, not by trauma of impact like a bullet. The thoracic region is highly vascularized, containing heart, lungs, and liver; therefore, when a projectile slices through these tissues, the resultant massive loss of blood can make the animal weaken, grow dizzy, and die within minutes.

The central nervous system is so well protected by bone that spear hits to the skull or spinal column are seldom effective. Likewise, thick limb muscles are not well enough vascularized to allow reliably fatal hemorrhaging—animals hit in these areas normally recover. Hits to the gut mean a slow death, a long pursuit, or possibly even a loss. Many Paleolithic images disclose the artists' keen awareness of the efficacy of thoracic shots and the risks to the hunter from wounded animals after improper spear hits.

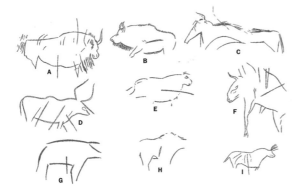

In Paleolithic art many large mammals are shown speared. These vary from poorly done (as shown here) to well drawn. **A**, Bison, Gabillou, Fr. **B**, Bison, Bédeilhac, Fr. **C**, Aurochs, Parpalló, Sp. **D**, Aurochs, Le Placard, Fr. **E**, Aurochs, Mas d'Azil, Fr. **F**, Bison, Les Combarelles, Fr. **G**, Bison, Hornos de la Peña, Sp. **H**, Bison, Enlène, Fr. **I**, Aurochs, Levanzo, It.

More speared-animal art from later Holocene hunting cultures: **A**, Sandia Canyon, New Mexico, U.S.A. **B**, Matopos, Zimbabwe. **C**, Ladybrand, R.S.A. **D**, Indwe, R.S.A. **E**, Assyrian. **F**, Ndema George, R.S.A. **G**, Harare, Zimbabwe. **H**, Sioux, U.S.A. **I**, Sinai. **J**, Cañada Remiga, Sp.

This kind of knowledge continues after the Pleistocene into Holocene times. For example, we have physical evidence from the Mesolithic (the period directly following the late Paleolithic), in the form of projectile point pieces embedded in bone and indications of point impacts on bone, that Mesolithic people also actively aimed for the thorax (Noe-Nygaard 1974, 1995).

Many Paleolithic paintings show blood spraying from the wounded animal's mouth and nostrils. This happens when an animal has been mortally hit in the thorax. To point out the obvious, people operating only as scavengers would never have observed this phenomenon. Paleolithic images most commonly show spears clustered in the chest or thoracic cavity. Thoracic wounds not only bleed from the entry hole, as other wounds bleed, but with significant lung penetration the bronchial tubes are flooded. Every time the animal breathes it exhales a shower of bright, bubbly, frothy-pink, oxygenated blood —a spoor experienced large-mammal hunters recognize. In Fitzpatrick's classic *Jock of the Bushfeld* he says: "There were smears on the long yellow grass, and it was clear enough, judging by the height of the blood-marks from the ground, that the impala was wounded in the body— probably far back, as there were no frothy bubbles to show a lung shot" (1984, 100). Lung blood is witnessed annu-

ally by many of the several million people who bow-hunt in the United States. It is the color of life, of death, the color of success, and a color of terrible beauty.

Some Paleolithic images include both a spear in the thorax and blood coming out the animal's nose and mouth. A parallel pattern is seen in Bushman art, Plains Indian art, Scythian art, and the art of many other groups using weapons which killed by hemorrhaging. Paleolithic art scholars have tended to treat these images as an enigma requiring special interpretation. One such interpretation is that these images picture the "breath of life" (Smith 1989) and are somehow tied to shamanism. Delluc and Delluc (1991) recognized that they probably represent blood, but then went on to propose that Paleolithic art was, in a way, morbidly focused on pain, blood, and death. Not only are animals in Paleolithic art portrayed as hit with spears and shown nose-bleeding, they are often shown urinating or defecating. This is a common autonomic response to a lethal hit.

For me, these scholars fail to appreciate the extent to which human well-being, survival, and happiness depend on the demanding and erratic successes of killing large mammals. I suspect Paleolithic artists included these details as integral parts of the ensemble as an expression of beauty and excitement. A wounded animal bleeding through the nose had to be a welcome sight for hunters using hemorrhaging weapons. It was indeed the breath of life and the breath of death on many levels.

A Taste for Meat

I would like to swing back and pick up our story in the trees. Primate life was constructed around trees: trees for food and trees for escape from predators. A short description of primate diets is that they prefer high-quality resources. True to that pattern, the stem-stock of the great apes seem to have been fruit-eating specialists, living mainly on modest-sized fruit from tall forest trees. Today, over 75% of the diet of chimps, bonobos, gorillas, and orangutans is fruit (Leach 1997). One gorilla subspecies is a little different due to the relative lack of fruit in its cool upland habitat. That mountain gorilla feeds predominantly on new-growth leaves.

RED, YELLOW, AND BLUE PIE-IN-THE-SKY: OUR FRUIT-EATING ORIGINS

In a metaphorical evolutionary sense, African tropical tree species manipulated apes as one of their main reproductive organs. Both trees and apes had something to gain: apes the food, and plants the vectors to disperse their seeds, fertilized with steamy rich poop. Flowers and insects are also important in ape diets, but these are hostile fare, being well defended with some noxious or toxic chemicals. Evolution saw to it that fruit entices and insects fight back.

The wealth of fruit in tropical forests is a fairly stable and predictable resource, and our ancient ancestors probably enjoyed a good life in the trees. The short stocky legs and elongated powerful arms of the great apes allow them a smooth "telephone-lineman" climb up vertical trunks of large trees where fruits are located. Chimps manage this maneuver handily—it is their forte, and it is an impressive maneuver. Long arms let them reach around past the trunk's midline, from this position the animals lean backward, pressing their flat feet into the trunk's surface, and hand-over-hand up they walk. Their whole body is made for this process. But this tree-climbing grace is purchased by a peculiarly awkward amble on the ground, where they actually spend most daylight hours, resting and traveling between widely scattered fruit trees. The thick and powerful finger tendons that work so well holding onto the tree do not allow the chimp's hand to open flat like ours or monkeys', so they must walk on the backs of their knuckles. Judging from ape analogies, knuckle walking was our ancient ancestral mode of locomotion as well.

Analogies with the living great apes also suggest that in our chimplike past we ate a fruit-based diet, and that is why, unlike most mammals, we cannot synthesize vitamin C. There was no need to synthesize a nutrient so abundantly consumed every day. Fruit's pulpy sugars (fructose mostly) are cheap for plants to photosynthesize from ubiquitous CO_2 and provide an inducement or exchange of sorts for inadvertent dispersal by birds, rodents, and primates. Once the developing seed matures, the surrounding starches are turned into sweet sugars, and the fruit signals its attractive ripeness by changes in color. Color vision evolved among tree lizards, birds, arboreal rodents, and primates as a link coordinating seed dispersal with the plants' signals of fruit location and degree of ripeness. Thus, Paleolithic cave art in its shades of reds, blues, and yellows relates indirectly to our ape-old connection with tree-fruit evolution.

The downside to a fruit-filled diet is that many fruits tend to be rather "empty calories," high in energy and very low in most essential nutrients, especially the amino acid constituents of protein. A strictly fruit diet is sometimes a recipe for kwashiorkor. Great apes have always eaten nonfruit items to obtain essential fatty acids, amino acids, and vitamins. Yet these important supplements are rarely easy to come by, and many chimp behaviors, the ones we find most creative and interesting, such as using sticks to obtain small termites or their use of rocks to crack nuts, are to get essential fats and protein. This also explains their occasional hunger for meat and their occasional hunting, such as a group of chimps combining forces to catch a young monkey. Ecologically, apes are protein limited (like the tropical forests around them). For the earliest forest-edge hominids, nuts, ants, grubs, and other small high-nutrient packages were equally available to all, but a large-mammal carcass was a nutrient package too ample not to be shared—the first public property. But its acquisition was not easy and so they relied on a powerful appetite for meat.

THE NEW ENTRÉE: MEAT

Most animals are not fond of meat. Animals have specializations, and niches of carnivory are rare. All animals are constrained by time, and reproductive success is negatively correlated to spending lots of time searching for something that one is highly unlikely to obtain. Most primates occupy niches that involve spending time in inquisitive rummaging, and when this occasionally affords an opportunity to kill and eat small animals, they often do so. In short, their tastes have evolved to be quite eclectic; that was our original background as well.

Mitochondrial evidence suggests that some 5–7 million years have past since chimps and humans shared a common ancestor, but we can glean hints about the nature of our distant past from studying chimps. Chimps easily learn to hunt and kill for meat and readily establish this as a cultural tradition for following generations. Although both sexes participate, it is predominantly males who kill young monkeys and antelope. Male chimps particularly appear to relish the process of hunting. In hunting forays they exhibit unbounded excitement as well as intense relish for mammalian tissue (Wrangham and Peterson 1996; Shepard 1995). Though chimps are certainly not sophisticated carnivores, they do have a marked appetite for fresh red meat.

Image of an isolated hind limb of cloven-hoofed animal from Massat, Fr., engraved in the round. My reconstruction at right. I see this as a boned-out "hindquarter." Backpack hunters today leave the bones and skin behind and only carry out the meat. This is done by filleting the tissue from the femur and lifting it off as one piece. I bone out wild large mammals like this every year (if I am lucky).

Even before they first looked out over the savanna, ancestors of both humans and chimps may have begun to expand their taste for meat (beyond the protein afforded by grubs, eggs, and lizards) toward making it a priority in their diet. Evolution is no dietician specifying "go out and increase your dietary percentage of protein and fat"; hunting behavior is evolutionarily linked in a shortcut route via appetite—developing an attraction to the taste of viscera, muscle, and fat. Sheer calories or energetic content of foodstuffs often fail to disclose significant differences in dietary strategies. Studying both preference and indifference curves (food that hunters ignore rather than acquire) of representative hunter-gatherers, Stephens and Krebs (1986) showed that protein and fat from game were more highly regarded and sought after by male subsistence hunters than simple energy foods (also see Hill 1988).

The seek-and-kill behavior, the urge to go after meat on-the-hoof, can be most simply evolutionarily encoded by a taste craving. We can infer that chimps fight, prostitute themselves, and beg other chimps for small morsels of monkey meat, even a fragment of bone, because it tastes so splendidly delicious. These taste pleasures rooted in evolutionary dynamics regarding nutrients, and chimp social nuances, including any symbolism attached to meat, are derivatives. We can say from the archaeological record that our taste for animal tissue has been honed for more than 40,000 generations, but probably many more.

Another collage to bring to your attention the hunting scenes in post-Pleistocene art. **A**, Bowmen, dogs, and wild cattle, Yeniu Valley, Inner Mongolia. **B**, Bushman with bleeding buck, Tanzania. **C**, Red deer and bowman, Castillón, Sp. **D**, Aoudad, dogs, and spearmen, Tassili, Sahara. **E**, Bowmen and red deer, Cueva los Caballos, Sp. **F**, Skiers and moose, Zalavruga, Siberia. **G**, Bushman and buck, Brandberg, Namibia.

Allowing 25 years per generation for 40,000 generations, that is only 1,000,000 years. In the face of such evidence that large mammals have provided key nutrients for growth, body condition, and health for so many generations, surely we can imagine that our very tastes for meat have also been shaped by selective forces across such a span of time. Presumably, selection favored individuals who experienced the most scrumptious pleasure and attraction to the taste of meat and thus were more motivated to obtain it directly, or indirectly even if that meant major social obligations.

Just as sensory structures in our eyes, tongues, noses, and brains delight in sweet essences from our fruit-and-berry past, we are predisposed to also enjoy the salty richness of meat and fat. Tastes and scents are not only learned. Ecological niches provide differently highlighted menus. You do not buy dog and cat food in flavors of cranberry and avocado but in lamb and chicken, not because of some manufacturer's whim but because of the long time the ancestors of dogs and cats were wild carnivores. Niches of carnivory include an appetite for animal tissue. Meat craving evolved among carnivores in association with the anatomy of fang-and-claw and complex predatory behaviors.

Our ancestors weren't carnivores but they became carnivorous, apparently a long time ago, and this past has left its mark on our tastes. As a guest for dinner most anywhere on the globe, you are likely to be served some kind of meat. It is the feastly dish. Cross-culturally the sharing of food, and especially the sharing of meat, is a practice of hospitality and friendship. We have eclectic tastes, but rich meat is the nourishing entrée, not yams, parsnips, mopane nuts, or tapioca. As people, we love the delicious taste of other animals, big ones if in season. We may, for various reasons, elect to suppress these Pleistocene tastes, but they are ours by birth.

COOKING ARTS, BUT NO ART OF COOKING

Some authors have presumed that fires were first used to cook tubers and that this combination was a central force in the early evolution of our genus (Wrangham et al. 1994). There is reason to be skeptical of the tuber theory because clear records of hearths do not occur in the fossil record until after 500,000 years ago, and *Homo* was well on its evolutionary carnivorous way long before this (e.g., Carbonell Roura 1999). As we have seen, bone middens suggest that by this time people had been devoted meat eaters for hundreds of thousands of years. It is true that meat eaters are often plagued by a variety of internal parasites from eating raw viscera and muscle. I was hired by the University of Alaska years ago to fill a position left vacant after a pioneer Alaskan paleontologist, Otto Geist, died from parasites in uncooked game meat, probably bear. And raw meat can also present extra problems of food poisoning.

Roasting meat had numerous benefits. The degradation of collagen fibers that occurs at high temperatures tenderizes cuts rich in tendon and gristle, cuts that would otherwise be almost unchewable. Heat, more importantly, kills parasite eggs and cysts and denatures toxic by-products of rot. With all these benefits it is easy to imagine now that preferences for the taste of cooked meat

Steak for Breakfast, Lunch, and Dinner: Is a Diet of Meat and Fat Physiologically Sound?

Some researchers have questioned the physiological feasibility of a diet low in carbohydrates. Others have wondered if it is even possible to process so much protein. Speth (1991), for example, argues that the human liver has difficulty when over 50% of calories are from protein, and therefore Paleolithic peoples must have had some other basic food than hunted animals.

There is some truth to these objections: however, lean meat has so very few calories that when one compares fresh muscle and fat, the actual ratio of protein to fat calories for equal amounts of food mass consumed is close to 1:30. Protein, carbohydrates, and fat have respective caloric values that round off to a ratio of 1:5:10 dry weight, but because lean muscle is over two-thirds (65–75%) water and fat contains very little water, a diet of 50% calories from meat and 50% from fat is actually achieved with consumption of about 96% fresh lean meat. In another comparison, a ratio of 25% of calories from meat and 75% from fat is approximated by eating 93% lean bison muscle and 6.6% bone marrow (for some sense of what this means, a 7% fat hamburger or bratwurst is experienced as incredibly dry). Since most fresh lean-looking muscle contains some fat (5%), a lean-meat diet would be even more skewed toward fat. For example, a diet of modestly lean, summer bison would mean less than 30% of calories from protein. My calculations do not take into consideration that roughly half the fat is normally lost in roasting. Another factor is that compared to meat from most domestic livestock, lean cuts from

Left, image of horse hit with multiple spears, bleeding from mouth and nose; Marsoulas, Fr. *Right,* woolly rhino with blood streaks coming from mouth and nose; Chauvet, Fr.

wild game are comparatively healthy; an Alaskan moose, for example, is high in the nonsaturated fats (Nobmann 1993), about 65%, similar in that regard to the well-publicized "healthy-heart" diets. Among northern natives on diets heavily dependent on wild meats, cardiovascular diseases were almost unknown, but all that changed with the coming of grocery stores (e.g., Appavoo, Kubow, and Kuhnlein 1991).

Therefore, there is no physiological necessity to presume that extensive supplements from plant sources were required by Paleolithic people during the long winters. A diet of large mammals with some smaller mammals, a few birds, salmon, and occasionally rumen contents would do fine. Rumen contents were certainly a part of the diets of hunting groups surveyed in modern ethnographic studies. Recent northern hunter-gatherer groups demonstrate that it is possible to exist on a diet almost devoid of carbohydrates. But one does not have to go to the ethnographic literature to test this. High-protein diets are now being used by millions of Americans for weight loss, buffering emotional stress, intestinal yeast infection, and type II diabetes control. These diets include few carbohydrates—often less than 30 grams per day, which is equivalent to half of a small potato (e.g., Eades and Eades 1996; Atkins 1992).

would have been highly favored by selection, and such strong selection pressures for cooking meat, exerted for hundreds of thousands of years, have diverted our tastes from still-twitching muscle to the aromatic appeal of crispy cooked rashers with crackling edges. A taste for cooked meat is one of the universal human attractions (Brown 1991).

There is ample evidence in the form of thick hearth deposits, charred bones, and indications of marrow extraction by boiling (probably by adding hot rocks to water in green [untanned] skin containers) that European late Paleolithic people cooked their meat. Yet images of cooking have not been found in the preserved art. I imagine Paleolithic people took pleasure in cooking and eating meat, but the makers of our preserved art chose not to portray cooking, or even eating, but rather produced images of the pursuit and killing of the animals. In Paleolithic art, animals are not pictured cooked, or deliciously processed; they are wild and beautiful beings—possibly available to a strong and talented hunter. While meat preparation can be a fine culinary art, the fact that it was not portrayed on Paleolithic cave walls reflects another evolutionarily honed motivation for hunting that extends beyond culinary pleasure: it is the jubilation of hunting itself that saturates this old art.

FROM CRUMB-FEEDING TO HIJACKING THE BREAD TRUCK

Although all men complain about the onerousness of making gardens they never gripe about hunting.
K. M. Kensinger, "Hunting and Male Domination in Cashinahua Society"

Carnivorous humans are the main exception to the "crumb-feeding" strategy of primates, but it is not a taste for meat alone that drives carnivores or human hunters, but the appetite for hunting itself. This special appetite for hunting is sometimes not recognized or acknowledged: witness the ethnographic studies that discuss hunting as yet another "division of labor." This is a mistake akin to assigning the pleasures of sexual intercourse to a tally called "reproductive tasks."

I wonder if field-"workers" were really listening when stories were told around the campfires. Athabascan men I know have a connection to hunting beyond comparison to their other activities. Their year is marked by seasonal hunting events—the arrival of the first geese or when the caribou are moving—and hunting is the subject of endless discussion. School and official jobs pause at these times because hunting is too important and just too much fun to miss.

Male Bushman also never seem to tire of talking about hunting (Lee 1979). They give graphic descriptions of their most recent hunts, which remind them of incidents

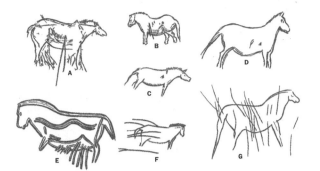

These Paleolithic images of speared horses are done in several styles and rendered with different levels of technical skill. **A–D**, Trois Frères, Fr. **E**, Chauvet, Fr. **F**, Tuc d'Audoubert, Fr. **G**, Niaux, Fr.

from past hunts, and then of tales their ancestors told. These discussions go on hour after hour and are captivating to younger boys. Though male Bushman do gather plants for food while out from camp, they regard this activity as monotonous and uninteresting compared to hunting (Marshall 1976).

This Appetite for Hunting

Male chimpanzees everywhere hunt and kill mammals. . . . They can kill often. In one extraordinary two-month period, the main community at Gombe killed seventy-one monkeys in sixty-eight days . . . 30 percent of the colobus population was eliminated each year. And in every place the visceral reaction to a hunt and a kill is intense excitement. The monkey may be eaten alive, shrieking as it is torn apart. The forest comes alive with the barks and hoots and cries of the apes, and aroused chimpanzees race in from several directions. . . . For one or two hours the thrilled apes tear apart and devour the monkey.
R. Wrangham and D. Peterson, *Demonic Males*

Some appreciation of the evolution of this appetite for hunting might help in understanding the reasons behind the main themes of Paleolithic art. In the evolution of hunting the need for nutrition is reinforced not only by an appetite for meat but by a thirst for the jubilation of the seek-and-kill experience. Though carnivores evolved a deep attraction to the taste of meat, the forces that drove hunting behavior did not stop there. Their food does not hold still; it hides and fights back. Therefore, in addition to the delicious taste of red meat, natural selection added a predilection to hunt in the form of a special passion—which takes very little experience to activate. Among carnivores, we can see that individuals who have this passion perform better than their compatriots who hunt for hunger alone. And hence virtually no carnivores are without this ardor. Before we talk about humans, that point—that carnivores are genetically prone to developing a special delight in hunting—has to be made.

A reindeer walking across the tundra chooses its food carefully; it must balance its intake of energy and complex nutrients against the plethora of toxic compounds that plants use for defense. These decisions are guided by a few simple clues of smell, sight, and taste alone: healthy food tastes delicious, while toxic food tastes repulsive. Those pleasure and avoidance centers in the brain are educated by experience and some guidance from parents. For herbivores these mechanisms are enough—they work. Meat eaters benefit from an additional appetite not obvious in a zoo or backyard.

Technically, wolves are opportunists; that is, if you examine their feces, you can see that they also eat vegetable foods. But, make no mistake, large-mammal hunting is their forte, and hunting is built into their anatomy, physiology, and behavior. The fact that a wolf pack often stages a "pep rally" before the hunt makes this clear.

Of course, for many carnivores, there is a learning curve. Wolves require a context and experience before they learn to hunt successfully, whereas hunting behavior among weasels and foxes is more innately directed. A tiny arctic fox kit, eyes barely open, automatically grabs the first lemming it sees with a killing neck bite. A four-month-old wolf, however, best distinguishes a sheep as food with some tutoring. But wolves are selectively predisposed to hunt and learn easily and with great pleasure—moose simply don't.

I propose that the repeated portrayal of so many aspects of hunting in Paleolithic art is evidence of selective pressures that were producing human males who (in

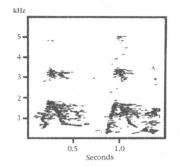

Sonogram print of a chimp hunting call: a special vocalization used for no other purpose but to announce and arouse the group to participate in a hunt. After Mitani and Watts 1999.

the Paleolithic context of hunting exposure) were predisposed to get an incomparable thrill out of the chase. Reproductive success was associated with men who were keenly attached to the search-and-kill experience of hunting. Further, I believe that the essential unity and character of Paleolithic art remains opaque without this appreciation. Again, we are considering predispositions toward sorts of learning, toward sorts of pleasures. In a way these predispositions might be thought of as cheap evolutionary shortcuts to complex, hard-wired behavioral programs. Our ape relatives exhibit a range of behavioral patterns that clarify this point.

Gorillas do not seem predisposed to hunt; at least they are not known to do so. In contrast, our nearest ape relatives, chimps, often pursue any susceptible source of fresh meat when the opportunity arises, from young monkeys to termites. Male chimps, particularly, appear to enjoy the exhilaration of chasing and killing young antelope and monkeys. In fact, they have a call, used in no other situation, a "call-to-hunt," used prior to a monkey hunt or when monkeys are sighted (Mitani and Watts 1999). This call mobilizes other males, and the success rate increases with the number of male participants. Adult male chimps have been observed in hunts in which they walk along quietly in single file looking for monkey groups that contain numerous young (Mitani and Watts 1999). Historic

Evolution's Outlandish Consigliere

Evolution is not guided by some all-wise mafioso Don-in-the-sky making optimally rational design decisions. A better metaphor might be to envision evolutionary adaptations as though "consigned" to a pragmatic agent, let's say a Consigliere, who gets things done with what is at hand, though the work consists of cobbled-up expediency in which rough approximations outnumber optimal solutions.

Despite their often remarkable beauty, evolutionary solutions are often radically ad hoc and proximate. A behavioral trait, an anatomical feature, or a seasonal color change may be once or twice removed from what we would consider a directly targeted link to an evolutionary problem. For example, among mammals the timing of many life events (like rut or molt) is determined by distant extraterrestrial forces that control day length. Snowshoe hares and ptarmigan in my lower field both molt to white in winter and to brown-gray tones in summer, thereby assuming seasonally apt camouflage. This seasonal change of fur and feather camouflage is not timed by melting snow or autumn foliage color but to the autumn and spring equinoxes. In fact, these species use day-length cues for the timing of mating behavior and dispersal as well. Day length was an evolutionarily cheap and ready-at-hand component for timing a physiological clock. Autumn and spring day length are indeed secondarily related to snow arrival and spring melt, but the crudity in this correlation means that some hares and ptarmigan die each year when, for example, snowfall is late and thousands of individuals are left nakedly exposed to predation—white ptarmigan really stand out on autumn brown tundra.

Natural selection has most influence on existing individual variations; the Consigliere makes do, sometimes simply, but often obliquely—red fruit as ripe, red rumps as erotic. In spite of it all, his solutions generally work, or at least did so in their context of origin. Appreciation of this indirect evolutionary consignment of regulators is also critical when looking at human behavioral propensities and hence Paleolithic art. For example, a better appreciation of the Consigliere's methods can give us a new eye for images of big-breasted, full-figured woman and spirited animals of the hunt.

---

and contemporary human evidence suggests that men are farther along a route of innate proclivity to hunt, particularly if exposed to hunting opportunities during youth. My point is that this proclivity to take pleasure in hunting and in skills related to hunting excellence has been shaped over millennia in which the search-and-kill portion was a part of the human lifeway.

IF THE THRILL OF THE CHASE HAS A GENETIC BASIS, WHY DON'T ALL MEN WANT TO HUNT?

If the appetite for hunting, for exercising hunting skills and taking pleasure in the chase and kill, was in the genetic makeup of Pleistocene males, why don't we see a universal desire to hunt expressed among men today? Why don't all men still hunt? A response to that question is probably similar in principle to the answer to the question "If there is a genetic propensity to become a good parent (which has been so crucial in human evolution), why do we find many individuals and couples today choosing not to have children and so many botching the job if they do have children?" I think the answer about parenting is complicated and has several dimensions: (1) Until modern times, lust quite sufficiently promoted pregnancy. Modern contraceptives have decoupled the age-old link of sexual desire and conception, allowing us considerable choice as to when, or even if, to connect the two. (2) Becoming a good parent depends to a considerable degree on proper "imprinting," that is, being raised in a loving family with good parenting skills. So failure here often breeds more failure. (3) One can substitute surrogates to satisfy innate child-caring needs, like caring for

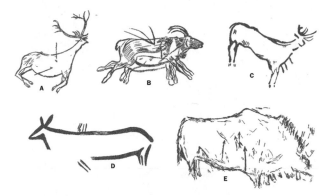

What do you always include in your drawings of animals: ears, hooves, horns, tail, eyes? Paleolithic hunters liked to include a spear. A sizable percentage of animals drawn over tens of thousands of years, discovered over millions of square kilometers, have spears sticking out of them. The people who made these images were not preoccupied with berries and mushrooms or collecting spring snails. Their preoccupations were with large mammals, speared large mammals. **A**, Red deer, Lascaux, Fr. **B**, Ibex, Trois Frères, Fr. **C**, Red deer, Minateda, Sp. **D**, Red deer, Cueva Silatre, Sp. **E**, Bison, Mas d'Azil, Fr.

A Pleistocene horse done with fingers on the mud wall of Montespan, Fr., with numerous "hits." A picture made thousands of years later and thousands of kilometers away on an open-air rock surface in the Atlas Mountains, at Guerar el-Hamra, shows similar repeated hits. Both of these seem to be the kind of images young people would make, not seasoned hunters.

pets. This surrogate-human role is one of the main uses these days for cats and dogs. (4) Modern life does not always present the right context in which to have and care for children, in the form of appropriate spouse, sufficient resources, sufficient time, and reduced stress. One could go on adding to this list, but you get the idea. In principle, most of these apply to why all men do not follow the natural propensity to hunt: missed critical periods for "imprinting," surrogate substitution, improper context, and so forth.

There is evidence that men's brains differ subtly from women's in those areas involving "targeting" activities (see Kimura 1999 for a review of the experimental evidence). These activities involve aiming objects at a target—throwing or intercepting a projectile. Kimura found that statistically women excel on tests involving stereoscopic perception at close range and fine motor precision and speed; whereas, on average, she found that men score higher on large-scale muscle activities and rapid spatiomotor analysis away from the body, even when corrected for body size and muscle bulk. These differences are marked early in life before boys and girls differ in muscular strength or targeting experience (Lunn 1987). And they seem to be universal cross-culturally, with sexual dif-

ferences as large as one standard deviation (Kimura 1999). She proposed that these particular sexual differences we measure today could be most reasonably explained by natural selection acting within the context of Pleistocene sexual role differences.

Under the public-park shade of dark chestnuts across southern Europe one can find clusters of six or more males, of all ages and vocations, intensely absorbed in throwing steel balls in a game of immense precision, boules. As a boy in rural America I caught the last edge of a similar tradition with the game of horseshoes. Today, throughout the world, grand stadiums in every city are devoted to the games of rival teams testing their agility, speed, and accuracy with projectiles. A Martian might find all this nonproductive activity with balls bizarre, unless she was briefed about our Pleistocene past and our sexual differences here on earth.

IT TOOK MORE THAN APPETITE AND ENTHUSIASM

Motivation alone was not enough to turn the physically challenged *Homo* folks into successful hunters. The emergence of *Homo* as a hunting specialist relied on a unique social structure interlinked with sophisticated intelligence. The older primate troop of small-item crumbfeeders had to become an organized team. This new organizational level required creative individuals, male and female, who could manage the complexity of human-style interactions and alliances. How did such individual

Context, Genes, and Genetic Predisposition

Contextual exposure is critical for proper development of many behaviors, including those for which there are strong genetic predispositions. Leyhausen's (1973) work with carnivore development and hunting behavior provides many insights from other species into the critical periods involved in the love of hunting. Without early exposure cats make poor mousers or no mousers at all. They are left with a disjointed attentiveness to watching birds out the window or pouncing on movements under the bed sheet. In a heritability study of over 1500 dogs, Vangen and Klemetsdal (1988) found that individual behavioral traits having to do with hunting (hunting eagerness, style and speed, tracking, sense of smell, seeking, fieldwork, and following birds) each had a significant heritability. These authors also observed that mongrels produced by

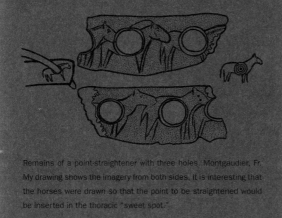

Remains of a point-straightener with three holes. Montgaudier, Fr. My drawing shows the imagery from both sides. It is interesting that the horses were drawn so that the point to be straightened would be inserted in the thoracic "sweet spot."

crossing hunting with nonhunting breeds frequently possessed disrupted or rearranged elements of the predatory sequence or were missing elements altogether. In later dog studies Hart (1995) and Willis (1995) found similar heritability in hunting and related behaviors.

It is true that humans are not cats or dogs, but some of the same principles apply. Bouchard and his team (1990), in what is now known as the Minnesota Twin Study, were able to show that occupational-vocational and leisure-time interests are heritable: 0.40 heritability on the Minnesota Occupational Interest Scale and 0.43 on the Jackson Vocational Interest Scale. These heritability figures do not directly address hunting, but they do show that similar things have a significant heritability. This is the heritability range that in dogs, for example, provided the basis for selective creation of various breeds with their different physical appearances and behaviors, including breed-specific levels of hunting enthusiasm and kinds of hunting ability.

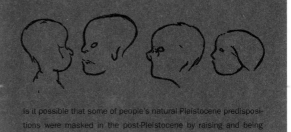

Is it possible that some of people's natural Pleistocene predispositions were masked in the post-Pleistocene by raising and being raised in such altered contexts? Pleistocene children, La Marche, Fr.

capacities and complex sociality arise? Like stones in an arch, the evolutionary role of each aspect was critical, but if any could be called the keystone I would say it had to have been the evolution of the human family. I focus there because the family creates the necessary space required to raise human-style, high-quality kids (chapter 4). Uniquely aligned family bonds interactively allowed the development of bonds and intimacies within the human band that are not found among chimps, nor probably were they present in some ancestral early hominids.

New Social Bonds and the Hunting Revolution

In our battle to capture virtue—the division of labor and opportunities of co-operative synergy—it was hunting for meat that granted our species its first great opportunity.
M. Ridley, *The Origins of Virtue*

In the next few pages I would like to sketch out the evolutionary story of human social bonding as it relates to the hunting enterprise. It is going to be the guy rope that will help us ground Paleolithic art. Please understand that

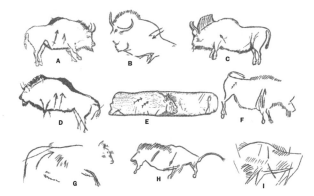

Images of speared bison from a variety of Paleolithic sites: **A** and **D**, Niaux, Fr. **B**, Lascaux, Fr. **C** and **F**, Trois Frères, Fr. **E**, Isturitz, Fr. **G**, Bois du Cantet, Fr. **H**, Bara-Bahau, Fr. **I**, La Madeleine, Fr.

these suggestions about core patterns are not insensitive to the immense complexity of human variation. We know from historic human analogs and chimp societies that raids, rape, adultery, child abandonment, promiscuity, infanticide, murder, inbreeding, and such occur. Likewise, in some Paleolithic localities human groups may have specialized on waterfowl or hares. Others may have shifted to matrilocal traditions. And still others may have stabilized at village size instead of band size. My aim is a profile of the central story.

THE BOND TO CHILDREN: MAKING QUALITY INSTEAD OF QUANTITY

The most fundamental bond in every mammalian species is between a mother and her offspring. The new demands that the hunting niche made upon the first members of our genus not only intensified that bond but added participation and protection by the father. Paleolithic children had to have spent a long apprenticeship in a wide range of disciplines. Quality education mattered here; the evidence of that story forms the spine of this book. The radically new thing about the Pleistocene band may have been its carefully nurtured children with years of rich and intimate experiences, able to achieve new plateaus of individual and social complexity. An extended childhood in particular allowed long periods of play and exploration. It

all depended on long-term parent-child bonds with both the father and the mother: the intimacy of sleeping in each other's warmth and long talks during shared chores and time together around glowing coals.

THE FEMALE-MALE BOND: INTERDEPENDENCE AND ASSURED PATERNITY

Mother apes have an amazing and enduring attachment to their young, but male chimps do not. Neither bonobos nor chimps have enduring pair bonds, though one can see hints of its precursors in temporary male-female consorts during estrus. A few other primate species do have mated pairs and these species allow us to examine the different faces of pair-bonding. Several primate groups live in adult male-female pairs, but very few show the criteria of evolved monogamous bonding as discussed by Fuentes (1999) and Anzenberger (1992):

- high rates of separation anxiety (both physiological and behavioral)
- paternal care (especially after weaning)
- aggression toward extragroup adults
- considerable time spent in joint grooming
- joint displays (such as duetting)
- frequent physical intimacy (behaviors like tail-twining)
- relative copulation exclusivity

Primate groups that do exhibit these patterns to varying degrees include South American titi monkeys (*Callicebus*) and night monkeys (*Aotus*), Madagascar indrid lemurs (*Avahi* and *Indri*), and Southeast Asian gibbons (*Hylobates*). These species normally live in "nuclear-family" groups consisting of the mated pair and growing young. But unlike humans, male participation in fatherhood among these species is not so much targeted at increasing the quality of young as it is in increasing the quantity of offspring. Male care of offspring in these species seems a simple replacement of female care, freeing the female to have more young. Male participation does not appear to be associated with increased quality of parenting (e.g.,

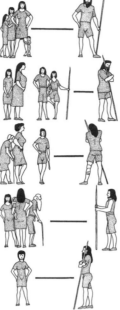

Image of Pleistocene stallion with foal. Unlike most other male ungulates, wild stallions recognize and protect their foals in the harem with an energy equal to that of the mares. This Paleolithic image occurs as a small engraving "wrapped around" a point-straightener from Teyjat, Fr. As an aside, note the neck striping in both animals, discussed earlier.

Unlike our nearest living related species, chimps, there is a distinctly human biological tendency toward male-female bonding as a family unit. It can take various forms but the mainstream is that the family unit is headed by one male and one female.

elaborating skills or increasing years of dependency). The human capacity to pair-bond traced a different evolutionary route and focused more on family and quality offspring, not only increased quantity.

Human pair-bonding also differs from the above examples of monogamous or monogamous-like primate pair-bonding in that human nuclear family groups are the building blocks of a larger band (Lovejoy 1981, 1993), a band consisting of diversely related individuals who cooperate in most activities. Thus, the human pair-bond and nuclear family appear profoundly involved in the human capacity to live in larger social groups. Apparently both the family and the band were necessary to create uniquely human offspring, those high-investment children.

Many aspects of the monogamous or near-monogamous character of human pairing are controversial when we seek modern comparisons (see Fuentes 1999). But modern cultural diversity may not always be a fair representation of our Pleistocene past. Accumulations of wealth and power, technology-based economies, disen-

franchisement, subservience, and poverty create diverse imbalances of older norms. To pursue a theme of monogamous tendencies is not to deny forces that result in promiscuity, adultery, divorce, bigamy, and much else. Still, the predispositions we do have toward near-monogamous patterns are suggestive of deep roots (Ridley 1993; Wright 1994).

THE FEMALE-FEMALE BOND: CREATING HEARTH AND HOME

Generally, social organization among social mammals, including Old World primates, centers on ties between young and mother and on female-female bonds, but the social lives of great apes are usually organized by a patrilocal strategy in which males hold and defend an area while many of the females leave their birth area and join adjacent groups at puberty. This is particularly striking among bonobos and chimps, our nearest relatives. A similar pattern is observed in humans who live in small bands. Almost all societies dependent on large-mammal hunting (Eskimo, Bushman, etc.) are patriarchal and patrilocal. Matriarchies are unknown among human groups in either history or modernity.

Many primate females are very hierarchical and competitive, because breeding success, health, and longevity of the young depend on the mother's relative status. Adult females are known to kill young of other females when the opportunity presents itself (evidence reviewed in Hrdy 1999). Perhaps the stability afforded by a long-term male

Happy Marriages and Honor-Roll Kids:
How to Get There from Promiscuous Chimps?

While human-style hunting may be linked with the complicated process of developing quality young, the evolutionary route to this process is not obvious. We can track backward and propose a likely scenario. Evolutionary solutions often have one or more intermediate functional stages that are not the same as the final solution, and those are what we want to look for. For example, how to get to flying from nonflying? Fossils and modern analogs of several groups show that the intermediate step was likely gliding. What then was the intermediate step from chimp-style life history to that of humans? Things like dual-parenting, mate love, and fidelity do not arise de novo.

A male's investment in an offspring cannot come before the evolution of some behavior that ensures paternity (behaviors that result in attentive fathers being victims of cuckoldry are selected against, for obvious reasons). Extensive consorting with a female is the one way a male can be more certain of paternity. But the emotion of mate love that drives the consorting had to come first. This sequence could not work backward. What forces could start that process? How to fly from walking?

Early theorists on this subject (e.g., Washburn and Lancaster 1968) proposed that the romantic pair-bond originated from reciprocal resource sharing between a male and female. What may have been involved in such trade? Chimp behavior helps us reconstruct this. A female has something a male seeks above all else: all the sex he wants, in the form of exclusive copulatory rights around the clock, any month of the year,

year after year. Male attachment and male trust could grow on a guarantee of access—exclusive access granted by the female.

What would induce a female to make such an extreme pact? We can hypothesize two crucial things: protection from other marauding males or predators and provisioning, especially with nutrient-rich meat. These would directly contribute to her reproductive success and the preservation of health and life for both herself and her young. Is there any evidence for such a scenario?

Again, chimp biology is helpful. Chimp mothers in the wild are always single parents, and field studies show that female chimps are vulnerable to attack by strange males or even by other females in the band. These attacks can be so serious as to lead to the death of young or even the death of adult female chimps (Wrangham and Peterson 1996; Hrdy 1999).

Evidence for an intermediate stage of male nutrient provisioning is twofold. The first clue comes from the fact that chimp males exchange sought-after meat in return for copulatory privileges with females (Tutin 1979; Stanford et al. 1994). Second, some of our present patterns in gift-giving must be, in part, behavioral remnants of such an intermediary stage. Courtship rituals, in which men give prized food (chocolates, restaurant dining, etc.) or other valuable gifts are familiar, not-so-symbolic hints of older behaviors. Bride-price is another kind of example; Bushman provide a freshly killed large mammal as a symbolic bride-price. Prostitution can perhaps be seen as an analogous form of exchange, one emancipated from bonding by money, simply sex for cash to pay the grocery bills.

consort allowed females to turn their energies from coarse competition to rearing their young in a more secure and superior setting. In fact bonobo communities illustrate nascent aspects of female-female cooperation (De Waal and Lanting 1997). Genetic and kinship lines would have linked adult women to their original home groups among neighboring bands, and thus, females may have taken the leading role in maintaining peaceful interactions among groups (Hrdy 1999).

Modern hunter-gather analogs testify to the intensely communicative network women maintain inside a band. This communication promotes individual, family, and

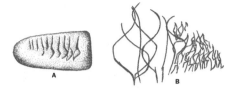

A, Carved stone from Niederbieker II, Ger., showing female-like images. **B**, Similar images on a stone plaquette from Gönnersdorf, Ger. This plaquette contains the largest number of female images drawn together in Paleolithic art. I am not sure numbers mean a lot in these cases, but the maximum number of females in a viable Paleolithic band was probably ten to twenty.

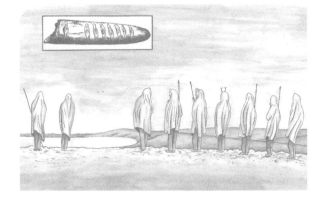

Box: Scene of nine people engraved on an ivory fragment from Gourdan, Fr. The engraving was done at a quick, elementary level. The broken-off part may have had details that would allow us to better interpret this scene. *Below,* my reconstruction as a group of adults facing away from the viewer, with one person wearing an antler cap, the kind of disguise common among hunters who use hemorrhaging-type projectiles.

group well-being, helps resolve conflicts, and aids in cultivating encyclopedic know-how. Thousands of things are tested, created, modified, and added to. Such developments made people healthier and longer lived, work more efficient, and camps more livable and comfortable. As with chimps, human females normally live longer than males (Allman 1999); thus, we can expect that women had significant roles as elders and transmitters of knowledge, passing on knowledge of how to endure rough times and to best capitalize on bountiful ones from generation to generation—a behavior clearly linked to evolutionary fitness.

THE MALE-MALE BOND: BROTHERHOOD OF RISK AND VIOLENCE

Human males are not strong-armed boar bears or silver-backed gorillas who make it on their own. Our niche was not that of a solitary male living all on his own. Human hunting required close group cooperation; that is our nature. A search-and-kill hunting party of three to four adult hunters was likely a minimal number that could function well and still have been effective against a wounded bison and an intimidating defensive shield against dangerous predators.

Such life-and-death stakes required loyalty and profound commitment, the sort of mutual reliance we call brotherhood. This kind of cooperation would not have been demanded of tuber-diggers or scavengers. Coopera-

tive hunting of large dangerous game with slow-killing weapons demanded degrees of self-sacrifice or at least risk taking for others. Genetic kinship is the best way to underwrite such commitment and trust, and that, in turn, is best obtained with a patrilocal tradition.

Using historic societies as analogs, a number of anthropologists (e.g., Birdsell 1968; Steward 1968; Williams 1968) have proposed patrilocal organization as a Paleolithic standard. Selection for committed teamwork, for brotherhood behaviors, is clearer cut when the other guys are near-relatives—sharing more than a few of their genes. The hunting lifeway depended on cooperation, but if males were competing for sex, they were less likely to fully cooperate for hunting. So what was the evolutionary patch to this age-old pattern of fighting over women? Two routes were available to decrease male-male sexual competition. One route is exemplified by the more free and frequent sexual exchanges we see among chimps, especially bonobos. The second avenue involved delimiting copulation, primarily to a partnered pair via behavioral bonds of love and devotion. Human-style male cooperation was made possible by this route toward monogamy (or near-monogamy), which ensured that most adult males either had a wife or had prospects of one. Unlike chimps, human males are not perpetually competing over each female coming into estrus. The new human style of pair-bond with its full and frequent copulatory privileges changed male-male competition. Male-female bonding kept the lust of adult males relatively satisfied, enabling them to set aside copulatory obsessions long enough to cooperate creatively and focus on the other obsession of large-mammal hunting. Monogamy or monogamy-like arrangements changed the face of male life, allowing men to cooperate with one another and simultaneously fostering new male behaviors such as being an intimately present father, teacher, and provider.

Gorilla groups are dominated by a single, naturally fascist male, and chimp societies are something like an oligarchy, ruled by a coalition of powerful males. Ethnographic analogs suggest that early human hunting groups were, in sharp contrast, markedly democratic. Perhaps seniority, especially the experience and wisdom that seniority brings, weighed heavily in field decisions, but the capacity to act cooperatively with other males over long periods of time is the hallmark of hunting success among humans. There were undoubtedly exceptions to such cooperative interaction, but genetic kinship of adult male band members would have provided some natural glue. A number of Paleolithic skeletons of people interred together appear related (Ullrich 1996); the skulls are more similar than one would predict of a random group—added evidence that the bands were small, family-based groups.

GREATER GOOD AMONG THE BAND

Unlike some vegetarians, carnivores high on the food pyramid are adapted to life at low densities, both within and among groups. Each group has comparatively large home ranges and defended territories. This is because the opportunities for getting food are spotty and occur errati-

Even though the major bond in the Paleolithic must have been within the family, there must also have been bonds within age-groups and within the sexes. Of course, we can also imagine that they were all bonded together as part of the greater band's unity.

cally, despite the fact that potential prey may be common. This pattern helps us envision Pleistocene hunters.

A highly interdependent large-mammal hunting lifeway combined with nuclear-family structure meant that the fission-fusion pattern of a large chimpanzee community (150 or so), which fostered much movement and shifts in social affiliation among small group segments (primarily sexually based), would not have worked. A change to a more permanent attachment within a smaller group was required.

As I discussed in the previous chapter, a band of roughly twenty-five to forty people fits our best guess for the average size of the Paleolithic social unit above the nuclear family. Selection for trust, interdependence, empathy, and a strategy of general goodwill outside the nuclear family was based both on degrees of nepotism and on insistence on sensitive reciprocity that women added as members from outside (Ridley 1996). One's fate certainly depended on the concerted performance of the whole band on a mutualistic and integrated level never seen in the rest of nature, even among the eusocial termites and bees. The forces driving such new levels of cooperation and communication in such a hunting lifeway had to be very powerful. Yet individual stature from hunting excellence also had to be important; again, our analogs don't fail us. Ethnographers report that all hunters do not have to be of equal stature to cooperate. Some gradient of stature seems inherent. We cannot exclude violence in our model here, but it had to be infrequent and mostly low profile.

WIDER ALLIANCES: TRADE AND PEACE

Of course, a Paleolithic hunting band did not live in complete isolation. Analogies with recent hunting groups suggest that bands may have had peripheral connections with five to ten other bands, which might mean in the vicinity of 200 to 400 people who were known by name as more distant relatives and acquaintances (Birdsell 1968; Dunbar 1996). Evidence from Paleolithic art as well as the wide geographic dispersal of raw stone materials suggests that through trade these late Paleolithic connections among bands may have extended to other less proximate bands and kinship groups (Gamble 1982). Again, modern analogies do show such a broad pattern. Trade and information sharing contributed to the shared pool of unwritten memory and to overall security.

These wider alliances were likely a complex mix of competition and cooperation, and some conflict must have been present. I doubt that peace among groups could always have prevailed. But there is a largely unremarked-upon clue about Paleolithic intergroup relations that is hidden in Paleolithic art and is a little like Sherlock Holmes's "dog that didn't bark." We have drawings galore of weapons but something is missing in Paleolithic art that occurs widely in later prehistoric tribal art. Paleolithic art lacks depictions of shields and scenes showing violent intergroup confrontations. This lack is suggestive of a Paleolithic standard of good interband relations. I will have more to say on these missing shields and the lack of portrayals of intergroup conflict later.

FORGING THE ALLOY OF AMBITION AND ALLIANCE

Another important wheel spoke in the story of large-mammal hunting and human behavior starts with the size of the prey itself, the package size. Though a dead large mammal was off-the-scale abundance for a meat-hungry primate, it came with problems. Imagine, five of you sweaty and excited, standing over a 1000-kilogram bison

How to cooperate and yet be ambitious? It is not just climate and diet that affect natural selection. A lot is at stake in things like the choice of a husband, both in day-to-day proximate terms and in terms of evolutionary fitness. Mate selection, generations after thousands of generations, is a strong selective pressure. The Pleistocene males incised on stone from Addaura, It., were not totally equal as potential mates.

coughing its last breath. There is an enormous load of meat to carry a long distance to camp. Who can claim it and who gets a portion—how much and what part? Not all carcass parts are equal, nor perhaps are all people equally worthy.

Hyenas and lions go about dividing a fresh kill with laid-back ears in a noisy frenzy of competitive snarls, growls, bites, and cuffs that one can hear from a long way off. Low-status individuals often come away torn and bloody. Ethnographic analogs suggest that early humans avoided such aggressive violence over carcass distribution. Unlike hyenas and lions, the more intensely cooperative style of humans required more egalitarian payback, which could take place only within a low-profile social hierarchy. So, not only did the band have to cooperate in new ways to take large prey, but the large packaging itself encouraged sharing and distributing the rewards amicably. This cooperative spirit had to be underwritten by related families, among which the distribution of the bounty at dinnertime was not very lopsided.

But we must allow for a little lopsidedness. Indeed, evolution is about lopsidedness, and it is this slight imbalance that is going to figure in our understanding of much of Paleolithic art. Individual excellence and dedication were essential, and that may have been no problem, because with such a small group, any advantages accruing to an individual's competitive edge are basically built in. By that I mean that individuals consistently did "get what they gave." Later I will show some ways that ambition leaked through into Paleolithic art. The key was to balance individual ambition and cooperation. The optimal mix of hunting excellence and propensity to share would likely have resulted in the highest stature.

We can easily imagine forces that maintained this balance between hunting excellence and sharing. A swing too far toward individual reward would have endangered the very cooperation such hunting success required. A swing in the opposite direction, toward "millimeter" sharing and lack of recognition and reward, might have dampened effort and reduced success. The more cooperative Paleolithic human context required older kinds of ape ambition to be checked and redirected—transformed by the new context and its possibilities into ambitions unavailable to our ape cousins.

The emerging capacity to love, to create and enjoy the romance of pair-bonding, was related to not having to mate all the females or be irresistibly attracted to the brawniest thump-chest male. Lust was not in any way eliminated, but there were new emotional domains and combinations to inhabit, and in one of these new combinations, personal glory could mesh with group service. And these newly amalgamated qualities were there to be admired, celebrated, befriended, and if possible married. Glory could now arise from providing, sharing, and setting things right—modern ethnographic analogs tell that story. These emergent kinds of ambition had to be important. And certainly for men, personal ambition and recognition were entangled with the central enterprise of hunting, but they were not spread evenly.

And that, I propose, is the substory to much of the imagery in preserved Paleolithic art. We do not find the celebration of cooperation, family games, camp making, wood gathering, dancing, flowers, or chasing delicate insects depicted in the art. Taphonomic biases distort our collections, and work in the most physically durable materials was largely done by males. Their attraction is to most forms of glory—the dynamics of young male attraction to risk. The preoccupations with excelling in hunting lend themselves to visual portrayal—all these forces shape what is left to be seen in Paleolithic art. This does not mean that hunting success was necessarily the most influential or greatest service in the band. But it does suggest that large mammals and their successful hunting were the most tangibly sought-after goal of the artists whose work we happen to have. To use an oblique analogy with today, few adolescents fantasize about becoming loving fathers, business magnates, statesmen, or great thinkers; rather, images of rock stars, actors, and athletes line the walls of their rooms. To our youth, these high-profile glamorous figures more directly embody achievement, reward, and glory.

EVOLUTION, COGNITION, AND THE HUNTING LIFEWAY

I was struck by how much the Eskimos know about animals and their environment. I had never encountered that level of knowledge—especially not in the biology department of the university. Eskimos study animals as intensively as any biologist, but their knowledge is not esoteric. It is based on hunting these animals for survival. I was also impressed by the passion with which the Eskimos pursued animals, not just in the hunt, but in their desire to learn about them. I had never experienced anything like the intensity of their relationship to animals. The greatest hunter in the village was an old man named Wesley Ehak. His sense of animals was so profound that the distinction between his humanness and the animal's animalness seemed blurred.

Richard Nelson, "The Way of the Hunter"

Pleistocene people must have chosen their mates carefully. Of course, signs of likely fidelity, physical attractiveness, youth, and health have always been important (Buss 1989, 1992), but people who were perceptive, thoughtful, and creative in meeting life's challenges would surely also have been desirable as mates; these characteristics certainly figure into mate choice in virtually all cultures (Buss 1989; Brown 1991). This is because, as we have already seen, quality child care as opposed to simply having more children is associated with greater net reproduction among most hunting cultures (e.g., Blurton-Jones 1987). Choice of husband or of wife would have been equally important, even though the most sought-after qualities may have differed in detail.

Stamina, social adeptness, health, strength, kindness, and much else are likely to be qualities of a good hunter, husband, and father—the prospective parent. But all else being equal, should women choose brainy husbands? In a hunting-dependent economy, where all males hunt, one good predictor of intelligence may be long-term success in hunting. The varied nature of large-mammal hunting requires great cognitive skills in addition to physical assets. There is ethnographic evidence that the top hunters are indeed the smartest men; by administering tests of cognitive skills to Bushman, Reuning (1988) found that the top scores indeed came from the most successful hunters. Along with a male's choice of a creative and thoughtful woman stands a female's appreciation of a mate who is proving to be a successful hunter. Thus, men's and women's competition for the best mates may well have inadvertently selected for creative opportunism, intellectual perception and reason, and many other human characteristics.

In the Paleolithic, differences in men's hunting behavior would have been closely linked to fitness. Marks (1976) found that among the Bias of Zambia over half of the meat was killed by only 20% of the hunters. Laughlin (1968) too observed large differences in hunting success among Aleuts. Lee's (1979) sample showed that among the !Kung Bushman 30% of the adult hunters produced 80% of the meat. Among the prime-aged groups, half of the hunters accounted for almost all of the kills. The few Bushman males who could not hunt successfully were not even initiated into manhood. For a man to marry he had to be a proven and reliable hunter, and whether he could ever take a second wife depended on his hunting excellence (Wannenberg 1979). I mentioned earlier that not only must a Bushman have been an experienced hunter to marry, but he had to bring a large mammal to the prospective parents as a gift to prove his ability. Interestingly, he could kill hundreds of steenboks, duikers, aardvarks, springhaas, and even warthogs, but none of these counted

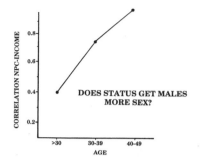

Status and wealth make a difference when it comes to single males getting sex. Is this an old Pleistocene behavior in modern guise? The correlation coefficient (with a range of 0.0–1.0) between income and number of potential conceptions (NPC) was highest in the mature ages, particularly among men in their forties. French Canadian unmarried males were used in this study (Alcock 1993).

toward being a real hunter; they were not defined as large mammals. The marriage gift must be in the gemsbok, kudu, eland, or buffalo class.

A behavioral predisposition toward enthusiastic hunting directly affects how much or how long one hunts. And from this one would guess that how much one hunts affects overall success. Hill and Hawkes (1983) found that high-return hunters hunted more than low-return hunters among the Ache, a hunter-gatherer people in South America. And indeed, the high-return hunters had a greater survivorship rate among their legitimate children and sired more illegitimate children. That is how one describes the force of natural selection. See Hill and Hurtado 1989 for a review.

Unlike more inegalitarian societies, the competition between Bushman (and Australian Aboriginal) males is extremely low profile with regard to hunting. One never brags about hunting prowess or success. However, as with every society, the competition is keen with regard to female favors and marriage—and this, by and large, is related to Bushman hunting success (Gowaseb 1992). According to Gowaseb, "Every parent seeks the most productive hunter for a son-in-law. The girl's parents address the boy's parents with 'Your son is hunting very well and

we want him to marry our daughter'" (1992, 27). Thomas comments, "Bushmen are polygamous, and a man is allowed by custom to have as many wives as he can afford, depending on how well he hunts" (1988, 23). And husbands insist on fidelity. Lee (1968) found adultery was the most common factor resulting in Bushman fights and the most common cause of killings. Three times as many fights were started by males as by females. Homicide levels were high compared to industrial societies. Homicide among Bushman in general is a male endeavor (Daly and Wilson 1988).

One can easily see why the intense effort at hunting excellence which creates differential evolutionary fitness is not elevated into win/lose competition models in Bushman, Ituri, or Australian Aboriginal society. Directly competitive social formats were likely avoided in the Paleolithic as well. Excellence does not necessitate a win/lose structure, and the interdependence of the members of small Paleolithic bands likely led them to develop social forms and practices to moderate jealousy. As one increases in excellence, it is incumbent to share even more. One might say that one has to share good luck in order to get a share in times of bad luck. This explains the taboos in many hunting societies against keeping most (sometimes any) of the meat for oneself. Even so, gifts, especially of the largest mammals, tend to be skewed along lines of nepotism and reciprocity, favoring individuals upon whom the hunter during less favorable times may have to depend most for assistance.

In hunting economies, an excellent hunter has high social status among his peers. Seeking status is one of those behaviors, like lust, that has seemingly unexplainable aspects unless you realize it is a secondary trait in its relation to reproduction. High status does not always mean high reproduction—the currency of evolutionary fitness. In fact, status, like the degree of lust, is only slightly correlated with reproduction, but the correlation is positive in both cases (i.e., the higher the status, the higher the reproduction, and vice versa). Our striving for status, like satisfaction of lust, is a little crazy unless you understand its connection to reproduction.

THE SELECTION DYNAMICS

If large-mammal hunters are obliged to share with the entire group, why not selfishly concentrate on smaller creatures and let others engage the dangerous large mammals? The answer is that selective benefits other than an interest in dinner are involved. Cooperation to get the large-mammal bounty does not mean that individual abilities were obscured, any more than team sports hide individual performance. Selective pressures and rewards promoting seek-and-kill hunting excellence in males would have included the following:

▶ The first to benefit would have been the family of origin. A young boy or an unmarried young man would have provided resources for his mother's hearth (and his valuable reputation as a good hunter), enhancing both the quality and quantity of living (and future) siblings via his mother's reproduction and parenting. Remember that siblings and parents share many genes; the young hunter's genetic relation to them is the same as it will be to his own children, that is, 0.5. Of course, more generally, when an adult hunter distributes meat in a patrilocal band, the families of all his male relatives will also be favored.

▶ The most successful young hunters would have been the most sought after as husbands and thus would have married earlier than poor hunters (Lee 1979). Early reproduction is even more important to evolutionary fitness than continued reproduction into old age. The wife and children of an outstanding hunter would likely have been the most direct and indirect beneficiaries in terms of relative access to resources (Thomas 1988). Both adult fecundity and children's survivorship are necessarily linked to resources.

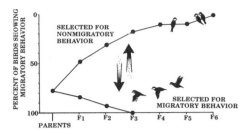

In addition to examining heritability by plotting relatives, one can actually estimate it from selection response. If there is no response, there is likely little heritability. In this experiment one sample of blackcaps was selected for migratory tendency (migratory restlessness), and the other sample for none. In three generations all the former line were migration-prone, while in six generations the latter approached 0. After Berthold et al. 1990.

Modified after Zamiatnin in Delporte 1993. Reconstructed from fragments fallen from a wall surface (shown in stipple) and found at Laussel, Fr. Three weighty gals stand, sipping their drinks from horn containers and watching a lean male spear thrower.

▶ The best hunters would have been, on average, more likely to have both the highest-quality, hardest-working, youngest, and fertile wives (Hawkes 2001), as well as possibly multiple wives, and, hence, more children (Lee 1979; Blurton-Jones 1967). In fact, Mitani and Watts (1999) found a similar phenomenon among chimps: the most dominant males (those with greater access to estrous females) were the best hunters (killed more monkeys and antelope).

▶ The high reputation and hence high social stature associated with being an outstanding hunter would allow one to accrue reciprocity credits on which to draw during periods of illness or injury, thereby ensuring greater

Statistically, cross-cultural studies show that the best hunters seem to marry earlier, appeal to the choicest wives, get more wives, father more children, and have more children who survive to maturity. A Holocene Australian Aboriginal painting of a man, a child, and two women. Upper Alligator River, Australia.

These illustrations are from later prehistoric rock art scenes by hunting cultures from North Africa: **A**, Tin-n-Lalan. **B**, Fezzan. **C**, Atlas Mountains. Pictures make the point better than words—sexual access and hunting success were connected.

personal and extended family security and hence higher reproduction and survival (Thomas 1988).

► Men choose to accompany, make alliances with, and become neighbors of individuals with high reputations as hunters, which in turn affects cooperation and hunting success (Hawkes 2001).

► The benefits of being a good young hunter would likely have been continued into old age. Ethnographers tell us that the alliance of old hunters is sought with gifts (Lee 1979; Cook 1980). The meat used as gifts would not only help the older hunters personally but serve as resources for their wives and children, enhancing survival and further reproduction.

► The best hunters are apparently more likely to be successful in their pursuit of extramarital liaisons, or so Kensinger (1989) found among the Cashinahua. There, the best hunters do have more illegitimate children than lesser hunters (Kensinger 1989). Anthropologists studying the Ache, a hunter-gatherer people in South America, found that the best hunters do share their meat selectively with other women and obtain sex in return (Hill and Kaplan 1988). Likewise, among the Aka Pygmies of central Africa, the best hunters enjoy sex with more women: they have more wives and more extramarital liaisons with unmarried and married

women (Hewlett 1988), and consequently more offspring. Forces such as these are not selectively neutral.

Reconstructing Some Textures of Paleolithic Hunting Lifeways from the Art

Having told me about all the old methods of hunting the caribou, Igjugârjuk proceeded to praise the white man . . . particularly such a wonderful invention as the gun that occupied his thoughts. In the old days it was only rarely that the people lived in a state of plenty. This happened only when they succeeded in driving a flock of caribou into a lake or river, so that they could be killed by the score. All other methods of hunting demanded great exertion, great perseverance, and never yielded anything much.

K. Rasmussen, *Intellectual Culture of the Iglulik Eskimos*

THE FAR-FROM-IDYLLIC PALEOLITHIC LIFE

Paleolithic images afford scant access to many aspects of late Paleolithic life; they don't tell us about gatherings or celebrations or about the variety of dances and songs, and they don't flesh out the wealth of stories and myths. Tens of thousands of years are more than we can imagine, but we can wonder, based on what we do know from people today, at what intimacies must have arisen from living among a band of extended family, and how broadly expert one must have become to live in such challenging climates with Paleolithic tool kits.

Among the graves and scattered in the art images are some hints about general patterns of life in the late Paleolithic. For example, the portrayals of risky situations bear out what one could imagine—that Paleolithic life was not always idyllic. In the next chapter we'll see how the full-figured Paleolithic images of women may paradoxically indicate frequent lean times, because fat is a way of storing energy for periods of food deficit. Skeletons in Paleolithic graves let us guess at mortality patterns and life expectancy. Such features of the life history figure importantly in our interpretation of the artists' lives and the emotional context of their art. While we reach for the big picture, it is a good time to remember that there would likely

How Could Hunting Appetites Have Evolved If Hunting Success Is Almost Random?

Some scholars have intimated (e.g., Pinker 1997) that selection pressures affecting human hunting have been nonexistent or very weak because hunting success has a high component of randomness. This element of chance brings to mind small-town newspaper photos of a twelve-year-old boy with his huge-antlered buck taken at first light on opening day. But to universally extend this fortuitous aspect of hunting is like saying chance plays a large role in whether a baseball player will hit a home run or simply strike out, and therefore it doesn't matter who plays on which team, because it won't affect the final score. As with baseball players, stochastic differences between an accomplished and a poor hunter can be extreme.

Outstanding hunters have developed an intimate knowledge of game behavior and local landscape and how they all relate to weather, weapon choice, use, etc. They have integrated an appetite for action with patience. And like professional baseball players, they have usually spent years honing hand-eye coordination skills. Paleolithic hunting demanded physical stamina, tolerance of discomfort and pain, knowledge and cleverness, and the long view in which mistakes as well as successes are synthesized into wisdom. Such talents are not acquired quickly or without great attention. Of course, these talents relate to one's health, sensory clarity, physical fitness, and internal motivation. Results may show considerable variation, but at issue are long-term patterns of consistently superior performance.

Today, most people do not actively hunt and many have never had occasion to even go out alongside experienced hunters and trackers. Slipping along quietly in a skin boat with Eskimos in among the pack ice looking for seals or tracking wounded game with Bushman are enlightening experiences. A few years ago I was out with a native Yakutian hunter getting food for our field camp of researchers in northeastern Siberia. The tundra was wet and difficult to negotiate, so he and I had taken a small boat down a narrow river, concentrating on places reindeer might cross. About midmorning two reindeer appeared over the riverbank, then turned and ran at full speed down the sandbar. He cut the motor, grabbed his old World War I vintage military rifle, and from a standing position in that small tippy boat dropped both animals dead with head shots. As we stepped out on to the sandbar, I asked why he had not used a traditional lung-heart shot? He smiled as he showed me the old surplus military cartridges with full-jacketed bullets. I understood. The complete jacket of copper meant that the lead bullet in the animal's thorax would not mushroom and would not result in a quick-killing shot. I was impressed. The boat was still moving when he had fired; the reindeer were at 80–100 meters and running away at an angle. I am a good shot, but not in that class. I watched him take a moose later that trip with an equally challenging shot. Excellence is closely related to hunting success.

have been great variability from group to group across these many thousands of years and tens of thousands of kilometers.

Overwhelming archaeological evidence for small camp sizes corroborates other evidence that hunting large mammals with limited technology was a difficult proposition, even with the cooperation of a close-knit band that was ready to undergo the hardships of long forays, camp mobility, and occasional hunger and to use other, opportunistic resources. Paleolithic art is informative about the difficulties encountered; a common scene in the art shows individual animals with protruding spears, sometimes mortally wounded and spewing lung blood and sometimes not so seriously wounded and threatening. Never are mass kills portrayed. Even with an atlatl one has to get close to a large mammal, within 30 meters for some reasonable likelihood of a hit. And even then, the lethal target area on a large mammal is not so big. This is not to

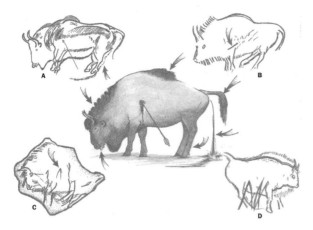

Large mammals mortally speared in the trunk behave in a characteristic manner, from autonomic discomfort. Bison so hit tend to hang their tongues out, pull their hind legs under them as they hump over, arch their backs, lower their heads, and often raise their tails to urinate/defecate. Illustrations of bison behavior from Paleolithic hits: **A** and **C**, Trois Frères, Fr. **B**, Montespan, Fr. **D**, Bruniquel, Fr. *Center*, my reconstructed image.

say that a hunting group may not occasionally have taken the opportunity to throw into a running herd 70–100 meters away.

The mix of species in Paleolithic middens lets us surmise that people were able to hunt in diverse locales, varying their hunting methods and tools. This kind of opportunistic hunting is not always formulaic. It would have required considerable experience, quality education, and years of intensive practice. From what we know about hunting today, Paleolithic hunting appears as the ultimate challenge. My bow-hunting equipment has a longer range and is considerably more accurate than any atlatl. Bow-hunting moose in woodlands is difficult, but hunting in the open is more difficult by an order of magnitude. The late Pleistocene European landscape was a much more open grassland than was characteristic of those same regions in later times. It is simply naive to portray Paleolithic life as a romantic idyll, as if one could spend most of one's time preoccupied with social and mystical concerns and only casually head out and kill game whenever the larder became empty. Hunting could not have been so

easy, or so boring. Periodic dearth and even starvation (Hayden 1981b) appear in ethnographic reports of many hunter-gatherer cultures. Such bottlenecks seem to be the hand that places upper limits on population numbers. These are potent selection pressures for keeping one's mind in touch with everyday reality, and of course sometimes playing with that reality.

The hours hunter-gatherers devote to subsistence hunting and gathering efforts as quoted in textbooks can be extraordinarily misleading. In many situations more hours spent hunting or gathering may cause a net reduction in well-being and fertility. Time spent in alternative nonhunting activities may have a greater positive effect on reproduction and children's survival (Hill and Hurtado 1989). Estimates of time spent foraging may be a poor indicator of how much time is required to deliver the amount of food people would actually prefer to have. For example, Ache women are reported as spending 2 hours per day on food gathering, but this is because this work must come on top of a demanding day filled with other tasks (Hill and Hurtado 1989). Just because subsistence hunters do not spend many hours per day hunting does not necessarily mean they could not use more food. They may not be hunting because opportunities are poor or weather is dangerous or not conducive to hunting success. Both Bushman and Australian Aboriginals often lay up (as do the animals they hunt) during the sweltering heat of summer midday, leaving only a few hours of prime hunting time at dawn and sunset.

Late Pleistocene life was likely both unpredictable and risky. Mature women would have faced particular health risks associated with the increased energetic and nutrient demands of pregnancy, parturition, and lactation. Men too faced demanding episodes. And ethnographic studies show that long serious hunts are risky and physically demanding for men. Kensinger (1989) found that among the Cashinahua men seldom returned from such hunts without having suffered some wound, and usually the hunters sat around for a day or two to "heal up" between hunts. These and other things made for a short life. If you imagine that Paleolithic life was idyllic or that early herbal medicines were potent, the mortality statistics of any subsistence society can be disillusioning.

It is worthwhile to look closely at the timing of death in the late Paleolithic. From studies of late Paleolithic skeletons Collins (1986) concluded that child mortality was about 30%, and he estimated that infant mortality must have been around 50%. This mortality pattern is strikingly similar to that of many wild Alaskan large mammals. It is also about average for other human cultures living without domesticated foodstuffs. Adult life expectancy throughout much of the late Paleolithic was roughly comparable to historically recorded mortality patterns for Bushman and Eskimo groups. Collins's review of late Paleolithic skeletal remains revealed 22 infants, 126 non-infants younger than sixteen years (let me remind you that skeletons of young animals are underrepresented taphonomically because of their fragility), 207 remains aged between sixteen and forty, but only 15 individuals who were over the age of forty when they died. That is, only 4% of the people lived past forty. (Compare that to the generation being born today, of whom at least 4% will reach almost 100 years of age.) We see from these Paleolithic data that knowing one's grandparents must have been rare, and knowing great-grandparents is a rather recent experience in human history.

Male Bushman are reported as starting to hunt seriously between the ages of seventeen and eighteen, reaching a peak in their twenties, after which hunting stamina declines significantly by thirty-five, and by forty their hunting abilities are severely limited (Silberbauer 1980). Female reproduction among Bushman is considerably slowed by thirty-five and all but ceased by forty. Of course, we cannot simply presume a similar pattern during the Paleolithic, but known survivorship curves for recent hunter-gatherers and the Paleolithic graves we have found suggest similarities.

Today, the performance of professional athletes in physiologically demanding sports declines with age, and

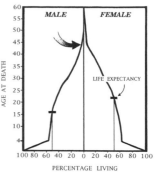

Demographics are important to keep in mind in understanding Paleolithic life, particularly art. The scattered sample used to imagine a survivorship curve for late Paleolithic peoples seems to be roughly similar to that of prehistoric Eskimo. Here are survivorship statistics from an old graveyard at Native Point, Sadlermiut. Data from Merbs 1983. T-bar marks the age of life expectancy (a time when half that cohort are dead). One can see that males have a high-risk life as measured by mortality. My arrow is meant to draw attention to the fact that at age forty-five virtually no males are alive.

most such athletes retire well before thirty-five. We also know that physiological fertility declines rapidly after thirty-five in modern Western women; by forty, the decline is clearly marked (Overfield 1985), though actual menopause does not occur until about fifty. On low-nutrient and low-calorie diets, fertility declines even earlier. I suspect these statistics echo a life history and mortality curve from the Paleolithic.

While our demographic information points to a short Paleolithic life, I do not want to suggest it was nasty or brutish. Good times may have been frequent, and one's efforts often successful. There is every reason to imagine they enjoyed some leisure, not mere rest but true leisure, no fences to mend, no rows to hoe—leisure to weave events into stories, to sing and dance, to draw and carve, to make life more elegant, comfortable, and entertaining. Paleolithic art offers little evidence of worried preoccupation with visual symbols; its expressions are animate, vivid, often poetic, vitally individual, and frequently erotic.

Such creativity requires a certain kind of energy, a particular combination of relaxation and attention. Ask any practicing artist. Their most profound enemies are forces that sap this vitality. A profusion of creativity comes from times that generate such energy, including deep involvement in high-arousal situations. The life risks of the late Paleolithic seem to have included such situations and to have occasionally provided episodes of abundance unharried by want or stress—times when one's needs were met, ample time to talk, to play, to make art. But can we take the art images and the midden contents at face value in assessing all this?

DISPARITY BETWEEN THE SPECIES IN THE MIDDENS AND THOSE IN THE ART

There is often a significant difference between the proportions of animal species pictured by Paleolithic artists and actual proportions of those species' bones in the food refuse piles. Some scholars have proposed that this disparity means that the subjects in the art had little to do with day-to-day hunting and instead were more closely aligned with unrelated social rituals. Certainly, the disparity exists. For example, in Franco-Cantabrian Paleolithic middens one finds mainly bones of reindeer, red deer, and ibex, while the art of that region is mainly pictures of horses, bison, and mammoths. This lack of correlation between the bones and the art is a common phenomenon (Klíma 1990; Altuna 1983; Delporte 1984). Dating to the same general period as Lascaux's artworks is an archaeological site at the entrance of the cave. Most bones are from young reindeer, but only one reindeer appears among the more than one thousand Lascaux drawings (Leroi-Gourhan 1982b). Does this disparity mean that the art had little to do with hunting? I don't think so. Rather, it could well be explained by two forces: one is a taphonomic skew, and the other is the difference between desire and implementation.

A statistical comparison of bones of mammal species in the archaeological sites with images in the art is not as straightforward as it might seem. First, most Eurasian sites are not kill-sites but campsites, and there is a strong bias as to what one carries back to camp. Bones from quite large mammals are heavy, so few would have been carried home. Bones from smaller mammals—hares, birds, and furbearers—apparently were. The simple reason for this has to do with the range of weight a person can pack. Small animals, like chamois and female ibex, could be carried whole. Intermediate-sized animals, like reindeer, can

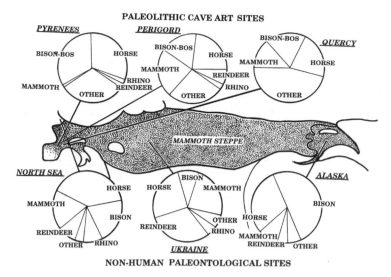

PALEOLITHIC CAVE ART SITES

NON-HUMAN PALEONTOLOGICAL SITES

Species pictured in Paleolithic art occur in very different proportions than the species percentages found in Paleolithic middens. However, there is a rough correspondence between species in the art and in the (nonhuman) paleontological sites. There seem to be two taphonomic processes at work. First, there is the artists' preference for drawing larger animals, whereas hunters mainly bagged the smaller ones. Second, in the paleontological sites large species (bison, horse) with more rugged bones preserve more easily than the smaller ones (saiga, reindeer). So in the art and in the paleontological sites an aggregate of horse, bison, reindeer, and mammoth predominate. (Data from Guthrie 1968; Pidoplichko 1956; Delporte 1990; and with great thanks to Dr. John de Vos, curator, National Museum of Natural History, Utrecht, Netherlands, pers. comm., with regard to North Sea fossil assemblages.)

be quartered (in some respects it is easier to carry a carcass when muscle mass is still attached to the bone). But very large animals are simply too heavy to quarter and carry, and these are often boned out into smaller, manageable pieces. A bison quarter, for example, may weigh 50–80 kilograms (about 110–176 pounds). That is simply too much to carry for many kilometers. Such large mammals were almost certainly boned out, and many of the bones left behind. Of course, if the kill was near camp or if the desire for marrow fat was sufficient, some long bones could also have been carried back home.

A similar sorting of bones and meat goes on every autumn here in Alaska. Moose that hunters kill near rivers, roads, or lakes are often simply quartered and brought home for future butchering. Backpack hunters, however, bone out large game, leaving the bones behind. My family and I hunt moose each year. We are not always successful

There are also notably few Pleistocene images of speared woolly mammoths. Here are a couple of possible exceptions: **A**, Bernifal, Fr. **B**, Gönnersdorf, Ger. One could argue that people hunted mammoths only on rare, opportunistic occasions.

There are virtually no Paleolithic images of speared rhinos. Here are a few possibilities: **A**, La Mouthe, Fr. **B**, Colombière, Fr. **C–E**, Rouffignac, Fr. Guerin and Faure (1984) reviewed the paleontological evidence and concluded that people did not regularly hunt rhinos in the late Paleolithic. Remember, woolly mammoths and rhinos were formidable creatures, against which Paleolithic hunters had no good defense if charged. Probably people and pachyderms generally practiced a peaceful, if tense, mutual avoidance, like Bushman with African elephants and rhinos. Rhino hunting was undoubtedly very rare and highly opportunistic.

and when we are fortunate enough to get a moose, the kill may be miles from the nearest road. So, faced with the arduous task of carrying heavy packs over long distances of challenging terrain, we avoid any unessential weight and extra trips. Fresh moose bones add an extra hundred kilograms, and we choose to leave them and other scraps for wolves, bears, and ravens. Judging by their middens, Paleolithic hunters often acted similarly. Crader (1983) observed that when the Africans she studied killed elephants, they never brought the bones back to camp but carefully removed and transported only the soft tissue. Paleoindian mammoth and bison kill/butchery-sites in North America show that most meat was boned out; the skeletons were left behind (Frison 1978). Ethnographic studies of caribou hunters, on the other hand, show that they usually take the eviscerated carcasses back to camp, bones and all (Spiess 1979), rather like most hunters do today with white-tail or roe deer.

Another detail to observe when comparing bones with art images is the problem of numbers versus mass. González Morales (1997), working with archaeological data from Altamira, found that although bison are the most common animals in the art, bone scraps excavated from the associated archaeological site were primarily from red deer. However, when the biomass of the respective species was accounted for, González Morales determined that bison and horses would have provided most of the meat.

An even more likely explanation for this discrepancy in species is that hunters are more keen about some species than others, and they choose to draw and talk about what is most interesting or "sought after." These latter species may or may not be the most numerous or the most commonly killed. Eating and hunting thrills are distinguishable and can be different. In historic times, little roe deer (*Capreolus capreolus*) far outnumber the larger red deer, or *Hirsch* (*Cervus elaphus*), in Europe. But it is red deer that figure most prominently in historic European hunting art and legend. Similarly, bighorn mountain sheep are relatively rare in North America, but in North American hunting art and hunting tales, they hold a place overwhelmingly disproportionate to their numbers. Much the same is true for wapiti and moose. American hunters annually kill large numbers of rabbits, quail, tree squirrels, doves, and white-tailed deer, yet the pictures that most often adorn their walls are of wild rams on wind-swept mountains or of a bull moose in a woodland lake at dawn. Of course, we cannot simply extrapolate this back to the Paleolithic, but evidence from many cultures does show that this phenomenon is very widespread. In an analogous fashion, the vehicles young boys draw are usually sports cars and large-wheeled trucks (far out of proportion to the percentages registered by the Division of Motor Vehicles).

In brief, most sought-after species are not necessarily "the most often got." The hunter's sense of nobility relates to challenge, risk, size, and passion. Woodhouse (1978) suggests that Bushman art is often "heroic"; the artists selected special subjects for inscription and rarely portrayed their daily activities of trapping small game and digging edible roots. Likewise, kangaroo and wallaby dominate in Australian Aboriginal art, not witchitty grubs, budgies, grass seeds, fruit, lizards, etc., which were their central dietary staples. Art is about value, and so indeed is hunting. I don't think that the lack of straight numerical congruence between relative numbers of particular species in Paleolithic art and Paleolithic diet requires sophisticated explanation. It is rather predictable—art is seldom preoccupied with statistical truth.

It may be that reindeer and red deer did provide most of the large-mammal meat during the late Paleolithic in the regions where most of the art is preserved, as a result of some circumstance that allowed the hunters' methods to be especially effective with these species, perhaps due to some aspect of the animals' behavior. This does not mean that reindeer and red deer were necessarily the most expressive of these hunters' passions; in fact, it may suggest the opposite. Van Noten (1982) drew just such a conclusion from the disproportionate frequency of eland in South African art; eland are never very common in nature (or the Bushman diet) compared to other antelope.

These choices could also have differed regionally depending on the prevalence of surrounding animals, which in turn could have locally affected hunters' regard or heroic passions. In the Périgord, for example, bison and horses predominate in Paleolithic art, while in northern Spain (now only an afternoon's drive away) it is mainly red deer that dominate the art. The independent fossil record in this case suggests red deer did actually predominate within the large-mammal community in Spanish Cantabria, in contrast to fewer red deer and more horses and bison in the Périgord.

Heroic regard can also flow in reverse, toward disregard. Hyenas are rare in Paleolithic art, perhaps depicted

Hyenas live in matrilocal, matriarchal groups and specialize in hunting large mammals. Though their bones and gnawing marks are common in the Pleistocene fossil record, images of European spotted hyenas are missing from Paleolithic art, with one or two possible exceptions. **A**, La Marche, Fr. (it is not certain that this is a hyena). **B**, My reconstruction.

in one or two enigmatic representations. Yet the paleontological record is quite clear: spotted hyenas (*Crocuta crocuta*), now found throughout much of Africa, were rather common in Europe during the late Paleolithic; hyenas occurred as far north as central England. Some of the most productive late Pleistocene fossil mammal sites are bones brought back to dens by hyenas (Sutcliffe 1969, 1970). We don't often imagine European Paleolithic people listening to the whooOOps of spotted hyenas at night, but that must have been one of the more familiar night sounds. The virtual absence of spotted hyenas in our collection of Paleolithic art is thus both curious and informative. Why weren't hyenas engraved or painted? Again, Bushman art provides an analog, as hyenas occurred in the regions where Bushman did their art, but they almost never painted hyenas. Thomas (1988), asking Bushman about hyenas, received the response that "hyenas are worthless animals." She took this to mean that hyenas were neither desired for food nor feared. This category of "noted as present but irrelevant" fits scads of things which were never or rarely included in Paleolithic art or Bushman art: dung beetles, spiders, mosquitoes, flies, lice, ticks, warblers, and so on. Hölldobler and Wilson (1994) reiterated what other researchers had seen, that native New Guinea tribesmen, who prize birds for their plumage and meat, know every bird species by a specific name; whereas they lump the dozens of local species of ants into one group with one name, equivalent to our "ants." In short, the idea that Paleolithic art cannot be about hunting because there are "discrepancies" in what they drew compared with what they ate may be misconceived.

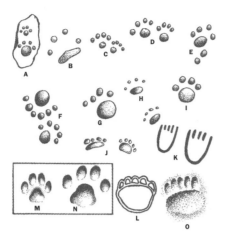

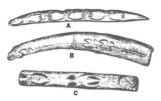

Tracks carved into osseous pieces: **A**, Bear tracks, La Madeleine, Fr. **B**, Artiodactyl tracks, Le Placard, Fr. **C**, Artiodactyl tracks, Lourdes, Fr.

There are a few images of tracks in Paleolithic art. The idea that senior males used cave walls as educational slates for young hunters is discredited by these drawings of tracks. They are too stylized and lack the necessary detail a teacher would have highlighted. It is interesting that most of these tracks we do find are of carnivores—wolves, lions, and bears—that in real life would have elicited excitement. **A–E**, Abri Blanchard, Fr. **F**, Laussel, Fr. **G**, Le Poisson, Fr. **H**, Gourdan, Fr. **I**, Castanet, Fr. **J**, Abri d'Oreille d'Enfer, Fr. **K**, La Pasiega, Sp. **L**, Niaux, Fr. *Box:* These are my sketches of real tracks: **M**, Hind foot of a modern wolf. **N**, Hind foot of a modern lion. **O**, Actual track of a cave bear, Chauvet, Fr.

TRACKS, IN PALEOLITHIC ART AND LIFE

Part of a Paleolithic lifeway depended on being able to "read" the surrounding world. Years ago, I was trying to drive to a tent-camp in the rolling scrub savanna of the southern Kalahari and had gotten lost in a crisscross of old and new sand tracks (I never did adjust to the noonday sun being in the north). One of the tracks led to a remote ranch house in a land where there were few, so I pulled up to ask directions. The owners were not at home, but a Bushman worker understood the name of the place where I was to go. I could not understand his native Bushman or much of his second language, Afrikaans. He paused thoughtfully for a moment, looking at the distance— then came the spark of a solution. Taking me by the sleeve, he walked me out to a spiderweb of vehicle tracks in the sand, pointed to some heavily lugged tractor marks, and smiled and said, *"Spoor,"* the Afrikaans word for track. Ah! I understood. The tractor driver was headed to where I was going. I had only to follow the spoor. Maybe we can ap-

proach Paleolithic art by using a similarly contrived spoor for direction. In the Netherlands *spoor* can mean dirt track or railway, but in English it means animal sign, mainly in the form of tracks, feces, urine, and blood drops, and such spoor is critical information for large-mammal hunters. Let's look at spoor in Paleolithic art.

The legs of many animal images in Paleolithic art are twisted so that the artist/observer can see the underside of the hooves. This tends to make the animals seem to float in the air. Early scholars have made much of this style, and interpretations range from a portrayal of floating magical symbols to ideas about animals only being drawn when they were dead, with the artist looking at the underside of the animal—hooves off the ground. I think a better place to begin is to realize the importance of footprints to a hunter/tracker. Footprints are as much a part of an animal's identity as the contours of horns or tail. Twisting the feet around to clearly show what makes the track is like including both horns or both eyes in a picture whether or not the head is successfully rendered in three-quarters view. These are key parts to identify an animal (Bahn and Vertut 1997). Australian Aboriginals also pictured some of their animals in this way. Walsh commented on Aboriginal art: "Feet are depicted in track form. Depicting feet hoppers and paws in plan view is a common practice in many areas of Australian rock art, even when attached to vertical figures. This style emphasizes pertinent characteristics of specific species" (1988, 92).

Tracks are an unmistakable signature. They can also be a running documentary. A hunter relies on tracks to determine which species were in the vicinity, how long ago, what direction they were moving, how many of each

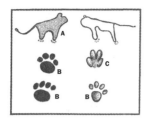

Many other prehistoric cultures since the Paleolithic have chosen to make tracks part of their art. These are from much later rock art in the Sahara: **A**, Twisted paws on lions, Taghtna. **B**, Dôrel-Gûsa. **C**, Wâdi Zrêda.

kind, and their age and sex. A skilled tracker uses tracks to actually picture the moving animal—not the dot-dot-dot of tracks but the animal itself. One can see its speed, tension, and gait. A trot leaves a different signature than a gallop, and an animal turning to look over its shoulder rides the track on that side more deeply. Bushman are able to interpret and describe the copulation patterns of nocturnal animals that they never see by day. A hunter-artist might well know tracks even better than some body contours. Tracks, like a name or insignia, are an inseparable part of the animal's identity and form. Twisting the legs in a drawing to show the underside of the hooves includes this important diagnostic character that is otherwise missing.

THE SCIENCE OF ART AND TRACKING

The cinema and stage suggest that people fall over stone-dead when they are lethally stabbed or shot, but it seldom happens that way in real life. Bodies can sustain considerable damage and still function, especially at high adrenaline levels. After being struck by an arrow or spear, most animals are still functional for a considerable time. Even when solidly shot with a bullet, which causes considerable trauma and tissue shock, an animal can often travel remarkable distances. African hunters work with experienced trackers, not so much to initially find huntable animals, though that is often the case, but because the tracker is so often essential in recovering mortally wounded

game. As I said earlier, spear-hunting in the Paleolithic would mean a lot of tracking.

I have tracked large mammals a great deal in hunting and nonhunting situations, but I stand as a babe compared with some Bushman trackers I have accompanied. Outstanding trackers go beyond sex and age and can actually identify tracks of particular individuals. It is impressive to see a good tracker discerning the barely visible tracks of a particular animal among the interwoven pattern of a herd, across long distances and irregular terrain.

Tracking teaches cause-and-effect reality and it is also a creative game. Profoundly empirical and reasoned and at the same time using imagination to visualize an image never seen, in every way tracking is science (Liebenberg 1990a); one is constantly formulating hypotheses and testing them. It is exemplary of other aspects of large-mammal hunting in that logical deductions have to be complexly combined with intuition for it to work well. But it is also similar to art as well as science. Trackers can work well as a team, discussing and debating interpretations and trading observations with one another. Usually, there is little exertion of authority, since tracking is probabilistic and statements will always be tested. It works best when conducted openly and democratically; no one professes the revealed truth or a sure answer (Liebenberg 1990a). Like science or art the key elements are observation and creative response, a free and interactive reasoned discussion among players, and then a return to observing the evidence at hand.

One reason hunting can be easier during winter is due to the better tracking. Most familiar Eurasian Paleolithic sites had snow on the ground for a number of months of the year. Snow not only increases the hunter's ability to see animals at extreme distances but also makes tracks, sometimes kilometers distant, stand out. Recent happenings are all recorded with blueprint clarity. Also, snow improves a hunter's recovery of wounded animals, as red marks on snow leave such a well-defined spoor whether the animal is alone or in a herd.

Spencer and Gillen (1968) emphasized how excellent Australian Aboriginals were at tracking and remarked that children recognized the tracks of all the animals. Moreover, most Aboriginals could recognize tracks of every person they had ever met. Liebenberg spoke to African Bushman about knowing one another's tracks: "When I asked a group of !Xõ trackers if they could identify the spoor of individuals, they found it very amusing that I should ask them such a stupid question. To them it is difficult to understand that some people can not do it" (1990a, 72).

THOSE MYSTERIOUS RED DOTS

One of the most puzzling aspects of Paleolithic cave art has been the occurrence of dots, usually in red ocher, often in horizontal rows, sometimes in two or three parallel rows. Such series of dots are apparently not concentrated in time or place. They are found in Chauvet Cave, 32,000 years ago, and in Lascaux, which dates 15,000 years later. These enigmatic dots have occasioned lots of explanations, from being Paleolithic "signs" of some mystical symbolic language (Leroi-Gourhan 1964) to being religious symbols that were part of a prehunt cave ceremony involving drive fences and corrals (Kehoe 1996). These ideas could perhaps be correct, but most explanations have left me feeling that we were still missing the real story. They may have been made by young people walking along with mouths full of chewed ocher, making simple spray patterns, but the ubiquity of the repeated dots suggests significance above random marking. But what? They must relate to some persistent aspect of Paleolithic experience given their widespread occurrence. The red spots baffled me. And eventually, the enigma began to get to me. Over the years of climbing in caves, I started to greet these images with an explicative of "Oh crap, some more of those danged red spots."

One fall, not long ago, when my mind was far from Paleolithic art, I was trailing a wounded caribou under low autumn skies. I had hit the young bull solidly; by now it

should be dead, somewhere up ahead. But the spoor was difficult to follow. A fine mist and wind from the Arctic Ocean raked the scatter of crimson bearberry leaves, making any blood drops difficult to see. No blood and too many tracks; I had lost the trail and was almost ready to give up and return to my point of origin and begin tracking again, when . . . there it was, a clear red splotch. I knelt to make sure, Yes, then up ahead another, and another, in a distinct trail across yellow-lichen-covered stones. Ahh, whew, it was beautiful. I have had this experience a number of times over a lifetime of tracking and I wondered how many Paleolithic hunters had had that same sense of relief.

At that precise instant it hit me, kneeling in the lichen I was jerked back to the caves—those mysterious red dots. I slumped, wind whipping my anorak, wet-eyed with pleasure as certainty of the story behind the red spots fell into place, like that caribou's whereabouts. It was truly like a broken code, across tens of thousands of years. Fellow tracker to fellow tracker, reindeer hunting had linked us . . . those wonderful danged red dots.

Blood trailing as well as tracking is a fine skill, best practiced with quiet confidence as an enjoyable, even addictive, puzzle. Splatters of red blood, far from being repugnant, become linked to the beauty of success, become the most welcome and exquisite thing one can imagine right then and there. The agony comes if they disappear. A small droplet of blood falling into lichen, moss, silt, sand, short grass sward, or other absorbent material leaves little mark. The blood drop is most visible when it strikes a flat rock or a broad leaf and disperses into a splotch a centimeter or more in diameter. One may spend hours scanning and reconstructing directions, walking stooped until the back aches, searching in the profound hope that the blood dots will reappear—that one will be back on track. After hours of such searching, the mind's eye does not see trotting reindeer after closing one's eyes at night but rather—red dots.

Once I experienced this connection, I could see Paleolithic art with new appreciation for its depiction of blood in the context of the hunters' experience. Among those

A New Tracking Partner   Unlike later Bushman and Australian Aboriginal art, Paleolithic art contains no evidence of domestic dogs. This absence of dogs fits other sources of information that suggest that the beginnings of wolf domestication coincided with other large-scale cultural and climatic changes at the end of the Pleistocene. The reasons behind wolf domestication and its rapid spread at that time are not very clear. Common wisdom assumed a dog's worth would have been in locating game for the hunter and chasing the animal until it stopped to defend itself, the way elkhounds are used today (in northern Europe moose are known as elk). Certainly, this could have been important, but dogs could also have assisted human hunters to locate animals that did not die immediately after being hit by spears or arrows, for even lethally hit animals can travel far.

So the key to the dog's value and its rapid spread may have been this unusual ability of canines to scent-track wounded game. This would have been increasingly valuable as expanding Holocene forests made visibility poorer and tracking more difficult. Even the best human trackers often lose hit game in thick forests. Wolves and dogs have exceptional abilities, adapted to follow the smell of blood. We know from German trainers of blood-trailing dogs (availability of such dogs is required in Germany if you are to hunt large mammals) that blood has a very strong odor to dogs. Field trials for such dogs are held with a trail of blood droplets that is 24 hours old. We are comparatively blind in our olfactory sense, and especially insensitive to blood odors; dogs, however, live in a world full of scents. A tracking dog would have allowed hunters to take more risky shots and found many kills that would have otherwise been lost: a blood-trailing dog would more than have paid for its keep.

images, I noticed not only red blood splotches gushing from wounds but also animals with ocher red dots coming out of their mouths and red dots splotching near wounded animals or trailing behind them. How poignant that Paleolithic artists' ocher pigments and blood's hemoglobin are made red by chemically similar oxides of iron.

DEFECATION CULTS IN PALEOLITHIC ART?

The tail-up posture is a common theme in Paleolithic images, as discussed in chapter 2. Tail-up postures are associated with elimination (the tail is lifted to prevent soiling from urine or feces) and, via that, with states of alarm, because alarmed animals often quickly urinate or defecate. Indeed, quite a few animals in Paleolithic images are shown defecating, some with feces shooting out the back end. In fright (of any origin) there is a physiological tendency among vertebrates to empty the bowels and bladder. Presumably, this is an adaptive lightening of excess ballast; that little bit may be the bit that allows the fraction of a second or few meters separating escape from capture. Carnivore chases are often just such close calls—as the frequency of lion scars on zebras' rumps testifies. Being a body length ahead of death is selectively significant.

Late Paleolithic hunters, whose anatomical reach was so magically extended by spears, were probably an alarming presence. These artists were not welcome associates anywhere near a mixed group of grazing large mammals, and most of the large mammals they saw would have already seen them—and would have had their tails up in mild alarm, anxiously defecating. That is likely why the tail-up posture is so common in the art.

There have been articles written about a "Defecation Cult," proposing a mystical symbolic meaning to Paleolithic feces (e.g., Camps 1984). I find such proposals unnecessary, because surely in this case the simplest explanation is also the most apt. The sense a naturalist often gets from Paleolithic art is that of an individual animal portrayed as aware of the artist's presence, and alarmed by him as a potential predator. I think this is a reflection of the Paleolithic artists' experience, not a magico-religious drama. But not all the animals a Paleolithic hunter saw were potential prey; some were predators.

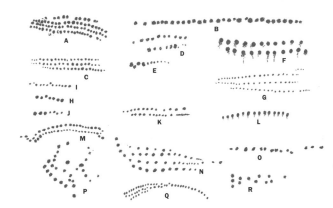

Those mysterious red spots. A sampling of Paleolithic red-ocher dots repeated on cave walls: **A**, Navarro, Sp. **B**, El Castillo, Sp. **C** and **G**, Llonín, Sp. **D**, Porquerizo, Sp. **E**, Marranos, Sp. **F**, Niaux, Fr. **H–J**, Lascaux, Fr. **K**, Marsoulas, Fr. **L**, Quintanal, Fr. **M**, Grotte d'Oulin, Fr. **N**, Pech-Merle, Fr. **O**, Travers de Janoye, Fr. **P**, Pradières, Fr. **Q**, Altamira, Sp. **R**, Merveilles, Fr. When a speared animal runs, it leaves, not one row of red blood spots, but often a scatter, sometimes in parallel rows.

Animals associated with red dots occur in some of the more well known caves as well as in some of the more obscure: **A**, Horse, Pindal, Sp. **B**, **D**, and **J–K**, Horse, Lascaux, Fr. **C**, Horse, Pasiega, Sp. **E**, Horse, Pileta, Sp. **F**, Horse, Altamira, Sp. **G**, Horse, Trois Frères, Fr. **H**, Horse, Nerja, Sp. **I**, Ibex, Parpalló, Sp. **L**, Red deer, Doña Trinidad, Sp.

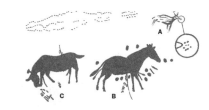

Some rows of red dots from later Bushman art are very similar to those from the Paleolithic. Three different rows from eastern Orange Free State, R.S.A.

Speared animals dripping blood are not limited to Paleolithic art. **A**, Deer, Huerta de las Tajadas de Bezas, Sp. (probably mid-Holocene), note the dots around its muzzle. These zebra are from more recent Bushman rock art: **B**, Mutoko, Zimbabwe. **C**, Bindura, Zimbabwe.

Red dots associated with animals: **A**, Ibex, Altamira, Sp. **B**, Horses, Pech-Merle, Fr. **C**, Aurochs, Chauvet, Fr. **D**, Reindeer, Chauvet, Fr. **E**, Woolly rhino, Chauvet, Fr. **F**, Travers de Janoye, Fr. **G**, Ibex, Pech-Merle, Fr. **H**, Person, Cougnac, Fr.

Part of the evidence that these mysterious red spots represent blood drips comes from the fact that the art shows them coming from a spear point, around the snout, or spewing from the mouth. **A** and **D**, Red dots on muzzles of horses, Chauvet, Fr. **B**, Red deer, Marcenac, Fr. **C** and **E**, Lions, Chauvet, Fr.

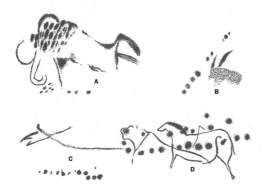

More large mammals with red dots: **A**, Mammoth defecating with red dots splattered around it, Pech-Merle, Fr. **B** and **C**, Ibex(?), Travers de Janoye, Fr. **D**, Lion and horse, Pech-Merle, Fr.

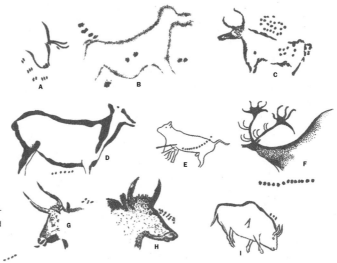

A few more large mammals in Paleolithic art with what seems to be blood splotches: **A**, Aurochs, Pasiega, Sp. **B**, Red deer(?), Navarro, Sp. **C**, Aurochs, Bidon, Fr. **D**, Red deer, Pindal, Sp. **E**, Aurochs(?), La Madeleine, Fr., with a trail of red spots leading from a spear wound. **F**, Red deer, Lascaux, Fr. **G–H**, Aurochs, with red splotches, Lascaux, Fr. **I**, Speared bison with red dots, Pindal, Sp.

Red dots, though a few here are in black, are scattered around a number of large mammals in Paleolithic art: **A–C**, Familiar horses, Lascaux, Fr. **D**, Bison spewing blood, Le Portel, Fr. **E**, Aurochs dribbling blood, Covalanas, Sp. **F**, Red splotches from a red deer, Lascaux, Fr. **G–H**, Red dots around aurochs and horses, Pileta, Sp. Some of the latter are speared.

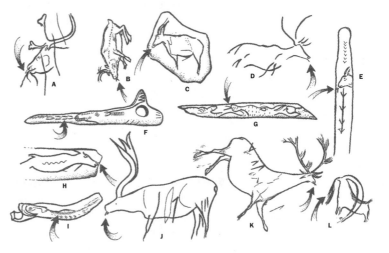

Many Pleistocene images have lines representing blood coming out of the snout: **A**, Reindeer, Tuc d'Audoubert, Fr. **B**, Reindeer, Trois Frères, Fr. **C**, Ibex, Parpalló, Sp. **D**, Reindeer, Gabillou, Fr. **E**, Reindeer, La Madeleine, Fr. **F**, Reindeer(?), La Madeleine, Fr. **G**, Ungulate, La Madeleine, Fr. **H**, Ibex, Bruniquel, Fr. **I**, Musk ox, Arudy, Fr. **J**, Reindeer, Les Combarelles, Fr. **K**, Red deer, Lascaux, Fr. **L**, Ibex, Saint-Martin, Fr.

Ibex drawn on a cave wall irregularity with dramatic lines of pigment coming from its mouth and nose. Pileta, Sp.

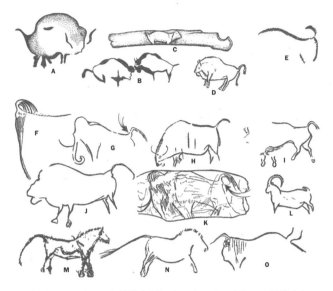

Large mammals usually lift their tails when alarmed, and they would likely have been alarmed when Paleolithic hunters saw them; therefore, hunters probably saw many animals with their tails raised. This tail-up posture gets into Paleolithic art: **A**, **F**, and **I**, Bison, Lascaux, Fr. **B**, Bison, Santimamiñe, Sp. **C**, Ibex(?), La Madeleine, Fr. **D–E** and **H**, Bison, Trois Frères, Fr. **G**, Mammoth, Pech-Merle, Fr. (note anal flap at base of tail). **J**, Bison, Gargas, Fr. **K**, Mammoth, La Madeleine, Fr. (again note anal flap). **L**, Ibex, Rouffignac, Fr. (note arcing curve to horns and perspective problem with ears). **M**, Horse, Niaux, Fr. **N**, Horse, Gönnersdorf, Ger. **O**, Bison, Trois Frères, Fr. (note twisted anal perspective).

OUR HUNTING COMPETITORS IN PALEOLITHIC ART

Few Paleolithic images have a distinctly agonistic air. Most hunting behavior is not at all agonistic and I think these particular agonistic images record the artists' occasional competitive relations with other hunting species. The intensity with which a few of the carnivore drawings are pitted with projectile marks is different from the few marks or spear checks that appear on most images of the hoofed animals. The former suggest agonistic behavior rather than hunting scenes. The number of "wounds" indicates a "#&*!!$%#&!& take that, and that, and that!!!" until the animal is filled with holes and blood is spewing out its mouth. Paleolithic engravings of bears attacking men were probably not illustrating a mythical incident, as

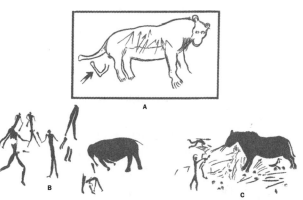

Speared, mortally wounded animals figure in the prehistoric art of a number of cultures: **A–B**, Baja California. **C**, Christopher's Kraal, Zimbabwe. **D**, Libya. **E**, Lion's Head, Zimbabwe. **F**, Egypt, Nile Valley. **G**, Cañada Remigia, Sp.

A, Lion engraving on stalagmite flow in Trois-Frères, Fr. Note the spearlike line in the neck-and-shoulder area and the many spears in the chest area. What is interesting here is the detached human arm behind the lion. One sees detached body parts in Holocene scenes of animal attacks. Here are two portrayals in Bushman art: **B**, Queenstown District, R.S.A. **C**, Matopo Hills, Zimbabwe.

Leroi-Gourhan (1983) has suggested, but a tragic incident, as bear encounters can be.

Lions and bears must have posed some of the more dramatic risks in Paleolithic life. We know hints of that here in Alaska, where every year people are attacked and often killed by bears. People here do not disregard the possibility of a bad bear encounter, and many can relate their own bear stories. Such experiences would have been more intense if their weapons could not as reliably stop a lion or bear. Still, Paleolithic hunters carried weapons that could almost guarantee death, and that made the difference. Bears and lions are not dumb, and most would have had strong traditions of avoiding such confrontations. I imagine Paleolithic hunters experienced a tense truce with those other large carnivorous mammals. But it would have been a truce that was broken at times: in competition over carcass ownership, over the bounty of a rack of drying meat, or the best fishing shallows. And there were, no doubt, occasional provocations of bravado by testy young males of several species, including our own.

Bears and lions in Paleolithic art are not usually pictured frolicking or lolling about as you may see them in zoos or animal preserves. Most are shown alert and some have an alarmed, threatening posture. For example, a bear's shoulders may be raised as high as possible and the head lowered. Again, I think this most logically reflects the actual experiences of Paleolithic artists. An artist close enough to observe a bear's contours would most likely be looking at a bear that had also observed the artist, and upon doing so would have assumed an alert or threatening posture. Compared to the images of lions and bears, Paleolithic artists seldom portrayed hyenas, canids, mustelids, lynx, sabertooths, and other carnivores. The potentially dangerous and ever-present bears and lions had to have added a tang to Paleolithic life that we seldom experience today.

SIZE OF THE PALEOLITHIC HUNTING PARTY AS PORTRAYED IN PALEOLITHIC ART

There is no reason to envision a single pattern of social organization for all of late Paleolithic life; after all, such uniformity does not happen in other animals. For example, social carnivores like wolves, spotted hyenas, and lions switch back and forth from small groups to huge ones, adjusting social forms and sex mixtures. That being said, we do observe species-typical norms—recurring forms of social organization that generally fit each species' lifeway and ecology. What does the archaeological record suggest about such a species-typical norm for humans in the late Paleolithic? In particular, how large were the groups of men on seek-and-kill hunting forays in the late Paleolithic? And how can we find that out?

Operating within the magico-religious paradigm one might see a shaman with a magic scepter standing before a sacred stone ring. But a more parsimonious explanation would be to say that a beginning drawer painted this scene of three males (sex is clear) with a long object (the most common long objects males dealt with were probably spears, a tool they would have kept within reach most of the time). El Castillo, Sp. Note how all are standing over red dots.

Maybe Paleolithic art can help. A few images give us a glimpse at Paleolithic hunting. Possible hunting scenes include images of a single man (identified by penis) with a wounded animal or engaged in a dangerous-beast encounter and images of modest-sized groups of people with a single or a few large mammals. One engraving shows a group of people butchering a single bison. Some images include people carrying long spears, which appear to be about 2–2.5 meters in length (using the body for scale). Some figures carry more than one spear. I've interpreted twelve of these images from Paleolithic art as representing hunting parties of individuals. I did not include the scene from Addaura, Sicily, which may date from the early Holocene and does not seem to represent a hunting incident even though most males carry their spears (could it be a wrestling match?). My identification of scenes as being hunting parties depends on no women, infants, or very small children being present. Here are the numbers of individuals in the different scenes:

3   Bruniquel, France
10   Cueva de Valle, Spain
3   El Castillo, Spain (*a*)
5   El Castillo, Spain (*b*)
9   Gourdan, France
3   La Vache, France (*a*)
6   La Vache, France (*b*)
9   Les Eyzies, France
3   Pechialet, France
7   Raymonden, France
3   Teyjat, France

This is an average of 5.5 people (hunters?) per scene. I do not want to insist that every one of these images is definitely a hunting party, but such an interpretation is plausible and I am working with what we have. These numbers generally align with anthropologists' reconstruction of a typical Paleolithic hunting party. Ethnographic analogs as well as Paleolithic archaeological sites suggest an overall camp size of thirty or so people. A camp of that size could regularly field a group of five adult males, perhaps occasionally including a teenager or two. The numbers of figures in these scenes are also consistent with Paleolithic demographics discussed in the last chapter.

A hunting party of three to seven men would have been able to take advantage of hunting methods that would not work with one or two hunters, and a group can compensate for slight individual deficiencies in speed, strength, eyesight, experience, etc. Such a party also constitutes a powerful defensive group, able to lethally threaten belligerent lions, a large bear, a leopard, a saber-toothed cat, hyenas, or wolves. The smell of blood is attractive to carnivores, and defending a fresh kill would have entailed higher-than-normal risks. The presence of several well-armed, strong, and experienced people would have meant the carcass could be more safely defended from other predators along with being more quickly butchered and carried back to the main camp. This latter is a big job. It would have been impossible for one or two men to pack home the meat of a bison or horse in a single trip. Five to six men can just about do so. And other carnivores would likely claim a carcass left for any period of time. Finally, a larger party could more successfully get injured or ill members back to home camp.

Ethnographic studies of groups dependent on large terrestrial mammals show that men seldom hunt alone; rather, they go out in small- to modest-sized groups. There are several images in Paleolithic art of a bear or a bison attacking a single man. Though these do not portray a whole party, these are the "frames" that would have occurred even when the encounter involved a larger hunting team, because a bear cannot attack five people at once.

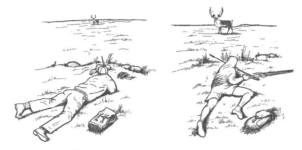

Paleolithic artists were probably able to get much closer to wild mammals than we are today. In the Paleolithic, large mammals, even those regularly hunted, were probably a lot less "flighty" around humans. Reindeer can estimate their flight or escape distance in relation to the particular threat. We can also see this aspect of calculated composure in Africa. Impalas, for example, treat lions with casual interest until lions cross the radius of critical distance that impalas need for a head start. Whenever long-range rifles are in common use, game quickly responds with longer flight distances. Hunters constantly experience empirical evidence of large-mammal smarts.

There are very few clues as to the exact Paleolithic hunting techniques. We have nothing like this more recent prehistoric Bushman drawing from Mutoko, Zimbabwe, showing two males using a limber pole to flush out a warthog-looking mammal from its burrow. Bushman use such long sticks to twist into the fur of several different burrowing mammals, like springhaas, and pull them out of their dens.

Bushman refer to two main kinds of male hunting-group forays: (1) day hunts and (2) biltong, or dried meat, hunts. The names are self-explanatory. Day hunts radiate out from the home camp for shorter distances, and women are often important informants and assistants in reporting animal presence and kinds of activity in the day range from camp (Silberbauer 1980). Biltong hunts range farther from home camp, and, if successful, the party may take time to air-dry the meat. Making biltong, or dry jerky, of the muscle mass makes it possible to carry more meat for longer distances. Hunters on these hunts traditionally eat liver and other viscera, rib-racks, tongue, and other parts that do not preserve or dry as well as does muscle.

Sometimes, a third sort of hunting is practiced, which directly involves almost all people in camp: game drives. Gordon (1990) has worked with the age-structure of rein-

deer remains in Paleolithic sites, and he has proposed that these animals were taken by drives. Many hunting cultures do use some sort of drive technique. In the Tanana Hills, here in central Alaska, one can find weathered remnants of Athabascan drive-fences used in caribou drives. Spruce poles and stone cairns still appear on ridgelines, where they presumably helped direct the migrating herds into the best positions for the hunters. Similar structures were used by inland Eskimo farther to the north. American Plains Indians used bison drives throughout the High Plains, and Bushman, too, occasionally used drives of sorts; their stone cairns still stood in the 1830s and were noted when Andrew Smith made his survey of the interior of South Africa (Lye 1975).

Because there simply are very few late Paleolithic kill-sites known in western Europe, we face persistent taphonomic problems in assessing Paleolithic hunting techniques on the basis of evidence from camp middens or processing stations. With only middens to work with, it is almost impossible to differentiate the instantaneous mortality distributions one typically obtains by bringing home animals from a mass drive from slower accumulations of, for example, September hunts spread over many years.

The dramatic cliff of Solutré, along the Rhône in southern France, has long been a presumed Paleolithic drive site. There, a tremendous mass of horse bones occurs in the processing debris 100 meters or so from the base of the famous cliff. But whether Solutré was a drive site or not is somewhat controversial.

Paleolithic art provides several hints about hunting techniques. One is that the images of large mammals are often portrayed hit by more than one spear. This has several important implications; most of all it corroborates the idea that hunting was indeed cooperative. Large mammals do not die easily and multiple hits with the kinds of weapons available during those times would have been desirable to prevent escape. There are few archaeological kill-sites in Eurasia, but Mesolithic carcasses of wounded elk (moose) that escaped and were preserved in bogs in En-

A

Small Paleolithic engraving from Eglises, Fr. (*box*) showing a person by a netlike lattice of uncertain identity or function. This could be a fishnet, but it is just as likely to have been a net into which small animals were driven. Hunters all over the world use something like this technique. Alaskan Inland Eskimo and Athabascans made netlike fences, with snares at the openings, into which caribou were driven. Recent engravings: **A**, Koyukuk River, Alaska. **B**, Saint Lawrence Island, Alaska. **c**, Norton Sound, Alaska. **D**, Bushman painting from Wolwedans, R.S.A.

gland and Scandinavia around 10,000 years ago contain multiple bone projectile points. Likewise, archaeologists have found more than one projectile point per animal in Paleoindian sites in America: of mammoth/mastodon in Clovis times (around 11,000 years ago) and bison in Folsom times (around 10,000 years ago), indicating multiple hits.

Whatever the diverse hunting techniques during the Paleolithic, they probably varied seasonally within the year for each different species and also changed over long time scales. From the art, we do know that Paleolithic hunters had to have been good students of animal behavior, which must have figured importantly in their hunting patterns.

DISGUISE AND OTHER ETHOLOGICAL TRICKS AS PALEOLITHIC HUNTING TECHNIQUES

I have heard many people express wonder at how Paleolithic hunters could have regularly found, stalked, and hit enough large mammals to provide a significant and reliable resource. It is a puzzle; no skilled hunter I know could do it with a simple spear. But as I have repeatedly empha-

sized, our similarity to other large mammals means that hunting them is pitting wit against wit. This is the basis of our advantage, for example, when utilizing an animal's behavioral idiosyncrasies and when disguising ourselves. Before I talk about disguises, let me give you a sense of the ways other large mammals differ from us, and how that difference can potentially be exploited. Perhaps the most familiar example is the modern symbolic dance of hunting seen in the bullfight.

Hemingway (1939) commented that the most common response to one's first bullfight was that it seemed incredible that a bull would be so dumb as to not go after the matador instead of the cape. But this ethological pattern was discovered long ago in Spain, and it is a pattern the matador knows and must employ with practiced discipline. Evolution has gifted the bull with a decisive sense for detecting and charging the fastest-moving object or part of an attacker (another of the Consigliere's cost-saving devices, remember). This focused stimulus-response pattern works well for the bull in battles with other bulls or against attacking predators, but it lets the matador control the bull's attacks, providing he moves the cape faster than his own body. If in the slightest feint he fails to do so, he will be gored. Bullfight rules guarantee the game is tilted toward the matador's success by requiring that all bulls be virgin to the cape, and that a bull be allowed only 15 minutes in the ring. A bull cannot learn in less than 15 minutes to disobey its innate propensity. Given a little more time, a bull does learn, and the rules of the ring require a lethal ending so that a bull can never be fought again on a different occasion. After about 15 minutes, bulls become deadly dangerous—they discover the trick and can override their set stimulus-response path.

Similarly, it is possible to trick caribou with an antler and cape disguise, even when worn by a two-legged hunter. Why is the reindeer so dumb as to not see through this "false-front" disguise, which does not even attempt to have a posterior half? Hunters have learned that the caribou's innate means of visually identifying species, age, and sex is determined by an appraisal of, not the entire caribou form, but only the anterior end, primarily face pattern, size of neck mane, and antler shape and size. Hunters can employ this behavioral pattern of caribou to get close to them. Like the bull in the bullring, caribou do learn to see past their automatic responses. Large mammals are not dumb, but for the hunter, that few minutes of trickery may be enough. We know that hunting cultures the world over have used disguises to approach fleet game, and sheer survival is reason enough to presume Paleolithic peoples were not only consummate spear-throwers but also skilled in using many ethological tricks to get closer to their prey: aware of animal calls to use, having strategies to avoid being scented, and much more.

Certain enigmatic man-beast figures in Paleolithic art may in fact be depictions of hunting disguises. Prehistoric Bushman art from a much later time has several drawings of hunters in ostrich disguise, a Bushman technique described by early European explorers (Thackeray 1983). In Australia, Spencer and Gillen recounted a similar technique used by Aboriginals: "A native will carry something which resembles the long neck and small head of a bird in emu hunting as a false image" (1968, 20). Eskimo also occasionally used disguises and decoys when hunting caribou (Gordon 1990). These sorts of questions about the Paleolithic are unlikely to ever be definitely answered—

Hunters capitalize on mammalian and avian species-recognition "insignia" by using mimicry and disguise to get within hunting range. These drawings from a photograph by Antony Bubenik (1984) show hunters approaching a wild reindeer and moose in Alaska using model heads. It is interesting ethologically that the head, antlers, and mane are focal points for recognition; the rear part of the body is almost inconsequential.

My drawing from a photograph taken by William Rudd in Kenya after the turn of the century, showing two people using a zebra skin as a hunting disguise (Wilcox 1982, 1985).

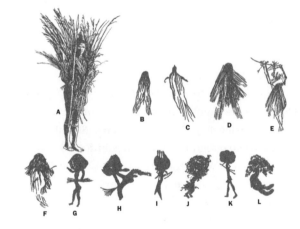

Hunters have often disguised themselves as other animals, but the most common form of disguise today is camouflage. Every year in the United States millions of garments with leaf and limb patterns, in a variety of colorations depending on the kind of hunting, are sold. Most hunters have several garment patterns for different background conditions. **A**, An example of Bushman hunting camouflage from photo. Paleolithic images: **B–C**, Ojo Guareña, Sp. **D–E**, Lascaux, Fr. Those below are from Spanish sites that date later than the Paleolithic: **F**, Bojadillas. **G**, Solana de Los Covachas. **H–I**, El Civil. **J**, Hornacina de la Pareja. **K**, Fuenta del Sabruco. **L**, Bojadicallas, Sp.

A, These little chamois with human legs from Teyjat, Fr., have been thought of as shamans or mystical images, but it is just as likely that they are dancers or even hunting disguises. **B**, One would need something like this (my reconstruction) to get close to such a fleet and wary species.

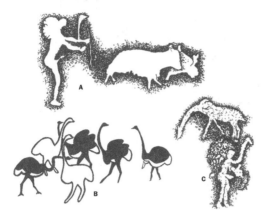

Bushman hunting disguises used in life and shown in the art. Rather than portrayals of ostrich-human shaman trance visions, we know these to be hunters in disguise (Woodhouse 1984). It was a good technique for approaching other species to within bow range. Art from R.S.A.: **A**, Bushman Fountain. **B**, Hershel District. **C**, Klipfontein.

again, we're simply looking at yet another aspect of life not amenable to physical fossilization. Still, this is such a central part of hunting that we would do well to keep alert to it when viewing Paleolithic art. Under the disguise the Paleolithic hunter would have carried his normal kit. If only we could see what he kept in his pockets.

WHAT DID PALEOLITHIC GUYS KEEP IN THEIR KIT BAGS?

Was it possible to find a color crayon and hunting tools in the same pocket of a Paleolithic young man? Or maybe we could conduct a random search of another guy and find a pocket full of seashells, the kind used in ornamentation.

There is so much we simply cannot know about these hunter-artists, but small fragments of information such as burials can charge our imaginations. Fortunately, one Paleolithic grave excavated in a cave in northern Italy may be just what we need. It is called Villabruna A Cave and dates to 12,000 years ago. At least that is the interpretation made by Broglio (1995), who suggests a "hunter's poke," or kit bag, was included in the grave of a twenty-five-year-old male at that site. Whether these were contents of the jacket pocket or perhaps of a bag tied to a belt, six objects were preserved in a cluster between the left arm and the body: two knives made from flint blades (one retouched or sharpened and another not), a flint core, a bone point, and an elongate pebble like those used today in flint knapping or retouching. The sixth item was a peculiar object about the size of a tennis ball. Chemical and palynological tests showed it to be something like a color crayon made of ocher and beeswax.

The preserved objects were apparently personal, everyday belongings—essential stuff for repairs, skinning, butchering, coloring, and perhaps engraving. Remember, more preserved Paleolithic art was produced with a sharp stone than any other means (Bahn and Vertut 1997). We also know that comparable tools could be found in the kits or pockets of many other men from hunting-dependent cultures. Of course, a ball of sinew thread, a coil of twine, a wood whistle, dried meat, and other soft-tissue items could possibly have been present in our young man's pocket—but these materials are almost never preserved.

Another male in his midtwenties, excavated from a cave in England and once dubbed the "Lady of Paviland" (the skeleton was originally thought to have been a woman), provides more such evidence. In the last century, Buckland excavated this grave and described a collection of "two-handsfull" of seashells of *Narita littoralis* in a cluster close to the upper thigh bone, "where the pocket is usually worn" (discussed by Roebroeks 2000). Not far from this, Buckland found another cluster of small, cylindrical ivory rods. The preserved contents of these two "bags"

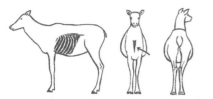

Hemorrhaging weapons must hit highly vascularized tissue for a sure kill. There are only a few areas of the body that make this possible. These are primarily within the ribcage, which houses the heart, lungs, and liver (the latter fits closely up into the ribcage under the concave diaphragm). Only a lateral impact or thrust is suitable; other angles are protected by thick muscles.

These two drawings have been explained by a variety of magico-religious "heart" theories. However, the highly vascular center highlighted in red ocher within these images is a preferred focus of hunters. Hunting is about life and death, work and wonder. *Left,* mammoth, Pindal, Sp. *Right,* horse, Pileta, Sp.

stand as paragons for pocket contents in the late Paleolithic, and they enrich our imagination about the lives of other late Paleolithic young men. And now, what about the weapons they carried?

Paleolithic Weapons and Art

For hundreds of thousands of years prior to the late Paleolithic, hominids probably used sharpened wood poles as thrusting spears, also called pikes, as their basic weapons. Such a pike can be seen as a biological extension of hominid anatomy, somewhat analogous to the hermit crab's adaptation to fit gastropod shells or a sea otter's armpit, where it carries a pebble for shell cracking. Hominid anatomy is well suited to carrying a sharpened pole (perhaps this underlies the reason for our strong version of the opposable-thumb grip and its diagonal crease across our palms, unlike the weak oppositional grip and the right-angled creased palms of climbing apes). With a pike in hand, hominids were the longest horned and longest fanged beast to walk the earth. Without it we were soft, slow, and vulnerable—armed only with vestigial canines and a hand full of pebbles.

An air-dried, sharpened wooden pole makes a better weapon than one might first guess. It gets the action out away from the body. The point is not constructed just to cause pain; it concentrates energy in order to penetrate

through the overlying thick skin and taut intercostal muscles of the thorax. Recall that a deep puncture of the thoracic cavity would have meant sure death, though not an immediate one. And it would have been an easy transition from wielding a thrusting spear to heaving a lighter version at an animal. When this transition to a projectile weapon occurred is unclear. For our ideas about the time depth of this kind of weapon, we once used ethnographic analogs, but more recently remnants of wooden weapons have been unearthed at the early to middle Paleolithic English site of Clacton (Oakley et al. 1977) and at the German sites of Lehringen (Movius 1950) and Schönin-

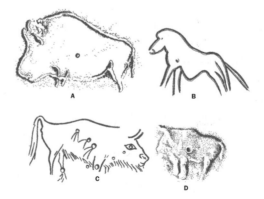

In the first three of these portrayals the artists used natural spots or cupules as spear hits; the hole in the fourth image seems to have been made in mud with a finger. **A** and **D**, Bison, Bédeilhac, Fr. **B**, Horse, Roc de Sers, Fr. **C**, Bison, Niaux, Fr. Again, here is an indication of the subjects that occupied the minds of these drawers. What would you be inclined to make out of a small pockmark in a cave wall or floor? These Paleolithic artists saw the "sweet spot" of horses and bison.

More animals in Paleolithic art showing lung blood coming out of the mouth and nose, a Pleistocene aesthetic from spear-hunting traditions. **A** and **I**, Bison, Hornos de la Peña, Sp. **B** and **C**, Bison, Font de Gaume, Fr. **D**, Bison, Labastide, Fr. **E**, Aurochs, Gabillou, Fr. **F**, Ibex, La Croze à Gontran, Fr. **G**, Red deer, Lourdes, Fr. **H** and **Q**, Bison, La Mouthe, Fr. **J**, Horse, Altamira, Sp. **K**, Horse, Arudy, Fr. **L**, Bison, Bernifal, Fr. **M**, Bison, Isturitz, Fr. **N**, Bison, Fontanet, Fr. **O–P**, Bison, Trois Frères, Fr.

gen (Thieme and Veil 1997). At the Schöningen site, dating around 300,000–400,000 years ago, eight preserved spears, each about 2–2.5 meters, were recovered. They were made from lightweight spruce and were used without hafted stone points. The point end was strategically made from the very dense wood that occurs near the tree's base. Tests with reconstructed models show that the size and balance of these spears allowed them to be either thrust or thrown. Olympic javelin throwers used replicas and expressed approval of their flight characteristics—their flight exceeded 100 meters. Note that these hominid hunters preceded human entry into Europe by hundreds of thousands of years.

Certainly, by the time the first humans appeared, the thrown spear may have been a quite refined weapon. But the pike, or thrusting spear, is such an effective tool in close-contact hunting or defensive situations (it was used into modern times by boar hunters across Europe and in the circumboreal tradition of impaling bears when they were flushed out of winter hibernation) that it was not given up totally. A pike and thrown spear may have existed together in the same groups as standard armament. This dual ordnance may have existed at least throughout the late Paleolithic, if not well before.

A sharp and dense wooden spear point can work, but it is made more effective by adding a tip of harder material that possesses a sharp cutting edge. A cut opening is more friction-free, letting the projectile pass in with less resistance, and a sharp-edged point severs more blood vessels than does a wooden point. Ultimately, this means a deeper wound with more rapid hemorrhaging. Some of the Neanderthal stone tools look as if they could have been hafted to a thrusting spear. The first anatomically modern people in Eurasia definitely used spears hafted with stone or osseous materials. Antler, ivory, and bone points were a part of this technology, and in the late Paleolithic small inset microblades, or microliths, were often used (Bader 1984). Adding these sharp stone or bone edges dramatically increased the effectiveness (or at least the rapidity) of the projectile's killing power. The change from dependence on a thrusting spear to the predominance of thrown spears meant the latter had to be lightened considerably, but many remained relatively long. The 2.5-meter-long slender ivory spears at Sungir in Russia date to around 22,000 years ago, and these were apparently made for throwing. There is also a wooden spear reconstructed from that site that measured 1.7 meters in length and had small inset stone blades (Bader 1984; Bosinski 1990). Both these kinds of spears were found in graves of young boys, so we don't know if spears used by adults were different.

My discussion centers on these weapons not because other weapons and specialized techniques for taking vari-

A plot of entry points of spears shown in a random sample of Paleolithic art drawings. Despite the fact that many pictures appear to have been made to show that the animal was wounded, the general cluster is still in the thoracic area, the logical "target zone" for people who hunt with spears and/or arrows. Black dots represent lethal hits within minutes; white dots represent nonlethal, sublethal, or prolonged death. Bear in mind that the spear usually enters at a descending angle.

There are several carnivores portrayed in Paleolithic art with protruding spears, and people as well. This is a composite plot of the entry points of the spears for a random sample of people, lions, and bears in the art. As with the previous illustration, these show a pattern of mortal wounds in the thoracic area, despite the fact that several drawings may have meant to portray the testosterone-charged scene of a wounded animal. (Note the large number of spear hits portrayed in the butt in a number of drawings of people. Now what age and sex would have been most likely to be thinking about such things and draw them?)

ous kinds of game were not used, but because we happen to know something about spears and atlatls (spearthrowers) due to their occasional preservation in archaeological sites and their portrayals in Paleolithic art. Apparently, this combination of a fast projectile and hunting opportunities provided by the diverse large-mammal fauna gave late Paleolithic cultures living in the regions of the art caves their unique character.

An Arsenal—Not Simply Single Weapons

I stress that each spearlike weapon design has its own range of strengths and weaknesses, which relate to an animal's size and speed, the hunting situation and technique, needs for defense against dangerous predators, and much else. Just a few generations ago Alaskan Eskimo used bows, atlatl-darts, thrown spears (and harpoons), and thrusting spears, each specialized for slightly different situations. We know that different projectile points were employed for birds, small game, fish, seals, whales, caribou, and people. Taking this "arsenal" approach can help us envision Paleolithic hunting. There was probably no single hunting strategy. In lithic studies archaeologists should always be alert to the likelihood that different kinds of projectile points from a single camp floor may have been used for different weapons in the arsenal and for different prey. This would explain why in the same population, even in the same year, lithic styles can vary considerably from site to site.

THE THROWN SPEAR IN PALEOLITHIC ART

Most scholars now dismiss the labeling of those motifs by what they look like to our eyes, and avoid words such as "arrow" in favor of more objective terms, descriptive of shape (e.g. chevron with a median longitudinal line).
P. Bahn and J. Vertut, *Journey through the Ice Age*

We find in Paleolithic art several images in which people are portrayed carrying what must certainly be spears or spearlike objects. Actually, a number of weapons sometimes go under the name of "spear": (1) A long, hand-held thrusting spear is sometimes called a "pike." (2) When held by a horseman or charioteer, it is called a "lance." (3) A spear thrown with the hand held just behind its center is usually referred to as a "javelin." (4) A spear thrown with an atlatl is called a "dart" and is usually, but not always, fletched. (5) Such darts grade downward in size to the point of overlap with fletched "arrows," which are shot from bows. (6) "Harpoons," used primarily to take water animals, may incorporate one of the above patterns

Images of large Pleistocene carnivores speared and bleeding. **A–B**, Lions or wolves, Los Casares, Sp. **c**, Lion, Lascaux, Fr. **D**, Bears, Le Portel, Fr. (note how this bear is both bleeding through its mouth and defecating). **E**, Lion, Gourdan, Fr. **F**, Bear, Les Combarelles, Fr. **G**, Bear, Massat, Fr. **H**, Bear, Trois Frères, Fr. **I**, Lion, Gargas, Fr. **J**, Lion, Lascaux, Fr. (again note speared lion wheezing blood through mouth and nose and defecating). **K**, Lion, Les Combarelles, Fr. **L**, Bear, Trois Frères, Fr.

Hunters growing up with the ideal of large animals spear-hit in the chest cavity would have had a common aesthetic about bleeding at the mouth/nose, and also they would know that animals hit in these ways tend to urinate and defecate. These images are found in one cave, Pech-Merle, Fr.

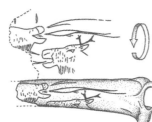

Engraving done in the round on bone from Torre, Sp. Images of two reindeer shown with what appears to be blood coming out of their mouths.

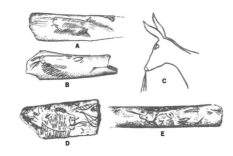

I suspect these vignettes were simply sketches on bone scraps underfoot from past meals. What subjects would you choose to sketch? Here Paleolithic people chose heads of large mammals with lung blood spewing out the mouth and/or nose. **A**, Horse, Trois Frères, Fr. **B**, Bison, La Madeleine, Fr. **C**, Red deer, Pergouset, Fr. **D**, Bison, Arudy, Fr. **E**, Ibex, Lortet, Fr.

A, Horse, Saint-Cirq, Fr. **B**, Bison, Cosquer, Fr. **C**, Bison, La Marche, Fr. **D**, Ibex(?), El Linar, Fr. **E**, Horse, Bize, Fr. **F**, Horse, Roc-la-Tour, Fr. **G–H** and **v**, Horses, Labastide, Fr. **I**, Red deer, La Vache, Fr. **J**, Red deer, Cosquer, Fr. **K**, Red deer, Parpalló, Sp. **L** and **P**, Horse, Bara-Bahau, Fr. **M**, Horse, El Castillo, Sp. **N**, Bison, Trois Frères, Fr. **o**, Horse, La Madeleine, Fr. **Q**, Horse, Isturitz, Fr. **R**, Horse, Niaux, Fr. **s**, Horse, Arudy, Fr. **T**, Horse, Montespan, Fr. **u**, Horse, La Madeleine, Fr. **w**, Horse, Lascaux, Fr. **x–y** Horses, Laugerie-Basse, Fr. **z**, Bear, Gönnersdorf, Ger. **AA**, Horse, Gabillou, Fr.

but are usually barb-tipped and guyed to secure the animal from sinking or otherwise escaping. Of course, there is some intergradation among these projectile types, in design and use. For example, some arrows are quite long, more like darts in design; likewise, many spears are made to be either thrust or thrown. As it is impossible to confidently distinguish these various types and uses in the Paleolithic images, I keep to the more inclusive meaning and simply call these objects "spears," even though we suspect Paleolithic hunters may have made use of categories 1, 3, and 4 in their ordnance at any one time.

A thrown spear's special effectiveness arises from its light weight and great length in proportion to its small cross-sectional area. This combination produces what ballisticians call a high *sectional-density*. A high sectional-density reduces drag (producing a flatter trajectory) and allows more energy to be delivered on impact (high number of kilograms per square centimeter), thus producing deeper penetration. A spear of the same weight as a given rock travels farther, retains its impact energy longer, and focuses its energy into a smaller surface upon impact—indeed, using Bahn and Vertut's terminology, we have a median longitudinal line converging its energy on the chevron.

A thrown spear can kill all but the thickest-skinned pachyderms; whereas damage from hurled rocks depends solely on concussion. Soft body tissues and springy ribs will tend to dissipate the rock's energy over a larger surface, so unless the head is hit where the skull bone comes near the surface, rocks can fail to inflict serious internal damage, even though they may produce a lot of pain and bruising. Deceleration of the spear occurs not from diffusing its energy over a large surface, like a rock, but from side friction: the squeeze of surrounding tissue, mainly skin, as the spear penetrates deeper and deeper. There is a special kind of sound when a spear or arrow hits the targeted thoracic region, a sort of drumhead thump. The intercostal muscles stretched between the ribs provide a taut backing to tough overlying skin; they do not give much with the

How a Dart Works I will show how the atlatl is designed and weighted to store energy throughout the early phases of the throw, which is then transferred to the dart just before it leaves the atlatl. That same principle works for the dart. The flexibility of the dart means that during the initial phases of the throw, the rear end is accelerating faster than the point, and this causes a flex in the dart's shaft, like a spring. At the end of the throw, a properly tuned shaft will release the energy stored in this spring against the atlatl. Picture a diving board (atlatl) springing at the same time the crouched diver (dart) springs away. As the thin dart races toward its target, it wobbles or flattens a bit, rather like a swimming fish, and not at all like the flight of a stiff javelin. The first time someone unfamiliar with an atlatl-thrown dart witnesses a dart's remarkable speed and flexing, it seems counterintuitive.

Ensuring the right amount of flex in the dart's shaft is not easy. Not only is the diameter critical, but so is shaft length. The longer the shaft, the greater the relative flexibility (remember, a short match stick is quite stiff). The weight of the point also influences the relative stiffness of the shaft—the heavier the point, the more flexible the shaft. Fine-tuning like this makes very real differences in actual hunting, and it is more than likely that Paleolithic peoples, whose very lives depended on it, had this tuning of darts down to a fine art.

impact of the sharp spear point. It is thus between the ribs that thrown spears penetrate most deeply (Guthrie 1983).

The lightweight thrown spear was a hunting breakthrough. A thrown spear allows hunters to strike from a distance beyond an animal's traditional flight zone (or attack zone). The thrown spear could travel a short distance faster than any mammal could run, enabling people to take fleet medium-sized mammals, like horses or reindeer, that were not easy to approach. The reindeer's age-old behavior of being able to watch out for predators and accelerate out of their reach, putting on an extra burst of speed

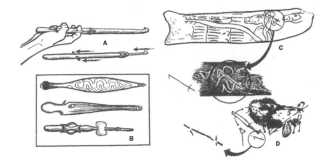

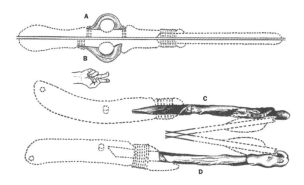

Using an atlatl. The propelling arm is extended backward to lengthen the reach of the throw; at the same time, the other arm is extended forward as a counterweight to the throwing arm. During the throw, the body weight is shifted from the back foot to the front foot, and the whole body is thrown forward, further lengthening the reach. Kids had to throw thousands of times to reach a plateau of precision.

A, Atlatls often have finger and/or thumb hooks, holes, or bars to help hold the weapon. **B**, Atlatls (*top to bottom*): Australian, Eskimo, and Hopewell. **C**, One can see the crosspiece for the finger hold in the atlatl being held by the Pleistocene figure on the engraved antler from La Madeleine, Fr. (Enlargement is circled.) **D**, The atlatl in this famous scene from Lascaux, Fr., is enlarged to the left, showing its crosspiece finger bar.

Paleolithic atlatl parts. **A–B**, Le Placard, Fr. (note how these pieces seem to have been mounted on either the side of the handle to form finger-holes). **C–D**, Engraved atlatl parts with hooked tip. These apparently inserted into a handle. **C**, Ibex, Mas d'Azil, Fr. **D**, Horse, Courbet, Fr.

as harm came close, was less effective against the acceleration of the thrown spear.

I illustrate many of the Paleolithic images of spears in this book (for some of these I have made an interpretive drawing beside the illustration of the original), and for the most part we can be assured that the Paleolithic artists' lines are meant to represent spears—some images even show feather fletching. Comparable images of projectiles are found in art scenes of most prehistoric hunting cultures. Often images include large mammals and clearly depict a hunting episode. Such highly charged portrayals of the precise moment of violent contact have been created for emphasis and celebration by male hunters of many cultures. Despite Diana, such images seem very much to be about men's weapons and male thrills—it is a kind of male art.

ATLATLS: HUNTING TOOLS AND ART FORMS

I am going to devote quite a few pages to atlatls and point- (or shaft-) straighteners, because they are such important Paleolithic tools and art media. Interestingly, the portions of the point-straightener and atlatal upon which art is made have very significant properties that relate to the tools' effectiveness. These are cases where utility and aesthetics come together, for velocity and art.

In North America we refer to spear-throwers as "atlatls" (a Uto-Aztecan word) and the lightweight kind of spear designed to be thrown with an atlatl we call a "dart." We don't know when atlatls were invented, because wood does not preserve well; yet we know that historic Aboriginal Australians and American Indians used hardwood at-

latls very effectively. It is possible that atlatls were around long before we can document their presence. We can presume that atlatls were not only present but were common during much of the time that late Paleolithic people occupied Europe, but that is not certain. We surmise this because at least some atlatls were made using antler, ivory, and bone materials that do preserve relatively well. Furthermore, osseous materials were probably preferentially used once it became clear that "weighting" helped atlatl function. I will return to that point shortly.

I suspect that the repercussions of the invention of atlatls have been underemphasized. A spear thrown with

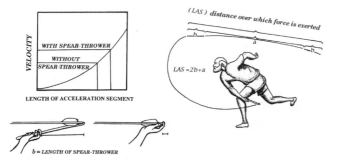

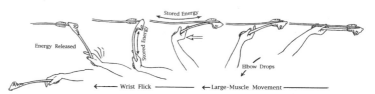

Advantages of a weighted atlatl. The shaft of the atlatl flexes during the throw, storing energy in this initial acceleration that is released just before the spear disengages. The flex of the spear also stores energy, and this is released as it springs away from the atlatl.

Simple physics of atlatl advantage. The throwing speed of the human arm can be enhanced by mechanical means. By adding length to the distance the arm travels along the line of acceleration, a projectile will have longer to accelerate. (Remember, this is not an arc but a line.) The atlatl lengthens this distance by twice its own length, that is, at the beginning of the throw and at the end. That is, LAS = 2b + a. See difference from a hand-held throw in lower-left comparison.

the bare hand could be made light and fast, but the human arm has limits as to how fast it can move, and atlatls were a way to surpass those limits; they artificially extended the arm. By effectively lengthening the reach of the arm, force could be exerted on the spear for a longer distance during the course of the throw. This increased the speed of the spear, much as a cord sling allows us to throw a small stone farther and faster. An atlatl changed not the strength but the leverage of the human arm. However, to take full advantage of this leverage, darts generally had to be lighter in weight than spears thrown by the arm alone. Greater speed, distance, and accuracy of projectiles meant a flatter trajectory, and often a greater penetration on impact—resulting in greater killing power. Increased speed also meant less time for the animal to move after the dart left the thrower's hand. All these would have contributed to a hunter's effectiveness.

It takes a lot of skill to make effective projectiles. Both darts and atlatls have to be limber, but not too limber. Just as bow-hunters today carefully select a bow appropriate to their build and strength and then match the right arrows to that particular bow, darts must be matched to a given person and a given atlatl. Archery companies now manufacture arrows in some thirty to forty combinations of diameters and stiffness, or "spines." Archers select the ap-

propriate combination of arrow length, spine, fletching, and point weight as part of figuring out what works best for their particular bow weight and cast. Any kind of bow and arrow will work but some work much better than others, and likewise, a long stiff stick was just the beginning step in fashioning an effective Paleolithic spear or dart. Tradition would have incorporated much past experience as to appropriate design. Within that, one's own experience of what constitutes an effective spear or dart would have been based on a particular feel and balance, that is, an underlying intuitive sense of highly complex engineering physics. After the point was affixed to the shaft, the Paleolithic hunter would have finely tuned the dart shaft by scraping or shortening and frequent test trials until the shaft was just right. Atlatls required similar tuning to fit general classes of darts and the throw of the owner. As now, guidelines and traditions help one locate the ballpark, but fine-tuning is largely experimental.

I suspect that most Paleolithic atlatls were wooden and thus did not preserve. We find a few osseous ones, but these are not very long. A few of these appear to have been hafted to a wooden handle, which was not preserved. Atlatl size and shape may have changed with different hunting strategies and/or with the species of game customarily hunted. Size may have also related to dart materials that were available and varied with each individual hunter's strength, build, and preferences. In general, the longer the atlatl, the lighter the dart must be. Additionally, there is a tradeoff of mass for velocity, and one cannot have the best of both.

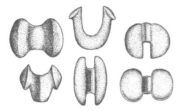

Mid-Holocene hunters of the Mississippi Valley produced beautifully carved rock objects called "bannerstones" by archaeologists who thought these were sacred ceremonial pieces. More recently, people have realized that bannerstones were fully functional, beautiful atlatl weights.

A   B

For Pleistocene atlatls, the most stress was experienced just beneath the weight—the spring region in which most of the energy was stored. Breakage thus occurs most often at this point (**A**), and that is exactly what we see in the breakage pattern of Paleolithic atlatls. In the Holocene weights were moved down the shaft (**B**), perhaps to try to resolve this breakage problem.

The atlatl itself actually flexes slightly during the throw, and this flexing stores energy that is released in the later stages of the throwing maneuver, like a bow's limb. The physics of this involves the wavelengths produced in the dart as it accelerates along the arc of the throw; a slightly flexed atlatl, tuned to complement the flex of the dart, helps transmit more energy into the nock of the dart, at the right time. Some additional weight optimally placed on the atlatl enhances this phenomenon as well.

Atlatl weights are common throughout the Americas. Prehistoric Indians of the Mississippi Valley used beautifully abstract stone weights on their atlatls. Later, when these weights were found as artifacts, no one realized just what they were, and for decades they were misinterpreted as some sort of ceremonial/religious object and were called "banner-stones" or "charm stones" (the magico-religious paradigm was at work there, too).

How a Paleolithic Atlatl Weight Worked

Atlatls not only extend the arm's reach but act as a spring—like a diving board that propels a diver. Just how a well-designed atlatl spring works and how it can be affected by a weight is not easy to envision, so let me start with an analogy from baseball. It is highly illegal in baseball to insert a small lead weight into the heavy end of the bat. Why? Because such a weighted bat can knock a ball much farther than unweighted pure hickory. The weight of the lead allows more energy to be stored in the bat as it is swung, increasing the flexibility of the bat. At the end of the swing, this energy in the flex is released, and the ball is not just hit but swatted. A weighted atlatl operates similarly in that at the beginning of the throw, when large body muscles are providing the main acceleration, the weight at the end of the atlatl makes the shaft flex more, storing energy that will be released at the end of the throw, when it is mainly the smaller forearm muscles, the "flick of the wrist," which provide the last addition to the dart's acceleration. Instead of adding a stone weight, Paleolithic Eurasians simply carved some of their atlatls from antler, leaving an extra portion of antler near the tip (distal) end. This extra lump of antler offered an opportunity for decoration, for art—another example of how Paleolithic folks interwove aesthetics into their everyday lives.

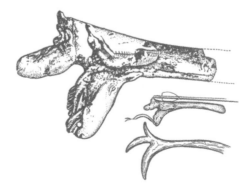

Fragment of atlatl weight from Mas d'Azil, Fr. Three horse heads, one partially skinless.

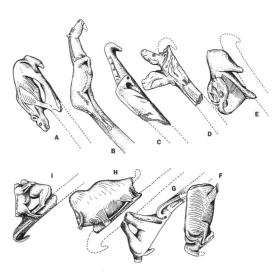

Broken Paleolithic atlatls showing how the weight was used as a medium of decoration, traditionally with large-mammal images: **A** and **E**, Madeleine, Fr. **B** and **G**, Bruniquel, Fr. **C**, **F**, and **I**, Enlène, Fr. **D**, Mas d'Azil, Fr. **H**, Canecaude, Fr.

As with other archaeological objects, we need to be aware that atlatls may not always have been the work of adults for adult use (recall the "moose antler effect"). Children undoubtedly did make atlatls, and kids' versions of these and other tools were probably also made by adults expressly for children to use. This likely accounts for some of the smaller and more fragile Paleolithic atlatls as well as some that are crudely made.

Paleolithic atlatls apparently were not disposable items. Ethnographic work indicates that atlatls in most later cultures were personally prized, semipermanent tools, and judging from the care with which most were made, this would seem true of Paleolithic atlatls as well. Indeed, the majority of preserved Paleolithic atlatls are superbly decorated with sculpted or engraved images of large mammals. For example, the famous bison from La Madeleine in France with its head turned to the left grooming its flank is part of an atlatl, as are a well-known mammoth and horse from Bruniquel and the lion from La Madeleine. There is even an atlatl carved with waterfowl found at Les Trois Frères. The carvers of these pieces aptly incorporated their designs into the antler forms they care-

fully chose for that purpose, making beautiful use of their unique shapes.

Weapon decoration in historic times tends to reflect a weapon's use (crossbows used for red deer were not decorated with hares), so it is credible to imagine that Paleolithic hunters might also have chosen imagery that related to the desired uses of their weapons. This thread of logic is supported by the fact that hunted large mammals are the main decorative theme on Paleolithic atlatls, arising again and again in the different cultures and geographic regions. In a few cases motifs are repeated regionally. For example, in the central Pyrenees several Magdalenian atlatls have a young ibex with upright tail and feces (or birds eating the feces) forming the hook for the spear nock. Paleolithic atlatls include images of bison, horses, mammoths, reindeer, and other animals, done in bas-relief, fully sculpted, or as fine engravings.

One engraving, from La Madeleine, shows a hunter walking with an atlatl over his shoulder; it not only has the hook on the distal end but also a hooked crossbar on the handle end for the second and third fingers—a common atlatl design in later cultures. The possible existence of a crossbar finger hold on Paleolithic atlatls may clarify an ambiguous image from Lascaux. This painted scene appears in a lower level of the vertical well-like depression called "the pit" and portrays a prostrate hunter being threatened by a wounded bison. The object on the ground beside the hunter has a crossbar and a hook at the end of

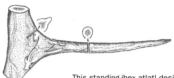

This standing-ibex atlatl design, carved from reindeer antler, was common for a short while in the northern Pyrenees, Fr. The "engineering" problem was how to use as much of the external dense antler cortex as possible and as little of the more fragile medulla (especially for the fragile projecting elements in the design). These constraints are involved in the engineering of a durable yet appealing design (Guthrie 2002).

Another problem with the original ibex design was that the little tail was too fragile as a spur with which to engage the dart. This was circumvented by avoiding the tail altogether (**A**) and instead using a thick projection of feces (**B**). On some of these atlatls the tail was lifted forward (**c**) in characteristic ibex posture. Curving the feces to make the spur for the dart made it look like a perched bird. This upright perch was characteristic of one main group of birds, woodpeckers—and the designer made this explicit. Two of the most widespread woodpecker species in Europe today are barred across their backs as on the Paleolithic atlatl: *Dendrocopos minor*, the lesser spotted woodpecker, and the larger *D. leucotos*, the white-backed woodpecker (**D** and **E**). The woodpecker perching on the feces combined with the ibex's head turned in that direction makes for a touch of humor. The lines of all this action combine to make a thing of balance, heft, and beauty.

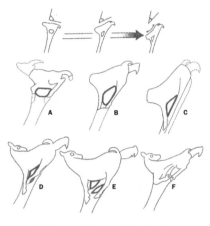

Atlatls are high-energy weapons of violence and thus easily broken. One can reconstruct the design stages that made this ibex atlatl weight more durable. The pattern to the left (**A**) is reconstructed from various fragments at different sites. It had several problems. One was that the upright legs were too fragile a connection between the shaft and weight. The shaft-weight contact could be strengthened by artfully angling the mass slightly down the shaft and by making the opening between the legs more angular or eliminating it altogether: **B**–**C**, Arudy, Fr. **D**–**E**, Mas'd'Azil, Fr. **F**, Bédeilhac, Fr.

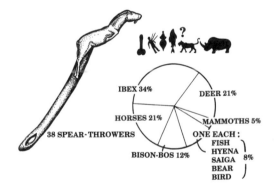

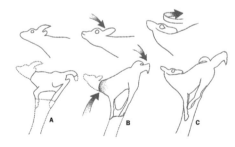

The fragile protruding head was strengthened by portraying a young hornless ibex or by rounding the shoulder and making it headless (some of the latter are probably repairs of weapons with heads broken off). And finally, the designers circumvented this whole problem by artfully twisting the head rearward and incorporating it into the shoulder structure. **A**, Reconstructed early form of this ibex design. **B**, Arudy, Fr. **c**, Mas d'Azil, Fr.

The majority of preserved atlatls are decorated with representational images. What images does one put on such a tool? Here is a Paleolithic sample of thirty-eight atlatls. Most of the images are of commonly hunted large mammals (as we know from archaeological middens). Images of mammoths, fish, rhinos, and carnivores are rare, and it is quite possible that atlatls were not regularly used on those species. Speared humans or war scenes are unknown on atlatls. I surmise that this means something—that weapons were made only with hunting in mind and not hostility. Erotic images of women, vulvae, and penises are also absent. This tool was carried publicly, suggesting that flagrant erotica was discouraged. Such aesthetic constraints are not merely modern cultural products but persist because of deep tensions over paternal uncertainty and incest taboos.

the shaft, which I suspect was meant to portray an atlatl, dropped after the hunter was gored by the bison. The bison is shown with its intestines coming out from a hole in its abdomen, from which a spear also protrudes. This vivid image is very likely recording a quite real event.

Unlike carefully made atlatls which a hunter might hope to use for many years, spears and darts, even those tipped with durable stone and osseous projectile points, would not have lasted long (Guthrie 1983; Arndt and Newcomer 1986). Among thousands of preserved Paleolithic osseous hunting points, few are decorated and none have complex representational images. Most decorated points have but a few schematic grooves. Again, this pattern of decorated atlatls and undecorated projectiles is consistent with ethnographic parallels, where we observe that the more permanent a hunting tool is, the more likely it is to be decorated or embellished. It is not labor intensiveness that mediates this, but durability.

The first spears children used were probably not tipped, or at least not tipped with labor-intensive points. But once a youthful proficiency was achieved, it would have been foolish to miss a hunting opportunity because one did not have among one's repertoire a well-tipped point.

FLETCHING: VANES OF DEADLY PRECISION

Thrown spears don't always require fletching, because there is enough front-heavy balance to keep the javelin-like spear's line-of-flight true. Javelins used in today's track-and-field sports, for example, are thrown with the hand held just behind the balance point to guide it to the target. Australian Aboriginals use a spear-thrower to hurl long slender spears designed more like javelins, which maintain their flight paths because of a front-heavy balance. A lightweight dart propelled from the shaft's butt end, however, is inherently unstable. The slightest deviation from the line of trajectory of a slender dart causes it to lurch sideways. The butt end needs some drag to hold it back or a fin to guide it and thus stabilize the dart's flight. The innovation that achieved this was fletching.

Amazingly, we have Paleolithic images which show fletching. In these images each feather is drawn as

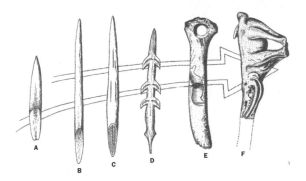

Generally, more ephemeral tools are less ornamented. Projectile points, for example, are seldom decorated with complex representational images. Point-straighteners and atlatls, on the other hand, are often highly decorated. **A–D** are typical antler projectile points. **E**, Point-straightener decorated with a horse, Kesslerloch, Switz. **F**, Atlatl decorated with a mammoth, Bruniquel, Fr.

Prehistoric (but non-Paleolithic) Native American males with their atlatls: **A**, Mayan stone carving of warrior with war club in right hand, atlatl in left. Note atlatl has two finger-holes. **B**, A portrayal of two people, darts, atlatls, and atlatl weights from Sierra Kilo, Chihuahua, Mexico.

rounded fore and aft, symmetrically (like a half-moon)—a fletching pattern in use today on many arrows. Fletching is mainly about accuracy and distance. For accurate long shots, fletching needs to be trim and refined, and surprisingly little is required to do the job. Indeed, most cultures seem to overfletch. The long rectangular fletching found on American Indian arrows meant that they were mostly for short-range shooting. This was particularly true among the equestrian bison hunters of the Plains (Hamilton 1982) and Eastern Woodland deer hunters. For longer shots, say of 20 meters or more, vanes need to be trimmed and refined so that their drag does not unnecessarily compromise the effective distance of the weapon. Thus, the streamlined contours of feather trim that we see in Paleolithic art suggest that their spears/darts were light in weight and capable of being used at moderately long distances.

THE MYSTERY OF THE MISSING SPEARS

One of the puzzles I find in Paleolithic art involves the number of animals portrayed with what appears to be a bleeding puncture wound but with no protruding spear or dart. Another puzzle is why hunters are portrayed carrying only one spear, sometimes two. I would have expected a small bundle of spears for backups, to use if one misses, if a spear is broken, or if more opportunities present themselves. I would hate to carry only one or two arrows in my quiver while bow-hunting. Carrying a bundle of spears would have been inconvenient, but surely a hunter would normally have needed more than one. That so few spears are portrayed may, then, be a clue about Paleolithic hunting methods.

One solution to these problems, arrived at by looking at some other spear- and dart-throwing cultures, is to carry extra points which can be hafted to replaceable foreshafts. Replaceable foreshafts have obvious advantages. Breakage on thrown spears usually occurs near the tip or to the tip itself (Guthrie 1983; Arndt and Newcomer 1986). A separate point/foreshaft also means that, if a hit is made, the dislodged shaft can be quickly retrieved and rearmed. If the throw missed and the point was broken, then a previously prepared tip (taken from the hunter's kit bag) can be substituted on the spot. A foreshaft with its hafted tip could have been friction-fitted (maybe with some gum stickum) onto the main shaft, allowing speedy replacement (or held more loosely with replaceable hafting materials). There are still other advantages to this foreshaft approach (Guthrie 1983).

Another interpretation of this "mystery of the missing spears" relates to the artist making these scenes. Unlike javelins, pikes, and spears, darts are quite slender, so carrying six to eight of them in one's hand is very easy. Such a bundle appears from a distance like one spear. An artist using a stone engraving tool can accomplish this impression

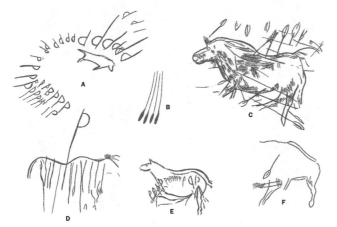

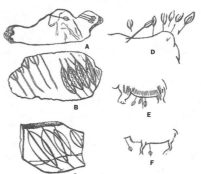

Paleolithic drawings of fletched spears: **A**, Tuc d'Audoubert, Fr. **B**, Polvorin, Sp. **C**, Paglicci, It. **D**, Trois Frères, Fr. **E**, Trois-Frères, Fr. **F**, Bara-Bahau, Fr.

One can see fletching portrayed in Paleolithic art in a number of works: **A–D**, Polesini, It. **E–F**, Colombière, Fr. It is difficult to see whether these were tangentially or radially fletched. But one can see that the fletch was trimmed oval, not left rectangular.

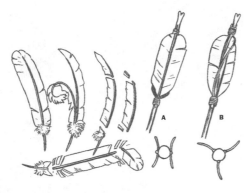

Fletching is crucial for flight orientation on a light stick-projectile; otherwise, the projectile tends to fly erratically, losing energy and accuracy. Feathers are the best natural material for fletching because they are light, durable, and thin. People in many cultures have discovered this use and so apparently did some Paleolithic peoples. There are two kinds of fletching. **A**, Tangential fletching involves mounting whole segments of the intact feather. **B**, Radial fletching involves splitting the vane and mounting the split feather on the shaft.

with the mark of a single line. Whichever explanation is correct, it is likely that hunters did not have just a "one-throw" capability.

POINT- (OR SHAFT-) STRAIGHTENERS AND THE ART UPON THEM

While projectile points made from bone, antler, or ivory do not break as easily as stone or wood, their strong tendency to warp is a glaring disadvantage. This is because the source material from which they are made is seldom

straight. Newly made points must often be straightened before they are used, but over time these materials have a persistent tendency to return to their original arcs. This warping can be remedied by using a wrenchlike tool to lever the point straight again. Such a tool allows one to apply more pressure on specific parts of the osseous point than is possible using hands alone. If the warp is serious, the point must first be soaked in water and then affixed to the handle of the straightener in a straight position to dry. When dried straight, it will remain that way for a considerable time.

Reindeer antlers were a favored Paleolithic material for projectile points, because the dense cortex is thicker than that in antlers of other deer (Guthrie 1983). But even a blank taken from a straight piece of reindeer antler has an inherent tendency to warp. Antler tines are usually too thick to be used whole, so blanks are normally cut from the thick cortex of the main antler beam. We have Paleolithic sections of antlers from which blanks were removed, so this process is well documented. The inner part of the antler is spongy but the cortex is dense; the cortex from a large bull's antler averages 1 centimeter in thickness. However, even within this dense cortex the inner portion is less dense and this difference alone inclines even a straight point to warp, particularly with changes in moisture. Since projectile points need to be straight, this chronic tendency to curve must have meant that straightening points was a recurrent activity for Paleolithic hunters. That probably explains why straighteners are relatively common in the late Paleolithic archaeological record. These implements have also been called *bâton-de-commandment* (staff of command) in French and *Lochstab* (simply "holed bar") in German. Both names reflect the fact that earlier researchers weren't sure what these objects were or how they were used. Indeed, many uses have been proposed, from a leather-rope softener to a piece of horse bridle tack that held the bit-like muzzle constrictor (Bahn 1980). The older name *bâton-de-commandment* even has overtones of a chief's or shaman's scepter of power.

As yet no Paleolithic images have been located showing these tools in use — hardly surprising as point straightening was undoubtedly not a very exciting or picturesque job (very little of our hunting art features gun cleaning, though this task is sweetly familiar to most hunters). Ethnographic analogs and circumstantial evidence do support their use as point- or shaft-straighteners. Ethnographically equivalent tools are common; Eskimos used a nearly identical tool for this very purpose. It is more than an interesting aside here that Eskimo atlatls are rather similar to those from the Paleolithic as well. Eskimo used atlatls for large-mammal hunting and the straightener for

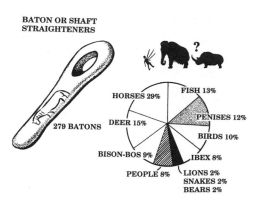

HORSES 29%
FISH 13%
DEER 15%
PENISES 12%
279 BATONS
BIRDS 10%
BISON-BOS 9%
IBEX 8%
PEOPLE 8%
LIONS 2%
SNAKES 2%
BEARS 2%

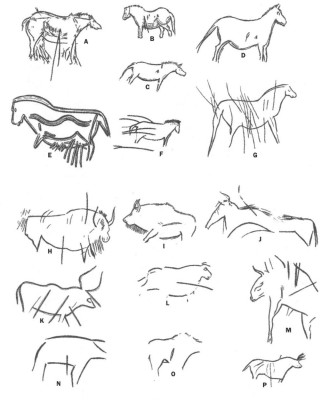

As with atlatls, representational imagery on Paleolithic shaft-straighteners might provide clues about the uses of these tools. Fortunately, Noiret (1990) has already surveyed this imagery in detail. He found that over 60% of the preserved pieces bore images of large mammals. Mammoths and rhinos were rare to absent. As with the atlatls, scenes of human violence were absent, maybe for the same reason. Also, carnivores were rare. Perhaps straighteners would not have been necessary for the long pikes or spears that were probably used against bears and lions. There were lots of bird and fish images, so it is very likely that these straighteners were also used for adjusting weapons for small game and fish. Finally, many had images of vulvae, penises with full erections, or nude women. This suggests that these tools, unlike atlatls, were not worn exposed but kept in handy personal bags or packs, whose contents were seen mainly only by the guys. The social use of erotica does have some biological constraints.

As we near the end of this chapter, I want to remind you that every time you look at Paleolithic art you should notice how often the images show protruding spears: A–D, Trois Frères, Fr. E, Chauvet, Fr. F, Tuc d'Audoubert, Fr. G, Christian, Fr. H, Gabillou, Fr. I, Bédeilhac, Fr. J, Parpalló, Sp. K, Le Placard, Fr. L, Mas d'Azil, Fr. M, Les Combarelles, Fr. N, Hornos de la Peña, Sp. O, Enlène, Fr. P, Levanzo, It.

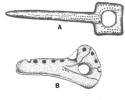

Most shaft-straighteners are decorated in representational style, but not all: A, Sungir, Rus. B, Isturitz, Fr.

Historic Eskimo shaft- and point-straighteners. Many of these are carved with images of the animals on which the weapons were used: caribou, polar bears, etc.

maintaining the darts, arrows, and their points. Also, Paleolithic projectile points fit in the grooves across the hole in Paleolithic straighteners. The taper of the hole angles upward toward the handle butt in an ergonomically appropriate manner to gain leverage to straighten a point. The hole diameter (distance between fulcrum and brace) corresponds to the physics of optimum tool design. There is a use-polish on some of these tools congruent with many straightening operations. The observed tendency of osseous points to warp implies the need for such a tool for construction and maintenance. And, finally, these Paleolithic *"bâton"* specimens are commonly broken at the very place that would receive the greatest stress when employed in straightening osseous points.

A typical Paleolithic point-straightener is made of reindeer antler, with a handle around 25 centimeters long and a palmate distal end. The hole bored through this end was apparently done with a special triangular-bitted stone borer in the lithic tool kit, found in archaeological sites. Holes were either bored at an angle to the handle or dressed that way later. An osseous point of slightly smaller diameter can be inserted in this hole and bent against its curve with a pliers-like grip on the handle and the point. Not only can osseous material be wetted and lashed to this handle until dry (Guthrie 1983), but so too can soaked pieces of hardwood or horn points (keratin) from bison, ibex, or chamois.

Since straight points and shafts were essential, it is likely that each hunter had such a tool in his personal kit as a fairly durable piece handy for frequent use in maintaining weapons, both in camp and in the field. Permanence is implied by the durable materials from which they were made and by the great care shown in their construction, including the fact that straighteners were almost always decorated—their osseous surfaces were an ideal art medium. These point-straighteners are one of the more common of the decorated osseous finished tools that we find in late Paleolithic archaeological sites (Noiret 1990).

I made this detour because it seemed worthwhile to grasp the most likely uses of the tools upon which so much Paleolithic art is carved and engraved, and not least because it makes some difference in how one interprets that art—as to whether we call this particular tool a scepter, a rope softener, a bridle piece, or a straightener of hunting projectiles. Representational images on these tools tend to corroborate the idea that atlatls and point-straighteners were used in large-mammal hunting. The subjects of their decorations are overwhelmingly of large hunted mammals, many showing spear hits and some bleeding from the mouth and nose (Noiret 1990). This is wholly congruent for a tool involved either primarily or secondarily in hunting.

Paleolithic Fish Hunting

The exact role of fish in late Paleolithic diets has been controversial, but certainly they ate fish and included them in their art. Julien (1982) and Jochim (1983) have argued on the basis of the abundance of harpoons that Magdalenians ate considerable amounts of salmon, at least seasonally. Others, like Bahn (1983) and Mellars (1985), have argued, mainly on the basis of bones remaining in the middens, that salmon were not a big part of late Paleolithic diets. Stable-isotope studies of Paleolithic people's bones seem to show little use of marine resources until the latest Paleolithic (Hayden, Chisholm, and Schwartz 1987). But the controversy continues.

The fish images rendered in Paleolithic art are mainly of meaty-fatty species, like salmonids. Salmon are anadromous; that is, they hatch in the upper parts of streams, where predation is low, migrate to the sea as tiny fingerlings, where they grow to maturity in a high-nutrient environment, and then return to the freshwater brook of their birth to complete the life cycle. This loop-of-life takes several years to complete. The appealing aspect of salmon for humans is that they import energy from the sea in the form of large quantities of fat and grow thick muscle for their trip upstream. During this trip their stomachs shrivel and they do not eat. The stored reserves are

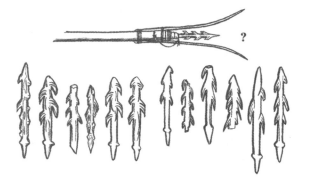

These heavily barbed antler points are characteristic of Magdalenian, especially late Magdalenian, cultures, almost post-Pleistocene. These seem to be specialized fish points. Fish flesh is soft and easily torn, so barbs must be large (especially for a large fish like Atlantic salmon). As the tip tends to roll off a slippery fish, or push the fish aside, something has to hold the fish. I suspect Paleolithic people used some sort of three-pronged device like a leister, where two outer, smooth tines hold the fish firmly and guide the barbed point. Such guides would most likely have been made from wood, which would not preserve. The beveled base allows the point to be friction-hafted directly into a cavity in the tip of a spear shaft. Located at the base, the swollen "belt" must have secured a detachable harpoon line. A detachable harpoon line protects the shaft from being broken by the fish's powerful thrashing because it does not allow the fish to exert force directly onto the stiff shaft (it is the kind of device used historically on sea mammals until quite recently). Points illustrated are from a variety of localities in France (almost always found close to Pleistocene salmon streams).

While there are no preserved fish images on atlatls, they are incorporated into shaft-straighteners. The bone harpoons had to be straightened, both in their making and as a product of dry-wet-dry warping. One straightener tool (A) from La Madeleine, Fr., even contains two images that seems to be barbed points, the kind shown in B. An example of fish on a straightener tool is shown in C.

used up during the trip and in reproductive bouts with other salmon. After breeding they are an emaciated, almost gelatinous shell of their former selves, referred to as black salmon. Pacific salmon inexorably die at this time, but Atlantic salmon retain just enough bodily resources to occasionally make it back to the sea as "kelts" and may recover, but the odds are not good. Only about 5% of wild Atlantic salmon subsequently return to breed again (Netboy 1968). In historic England the dark gray spent salmon were often fed to pigs and poor servants.

Hunting versus Fishing—Art and Psyche

Images of fish are included in Paleolithic art using the same media, tools, format, and styles as the artists used with mammals. It is curious that in historic times we have made the dichotomous distinction between hunting and fishing. One hunts for mammals, birds, reptiles, and amphibians, but fishes for fish. Throughout the world one purchases separate fishing and hunting rights. This is curious, since all of the above species are vertebrates, with basically similar anatomical organization, especially their nervous and sensory systems. Meat and fish are not logical dichotomies. It is likely that a distinction of this degree between hunting and fishing was not apparent to a Paleolithic person standing up to his thighs in the cool clear water trying to get a shot at the large salmon working its way past him.

Not only were the tools used for spearing fish only slightly modified from hunting tools (Hayden, Chisholm, and Schwartz 1987), but the psychology behind spear-fishing almost seems to be the same as in hunting: stealth and adroitness to approach the prey and practiced skill in hand-eye coordination to hit it. Unlike many kinds of modern pole-fishing, spearing fish is not a passive activity. Spearing was certainly a "blood sport," differing little psychologically and operationally from small-mammal or bird hunting. But although these are fascinating activities in a hunting society, they are admittedly not in the same class as serious big-game hunting, where animals larger than one's self are taken. Indeed, we need not be reminded that bison are far more common in Paleolithic art than are salmon.

Unlike prehistoric Bushman art or Aboriginal art there are no images of Paleolithic people netting anadromous fish, nor are there characteristic net-sinker artifacts in Paleolithic sites. The widespread abundance of barbed harpoons, particularly after about 15,000 years ago, suggests that concentrated "runs" of these fish were speared when

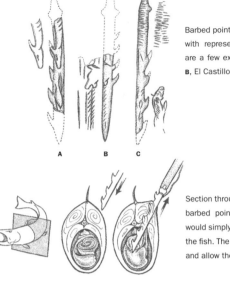

Barbed points are almost never decorated with representational images, but there are a few exceptions: **A**, El Rascano, Sp. **B**, El Castillo, Sp. **C**, El Pendo, Sp.

Section through a salmon to show how the barbed points work. An unbarbed point would simply slide out, and one would lose the fish. The barbs catch on the tough skin and allow the fish to be retrieved.

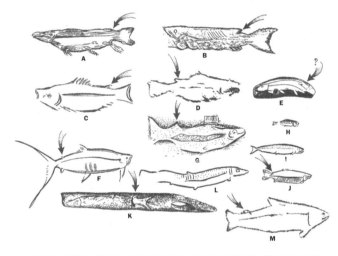

Images of fatty and tasty salmonids (e.g., salmon and trout). Note the small posterior-dorsal fin-lobe characteristic of these fish. **A**, Enlène, Fr. **B** and **K**, Les Eyzies, Fr. **C**, Niaux, Fr. **D**, Trois Frères, Fr. **E**, Mas d'Azil, Fr. **F**, Pindal, Sp. **G**, Abri du Poisson, Fr. **H**, Lourdes, Fr. **I**, Montgaudier, Fr. **J**, Laugerie-Basse, Fr. **L**, Pech-Merle, Fr. **M**, Ekain, Sp.

their numbers rose as an indirect result of increased stream flow from postglacial melting (Julien 1982).

Fish flesh is so fragile that a large barb is needed to impale the fish; otherwise, it will tear out and the fish will escape. One clue as to how these harpoons were used is that portrayals of fish seldom occur on atlatls. However, fish are sometimes portrayed on the point-straighteners (a harpoon made from antler would have warped from wetting and drying and require frequent straightening). This suggests that the harpoon may have been thrust at the fish by a hunter standing in shallow water (most of these harpoon points are found in sites near the shallow upper reaches of feeder streams). In fact, today a few seals follow salmon far upstream, and in the past these were probably speared along with the salmon (as shown by midden bones and images in the Paleolithic art of sites far inland).

Spear-fishing is an active pursuit in which, during daylight, the individual uses stealth or, at night, sometimes a torch to dazzle the fish (we used to fish this way, with a harpoon-like gig, for migratory whiting in the streams around Fairbanks, Alaska). Salmon require shallow water for breeding, and this aspect of their behavior gives the hunters (and bears) a needed edge for taking these powerful fish. Recall that most theories of Paleolithic art ignore the fish imagery, but these images do fit into the diverse portrayals of exciting hunting times.

The Evolutionary Legacy of Our Hunting Past

"Hunters" is an appropriate term for a society in which meat, the best of foods, signifies the gift of life, the obtaining and preparation of which ritualizes the encounter of life and death, where the human kinship with animals is faced in its ambiguity, and the quest of all elusive things is experienced as the hunt's most emphatic metaphor.

Paul Shepard, "Virtual Hunting Reality in the Forests of Simulacra"

Preserved Paleolithic art tells us that hunting was done by people who viewed large mammals with passion—not just with a passive appreciation of large-mammal beauty. The Pleistocene was a time when these large mammals meant life and death: food, clothing, tools, and social status. But they meant even more—something limbic, not easy to capture in words or dissect into economic flowcharts. These big warm creatures were part of a profoundly ancient and earthly splendor, elegance, power,

Seals on cave walls from Cosquer, Fr. Note that many are shown speared. Though seals reach far inland up the main rivers in Europe and become part of Continental art, these were engraved on a coastal site of the Mediterranean, where they were probably killed as they hauled out on the beach.

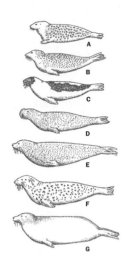

There are several phocid seal species along the European coasts and waterways that may have been seen by Paleolithic peoples, either as live animals or when their carcasses washed up on the beach. **A**, *Pusa hispida*. **B**, *Phoca vitulina*. **C**, *Pagophilus groenlandicus*. **D**, *Cystophora cristata*. **E**, *Mouachus monachus*. **F**, *Halichoerus grypus*. **G**, *Erignathus barbatus*. After Van der Brink and Barruel 1967.

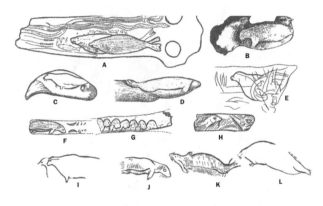

Seals haul out on land and can occasionally be taken by hunters. They were probably not dietary staples for any Paleolithic community, but they do appear occasionally in Paleolithic: **A**, Montgaudier, Fr. **B**, Brassempouy, Fr. **C**, Duruthy, Fr. **D**, Isturitz, Fr. **E**, La Madeleine, Fr. **F**, Gourdan, Fr. **G**, Morin, Fr. **H** and **J**, La Vache, Fr. **I** and **L**, Gönnersdorf, Ger. **K**, Abri Mège, Fr.

and bounty. I know of no better way of putting it than by saying that hunting lets one partake in a biological grace. Certainly, this passionately appreciative dimension is a central part of hunting. But step back and imagine the Pleistocene forces under which we once lived. Are 10,000–20,000 (or more) generations of human hunters enough to result in a propensity to hunt—a genetic inclination?

Paleolithic art and Paleolithic archaeological sites provide unanimous and eloquent evidence that hunting was a central aspect of our human heritage—so central, for so many years, that it is a part of our organismal history. As we have come to see, human hunting of large animals is profoundly related to our sociality, communication, and cooperation, to family bonds, and to conscious creativity, as well as to such traditionally noted human activities as elaborate toolmaking and the refined manipulation of objects. Our altricial (almost embryonic) birth, hugely prolonged childhood, and rich dual-parenting that emphasizes nurture and cultivation of quality-plus children are interrelated. They were both the outcome and the means of a lifeway in which the qualities of uniquely human cognitive and creative skills were again and again selectively successful. Our human niche also resulted in the evolution of a potentially prolonged life in which the opportunity for developing wisdom and experience was cherished.

In keeping with the preservation and artistic biases in Paleolithic art and other parts of the archaeological record, I have focused in this chapter on what I call the "seek-and-kill" part of hunting. Evidence from preserved Paleolithic art indicates that certain aspects of hunting were differentially emphasized in men's and women's lives; but there is no doubt that this lifeway made stringent demands upon and offered equal scope to both women and men.

The Missing Bows in Paleolithic Art

What is not in the art can also be informative. If a strong sharp pike helped put us on a par with other large carnivorous mammals, a thrown spear or its fleeter version, the atlatl and dart, afforded remarkable new possibilities. But hunting with a thrown spear is still tough business, and though it was a revolutionary weapon in terms of human evolution, the advantages of a thrown spear seem never to have guaranteed long-term stored surpluses of food. The technologies to regularly produce large surpluses of food seem to have come only in the Holocene—with the bow and of course with dogs, gill and dip nets, fish traps, toggle-harpoons, and domestic livestock and plants, more on all that in the penultimate chapter.

After the atlatl, bows were the next great innovation in hunting projectiles, and though various proposals and theories have been advanced about bows being used during the Paleolithic, we still lack solid archaeological evidence for them at that time. Certainly, there are no images of bows in Paleolithic art,

so one can say with some confidence that, in those vast regions where Paleolithic art is found, the bow definitely appears to be a Holocene invention. Bows are portrayed in Holocene art throughout much of the world, yet it is not clear where bows originated, partly because their use spread so very rapidly and widely. Of course, bows may have been invented independently in several places (as we see, for example, in the firing of pottery, domestication of plants and animals, and shipbuilding). Evidence for the use of bows can be detected indirectly from archaeological sites by the appearance of very small projectile points, but even that can potentially be misleading, as many light atlatl darts had rather small points—and of course there is a high likelihood that small points were made for children's toy spears (Dawe 1997).

Bows are used by many post-Paleolithic groups and were often portrayed in art: **A**, Remigia, Sp. **B**, Central Himalayas. **C**, Valltorta Gorge, Sp. **D**, Yenesi, central Asia. **E**, Western Cape, R.S.A.

While the bow can be quite accurate, its range is limited. Bow-hunters often use disguises to get within less than 30–40 meters. **A**, Reconstruction of aurochs head disguise. Holocene rock art: **B**, Wādi Matkhendûsh, Sahara. The remainder are from Holocene Spain: **C**, Rahcho del Molero. **D**, Cingle de la Mola Remigia. **E**, Molino de las Fuente. **F**, Mas D'en Josep. **G–H**, Peña del Escrito.

Paleolithic images of hunted animals were expressions of an intimacy colored by love and passion—a combination that is central to art. Preserved art is replete with evidence that the passion these artists brought to animal form was inseparably linked to experiences central to their lives as hunters. I also tried to move back to the time prior to Paleolithic art in order to address our older hominid legacy as hunters, and ponder where it came from and why, and along the way reviewed some objections to the view that hunting has played such a pivotal role in our

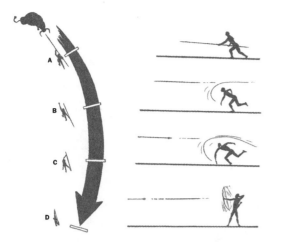

Each kind of projectile weapon has its own strengths and weaknesses. But one gains distance with the technological shift through this sequence: **A**, Pike. **B**, Spear. **C**, Spear-thrower (atlatl). **D**, Bow. The bars across the bold black arrow roughly indicate increasing effective distances to potential target.

evolutionary heritage. I think most of these objections arise from a mistaken sense of correctness rather than from archaeological and other evidence. Throughout I have assumed that the hunting themes in Paleolithic art are best understood via an appreciation of underlying biological drivers of hunting and predatory behavior in general. I'll take a similar route in the next chapter; there, we will explore the evolution of sexual attraction as a foundation for appreciating another important theme in the imagery of Paleolithic art.

Can we divine these old souls from bony refuse and incised line? Borne on the roll of chase-driven lust and comradeship of the pack, foray after foray, hunting with risk, chance, risk, success. Grilled heart and liver at the kill, not so much feast as toast. Packing back to camp dry-crusted magenta bounty, sustaining noisy kids and warm bonds. Hanging in the tents, fat and meat fueling a new elegance. Resting, drawing lines of animal beauty, watching them spread on the smooth antler surface like magic reincarnation—yes, incised lines from the soul.

A, Pleistocene point-straightener decoration on engraved antler. La Vache, Fr. **B**, My guess at the experience behind the art. Three figures have made their hit; they now must not push or excite the animal but let it go quietly, until it bleeds to death. They watch a stag red deer walk away bleeding out of its mouth. This nose-mouth bleeding signifies a lung hit, a beautiful scene for hunters who use piercing weapons like arrows and spears.

This small piece of reindeer antler from La Vache, Fr., was carved with a repetitive pattern of horse heads, as I illustrate in **A**. However, during the carving, or later, the carver saw some additional creative potential (**B**). He added a small line (**C**) from the horses' throats. This both looks like a spear, but also, when flipped (**D**), this line makes a vulva from the negative space, the horses' manes forming the pubic hair and the upper neck line completing the pubic triangle. This piece combines two important themes that contribute to the integrity of Paleolithic art: large mammals (**E**) and erotic imagery (**F**).

Full-Figured Women—In Ivory and in Life

LOVELY LIPIDS

Stone Age codes,
Have my eye
On Laussel swells.
Silky to touch,
Your own beauty's
Plethora designed
Long ago.

Lipid wealth,
Grimaldi ovals on
Ovals charging desire.
Their rotund sash,
A fertile bond,
Wrapping me closer
To you.

La Magdeleine, Fr.

On Love, Lust, and Art

Ultimately this chapter is about love, about the natural history of love. My proposition in this chapter is that looking into the evolutionary backdrop of human love will help us gain insights into many Paleolithic images. I think a grasp of our human nature is important here, because we can't truly go back and research most details of extinct cultures. Fortunately we can lean on the patterns from the diversity of human cultures to help us understand more about our nature, that core of fundamentals that unite all cultures. And there is a world of fellow species whose histories and natures can help us better realize what we are and are not. As organisms we share our behaviors of "love" with many other organisms, but we have some kinds of love that are more singularly human.

The figurines, those lovely full-figured statuettes, are some of the most famous of Pleistocene images, but there also exist many less familiar drawings, carvings, and engravings that feature salient womanly curves and male and female genitals. We will survey those images and try to account for their presence in so many different places and times throughout the late Paleolithic. Again, ethology, evolutionary biology, ethnography, and other aspects of natural history will be our guides.

As we have seen, Paleolithic images of reindeer, bison, horses, and other large mammals are clear expressions of the artists' hunting preoccupations. And yet the art we possess portrays that lifeway with notable biases. We find few images of social cooperation, kids at play, parenting, food and skin preparation, and any number of other aspects of that life. This chapter will explore biases in Paleolithic art that are both artistic and taphonomic. The nutshell story about Paleolithic images of nude females, penises, and vulvae is that such images seem to portray one omnipresent side of love, one that is readily translated into drawings and carvings. Indeed, part of life thrives on visual imagery.

Two aspects of love are often intertwined in our experiences and actions, but they are rather distinct in terms of biological origins, hormonal regulation, and neural wiring. Despite the fact that mate-bonding and parental love were—as we shall see—important to the origins and making of this first visual art, those aspects are seldom explicitly portrayed there. What Paleolithic art does portray is erotic love via images focused on sexually charged features of (mostly) female anatomy. Bulging breasts and hips, curvaceous torsos, and graffitiesque genitalia reflect an active (and overwhelmingly male) erotic impulse (Stoller 1985).

I may be in hot water here, and I hope you will bear with me. First, I shall ask you to entertain an explicitly erotic view of certain Paleolithic images which have been thoroughly mystified and politicized. This distortion of the art and our conception of the past deserves a candid reexamination. Second, I shall ask you to consider some rather broad, and decidedly unfashionable, ideas. Your forbearance will be rewarded, for the trail of lust takes unexpected turns. Our species' hypersexuality is, in origin, intimately linked to developing bonds between men and women and to greater care and treasuring of children. We will see how certain lust-promoting, fat-filled anatomical elaborations are both biological symbol and evidence of the male inclusion into human parenting. Sensuality and

Many images of women in Paleolithic art are not familiar to the general public. This one is carved from the roots of a horse incisor tooth. Mas d'Azil, Fr.

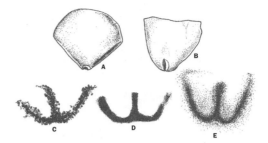

On first exposure you might not appreciate the representational identity of these little carved stones, made over a thousand kilometers apart, nor the isolated W shapes on cave walls. We will look at these images and similar ones and try to account for this pattern. What did the makers, tens of thousands of years ago, have in mind? **A**, Cejkov, Slovakia. **B**, Gouy, Fr. **C–D**, Chauvet, Fr., **E**, Angles-sur-l'Anglin, Fr.

the erotic are essential dimensions of being human, and Paleolithic art can be honestly informative in this, but our subject is hedged with taboos, and I want to pay my respects to them now.

Social mores normally prevent us from casual frankness about the slice of experience identified with lust. Such reticence and limits serve important social functions, but in the case of Paleolithic art study, this observance has inadvertently contributed to significant problems. It has obstructed the asking of appropriate questions and precluded recognition and insight. The erotic and lusty aspects of many Paleolithic art images are not incidental, and our more general sense of what Paleolithic art includes and what it means has ramifications far beyond appreciation of specific art pieces. Paleolithic art holds evidence crucial to students of human evolution, human history and religion, the evolution of art, and certainly to investigations of human nature. Therefore, I ask for clearance to disregard some conventions in order to follow where the art takes us. First, we have to talk about love.

Evolution of Quality Children

All species of mammals experience some kind of lust and sexual drive. Sexual attraction goes way back in animal evolution, ensuring abundant reproductive activity. Its simplest setting was once evolutionarily aimed at having as many low-investment young as possible, as quickly as possible, and thereafter as frequently as possible, several litters per year. This hyperreproduction was moderated in most niches. Many species evolved in the direction of making considerable investments in their young—sacri-

ficing immediate quantity for novel dimensions in quality. One route to increased quality is offering active male parenting, thereby doubling caretaking. That is where loving one's spouse, a bonding kind of love, comes in. However, there are evolutionary tensions between the different kinds of love—lust and romance—and understanding these helps us see their expressions in Paleolithic art.

The Pleistocene hunting lifeway required thoughtful mate choices and pair-bonding because so much depended on the long process of raising these slow-maturing kids. The lusty emotions remained strong but they had to be directed, controlled, and sometimes made reticent. The selective balancing of the two evolutionary tugs and tensions of quality and quantity goes on in every species in every generation. The balance of the tensions shifts back and forth as situations change, and the best balance varies with one's age and sex. How all this gets braided in with the kinds of things we find in Paleolithic art is rather a long story.

In the Pleistocene, individuals could make a greater genetic contribution (more and higher-quality kids) by carefully choosing mates than by breeding at random. First of all, genes in any population vary in their quality (defined in terms of evolutionary fitness) in every generation and across different environments. So, in addition to its other roles, sexual reproduction offers an opportunity to in-

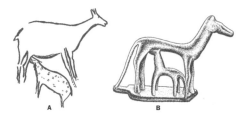

Among red deer it is only the female that cares for the young. **A**, Female red deer nursing her young. Young red deer are cryptically spotted for the first few weeks of their lives (fawns do not follow hinds but "hide out" and only show themselves for nursing). **A**, Parpalló, Sp. **B**, Small bronze figurine of mare nursing foal, Peloponnesian, first century B.C.

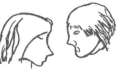

In the Pleistocene, rearing quality children required thoughtful mate choices, just as it does today. Paleolithic image from a stone engraving, La Marche, Fr.

crease one's fitness by tying one's genes to better ones. That is what much of selective sexual attraction and animal courtship is all about—assessing the genetic quality of partners.

Generally speaking, the more investment one makes in rearing one's young, the more discriminating one should be in trying to improve on randomness in mate choice (Trivers 1972). The problem is, what criteria to use? What are the best estimators? The clues that we use are not obvious, not always explicit. Most are so integrated that we are unconscious of their changing directives, but they are there as intuitive feelings. Looks, social position, communication skills, health, parasite and disease resistance, sexual fidelity, experience, knowledge and wisdom, a sharing-giving nature, emotional stability, and much else figure into our choices, which vary with our sex, age, and situation.

The Natural History of Mate Selection

In the following I shall develop points from earlier chapters on the evolutionary dynamics of sexual attraction between male and female mammals, including us, particularly as these relate to respective patterns in rearing young. Next, we shall look at the anatomy of erotic attractions in humans and some of the ways in which our attention is biologically organized. Finally, we shall return to examine some Paleolithic images that are preoccupied with this sig-

nificant part of human experience. But first, with whom do females choose to make love?

THE FEMALE'S VIEWPOINT

Choosing the Best Stud   The evolutionary dichotomy between natural selection and sexual selection has always been a false one. Ultimately, there is only one category of selection in evolution, and that is *fitness:* reproducing more young that reproduce, and thus more of the genes of which one is composed, than others do. Those courting to get that edge must be attracted to certain predictors of reproductive superiority. But the specifics vary greatly for each species, especially for the female.

Most female mammals rear their offspring alone. In these species males contribute only a squirt of sperm. This was true, for example, of woolly mammoths, woolly rhinos, bears, reindeer, red deer, ibex, bison, saiga antelope, and aurochs—species portrayed in Paleolithic art. Females of these species bear, birth, and raise the young without further male participation.

The first step to quality offspring for such females is choosing a blue-ribbon stud. Generally, this means selecting a mature and dominant male, because longevity, sleek pelage, confident behavior, energetic movements, and high social status are desirable evidence of a male's health and fitness. Of course, this is a rather indirect method, but how otherwise can one judge good genes? A male's dominant stature thus serves as a shorthand "all-systems" quality check for the female.

Such a female does not have to calculate the genetic quality of her suitors consciously or explicitly, because intuitive clues in the form of "natural attraction"—that powerful ensemble of behaviors—favored females who reserved mating favors for the winners. So, let the males

Many of the qualities that make for a good mate are probably the same for men and women: health, cheerfulness, loving nature, loyalty, integrated erotic appetite, etc. However, it is important to understand that there are some sexual differences in mate choice. Masked(?) couple from La Marche, Fr.

Which male should the "evolutionarily savvy" woman choose? I wonder if some Pleistocene woman chose the guy in this engraving from La Marche, Fr.

slug it out. Although young male horses, bison, reindeer, and red deer are sexually fertile during their first rut, it takes them a number of years of growth, experience, and testing to become socially dominant. Genetic quality is vetted by this process; dominant males get most of the copulations, and subordinates little or none—males do not fight among themselves for nothing. This rivalry reveals to the females who is the best stud, and it is almost always the females in such species who have the ultimate say. In a way of speaking, it was females who selected for the males' high testosterone titers.

Trivers (1972) found that mating competition is always most intense in the sex that invests least in the rearing of the young. It is the bulls who mostly compete for the cows. Among species in which males are not involved in raising the young, male social hierarchy is mainly about reproductive rights. Generally, this favors males who recognize one another's clues of status (strength, confidence, age, etc.) and either challenge or give ground accordingly. But what is important here is that this process also selects for *females who recognize those same clues of male social station.* In short, male power becomes attractive. For humans, "power" can mean not only strength or athletic performance but wealth, notoriety, status, and coming from the right family.

We humans do not have this old mammalian "love-'em-'n-leave-'em" mate selection dynamic, but the attractive power of the "big-stag-on-the-mountain" emotion is not completely alien. We don't have a name for it, but it could be called the "Wilt Chamberlain effect." There is often quite an entourage of "camp-followers" attracted to the limelight enjoyed by male entertainers and sports

figures. The late basketball superstar Wilt Chamberlain, on the road most of his ball-playing life, boasted in his autobiography of "laying 20,000 women" (Chamberlain 1976); though this might be an exaggeration, many women do find superstar status a potent sexual attraction. While all that is true, some guys make good dads, and throughout the long human past most women have preferred those kinds of men.

Family was an important evolutionary invention. It is likely that there were few single playboys and fewer playgirls in the Paleolithic. Pleistocene rabbit engraving on bone from Polesini, It.

Bonding: Evolutionary Guidelines for Choosing a Husband

The mother's nurturing tie to her child is apparently so deeply rooted in the actual biological conditions of conception and gestation, birth and suckling, that only fairly complicated social arrangements can break it down entirely. . . . We have no indication that man the animal, man unpatterned by social learning, would do anything of the sort.   Margaret Mead, *Male and Female*

We can appreciate the smidgen of truth in Mead's pessimism about men's innate bent toward fatherhood. But she is clearly wrong if we compare humans to the great apes. Good fathers and loving husbands are more the rule among humans than not, and social learning is not the only mediator of these characteristics. Where Mead is correct is that the evolutionary dynamics of spousal bonding, motivated by child care, are not the same for men and women. But, as we saw in the last chapter, the chances of producing more young of higher quality can be greatly increased, in some niches, with the help of a dedicated male mate. In fact, many niches are not accessible without such

So how is a woman to choose a husband? Ability to provide is crucial; that is, males should have personal resources or the ability to access resources. And, more important, the ideal man will expect loyalty in return for sharing those resources with his mate. Loyalty and bonding thus largely overrode older qualities of studship, the metaphorical equivalent of large antlers and big manes. Pleistocene husbands or husbands-to-be from Addaura, It.

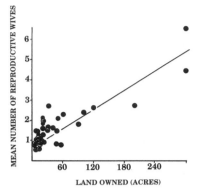

Tribal Males' Wealth and Reproduction In most tribal situations male wealth greatly affected one's "reproductive fitness." In this case, among the Kipsigis of Kenya, it is number of reproductive wives plotted against the amount of land owned (Borgerhoff Mulder 1988a, 1988b; Betzig 1988).

a pair-bond; this was probably the case in the Paleolithic human lifeway.

Wild mare horses profit from a husband. Reindeer don't. Imagine yourself out on the snow-drifted tundra in winter. You will see that an antlered cow reindeer can better defend feeding craters against competitors than can shed-antlered bulls, so having an unhelpful bonded male follow her around sharing her craters may not be a net benefit when food is scarce. It is far better to have the big lug move on and to raise the young yourself. Unlike reindeer, a stallion has a lethal kick and is alert and vigorous in using it to defend his mares and foals from predators or competitors. His power and dedication so contribute to their defense that well-being is increased; he is the kind of guy you want to follow. But not all male-female bonds are based on power. Some also include attention and help.

We can see some nascent shadows of male helpmates in chimps. For example, De Waal (1998) studied male-female social interactions among a group of chimps kept semiwild in a large enclosure in the Arnhem Zoo, Netherlands. Males there strive for hierarchical dominance and thus mating privileges, but their attraction to some females seems to extend to "attentiveness and food sharing" as well. The same is true among baboons; male tenderness and attentiveness to females counts (Strum 1987). In the right circumstance that kind of attention and protection is not evolutionarily neutral and can be selected for. Enter humans.

We need to acknowledge that human life in the Paleolithic was not idyllic. It is likely that women occasionally were exposed to threats of male violence toward themselves or their children; certainly that is the case with chimp females today. In such contexts personal choice likely reaffirmed the natural attraction to men of high stature. That is, a physically powerful and somewhat aggressive man would have been the best protector. The counterbalance comes with the emerging requirement that the protective male also be a faithful and loving spouse and involved father. Apparently, some mix of these qualities became the ideal.

An emerging human pair-bond would have affected the way both women and men approached mate selection. And this brings us to another feature of pair-bonding. It changed the evolutionary landscape of mate choice. When men began contributing to the rearing of their young, *women began to compete with other women for mates of choice—for the choicest providers and lovers* (Trivers 1972, 1985). This competition among young females over husbands was new. It was very different from looking for a good stud. Good studs were never in short supply: they are only needed for the moment. But alpha men who are also excellent lovers and show promise of becoming doting fathers are, by definition, likely already engaged. And, re-

The Evolution of Child Nurture

As we saw in chapter 4, brooding behavior and even parenting behavior in humans has a heritable component (Masson 1999). This means that genetically related behavioral variations in a population are continually undergoing selective editing and emphasis. And the process is not always unidirectional, toward more and more parenting, for instance. The most dramatic example of this is found in parasitic nesting birds, where both males and females have totally lost their direct parental inclinations; we can thus see the opposite side of the evolution of human quality-parenting in the extreme form of adaptive parental abdication among cuckoos. However, parasites cannot overuse their hosts, or the hosts disappear. Also, the cuckoo solution does not involve doing away with parenting; rather, it is just a way of getting better parenting from other species (all the other young are pushed out of the nest and the cuckolded birds concentrate all their care on just one chick—the big, hungry cuckoo).

Quality-Child Abandonment

Two syllables, cuckoo's lovely word.
Cuckoos, never seen, just heard.
What secret must her hiding keep?
Sweet sonnet's tale to make us weep?
Is this a "just so" medieval yarn?
Another mourning dove that doesn't mourn?

Truth is, he-bird sings, as he should.
She-bird keeps deeper in the wood,
Where an unguarded nest she spies.
Adds a quick egg, then away she flies.
Her egg hatches first, begs for worms,
And elbows from nest, unhatched, the rest.

Thus, noncuckoos are duped each spring
To make more cuckoos grow and sing.
That is the story behind her sleuth.
Not so valorous this harsh truth.
No nest, no clutch, no brood to beg.
Is she less a mother, for this slight-of-egg?

Evolution, neither virtuous or kind,
Winds a tentative order so we may find
Reason, balance, pattern, and form
Even in niches, like hers, outside the norm.
Tiny blackbird, your loss of egg must be
This bigger truth's hard currency.

No wilder tale could ten wizards spin.
Cuckoo's tricks on robin, tit, or hen.
Her secret, more fit than wrong.
Its strategy more elegant than song.
And richer now its "Kook-kooo" lament,
Our reminder of adaptive abandonment.

member, the physically strongest, healthiest, and most attractive young males may not be the best providers and fathers. Thus, some tensions and compromises always attend these choices. I will develop the point that evolution has played a role in our love life, from fantasy, to making-out, to romantic courtships, to bonding, and even to philandering.

And while it may be true that earlier Pleistocene genes are not destiny, they do still tilt the playing field. Our day-to-day decisions are often not "fitness maximizers" but "adaptation executors" (Wright 1994). Though we live in comfortable houses, watch TV, cruise along the paved freeway with the power of 300 horses, dine on ravioli and burgundy, and do not know most of the people we see every day, we are still physically and socially adapted as members of a small hunter-gatherer camp living out among the elements, like our ancestors. Our choices, conflicts, and mistakes about love are much the same as theirs were.

THE MALE'S VIEWPOINT

For Studs, All Estrous Females Are Gorgeous   Without pair-bonding and male involvement with offspring, there is no reason for males to discriminate among females. One ejac-

Budding love during the late Paleolithic?
La Marche, Fr.

Female Pleistocene shelks, the giant deer, chose their stags carefully. Although male shelks were exceedingly preoccupied with status, they were highly unselective about copulation partners. We can reconstruct these behaviors from the gigantic size of male antlers, the striking sexual dimorphism preserved in the fossil record, and the extravagantly patterned pelage pictured in Paleolithic art.

ulation into a less-fit female is a minor matter; therefore, it behooves males to impregnate any receptive female of reproductive age, irrespective of visual clues as to her potential success in raising offspring. Among such males, *every estrous female is gorgeous*. These males need only know that a female is the right age to reproduce and, hopefully, is in peak estrus.

Male display and fighting paraphernalia are most exaggerated in species within which the males provide no care for the young or females and focus all reproductive activity on male-male competition and mating (Trivers 1972). Ethologists use the tongue twister *polybrachygyny* to describe this extreme. Mammoths, reindeer, bison, shelks, ibex, musk oxen, saigas, and other species familiar to Paleolithic artists exhibited this elaborate male-specific threat and weapon anatomy, and we can be confident that they had little to do with rearing the young. This is in contrast to our own species and certain other social mammals from Paleolithic art, including horses and wolves. Physical appearance in these species tends to be far less dimorphic, and sometimes it can be a challenge to visually distinguish males from females. These same species bond to mates on a long-term basis.

Bonding: Evolutionary Guidelines for Choosing a Wife What happens to male choice in this new pair-bonding? The

The Consigliere's Shortcuts to Creating Loving Behavior If the evolutionary target was to have babies, why don't we all experience baby-lust, with everybody wanting more babies, trying to have more, stealing them and buying them on the black market? Well, there are evolutionary complications with the baby-lust approach. Apparently, it was just simpler to stick with the old Consigliere's shortcut directive from our early vertebrate ancestors—erotic lust. It secondarily generated the kids and served the purpose. The problem in this developing human niche was not just how to have more kids but how to increase their individual quality by creating a male bond to the mother of his children. Where was the Consigliere going to come up with a motivator for such a bond? What variations were available for selection to shape into this new male-female bond?

Core behavioral elements necessary for the evolving human male-female pair-bond were already programmed in the genome—the one the male shared with the female—in the form of the bond of offspring to their mothers and the bond of mothers to their offspring. Among males the latter bond had been unplugged (biochemically deactivated). The brain module had only to be reformatted with a modification of the former bond—to love a mate as one does one's closest genetic kin, as his mother had loved him. Innate gestures of that love were transferred as a block—hugging, kissing, nuzzling, caressing, nibbling, grooming, etc.—and given a different twist of meaning in the new female-male context. I'll review in a second how the genes for lust were kneaded into this reformatted mix.

studly appraisal that all estrous females are gorgeous doesn't completely disappear, but males must start to notice other things. For example, unlike bison and reindeer, wolves form mate bonds. Every wolf pack is based on a mated alpha pair who work as a team and share status. The alpha male is a good provider for pups, bringing food from afar to the nursing alpha female and their pups in

For males who focus their energies on supporting spouse(s), selection of wives from good genetic stock is important, but even more important in terms of reproductive contribution is youth. All else being equal, youth or youthful appearance thus predominates in assessing females, which ultimately selects for females who look younger than they are. (Of course, some physically less attractive women may be more appealing if they have compensatory assets.) From La Marche, Fr.

Because married men face the ever-present specter of uncertain paternity, a female who exhibited sexual fidelity might make a better partner than a fickle beauty. Stated in terms of the selection dynamics, males who chose less faithful wives would have tended to leave fewer offspring, thus selecting for males who were sensitive to fidelity. La Marche, Fr.

their summer dens. Unlike foxes, wolves go through several years of learning and dependence before adulthood, which is made possible by the protective and nurturing presence of both wolf parents. Young wolves need two parents, because they need a special kind of puppyhood, a longer and more developmentally open-ended one, to learn those distinctively wolf smarts that their social hunting demands.

Likewise, in the human Pleistocene niche our young required a two-parent investment. Being a good "chimp-style" stud was no longer sufficient. Men had to be dads—to desire a mate—to feel that special ache of the dizzying psychophysiological state called romantic love and to cast in their lot "till death do us part." All else being equal, males who failed to become caring parents left fewer survivors who were confident, well educated, and capable of their own successful reproduction.

A bachelor's assessment of a possible mate begins with more obvious physical signals. Such assessments do not have to be particularly conscious; our judgments of what is attractive and what is not have been roughly sketched in for us by natural selection. We gain some conscious independence in these matters only with time and repeated awareness of how very undeliberate much of this is. But our bachelor does not have to consciously weigh his choice. Being thoroughly and deeply smitten is evolution's gift.

For obvious evolutionary reasons, loyalty is a critical quality in his mate. This emotional bonding was selected for in the Pleistocene, contingent on the guarantee that those are indeed his genes in the offspring he will be tending and for which he will assume risk (Wickler and Seibt

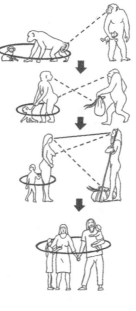

Among our ancestral hominids, males were attracted to females (and their attractive red rumps?) for copulation purposes only. However, greater access to copulation privileges began to include exchange of protection and provisioning. The erotic focus seems to have shifted to rounded rumps (fat depots), which indicated a prime reproductive state. Later, the male erotic focus expanded to include plump breasts. Permanent bonding increased male copulation privileges and better ensured protection and provisioning for the female and her young. With this male-female love-bond, the assurance of paternity allowed the male to expand his attraction from his consort to include her children, for they were likely his.

1983). Males in all human cultures select mates who behave in ways that increase confidence of paternity. Women always know their own children, but men have no such built-in guarantee—mommy's baby, daddy's maybe. Looking at marriage from this angle, one can appreciate the biological structure underlying men's preoccupation with assurances of paternity. It is another aspect of our natural history—for better or for worse (Wilson and Daly 1992). This in no way disputes the other pleasures of rearing children, even adopted ones not genetically one's own. That said, statistically, stepfathers remain one of the foremost hazards to children.

So, in an Ice Age context, carelessness or ineptitude in mate selection and bonding would have lessened a man's or a woman's genetic impact. The bottom line is that in-

The circle of love in the Pleistocene? A pendant of male and female back to back from Balzi Rossi, It. My interpretation at right.

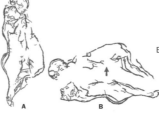

Because of the small band size and the unpredictable economic base, it is likely that Paleolithic men and women both chose their mates carefully. Here a Paleolithic couple is portrayed copulating, and it appears that the woman is in the top position. Most sex is conducted between lovers. If you wish to know a major driving force in human evolution, here it is engraved in stone in Paleolithic art, albeit rather rudimentarily. La Marche, Fr. **A**, Standing? **B**, Exploded view.

creasing investment in quality children upped the ante of mate choice and bonding behavior for both sexes. Bonding between human mates did not evolve primarily to provide companionship or financial security; it was about a better way to raise children. We don't experience bonding that way, but it is the Consigliere at work again.

UNDERSCORING MALE-FEMALE DIFFERENCES

Most older women would like to step back into a more youthful face and most young males would like to step forward to a more manly place.

Women and men are not the same, so there are no simple symmetries or neat patterns of parallels to their respective erotic and bonding experiences. Asymmetry in these dynamics is dramatically underscored in how many children one can have. Men can potentially have hundreds; women stop well short of twenty. This difference is not evolutionarily neutral. Short-term sexual relationships pose entirely different risks to men and women, and that is true cross-culturally.

These differences are subsumed in pair-bonding, but apparently aspects of their old tensions remain. There are other sexual differences in sexual attractions and behaviors. Males and females exhibit strong cross-cultural sexual asymmetries in sexual violence (Daly and Wilson 1988), sexual coercion (Symons 1979), and physical sexual attraction (Buss 1989). Men pursue more variety in sexual partners, and such behavior has probably paid off in fitness terms. Symons (1979) studied sexual differences in attraction to partner variety in pornographic literature and in

prostitute use and found that the appeal of "variety" is mainly a male phenomenon. He also studied gays and lesbians, finding that homosexual males tended to continue seeking out other males outside their pair-bond, whereas bonded homosexual females were less likely to do so.

Ethologists refer to the heightened erotic effect of a variety of sexual partners as the "Coolidge effect." When President Calvin Coolidge and his wife had separate guides on a visit to a model chicken farm, Mrs. Coolidge asked why there were so few roosters. Her guide informed her that roosters can copulate dozens of times daily. "Tell that to the president," said Mrs. Coolidge. When the guide passed on her message, the president asked, "Is it always with the same hen?" "Oh no, a different hen every time." "Tell that to Mrs. Coolidge," said the president.

In the last two decades research in animal behavior has outlined many issues underlying the dynamics of mate selection. It is almost a subdiscipline. In many monogamous animals studied, females actively select males who can best provide for them and their offspring. Alcock (1993) has suggested that evolution is responsible for the related predisposition in women. In Western cultures females consistently give high marks to "earning power," while males attach a greater value to "physical attractiveness" (Buss 1989). Buss's survey of thirty-seven countries showed that these patterns of choice were cross-culturally consistent. In *all* those cultures most women preferred older mates, and most men preferred younger mates. Numerous other studies have also revealed this marriage partner age skew (e.g., Bouckaert and Boulanger 1997). Symons (1979), Alcock (1993), and Mealy (2000) make the

Copulatory Desire and the Glue of Human Pair-Bonding

For a Paleolithic guy this switch to fatherhood did not decrease lust; it just focused it—or maybe even increased it. Let me reiterate a point made in the last chapter that the shift toward this new male-female bond resulted in increased sexual opportunities. If lust was central in brokering the attraction to bonding, then the proximate tradeoff of sacrificing philandering for being a good father was increased lust satisfaction—guaranteed by mating with a female who behaved and appeared as though she were in estrus at all times (Szalay and Costello 1991). For most men, traditionally, opportunities to copulate are scarce, and by increasing these opportunities with pair-bonding, they inadvertently increased their reproductive success. The same is true for the woman. Through her husband's sustained attraction, a woman increased her resources and those of her children. Romantic love and sexual attraction remain largely separate in the brain and in behavior, but their evolution has begun to intertwine.

A woman could transmit inviting estrous signals year-round to her husband, as Szalay and Costello have proposed, because there was an emerging pair-bond. And that pair-bond in turn made a band structure with multiple breeding males possible. Unlike a female chimp, an early human female had the protection of her mated male (and of the other band members, with whom she had signed the contract to the band ethos—look but don't touch). She no longer had to fear a constant free-for-all mating frenzy with male fights for violent access. We know well the sometimes fragile contingency which still marks our pairing, yet despite biological loose ends, it generally works well.

argument that the cross-cultural ubiquity of these differences is genetic in origin, the results of different selective pressures in the Pleistocene and even more distant past.

These respective male-female dynamics are also revealed in the ways men and women act to "enhance" their mating status. Girls in their early teens desiring more sexual allure generally use makeup and clothes in ways to appear older. Middle-aged women who are seeking long-term relationships with men tend to use cosmetics and dress the other way, to appear more youthful. Likewise, men looking for a wife tend to exaggerate their wealth, social status, kindness, and fidelity, and, if under thirty or so, try to appear older. These patterns are common in most cultures.

Kenrick and Keefe (1992) examined newspaper advertisements from Arizona and India that indicated maximum and minimum ages sought by people seeking marriage partners. Men sought younger women and women preferred older men. Interestingly, men past thirty-five set their *minimum* age difference for a wife to at least five years younger than themselves, and by age fifty it was ten years younger. This desire for comparative youth in one's bride is an evolutionarily coherent strategy because young wives have, statistically, the greatest potential to bear and raise children. Groups that use a bride-price set it higher for a younger wife (e.g., Borgerhoff Mulder 1988b). Shortly, we will see how these patterns can help us understand certain images in Paleolithic art.

Divorces and separations also provide insights into the dimorphic dynamics of pair-bonding. Men tend to leave older mates for younger women, whereas women often cite a man's inability to provide economically when they sue for divorce (see Betzig 1988 for a cross-cultural review). Inversely, bonding is statistically more successful when men provide amply and women retain a youthful attractiveness—in other words, when each embodies the evolutionarily engraved desires of the other sex (Buss 1997). As Mrs. Simpson, the duchess of Windsor, once said, "A woman can never be too rich or too thin." Thinness implies youth, and richness . . . well . . . her choice of mate speaks for itself.

The push and pull of these dynamics of mate selection are also detected in choices about extramarital copulation. For example, a study of the Paraguayan Ache found that

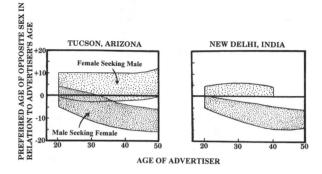

TUCSON, ARIZONA NEW DELHI, INDIA

PREFERRED AGE OF OPPOSITE SEX IN RELATION TO ADVERTISER'S AGE

Female Seeking Male

Male Seeking Female

AGE OF ADVERTISER

Women tend to be younger than their husbands. Is it because they themselves prefer it that way? One way to address this is to survey newspaper personal ads of people who wish to meet the opposite sex (newspapers from Tucson, Arizona, and New Delhi, India). The zero midline in these graphs is for a partner of the same age, the heavily stippled area represents the ranges of men seeking women, and the lightly stippled area is women seeking men. Women are advertising to meet men of the same age and older, but not younger males. Men prefer women younger than themselves, and this age disparity preference increases with age. Data from Kenrick and Keefe 1992.

Apparently, women of all cultures are, statistically, less attracted to much younger males for a long-term relationship (Buss 1989). Engraving from La Marche, Fr.

good hunters were more likely to produce extramarital children than were poor hunters. Additionally, Borgerhoff Mulder (1988b) found that among the Kipsigis of Kenya the amount of land owned by a husband was positively correlated with the number of his surviving offspring (Alcock 1993). Studies of old records from Europe show similar patterns of higher fecundity and survivorship of children among women marrying wealthier males. The more resources the male attained, the more offspring he produced, including more illegitimate children, and the more likely he was to marry more than once (Boone 1986).

To summarize the above sections about bonding we could say that women are *initially* attracted to a mate by some form of perceived excellence and outstanding status—which could be financial success, athletic prowess, political power, superior hunting success, etc. And in the same vein, we can say that a man's *initial* attraction is

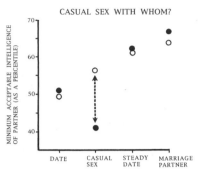

CASUAL SEX WITH WHOM?

MINIMUM ACCEPTABLE INTELLIGENCE OF PARTNER (AS A PERCENTILE)

DATE CASUAL SEX STEADY DATE MARRIAGE PARTNER

How does intelligence factor into sexual attraction? Men and women feel much the same about one another when it comes to a datable prospect, steady date, or marriage partner. But when it comes to casual sex, males are much less choosy—an old evolutionary pattern of differential investments at stake? After Kenrick and Keefe 1992. Black dots represent men's choice; white dots, women's.

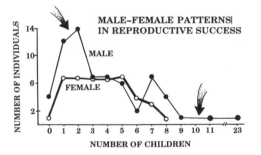

MALE–FEMALE PATTERNS IN REPRODUCTIVE SUCCESS

NUMBER OF INDIVIDUALS

MALE

FEMALE

NUMBER OF CHILDREN

The mean number of children born to wealthy and poor women among the tribal Yomut of Iran is about the same. However, the number of children a man may have depends on his status and wealth. The Yomut are a polygamous society, and individual males among the wealthier half have about twice as many children as the poorer half. After Irons 1979. Arrow on left points to poor males and right arrow points to wealthier males.

based mainly on youthful physical beauty. What we see next is that on these terms virtually all young women are beautiful to a degree, but all men are not of outstanding status. To enhance their at-first-glance mate value, then, it behooves males to take risks to become outstanding and prosperous and females to strive for youthful beauty. Though a complex mix of things, beauty does have a natural history (Eibl-Eibesfeldt 1989a).

Face and Figure: Two Evolutionary Pathways of Men's Physical Attraction to Women

Let's turn now to the evolutionary forces underlying physical attraction. Actually, I'll be mostly talking about women's faces and figures, but that is because I am going to focus on heterosexual male attraction to women. I take the male viewpoint because, as we have learned from previous chapters, it is so apparent in Paleolithic imagery. The forms of women's figures and faces are handy stuff for visual art, and since they have almost universal appeal, they may help us step with prudence across cultural variety and allow a certain access into Paleolithic imagery.

Face and figure—these two words summarize the locations of the natural attractors of *philos* and *eros.* We'll begin by talking about *philos,* with the understanding that, historically, evolutionarily, it is the newer addition.

PHILOS: REPRODUCTIVE POTENTIAL

The most potent evolutionary driver for males behind the romantic love ancient Greeks referred to as *philos* stems, as I said, from youth, because young women have the greatest number of potential reproductive years and the most time for rearing young. This is the evolutionary currency with the highest compounded-investment returns. Biologists calculate *reproductive potential* (some biologists use the designation "reproductive value"; Pianka and Parker 1975) as the average potential offspring a female animal could produce for the remainder of her life, depending on her present age.

In women, reproductive potential peaks just after puberty and declines rapidly each year thereafter, until it approaches zero at menopause. The caveat here, and especially in the Pleistocene context, is that statistically a seventeen-year-old girl has more potential offspring ahead of her than a seven-year-old girl, because the latter has a modest chance of dying before attaining sexual maturity. All this related directly to male evolutionary fitness. For example, a new wife at twenty has more than *triple* the (compounded) reproductive potential of a new wife aged thirty, assuming all else is equal and that on average fertility extends from ages twenty to forty. Few adaptive features come close to such a tripling of genetic fitness. One can see that selective forces jealously maintain men's attraction to fecund youthfulness. Such attraction doesn't require numerical literacy—only the recognition of visual clues. For example, evolution has not as yet turned on the "flashing-light" sexual attractants in a seven-year-old girl. Once sexually mature, a youthful (not underage) appearance is therefore key to initially attracting the arrows of *philos.* The age of a male is important to a woman but not so crucial (particularly in the modern context of greater life expectancy). The man's extended fertility is not in question—if a Rockefeller or Rothschild is twenty years older than his young wife, the usual attitude is, what does it really matter?

So, for marriage, men are attracted to young mature women, that is to say, to women *whose appearance most closely resembles that age.* That is why mature women strive to alter their appearance toward youth, and why someone beyond thirty might choose to hide her age. In evolutionary terms, it is crucial for males to be able to read the face of a female's age. Remember, these forces are deep and irrational; one does not rationally assess beauty in terms of more babies—here is another Consigliere shortcut. Visceral responses override rational ones: a youthful face on a woman aged thirty-five may make her more appealing than a twenty-five-year-old with an aged face.

The Face of Reproductive Potential   Reproductive potential is closely traced in a woman's face, and it is a woman's face

Faceless in the Paleolithic, La Marche, Fr.

At most sites the faces are missing in Paleolithic art or at least poorly done. The main exception is at the French site of La Marche, where many of the faces are done well enough to get some sense of the subjects' sex and age. Notice how often the hair has been engraved as wild and unkempt; however, in most cases it has been cut—interesting.

Two different cases of male and female hands being placed side by side on the cave wall. Gargas and Cosquer, Fr. Is this fossilized love?

a man looks at in assessing long-term bonding. Falling in love with a face is a special neurophysiological state. Males are finally smitten by faces, not feet, breasts, or shoulders. There is every evolutionary reason this should be so. The face is one of the best indicators of age, health, and genetic hardiness. Physical attractiveness depends on the face more than on any other feature (Bersheid 1981).

A first glance at someone's face indicates age, because as one grows older the facial features change proportion: relative eye size decreases as lids become more constricted around the orbit, eye-whites lose their clarity, bony angularity increases, noses enlarge, lips thin, skin sags, scalp hair loses luster and grays, and small facial hairs thicken and darken. The assessment of age from the face also relies on its being the area most exposed to the sun's rays and where skin irregularities accumulate with time. The thinning skin exposes underlying blood vessel varicosity,

wrinkles become exaggerated, surface texture coarsens, sun warts and tumors multiply. All the initial information a male needs to know is here, to motivate or discourage in the direction of loving. Young good looks are more completely products of biology and less an individual's artwork.

There is very little about *philos* in Paleolithic art. As with most points made in this book, there are interesting exceptions. Two exceptions to the lack of romantic love depicted in Paleolithic art are the two pairs of male and female hands, one set in Gargas Cave and the other in Cosquer Cave. One or both of the individuals sprayed ocher onto the backs of their hands while they were tightly pressed side by side against the cool cave wall. What wonderful stories undoubtedly connect the making of these linked prints. A little imagination makes them into poignant reminders that the same feelings we experience in our lifetimes were there over 1000 generations ago, and perhaps much farther back in time. But it left few traces in this old art. However, there is a side of love that *is* common in Paleolithic art; I refer to this as *eros*.

EROS: INSTANTANEOUS FERTILITY

"Figure" is the word associated with *eros*—erotic love for an attractive figure. There is another biological statistic relating to reproductive success that, indirectly, tells us something about the attractive tug that heterosexual men experience in seeing a voluptuously curvaceous female figure. *Instantaneous fertility* describes the likelihood that a female of a given species will bear young in that particular time (say, year) of her life. *This curve is not the same as the curve for reproductive potential.* The instantaneous fertility of a seventeen-year-old girl is rather low, about the same as for a woman of thirty-eight, as measured by hospital births in the United States, for example. This fertility curve varies with region and culture. A recent Canadian survey showed a mean instantaneous fertility of age twenty-eight (Daly and Wilson 1997). We can think of this curve as reflecting the age of women who predominate in

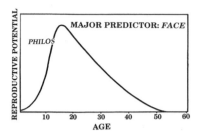

English speakers have one word, "love," for what the Greeks considered two phenomena: *eros* and *philos*. *Philos* is the emotion underlying male bonding to females. All else being equal, the factor of age in attraction is critical and can best be expressed in terms of "reproductive potential," that is, the lifetime potential for future reproduction of an average female of a given age. Once past puberty this reproductive potential declines almost exponentially with age. For good biological reasons the best predictor of reproductive potential is the face. Theoretical curve.

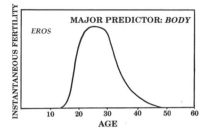

Another biological estimator of reproduction is time-limited, say for any given year, and is known as "instantaneous fertility." All else being equal, which year is the average female most likely to be most fertile, able to have young easily, and able to do the best job rearing them, etc.? This does not decline linearly after puberty but peaks in the late twenties or early thirties—much later than the peak of reproductive potential. Its best predictor is the body or, more precisely, the torso. Theoretical curve.

maternity wards. Statistically, a woman in her late twenties is more likely to bear and rear a healthy baby to maturity than are mothers aged fourteen or forty-eight. A woman of twenty-eight still has the resiliency of youth and ample life expectancy ahead, is at her lifetime healthiest, and has accumulated considerable experience that will help her in rearing young. This curve of instantaneous fertility would likely have peaked earlier during the Pleistocene, and perhaps the curve had steeper sides. This instantaneous fertility curve closely tracks the ages at which men find women's figures most sexually attractive just as the curve of reproductive potential closely mirrors a woman's facial appearance.

The overwhelming majority of Paleolithic figurines and female images engraved on bone and stone lack a beautiful, youthful face, and many have no face at all. Rather, these images emphasize full-figured torsos, the voluptuous curves of sexual attraction—the kind of love associated with instantaneous fertility.

The Curves of Instantaneous Fertility   Men find the curves of instantaneous fertility just as eye-catching from behind as from the front. Men's attraction to a voluptuous figure is something in addition to, or other than, the *philos* of bonding love. These curves are very dear to heterosexual male fantasy. Lust values most highly the curvaceous out-

lines statistically associated with the figure of twenty- to thirty-year-olds. This is the peak period of full breasts and buttocks, curvaceous body outlines, broad hips—all of which are produced by the body-modeling of fat depots. These are the figures businesses like to feature at their front desks, as stewardesses, as tour guides, etc. Shapely women of this age are highlighted in advertising, especially in advertisements directed at men—motorcycle, sports car, motorboat, and beer ads—and, of course, in the more explicitly erotic/pornographic media.

THE EMOTIONS OF *EROS* AND *PHILOS* AMONG HETEROSEXUAL MALES

Lust is an old neurophysiological driver of copulatory desire. As we saw in chapter 4, it is testosterone keyed in both male and female mammals. Its human version has been the subject of study in medical laboratories and clinics (e.g., Masters and Johnson 1966) and its symptoms are widely known.

In contrast, the emotion of romantic love is more of a breathlessly intimate fixation. We can better see the dynamics of falling in love by their artificially exaggerated renditions. For example, cinema and TV exaggerate our innate social program for romance. In real life we fall in love with some person who is familiar and has health, charisma,

There is no doubt that many people the world over put enormous amounts of time and energy into making themselves attractive and in seeking partners. People do not bond or have sex at random. Small engraving from Gourdan, Fr. My enhancement on the right.

Bodies predominate over faces in Paleolithic art, the extreme being a quick stylized figure of slender torso and large buttocks, thighs, and hips, no feet, arms, or head. Gönnersdorf, Ger.

Late Holocene art portraying male and female Bushman. Males living in situations with unpredictable resources should be most attracted to women who have a proven ability to lay up fat reserves. From Zastron, R.S.A.

and so on. The movies can bring that person to you in virtual, up-close, fine-grained, bigger-than-life intimacy. Top-billing actors and actresses are picked for their ability to trigger that response. It sells well. Who has not fallen in love with a star or starlet? On the face of it, it is ridiculous, falling in love with somebody who is portraying someone else and really is just an image of a person made from dots on a tube or a light shown through plastic fluttering through a reel. Ironically, stars have to have bodyguards because of the occasional pathologies of attraction produced by this phenomenon. Becoming zapped with cupid's arrow is more than a cultural construct.

In the previous chapter I listed the criteria that researchers use to recognize emotional male-female bonding among a few other primate species (Anzenberger 1992; Fuentes 1999). These same criteria can be lifted almost intact and applied to some of the oft-expressed outward symptoms of human romantic bonding:

- illness-like state when separated for extended periods
- ease of intense jealousy
- considerable time spent in direct eye-to-eye contact with lifted brows and smiling
- focus of attention on partner manifested in other diverse ways
- involvement with love songs, dancing, or poetry
- physical intimacy, such as cuddling, hugging, and kissing
- parental-like care for partner's comfort and well-being

Well, you know all the signs.

EVOLUTIONARY SHORT-TERM AND LONG-TERM MATING STRATEGIES

Much of the credibility of the "Mother Goddess theory" regarding a class of Paleolithic images has relied on the fact that quite a few of these curvy nude figures seem to be mature women, not young teenagers. We can agree that female body forms portrayed in Paleolithic art vary from pubescent to menopausal (Duhard 1993). Is it likely that images of older, "motherly" women might have served erotic purposes? There is a way of assessing this.

We have already noted that female age ranges to which males are attracted differ strikingly between *eros* and *philos*. At puberty, boys generally fall in love with girls roughly their own age. As we've seen, as men age, the preferred age of bridal candidates is lowered. *Eros* plots very differently about age. The age range of women to whom males are sexually attracted, whether for a quick fling or imaginative fantasy, is broad and reaches from puberty to menopause (fitting our evolutionary expectation as previously outlined). A man of thirty, say, might be wildly sexually attracted to a girl of sixteen or to a woman of forty-nine but find neither desirable as a bride. Young boys can readily have runaway erotic fantasies involving women twice and even three times their own age. In fact, almost any woman in her reproductive years might be sexually appealing for a *low-investment, short-term sexual relationship* (see Jones 1996 for a review).

Most teenage males are not attracted to middle-aged women for matrimony, even though such a woman may be the most luscious, sexually desirable woman a teenage

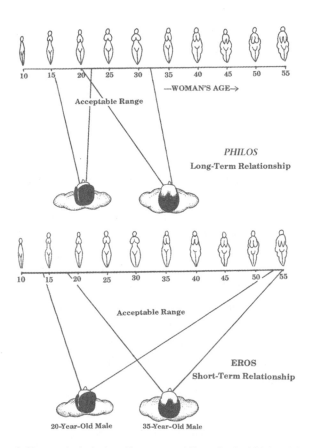

—WOMAN'S AGE→

Acceptable Range

PHILOS
Long-Term Relationship

Acceptable Range

EROS
Short-Term Relationship

20-Year-Old Male   35-Year-Old Male

As I have emphasized, when either young or middle-aged males fall in love, it is more often than not with women in a rather narrow age range, near their own age or usually somewhat younger, virtually never a decade older. That is almost universal among human societies (Buss 1989), with but a few special-case caveats. When either young or middle-aged males are attracted to a woman for just sex (a short-term relationship), the age of the woman is not as important; she may even be decades older than the man (Jones 1996).

boy has ever seen. Is there any reason to think a Paleolithic boy's sexual fantasies would have been limited to nubile girls? Remember what was said in the last chapter about Paleolithic patrilocal styles; since most wives were chosen from outside the band, boys were not closely related to most women in their own band, and not organically repelled by close genetic links.

It is very difficult to judge the "intended" ages of the Paleolithic images of women, other than to say they generally depict women in their prime child-bearing years, not prepubertal girls or postmenopausal women. Rice (1981) tried estimating the exact ages of these Pleistocene

figurines. Rice's largest class was between the ages of seventeen and thirty-five and not pregnant. This is consistent with the prediction of *eros*'s prime target. However, there is an inherent bias in this kind of analysis, because today we almost always equate major obesity with full maturity in human females—one of the main reasons modern women try to lose weight is to look younger. My female informants who weekly use communal sports shower-rooms at the university (and who happen to be observant sculptors) tell me that some nude women in their early twenties look amazingly similar to typical Paleolithic figurines. This may be one of those cases where anecdotal evidence from a trained observer is the best evidence one gets.

MALE/FEMALE *EROS* AND *PHILOS*: HOW THEY AFFECT TASTES AND BECOME ENTANGLED IN THE ART

While spousal attraction may be set in motion by a face or figure, it is also mediated by less physical features that may never come into play in short-term relationships or in fantasy. These include fidelity, compatibility, gentleness, stability, extended-family resources, and so forth. These aspects do affect spouse choice and do so in patterns that are consistent cross-culturally (Buss 1997). Still, beauty and outstanding status remain exceptionally important to men and women, respectively. Indeed, a statistical study by Urdy and Ekland (1984) found that the single best positive predictor of the relative occupational status of a man was the physical attractiveness of his wife; likewise, the single best predictor of relative physical attractiveness of a woman was the status of the man she had married. While this is perhaps not the science nugget to pull out for small talk at a dinner party, it is a principle that has been shown cross-culturally (see Buss 1989 and Jones 1996 for reviews).

These sexually bimodal patterns of erotic and spousal evaluation reverberate in all kinds of matters. Let's take, for example, the subjects discussed by members of the same sex. Young women can be expected to share more about their love problems than about their philandering or fantasies of short-term flings, because they generally gain more status from being sought after for long-term relationships than from one-night stands. Young men, on the other hand, seldom talk with the guys about serious girlfriends or long-term courtships, but they do brag or joke about their fantasized or real sexual exploits and the possibilities of specific females for potential short-term relations. Evolutionarily, it behooves men not to advertise or boast about the sexual appeal of their long-term partners (real or potential). This is what must underlie the taboos men generally observe against showing other guys nude pictures of their wives or close girlfriends. Exclusivity has to be protected. Expressions of love are private, reserved for a sweetheart.

But young men especially can happily share quite explicit images or erotic fantasies of women when bonding conditions are not involved. Again, it matters little to a couple of thirteen-year-old boys that the models in the bra catalog they are ogling are more than their combined ages. When bonding issues are not at stake, neither is exclusivity, and such male fantasies can be shared. Tensions and taboos most often enter when *philos* and *eros* appear together.

EROS, PHILOS, AND PHILANDERING

There is an asymmetry in the opportunities and challenges that philandering poses to mate fidelity and bonding. In evolutionary terms, the great peril to females is to be *deserted,* while the great peril to males is to be *cuckolded.* Thus, in interdependent bonding, males are keenly concerned with sexual fidelity and females with emotional fidelity. Neither biological selection nor social dynamics are insensitive to this difference. There is indeed a double biological standard. Men's fears of courtship competition and cuckoldry are evolutionarily deep and age-old (Buss 1988b). Asymmetric evolutionary pressures have promoted both female reticence and the male eye for a variety of possible copulatory partners and the male involvement

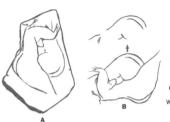

A, Plaquette from La Marche, Fr., that turned one way looks like someone on someone else's lap but turned the other way is someone lying on top of a woman. **B**, Exploded view.

with more explicit erotica. These asymmetries allow us to see that some Paleolithic art on cave walls is clearly about male *eros.* The erotic does not care about wives or husbands; it occasionally circumvents the social contracts we all make. It surely did in the Pleistocene as well.

Fidelity, however, was in the interest of a Pleistocene couple and their band. The reason is spelled k-i-d-s. Yet, there were undoubtedly lapses in fidelity. Ethologists working with new DNA identification techniques have shown that infidelity is present in some degree among all monogamously pairing species that have been studied. Ethologists refer to this as extra-pair copulation, EPC. It is known to occur in species we once swore (from behavioral studies using field glasses) were totally loyal.

If pair-bonding is important with regard to evolutionary fitness as I am suggesting, if it is in fact a centrally crucial part of our species' niche strategy, then one would think that EPCs would be evolutionarily selected against. Indeed, many bonding species have evolved elaborate behaviors and anatomical features to ensure genetic paternity. Wolves, for example, have inflatable side-swellings on the penis that serve as a plug, locking the male to the female for many minutes after ejaculation.

One might imagine how copulation in casual relationships might be selected for, especially among unmarried males. But what about outside marriage? Perhaps the persistence of EPCs at low levels of incidence indicates a balancing of individual genetic advantage with the interests of the family, in which the strong selective advantages of fidelity are very clear. Cheating affords some selective advantage only as long as it is not very common. It is one of those frequency-related kinds of selection, like parasitism or lying, where fitness value changes with incidence.

The bottom line is that natural selection has produced erotic forces so strong and broad, particularly among young unpaired males, that they result in a major desire for, fantasy about, and the occasional accomplishment of copulation with someone other than a bonded partner. This is linked to the fact that the consequences of promiscuity or infidelity are not the same for each age and sex.

A bonded male who philanders (even the Greek word implies male behavior, combining *philos* and *andros,* "man") can still rear his own young and at the same time let another male rear his wild oats. We see this sexual asymmetry in all other pair-bonding species, such as communal swallows. Permanently bonded male swallows continue to try, whenever the rare opportunity arises, to copulate with females mated to other, absent males. Yet to become the victim of cuckoldry is such a major risk of fitness loss for a male swallow that if he finds his mate consorting with another male, he will abandon her and their young and seek a new mate (Birkhead, Atkin, and Møller 1987). Thus, female philandering is associated with much higher risk of brood failure. Yet it is not necessarily to a female's advantage to abandon an attentive male because he also fertilized another female. This dynamic is broadly observable in pair-bonding species. Biologists consistently find more male than female philandering.

Paired females of bonding species of birds and mice copulate discretely with other males, but unlike the philandering males, female infidelity is not random. It is generally with males of high stature, or higher stature than her mate (Møller 1987). Møller explains the advantages of such female infidelity by the fact that if her mate dies, she is aided by the cuckolder, whom evolution has inclined to that behavioral pattern because of the chance that he is indeed the real father.

Those testosterone-flushed, high-libido, young Paleolithic males were following basic human directives, for their sex and age, of not only thinking about future wives but fantasizing about sex without consequence—seducing unmarried girls with no thought to marrying them,

An early Heimlich maneuver? In a modern art gallery we might expect a title like "Lust." A Pleistocene embrace from La Marche, Fr.

even perhaps widows and other men's wives. And, of course, Paleolithic married guys likely had roving eyes, if not deeds.

THE HISTORY AND HERITABILITY OF HUMAN LUST

Chimp females often offer sexual access for male favors and in some cases to reduce male aggression. Among bonobos, sex play and copulation are used for social facilitation, more like grooming. This trend toward liberating human, bonobo, and chimp sexual behavior from reproduction (Morris 1967; Eibl-Eibesfeldt 1970, 1989b; Wrangham and Peterson 1996) means that, as mammals go, humans are rather hypersexual (Morris 1969)—though well behind chimps. This hypersexuality, if not in action, at least in mind, is a component of the human daily aesthetic experience but varies with age and sex.

Lust is a very ancient vertebrate experience. Serum androgenic hormones activate a major change in sexual behavior in adolescent boys (Urdy et al. 1985), and testosterone production has a significant heritability. Our individual variations in erotic bent and degree not only are cultural but have heritable components too. In a study of 1500 twin pairs McGue and Lykken (1992) calculated a heritability of 0.52 for sex drive; that is, among this large sample about half of the variations in erotic feelings and behaviors can be best accounted for by genetic propensities. This supported similar findings of earlier studies (Eysenck 1976; Martin, Eaves, and Eysenck 1977). These studies formalize what we know to be true, that although there are individual and cultural nuances and flavors, the erotic is a persistent and universal human propensity. Indeed, we find ample evidence of the erotic throughout Pa-

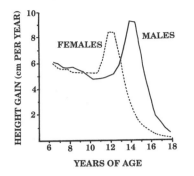

Adolescent Growth Spurt in Height for Males and Females Males of most mammals continue to grow well after females at the same age become fecund and cease their growth. These differences seem to relate to sociobiological factors. The low status of young males means they cannot compete with older males and instead have been selected to devote some reproductive energies to continued growth. (American population sample, after Bongaarts and Potter 1983.)

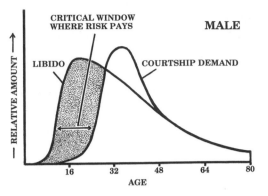

In men, testosterone and often its behavioral corollary, libido, peak almost a decade before optimum courtship potential (the point at which one is most likely to obtain a wife, especially a wife of the best genetic quality). This is the discrepancy I talked about in the last chapter, which selected for a mind bent toward risk, which included sexual matters. At thirty, a male is approaching his peak courtship power and so should theoretically be very discriminating. After Kinsey, Pomroy, and Martin 1948 and Masters and Johnson 1966.

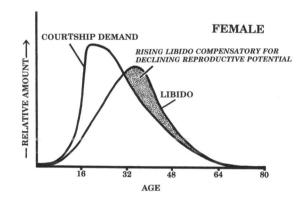

Among women, libido is also offset from peak courtship potential, but instead of preceding courtship potential, libido crests over a decade later. Women at sixteen have all the courtship power they will ever have, so in evolutionary terms, young girls should be cautious about flagrant libido; after thirty-five, a woman needs to be less cautious. After Kinsey, Pomroy, and Martin 1948; Kinsey et al. 1953; and Masters and Johnson 1966.

leolithic art. I want to acknowledge this presence and will rely in part on the more universal biological aspects of male (in particular) heterosexual erotic imagination, using historic analogs and studies of modern populations for insight.

Do not misunderstand; I am not asserting a single motivation for all the images of nude females or genitals engraved on walls and tools. Specific motivations for such a collection of art must certainly have been diverse, and we can only assume that both people and animals were portrayed for a number of reasons. The challenge is to discern themes or patterns that run through the imagery. I see an erotic leitmotif underlying the numerous images of plump female nudity and exaggerated sexual organs. There seems to be a natural, logical explanation for why these images occur and recur, one of the most important of which we shall discuss next.

YOUNG MEN AND DELAYED SEX

The incorporation of more ancient erotic emotions as additional glue to the human mate-bond worked well, but this evolutionary solution created one minor problem. As we have seen, the evolutionary dynamics of attraction and pair-bonding mean that young women usually marry somewhat more mature men, with the result that young males are frequently in a state of lots of lust and little action, as in most other mammalian species.

In subsistence groups men may be in their mid- to late twenties or even early thirties before they obtain their first wife (Irons 1983). This means that young men in their late

Huck Finns of the Paleolithic   In the past, books about Paleolithic art have tended to explain it in terms of formal themes: education, religion, puberty rites, and other ceremonies all in the public sphere. Less often do we acknowledge the many largely private aspects of our own or Paleolithic experience: what we do with lovers, spouses, family, close friends, and when alone. Most of this life goes unrecorded: warm nuzzling of nurture, quiet words of comfort, tears of panic attacks, sweaty lust, children absorbed in play, or the fooling around of feral boys. I am thinking of boys left to themselves for long hunks of time, not those with fully scheduled summer vacations whose main adventures occur on screen. Sam Clemens's marvelous imagination was fed by his nonliterary boyhood experiences. For a more contemporary example, just listen to E. O. Wilson (now a Harvard professor), who studies entomology, reporting on some of his "boy-scout"-aged experiences in his autobiography:

A substantial fraction of campfire and trailside conversation consisted of raucous jokes that dwelled on every imaginable sexual perversion and grotesquerie: homosexuals trying to have babies, necrophiliac undertakers carrying the severed genitalia of female corpses as trophies, sex with animals, impossibly large sexual equipment on both men and women, insatiable appetites and marathon infidelities and so on through a fantastical Psychopathia Sexualis. *Every teenage Alabamian male, it seemed, was a budding Krafft-Ebing. But of normal heterosexual relations scant was known. (Wilson 1994, 80)*

Scholars working with Paleolithic art seldom mention adolescent boys. Was the youth of Paleo-art historians so deprived? I doubt it. Like the rest of us, they have become conditioned to not discussing the great role of the private and unsanctioned. This may come as news to some, but Wilson's experience is not atypical of "free-ranging" adolescent boys. We must deal with the public face, but we all have a private side. This excursion into the properly private wildness of adolescent male imagination and sex fantasies is quite rightly edited out of normal public discussion.

With fresh testosterone percolating up through their behavior, these boys are less edited when alone or with others of their kind. Such young barbarians are apt to draw brains splattered on the sidewalk and chortle over drawings of giant whangers. They may fantasize about screaming tires and blowing away the enemy, and little of this is ever exposed to Franz Boas or his anthropological equivalents, only to brother adolescents, "the Guys." The rare mom gets a hint of this, but young girls could never imagine it. Fortunately, and appropriately, they are usually protected from its wacky coarseness. All but the most sheltered men know something of what can happen among feral boys left to their own devices.

teens and early twenties participate as adults in most ways but remain unmarried and unencumbered by the responsibilities of fatherhood. We know that testosterone levels rise almost vertically around ages seventeen to nineteen, which means a closely related peak in sexual appetites as well (these two are connected). So these young men are unwed and may remain so for a decade. The result is that for a number of years they experience mostly a fantasy sex life. That is the key operant sentence and I will return to it in a moment.

My point is that Paleolithic groups would have regularly included young men nearing and in their sexual prime—but not necessarily social prime, and hence not yet mated. Such young fellows had both responsibility-free time and hormones to support erotic interests. These unwed years were a time for males to advance and ripen those desires that were later to be incorporated as glue for the romantic bond when they mated. But in the meantime they were left desirous, left to their imaginations and perhaps to occasional nefarious actions. Studies of

If a significant portion of preserved Paleolithic art was done by young males, we might expect some themes not common among other ages and sexes. La Marche, Fr.

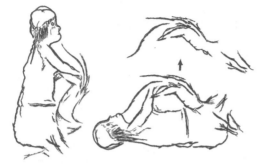

Another simple drawing from La Marche, Fr., of a seated woman. But, again, Pales (1976b) was able to tease out from among the blur of superimposed lines a mounted figure, but this mounted figure is not well done, hardly even recognizable if it were not for the pattern seen in similar drawings from the same site.

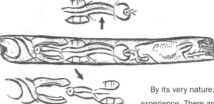

By its very nature, the erotic is a private experience. There are more erotic feelings, discussions, participations, and art than we admit to publicly. We must acknowledge that fact to make truthful sense out of Paleolithic art. A lion licking a penis and a penis between vulva lips, from La Madeleine, Fr. The two penises use the same scrotum. I have separated out the critical parts to make them more obvious.

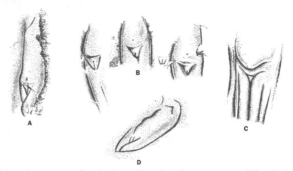

It is not just a matter of solving the problem of why there are so many little naked "Venus" figurines in Paleolithic art, because there are many other naked female drawings, carvings, clay models, engravings, etc., as well as copulation scenes and vulva images. Naked female images occur throughout Paleolithic art (Delporte 1993). A few examples: **A**, La Magdeleine, Fr. **B**, Angles-sur-l'Anglin, Fr. **c**, Bédeilhac, Fr. **D**, Commarque, Fr. The accounting must be much broader.

teenage males reveal that they think of sex unbelievably often (Baldwin 1993). They think of romantic love too, but less often. There is graphic evidence that Pleistocene young males thought about and made erotic images, playing all the while with the body's largest sex organ—the brain.

Postponement of the pressures of marriage and parental responsibility gave young men time to prowl, explore, and take physical risks, as we have already discussed, like exploring deep and dangerous caves and other mischief. Now, combine that with limited, or no, access to the real targets of their sexual desires, and what do you get? It is not hard to imagine several of these guys high on testosterone poking into a cave, breaking off stalactites, scuffing up previous images, spitting ocher on the walls, and making images of their own obsessions and interests—and, strangely enough, that aptly describes what we find in a number of Paleolithic art caves.

Was it sexual erotica for its own sake? Of course, no erotica is simply for its own sake; no philandering is just

for fun. In evolutionary terms, the play in "playboy" is not just play. These desires and fantasies have had significant evolutionary paybacks. The exact purpose for any particular Paleolithic image is, of course, unknowable, but consistently emphasized characteristics of these images do suggest that the artists were carving these images not with love in their hearts but with lust in their hands.

The portions of female anatomy occurring in Paleolithic art range from below-the-belt explicit erotica to abstract female curves; these are usually headless or faceless. The figures include many stooped-over, lordosis postures, breasts dangling, ready for penetration; bas-relief fig-

Human Males versus Females as Subjects of Paleolithic Art

Eros and *philos* are part of the biological reasons for men to watch female bodies closely, and be informed about them. Skimming through this book, you will notice that most images of human males are rather rudimentary, often little more than stick figures (other than at one site, La Marche, mentioned earlier). Such little attention is paid to rendering male form that we would not know some of the figures were males had there not been an erect penis, and even these are drawn more as an identifying symbol rather than as a realistic contour. Notably, male figures are occasionally presented as part of a larger scene: being threatened by wounded game or ferocious beast and groups hunting with spears. In contrast, Paleolithic images of women appear without much context.

Paleolithic images of male bodies lack the sophistication of distinctive line or relational form that characterizes most Paleolithic animal images and many renditions of women. Not only are many images of women rendered with more care and flair, but they far outnumber images of men. In 1976, Pales and St.-Péreuse calculated that there were 57 identifiable males and 171 females portrayed in all of Paleolithic art. This does not include the many images of vulvae or the hundreds of partial clay female figurines from

Expected Female : Male   Paleolithic Art Female : Male

One might expect that about half the people shown in Paleolithic art would be males and the other half females. In fact, the ratio in this old art from western Europe is closer to 1:3 (Pales [1976b] counted 57:171). In eastern Europe and Asia virtually all the figurines are women. The question is, why this discrimination against males as an image choice?

Eastern Europe, which would increase the skew of the numbers toward females. Discoveries of artwork since 1976 have continued to show this dramatic skew.

Remember our forensic principle that artists tend to draw forms they find most interesting and exciting and hence become more accomplished drawing those subjects. What can we make of the greater number of female images and their more carefully rendered contours? I believe we can use our forensic principle and say that the subject of a set of artworks will tell us something of the art makers' interests, and possibly their identity.

---

ures in a reclining position, legs spread invitingly; and isolated vulvae or many vulvae, some in flocks, and some gaping open. These are not the subtle curves of "fine art" but are of another genre, the timeless visual erotica of young guys.

Some Paleolithic work suggests an enjoyment of sexual stimulation that is unfulfilled, a certain edge of horniness not characteristic of mature men who are actually enjoying a full sex life. Although the latter may enjoy attractive female forms and figures, few produce sexual graffiti. Generally, it is younger, unattached guys who find pleasure in

the vicarious stimulation and gratification that pictures of the fundamental sexual releasers supply.

Perhaps some of the palm-sized Paleolithic figurines were used much as erotic magazines are today—whether passed around among the guys or enjoyed in erotic solitude. The small, curvy, nude figurines especially are portable, and easily tucked away. Such noncopulatory erotic behaviors are significant and persistent facets of human experience and behavior, and we should be able to give them their due in art history books, sex education, psychology courses, and, for that matter, human biology

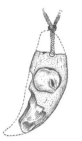

A vulva-like image on a bear tooth that seems to have been part of a pendant. Duruthy, Fr.

Another rather enigmatic stone showing nude body portions of two forms, from La Marche, Fr.

A, This little stone carving from Laussel, Fr., has been identified as a lot of different things, but it is clearly a couple copulating, woman sitting in top position, as per my reconstruction, **B**. Similar images with similar positions from other prehistoric cultures from later times: **C**, Prehistoric Swedish rock art. **D–F**, Niger, Africa.

texts. Noncopulatory sexual behaviors play a role in unmated people's time and energies, and they should be a part of any ethological-behavioral understanding of human sexual behavior.

Art as an Aphrodisiac:
An Evolutionary Perspective

Sexual arousal feels good, and there is a long history of demand for elixirs that promise to amplify sexual excitement, especially among men. All kinds of things have been promulgated, from oysters to powdered deer antlers. In Alaska, every summer, there are helicopter roundups of thousands of domestic reindeer so that the growing antlers in velvet can be cut off. These springy summer antlers are sold to Asian markets for their purportedly aphrodisiac qualities. But, of course, they only work if you truly believe they do. Viagra and its pharmaceutical relatives that aid male erection are highly popular, but Viagra targets erection physiology and not sexual excitement. Because of this it is not a true aphrodisiac drug. A potent aphrodisiac drug would probably eclipse street demand for other illegal drugs. As of this writing, other than topping up a deficient testosterone titer, there is no elixir that works, beyond the placebo effect. However, there is one effective, nonpharmaceutical aphrodisiac.

This elixir exception—the aphrodisiac with proven effectiveness—is the basis of a worldwide multibillion dollar industry. What is it? Erotic images—*erotic art*. Erotic appeal is designed into much of mainstream advertising as well as being the essence of explicit pornography. Advertisers create images with finely honed erotic appeal to sell cigarettes and cars; publishers splash it on covers to sell novels and newspapers. Fashion has always played with it. Aesthetics falls apart without it. Body lines are echoed in the design of many commodities. Various concentrations of this visual aphrodisiac are available depending on your taste and demand.

SEXUAL INEQUIVALENCY OF EROTICA

I suspect that differences in erotic tastes between the sexes are related to the very different repercussions erotic abandon has held for men and women. We know that women in hunting societies treated conception with serious concern (Silberbauer 1963). Women's sexual attraction to men evolved in the immediate context of potential conception; thus, the dynamics of sexual attraction and erotic behavior are much more complex for women. Male and female erotica are simply not identical. This is hugely complex, but women do appear both more broadly inclusive and more subtle in their erotic preferences: clothing patterns, nuances of color, fabric quality, shoe styles, body decoration, lacy undergarments, care in grooming, witty conversation, scents (scents are very important), music, and body movements. These can be more erotic to most

Creative double entendres: naked ladies, sans face and feet (the usual formula of the genre), but in these cases they are part of penis carvings. **A**, Gaban, Fr. (Epipaleolithic). **B**, Lespugue, Fr.

Erotic truth often spills into the public sphere in graffiti, a phenomenon not unique to Paleolithic art. A collage of giant erections from prehistoric rock art in the north Sahara: **A**, Ti-n-Teheb. **B**, Ti-n-Terirt. **C**, Ti-n-Amraren Dej. **D**, Ti-n-Teriat. **E**, Gûret. **F**, Wâdi Matkhendûsh. **G**, Wâdi Dejerât. This is young testosterone speaking.

women than the largely male mainstream pornography, with its images of flapping secondary sex organs, genitalia, and sweaty copulation close-ups.

Explicitly erotic art is intimately tied to fantasy. Not only does fantasy produce erotic art, such art further fuels fantasy. On average, men have more explicitly erotic fantasies than do women (Hessellund 1976; Kinsey, Pomroy, and Martin 1948; Kinsey et al. 1953; Knoth, Boyd, and Singer 1988). Studies in several different cultures have also found that on average men have more than twice as many sexual fantasies as women (Iwawaki and Wilson 1983). Men also report more sexually erotic dreams (Winget, Kramer, and Whitman 1972). Women's fantasies were found to incorporate elements of affection and commitment (Przbyla, Byrne, and Kelley 1983), and women were aroused by emotional factors more than simple physical appearances (Knoth, Boyd, and Singer 1988). Hessellund (1976) found that women's fantasies more likely emphasize themes of tenderness and emotionality. Diana (1985) listed women's fantasy themes of falling in love, marrying, and being desired for their physical and inner beauty.

Brickman's (1978) research contrasted men's fantasies as mainly explicit and overt, while those of women were embedded in implicit content, intimate, passive, and only implying sexual details. In general, male fantasy consists of much more graphic visual content focusing on genitals (Hass 1979; Follingstad and Kimbrell 1986). There is an extensive literature of published studies concluding that male fantasies differ from those of females. Men's erotic fantasies are more promiscuous and more adulterous, involve strangers or anonymous partners more often, and

include more multiple partners, exotic positions, etc. (see Ellis and Symons 1997 for a review). Visual prompting of fantasies is much more common among males than females (Gottlieb 1985; Ellis and Symons 1997).

PULPY SEX

We can see the extremes of these tastes at either end of the magazine displays in airport shops or news racks at local quick-stop gas stations. At one end are the highly visual, coarsely explicit, glossy pornographic magazines loaded with color photos, produced for and purchased by males. At the other end of the rack are the romantic paperback novels (without a single illustration inside the covers), usually written by and purchased by women. The romance novels typically portray a sensitive and beautiful woman taming a high-testosterone male (Symons, Salmon, and Ellis 1997). Both kinds of reading material, male and female, have remained fundamentally unchanged throughout the history of book marketing (Mussel 1984). Note that bright primary colors predominate on the covers of men's magazines. In contrast, the covers of romantic paperbacks tend to feature subtle fuchsia pastels of light blue and pink mixes—Barbara Cartland pinks. In the same way

On Inflatable Dolls, Centerfolds, and Stuffed Heads In the chapter on hunting we saw how decoys and disguise can be used to lure, distract, or otherwise fool other animals. Ethologists have long used mannequins to study and elicit basic species-specific behaviors. For example, the isolated stuffed head of a hen turkey is enough to stimulate tom turkeys, *Melaegris gallopavo*, to attempt copulation. For tom turkeys, a hen's head and neck are the key indicators of female reproductive condition, the main erotic releaser, even in the absence of the other 95% of the hen.

That may seem ludicrous and yet . . . men often become sexually aroused by miniature two-dimensional images of women on paper. A man knows he is looking at pigments on plant cellulose. But the tiny image nonetheless can produce an effective physiological and emotional charge. Are women less easily duped— less easily roused into orgasmic frenzy by 100-millimeter-tall ink-men? Additionally, it is difficult for women to believe that there is a thriving market in plastic, inflatable, life-sized, curvaceous dolls, but they sell by the tens of thousands, available in virtually every city in the world. I don't know if inflatable male dolls for women exist, but I doubt if this is a market opportunity waiting to be filled.

---

that the fast-food counter appeals to our old Pleistocene palate of fat-salty-sweet fixes, pulp publishers capitalize on our erotic predilections. It is more than probable that these deep male-female differences in what constitutes erotica were present within the communities that drew and observed Paleolithic art.

IVORY PROMPTERS

Imagination benefits from a prompter. That is the purpose of a doll. The figure in yarn and cloth makes it is easier to imagine a real baby. Why do kids play with toys: soldiers, tractors, rockets, planes, trains, robots, doctor-nurse kits, dolls and dollhouses, farm animals, etc.? They are aids to the imagination. My son was not just playing with a block of painted wood when he BRRRrrrrrrrmmmmm ran his "truck" around the floor; he was imagining a real truck. The wooden block was merely a convenient prompter.

Erotic fantasy and erotic play also benefit from toy prompters—be they in picture or three-dimensional form. We have a lot of prompters to the erotic in the modern world, pornography being only one of the more overt. We pick up on what the images imply, adding our own melodies. They are but private tutors to get the brain going on its own stories, using our own creative imaginations. I think certain Paleolithic carvings and images were used as erotic prompters—and some of them very clearly so. They are so erotically charged that they would be inappropriate in the display cases of your local library. They are deliberately the images they are because they are not end products but suggestive notes which lead the observer's brain to supply the melodic variations and chordal support.

TESTOSTERONE AND FANTASY

Testosterone (T) is a key hormone in both men's and women's erotic lives. With advancing age, T levels decline in both sexes, and the clear association of sexual fantasy and T is shown in the rapid decline of erotic fantasies reported following removal of the testes (Bancroft 1984). Erotic fantasies were reported to return rapidly after two weeks of synthetic T replacement. Likewise, surgically menopausal women administered synthetic T reported a marked increase in sexual desire and frequency of sexual arousal and sexual fantasy (Sherwin, Gelfand, and Bender 1985).

Today, a young male with a graffitiesque state of mind would know what this image was about if he saw it engraved into the paint of a toilet stall. Enlène, Fr. I suspect it may have had the same reference in the Paleolithic.

The human brain is the largest sex organ. The superposition of two engravings resulted in this humorous image from La Marche, Fr. Note how someone has modeled eyes over the nipples and gouged a large crater under the male's chin. It captures my point.

Kemper (1990) reviews evidence that sexual fantasies result in elevated T levels. Bancroft and Wu (1983) found that among males with low T levels, arousal was increased more by exposure to visual pornography than by using their own fantasy without physical cues. In chapter 4 I discussed the definite link among males between T production and sexual interest, suggesting that visual erotica can be an important part of the web of male sexual arousal. As T production is so basic a behavioral regulator, this repeated hormonal production as a reward for erotic fantasy and/or viewing erotic images can become analogous to an addictive fix.

These and many other studies, which clearly show that changes in physiological state are associated with erotic activity and vice versa, cast doubt on those who argue that culture alone is responsible for human behavioral sex dimorphisms (Follingstad and Kimbrell 1986). Of course, individual experience and cultural traditions are important variables in sexual fantasy. But, as Ellis and Symons (1990, 1997) conclude, differences between males and females in sexual fantasy form coherent, integrated, sexually bimodal systems. These behaviors fit the criteria by which we judge adaptiveness: they promote actions that positively affect reproduction, show a significant heritability, and are cross-culturally universal; considerable time is dedicated to these improbably complex activities; and there are elaborate physiological-behavioral connections

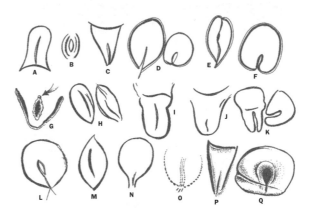

A sampler of just a few vulvae from Paleolithic art: **A**, Castillo, Sp. **B**, Trois Frères, Fr. **C**, Pergouset, Fr. **D**, Abri Blanchard, Fr. **E**, Eglises, Fr. **F**, Laussel, Fr. **G**, Bédeilhac, Fr. (note how some Paleolithic person stuck a stalactite fragment into the soft clay as a clitoris; now what kind of person would have done something like that?). **H**, Cougnac, Fr. **I**, Les Combarelles, Fr. **J**, Arcy-sur-Cure, Fr. **K**, La Ferassie, Fr. **L**, Maszysaka, Pol. **M**, Saint-Cirq, Fr. **N**, Gargas, Fr. **O**, La Pileta, Sp. **P**, Ölknitz, Ger. **Q**, Kostenki I, Rus.

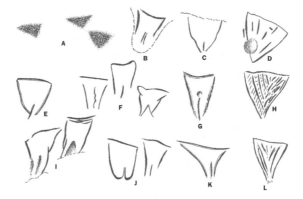

An extended sampler: **A**, Ojo Gareña, Sp. **B**, Cheval, Fr. **C**, Cazelle, Fr. **D**, Gouy, Fr. **E**, Deux Ouvertures, Fr. **F**, La Font Bargeix, Fr. **G**, Ölknitz, Ger. **H** and **L**, Gouy, Fr. **I**, Lussac-du-Chateau, Fr. **J**, Commarque, Fr. **K**, Fronsac, Fr.

associated with their expression. Wilson (1998) described cases like this as gene-culture interaction, each reinforcing the other.

FANTASIES OF FAST WOMEN IN MALES' HEADS AND IN PALEOLITHIC ART

As we have noted, heavy selection pressure would have always favored young males who were easily aroused and young females who were more discriminatingly reti-

Young male fantasy? La Marche, Fr.

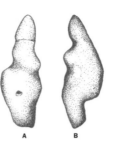

Two "full-figured" female-like forms:
A, Marsangry, Ger. **B**, Molodova, Ukraine.

cent. Brown (1991) noted this as one of the universal human traits. Evolutionarily, one would predict that young women should be much less likely to engage in unrestricted promiscuity than are young men, if not in fact, then in fantasy. Researchers have observed a related point, namely, that sexual fantasies of men and boys range widely beyond normally sanctioned outlets and are not limited to age-appropriate marital partners (Brown 1991; Ellis and Symons 1997).

DNA identification methods suggest there may be some real-life support for these broad-ranging male fantasies. Children of older married women do reveal higher EPC values than children of younger married women. Apparently, mature married women fool around more (Baker and Bellis 1995). I think that some Paleolithic images demonstrate such youthful fantasies of sexually attractive older women.

VISION, IMAGE, AND IMAGINATION

In their book *The Way Men Think,* Hudson and Jacot (1991) conclude that a central, and characteristically male, trait is that men show a tendency to treat persons as things and things as persons. For example, the technical details of computers or automobiles are experienced as being as fascinating as a friend. I think this phenomenon figures importantly in explaining why visual images can be such an influential erotic arouser to men. Abstractions play a role here.

Abstraction is a sort of distilled essence, which we acknowledge in the old saying "from a single thread the mind can knit a garment." In the case of visual art (and all visual art is an abstraction of some sort) what an artist is doing is establishing a focus or image that opens a cham-

ber in the mind, literally a microcircuitry file in the brain where individual experiences, both real and imagined, are stored. A painting of an approaching storm, thus, may evoke breathless memories of a lightning-raked dark sky, the air suddenly full of dust and ozone smells and the cool freshness of the wind.

Our brains do not record images projected onto the retina as a videocamera records a television program; they edit. This editing is even influenced by retinal organization, by the way our brain circuitry is laid out, and by our arousal levels. The brain reorganizes an image by highlighting what its visual memory bank deems to be the critical curves, the relationship of certain line shapes to other lines, and by fitting the competing particulates into a more stylized pattern. For example, when you first notice a human figure from a long distance, the brain attempts to pattern-fit critical curves to its memory bank to evaluate familiarity.

It almost seems as though the brain works with cartoons, making and matching visual data in stylized images. Newspaper caricatures of political figures are recognized, not despite distortions, but because of them. The distortions that exaggerate key features seem to match images in our memory banks more readily than the lines of an actual face do. Our recollection system apparently gives less emphasis to some features and overemphasizes others, particularly the relationships of lines. Our nervous system is set up to highlight lines, the edges of spaces rather than the spaces themselves. Photoreceptors on the retina fire disproportionately along lines. I suspect this is why a line drawing can be so potent in providing information.

The double sparking of recognition and response that exists between an effective image and the viewer is often

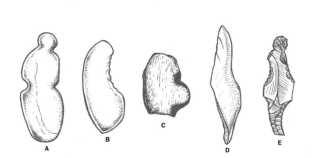

Several stones that may have naturally looked like naked women were modified to do so with little effort. A curve in the hand brings to mind a curve in the head. What people see in natural formations is an insight into some of the subjects on their minds. **A**, Pavlov, Czech. **B**, Ölknitz, Ger. **C**, La Ferrassie, Fr. **D**, Mas d'Azil, Fr. **E**, Russian Neolithic, Urals.

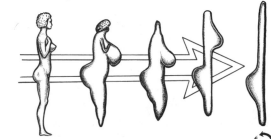

■ LEAST EROTIC
☐ MOST EROTIC

A, My illustration of a nude pose. **B**, Least erotic zones are shown in black. Exaggerate the least erotic and shrink the most erotic and you have **C**. Exaggerate the most erotic and shrink the least erotic and you have **D**, which is similar to images in Paleolithic art.

Gradient of increasing abstraction. A simple curve or bulge can sometimes convey eroticism, even though quite stylized. As shown it represents a rear; rotated top to bottom it can be imagined as breasts. We see all these points along this gradient in Paleolithic art.

near instantaneous and undeliberate. For example, although the lines of an erotic image may be elementary and impersonal—the ovals of breasts and buttocks—one's experiences, real or imagined, furnish the details of other erotic associations. It is that very capacity the image has for sparking the imagination, for arousal, that can lead to censorship.

LOADED CURVES: EVOLUTIONARY EXAGGERATION OF BODY FORMS IN REALITY AND IN OUR ATTENTION

We do not watch every person with equal concentration, nor do we watch all parts of the body equally. Usually, we first scan the features of a new individual that are most informative of status, age, power, fecundity, etc. These so-called *body hot spots* (Guthrie 1976) are featured in the automatic appraisals we fleetingly make in a waiting room or at a crossing light. A novelist or visual artist can develop these exquisitely, through more intense awareness and intensity of observation.

An artist interested in emphasizing the erotic dimensions of his or her human subject has a number of ethologically salient curves to reiterate and emphasize. These curves are so loaded that the artist doesn't have to present the entire form. It is often said that art is mostly a matter of deciding what to leave out. Heterosexual men are rather like the tom turkey in this regard: what can be left out is three-quarters of a woman's body. The erotically essential forms can be rearranged, exaggerated, or distorted and the

resulting image becomes more erotic than the original form. Less can indeed be more. The artist's image and the viewer's vision and imagination all work together to make something that is far more erotic than technical anatomical drawings or photographic pictures in underwear catalogs. This potency of particular body parts for yielding clues to individual fecundity, age, status, and so on has affected the evolution of both the contours of the observed and the emotions of the observer.

EVOLUTIONARY EXAGGERATION FOR EMOTIONAL EFFECT

Artists are not the first to shape human form for erotic effect. Biological evolution has exaggerated what were once subtle anatomical differences, creating a veritable "social anatomy" that we can enjoy in many species, including our own. Of course, this evolutionary shaping is always twofold. On the one hand, we note straightforward evolu-

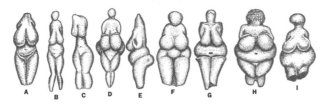

Looking at these Paleolithic figurines we can see a pattern: (1) Hips large. (2) Buttocks large. (3) Breasts large. (4) Usually no face. (5) Shoulders small and narrow. (6) Arms absent or atrophied. (7) Feet and hands missing. (8) Lower legs missing or atrophied. (9) Abdomen sometimes large. Figurines: A, Moravany, Czech. B, Avdeevo, Rus. C, Eliseevitchi, Rus. D, Lespugue, Fr. E, Savignano, It. F, Grimaldi, It. G, Dolni Věstonice, Czech. H, Willendorf, Aus. I, Gargano, It.

tionary changes in body parts which provide clues to individual fecundity, age, and status. On the other hand, there is a sometimes less observable but no less profound shaping of the attention and emotions of the observer.

We've already discussed these enhancements in other animals, such as enlarged neck muscles and manes in deer. Stallions and squirrel monkeys (Dumond and Hutchinson 1967) add neck fat, which beefs up the appearance of the neck. In species that fight by biting—tigers, lynx, and many primates—beards act as a similar supersignal by expanding the apparent size of the jaw and its muscles. That, of course, was the original role of the human beard, a socioanatomical device, retained long after we stopped fighting with teeth (Guthrie 1976).

Genitalia in many mammals are often decked out in biologically fashioned social displays. For example, inguinal white may be expanded into a full rump patch (Guthrie 1971b). Among primates, some lemurs have white rump patches, but the more common simian pattern is a tumescent rump supersignal created from the red lips of the vulva. Among females of many primate species the "sexual skin" around the red vulva engorges with blood and spreads out onto the buttocks region during the flush of estrus hormones. This huge red rump patch enhances the visual effect of the genitalia as part of the signal of peak estrus.

Humans do not have engorged red rump patches during estrus, but the anatomical differences between men and women have been just as biologically exaggerated

(Guthrie 1976). And these biologically emphasized social signals were picked up and emphasized again by Paleolithic artists. Feminine form is very largely shaped by evolutionarily selected depots of fat. And those female fat depots are key to many of the emotionally loaded curves in Paleolithic art as well. Numerous authors have commented on the abundance of female fat in Paleolithic art, and most have found it enigmatic (e.g., Breuil 1952; Leroi-Gourhan 1982b; Duhard 1993; Delporte 1993).

Full-figured womanly forms in Paleolithic art are not utterly mysterious and certainly are not trivial. But in order to appreciate the significance of these Paleolithic depots of fat, among both humans and other mammals, we'll need a bit of biology.

The Evolutionary Significance of Adipose Tissue Today and in Paleolithic Art

In our twenty-first-century view, human adipose tissue is generally considered extraneous, an unwanted and inadvertent extra, usually noted as a cosmetic problem and a health risk. Indeed, many anatomists and evolutionary biologists have paid little attention to fat (Pond 1978). But fat is essential to animal well-being and plays a large role in survival and reproduction. Physiologists who deal with ecological considerations have found that fat is critical in assessing how animals cope with periodic energy deficiencies (e.g., Myrberget and Skar 1976). Wildlife managers also use fat to assess body condition of both individuals and populations as a management tool (e.g., Franzmann and Arneson 1976). The biology of fat is becoming increasingly significant in the study of animal behavior, as fat seems to be what animals note in each other as predictors of individual quality. Fat is important in assessing fighting potential and mate choice (Pond 1978, 1998).

Along these lines, curiously little attention from researchers has been given to human body fat, even though there are striking variations in the way that people put on fat and in observable age, sexual, and racial patterns of fattening. The amount of adipose tissue and the location of fat depots can be very informative (Guthrie 1976, 1996, 1997; Pond 1998). Occasionally, fat is preserved in the fossil record and, as such, becomes an important forensic tool (e.g., Guthrie 1990).

Two fat reindeer scratched on slate, both from La Marche, Fr.

USING IMAGES IN PALEOLITHIC ART AS TRACE FOSSILS

Il faut tenir compte de la morphologie qui peut-être un élément essentiel de la traduction de la motivation.

Henri Delporte, in J.-P. Duhard, *Réalisme de l'image féminine Paléolithic*

Delporte was speaking about how the form of women's images in Paleolithic art might help us understand the motivations behind those who carved them. Occasionally, trace fossils often contain more information about the living creature than do direct remnants of the animal. For example, an imprint-cast of a Paleolithic woman in deep mud would give us information unavailable from mere skeletal reconstruction. We do not have such an imprint, though one very rough body cast has been found in Spain that is from a Paleolithic burial. What we do have are images of Paleolithic peoples—the wealth of Paleolithic art. These trace fossils allow us to study patterns of fat and obesity in the late Pleistocene. Though these images are neither a random sample nor photographically accurate, they can be informative, because we are able to identify and compensate for many of the underlying biases of these artists.

ANIMAL FAT AS STORED SURPLUS AGAINST COMING FAMINE

We all know too well that the consumption of surplus calories results in more fat, but you may not realize that the genetic *capacity* for prodigious fatness is not universal. The biological capacity to easily put on stores of fat is evolutionarily limited to adaptive contexts in which energy sources are severely restricted during certain seasons or unpredictable episodes. Fat is less important than people once thought it was as a direct insulator against cold; it is important in thermoregulation as an energy source, and hence a heat source, when food is scarce. Birds and mammals, for example, normally use more than 85% of their dietary calories simply to maintain a constant body temperature. The intense hunger, high satiety point, and metabolic allocation of energy to fat are not so much about immediate bounty; their very biological existence is tied to past episodes of dearth. The genetic ability to fatten prodigiously is an adaptive response to times of hunger and starvation.

Fat is a true organ system, occurring in various degrees and in different patterns in many animal groups. In both birds and mammals the quantity, anatomical location, and timing of fat deposition are under tight physiological control. Fat varies greatly in quality and character in its different depots. Lower-leg fat, for example, is composed mostly of a mix of low-saturated fatty acids with low melting point (these are the fats from which commercial neat's-foot oil for softening leather is made). Kidney fat, on the other hand, is more highly saturated with a high melting point (Irving, Schmidt-Nielsen, and Abrahamsen 1957); thus, it makes high-quality lard for stiff pastry, such as piecrusts. Some fat depots are easily marshaled for energy release, like brown fat, while other fats are slow to be tapped; bone marrow fat is one of the last to go, at least in most herbivores (Neiland 1970).

In the woods outside my house, northern tree squirrels remain active in the winter and yet they put on little fat. This is because they collect extensive stores of food, including conifer cones and dried mushrooms. In contrast, the Alaska arctic ground squirrels are true hibernators and they fatten prodigiously during the short Arctic summer. By autumn, most individuals have put on sufficient body fat to last 7–8 months. In these two kinds of squirrels we see opposite extremes of winter survival strategy. Both hoard energy: ground squirrels use fat stores and tree squirrels use food stores. Their very lives are dependent on these stores, and large numbers of both kinds of squirrels die every winter because their territories were insufficient to provide adequate stores.

The litter of tracks across the snow in my willow thickets are mostly made by snowshoe hares. Like most hares, snowshoe hares never become obese, even though they are the smallest mammalian herbivore that lives out in the open in the far north. Voles, squirrels, and shrews gain thermal protection by spending most of their time under the insulating snow. But these lean hares live with ambient temperatures ranging down to −40°F almost every winter, and as low as −60° on occasion. Hares are able to eat enough to stay warm in such cold because their food staples are both ubiquitous and energy packed: bud tips, sapling stems, and twig bark. Thus, snowshoe hares carry less than a day's worth of fat reserves. Why not more? Apparently, the cost of this weight in terms of speed and endurance is deleterious.

In hot climates, it is overheating that is particularly costly. Australian kangaroos are unusually lean for this reason. Water conservation is also an issue, as precious water would have to be used in sweat to cool an overheated animal. The need for extra fleetness and the high subtropical temperatures are probably the reasons most African antelope are also lean. Fat accounts for less than 5% of total body weight of African antelope (Smith 1970). African aardvarks and hippopotamuses are two informative exceptions to the rarity of fat among tropical-subtropical mammals. Both fatten prodigiously. Fat aardvarks spend the heat of the day in cool underground dens. Hippos lie underwater during the daylight hours and graze out into the savanna at night.

Domestic animals are especially informative about the genetics of obesity. Animal fats were prized for their flavor and sheer abundance of calories. People have selected for genetic "ease of obesity" in domestic livestock: pigs, cattle, chickens, goats, rabbits, ducks, and geese, in contrast to their wild counterparts. In zoo situations, wild animals do overeat as a result of boredom, stress displacement, or restrictions on movement, which sometimes torques the metabolic regulators to such a degree that species adapted to leanness may even become obese.

In summary, we can say that fat is a means animals have of transferring energy from a season of abundance to a season of scarcity. But the advantages of carrying reserves of energy come with considerable costs. The pull and push of these dynamics are amplified in highly seasonal environments such as that of the Eurasian Pleistocene countryside that was home for the people who made the art discussed in this book.

ENERGY RESERVES FOR THE WINTER BOTTLENECK ON THE MAMMOTH STEPPE

During most of the late Pleistocene the flow of air called the January Storm Track bore down the center of Eurasia from west to east. Climatic reconstructions show tough winters on the Mammoth Steppe, and there are multiple lines of evidence that most mammalian species needed large fat resources to help them survive the winter season. We know that in the boom-bust seasonality of today's boreal forest and tundra, no large mammals can obtain enough calories from wild forage to maintain their autumn body weight. At best, winter means a slowly descending curve in body weight and physiological well-being. For some animals, this declining curve reaches lethal depths. But for most, the decline is arrested short of death by the coming of spring. Looked at this way, the function of fat stores is to change the angle of that decline, allowing individuals to survive longer northern winters on a submaintenance diet.

Of course, African animals face serious seasonal bottlenecks, and African dry seasons also can be lethal. In most

Images of a horse and a mammoth from the Paleolithic site of Mayenne-Sciences, Fr. Both rendered in rounded curves.

Gaining weight in the Pleistocene. Enval, Fr.

A little image scratched on the cave wall at Les Combarelles, Fr.

years, however, such droughts are relatively short, only 2–4 months. In contrast, northern mammals regularly go 8–9 months between annual food flushes. This is a long time to be below maintenance levels, especially in light of the metabolic demands of cold weather. The evidence of large fat depots in the bulging abdomens and arcing rump lines visible among the Paleolithic images of horses, reindeer, bison, mammoths, red deer, ibex, and other Mammoth Steppe species is thus not surprising, and these body contours recorded by Paleolithic artists echo the body form of many extant northern animals at their full peak condition. What then can we make of the Paleolithic images which record fattening in our own species?

We have already noted that images of women are roughly three times as numerous as images of men in Paleolithic art. With only a few exceptions, these images of women are notably full-figured, even obese, while images of males are universally lean. This striking pattern is consistent across the whole span of Paleolithic art, both geographically and throughout time. What are we to make of this disparity? Were all Paleolithic males lean and all women fat? (One is reminded of the old children's poem of Jack Sprat.) Or are there biases that would lead to preferential portrayal of very full-figured imagery when most women were, in fact, probably not fat? If so, why would those biases not pertain to images of men? A look at the biological basis of human fat will enable us to return to these questions with new insights.

SOME NOTES ON THE BIOLOGY OF HUMAN FAT

We know that accumulation of some fat was important in the human past because ovulation is keyed to thresholds of fatty acids in the blood. As women become very lean, they cease ovulating. This is apparently an evolutionary safeguard; to conceive during a time of dearth would likely have resulted in death of the young and possibly of the mother as well. Suppression of ovulation, triggered by exceptionally low fat levels, protects a woman from risking debilitation and waste of reproductive time and energy (Wasser and Barash 1983; Frisch 1988; Neel 1992). This suppression of reproductive readiness at low levels of body fat is in high contrast to male physiology, which does not generally exhibit such sharply delimiting regulators.

Fat—both dietary and body fat—is highly esteemed among hunter-gatherers who have few stores (Hayden 1981a). Among traditional Bushman there was no such thing as being "too fat," and couples at marriage were symbolically anointed with fat (Thomas 1988). Most studies show a direct relationship between more food and higher rates of reproduction and lower child mortality (Hill and Hurtado 1989). Age at menarche in Kalahari Bushman groups averages 15.5–16 years, which is rather late by American standards. Blurton-Jones and Sibley (1978) suggested this was due to calorically marginal diets rather than inability of the mother to transport infants and toddlers, as other writers had suggested. Adolescent subfecundity in these groups tends to add another few years, so that the average age of women at first childbirth is 20–21 years. Blurton-Jones (1987), in a follow-up study, showed birth spacing was typically four years for Kalahari Bushman (Lee 1979). This also was thought to be the result of low caloric nourishment.

In the United States menarche presently occurs, on average, at 12.8 years of age, and by 16 most girls complete

Images of full-figured nude women (armless, headless, and footless) from rock art in central Arabia. Throughout this book I show many images from later prehistoric cultures that are similar to those in Paleolithic art. I intend this to be more than a simple aside.

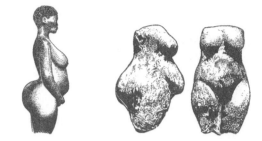

Fat depots in women are concentrated in the breasts, buttocks, and hips. Steatopygia in some Bushman women becomes more pronounced with increasing overall obesity. Though not so extreme, the same breast, buttock, and hip depots are clearly shown in this Pleistocene image from Brassempouy, Fr.

In life, well-rounded Bushman women were apparently unusual. Not only was female fat considered erotic, but no sexually mature decent female went about with her rear or genitals exposed. Thus, these portrayals from Bushman rock art were presumably erotic for Bushman artists. **A**, Brandberg, Namibia. **B**, Eland Cave, R.S.A. **C–D**, Tigerhoek Spruit, R.S.A. **E**, Post Catherine, R.S.A. **F**, Tripolitania, R.S.A. **G**, Rockwood, R.S.A. **H**, Griqualand East, Namibia. **I**, Tigerhoek, R.S.A. **J**, Camp Siding, R.S.A.

their growth and their subfecundity period. Menopause occurs at 51 years of age, on average, in well-nourished societies. Menopause occurs earlier where diets are calorically limited. Frisch's (1976) survey of nutrition and reproduction concluded that more-than-ample nourishment was associated with an earlier age at menarche, later menopause, and thus with a much longer reproductive span. As body fat drops much below 20%, menses tend to cease.

In most populations, adult males typically average below 20% and adult females well above 20% in body fat. While fat is distributed in much the same manner prior to puberty in both sexes, at puberty girls increase their fat

percentage to over 20% of body weight. Boys at puberty drop in fat percentage (particularly in peripheral fat) to a mean of 10% of body weight. In general, subcutaneous fat among males continues to, statistically, decline into their late twenties, but not in females. In general, postpubertal girls characteristically had 1.5–2 times as much fat as boys (Frisch 1976). This fat increase among girls is mostly an increase in peripheral fat (legs, hips, and breasts).

In summary, body fat percentages change in marked ways from infancy through adulthood. Differences between males and females are greatest during reproductive life. The greater female efficiency for fat deposition (Pond 1998) may reflect a survival-reproductive strategy (see Pond 1978, 1998, for review). The higher fat percentages among women of reproductive age are seen from an evolutionary perspective as consistent with the increased energetic demands of pregnancy, nursing, and nurturing, which can require a caloric increase of as much as 50%.

THE SARTORIAL ROLE FAT PLAYED IN OUR EVOLUTION

Let's shift now from these purely physiological factors and include the social dimensions of fat. While mechanical and thermoregulatory forces do affect the location of fat depots, a more complete understanding includes an appreciation of the way fat depots nonrandomly shape body contours for biosocial reasons (Guthrie 1976; Pond 1978, 1998). A few examples will help clarify this. Male gorillas

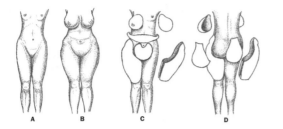

Fat depots are an organ system. Central depots vary somewhat in individual women but mainly are located in breasts, lower abdomen, a belt around the waist, buttocks, and thighs. **A**, Body with fat depots reduced. **B**, Same body with fat depots charged. **C–D**, Exploded views of common depots.

Adipose tissue is usually concentrated in genetically determined, hormonally mediated depots which relate to locomotor efficiency and to body modeling for social reasons. However, depot locations vary with species, populations, sexes, and individuals. The main depots of these two individuals are stippled.

(*Gorilla gorilla*) display their height when threatening opponents. Not only do adult males have erectile hair crests on their heads, but they also have a fatty mass there. This is a biosocial fatty structure, an image-enhancing fat depot. Orangutans (*Pongo pygmaeus*) have fatty masses on their cheeks that overlie their temporal-masseter muscles (Schultz 1969) and thus emphasize their powerful jaws. Fat depots on the necks of male squirrel monkeys (*Saimiri sciureus;* Dumond and Hutchinson 1967) and sea lions (*Zalophus californicus*) during breeding season (Pond 1978) likely enhance displays of fighting strength.

Young mammals are often clothed in special biosocial garments of fat and pelage or skin color that proclaim their noncompetitive, youthful status. Adult colobus monkeys are black and white, but their babies are totally white. Baboon babies have a jet black pelage with light skin in areas where adults are grizzled brown (see Guthrie 1976 for a review of this phenomenon).

Human babies are striking for their smooth, hairless skin and "Michelin-Man" rounded curves, thanks to deposits of thick subcutaneous fat. The round bodies and dimples of healthy babies seem to form the central releaser of our innate attraction to, and protection of, very young children (Morris 1967; Guthrie 1976). And the considerable subcutaneous fat of women in their peak reproductive years exists in this largely biosocial context. That is our main interest here.

The Importance of Erotic Fat—Location, Location, Location

The greatest fertility is amongst the strong stout women, the thin and weaker ones rarely having children.

B. Spencer and F. S. Gillen, *The Natives of Central Australia*

FAT AS A FLAG OF FECUNDITY

To menstruate, a woman has to have at least 20% body fat (Frisch and McArthur 1974), and so in a subsistence society a fat woman shows her state of fertility, which is not an evolutionarily neutral state. Betzig (1997) has estimated that on average a woman in a "natural-fertility" society would have roughly forty-eight fertile cycles in her lifetime. This is a net of only four years' worth of fertile menstrual cycles. The remaining lifetime is accounted for, statistically, by prefertile and postmenopausal years, pregnancy, and nursing. Evolutionary selection tilts the deck toward men who can recognize and be attracted to women who are passing through times of optimal fertility. How best to do this?

The fat depots of females are different from those of males, and fat depots differ with age as well as sex (Edwards 1951). Men look at curves, and the genes of men who were attracted to the right curves in the right places were more likely to be passed on, as were those of the women carrying those curves. And though culture and fashion play with details, the evolutionary standard is honored. This was not simply a matter of absolute amounts of fat, but its *location*. As we have seen, there are particular patterns of fat deposition in women of repro-

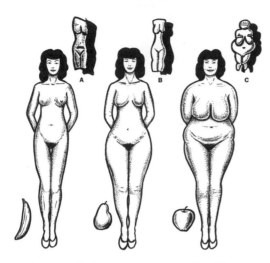

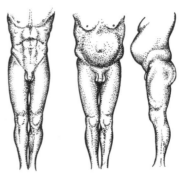

People vary considerably not only in their propensity to fatten but also in depot location. Physiologists who study human fat sometimes speak of the female body patterns as bananas, pears, and apples. Small Paleolithic figurines above: **A**, Laugerie-Basse, Fr. **B**, Eliseevitchi, Rus. **C**, Willendorf, Aus.

Fat depot location varies from male to male, but compared to females, men tend to put most fat onto their upper and mid-torsos, particularly the abdomen. Abdominal fat depots are internal as omental fat and external as subcutaneous fat.

ductive age. Two kinds of selection were going on here: one was sorting fat into particular depots, and the other was sorting male attention to these particular locations. So where are these critical locations?

Increasing estrogen promotes fat depots around two main centers. One is around the pelvic girdle and the other underlies newly developing mammary tissue. These are biological artifices, evolved social organs. There are other, much smaller, sexually dimorphic fat depots as well (Vague and Fenasse 1965), but these two critical "gynoid" centers are the key differences in body form we commonly note between adult men and women. There are of course individual, as well as subtle interracial, variations in male and female fat distribution (Guthrie 1976, 1996). But male fat in most racial groups is concentrated on the trunk: torso, neck, and shoulders. Some men center their fat in the greater omentum, resulting in a protruding abdomen on an otherwise lean body. Other male fattening patterns include depots between skin and torso muscles, and some men become broad across the back and shoulders. As men age there is a greater "roll" over the iliac crest of the hip (Garn 1954). Men tend to put little fat on their legs. Pond (1978) has reviewed these patterns and noted that, given our upright carriage, the mechanically most efficient place to carry large quantities of fat is on the trunk, espe-

cially internally near the center of gravity. She also suggested that additional torso mass might have social value for dominant males, as it increases apparent muscular mass, and modest amounts of weight may result in "sumo wrestler" advantages. Neck muscles are highly testosterone sensitive (probably as an adaptation to a more violent life, to protect the vulnerable head) and are also an important fat depot among adult men, creating a more formidable image.

Declines in estrogen at menopause are often associated with shifting fat depots from highly estrogen-sensitive pelvic-breast regions to the torso, neck, and upper arm. These shifts may confer a biosocial advantage by creating a more masculine outline (Pond 1978) and thus enhancing an image of power and authority consistent with a focus on leadership, extended caregiving, and protection rather than immediate attraction for further reproduction.

THE SWELL OF HIPS: PALEOLITHIC WAIST-TO-HIP RATIOS

Imagine yourself walking down to the post office and finding a scientist there polling people on which cardboard outlines from an array are most appealing. You are asked

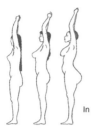
In addition to wide individual variation, racial groups tend statistically to have slightly different balances of fat depots.

Big hips and thighs, bas-relief on limestone, Laussel, Fr.

to choose, from a lineup, the most attractive silhouette. What results might you expect? In a manner not too dissimilar to this, researchers (e.g., Singh 1993, 1994) have canvassed large groups of people as to the most attractive waist-to-hip ratio. Female silhouettes with a ratio of around 0.7 were most often ideal (1.0 means waist = hips).

Constricted waist and broad hips have been known to figure importantly in female attractiveness (Guthrie 1976; Symons 1979). And Singh's (1994) research suggests there is some universal aesthetic angling toward this ratio. Such a ratio is not often found among women in their early teens or once past menopause.

I calculated the waist-to-hip ratios of a sample of fifty-three Paleolithic female images (using photos in Delporte 1993 and Duhard 1993). The average ratio was 0.655, with a standard error of the mean of 0.0188 and a standard deviation of 0.133. In other words, the Paleolithic artists' figurines have a slightly more exaggerated waist-to-hip ratio than the 0.7 found as a modern attractive ideal. Cartoon and cartoon-like figures, such as Barbie dolls, often push this ratio to 0.5 and beyond. For comparison, the average waist-to-hip ratio among today's women is higher than 0.7.

Why is this ratio of 0.7 significant? I think the answer is straightforward. It approximates very old and long-established visual clues to a woman's reproductive maturity. This ratio is rarely achieved by bony hip structure alone. Additional contouring via the fat depots we've been discussing is essential (absent a very tight belt or corset). Sexual maturity and many dimensions of good health, such as efficient metabolism, few parasites, and access to resources, all are signaled by this ratio. Not only did selection favor that shape, but it focused male attention on it. Men notice and become keen evaluators of these forms.

Remember that this 0.7 ratio was registered as an ideal preference. The perfect Miss 0.7 may be met only occasionally. I would further hypothesize that there is a slight difference between what waist-to-hip ratio is targeted in a long-term versus a short-term relationship. (Remember the previous discussions of face and torso comparisons, *philos* and *eros*.) For short-term relationships (torso focus) the mature fecundity of small-waisted and broad-hipped women is a potent signal. The fact that the Paleolithic figurines embody this ideal ratio of sexual attraction says volumes—more on that in a few pages.

Singh (1994) also asked women about the male shape they found most attractive. The statistically most preferred male waist-to-hip ratio was around 0.9. This ratio is usually achieved when narrow hips and waist are accompanied by broad shoulders. This contemporary preference is consistent with an imagined Pleistocene male ideal: well muscled, robust, and capable of rapid and sustained mobility in an active hunting life.

HERITABILITY AND THE SHAPING OF PELVIS STRUCTURE

Human hip circumference among women has a relatively high heritability of 0.66 (Cavalli-Sforza and Bodmer 1971). Therefore, its variations are available to natural selection. While woman have smaller shoulder, chest, and waist widths than men, their hips are proportionally wider to accommodate childbirth (Snyder et al. 1977), but there are locomotor costs to this wider pelvis structure. Walking or running are mechanically more efficient when the femur heads are close together (narrow hips), but birthing factors favor a larger pelvic aperture (and hence hip width). The resulting compromise tends to be slightly narrower than ideal for birth.

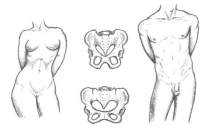

Sexual contours are modeled by hormonal titers. Testosterone swells the large muscles in the arms, back, shoulders, and neck. Estrogen affects the pelvic area, enlarging its bony structure and activating fat depots in that region. Upper pelvis, male; lower, female.

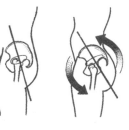

Apparently there is something in the birthing process that requires the female pelvic angle to be slightly tilted forward. This contributes to the different body postures and lines of women and men.

The wider pelvic aperture and more broadly set femur heads require female leg lines to slightly bow inward at the knee, producing a subtly different leg angle and gait from those of men (Muybridge 1887; Morris 1967; Guthrie 1976). Wider set hip sockets also cause more shifting of weight from side to side and more pelvic rotation up and down on each side during walking. Like anatomical features, gaits also can assume ethological significance. Gaits have been studied in a variety of mammals (e.g., Ewer 1968), and subtle differences between gaits of men and women are frequently exaggerated as an erotic signal, drawing further attention to the female pelvic girdle (Guthrie 1976; Morris 1997).

WOMEN'S BREASTS ARE NOT SIMPLY MAMMARY GLANDS

I am compelled to begin this section with the great Italian actress Sophia Loren's famous statement that "I owe all I am to pasta." Women's breasts are unique. No other mammal has enlarged breasts outside the lactation period. In a sense, large human breasts are counterfeit; they are not

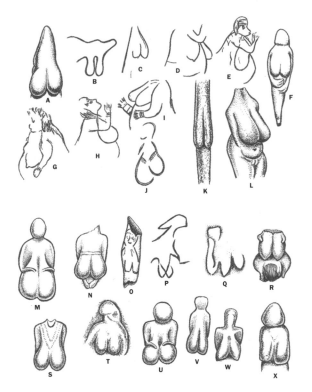

Paleolithic breasts: **A** and **W**, Dolni Věstonice, Czech. **B** and **P**, Pech-Merle, Fr. **C**, Gönnersdorf, Ger. **D–E** and **G–I**, La Marche, Fr. **F**, Parabita, It. **J** and **Q**, La Magdeleine, Fr. **K**, Rytirska, Moravia. **L**, Moravany, Czech. **M**, Lespugue, Fr. (reconstructed). **N** and **V**, Kostenki, Rus. **O**, Isturitz, Fr. **R**, Brassempouy, Fr. **S**, Kostenki, Rus. (reconstructed). **T**, Laussel, Fr. **U**, Gargano, It. **X**, Chiozza, It.

simply filled with mammary tissue as are breasts of all other female mammals but mainly consist of frothy fascia fat. There are very few collagen fibers in human breast fat, and the fatty acids deposited there are the more homogenous and oily form of low saturates (Pond 1998), producing a remarkable pillow-down softness. This unique breast fat is hormonally regulated, both in development of mammary tissue and in fat depot formation. This means breast development can be induced in men with hormone treatment (e.g., allowing male transsexuals to achieve breast-fat depots).

Even in our nearest primate relatives, breasts only enlarge just prior to parturition and are maintained by hormones stimulated by lactation. The presence of fat-filled

Imitation Buttocks, Hips, and Thighs

One of the Consigliere's cheap solutions to these conflicting forces of male attraction to broad hips and the reduced locomotor efficiency of such hips was to use fat depots to make the pelvis *appear* to be broader than it was. Much of "social anatomy" involves such changes in appearances. Evolution created the appearance of a wide pelvis with major subcutaneous fat depots on the lateral wings of the pelvic girdle and outer thighs (extreme versions of this are known as steatomeria). The subcutaneous fat depots over the gluteus muscles on the buttocks do the same (extreme versions are referred to as steatopygia).

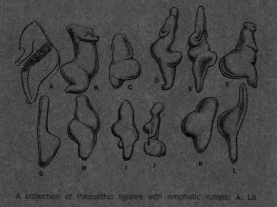

A collection of Paleolithic figures with emphatic rumps: A, La Marche, Fr. B, Sireuil, Fr. C, Weinberg, Ger. D, Monpazier, Fr. E, Savignano, It. F, Courbet, Fr. G, Ölknitz, Ger. H, Enval, Fr. I, Tursac, Fr. J, Grimaldi, It. K, Mauren, Ger. L, Petersfels, Ger.

A more sedentary strategy and enhanced ability to store fat may have been selected for among many women, who would have necessarily been engaged in closer-to-camp care of infants and children. The hypothesis is consistent with the pattern of larger fat depots on women's legs (particularly thighs) than on those of men (Snyder et al. 1977). Such fat depots would have been a subtle long-distance locomotor handicap for women with that genetic propensity.

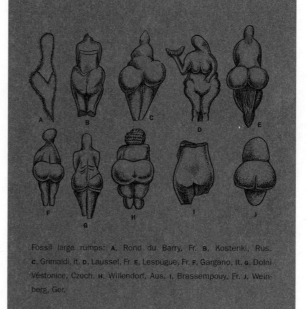

Fossil large rumps: A, Rond du Barry, Fr. B, Kostenki, Rus. C, Grimaldi, It. D, Laussel, Fr. E, Lespugue, Fr. F, Gargano, It. G, Dolni Véstonice, Czech. H, Willendorf, Aus. I, Brassempouy, Fr. J, Weinberg, Ger.

breasts, as a social signal that announces sexual maturity, has no counterpart among nonhuman animals. Enlarged breasts are a particularly human part of women's social anatomy.

Certainly there are cultural dimensions to eroticization of anatomy. Ankles, calves, feet, or the nape of the neck, for example, can be culturally supercharged, particularly when most biological signals of fecundity are traditionally covered. But not all variation in these matters is culturally determined, and the biological uniqueness of women's breasts is clear evidence. It has been suggested that breasts are not erotic in cultures where they are commonly exposed. Certainly, daily familiarity reduces aspects of eroticism, as on nude beaches. One is accustomed to thinking of breasts as once having been exposed throughout black Africa. Yet it was traditional among most Africans for married women to wear a blanket or cape that covered their breasts (Morris and Levitas 1987). But even out of Africa where people must all wear clothing against cooler weather, the bulge of breast can still be assessed—signaling the specific overtone for which enlarged prelactation breasts were evolutionary selected.

The simplest erotic objects from Paleolithic art must be the two lone protruding breasts, devoid of body, found at

Dolni Věstonice, Czech.

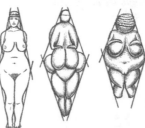

Spindle-shaped Venuses. Most women are naturally spindle shaped, and obesity increases the spindle effect. **A**, My sketch. **B**, Lespugue, Fr. **c**, Willendorf, Aus.

Dolni Věstonice and the pair of breasts protruding from a sticklike body shaft found at Rytirska. The idea is not too different from that behind the jewelry made from red deer stag canines mounted back-to-back like paired breasts. These work because the brain fills in all the other necessary details.

PLEISTOCENE EXAGGERATING: MINIMALISM AND MAXIMALISM

Women's thigh size is emphasized in Paleolithic art by decreasing the size of the calf and foot—or even omitting them entirely. Breasts appear enormous in these images because shoulders are thinned and narrowed, and arms and hands are either eliminated or minimized, sometimes looking like wet noodles draping over the breasts. Both breasts and butts are emphasized in most of the art by bending the female figure in such a way (lordosis posture) that these erotic loci are dramatized by protruding even farther.

Scholars once interpreted the spindle shape typical of many Paleolithic figurines as some traditional symbolic form, and the resulting spindle or diamond shape was presumed to have significant mystical implications (Leroi-Gourhan 1965; Gvozdover 1989). I agree with Duhard (1993) when he argues that it is a mistake to read some special meaning into the spindle-shaped female figurines in Paleolithic art, and I believe that this form, which he calls the "quadrilateral shape," echoes the real female figure when it is enhanced by fat deposits.

This "full-in-the-middle" form is the natural artistic outcome of exaggerating the female pelvic region, an important erotic releaser, and de-emphasizing the less-erotic head and feet. When feet are present, they are suggested rather than specifically depicted. Heads rarely include facial detail, at most only the designation of basic facial anatomy. Although these artistic female forms from different eras converge on the same general shape, the reading of mystical symbols here, where they likely did not exist, is typical of the magico-religious interpretation of much of Paleolithic art.

PALEOLITHIC FAT IN REALITY OR IN FANTASY?

The number of Paleolithic images of full-figured women suggests female obesity was at least not unknown, and the details of fat depot locations, fat fold characteristics, pendulous breasts, and so on appear based on actual observation. If we then accept that during times of plenty some adult women did become quite curvaceous, this conclusion has implications about Paleolithic life, implications that I will come back to in a moment. For now, let's look more critically at the Paleolithic representations of fat and lean people. Considerably fewer than 10% of Paleolithic images of women appear lean. Do we really want to assume that 90% of adult women were plump to corpulent?

I have already discussed the ways taphonomic processes have warped the record of the past. And I've suggested that in the case of Paleolithic art this has strongly favored the preservation of representational images made by males. Men making images of women would be likely to choose female forms that were sexually attractive—most curvaceous. So despite the fact that most females in Paleolithic art are made to look full-bodied, this representation may well be a gross distortion of reality.

To check this possibility, let's attempt an approximation of some Pleistocene demographics. Assume a reproductive rate sufficient to maintain a population. We can

Paleolithic Baubles and Beads—Faux Style

Beads and pendants seem to have been common in the late Paleolithic, and as more than an interesting aside, one of the more intriguing twists is the presence of imitations. People down through time have ornamented their bodies with the little fingertip-sized red deer canines. But access to this ivory material is

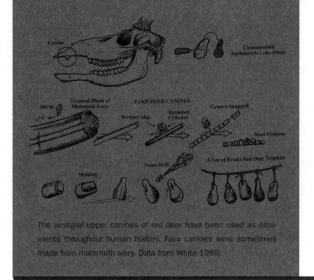

The vestigial upper canines of red deer have been used as ornaments throughout human history. Faux canines were sometimes made from mammoth ivory. Data from White 1989.

rather limited, a mature stag yielding two at most. It takes a while to gather enough for a necklace. However, an artist can take mammoth ivory and fabricate stag canines that are almost indistinguishable from the real thing. Though people probably killed few mammoths, the tusks were very durable and would not have been unusual as "found objects." Tusks were enormous packages of quality material, used often by Paleolithic artists. At one site, Pair-non-Pair in France, mammoth ivory was used for a pendant that imitated a cowrie seashell (Taborin 2000).

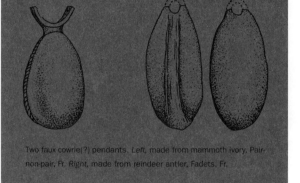

Two faux cowrie(?) pendants. *Left*, made from mammoth ivory, Pair-non-pair, Fr. *Right*, made from reindeer antler, Fadets, Fr.

---

model an average life expectancy of fifteen years (the age at which half of the individuals had died) and an average of 2.5 children surviving to adulthood. This would be consistent with ethnographic analogs and other archaeological evidence. Let us also assume that over half of the females in a hunting-gathering band would be under the age of puberty (age fourteen to fifteen or so), and say that half of the mature females would be nursing children under three years of age. Little girls and lactating women in the band would likely be lean. Thus, we see that, at any one time, fewer than 25% of the females, at most, would have been candidates for significant obesity. We would then conclude that the large fraction of obese women portrayed in Paleolithic art distorts the actual frequency of full-figured contours. Women were fat more in male fantasy than in reality.

MALE FAT IN THE PLEISTOCENE

It seems legitimate to say that, consistent with the ethnographic evidence from hunting subsistence societies, Pleistocene males would probably have been lean. Indeed, that is what the art shows. While this dichotomy of fat women and thin men pictured in the art may not reflect numerical accuracy, it may still reflect important differences in the selective pressures experienced by men and women. Men would have required a high metabolic "setpoint" for exploration and for hunting and packing out game. Wide-ranging hunting expeditions far from camp across diverse landscapes, river crossings, being out in inclement weather, and broken sleep on hard ground, among other hardships, would have used up calories and made obesity rare. But life is variable and complex, and it's quite conceivable that there were some fat Paleolithic

FULL-FIGURED WOMEN—IN IVORY AND IN LIFE **343**

males, and even that a number of men were fat during episodes in their lifetimes.

USING PALEOLITHIC ART IMAGES OF OBESITY TO RECONSTRUCT LATE PALEOLITHIC LIFEWAYS IN EURASIA

There were undoubtedly innumerable exceptions, but the above profile of most people being lean most of their lives was probably normal until Holocene technologies such as bows, dogs, fishhooks and nets, toggle-harpoons, domestic cereals, domestic livestock, and so on made dependable stores of food surpluses possible (Testart 1988). Stored surplus in the Holocene decreased mortality and increased recruitment, resulting in greater density and village size, and for the first time societies began to exhibit "macroparasitic" (McNeil 1980) hierarchies whereby some classes of people within the same village had greater access to food resources. In these situations some classes of nursing women were no longer energy restricted, and some classes of adult males could become sedentary and obese.

The bones from buried skeletons tell us that Europeans from late Paleolithic times were larger and stronger than later peoples (Ruff and Trinkaus 2000). The hard cortex of long bones was thicker and more dense, indicating a great deal of activity—as the human body responds to heavy activity not only with greater muscle mass but in bone development as well. This robustness required a good diet, high in minerals and protein. Cortex thickness of leg long bones, in particular, was much greater in Aurignacian times. However, near the end of the Paleolithic (Magdalenian times) body size declined slightly (Formicola 2000) and arm bones, more than leg bones, show evidence of more and heavier work (Holt and Churchill 2000; Churchill et al. 2000). Presumably, this is evidence of declining food quality and denser populations. In other words, people worked harder for less but did not range as far.

We can build on this information from bones and from the pattern of fat portrayed in the art and deduce that the following forces generally prevailed in the late Paleolithic:

▶ There is no evidence of obesity among the hundreds of positive and negative handprints in Paleolithic art caves. Admittedly, these handprints are a biased sample, made predominantly by young males, but within this sample there are handprints of mature adults, including females. The absence of significant fat on the fingers of all the people who went back into caves and left their handprints suggests that there were mostly lean people in the late Paleolithic. There are a number of other complicating biases here. For example, it is possible that the activities of climbing and crawling through difficult cave passages may have discouraged obese people. Also, the ubiquity of leanness among young people is expected in a Paleolithic-style subsistence economy. Nevertheless, *the handprints do suggest that, unlike today, neither food surpluses nor patterns of inactivity that promote obesity were common in the European late Paleolithic.*

▶ The anatomical accuracy of some details of Paleolithic images showing extensive fat depositions among adult women suggests there were at least occasional times and/or seasons of bounty. But, as we have noted, the existence of these energy stores in the form of body fat is also evidence of occasional dearth. We know this because it is dearth that creates the genetic-behavioral satiety levels and physiological predispositions that produce obesity.

▶ *Energy constraints, rather than nutrient quality, were the check to human population expansion in the Eurasian Paleolithic.* In particular, the scarcity of winter carbohydrate and fat resources may have forced people to obtain most of their caloric needs from animal sources: lean muscle, tendon, skin, fascia, with the availability being irregular. Episodes of plenty would have been punctuated with times of scarcity.

▶ *Late Paleolithic peoples regularly lived without substantial food stores.* Again, if stored food was a customary way of life, then why did evolution produce people who had a genetic predilection toward obesity? And what was it that restricted reproduction in the low-density Pleisto-

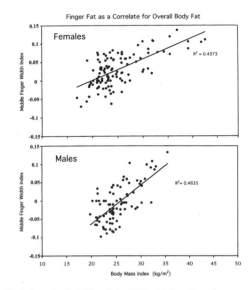

Finger Fat as a Correlate for Overall Body Fat

Females

$R^2 = 0.4373$

Males

$R^2 = 0.4635$

Body Mass Index (kg/m²)

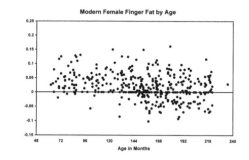

Modern Female Finger Fat by Age

Age in Months

In comparison to the previous graph (again using my Fairbanks school sample), one can see that patterns of finger fat among females of the same age differ only slightly. Though statistically quite variable, some females lose peripheral body fat at about 11–12 years of age, but, unlike males, over half maintain a preadolescent fat pattern of conical fingers. But it is a comparison with the fossil handprints in the next illustration that is important here.

A comparison of body fat, using Body Mass Index (BMI), with finger fat for a sample of male and female college students eighteen years and older. These plots document the statistical relationship between overall body fat and hand shape. I used adults because children in most cultures have a low, but quite variable BMI, for complex reasons (see *Amer. Jour. Disease of Child* 145 (1991): 259–263 for technical details). The Middle-Finger Fat Index is a comparison of finger width (A) at the ring location with mid-knuckle width (B). Finger Fat Index (FFI) = (A/B) − (1.0). Using that formula, FFI is expressed with a baseline of 0, the two measurements are the same. Thus, a positive number signifies the presence of more subcutaneous peripheral body fat; a negative number, less. As for shape, 0 records a columnar-shaped finger. A positive number means the finger is more conical shaped, and a negative number describes a knobby finger. In these two graphs one can see that the fingers of overweight people (BMI 25 or over according to U.S. National Institutes of Health) have a more conical shape, an FFI that is significantly greater than 0. These relationships indicate that the finger index is a rough indicator of body fat, subtly differing between sexes.

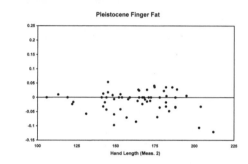

Pleistocene Finger Fat

Hand Length (Meas. 2)

As I showed in chapter 3, a large fraction of the Paleolithic hand prints are those of children. While it is difficult to overcome the irregularities of making absolute assessments of BMI using Paleolithic people's finger fat, we can reasonably compare their FFI with those of modern American children (the last two illustrations). We can conclude that there was little fat and certainly no obesity (most points showing an FFI near or below zero). That is, males and females, children and adults, who left their handprints in Paleolithic art caves were at lean weight. But remember there is an aspect of bias as to who went into caves and who did much of Paleolithic cave art.

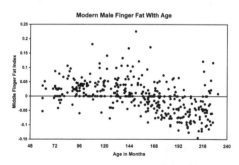

Modern Male Finger Fat With Age

Age in Months

Finger fat index plotted against age of Fairbanks Alaskan males from the age of six through adulthood. Most males appear to decline in body fat at around 11–12 years of age.

cene populations? Demographically, we can trace this population brake to energy limitations. Had they devised some system of "overkill" and extensive meat storage or a wealth of collected carbohydrates, populations would have eventually increased to village size, and such an increase is lacking in the archaeological record. There are a few fossil "food burial" pits in Pleistocene archaeological sites, but these are not large

Most males in Paleolithic art are not drawn well, but one can say that the majority are lean: **A** and **M**, Altamira, Sp. **B** and **K**, La Marche, Fr. **C**, Les Fieux, Fr. **D–E**, La Pileta, Sp. **F** and **S**, Hornos de la Peña, Sp. **G**, Le Portel, Fr. **H**, Minateda, Sp. **I**, Laussel, Fr. **J**, Roc de Sers, Fr. **L**, Sous-Grand-Lac, Fr. **N**, Geissenklösterle, Ger. **O**, Gourdan, Fr. **P**, Pergouset, Fr. **Q**, Pin Hole, England. **R**, Mas d'Azil, Fr. **T**, Lascaux, Fr. **U**, Brno, Czech. **V**, Nerja, Sp.

enough for the tons of meat it would take to keep a group supplied for months. Thirty people with high-caloric needs could use 2000 kilograms of winter reindeer in less than 10 days. The fossil food pits would have stored only a few days' food supply. A kinship-based band, with bands of relatives nearby, is probably better off storing social favors, by sharing episodic windfalls of food, rather than trying to process it for long-term storage. In a hunter-gatherer small-group setting in which the serendipity of gigantic large-mammal windfalls plays some role, sharing is a powerful insurance system, particularly among genetically related bands.

▶ *Quality of life was likely very uneven—perhaps experienced as good, but not idyllic.* We can infer from the preceding points that scarcity would lead to occasional premature births and/or stillbirths, episodes of infertility, childhood death from starvation or dearth-related illnesses, and possibly infanticide and perhaps the occasional abandonment of the ill or elderly. Everyone would have known what it was to go to bed hungry. Dearth did not have to occur often, only frequently enough to have held populations at maintenance levels—on average, each woman raising a little over two children to maturity. The shadow of starvation had to loom large enough to make it worthwhile to overeat when you could. Being fat had to pay off sometime—to give the

relaxed fat lady the edge over the thin energetic one—we have the art to portray that for us. And we also have the evolutionary documentation of our own bodies, relicts of an Ice Age legacy that provide flashes of understanding.

▶ Paleolithic images of men and women show a dimorphic pattern of storing reserves of energy on the body as extensive fat deposits. *These portrayals suggest distinct sexual roles, probably related to patterns of large-muscle activity in which men ranged farther from camp, while women's activities kept them closer to camp.* These activities may have been without a great amount of overlap, or the overlap may have been age, fertility, or ability related. Perhaps lame or older men participated more in women's traditional camp work. Likewise, childless women may have sometimes accompanied men hunting. Being human, there were probably diverse permutations, but our evidence suggests that sexual specializations of tasks are part of every traditional large-mammal hunting lifeway.

Saying that Pleistocene women were more sedentary than males must be understood on a relative scale; women in the late Pleistocene must have been quite active compared with their modern counterparts. Recall, there were no beasts of burden, no mechanical conveniences, no packaged prepared foods, etc. Every task was dependent on her own muscles. Pleistocene women would have had to work very hard, but at different kinds of work than men. The portrayals in the art are consistent with other evidence pointing to a Pleistocene skew, where males specialized in coarse motor activities and females in fine motor skills. Our modern legacy of this is that women score significantly higher on tests of coordination involving small-amplitude movements, whereas men score higher in large-amplitude movements involving high energy expenditure (see Kimura 1999 for a broad review of this subject).

The presence of sexually dimorphic fattening patterns among all human groups suggests that they predate the

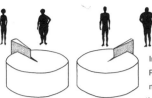

Images of lean women can be found in Paleolithic art but they are uncommon—less than 5%. Lean men, on the other hand, are the rule (there is one male image from Enlène, Fr., that could arguably be obese).

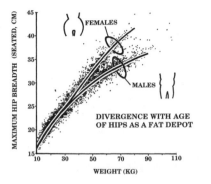

Males and females tend to have different fat depots. One of the best ways of seeing this change with age and weight is to measure seated hip breadth. In these hundreds of measurements of schoolchildren up until eighteen years of age, one can see the two lines (the two sexes) diverging. U.S. data after Snyder et al. 1977.

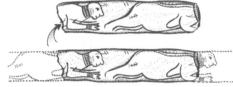

Nude women on a cylindrical rib fragment, Isturitz, Fr. Note bracelets, necklaces, and what appear to be tattoos.

late Paleolithic and were probably already elements of human heritage when the great diaspora out of Africa occurred and people separated into biogeographically different subgroups, many tens of thousands of years ago (Cavalli-Sforza and Cavalli-Sforza 1995).

EVOLUTION OF THE HUMAN "PROPENSITY TO OBESITY"

The main Paleolithic technique of food preservation and storage was: Eat It. In the last chapter I pointed out that a diet of lean muscle has few calories—lean meat has about 1000 calories per kilogram dry weight. Doing hard work in

I don't wish to be too simplistic here; mate choice is complex. Just as females scrutinized a male's resourcefulness in the Pleistocene, males (and especially their mothers) must have also given some consideration to female health, camp skills, strength, ability to carry heavy loads, teeth, etc. One portrayal from Addaura, It. (Sicily), on left, shows a woman with what appears to be a large pack. This is similar to some Bushman paintings, from much later times, such as the one on the right from Underberg District, R.S.A. (reversed for comparison). But the qualities of resourcefulness and strength are not necessarily what young men fantasize about in private.

cool conditions could easily lead to metabolizing 4000–5000 calories per day. That amounts to 4–5 kilograms (about 9–11 pounds) of lean dried meat just to maintain weight. Men working seven-twelves (7 days of 12-hour shifts) in the harsh Alaskan winter climate, constructing the Alaska Pipeline, consumed around 8000 calories per day—though few stayed lean!

A diet with much fat is a high-calorie diet, but in a lifeway dependent on northern large mammals, fat is available in quantity for only a comparatively short period of the year. Prime bull moose and reindeer put on fat only in late summer, but they soon burn most of it during early autumn rut battles. Female large mammals are not so fat. In late summer and autumn, quantities of fat are most available from fresh kills. It would pay to hunt intensively during this time and gorge on fat (Spiess 1979). Fat obtained from wild game can be stored, but it creates problems. Every other carnivorous mammal and bird is facing the same coming winter and is willing to take risks to obtain fat. Large stores of fat and meat make a small camp vulnerable to direct or secretive nighttime raids by powerful and sometimes starving desperate predators, along with the constant harassment by ravens and jays and smaller mammalian scavengers. Therefore, it would pay for a woman to eat all the fat she could and share all the rest. For her, obesity had to be not only critical insurance in pregnancy and the beginnings of nursing but sometimes the key to life itself.

The ability to become obese and the physiological capacity to lose fat with difficulty have significant heri-

People vary considerably in their genetic propensity to fatten. Women from French Paleolithic sites: **A**, Rochereil. **B**, Bruniquel.

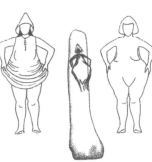

A bone fragment from Montastruc, Fr. This is a somewhat enigmatic figure, but the impression is of a rotund lady with her hands on her hips or one who is lifting her garment.

tability. While a large component of this is under the dominance control of just a few genes (producing many headlines on the "Thrifty Genotype" by the press), the additive, or continuous, variation has a heritability of 0.25 (Bouchard et al. 1990). Jaquish et al. (2000) found an even higher heritability value of 0.47 for body mass index (an indirect assessment of obesity) for people aged forty and over. But remember, obesity is only one part of the thrifty genotype. It also includes being able to binge-eat large quantities, to sleep longer, and to reduce metabolic rate (Nesse 1984). Benefits of famine resistance do not come free; the thrifty genotype is also associated with diabetes, cardiovascular problems, and increased accidents and injury.

Our environment has changed, but our adaptations still reflect those Pleistocene days when our appetites were formed by the years when food was so often limited, when fat tasted delicious, when the demands of raising a small child were always ready to drain the body of its fat, and when illness made insufficient fat dangerous. For millennia, well-being and love, sex and pregnancy, were directly tied to bulging, jiggling curves.

ATTRACTIVELY PLUMP OR AMPLY GRAVID?

Fertility, pregnancy, and fatness have often been rather casually identified in Paleolithic art, and there has been a tendency to see any image of a full-figured woman, as well as many images of rotund horses and other animals, as pregnant. But if one looks carefully, it is clear that only a few images of horses, bison, or reindeer represent a pregnant animal. Indeed, in many images, the large-bellied animals have male antlers and genitals and can only have

been meant to represent bulls in a pre-rut state. Some images do appear to represent pregnant animals, consistent with my earlier observation that animals are portrayed in a wide range of postures and states. Northern large mammals have enlarged abdomens only under two conditions: in the autumn, when males fatten prodigiously prior to rut, and in the spring, when adult females are in the late stages of pregnancy. Since parturition in northern large mammals is timed to coincide with the late-spring green flush of vegetation, we know that an animal that is visibly pregnant, carrying a late-term calf, represents a spring condition.

Research with frozen Pleistocene mummies (Guthrie 1990) and the physiology and ecology of contemporary large mammals that live in harsh northern climates substantiate this picture of intense seasonality. Northern large mammals regularly enter winter with as much as 25% of their weight in body fat (Spiess 1979), and this fact is what made fall bulls a favorite target of Pleistocene hunters. A fat autumn animal provides five times as much energy for the table as a lean animal in spring (Speiss 1979). This seasonal fattening makes the body contours of autumn-fat northern reindeer and wild horses quite distinctive, as back-fat gives the rump a rounded contour. Deep omental fat causes a sagging and distended belly line, not too different from that of a pregnant cow or mare. We can tell the difference between obesity and pregnancy because in spring other body contours are comparatively angular and gaunt. Hip bones show, hams are lean, and pelage is scraggly from winter's abrasions and wear. As most Paleolithic images of animals with distended abdomens also have other rounded contours, particularly along the back and

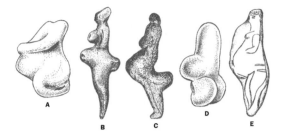

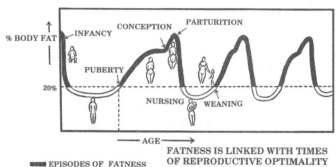

While I argue that most images of voluptuous females in Paleolithic art are primarily concerned with depicting the contours of distinctively female fat depots, there are some that could be interpreted as depicting pregnancy (Duhard 1993): **A**, Kostenki, Rus. **B**, Grimaldi, It. **C**, Monpazier, Fr. **D**, Transimène, It. **E**, La Marche, Fr. (reversed for comparison).

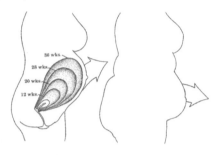

The contours of well-developed fat depots and pregnancy are not identical. One difference is due to the fact that the fetus grows upward in the uterus, causing the abdomen to expand over the navel, upward toward the breasts (*left*). Among simply fat women, omental and subcutaneous fat usually causes abdomen contours to sag (*right*).

FATNESS IS LINKED WITH TIMES OF REPRODUCTIVE OPTIMALITY AND LEANNESS WITH TIMES OF NONFECUNDITY

The Evolutionary Connection of the Erotic with Female Fatness Pleistocene males erotically attracted to voluptuously fat women were statistically more likely to leave more young than males attracted to lean women. Women were more likely to be fat after puberty and after weaning. This is a simplistic generalization, of course, that cannot take into consideration periodic lean times or illness.

rump, we can surmise that most of these are images of autumn-fat animals, not pregnant ones.

Now we can turn to the human images. Duhard (1989, 1993) examined all the human female figurines in Paleolithic art and declared most to be fat and many to be pregnant. But like the images of other animals, I think we can separate pregnancy from states of high fat deposition. Pregnant women carry their young high; the uterus/fetus lies deep against the inside wall of the back, and as it expands during pregnancy, it pushes upward under the viscera, causing a rising distension near the lower ribcage and beneath the breasts. This differs from simple deposits of subcutaneous abdominal fat, which normally sag downward. The contours of most full-figured women in Paleolithic art seem to indicate abdominal fat rather than pregnancy. Another key observation is that the swollen abdomen of an obviously pregnant woman is dispropor-

tionately large compared with the rest of the body bulges; in Paleolithic art the other body contours are consistent with portrayals of obesity. A figurine from Monpazier shows an abdominal distension that could be properly interpreted as pregnancy. Though this figurine is crudely done, the abdomen protrudes in a kind of forward arc, not downward.

THE TWO TIMES IN A PLEISTOCENE WOMAN'S LIFE SHE COULD BE FAT

In subsistence conditions the two times in women's lives when they might tend toward deposition of higher percentages of fat and even obesity corresponded to evolutionarily optimum episodes of sexual desirability: the first is postpuberty and the second is when not nursing (after weaning). On the other hand, the two times women were most lean—during the growth spurt leading to puberty and while nursing babies—were the times when the net reproduction outcome from copulation was very low. Evolutionarily, a woman at these times should be least sexually desirable and most sexually reticent. Our Paleolithic legacy for most girls on dietary plenty is to grow plumper at puberty and remain so until pregnancy. Once a woman becomes pregnant, hormones increase the appetite. This voracious appetite accelerates in midpregnancy. The exception is the sensitive stomach of early pregnancy, which is probably a mechanism to avoid toxins that could damage the delicate embryo's early development (Williams 1991). Hormonal shifts in mid- and late pregnancy direct energy allocation toward storing fat—and make every recipe taste sensational.

In the past, various forms of fertility fetishes or other ideas about magic and religion have been favored to interpret Paleolithic images. I want to show why I favor interpretations that are at least aware of natural-history elements. And I shall try to connect the points I have discussed—about romance and lust, fat deposition and long winters, fantasy and erotica—into a coherent view of the patterns we find in Paleolithic art.

Images of Women in Paleolithic Art: Is There an Erotic Emphasis?

The man who ignores the poetry of sex . . . finds the bare facts written on the walls of a privy, or is himself compelled to write them there.

Yeats, in A. D. F. Macrae, *W. B. Yeats*

Female nudity is clearly portrayed and ubiquitous in Paleolithic images of women. Nudity in the art, however, does not mean that Eurasian women customarily went unclothed when the Périgord was home to reindeer. We have evidence for the cold climate from fossil insects, vertebrates, and pollen and from the tools for clothing manufacture, such as punches, awls, and needles. These nude images are not good indicators of Pleistocene climatic conditioning. Rather, this nudity indicates the sex and age of the makers of these images.

We are the only mammal who intentionally conceals our sexual anatomy. Only a small fraction of aboriginal societies did not conceal erogenous zones in postpuberty individuals, and these exceptions occurred in hot tropical and subtropical situations where clothing tended to pro-

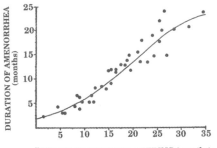

Breast-feeding and Postpartum Amenorrhea Generally, nursing women in hunter-gatherer cultures remain lean, causing their circulating fatty acids to be so low that they do not ovulate. Copulations during this time and prior to puberty, therefore, result in no children. Natural selection favors copulation during the most fecund episodes and so would tend toward reducing sexual attraction during lean times; thus, rounded female curves became a visual clue, a proximate erotic releaser. Data plot of U.S. sample from Bongaarts and Potter 1983.

vide a home to health-threatening and aggravating-itchy ectoparasites. In such situations clothing conceals skin irritations from sanitizing ultraviolet radiation. We can be certain that late Paleolithic people in the regions we are discussing were well clothed for most of the year.

GILDING THE STARK NAKED

With the usual one or two exceptions, women's breasts and genitals in Paleolithic images are never covered, and yet it is notable that many figures are not completely nude. That is quite interesting, because such partial nudity is traditionally associated with enhancing, rather than disguising or downplaying, the erotic. Partial nudity is a recurrent theme in historic and contemporary erotic pictures, in which strategic elements of jewelry, ribbons, bits of lingerie, boots, stockings, scarves, and the like serve to heighten the erotic effect *by emphasizing the absence of clothing* in the most critical spots.

For example, on otherwise nude figurines from the Ukraine and one from La Marche we find ornamented beltlike bands. Other figurines have bracelets. Some figurines from Dolni Věstonice have long stockings or boots.

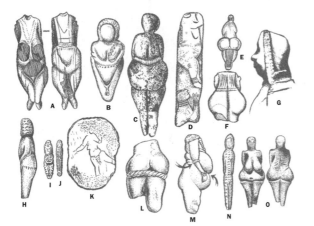

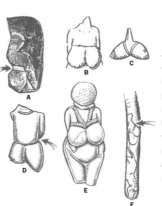

A few nude images in Paleolithic art do show bands over the breasts. This may be a kind of ornamentation or perhaps an indication of some restraint on the loose breasts, as a brassiere functions today. Most of these images come from eastern Europe: **A–B** and **E**, Kostenki I, Rus. **C–D**, Dolni Věstonice, Czech. **F**, La Madeleine, Fr.

Jewelry or partial dress often emphasizes nudity. Paleolithic portrayals of nude women wearing small bits of body decorations: **A**, **C**, **F**, and **M**, Kostenki I, Rus. **B** and **H–J**, Mal'ta, Rus. **D**, Isturitz, Fr. **E**, Lespugue, Fr. **G**, Mas d'Azil, Fr. **K**, Geldorp, Neth. **L**, Pavlov, Czech. **N**, Buret, Rus. **O**, Dolni Věstonice, Czech (two views).

In contemporary erotic art, stockings or boots decoratively de-emphasize the nonessential lower limbs, spotlighting exposed butt and genitals. Some female figurines have rather ornately coiffured hair. Our hairstyling industry did not invent the attractive significance of a head of healthy hair; they merely market it and find fashionable ways to amplify the underlying biological signal and the attention paid to that signal. These Paleolithic images of adorned nudity, I suggest, demonstrate the enormously rich and deep roots of heterosexual male attraction to female form that underlie contemporary and historic erotica.

ABSTRACT AND REPRESENTATIONAL EROTIC ART

There is considerable freedom and diversity in the subject matter of Paleolithic art, but the "style" in which a few erotic images of women and genitals are done is not quite the same as how other subjects, like the abundant large mammals, are usually rendered. Some of the naked women are, of course, rendered quite literally and figuratively like the other mammals, but others are quite abstract and stylized. Some of this can be explained by short-cut or rudimentary skills of a beginning artist trying to render the human body. For example, some rather sketchy Paleolithic copulation scenes are so crude that they take

time to puzzle out. But that cannot be the complete explanation, because some of the female images are beautifully abstract, like a Henry Moore. The artists who did this type of art were not only technically competent but extraordinarily talented. I have resculpted many of these Paleolithic female images and gained great appreciation for their flow of line and mass—in a different way from how I appreciate the horse-bison-reindeer end of the art. All classes of art subjects are, of course, not the same. Each presses differently on human emotions.

It is possible that there were, as now, some sanctions against flagrant erotic images exposed for all to see (as I mentioned in the preceding chapter in trying to account for the rarity of erotic images on atlatls). There are obvious biological reasons for not exhibiting a hypersexual profile. An image does not need to be overtly obvious or blatantly literal to fulfill all its intent, however. Creative distortion can in fact emphasize and exaggerate, deliberately amplifying the point of an image, enhancing its beauty and sophistication. I think this is exactly what is going on in a few of the more abstract Paleolithic images. It is true of much of our public art today and throughout history.

So, erotic emphasis can be overt, as in choosing to portray female forms displaying their genitals in sexually inviting postures, but it can also occur in imagery that is highly stylized and abstract. For example, the S shape formed by a lateral view of breast on one side and buttocks on the other can be so stylized that the resulting erotic reference in decorative pattern is almost unrecognizable

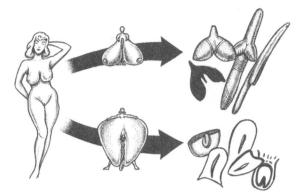

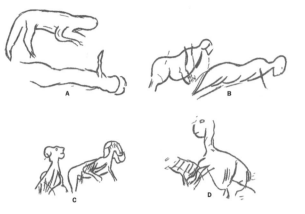

Four copulation scenes by beginning drawers? **A**, Limeuil, Fr. (front-to-front posture). The rest mounting from behind: **B–C**, Murat, Fr. **D**, Enlène, Fr.

More so than women, males respond erotically to coarse, direct, precopulatory signals. Because of this, male erotica often involves a reduction of complex female individual form into sexually essential elements. In Paleolithic art, as with art from many other cultures, the less erotic elements are often completely deleted—leaving only the vital imperatives.

Drawing of small sculpted image by Henry Moore, 1934.

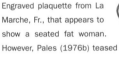

Engraved plaquette from La Marche, Fr., that appears to show a seated fat woman. However, Pales (1976b) teased a mounted person out of the many overlying scratches. So the woman can be placed on her back, legs in the air, and a partner is seen lying on top.

without the intermediate stages. And certainly the misidentified hoofprints, leaves, and butterflies of vulva labia in Paleolithic art are an example of this. Though nudity is the central theme in erotica, the best way to dramatize the eroticism of a nude figure is with an inviting body posture, even if rudimentary.

EROTIC POSTURES: "S" IS FOR SEX

The body positions of women portrayed in Paleolithic art are not randomly selected. There are, in fact, many parallels between female images in Paleolithic art and the poses chosen by photographers and producers of magazines like *Playboy, Hustler,* and *Penthouse.* Consider the frontal spread-leg position of three images from La Magdeleine and possibly others from La Marche. And the rear presentation is one of the most common postures in both Paleo-

lithic art and in modern erotic body posturing. Why should the rear be emphasized so?

Among primates, the female rump is a central focus of male attention. They keep a close watch on the rumps of adult females, because estrus hormones cause engorged swellings of brilliant colors to announce a female's estrus receptivity. This is true among chimps, our nearest hominoid relative, so it should not be puzzling that heterosexual men generally find a woman's buttocks and area surrounding the labia to be an erogenous-erotic zone. Gorillas, bonobos, and humans added belly-to-belly coupling to the older primate rear copulatory posture, but attraction to a female's rear remains. Among most mammals a position called *lumbar lordosis* is used by females to raise the rear, emphasizing the visual aspect of the genitalia and facilitating male intromission. Lordosis is the female primate posture of sexual invitation. In our more upright bipedal anatomy, the human counterpart to lordosis is a concave curve to the lower back, which dramatizes the woman's buttocks. As I said, this type of posturing can be

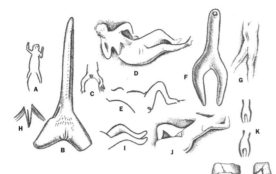

Rough approximations of spread legs in the Pleistocene: A, Fontalès, Fr. B and K, Le Placard, Fr. C, Fontanet, Fr. D and J, La Magdeleine, Fr. E, Gabillou, Fr. F, Pekarna, Czech. G, Angles-sur-l'Anglin, Fr. H, Clotilde, Sp. I, La Marche, Fr. L, Avdeevo, Rus. (two views).

An engraving on a stone from La Marche, Fr. A, This woman is normally illustrated in a sitting posture. B, But if the stone is rotated, she appears lying on her back with legs lifted and spread.

La Marche, Fr.

Praying, bowing, bad backs, or lordosis in the Pleistocene? A, La Marche, Fr. B–E, Les Combarelles, Fr. F, Gönnersdorf, Ger. G, Roucadour, Fr. H, Pech-Merle, Fr. I, Hohlenstein, Ger. J, Lalinde, Fr.

observed in many kinds of recent erotic imagery and fine art, including some of Rodin's torsos. Fashion plays with this lordosis-like curve as well. Many of the accouterments, armatures, and appliances of women's fashion highlight this S curve.

Lordosis squiggles are met with a number of times in Paleolithic art, ranging from small three-dimensional carvings to quickly done stone engravings; both occur in sites like Gönnersdorf. These images, lacking explicit head, feet, or arms, directly echo poses of models in the soft-core pornographic magazines. This posture claims erotic interest by emphasizing secondary sexual characteristics and a posture inviting copulation. The protruding rear exaggerates its size, while the chest is arched forward to emphasize the size and hang of the breasts. Legs bent at the knees further emphasize the rear.

Artistic traditions in southern Asia have developed and elaborated a frontal version of the S curve. This sensual bend is called *tribhanga*. I am not aware of an English equivalent, but I believe the French *déhanchement* comes close (Honor and Fleming 1982). The *tribhanga* torso is

bent at the waist while breasts are kept horizontal, a posture which emphasizes the breadth of the hips and the ball-shaped breasts. A rudimentary version of the *tribhanga* occurs when the weight on one hip is counterposed with a raised shoulder opposite—a posture present on one point-straightener from the Paleolithic.

These erotically charged postures and the shapes distilled from them are visual solutions to the problem of how to represent a sexually appealing and inviting image with the fewest lines. Of course, the counterpart to such erotic highlighting is omission or de-emphasis of less erotically provocative elements. Postures and shapes distill to the lowest denominator of sexual allure.

IMAGES OF PENISES AND VULVAE

Considerable numbers of two- and three-dimensional images of penises and vulvae occur in Paleolithic art. Almost always, penises are portrayed as erect, and when close-ups are shown, the foreskin is drawn back and the glans exposed. Penis images often occur by themselves, not as part of a more complete male body. Vulvae are likewise com-

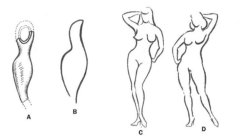

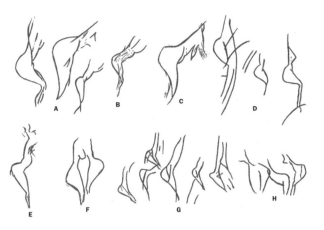

Another erotic posture is to rotate the pelvis with a bend at the waist, producing a lateral twist that emphasizes the hips. An extreme version of this is the *trib-hanga,* a common posture in ancient East Indian art. Pleistocene images: **A**, El Pendo, Sp. **B**, Rochereil, Fr. This posture is another way to exhibit the broad pelvic girdle as shown in **C** and **D** in the form of outline drawings from American models taking provocative positions using a laterally rotated pelvis.

S-shaped women from the Pleistocene: **A**, Fontalès, Fr. **B**, Courbet, Fr. **C**, Couze, Fr. **D**, Hohlenstein, Ger. **E**, Abri Murat, Fr. **F**, Gönnersdorf, Ger. **G**, Lalinde, Fr. **H**, Les Combarelles, Fr.

S-shaped, lordosis postures in Paleolithic art: **A–C**, Carriot, Fr. **D**, Saint-Cirq, Fr. **E–F**, Vielmouly, Fr. **G**, Font Bargeix, Fr. **H–J**, **M**, and **Q**, Gouy, Fr. **K–L**, Villars, Fr. **N**, Fronsac, Fr. **O–P**, Commarque, Fr. **R–T**, Les Combarelles, Fr. **U–V**, Teyjat, Fr. **W–X**, Pech-Merle, Fr.

Left, chimpanzee in exaggerated lordosis posture. *Right,* drawing of life-sized bronze by Rodin.

mon in Paleolithic art and are represented as exposed on nude women and as isolated triangles carved in three dimensions and engraved or drawn on bones, antlers, ivory, stone plaquettes, or cave walls.

Point-straighteners are occasionally decorated with erect penises and/or vulvae. Handles of point-straighteners are sometimes shaped to look like erect penises; one such tool has the handle made up as a penis and the hole is positioned between an image of two testes. Another point-straightener is designed so that the straightener-hole represents an open vulva, with spread legs on either side. Another has erect and decorated (tattooed?) penises jutting out in several directions. The most numerous genital images, though, are found as isolated insignia-like engrav-

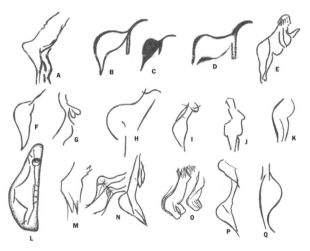

More lordosis images from Paleolithic art: **A**, Niaux, Fr. **B–D**, Pech-Merle, Fr. **E**, La Marche, Fr. **F** and **M**, Fontalès, Fr. **G–I**, Les Combarelles, Fr. **J–K**, Rochereil, Fr. **L**, Saut-du-Perron, Fr. **N**, Lalinde, Fr. **O**, Abri Faustin, Fr. **P**, Teyjat, Fr. **Q**, Gönnersdorf, Ger.

Lesbian Loving or Male Fantasy? There are a few Gönnersdorf engravings in which two nude women in S postures appear to be holding one another. In one image the female standing behind seems to be holding the breasts of the one in front. It is possible that these

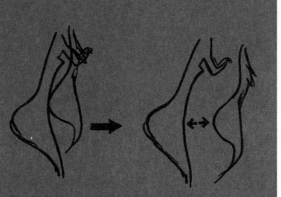

Two women in front-to-back posture, the one behind with her hands on the breasts of the woman in front (figures separated at right), Gönnersdorf, Ger. These could be the result of superimposition of drawings from different times, but perhaps not.

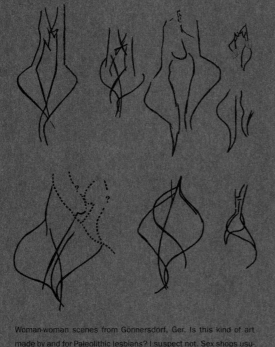

Woman-woman scenes from Gönnersdorf, Ger. Is this kind of art made by and for Paleolithic lesbians? I suspect not. Sex shops usually feature a large selection of woman-woman sex, which appeals to heterosexual males.

are superimposed fortuitously, but that seems unlikely, because this particular overlapping image was engraved several times. Few researchers have risked comment. Yet there is an entire category of modern heterosexual male erotica that consists of images of nude women portrayed in similar postures. It is indeed one genre of video-magazine display in "sex shops." Though male-male sex is offensive to most heterosexual males, for some reason female-female sex has a curious appeal. So finding naked women engaging other naked women among Paleolithic drawings does not necessarily imply true lesbian passion, or Ice Age mud wrestling, but perhaps a part of male erotica, some young male's wild fantasy.

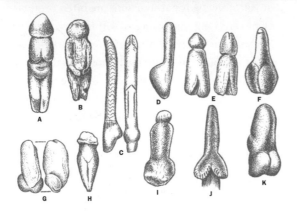

Creative double entendres in Paleolithic forms? **A**, Chiozza, It. **B**, Avdeevo, Rus. **C**, Mezine, Ukraine. **D**, Ölknitz, Ger. **E**, Mezine, Ukraine. **F**, Saint Marcel, Fr. **G**, Nab Head, England. **H**, Brassempouy, Fr. **I**, Trou-Magritte, Fr. **J**, Dolni Věstonice, Czech. **K**, Trasimène, It.

ings or simple drawings on cave walls.

Although men's bodies are not usually the prime focus of conventional heterosexual erotic art, an erect penis often is. I think that's because men's erotic emotions are normally accompanied by erections, so an erect penis has become erotic by association. And, as is often the case with potent associations, what originally was simply effect can become cause. Just as some Paleolithic penis images and dildo-like objects have survived, so has the behavioral urge and delight in making them. The presence of penis images scattered all through Paleolithic art should not require a religious explanation or interpretation as ritual paraphernalia.

Paleolithic images of vulvae sometimes occur in clusters, like flocks of butterflies. Similar clusters of vulvae im-

Paleolithic Dildoes? This is a rather delicate subject, but some of the penises may not be art objects but tools. Many of the penises carved from mammoth ivory, reindeer antler, and stone are almost identical in size and shape to a human male's erect penis. Taylor (1996) has proposed that in any other context we certainly would call these Paleolithic pieces dildoes, a type of sex toy. Such phallic look-alikes or dildoes are a well-known contemporary genre of erotica produced in varieties of materials, colors, textures, shapes, and sizes (double-ended, motorized, or belt mounted). Furthermore, the dildo has a long history in many cultures. Chimps have even been seen to insert objects into the vagina for erotic purposes. Though

What occurs to you when you see an oblong stream pebble? It takes a mind of a certain age and sex to have this brand of creativity in modifying one end. Kniegrotte, Ger.

today dildoes may be used by single women, their main erotic appeal seems to be to males, to be used on females. Is it far-fetched to see dildo-like objects tens of thousands of years old as part of that same phenomenon? Or perhaps these were just made by adolescent males as part of their erotic expressions. As I will show, they did some even wilder things, for example, with vulva images.

Prehistoric rock art, Tuxedni Bay, Alaska. Vulvae are common in prehistoric art all over the world, even in post-Pleistocene times in my own part of the world. Think about why vulvae, of all things, should be one of the images of choice.

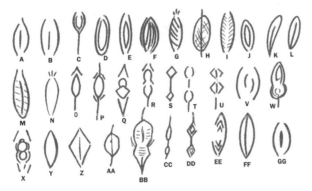

In addition to the more explicit ones, there are a lot of schematic vulvae and vulva-like forms in Paleolithic art, just little quickies, almost identical to what we see in modern toilet graffiti: **A**, La Madeleine, Fr. **B**, Abri Jolivet, Fr. **C**, Abri Morin, Fr. **D**, Saint Marcel, Fr. **E**, **H–I**, **R**, and **DD**, Laugerie-Basse, Fr. **F**, Mas d'Azil, Fr. **G**, **N**, and **P**, Marsoulas, Fr. **J** and **L**, Eglises, Fr. **K**, Les Combarelles, Fr. **M**, **U**, and **AA**, Isturitz, Fr. **O**, Le Placard, Fr. **Q**, Gourdan, Fr. **S**, Abri Morin, Fr. **T**, Laugerie-Haute, Fr. **V**, Abri Pataud, Fr. **W** and **BB**, Rochereil, Fr. **X**, Penne, Fr. **Y**, **CC**, and **EE**, La Madeleine, Fr. **Z**, Santimamiñe, Sp. **FF**, Polesini, It. **GG**, Bernifal, Fr.

ages are found in many later cultures. The spectacular cluster of vulvae among the prehistoric rock art in a remote gorge at Carnarvon National Park in south-central Queensland, Australia, is a good example. The wing or hooflike marks that occur in many places on Easter Island represent

vulvae. They were considered very erotic and some Polynesian men used similar images in their tattoo patterns, as evidence of their sexual prowess. In the case of Easter Island, the identity of the images is clear, and they were not part of a fertility cult; rather, sexual preoccupation was a ubiquitous element in this Polynesian culture. And, of course, this kind of thing pervades much of modern graffiti.

Much of Paleolithic art thwarts interpretation if we are not sensible to this stamp of male youthful humor and ardor. Trying to find adult motives may not always be appropriate. Marshack (1989), for example, has observed that Paleolithic vulva abstractions are often overmarked with pits and long gouges incised within the vulva. The interpretation has been that these are ritual markings, but of course they could have been made more casually, either by the artist who made the vulva or by later people walking by. Adults may need a symbolic reason or ritual context to make sense of such marks, but all who mark up walls are not adults.

Finally, to assume that some images in Paleolithic art are not erotic because a few of the nude figures lack visible genitals misses this broader point of erotica. Not even the hardest-core pornography magazines restrict their pages to genital detail. The absence of vivid genitals in *Playboy*, for example, does not exclude it from the erotica magazine section or make it obtainable at your public library.

Missing Pubic Hairs The presence of a thick hair mat on the pubic triangle of postpubertal women of all human groups indicates this hair patch was present at least during the last 100,000 years of human evolution—the mitochondrial DNA dating of human group divergence from a single interbreeding population. While men in some human groups are almost beardless, in no group are women without pubic hairs. Thus, there is no reason to think Paleolithic women lacked pubic hair. Nevertheless, female genitalia portrayed in Paleolithic art are hairless (with a few possible exceptions). This "clean-shaven" look often occurs in prehistoric art postdating the Paleolithic and also in vulva drawings in contemporary graffiti. Are there credible explanations for this discrepancy?

First, can we be assured that young Paleolithic boys knew about this hair patch on the pubic triangle? This is not always true today; I remember being with my buddies and seeing photos of nude women for the first time, aghast at how much more hairy this part was than we had imagined. But in the close quarters of Paleolithic life it is hard to imagine that Pleistocene people were not aware of the bodies of family members.

Another universal human trait is that men have, statistically, more coarsely haired limbs, torsos, and

Early weaving attempts or vulvae? Paleolithic boxlike openings with pubic hair–like squiggles around them: A–c, E, and i, Altamira, Sp. d and g, Parpalló, Sp. F, Buxú, Sp. H, Bédeilhac, Fr. J–L, La Pileta, Sp. M–N, Les Combarelles, Fr.

faces than women. Because of this, men generally find coarse body hair to be a more masculine signal than smooth skin. Women sometimes pluck, peel, or shave body hair to attain a smoother image. Especially in pornographic magazines, female body hair, even pubic hair, is often removed, suggesting its absence is more erotic than its presence. Perhaps its removal makes visible an even more potent erotic releaser? In short, it seems most likely that time and time again Paleolithic artists deleted pubic hairs for erotic emphasis.

Eroticism is complex, and more sophisticated forms of visual erotica normally operate back a number of notches from swollen genitals. That is precisely why the multiple vulvae and the occasional erect penis in Paleolithic art are so suggestive of unsophisticated, probably adolescent or juvenile, artists.

TECTIFORMS, QUADRILATERALS, AND CLEAVAGES

Paleolithic art includes some rather enigmatic designs, versions of which are found in different caves. I suggest that many of these are a sort of natural outline drawn by the ethologically literate heterosexual male brain—which is an avid reader of erotic images. The Paleolithic artist didn't have to complete the piece; their brains did that. This is especially true of Paleolithic images referred to as "signs," variously called *tectiforms* or *quadrilaterals* by art scholars. These have been interpreted as diagrams of lodges, animal traps, or religious symbols.

I propose instead that some of these Paleolithic "signs" are intended to represent a woman's crotch and/or genitals, drawn from a different angle than we are accustomed to seeing in art. Genitals of a standing woman are rather hidden, not really visible. An artist wishing to represent them can choose to do so in several ways. One is to draw a complex reclining figure, which involves demanding representational problems, especially for a beginner. Another is to simply move the vaginal opening around, where it can be presented visually in the same way that Paleolithic artists represented the feet of bison.

Some isolated carved penises are found in Paleolithic sites: **A**, La Combe, Fr. **B**, Laussel, Fr. **C**, Pavlov, Czech. **D**, Cueto de la Mina, Sp. (note vulvae). **E**, Bruniquel, Fr. Some would identify these as ceremonial wands, but I think a more straightforward explanation is that they are simply manifestations of a human, particularly male, aesthetic.

Simple carved image, Laussel, Fr.

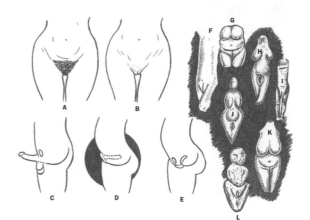

A number of Paleolithic images of women have the vulva opening at right angles to the body, in much the same angle that an erect penis lies. Boys make this same mistake in graffiti art today. **A**, Vulvae are not visible from the front of mature women because of the pubic hairs. **B**, Even without pubic hairs, a vulva is hardly visible on a standing woman. **C**, Naive boys know their erection points forward and presume the female opening should be the reciprocal negative match (**D**); In fact, a real vulva is angled very differently (**E**). Some "forward-pointing" Paleolithic vulvae: **F**, La Magdeleine, Fr. **G** and **K**, Moravany, Czech. **H**, Montpazier, Fr. **I**, Laugerie, Basse, Fr. **J**, Grimaldi, It. **L**, Mal'ta, Rus.

The mammoth tusk engraving from Predmosti, Czech., is rather enigmatic, but close observation reveals a woman's body; erotic parts have been emphasized, and non-erotic ones largely omitted. My drawings attempt to show a possible gradient of forms in that abstraction process.

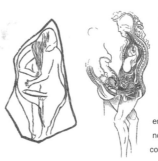

This Pleistocene engraving (*left*) from La Marche, Fr., illustrates my point in the previous illustration—an inexperienced adolescent anatomical mistake. Leonardo da Vinci made this same mistake (*right*) in adulthood, but perhaps for the same reason of inexperience. Some of his other drawings in his notebooks (da Vinci 1996) show this misconception even more graphically.

Unlike the frontal view of the pubic triangle (which is also common in Paleolithic art) with the small incision in the lower apex for the labia, this is a twisted-perspective view from underneath. As with the pubic triangle distillation, it paraphrases that underneath view and crops the image of all but the essentials. The resulting image is sometimes a vertically elongated diamond. Others are more complicated, with two or three outer lines running vertically as the ridges of the labia and a patch of hatch-marks at the crest representing pubic hairs (these are the possible exceptions to the Paleolithic pattern of failing to depict crotch hairs). Leg lines can be abbreviated by a frame-line or left hanging.

Quadrilaterals-tectiforms seen in Paleolithic art may not be meant as realistic crotch or vulva drawings. They seem to be rather quick visual guides, reminders to the imagination. As such, they are decorated with repeated lines paralleling the original lines and with crosshatch lines running at different angles. Stylization such as this is

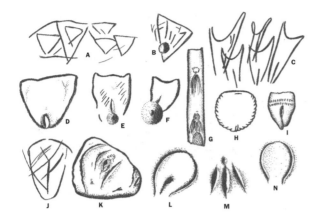

Another sampler showing the diverse variety of Paleolithic vulvae portrayals: **A**, Lluera, Sp. **c**, Micolón, Sp. **B**, **D–F**, Gouy, Fr. **G**, Le Placard, Fr. **H**, Bodrogkeresztur, Hung. **I**, Dolni Věstonice, Czech (may be lower part of venus figurine?). **J**, Les Combarelles, Fr. **K–N**, Abri Cellier, Fr.

Another Paleolithic vulvae sampler with different styles: **A**, Tito Bustillo, Sp. **B**, Castillo, Sp. **c**, Meaza, Sp. **D**, Réseau Clastres, Fr. **E**, Le Portel, Fr. **F**, Abri du Poisson, Fr. **G**, Romanelli, It. **H**, Abri Castanet, Fr. **I**, Planchard, Fr. **J**, Abri Cellier, Fr. **K**, Rochereil, Fr. **L**, Teyjat, Fr. **M**, Abri Pataud, Fr. **N**, Grand Grotte, Fr. **o**, La Ferrassie, Fr.

I wish to reiterate the point that Paleolithic vulva images are not restricted to those times but have a universal appeal to a certain sex and age-group. The same subject is  seen among diverse later prehistoric cultures: **A**, Lepenski Vir, Yugoslavia (eighth millennium B.P.). **B**, Bushman Fountain, R.S.A. **c**, Santa Cruz, Argentina.

a case where less is more, but there are examples of the opposite, where repetition is used for emphasis.

LUMPS AND BUMPS OF CLAVIFORMS

Some Paleolithic forms are not obviously identifiable until viewed in the context of related images. There is a continuum of imagery from clearly representational drawings to the rather cryptic lines of more abstract images, from, for example, a distinctly female figure to a strategically placed lump on an otherwise straight stick (whether carved, engraved, or drawn). Without the few S curves that have clearly defined breasts and arms, one could not be certain of the identity of the abstract ones.

Strategically placed lumps occur on otherwise enigmatic forms in Paleolithic collections from Spain, France, Germany, Hungary, Czechoslovakia, Russia, and the Ukraine. Fortunately, at the Gönnersdorf site, artists left

behind engravings of images that grade from definitely identifiable women with arms, breasts, and enlarged buttocks to very schematic representations. The simplest forms are basically sticks with an asymmetrical lump concentrating on the large swell of buttocks (or one can flip it 180 degrees and call this lump the breasts). This condensation of a male's appetite for sexual form also suggests, in a double entendre, an erect penis and tightened scrotum around testes, as occurs during male sexual excitement.

COPULATION SCENES

Copulation scenes are relatively rare in Paleolithic art, but they do exist, and like close-ups of genitals, they represent the more heavy-handed range of erotica. It is notable that while images of genitals are often engraved or carved into permanent tools, this is not true of images of copulation. In family settings incest taboos generally insist on covering genitals and at least censure free exhibition of copulation and imagery depicting copulation. Concealed copulation is one of the cross-cultural universals listed by Brown (1991). It is possible that there were Paleolithic restrictions on public displays of hard-core erotica just as

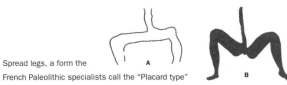

Spread legs, a form the French Paleolithic specialists call the "Placard type" (because Placard Cave, Fr., is the "type site"): **A**, Cosquer, Fr. **B**, A Postglacial image, Abri de los Toros, Sp.

Placard Cave, Fr.

Many of the otherwise strange "signs" in Paleolithic art from a variety of places and times appear as coarse, stylized vulvae or crotch views. *Top*, my more representational reminder. *Bottom*, some of a variety of Paleolithic female "signs" illustrated by Leroi-Gourhan (1964) and used in assessing the mystical-symbolic order of cave art chronologies and styles.

The following images are Paleolithic: **A** and **D**, Cougnac, Fr. **B**, Pech-Merle, Fr. **C**, Pasiega, Sp. We see something similar in many later prehistoric cultures: **E**, Chernovya, Rus. **F**, Dilukai, Rus. **G**, Manabi, Equador. **H**, Arnhem Land, Austrl. **I**, Northern Territory, Austrl.

The erotic significance of **A**, a Pleistocene spread-legged crotch display, is emphasized in post-Pleistocene drawings from Africa: **B–C**, Wâdi-Djerât, Sahara. **D**, Wâdi-I-Khêl, Sahara. **E**, Govalis, Namibia. **F**, Tassili, Sahara. **G**, Edjïj, Sahara. **H**, Akâkûs, Sahara. **I**, Tin-n-Lalan, Sahara.

there are in most societies today. Despite media reliance on images of suggestive and seductive beauty, copulation scenes and detailed images of genitals are rarely presented in public. This is true not only for Western cultures but for most others as well. In Paleolithic art the rarity of copulation scenes may also be in part due to their difficulty in execution. Representing two bodies in a complex assemblage of limbs and legs is demanding.

BESTIAL RAPE FROM LAUGERIE-BASSE?

Fragmentary engravings on a broken stone plaquette from Laugerie-Basse, France, rather like the one from Enlène,

Erotic Imagery: Where More Is More, Not Less

Often more stylized female images are shown in a "chorus line." Some Paleolithic specialists have called them "dancers." They could well be dancers, but one principle in ethology is that if one thing is

Chorus-line effect, as seen in an African dance. This is a Venda ceremony of puberty, rather like a coming-out rite, after which young girls are eligible for marriage. Sketch from photo. The "ethological" power of signals from women's figures is enhanced with repetition. People who buy erotica seldom purchase single images; rather, they buy magazines of images. Likewise, Paleolithic artists sometimes made multiples.

good, then several are usually better. Peacocks don't just have one "eye" image on their tail feathers but many, in the same way that dogs don't just go "woof"; they go "woof, woof, woof." Redundancy counts. Erotic magazines never limit themselves to one good picture but feature many images. Likewise, erotic fantasies can run to multiple partners, though one partner is likely sufficient. Multiples amplify the erotic signal (recall the Coolidge effect) in an almost additive fashion. In Paleolithic art female genital images are often found in clusters. Rows of "claviform" figures at Pindal, Niaux, and Gönnersdorf are such multiples of erotically stylized females.

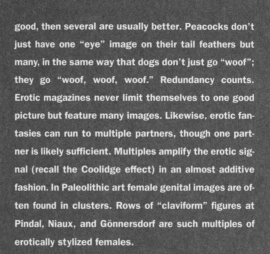

Erotic emblems or imagery are often repeated for impact. Flocks of Pleistocene vulvae: A, Estacion Cave, Sp. B, Abri Blanchard, Fr.

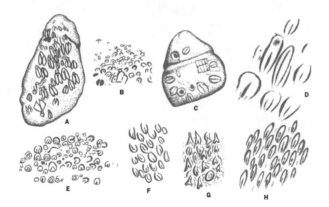

Flocks of vulvae are seen worldwide in prehistoric art much later in date than the Paleolithic: A, Easter Island petroglyph. B, Oliveiria de Prades, Portugal. C, Neolithic, Portugal. D, Solwezi, Zambia. E, D'Ulan Quab, Mongolia. F, Baja Mexico. G, Chatham Islands. H, Carnarvon Park, Austrl.

A, One finds single stylized females-with-breast in sites such as Chauvet, Fr. (reversed for comparison). There are similar figures done in "chorus lines" of parallel stripes, as seen in two Spanish caves: B, Pindal. C, La Cullalvera. These seem enigmatic if one is not aware of the other instances of stylized, repeated female body imagery in Paleolithic art.

have also been an enigma. The Laugerie-Basse image is definitely a fat and/or pregnant woman lying on her back with arms raised in what appears to be a gesture of protection. Apparently standing over her is a giant cloven-hoofed (thus not a horse), long-legged (thus not a bison) animal like a shelk or red deer. Some writers have proposed that this image represented the magic potency of the beast, mystic sexual virility, or even bestial rape. Pales and St.-Péreuse (1976), however, noted that when the plaquette

It should not surprise us that there are erotic elements in Paleolithic art. Similar erotic themes appear in the art of many later cultures: **A–B**, Bushman drawings from Zimbabwe. **C**, Carolinas. **D–E**, Babylonian graffiti. **F**, Israel. **G–H**, Atlas Mountains, Sahara. **I**, Egyptian graffiti. **J**, Fezzan, North Africa. **K**, Babylon. **L–M**, Inner Mongolia. **N**, White Sea, Rus. **O**, Sweden. **P–Q**, Onega, Rus.

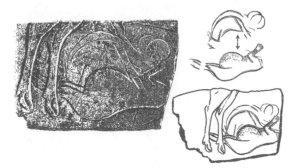

This little fragment of an engraving from Laugerie-Basse, Fr., has been a puzzle to researchers for a long time. What is the fat or pregnant woman doing lying under the legs of some cloven-hoofed artiodactyl? But if you look carefully, it is actually two people copulating; the man is just sketched in very lightly. I suspect it is rather like the piece from Enlène that had both a copulation scene and a bison; these "slates" were used for several different, often unrelated, images. And since erotica and large mammals are among the more common items drawn, they sometimes occur together on the same piece. Reconstruction at lower right.

was examined closely, another poorly drawn human figure could be discerned inclined over the supine woman in a belly-to-belly copulatory position. This is consistent with the pattern that images of men in general are usually quite sketchy in Paleolithic art, particularly those in copulatory scenes. And this certainly was meant to be a copulatory scene. Again, the large-mammal image on the plaquette may be unrelated, maybe even done by a different artist. We know many plaquettes from this and a number of other sites have been engraved over and over with different subjects, almost like reusing a slate tablet with chalk pencil. As I pointed out in chapter 4, there seems to be little intentional conflation of hunting and erotic images in Paleolithic art. These are usually just the fortuitous association of the two recurring choices of images.

HERMAPHRODITE IN THE PLEISTOCENE?

There is at least one Paleolithic image that is clearly hermaphroditic. This small figurine from Grimaldi, Italy, has female breasts and male genitals. The identification of the male genitals has been controversial; but if this little figurine lacked breasts, would there be any doubt as to what was being held between the legs? There is a huge

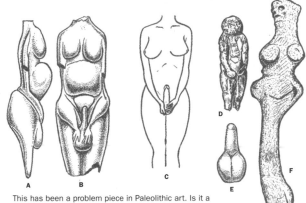

This has been a problem piece in Paleolithic art. Is it a hermaphrodite or childbirth? **A–B**, Side and front view of figurine from Grimaldi, It. **C**, My interpretation and reconstruction of the carver's attempted image. We can see from other, unrelated pieces of Paleolithic art that my reconstruction is legitimate. Having hands down near the genitals is not unusual. **D**, For example, a figurine from Avdeevo, Rus., shows this hands-down position. Likewise, we should not mistake the penis and testicles for some other object; as shown in **E**, a penis and testicles are sometimes represented with a vertical erection (Nab Head, Saint-Bride's, England). And from **F**, Petersfels, Ger., we can see that possibly other mixed-sex drawings occurred in Paleolithic art.

scrotum, and an erect penis points toward the navel—exactly as it should, just a little bigger than life. But the presence of structures, unarguably meant to be breasts, on that particular Grimaldi figurine has prompted strange interpretations about the male genitals.

The Missing Piece at Enlène Cave The mix of voluptuous women and large woolly mammals in Paleolithic art has been troublesome for researchers working within the paradigms of symbolism and ritual. This is highlighted by individual works on which both erotica and large mammals are incorporated. One fragment of an engraved stone plaquette, discovered in 1939 at the French site of Enlène, provides a telling case. The small, engraved, stone plaquette was broken, so the image was incomplete. The engraving had parts of what appeared to be two people and a large mammal. Central figures in Paleolithic art research (Breuil, Leroi-Gourhan, Pales, and Graziosi) provided mystical interpretations of this fragment. One could see the hairy underside of a large mammal and the rears, abdomens, and legs of what appeared to be two people, the large one interpreted to be a woman in a lordosis posture, because of her "Venus"-like obesity, and a smaller individual, probably male, almost superimposed. Foreparts were missing.

In 1980 Bégouën et al. (1982) discovered two more pieces at the site which fitted the well-known original fragment and the imagery was now clear: there was an elegant bison and there was an image of two people on their knees (Bégouën et al. 1982). As it turned out, the thick-chested figure was a man, identified by a hatched beard. The smaller figure was a woman, long hair falling over her face as she kneels with the man bent over behind her. Neither are dressed, but the woman is wearing what looks to be a belt. These authors concluded the obvious, that this was a couple copulating front-to-back.

Bison and sex, Enlène, Fr. This sketch of a couple copulating was done by someone with elementary drawing skills. Drawing two completely intertwined bodies from one's imagination is difficult. This drawing positions the woman kneeling and the man mounting from behind. Note the details. There appears to be a crudely done witness to this event. The woman has long hair and the man has a bristly chin.

The subject and its execution parallel the kinds of imagery one might see scratched into the paint of a boys' toilet booth in a middle school. The bison scene and copulation are independent images, possibly done by different artists, at different times. The two drawings overlap and are drawn from different angles of perspective. A third, also poorly drawn, human image can be seen superimposed near the posterior of the bison. This image does not seem related to either the bison or the copulation imagery.

The elegance of the bison suggests a more experienced artist, while the rudimentary copulation scene suggests a marginally competent artist or one in a rather early stage of artistic development. Still, the final product does carry the essence of his intent. I say *his* because this crude copulation scene bears the forensic stamp of a male artist's brain, just as surely as if he had left a print of his hand.

The hermaphrodite image from Grimaldi, It., is not necessarily bizarre. Similar images are found in later prehistoric art: **A**, Tin-n-Terit, Sahara. **B**, Bombala, Sahara. **C**, Bushman, Stowlands, R.S.A. **D**, Anasazi, Mesa Verde, U.S.A.

Devotion to the magico-religious paradigm, particularly to the notion of mystical fertility rites, can cloud judgments as to what people see in Paleolithic images, and some "fertility magic" theorists even see this figurine as a mother giving birth (Duhard 1989). But the Grimaldi figurine clearly combines male genitals with a body that is otherwise female. There is nothing in the Grimaldi piece to suggest artistic incompetence or technical mistake. Nor

Small female figurine pendant from Balzi Rossi, It. It has been called the "nun" because of its apparent robe (Mussi, Cinq-Mars, and Bolduc 2000). But it could equally be named the "flasher." The robe hangs open, exhibiting a well-rounded nude female body with exposed genitals and breasts. The lower portion is apparently broken off.

Even beginning artists can distill an erotic signal to its essential parts. Such little forms provide the kick-start for one's imagination and sexual fantasies. **A**, My distillation. **B**, The kind made by a Paleolithic artist, Andernach, Ger.

does it seem to have been made by an artist misinformed about normal male and female anatomy—the craftsmanship of the torso curves is too competent. Can we suppose that the artist deliberately mixed these male-female sexual images, as Pales and St.-Péreuse (1976) suggested? Taylor (1996) has proposed that it is a woman using a dildo. This may be correct, but one would imagine that in such a case an artist would place it coming up from below, disappearing into the vulva opening.

Or does the Grimaldi piece possibly represent an actual mixed-sex person? Hermaphroditic individuals do occur at very low frequencies, due to a developmental mix-up in regulatory hormones or their receptors. One form (Silber 1981) is the result of a typical XX chromosome female producing slightly too much testosterone, in which case secondary sexual characteristics are within the normal range, but the clitoris can be quite large, like a penis, and the seam of the vulva is often closed or partially closed and the thickened labia majora hang like a scrotum (without testes).

I suspect this little Grimaldi female-male figure was fantasized. Remember, the erotic is mainly about imagination. Could this exotic intersex be erotic for males? This is an open question, for sexual appetite can lead in diverse directions. But one would suspect that if such a hermaphroditic image was inherently erotic, then something similar would appear in erotic literature today. Indeed it does. For example, sex shops feature publications about transsexuals and hermaphrodites combining female bodies and male genitals. Acknowledging the obvious in this case need not threaten our appreciation of the various beauties and values of these Paleolithic images. Are these little figures less magical if they testify to complex earthy feel-

ings, to bittersweet, even quirky notions of human experience in deep antiquity?

A SUMMARY: EVIDENCE FOR EROTIC IMAGERY IN PALEOLITHIC ART

Some researchers have argued that Paleolithic artists were not really involved with erotica or sexual matters. Gvozdover (1989) sites the rarity of genitalia in Paleolithic art, and Bahn and Vertut (1988, 1997) have also argued that sex is not a significant theme, noting as evidence the rarity of Paleolithic depictions of copulation. Certainly, among representational art, images of large mammals numerically predominate. Nevertheless, as we have seen, images of nude women and the fairly numerous images of genitalia suggest erotic intent. Let me review nine points we have covered:

▸ We observed that Paleolithic artists were careful to make the lack, or near lack, of clothing very clear in all imagery of women. Further, this explicitly portrayed female nudity occurred in a climate notably unconducive to "back-to-naturism."

▸ Where there is enough detail to assess age, these images portray women in prime reproductive years, from seventeen to forty. There is a virtual absence of infants, underage girls, and very old women.

▸ There are numerous Paleolithic images of erect penises and florid vulvae. These primary sex organs are visually laden with erogenous impact in all cultures.

▸ We noted that most women are portrayed as full-figured and sometimes even corpulent. Such curva-

Could these be just meaningless abstract designs on rounded pieces of ivory? **A**, La Madeleine, Fr. **B**, Lortet, Fr. **c**, Gourdan, Fr.

Nude figure from Kostenki I, Rus., showing a ropelike band between wrists. Bondage in the Pleistocene?

ceousness biologically underwrites and socially signals fecundity. Parallel evolutionary processes have tuned the attention of men to take note of and read these signals with keen expertise. Such curves today retain their vitality as releasers of erotic appeal.

▶ Paleolithic artists dramatized female hips, thighs, breasts, and buttocks, enhancing the same fat depots evolution had already exaggerated in-the-flesh. These female body "hot spots" are areas of heterosexual male erotic interest.

▶ The reciprocal of the above pattern is the de-emphasis or omission of non-erotic (or less explicitly erotic) elements. We find many images that omit feet, hands, arms, faces, or such details as ears or eyes.

▶ The body posture of many images in Paleolithic art dramatically exposes genitalia and/or secondary sexual traits. Many of these postures convey sexual invitation.

▶ The kinds of imagery that form the typical genre of erotica today seem to have equivalents in Paleolithic art. These portrayals range from the typical (e.g., erections, enlarged breasts and buttocks, erotic female postures, exposed vulvae, shaved or omitted pubic hairs, ornamented nudity, copulation scenes) to the more exotic (e.g., woman-woman sex, transsexuality) and from the more sophisticated (e.g., beautifully carved figurines) to crude graffitiesque scribbles (e.g., stylized vulvae, coarsely scratched copulation scenes).

▶ Finally, there is a consilient link to the fact that in all cultures young males are the age and sex who physiologically have the highest libidos but are most restricted in their access to sex. The amateur artists of coarse erotic images and sexual graffiti on all continents of the world today are young guys. There are theoretical and evidential reasons to think this link prevailed in the Paleolithic as well.

In conclusion, there is ample evidence of erotic emphasis in a number of images from our collection of Paleolithic art. Then why has this not been widely acknowledged? Perhaps it is because this thread, which often transgresses into crudity, may not always be experienced as erotic but rather as strange or offensive. After all, we tend to look for some kind of beauty in art. But I submit to you that among the dramatic beauty of horse and bison so present in this old art, there also lie earthy and poignant insights into our human kinship. Occasional crudity is part of that array and may be a critical piece of the complex dynamic that eventually leads most young males to more mature sexual attraction, to good loving, and ultimately to good fathering. This thread of sensuality, and sometimes crude coarseness, discernible in some of the Paleolithic art is a normal part of male development. We do not need to mystify, deny, or idealize what it is, just recognize some traces of its presence. And that recognition may still be appropriate even in museum displays, glossy art books, traveling art exhibits, or other rather sanctified settings where it may now seem highly incongruous.

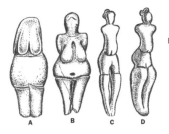

Erotic images of women often include partial dress, which seems to be more erotic than complete nudity. Pleistocene women wearing only long boots or stockings: **A**, Pavlov, Czech. **B**, Dolni Věstonice, Czech. **C–D**, Two late prehistoric Eskimo carvings from Thule.

Some caves contain a variety of quick-scratched vulvae, and one of those caves is Les Combarelles, Fr. Triangles are a repeated genre in graffiti and are often salted in among other common images found in Paleolithic art.

Next we will review some other explanations for the full-figured women in Paleolithic art and give some historical context to these different ideas as well as identify some of the political-ideological positions at stake. And finally, we will return to our theme of human evolution, pair-bonding, good parenting, and quality-plus kids.

Controversies behind Sex, Nudity, and Genitals in Paleolithic Art

Wishful thinking, therefore, permeates the search for human sexuality in Paleolithic art.   P. Bahn and J. Vertut, *Journey through the Ice Age*

Images of nude women have long been recognized as a part of Paleolithic art. Nude figurines were found at the French sites of Laugerie-Basse and Trou Magrite-Suscite in 1864. Since then, dozens more nude images of women have been recovered from the Paleolithic, from a wide geographic area beyond France: Germany, Russia, Czechoslovakia, Ukraine, Italy, Austria, and The Netherlands. Many authors have proposed different interpretations to account for these images in a wide assortment of scientific papers and books.

The most influential interpretation has claimed that the nudes were goddesses, and this magico-religious paradigm commandeers much of the limelight even today. But there are other interpretations. In fact, there are at least five books specifically directed at interpreting Paleolithic female images, four from France (Delporte 1979, later version in 1993; Duhard 1993; Nougier 1984; Cohen 2003) and one published in Belgium (Lansival 1990). Several others treat the topic more obliquely. In his first book, Delporte (1979) reviewed a number of hypotheses but did not accept one over another. Duhard (1993) proposed that Paleolithic art is a lost language whose symbolism is unknown and noted the interesting realism in much of the imagery, particularly images of women, which he interpreted as fat and/or pregnant. Nougier (1984) placed Paleolithic images of women in a context of magic and sexuality. Lansival (1990) concluded that these images were part of a symbolic language about the religious and sacred.

I explored the underlying erotic character of certain Paleolithic images (Guthrie 1984b) and only later discovered that others had done so before me (e.g., Absolon 1949). In his last book on the subject, Delporte (1993) also seems to lean more toward recognizing some aspects of eroticism. Actually, erotic interpretations of Paleolithic art have been mentioned in a number of publications. Studies of eroticism and sex in history and prehistory have often used Paleolithic images as illustrations of prehistoric erotica (e.g., Taylor 1996). Still, this erotic angle, and its implications, generally tend to be avoided in broad discussions about Paleolithic art, and popular treatments pay their respects to some vague goddess idea.

THE MAGICO-RELIGIOUS PARADIGM AND FAT, NAKED VENUSES

Many art historians and anthropologists have assumed that Paleolithic figurines were made and used as part of widespread cult practices or worship (the "Venus" label, of course, inherently implies that). It has also been assumed

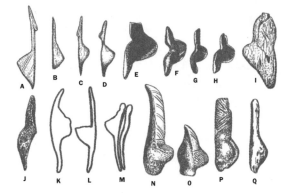

Some Paleolithic figurines are so highly abstracted that they are hardly recognizable unless you are familiar with this gradient of erotic distillation. **A**, Gönnersdorf, Ger. **B** and **I**, Andernach, Ger. **C**, Nebra, Ger. **D**, Thuringe, Ger. **E–H**, Petersfels, Ger. **J**, Mas d'Azil, Fr. **K–M**, Altamira, Sp. **N–Q**, Mezine, Ukraine. Though abstract the crucial curves are retained.

Steps in the carving of Paleolithic figurines (at least in one region) are revealed in this unfinished blank of ivory from Gagarino, Rus.

Forms similar to those from the Paleolithic are found in Holocene age rock art in Kom Ombo, Upper Egypt. They are the product of an entirely different culture, but I propose that they were made by people of the same age and sex, driven by similar pleasures, as were comparable Paleolithic images.

that these little figurines were made only during a short episode in Paleolithic history. Gamble (1982) proposed that European Paleolithic figurines occurred for only 2000 years—between 23 and 25 thousand years ago (ka). While many figurines date within this bracket, not all do. Bednarik (1995) emphasized that the Galgenberg figurine dates from an earlier time, around 30 ka. Soffer (1987) pointed out that the Eliseevichi figurines date from much later, 13–17 ka, and that those from Kostenki I date from 14 to 24 ka and those from Avdeevo from 12 to 23 ka. More recently, a very small figurine (31 millimeters), dated between 13.5 and 13 ka, was found at Enval, securely in the Magdalenian. So, these little figurines do scatter throughout the time range of other Paleolithic art.

This implies that the emergence and reemergence occurred because female nudity was an inherent and recurring interest to Paleolithic artists, just as were bison and horses. We do not need to assert an unbroken 20-millennium-long Paleolithic cultural tradition of drawing bison and horses for some secondary purpose, because for generation after generation the lives of people revolved around horses and bison. The same principle holds for erotic images.

Soffer (1987) has remarked on the widespread occurrence of diverse forms of nude female figurines among other cultures, images that are similar to those from the

Paleolithic. She proposed that this "diachronic fidelity" might represent some kind of cognitive or symbolic female category. I think it does—a rather elemental one—the sociobiology of which we've just retraced.

As for the possible functions of Paleolithic figurines, one can find many to choose from in the literature. Hancar (1940) argued that the figurines lacked any indication of erotic form. At the other extreme, Fisher (1979) proposed that researchers have concealed the high frequency of female sex organs represented in Paleolithic art. Instead of interpreting this as a puritanical attempt to conceal erotica, she thinks that many of the Paleolithic artists were, in fact, women and that later male researchers suppressed the extent of female imagery in an attempt to conceal the role of females as artists. McCoid and McDermott (1996) proposed that the exaggerated size of the breasts and buttocks of Paleolithic figurines reflects the distorted perspective of the female artists' self-inspection view—over their shoulders or behind their backs. They suggested

These are possibly abstract versions of the female figure. From Paleolithic art caves: **A**, Nerja, Sp. **B–C**, Le Portel, Fr. **D**, Altamira, Sp. (reversed for comparison). **E**, Pileta, Sp. **F**, Chufin, Sp. **G**, Tito Bustillo, Sp. (Compare to Henry Moore on p. 352.)

that the figurines document women's seeking to gain and preserve knowledge of their own bodies.

Parallel to the above, little-noticed, scholarly discussions, a major public drama has been unfolding, centered on using these little figurines from prehistoric art as symbols of a lost past when women were all-powerful keepers of order, when matriarchies dominated, and when the gods were mothers.

MUTTER GOTTESS AND THE MATRIARCHY MOVEMENT OF THE NINETEENTH CENTURY

It is true . . . that all the claims so glibly made about societies ruled by women are nonsense. We have no reason to believe that they ever existed . . . men everywhere have been in charge of running the show . . . men have been the leaders in public affairs and the final authorities at home.
    Margaret Mead, in S. Goldberg, "The Erosion of the Social Sciences"

Why are mother goddess ideas so persistently associated with these Paleolithic women figurines? I think it is because it is the most potent and direct way to mystify them. The result is a comfortable fuddle. There is certainly little empirical evidence for mother goddess interpretation. Rather, it seems it is tied to an old tale that won't die. That tale dates to early-nineteenth-century theoretical historians who proposed a distant matriarchal golden era. These historians saw human development progressing from an original disorder of roaming hordes with unconstrained promiscuous sexuality to a first-stage social order characterized by matriarchy.

Early writers liked the story of the Amazons. Both Hippocrates and Herodotus mentioned them. Building on this and other ideas, a Swiss jurist, Johann Bachofen, in an 1861 book entitled *Das Mutterrecht* (English translation, 1967), espoused an early matriarchal stage in human history. Subsequent discoveries of Paleolithic figurines nourished these ideas, which were taken up by Lewis Henry Morgan, who included a matriarchal stage in his grand view of historical development. Friedrich Engels leaned heavily on Morgan's ideas, and these in turn were used by Karl Marx, who postulated a matriarchal order as the original social structure. Versions still thread through postmodern Marxist-influenced ideology.

Anthropological and archaeological evidence does not support the universality of a matriarchal phase in human societies (Goldberg 1996). While matrilineal and matrilocal societies do exist and have existed widely, there are no documented matriarchal societies (Hrdy 1981). Analysis by anthropologists has illustrated the illogic of using figurines to argue for matriarchy (Childe 1951). But with Marx's blessing (Fluehr-Lobben 1979) notions of a golden age of matriarchy remain indelibly writ in many popular views of human history. Books by Gimbutas (e.g., 1982) and Ann and Myers-Imel (1995) have led many lessinformed readers to take these purported mother goddess/matriarchy ideas as a matter of faith and fact. Such ideas have become the central metaphor in some narrowly feminist rewrites of history.

Baring and Cashford (1991), in their book *Myth of the Goddess,* review the history of the mistaken idea of the universal goddess of presumed past matriarchal societies. The idea of a historic stage of a universal goddess and/or matriarchy has been abandoned by most scholars. Anthropologists such as Fluehr-Lobben (1979) and Hrdy (1981) have concluded that matrilines are the product of Holocene tribal horticultural economies, where women worked the land and kinship logically passed from mother to daughter. But this is not matriarchy.

POST-PLEISTOCENE "VENUSES"

Ucko (1968) studied miniature female figurines from Predynastic Egypt, Neolithic Crete, the prehistoric Near East,

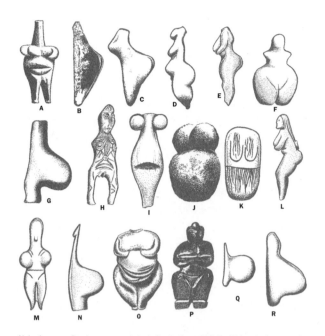

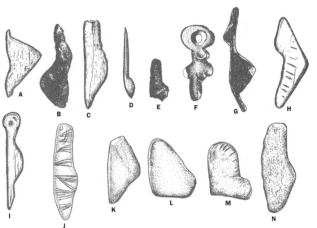

Naked-women figurines somewhat similar to those in Paleolithic art also occur in later cultures: **A**, Cernavoda, Romania (ca. 7000 B.P.). **B**, Predynastic Egypt. **C**, Macedonia (ca. 7800 B.P.). **D**, Prehistoric Eskimo, Southampton Island. **E**, Hagar, Malta. **F**, Tell Azmak, Bulgaria. **G**, Vinca, Neolithic. **H**, Okvik Eskimo. **I**, Cernica, Romania (ca. 8000 B.P.). **J**, Asturias, Sp. **K**, pebble from Kamikuroiwa, Japan (probably Paleolithic). **L**, Podolina, Ukraine. **M**, Cyclades (ca. 8000 B.P.). **N**, Cavdar, Bulgaria. **O**, Neolithic Turkey. **Q**, Lepenski Vir, Yugoslavia. **R**, Crete, Neolithic.

As I said earlier, many erotic Pleistocene figurines are highly stylized. These afford a test as to whether the emphasis in these "Venuses" is pregnancy or fat. Most of these figurines have protruding buttocks and occasionally large breasts, but seldom protruding abdomens. The emphasis is clearly on erotic appeal, not pregnancy. **A**, Ölknitz, Ger. **B**, **E**, and **G**, Gönnersdorf, Ger. **C**, Hohlenstein-Stadel, Ger. **D**, Koenigsee-Garsitz, Ger. **F**, Grimaldi, It. **H**, Krasnÿi Yar, Rus. **I**, Fontalès, Fr. **J**, Byci Skála, Czech. **K** and **N**, Dobranitchevka, Rus. **L–M**, Pilismarol, Rus.

and mainland Greece and found no evidence that these post-Pleistocene figures functioned in religious roles. These figurines of women, constructed from a variety of materials, were found in different contexts (household, outside household, tomb, etc.) and were quite variable in form. These figurines are generally plump and frequently obese and some are in a bent-knee position (close to the lordosis posture). Virtually all of these Neolithic images are nude. He recounted the nineteenth-century origins of this widespread misconception about matriarchy and its influence on explanations of the "Venuses" in Paleolithic art as well as in later prehistoric art. He found no evidence for these female figurines functioning in a religious role.

In sum, while I am inclined to agree with Gimbutas (1982) and many other authors in seeing similarities between Paleolithic and later female figurines, obviously I would attribute this "continuity" quite differently.

Meskell (1995) reviews this controversy in "Goddesses, Gimbutas, and 'New Age' Archaeology," pointing out a considerable lack of evidence and discrepancies in the matriarchal/goddess ideas.

TALISWOMAN OF DESIRE: PREGNANCY OR LUST?

Second only in popularity to the goddess theory is the explanation that these little figurines represent fertility magic—that they were used in some way by people trying to remedy an inability to become pregnant. However, Ucko (1962, 1968) contends that most archaeologists who have attributed fertility magic to figurines from post-Pleistocene archaeological sites have done so without much evidence. Certainly, there is no evidence at all that Paleolithic figurines were used to induce pregnancy. In fact, it looks as if the social preoccupation with fertility and its imagery came after the Pleistocene. Stored grain surpluses in the Holocene ensured more reliable calories; however, a dependency on carbohydrate staples gave rise to new nutritional deficiencies. For example, balanced amino acids are required for successful reproduction, and apparently both the Zuni from the Southwest United

States and the Snufo from West Africa had nutrition-related fertility problems on a carbohydrate-rich maize diet (Armelagos et al. 1984). It is probably not coincidental that fertility images were used among the Zuni and Snufo (Ehrenberg 1989).

Increased fertility is not a universal desire, however. In a hunting economy dependent on large terrestrial mammals, children require great amounts of time and investment before they are productive members of the society, and until that time they are a significant drain on limited resources. Lee (1979) found that Bushman women did not regard high fertility as an asset. Proper birth spacing is particularly important (Blurton-Jones 1987). To achieve this !Kung Bushman have stringent postpartum sex taboos during the first years of a baby's life. A pregnant woman who already had a child under two would often kill the new baby at birth.

Barrenness is a sorrow among most peoples, but extravagant production of a large family in a hunting society is definitely not an unqualified windfall. Forager societies may have the occasional need for a cure for barrenness, but it is not institutionalized as in tribal communities (Treswell and Hansen 1976; Howell 1979).

The tribalist formula is about population expansion and growth. Among most agriculturists or pastoralists, because of the different kinds of work to be done, even small children can be economic assets. Large families are sought after, and fertility of the land and the family are almost identical in net effect on increased stores of surpluses, so it is little wonder that large numbers of wives, children, and livestock are equated with wealth among traditional herders and farmers. Both women and men are obligated to produce. In most Bantu-speaking African groups marriage is not considered sealed until the wife bears children; if she proves barren, both the bride and the bride-price may be returned. Rather than encouraging fertility, the main intervention in a Paleolithic economy would have been to actively reduce reproduction and to emphasize quality children (Colinvaux 1979).

Sexual appetite is a much greater proximate driving force in human behavior than desiring pregnancy. We can reject the explanation of "fertility" as a major motivation of late Pleistocene artists. Of course, to acknowledge an erotic emphasis in these little Pleistocene figurines does not mean they were only and always used as someone today might use erotica or pornography. Other cultural expressions, even religious rites, are possibilities. Acknowledging the figurines' erotic potency does not specify their exact use. Just as today, attractive images of women of reproductive age are enlisted in a variety of settings—where each employs the associated appeal of erotic punch.

On Love and Lust—and Good Parenting

But if they cannot contain, let them marry: for it is better to marry than to burn.

Corinthians 7:8

In the last four chapters we have looked at the ways in which evolutionary drivers of human nature revolved around quality parenting of quality children. Now, it is time to reiterate and connect these threads of love and art with that larger theme. Love is the special bond that supports a couple in their parental role. The evolving human-style hunting niche depended on such a bond because it required cultivated individuals with the capacity to raise equally nurtured and able offspring. Szalay and Costello (1991) picture fat-filled breasts and buttocks as supporting a persistent erotic signal of attractiveness—not a concealed estrus but rather a *perpetual* estrus. These were organs to hold a mate, and this is something rather new among primates.

Most researchers trace the evolution of this perpetual estrus to females' influence on male behavior (Wrangham and Peterson 1996): to gain the favor of and protection by/from males. If that was the beginning, human bonding added something else. No longer was bonding built only around provisioning and sex. The focus evolved to en-

Kids, stooped postures, large breasts, and love and lust intertwine in human evolution and in Paleolithic art. Two figures from La Marche, Fr.

Smiling Pleistocene lady, Veneri (Parabita), It.

compass the pleasures of marriage and parenthood. For humans, sex was then transformed from the entrée to the dessert of bonding. But desserts can be important. Sexual attraction and sexual pleasures are a sustaining ingredient in the mix that made two individuals a couple, and this pleasure ultimately became an integrated symbol of romantic love.

Thus, strange as it seems, the uniquely human bio/ social organs of female breasts and shapely buttocks are linked to greater marital interdependence and a greater devotion to child care and the preparation of children for adulthood. These fat-filled erotic releasers are symbols of male involvement in quality parenting. One has to catch the light just right to see all this written in the little figurines, but I propose it is there.

Similarly, we can imagine Paleolithic erotic imagery as archaeological fragments—the shards and litter of individuals on their way to developing that special way humans love. If not yet, then soon that young boy who is scratching the coarse vulva onto the cave wall is going to be smitten with something even more powerful than his playful fantasy: it is the mighty blow of serious romance. Solid bonding relied on the powerful clutch of that wonderful and disturbing emotion, the wellspring of which came from growing up with good parents and from genes dedicated to the capacity to love. But that wasn't all. Human mate-bonding grows from the core ache of deep organic attraction to another person's body lines, soft touch, and sweet musky smells. Those sensual attractions do not come from nowhere—they start early and begin to blossom long before they can be put to serious use. Their de-

velopment depends on years of nurturing hope and fantasy. Vulva outlines on yellow cave walls and figures with pendulous breasts carved from flakes of creamy-white ivory portray the emotions required by that development. These erotic relics afford a glimpse into a part of life that ties us to people throughout time and, in an indirect way, to the long history we share with other mammals.

So these distant ancestors, in good humor, made marks of passion and desire in ivory and on limestone walls. We have these incidental trails of overwhelming obsession. They are not the refuse of illicit orgies nor are they the accouterments of holy shrines, just casual breasts and vulvae scattered in among lines of tail and antler—marks that played with the brain and made life more interesting.

❧

No bigger than my palm, you emerged from a white tusk flake, little trollop of lust. The warmth of your ivory curves gave delight. And polished from tender touching, you were gifted, hand to hand, a scarlet maiden for many seasons. Until, out of grasp one night, little lady, you slipped the ties of men, and were lost, trampled into the rock shelter's red earth. Buried and untouched in your rosa bed, you were a silent witness beneath the berths of generations. Who among your old lovers would have guessed that, resurrected and reformed, you would today rest, a Museum Goddess, on the finest velvet bed, a steel vault your wall of chastity, virgin art, Treasure of the State.

The Evolution of Art
Behavior in the Paleolithic

One of the great mysteries of human evolution is the sudden outburst of art
of a very high quality in the Upper Paleolithic.

Julian Huxley, in D. Morris, *The Biology of Art*

Homo aestheticus né *Homo ludens*

The origins of art making have always been a mystery.
Art is such a marvelous human peculiarity, so distinctive of our kind, and yet it is remarkably unillumi-
nated by a century of evolutionary inquiry. The latter
has generally exhibited a blind eye to the organic nature of art making and has tended to stall out when
faced with this aspect of human life, stiffly saying art
must be an epiphenomenon, some inexplicable evolutionary spin-off of being human. But let us look again
at the *nature* of human art making, this time through

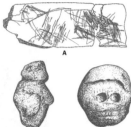

II have emphasized the bloom of visual art in the last 40,000 years, but that is not to say that some underlying dimensions of this behavior were not there long before. There are small scraps of early fun among artifacts from hundreds of thousands of years ago. **A**, Bilzingsleben, Ger. **B**, Berekhat Ram, Israel. **C**, Makapansgat, R.S.A. The subjects chosen even back then should be familiar to you.

We have seen that people drew what was on their minds, a stone to fit every bison, or a bison to fit every stone. But why engrave bison on stones in the first place? La Marche, Fr.

At a different level we can ask why were these people of all stages of development and experience making any kind of art? **A**, Rochereil, Fr. **B** and **E**, Gabillou, Fr. **C** and **H**, Altamira, Sp. **D**, Niaux, Fr. **F** and **K**, Isturitz, Fr. **G**, Villars, Fr. **I**, Abri de la Souquette, Fr. **J**, Montespan, Fr. **L**, Mayenne-Sciences, Fr. **M**, Vogelherd, Ger. **N**, Nancy, Fr. **O**, Labastide, Fr.

the wider aperture of natural history's lens. This approach has provided insight into organismal order underlying human patterns in courting and mating, nurturing babies, raising children, securing food, competing, and cooperating and sharing. We can readily see links to genetic fitness as well as ways in which our patterns in these matters are related to counterparts in other mammals.

Approaching the problem from that angle may reveal that art making has adaptive roots. Can we talk about an evolutionary history of art making as we might trace the history of gall bladders or nesting behavior? Is there anything a natural historian can contribute to the discussion of why Paleolithic folks were scratching forms in ivory and mixing ocher to paint on walls, decorating their clothes and tools, and coiffuring their hair? A natural historian's presumption of some coherence in these choices is not based on ideas of natural perfection nor is it a reductive nothing-but-biology view. It is rather a respect for the deep consilience which only time can render.

The abundance of art from the late Paleolithic challenges more utilitarian notions of productive and purposeful activity. Couldn't those painters have been making a warmer house or taking out the garbage to make a healthier campsite? Surely, there was more directly productive work always waiting to be done. Perhaps our attachment to practical activity is why scholars have so repeatedly sought and speculated on the *purposes* of this old art—wondering whether these images were made to please the gods, to bless hunts past or those to come, to dramatize a shaman's visions and hallucinations, or to initiate youngsters. Could this insistent pursuit of art's purpose be mistaken? Is it conceivable that art making advanced reproductive fitness in a different way from time spent repairing the weirs or producing extra raingear for emergencies?

I think so, and propose to sketch from my perspective the immense evolutionary importance of art making and its enjoyment in our human lineage. Indeed, those behaviors are so much a part of our experience that they are not readily apparent. Therefore, I will try to lay out the case that we are an art-making animal.

By "art making" I mean a certain class of actions that are not overtly necessary for the operational demands immediately linked to reproductive fitness. This broad sense of art would include many activities that appear to be just "playing around." And, in fact, that is my thesis, that art making is a uniquely evolved offshoot of play. Ethologists

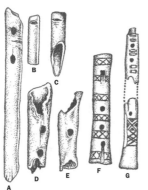

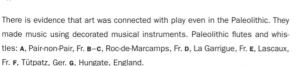

There is evidence that art was connected with play even in the Paleolithic. They made music using decorated musical instruments. Paleolithic flutes and whistles: **A**, Pair-non-Pair, Fr. **B–C**, Roc-de-Marcamps, Fr. **D**, La Garrigue, Fr. **E**, Lascaux, Fr. **F**, Tütpatz, Ger. **G**, Hungate, England.

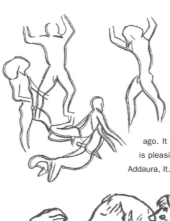

A Paleolithic wrestling match? We do not need images like this to know that young men played rough games of fun and power tens of thousands of years ago. It is one of the human universals, but it is pleasing to see that truth engraved so boldly. Addaura, It.

Pleistocene players? La Marche, Fr.

recognize that play is a complex adaptive trait and is an important feature in the biology of many species.

We know that some human play is similar to the play of other animals: rough-and-tumble fighting play, playing with objects, sexual play, locomotor play, social play, and so forth. But human play ranges wider and is very diverse. By human play I include not only the many things we recognize as child's play but also team and solo sports, humor, perhaps recreational shopping, and even daydreaming—particularly daydreaming, that rich fantasy world which consumes so much of one's day. In fact, new evidence might even include night dreams.

Later we will look at how play occurs in specific adaptive modules, or clusters (e.g., social play, locomotor play), that activate innovation and serve as practice for adult behavior. The human niche demanded a whole new level of innovation and imagination, requiring a radically new module beyond play. I will propose that art making in its most comprehensive sense is that module. In that role, though it apparently evolved as a transformation of more familiar primate play modules, art making functioned to activate and flex uniquely human creative capacities.

Though art making can appear to be closely related to other kinds of human play, and perhaps can arise in hu-

man play at any moment, I would like to distinguish art making as a kind of magnified play; it is play that creates and inhabits, as it were, a new and distinctly human dimension. The adaptive forces we see in play are magnified in art—you might imagine it as play-squared. Art making entails a vivifying awareness of the stuff of life. It is the concrete expression of aware experience and imagination, creating unique "art-stuff" that can be oil on canvas, music or story, sculpture, dance, fine food, play, poem, novel, movie, or a body made more interesting by dress, grooming, and other adornment. Much art is also involved in designing, making, and maintaining a pleasant shelter and surroundings. Architecture creates a "place" or fails to create one. And, certainly, art making is present or fails to be present in the sciences and other scholarly fields.

Let me add the obvious, if less easy to articulate, corollary: there is another sort of creative-vivifying event going on whenever we receptively engage a form of art-stuff—when we listen to another's story or music, when we appreciate someone else's good meal, a wonderful streetscape, or a scientific or historical insight, when we read a poem or enjoy a novel. Art making and art appreciating feed on one another; the capacities of each become static and stunted without their counterpart.

Let us acknowledge that most of one's day is made up of a collection of more or less elaborately artful activities,

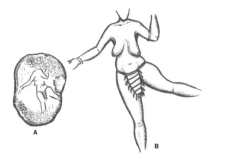

A, Scantily clad woman apparently dancing, Geldorp, Neth. Note design of G-string and bracelets. **B**, Reconstruction. Dancing, like other arts, is universal, but as with drawing the practice and expression of dancing vary considerably between cultures and individuals.

I have made the point many times already that much of Paleolithic art was done by people at an early stage in their artistic development, the very time when play dominates waking life. Here are a few lion images to keep reminding us of that point: **A**, Gönnersdorf, Ger. **B**, Bruniquel, Fr. **C**, Labastide, Fr. **D**, La Mouthe, Fr. **E**, Trois Frères, Fr. **F**, **G**, and **K**, Font de Gaume, Fr. **H**, La Marche, Fr. **I–J**, Dolni Věstonice, Czech.

Play has considerable costs of risk, time, and energy. Foals frolicking are a metaphor for those costs, and so are things like humans drawing frolicking foals. **A**, Paleolithic frolicking, Altamira, Sp. **B**, A much later Bushman painting, Brandewyn River, R.S.A.

often with scant direct or obviously productive components. For example, a strictly adequate meal might consist of nutritionally well-balanced, bite-size pellets of lab chow. But we don't stoop to that even when mountain climbing or in jails. Likewise, we don't all dress in a utilitarian norm but spend time tweaking our appearance for a blend that suits our sense of fashion, function, and fun—Mao's experiment in uni-dress failed for ethological reasons as much as for political ones. We are entertained by music, TV, reading, or games. We spend time decorating and maintaining our shelters and yards, even our offices at work. Expensively designed and marketed autos, computers, and other goods compete on many levels, and strict utilitarian function is a chimera. The examples can go on and on; in little or big ways, we play throughout much of our day. Art-making awareness and creativity can and do arise at any moment in this play—they are the next-of-kin—but it is the difference between art making and play that I want to emphasize here, and it is from their different evolutions that we can best see this.

Play is a biological emotional state separate from old utilitarian functions linked to our deeper evolutionary past. It is important to think in terms of play's several interrelated modular states. Play in species like ravens, turtles, and chimps can be informative about these modular states. If art making did evolve, its initial variants had to develop from somewhere. Perhaps when it comes to uniquely human capacities we may profit from taking a moment to see ourselves as an organism among other organisms. To do so here, we must start with play. Play is something we share with many other animal species, where it has the same origin and accomplishes similar functions.

The Adaptative Nature of Play

Here in Alaska ravens are always at home. And during the cold months, particularly, they seem to witness everything. Their wings whoosh and hiss as they row through the heavy air, faces frosted with the moisture of their breath. Everywhere I go, there they are, wheeling, doing

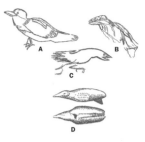

Many corvids (ravens, jays, etc.) hang around human encampments and follow hunters to glean the scraps. They are facultatively versatile creatures. **A–B**, La Marche, Fr. **C**, Gönnersdorf, Ger. **D**, Mal'ta, Rus.

Other cultures sometimes chose corvids as the subjects of their images: raven or crow from later prehistoric Hopewell culture of the Mississippi Basin, done in native beaten copper with pearl eye.

rolls and loop-the-loops. They jabber with weird clicks, honks, and burrs. Unlike the tiny red poll finches, intent at my feeder, ravens do a lot of fooling around. They show up in odd places, doing odd things. By any definition, ravens play a lot, both socially and individually. They are even known to roll down snowbanks sideways or slide otter style. Their aerial acrobatics are magnificent. Ravens are a daily reminder that play is not a uniquely human enjoyment. But why ravens? Why don't red polls play too?

THE PARADOXICAL PRACTICALITY OF PLAY

The short answer is that playing is observed in animals whose niches require versatility. Versatile lifeways seem to require a mode of learning that allows individuals to build on a genetically given behavioral base. The raven's genetic program itself has to do with refinement, flexibility, and opportunism. A red poll, on the other hand, keeps closer to a strict agenda. Bent on one main pursuit, it must find and eat birch seeds that have dropped in the snow, scrapping with competitors for this bounty and stuffing its crop for the cold night ahead. A raven's day is not so closely defined. Most primates, likewise, have a rather open-ended day. Ravens are to other birds what primates are to other mammals.

Primates simply play more than other mammals, and they excel in the business of versatility. Among primates, we humans are the big players. We are an opportunistic, innovative, and improvising organism par excellence. I have already spelled out my argument that the many interconnected traits surrounding that intelligence came from a unique style of large-mammal hunting. As I see it, we evolved as organisms that solved some highly rewarding problems *creatively*. Somewhat fortuitously, key human capacities that originated in solving Paleolithic-style savanna challenges were later applicable in other contexts. Our evolutionary line was progressively founded in situations characterized by change; that is, it was repeatedly subjected to novel problems requiring enterprising accommodation. Our evolutionary uniqueness is thus intimately linked to our biological potential to exploit unprecedented, newly minted opportunities.

But how does a species become biologically adapted to new horizons? What is biological flexibility of this sort? Adaptive processes are always a posteriori: present life is the legacy of what has worked in the past. There was—there is—no ready-made evolutionary module that creates a flexible and opportunistic animal. The roundabout adaptive solution was the modeling of some behaviors that indirectly facilitated mental and physical ability for sophisticated learning. The caveat was that the learning must be renewed every generation. The biological signature of this sort of program for individual education is *play*. Remember, this is characteristic of the Consigliere's indirect style: one doesn't eat to stay healthy but because food tastes so good; one copulates out of lust, not because one is dutifully following a set reproductive regimen. We learn and innovate best when we experience the added zest of delight, not from grim punch-the-time-clock determination. This may seem rather obvious, but a quick look around at the earth's other animal species will show how comparatively rare play is.

A PLAYLESS LIFE IS THE ANIMAL NORM

Most species do not play. No invertebrate plays, not bees, ants, scarab beetles, or mosquitoes—insects do not play.

Indeed, even relatively few vertebrates play. One might expect it of some fish; they are so diverse in almost every way that one might imagine that some ethologist would have discovered at least one fish species that exhibits play, but not so far. Nor do any amphibians play. And only a few unusual reptiles do so. Turtles, the most intelligent, slowest-maturing, and longest-lived reptiles, are known to play on occasion (Burghardt 1998).

The pattern is similar among birds. Very few species play, and, again, it is mainly the most opportunistic, the most facultative, and longest-lived birds—the parrots and corvids. Ravens are one of the corvids, along with crows, jays, magpies, and jackdaws. The raven niche in the north is remarkably enterprising. In the wild, ravens specialize in searching for large-mammal carcasses to scavenge or in following animals like wolves to feed off their leavings and feces. Traditionally, ravens often followed human hunters for the same reason. Today, ravens rely mainly on human camps, villages, and towns, an association I suspect is quite old. Corvids must have been the main camp followers in the Paleolithic. And in addition to pilferage and scavenging, ravens are fair predators of small game when given an opportunity.

FOOLING AROUND FOR FUN AND PROFIT

In contrast to the above groups, mammals are exceptional because all mammalian species play, though most mammals play only when young. Carnivores and primates exhibit the most play. And, notably, play is most highly correlated with opportunistic, facultative flexibility, and only secondarily with sociality. For example, bears and most mustelids, like mink and otter, are very playful, but they are not very social outside the nuclear family. The most elaborate play, however, seems to occur among social species.

Our nearest relatives, the chimps, are great players, but nothing like humans. Humans are distinguished both by an incredibly long and playful childhood and by the continued presence of play in adults. In fact, it is possible that

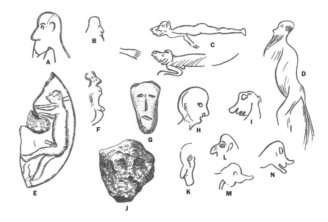

Were these rather elementary Paleolithic images done by people who were just fooling around? How can we account for so much playing in human behavior? **A** and **L**, Marsoulas, Fr. **B**, La Colombière, Fr. **C**, La Madeleine, Fr. **D**, Lourdes, Fr. **E**, Mas d'Azil, Fr. **F**, Pileta, Sp. **G**, Dolni Věstonice, Czech. **H**, Saint-Cirq, Fr. **I**, Gare de Couze, Fr. **J**, Romanelli, It. **K**, Font de Gaume, Fr. **M**, Isturitz, Fr. **N**, Rouffignac, Fr.

adult play is central to the adaptations of our species. It may be very literally true, not that adult humans play because we are young at heart, but rather that we remain young at heart because we must play. Our long developmental time seems to be tailored to foster the exercise of trial-and-error learning through imagination, driven by self-rewarding delight and interest—in short, fun, all the behaviors that we can best collect under the word "play." Many years ago Huizinga (1938) wanted to call us *Homo ludens,* the playful ape.

In sum, the ethological evidence suggests that the fun of play was the evolutionary answer to developing an animal that is intelligently flexible and opportunistically able. Play works this effect with limbic incentives, that is, enjoyments and pleasures. Playful species enjoy self-rewarding aspects of targeted kinds of play, because these potential enjoyments of playing entice and encourage an animal to do something, to be curious, to fool around. Of course, this kind of acquisition, trying out new moves and responses, involves making mistakes. Play is designed by evolution to diminish the effects of those mistakes. But not only does play exercise versatility, it also seems to in-

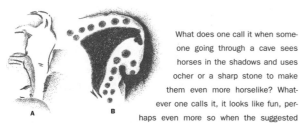

What does one call it when someone going through a cave sees horses in the shadows and uses ocher or a sharp stone to make them even more horselike? Whatever one calls it, it looks like fun, perhaps even more so when the suggested horse was standing on end as in **A**, Pergouset, Fr., or when shadows allowed one to make a horse image within a natural horse image as in **B**, Pech-Merle, Fr.

People from every culture play. In more recent times an Australian child stood straight up against a stone wall, arms outstretched, and another person spit ocher around the periphery, producing a prehistoric full-body print. The child stood 1.1 meters tall, so we can say he or she was most likely less than ten years of age. Eastern Bigge Range, Queensland.

herently *activate* experimentation. Play contains the seed, as it were, of flexibility and experimentation.

Ethologists discern behavioral modules, or clusters, of play activities. These are genetically tailored to the adaptive demands of each species, as in climbing play among goats and in biting play among carnivores. However, it is interesting that most kinds of play secondarily involve the whole brain, and certain play apparently integrates parts of the brain that are otherwise used for different specialties (Brown 1998).

Though play may have seemed to a Victorian Darwin as merely biological waste, we understand now that it is an essential and adaptive biological route to enhanced biological capacity. Play is keenly practical, but in a very roundabout way. The remarkable, two-decades-long dependency of human offspring is not meant to be spent in waiting for adulthood or in boring drill. Play may be "fooling around," but fooling around counts. Most juvenile learning and probably the best of our adult learning come from playful effort. Play is the writer, producer, choreographer, director, and actor of learning. The metaphorical cast, of course, are one's playmates, hence this book's dedication. And, just to reassure you, I am not wandering off from the pursuit of Paleolithic art; we are still on track.

We are evolutionarily tuned to learn best through playful activities that provide internally driven, self-rewarding fun. Games and play shape hand-eye coordination, nimble feet, endurance, strength, memory, word skills, reasoning ability, and other skills that activate and cultivate a sharper adult edge. Dolls and other toys let children recreate social and familial roles, to be explored later as adults. Rough-and-tumble play, wrestling, and tickling are more than calisthenics for adult fights. Among mammals sexual play is very important—young animals tease, feel, sniff, and mount, irrespective of gender. Group sports hone cooperative and physical skills for life's real contact sports. Selective forces shape deep patterns in human play, including social/team play, just as they do sparring play among bucks and fauns (Miller and Beyers 1998).

THE COSTS OF PLAY

I would like to have you understand the biological significance of play in a bit more detail before we return to our theme of art making. Play is so "natural" to us, so much a part of our way of life, and particularly our children's lives, that the challenge here is bringing it up to the forefront of our focus for some serious attention. Let's do that for a moment by examining some of the costs of play.

I was observing a ewe band of Dall sheep through binoculars in midsummer once and saw two lambs chasing back and forth across a precipitous rimrock above me. I was thinking what a beautiful lesson this was of how they come to be such agile adults. Then, my throat caught as one slipped and fell to its death. Not only does mammalian play require energy costs of some 4–10% of calories consumed (Martin and Bateson 1984), but many kinds of play also carry the risk of injury or even death (see a more complete review in Beyers 1998). For example, Harcourt (1991) found severe mortality costs associated with

Some young animals die in play accidents, and others use up precious energy that might have sustained them over difficult episodes. Two images from Paleolithic art that appear to be of young mammals: **A**, Arudy, Fr. **B**, Mas d'Azil, Fr.

play among South American fur seals, which were much more likely to be eaten by other seals when they were playing away from their mothers. Beyers (1977) found that ibex kids frequently had play injuries. Caro (1987) noted the indirect costs of play to cheetahs, as playing cubs reduced maternal hunting success. Such costs of play are noted in study after study of play in mammalian species. The persistence of play in the face of such strong selection pressure against it is itself a robust argument that play provides positive fitness advantages.

Consigliere solutions are often sloppy and approximate but they can never be far off target for too long. Natural selection would not have turned such a blind eye, tolerating this degree of waste. So it is legitimate to look for biological paybacks for play, understanding these may not be immediately apparent in the short term or even in every individual's lifetime.

In a broader sense, behavioral mistakes among adults are likely to diminish fitness; thus, selection favors adults who get something right on the first go (Frank and Frank 1987). Of course, adult mastery is one of the benefits of certain kinds of juvenile play. The developmental time and energy costs associated with play are so inordinately great that play would have been selected against were it not offset by substantial benefits. There is no other explanation of play behavior that is a credible contender to the hypothesis that play allows accumulation of developmental skills to cope with a more unpredictable adult future (Ewer 1968; Symons 1978). Earthworms and fruit flies mature quickly and never pause to play. But being a mammal means very high costs devoted to rearing each young, and we furry creatures must afford the expense of play to develop individual adult facility and capacity, thus the prodigious extravagance of human childhood.

Like the Paleolithic youths who climbed back into the dark caves, our early ancestors were, evolutionarily, given the time to play. Almost twenty years of support are demanded of human parents, and this is only part of the cost because childhood is demanding on the young themselves. During that time, in most subsistence societies, over half of the children die from mishap or disease. Baboons, in contrast, raise their young to maturity quickly, and their young are grandparents by the time we are teenagers. Natural selection strongly favors baboon-style rapid turnover unless there are considerable extenuating benefits. Our line paid—and pays—the price of the extravagantly long human childhood because all that playtime returns dividends applicable to our niche—in fact, they are requisite for our niche. My aim is that you value these evolutionary dividends—our human capacities—all the more by understanding just how dear is their biological price.

THE GENETIC COMPONENT OF THE PROPENSITY TO PLAY

This evolutionary tack of more learning gained through a long childhood was a difficult route because it involved acquiring facility and wisdom through many mistakes—and mistakes can be costly. The partial evolutionary fix for this was to create a sort of virtual world, paralleling the adult world, a vital playground of make-believe, where the penalties of failure were reduced, and yet successes were still rewarded. But how to develop this play behavior? As with most evolved traits, when it comes to propensity to play, all are not created equal.

As we have noted, mammalian species vary in amount and kinds of play, and these different propensities seem to be genetically specified. Furthermore, within any one species, all individuals do not play alike; some play more, others less. If we were to take one population and artificially

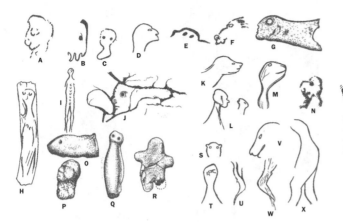

I need to reiterate and reiterate this theme: there are many rather crude attempts at people's faces and bodies done by Paleolithic folks who were just getting started in the arc of art development. **A**, Rouffignac, Fr. **B–C**, Font de Gaume, Fr. **D**, Los Hornos de la Peña, Sp. **E**, Lascaux, Fr. **F**, Villars, Fr. **G**, Roc-de-Marchamps, Fr. **H**, Laugerie-Basse, Fr. **I**, Bruniquel, Fr. **J**, Mas d'Azil, Fr. **K** and **P**, La Madeleine, Fr. **L** and **T**, Les Combarelles, Fr. **M**, Los Casares, Sp. **N**, Fontanet, Fr. **O**, Meersburg, Ger. **Q**, Dolni Věstonice, Czech. **R**, Maininskaya, Rus. **S**, Trois Frères, Fr. **U**, Niaux, Fr. **V**, Commarque, Fr. **W**, Courbet, Fr. **X**, Lourdes, Fr.

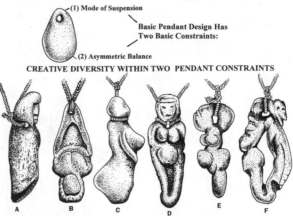

How to hang a pendant? Pendants consist of a mounting fixture and an asymmetric weight, as seen in this simple Paleolithic ivory pendant (*above*) from Geissenklösterle, Ger. But beyond this there are numerous design options (note suspension): **A**, Bédeilhac, Fr. **B**, Mal'ta, Rus. **C–F**, Balzi Rossi, It. (called "Innominate, Janus, Bicephalous, and Doublet").

select for the propensity to play, would there be a genetic response? Remember, one of the best ways to estimate heritability is from *selection response* (Alcock 1993), and here the outcome of domestications can be informative. Domestic animals, both pets and livestock, have undergone intentional selection (and perhaps inadvertent selection as well) for individuals that were more affectionate, tractable, and playful than ones we chose to cull (Morris 1986; Thomas 1993).

Wolf pups play during most of their nonsleeping hours, but as they grow older the amount of play decreases to where there is very little play among adults. But domestic wolves (dogs) are very different. Individual adult dogs of most breeds would be content to play all the time, even into old age. We train them via play by making games out of retrieving, search-and-rescue trials, herding, etc. Indeed, the zest that cats and dogs exhibit in their play is one of the most rewarding things about having them as pets. And it is their playfulness as well as affection that makes pets a bit like having children (Morris 1986).

Thus, while we don't know the heritability fraction for play behavior, we can see that selection has created a genetic response in a number of different lines of our domestic pets—and in our line as well. All this is strong suggestive evidence that the heritable fraction of play is significant among mammals, including us.

Social Invitations to Play

One characteristic shared by many kinds of play is a certain loose elasticity, even though play occurs in particular modes. In social play this elasticity is often paired with and preceded by a very specific gesture that signals "come play." In contrast to the play itself, these play signifiers or invitation gestures are quite stereotyped. It is as if these gestures not only signal "come play" but perhaps more properly "everything from here on is not for real, it is just for fun." Forms of play solicitation differ among species, but there is some cross-species continuity, especially among primates. Who could fail to recognize the monkey signals of a hidden peek (it will make a human baby smile more than any other gesture!) or the play face made toward babies, with wide eyes and a tight O mouth? Locomotor intention movements are also important play releasers; the gamboling, galumpfing gait, tagging, waving arms, and rolling over on the back invite wrestling. Many species use an open-mouthed play bite, a special controlled nibble.

Canids use specific behaviors to delineate social acts of play from serious reality. Darwin described the play bow, a shoulders-down, rump-up display among dogs, which both invites and demarks play. One might imagine it as built on a mixed metaphor, combining gestures of erect aggression and supine submission. Bekoff (1974) described a high leap and face-oriented pawing as another play marker for canids. Lions use a play bow similar to that of canids (Schaller 1972). There are many other forms of mammalian play invitation: a mongoose whips its tail, voles and field mice use a play pheromone, bears wobble their heads, and polecats have stiff-legged jumps (Wilson and Kleiman 1974; Morris 1990). The primate play invitation employs an open-mouth display with the face relaxed and the lip covering the upper teeth. Again, this signal combines mixed-metaphor elements characteristic of aggressive and submissive signals.

What are our own play-signifying behaviors? We mainly smile and laugh. These gestural metaphors com-

Bushman painting of two sparring young antelope playing at fighting. Most preserved Bushman art is later than Paleolithic, but it contains some similar features of subject choice and rendition. Worchester District, R.S.A.

A bronze pup in play-invitation posture. The sculptor used this familiar gesture to decorate a fountain in a public park.

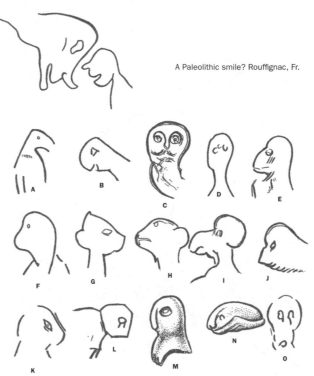

A Paleolithic smile? Rouffignac, Fr.

Paleolithic faces made by those not far along in their drawing development: **A–B** and **O**, Marsoulas, Fr. **C**, La Marche, Fr. **D–J**, Les Combarelles, Fr. **K**, Los Casares, Sp. **L**, Gabillou, Fr. **M–N**, Roc-de-Marcamps, Fr.

bine elements of aggressive and submissive signals. Primates and other animals that use teeth to bite their opponents have a reflexive aggressive gesture of a snarl, in which the top lip is lifted to expose the canines. We have the opposite metaphoric gesture for submission—pulling the mouth corners back to reveal the molars in a grimace, while hiding the canines. Just try it. Our play invitation gesture is a mixed metaphor of anger and grimace, a loose-lipped show of teeth, both the molars *and* the front teeth. It is our smile.

Active play among children is normally done from a high-arousal state. Apparently, this high arousal activates brain areas that facilitate learning. High arousal is also usually accompanied by heavy breathing or panting. Indeed, most primates include heavy panting, a metaphor of "vigorous play to come," as a play releaser. Chimps use the old primate open-mouthed inhalation-exhalation cycle, ha-huh-ha-huh (Aldis 1975). Humans use a derivation of this panting cycle, by deleting the inhalation portion and keeping only the repeated exhalations, ha-ha-ha-ha, of laughter (Guthrie 1976). Laughing and play go together. Children laugh more than adults, probably because they play more. Laughing kids are healthy kids; the cacophony

from school yards is dominated by laughter. Laughter is our main social signifier of the fun of play. At least one Paleolithic image shows a smile. And there are many that should elicit our smiles, if not laughs.

The *Nature* of Play

Behaviors can have specific smells: a smell for love, another odor for follow me, go where I have been, a smell for fight or panic, and so on. What is it like to communicate with smell? Consider the steamy traffic in an anthill or termite mound. Here, thousands of individuals in a giant family carry out intricate duties with great industry but with no leisure, no fantasy life, no holidays, and no jokes.

Play Addiction   Like most other vertebrates we have a pleasure center in our brains. Fun is the emotional experience when that center is activated by certain kinds of neural activity. The chemical at the center of this activation is the neurotransmitter dopamine, which can act as an addictive substance promoting learning. Some forms of addictions are adaptive. Kids go back again and again for things like carnival rides and often play at a favorite game over and over, beyond the point of parental patience. Insatiability is a frequent feature of play, providing such a charge that one does not want to give it up, cannot put it down, cannot stop. We should note that young people often become playfully addicted to aspects of art making as well. They can enjoy the same song over and over, redraw a favorite image with the subtlest of variations, or perform a favorite dance, read a favorite book, or watch the same video again and again. All the while parents must remind themselves: "It is normal for my child to do this. It is normal for my child to do this. It is . . . " What does this have to say about the taphonomy of art? It says that kids tend to produce their art in a continuous stream, and because of this, kids tend to do more art making than adults. And we should be alert to these patterns when we look back into the Paleolithic.

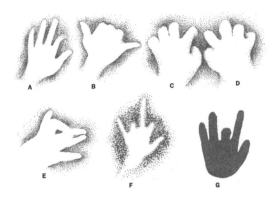

Lamp shadow games using hand images are a common children's game. It is but a slight shift to make a silhouette in ocher. **A–B**, Black Palace, Queensland, Austrl. **C–E**, Aztec, Yucatan. **F**, Baracoo River, Queensland, Austrl. **G**, Canyon de Chelly, New Mexico, U.S.A. (probably the hand was traced and then the interior painted), similar to Pleistocene hand prints.

Play addiction. Parents did not have to force Bushman boys to play at shooting straw dummies. Late Holocene painting, Epiphany Mission, R.S.A.

Yet they are successful beyond our imagination—these groups have dominated the earth's landscape for the last half a billion years. By weight they exceed us and our livestock. In fact, there are many more of these social insects than all vertebrates put together, may always have been, and perhaps always will be. Such lives, fully orchestrated by genetic prescription, are not passé; they are, quantitatively, the mainstream. And we should give due regard to their pheromonal perfections. Compared to them, we long-lived players operate at the margin of earth history, but the evolution of our costly flexibility out on the periphery involves other fascinating adaptations.

Let me review the argument that play, and art as a special kind of play, are adaptive. Recall that there are some basic criteria traditionally used to evaluate whether or not characters are biologically adaptive. In this instance the list might read as follows: (1) There are causal linkages between facultative ability and play, and the peculiarly human extension of play, art making, is linked with creativity. These connections are, in short, not mere behavioral epiphenomena. Rather, (2) play and art are improbably complex and coherent sets of behaviors. (3) Empirical evidence substantiates the logic that they result in reproductive fitness advantages, which (4) override significant evolutionary costs in time, risk, and energetics. (5) Their

Parpalló, Sp.

individual and group variations have a genetic component. (6) Play forms part of an evolutionary gradient and pattern among related organisms. (7) Play and art are universally distributed among all human groups. (8) In a larger way, this theory has broad explanatory powers superior to those of competing theories. If these propositions are credible, they can provide a unique context for viewing Pleistocene art and can help us understand the place of art and play in our lives.

My attachment of the evolution of play to behavioral flexibility is not new. A century ago, Groos (1901) proposed that play was an innate mechanism which directed adult development. Many ethologists and psychologists (e.g., Piaget 1964; Alland 1977) have clearly articulated connections between flexible behavior and play. I simply want to pull this thread out a bit farther and more explicitly link our remarkable art-making and art-enjoying abilities to those evolutionary roots. But before we go any further, I want to say that one problem in studying play and art making is that so many forms of these activities are not directly observable.

More examples to illustrate the childlike character of the artists responsible for much of Paleolithic art: **A** and **J**, Les Combarelles, Fr. **B–D**, Marsoulas, Fr. **E**, Labastide, Fr. **F**, Le Portel, Fr. **G**, Gabillou, Fr. **H–I**, Laugerie-Basse, Fr. **K**, Gönnersdorf, Ger.

Another sampler of the abundant drawings from early stages in art development: **A**, Mas d'Azil, Fr. **B**, Gönnersdorf, Ger. **C**, Gargas, Fr. **D**, Parpalló, Sp. **E**, Pair-non-Pair, Fr. **F**, Isturitz, Fr. **G–H**, Altamira, Sp. **I–K**, Los Casares, Sp.

IMAGINATION: THE BIGGEST PLAYGROUND OF ALL?

Much of human play, perhaps even most, remains unseen. I mean, of course, the play of imagination, daydreaming, or fantasy. This fantasy does sometimes leave traces. Is that what we see in Paleolithic art? I think so. It had to be the nucleus that generated most of Paleolithic art, as indeed it must underlie most art. That is why their art allows us a glimpse into their fancy, their imagination itself. Like them, we live amid relentless internal fantasy, not the TV show or mystery novel kind with rational flow but our own storytelling, story-making, disjointed commentary. Our brains are seldom still. They nimbly roll out the most pedestrian or Walter Mitty scenarios and run situation replays of what was, or should have been, said or done. We have considerable conscious control over these fantasies, retailoring and rewriting them to be more interesting, but they often take the bit and chase themes of their own making. This must be why so often when we talk with another person we are only half-listening. The rest of our attention is catching snippets at the cinema of the mind. We are, in essence, more playful than we think. The perspective of natural history reveals us as profoundly creative animals.

It is straightforward to propose that daydream fantasies evolved as calisthenics for creative thought, internally driven enjoyable play, a theater that keeps us in shape to function well in our unpredictable life as a truly facultative organism. We don't have to work at fantasizing; it is difficult to turn off. Fantasy seems to be important for our biological upkeep, like circulating blood or bone calcium turnover. This perpetual theater gives us a lot more experience and allows us to create ever newer and more elaborate stories than we could ever get in our "for-the-record" portions of the brain. These fantasies contribute to the brain's high metabolic rate, about 20% of our daily energy budget. When we stop fantasizing (as during successful meditation), our pulse rate and blood pressure drop noticeably, another reminder of the expensiveness of play.

Fantasy tends to throw a wrench into simple psychological studies that would associate play and creativity. Theoretically, we could test the association of art and creativity by examining the results of play deprivation—are people who live without play very uncreative? And we could ask whether artists are much more creative than nonartists. The answer to these questions from several studies seems to be yes (Brown 1998), but the problem is how to measure even less accessible dimensions of art or creativity, such as night dreams.

PLAYING, ON AUTOMATIC

As it was with art, for most of the twentieth century science was utterly lacking in insight into sleep and dreams, dismissing sleep as an epiphenomenon or mere byproduct. Experiments in the past decades have shown that dream sleep has important functions for health and well-being. We live in the theater of the mind all night (well not exactly all night—we take intermissions); during bouts of "rapid-eye-movement" (REM) sleep we run through the equivalent of a condensed week of surrealistic TV soap operas. As a daytime-adapted primate we have an average of 12 hours of downtime after dark. Why not put it to use?

We do. Researchers argue that dreams lubricate our learning processes and are critical for healthy mental

A collage of bears in Paleolithic art found at different sites. Note the varying levels of drawing development. **A**, Trois Frères, Fr. **B**, Venta de la Perra, Sp. **C**, Les Combarelles, Fr. **D**, La Colombière, Fr. **E**, Gazel, Fr. **F**, Lascaux, Fr. **G**, Massat, Fr. **H**, Dolni Věstonice, Czech. **I**, Laugerie-Basse, Fr.

Horses from one Paleolithic site, Les Combarelles, Fr. Most seem to have been done quickly in passing by people of an age-group who were not experienced drawers.

function. It is probably no coincidence that the animals most familiar to us, dogs and cats, who also depend on opportunistic learning, obviously have vivid dreams. Anyone who has lived around dogs or cats is familiar with their eye twitches, little whimpers and growls, and leg motions of running, all while they are asleep. Carnivores are opportunistic mammals that demand a lot of daytime play in their development. They go to night school as well, and this expends more energy than nondreaming sleep, at approximately the same rate as waking periods. Of course, young animals have much more REM sleep, and hence more dreams.

A Pleistocene bison calf apparently playing with its mother. Most play occurs among the young. Adult females usually play more than adult males, and you can see why by looking at this drawing— you have to have a sense of humor to raise kids. Which is to say that playing is crucial to development, and mothers often encourage it by being players themselves. Brassempouy, Fr.

A young artist from La Marche, Fr.?

Youthfulness and Playfulness

The lens of natural history throws a spotlight on the uniquely prolonged human childhood and on the neotenic extension of childlike elements into later, adult phases of life. A big part of that extension concerns play, and the specialized kind of play we call art. One seldom plays or makes art without expending time and energy, and the greatest free time and most abundant energy are always found among the young. Indeed, this is when most art is made now, and this was likely so in the Paleolithic as well. And little parental inducement is needed. Like all other forms of play, art is self-driven, self-rewarding. The natural history of youth and play thus becomes more important to our understanding of Paleolithic art because young people likely accounted for more of the preserved art than we usually imagine.

PLAY AND ITS CRITICAL PERIODS

One thing that strikes people who study animal behavior is the importance of developmental timing. Neural pathways in young animals have critical periods of maturity that correspond to the activities characteristic of a particular phase of development. Socialization, compass orientation, bird song, language, and many other features are formed during sensitive periods in a young animal's life. If not properly activated during that window, expected behaviors often do not develop in a typical fashion. Physical growth, the connection of neurons, synapse formation and elimination—in short, numerous aspects of brain development—are exquisitely time sensitive.

Among animals, play also seems to have just such distinct developmental periods, and some have been mapped (e.g., see Beyers 1998 for a review). Generally, mammalian play peaks in youth; however, newborns play little—at that age survival is tenuous, and meeting necessities seems to have been the main competitive focus of natural selection among newborns. Competition within the litter is most lethal at this point—for example, among owl nestlings and among fox and hyena littermates. That changes with time and play begins to increase. In a related way, a human infant's energies are focused on growth and nourishment in the first few months, and human mortality at that time is at its highest. Once past six to nine months, survival becomes more assured, and play continues to rise after that. For example, children peak in rough-and-tumble play between five and ten years of age (Ornitz

Trial and error. Though drawing involves getting down something that is on one's mind, often our drawings reveal that the details of our mental imagery are unclear. This look-draw cycle sharpens the mind's ability to see differently. Here are some redrawings from the Paleolithic . . . let's see, exactly how does this leg go? **A**, Teyjat, Fr. **B**, **E**, **G**, and **J**, Limeuil, Fr. **C**, Laugerie-Basse, Fr. **D**, Mas d'Azil, Fr. **F**, La Marche, Fr. **H**, La Colombière, Fr. **I**, Altamira, Sp.

1983). The percentage of the day devoted to other kinds of play continues to rise. Most forms of play generally decline on into adulthood.

It is obvious why play declines after adolescence among most mammals, especially among males. Serious things are at stake, and a frivolous miscommunication cannot be regularly risked. That is to say, the cost of that kind of play begins to outweigh its benefits. On the other hand, female mammals are more likely to play as adults, probably as part of caring for the playful young. For example, adult lion males virtually never play; whereas lionesses often do with cubs (Rudnai 1973). Humans, of course, continue playing into adulthood, but even there, many kinds of play characteristically peak during adolescence: competitive sports, exploration, adventure seeking, sexual fantasies, etc.

Csikszentmihalyi (1975) examined kinds of human play and how these changed with age: adventure-seeking, kinesthetic, object-fiddling, social, sex, creative-imaginative, and attentive play (people watching, watching TV, listening to radio). He found that all kinds of play declined after adolescence except social play. Kinesthetic play decreased most—do you like to go on breathtaking carnival rides as much as when you were fifteen?

Such observations, remember, were important when we tried to determine who went back into caves; adventure play peaks between eleven and seventeen. Recall those numbers from chapter 3? Play in youth seems crucial for healthy adult development. Sometimes the negative side of this is quite apparent. Deprivation of locomotor play during critical periods seems to affect adult abilities across a wide front (Beyers 1998). Play deprivation and/or play abnormalities when young are often noted among adults incarcerated as criminals and among those who become violent adults, alcoholics, and injurious parents (Brown 1998). More important for our concerns here is that experiments have shown that play among schoolchildren influences their ability to innovate (e.g., Dansky 1982; Dansky and Silverman 1973).

EXPANSION OF CHILDHOOD, EXPANSION OF PARENTHOOD

The natural history of play and art adds yet another angle to our view of the evolution of human parenting. Of course, the other side of the evolutionary coin of an expanded human parenting is an expanded human childhood. I have emphasized that one of the chief trends in human evolution must have focused on parental protection and care—a high investment in each offspring over an extended period of their lives. This neotenic trend kept children from reproductive responsibilities longer and longer. As with some social carnivores (lions, hyenas, wild dogs, suricates, wolves, and jackals), older sibs stayed with the parents and helped with the younger children, and a cohesive band of these families was formed, glued with genetic cement. Looking at desert kit foxes playing among parents and sibs, the term "family" for these groups is not stretched too thin.

Of course, the extensions of childhood and parenting were back-to-back, evolutionarily linked dynamics. They allowed more preparation for adult reproductive responsibilities and more time to absorb and retain vast quantities of information and hone problem-solving skills, especially aided by verbal communication. A complex language was undoubtedly the key catalyst in all this. Reproductive success increased with the direct help from older offspring, and parents added to their fitness by fledging increasingly quality-added young. Furthermore, human modes of play meant offspring became individuals with the plasticity to think for themselves, which was fostered by past success in decision making, which in turn was promoted by prolonged trial and error in the freedom of play.

LOVE AND PLAY

Pair-bonding, as well as parent-offspring bonds, probably feeds on this play process. There is something in the bonds between humans that is akin to play: smiles and giggles, expanded awareness, delight in one another, and the ability to enjoy imagining another's enjoyment—in short, the ability to love. The evolutionary extension of play into

Much of Paleolithic art at La Baume Latrone, Fr., has been described as modernistic Picassoesque greatness, but if similar images were found in any other place they would be called children's art. At La Baume Latrone dark terra rosa mud from the cave floor was picked up and smeared on the white limestone walls with fingers. Fortunately, we do not have to argue over the artists' identity because the mud smearers also pressed their whole hands against the walls, leaving positive prints. These clearly are handprints of adolescent boys.

Prehistoric target shooting, a form of Bushman archery play. Late Holocene, Epiphany Mission, R.S.A.

adulthood must have been linked to greater attachment and involvement of parents with children—simply delighting in playing with children and in child's play. We can see how that works in happy families today. And we can imagine that Pleistocene children who enjoyed a social context which featured bonded parents who were able to live among similar adults and children grew up to fledge offspring themselves who were better suited to the demands of the human niche. Indeed, it was a niche that required confident and creative intelligence and loving loyalty on the part of this increasingly novel animal, the human hunter.

Learning and Creating

The creation of something new is not accomplished by the intellect but by the play instinct acting from inner necessity. The creative mind plays with the objects it loves.

Carl Jung, quoted in E. Dissanayake, *Homo aestheticus*

Learning, or mastery of information, and creativity are related but different. We must remember to distinguish these related and easily confused siblings of mind. Teachers use methods that help students to learn certain material; teaching students to be more creative is a different

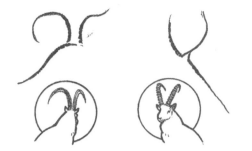

When an artist begins the risk of drawing, the results always fall short, to some degree, of the image he or she had in mind. The artists who made these two ibex from Niaux, Fr., experimented with some demanding perspectives. In the two circles are something like the perspective views I think they were trying for.

Experimentation in Paleolithic art. Some unusual Paleolithic images of head positions: **A**, Limeuil, Fr. **B**, Mas d'Azil, Fr. **C**, Trois Frères, Fr. **D–G**, Gourdan, Fr. **H**, Marcenac, Fr. **I**, Caldas, Sp. **J**, Levanzo, It. **K**, Les Combarelles, Fr. **L**, Chauvet, Fr.

matter. Report cards record learning, as IQ tests reflect the ability to learn. Creativity, on the other hand, has an aspect that is strangely antilearning. Learning, more often than not, includes an acquiescence to past paradigms, which can sometimes get in the way of new visions. Among other animals that do play, this play is largely about tailored learning, not about creating. However, extremely playful species, those with strongly opportunistic adaptations, not only share an ease of learning but can be very imaginative as well. Indeed, this is why ravens and monkeys make terrible pets. They are too inquisitive for most households, and these capacities in our domestic settings translate into trouble.

Despite some overlap between learning and creativity, the two have different qualities. This duality is often hazy to educators and can be downright opaque to administrators and politicians. The qualities of intuitive play—its creativity and, at times, breath-catching new vision—are elusive and very difficult to talk about. They may be impossible to define and yet remain essential to scholarship, to art—indeed, to being human. Creativity may be something we must catch as shadows or reflections, like a floater in the vitreous humor, as its processes cannot be captured by a direct gaze. But we can often recognize its products, and that is certainly what we see in ocher and ivory shaped by Paleolithic hands.

Generally speaking, learning has a different intensity from creativity. Most mammalian play, and its well-embedded learning, are often associated with such later, real-life, high-arousal activities as predation, flight, fight, copulation. During these high-arousal events it is very difficult to learn everything "on the job," particularly on the first job—thus the importance of play rehearsals. Gold's (1987) research showed that memory, and hence learning, are greatly affected by high adrenaline levels. This means that exaggerated high-arousal play is a much more effective learning path than tenuous, nondirected activity. Arousal itself accelerates the learning processes. Exciting fantasy gets entangled with the kinds of art kids make, as part of enhancing their learning processes.

While high adrenaline may sear lessons home, creativity does not necessarily benefit from high adrenaline. Rather, perceptive breakthroughs seem to occur more often during quasi-meditative states associated with walking, relaxing, reading, and sometimes even sleeping. Art making seems associated with quasi-meditative brainwave status. The heart of art making is particularly timeless. The combination of heightened awareness and full attention, this vivified state of being at creative play, is a fundamental part of the human character. Dissanayake (1992) has even proposed that we change the Latin name of humans to *Homo aestheticus,* the artful ape.

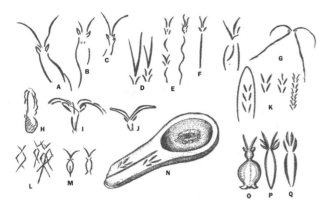

A single line playfully used as part of two images: **A**, Les Combarelles, Fr. **B**, Forêt, Fr. **c**, Gourdan, Fr. **D**, Laugerie-Basse, Fr. **E**, Gargas, Fr.

Some creative looseness can be seen in Paleolithic art that pertains to ibex. Those gigantic chevron-shaped horns almost begged to be integrated into abstract form. **A**, Otero, Sp. **B** and **E**, El Pendo, Sp. **c**, Urtiaga, Sp. **D**, Cueto de la Mina, Sp. **F**, Paloma, Sp. **G**, Niaux, Fr. **H** and **M**, Raymonden, Fr. **I**, Montgaudier, Fr. **J**, Morin, Fr. **K**, Lascaux, Fr. **L** and **O**, Laugerie-Basse, Fr. **N**, Lamp, Lascaux, Fr. **P–Q**, La Madeleine, Fr.

Now, Back to Art

This causal entanglement between art and play and creativity has been noted by ethologists and evolutionary biologists. For example, in his discussions of art as a kind of play, Fagen (1981, 1984) stressed the interrelations between behavioral plasticity and play, creativity and art. Olins (1992) pointed out that there is indication of play in Paleolithic art and emphasized the role of creativity in the play/art process. Here I make the additional proposal that natural selection for human creative plasticity was driven by our particular hunting-style lifeway.

This is not a mainstream idea. Though natural historians have seen that art could have evolutionary ties, there is disagreement as to how art and evolution are linked. Dissanayake (1992) reviews some of the ideas about the evolutionary role of art: to enhance communication (Alland 1977; Eibl-Eibesfeldt 1989a; Tiger and Fox 1971), as a means for individual display (Geist 1978; Harris 1989), to aid sexual selection (Low 2000), or to confer prestige (Harris 1989; Eibl-Eibesfeldt 1989a). Fagen (1981), as I said, proposes a direct link between art and creativity and, in a way, so does Dissanayake's idea (1992) about "making-

special" (see Bekoff and Beyers 1998 for critiques of these theories). My own view presented throughout this book is that play, art, and creativity are all linked to the process of our becoming large-mammal-hunting specialists. And, of course, in that context, childhood has a special importance.

THE ADAPTIVE ROLE OF ART: ARE ART ENERGIES SPENT PRODIGALLY?

For twenty-five hundred years of Western culture, the question, "What is art?" has been under constant consideration. Within the past two hundred years a major branch of philosophy has emerged, aesthetics, devoted solely to the attempt to answer that question. Few intellectual enterprises have so utterly failed; and to-day, it is seriously wondered if the question, "What is art?" can be regarded as a meaningful philosophical question at all.

M. Peckham, *Man's Rage for Chaos*

Throughout human evolution we retained most of our older primate play modules, but we evolved an additional kind of play. The whole lifeway of outwitting large mammals demanded not only that we be smarter but also that we be more imaginative, more creative. Creativity, the central part of humanness, is the activity in which we excel. But it does not emerge de novo: it has its special activator kind of play, a specialized kind of play module that more directly taught, and delighted in, true and beautiful innovation. What was that kind of play? It was art making. Art behavior evolved for creativity, the same way that lungs evolved for breathing.

Let me review an aspect of human origins as it relates to this topic. Before human ancestors began to play in this

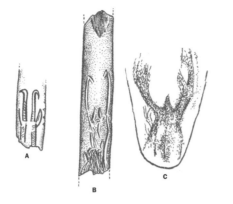

Creative foreshortening as viewed from behind: **A**, Chamois, Isturitz, Fr. **B**, Chamois, La Vache, Fr. **C**, Red deer, Mas d'Azil, Fr.

A, Playing in the Paleolithic? Fadets, Fr. Although nudity in this engraving on a stone fragment may suggest an erotic intent, this is a girlish figure with leg raised, apparently dancing. Dancing is a kind of play. Time spent playing generally declines with age in all mammals. To a degree this applies to humans as well, but we are different from virtually all other mammals in that adult humans still spend considerable time playing.

art module they must have been extremely committed players in the more conventional senses. From comparing our behavior today with that of other primates we can guess that early hominids played more than other apes when young but may not have brought much of that intensity of play to later life. Judging from complex anatomical evidence (brain development, the timing of tooth eruption, and body growth stages), researchers such as Bogin (1999) have documented the pattern of the lengthening childhood in early fossils of our genus (*Homo habilis* and early and late *Homo erectus*). I discussed possible reasons for that elsewhere, and will return to it later.

Whatever the reasons, this new species, *Homo sapiens*, apparently was subjected to greater biological demands on (or opportunities for) creativity than had existed prior to that time. But how could flexible opportunism be upgraded into genuine creativity? Apparently, the Consigliere could not find direct variations in some brain component for creativity. The problem had to be solved very indirectly. I think we can reconstruct the story of what happened. As it turned out, some play modules were already indirectly activating a facility for flexibility and exploration, and that was in the direction of creativity. So parts of these play modules were co-opted, reorganized, and retrofitted in the cause of pure creativity.

Apparently, the ability to obtain and communicate new insights demanded its own kind of virtual-reality module—a new kind of play, not like wrestling play, which developed various fighting abilities, and not like

object play, which helped us manipulate an array of tools. Rather, it was a kind of play that was specifically targeted and specifically dedicated to exploring and sharing new perceptions. For that, only the playfulness of art would suffice.

SELECTIVE ADVANTAGES OF ART BEHAVIOR

What does art do? . . . If the history of the human race is an epic of self preservation under adverse circumstances, of securing enough food to sustain our (and our children's) bodies, and of defending an area of land to live in, then how is it that all societies have been able to afford the luxury of art?

R. L. Anderson, *The Art of Primitive Societies*

If one can categorize art as a kind of play, then in that regard the case for a selective advantage for art would be a special extension of the case presented in the previous examples for play. But it is a dramatic extension; it deals with the frontier of our humanness. Given some individual variation, and a heritable component, it is easy to see how the arts—as in role-playing or acting, the buffer of humor, playing with and constructing fun objects (like doll clothes and forts), and making up stories—would have repercussions for later performance in critical utilitarian functions where imagination became crucial. Art, after all, is an exercise in magnifying life, exaggerating, distilling, recombining, and trying new recipes.

These drawings from Trois Frères, Fr., show animals with either two sets of horns (bison on the left) or both a set of horns and a set of antlers (reindeer on the right). Such outlandish images are not part of a pattern in Paleolithic art but appear to be made by drawers playing with imagery.

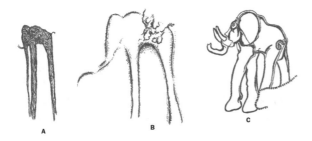

A, In the twentieth century, a mammoth carved on ivory turned up in a Siberian village. It reportedly came from the Berelekh paleontological site, from which hundreds of mammoth bones were removed. Its Paleolithic authenticity has been questioned; the unnaturally long legs, especially, have led some to consider it a forgery. However, a few other Paleolithic pieces do show mammoths drawn with unnaturally long legs, for example, the image (**B**) from Grèze, Fr. Later prehistoric art also shows similarly long-legged proboscideans: **c**, Elephant rock art drawing from Fezzan, Sahara.

A number of psychologists have documented that opportunities for artlike play enhance creative potential (e.g., Greenacre 1959; Torrance 1964; Lieberman 1965; Sutton-Smith 1967; Ellis and Scholtz 1978; Tower and Singer 1980; Cohen 1987), but data are not plentiful because traditionally the study of art and/or play as an important adaptive force has been neglected (Dolhinow and Bishop 1970). What is clear is that artistic kinds of play broaden brain function and activate a wide array of neural networks (Brown 1998) and brain regions. One can see that art may have enhanced communication as well as imagination. Though the direct utility of language has an obvious selective force for communication, art may have also played a role in the expansion of language capacities.

Certainly, creativity is universal among all human groups. But like most other traits, the advantages of cre-

Play in Prehistoric art. Paleolithic animals without a head in their brain: **A**, Les Combarelles, Fr. **B**, Addaura, It. **c**, Isturitz, Fr. (these two bison overlap, with their mirror-image rear portions emphasized). **D**, A similar two-rear image from Holocene Bushman rock art, Kinderdam, R.S.A. During the Holocene the reverse images were drawn in the Sahara, probably with humor: **E**, Palate de la Chasse. **F**, Suse. **G**, Wan-Bender. **H**, Sefar. **I–J**, Wâdi-Djerât.

ativity are not totally pervasive in every context. There are times and occasions where creation is crucial and times when not-rocking-the-boat, conservatively repeating what works, is the best solution. Creativity is not always beneficial or appropriate. But lots of evolutionary products are like that—held in reserve for appropriate expression. As an extreme exemplary reminder, the whole tail of some lizard species has an adaptive connection that allows it to snap off when it is grabbed by a predator. This may not happen to every individual, or even for several generations, but when it does happen, that complex anatomy more than pays for itself. Though not so simple as a snap-off tail, the propulsive dynamics of creativity stood a chance of occasionally jumping the chasm of change.

The human lifeway of a complexly social animal that lived as a physically rather inferior predator of large mammals necessitated creativity—and not just in weapon and shelter construction or food preparation. Our ancestors had to be able to cook up new recipes in all facets of life. Effective communication and logical analysis, the ability to imagine a future that was different, the flexibility to accept new political formats for decision making, to assume novel roles, and to negotiate complex situations with strangers, and the ability to look at old ideas with a fresh, new appraisal were all handy. Our niche needed people who got a kick out of pondering effects and causes. It favored persons able to tell a story or make a joke when the situation demanded a diffusion of tension or worry. Such

Paleolithic cave art includes some images of large quadrupeds that are presented vertically. These have elicited a variety of interpretations of mystical flavor. Some standing images have been interpreted as anthropomorphic shamans. But an item-by-item examination shows that there are more straightforward explanations. For example, many of these vertical quadrupeds are elaborations on natural contours that happen to suggest an animal in a vertical position: A, Le Portel, Fr. B, Santimamiñe, Sp. C–D, Altxerri, Sp. E, La Mouthe, Fr. F–G, Niaux, Fr.

traits are not selectively neutral; they distinguish more desirable leaders, friends, mates, or potential mates.

Oddly enough, we have no study of art making from that perspective, or of play for that matter. The reasons are complex, but they probably relate to the fact that potentially fascinating topics become invisible when we conceive of humans only as reproductive-age adults—children being unworthy of intellectual consideration. Aristotle, Locke, Leibniz, Spinoza, Hobbes, and Hume, who devoted their adult lives to seeking how human minds work, never even mentioned play. Plato, in his *Republic,* discussed how to educate philosopher-kings but never once referred to how they should play or make art. In fact, from Plato to Kant, philosophers have mistrusted both art and play (Murdock 1977) as a kind of lying. Nor is there evidence that it ever occurred to Darwin that either play or art could be adaptive, but he came close in one metaphor: "some instincts can hardly avoid looking as mere tricks or sometimes as play" (1859, 197).

Why has not the idea of art as an adaptive trait, which activates and exercises our creativity and ability to innovate, seemed more obvious or more popular? Perhaps it is one of those things that loom too close—the subject is too

familiar for the objective eye to see behind it, just like the difficulty in art classes in coaxing people to draw a realistic human eye instead of that almond-enclosed circle symbol. It is the difficulty of conscious analysis to penetrate that part of the brain directly. There are numerous objective aspects about ourselves that are not easy to grasp because we are the subject.

It is a challenge, for instance, to objectively observe and interpret a smile or a laugh as an ethologist would, because we are usually engaged in the firsthand living of our lives and connecting with each other. To also be an aware objective observer is an awkward double role. Perhaps that is the reason it is so difficult to see play. Because art is right under our noses, we often fail to see the way this art making activates interest, intelligence, attentiveness, and flexibility. Also, the "official" role of visual art today does not help. ART, as in the idea of modes of visual art, is such a tangle in art schools, professional identity, and entertainment, not to speak of its commodification, that we start to wonder what is going on.

Finally, we are critical of slackers. In jobs of direct utility it is easy to assess whether people are carrying their share of the load. Other situations are less clear and the line between slacker and innovator may sometimes be very fine. It is a subject familiar to most parents of teenagers; remember the kids playing in the garage in the 1970s with all that junk which would eventually become personal computers. Neighbors of the Wright family bicycle shop undoubtedly thought at some point that these two bachelor brothers should give up their boyish interests in airsailing and get on with useful lives.

How is all this relevant to the natural history of Paleolithic art? First of all, it highlights that the drawings were not labor and, further, that much of the art may have lacked an explicit, formal purpose. There is too much that is simply lighthearted, individualistically diverse, and too delightful. Certainly, attractive or technically excellent pieces in Paleolithic art do testify to the skills of people who spent many rewarding hours making art. But most of

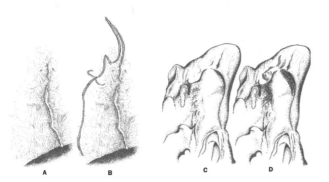

A, Chauvet Cave, Fr. A crack in the cave wall reminded someone of the lower contour of a rhino. B. C, A rock from El Castillo, Sp., with natural forms that suggest a vertical bison. D, The Paleolithic artist enhanced these with pigment. The vertical bison or rhino has been described as some mystical "anthropomorph," but one can see how the humped rocks might suggest a familiar image.

Lorblanchet has proposed that the aurochs image under the stone overhang at Pech-Merle, Fr., was done vertically because the artist (the one shown here on the right) had to twist into a sideways position to be able to make it. My drawing, after Lorblanchet 1991.

all, this old art testifies to the evolution of a major human quality, the very essence of humanness. Entangled in fantasy, it was done in play, yet something serious and fundamental was occurring. Underlying the colored bison, the red splotches of hand outlines, and the scratched images of swollen genitals we can surmise something besides the momentary expression they provided the doer or the impression they have on the viewer. Art making appears to be in our genes.

ARE THE VARIATIONS IN ART OR CREATIVITY HERITABLE?

We can see behaviors among ravens and chimps that certainly are related to human creativity, and we can be confident that evolutionary differences among organisms are derived from genetic differences. But within any one group what fraction of these behaviors is heritable? This question is almost unapproachable, and if we try to find appropriate data, all that is available will seem both simplistic and reductionistic. Creativity, by its own definition, involves coming up with something new. Any contrivances we make to test something so complex are going to be incomplete. There are, however, some oblique approximations available, obtained by working around the edges. For example, we know roughly what creative versatility is not. It is not an unshakable adherence to the given, the received, and we can measure that. That adherence is

called *traditionalism* in psychological testing. It is characterized by going to the same church you were born into, preferring the same general region in which you were raised, believing in roughly the same things as your parents, having basically their same tastes, etc. People vary in this resistance to personal change and considering new paradigms. The Minnesota Twin Study (Bouchard et al. 1990) measured the heritability of traditionalism at 0.53; that is, about half of the variation can be accounted for by genetic propensities. This "backside reflection" gives us some approximation of versatility, which at least is an aspect of creativity. It indeed seems moderately heritable.

But does human artistic propensity or ability have a heritability? Do people vary genetically in their propensity for art involvement, ease of art skill development, and range of ability? Common experience with musical ability and drawing skills within families suggests specific kinds do, but to my knowledge there has been little work on some approximation of heritability.

THE SELECTIVE COSTS OF ART

As with play, there are costs to art making. Indeed, art and direct utility seem to be at opposite poles, yet art is such a central and natural part of our lives, universal to all human groups, that it deserves a better accounting. We confidently assign the highest profile to utility and industry. Yet this may be a double blindness—both underestimating the vital role of creative endeavors in our own lives and the playful touch that created so much of what we proudly tout as progress and no-nonsense functionality.

The little burrs and projections near the base of shed antlers suggest all kinds of images that can be modified to highlight them further. These are all from Holstein, Ger.

So many things we take for granted add indirectly to our reproductive fitness. Our days are largely taken up with activities that ultimately arise from our art-making capacity. These activities are costly in time, money, and energy. Our ideas about and appreciation of art are given birth in hobbies, travel, beautiful gadgets like baked-enamel cars, comfortable and attractive clothes, homes with appealing architecture and furnishings, sports, books, electronic entertainment, and so much else. In the scales of evolutionary fitness there must be some counterbalancing force that counteracts these costs. In the end it has to be the powerful human imagination that is activated and honed by these pleasures. Shards of carved antler, engraved ivory, and the painted cave walls inform us that pleasure in art has been with us for many tens of thousands of years.

Apparently, lots of energy was devoted to art then as well. Many hundreds of these art pieces have survived from the Paleolithic. Imagine the scene: someone is sitting cross-legged on the ground carving an atlatal while he listens to and chats with others, among the noises of the small camp. Smoke shifts back and forth on the wafting breeze, which also conveys the odors of unwashed bodies, greasy leather clothing, decaying bone refuse and fly-blown debris, and the sweet smell of roasting meat. Scrrrape, Scrrrape, the sharp stone takes off a little of the water-softened antler at each stroke. Many hundreds of strokes lie ahead before the carver is finished. Such construction is not just a matter of naked utility. Looking back from his future, we are privileged to know the outcome in this case—the atlatal will take the shape of a leaping horse, the spur to connect with the dart is already protruding from the roughed underside of the jaw, like a tuft of beard. The finished piece will be something very different from a strictly utilitarian tool.

Thousands upon thousands of precious hours were devoted to such art making. And of course our preserved slice records the merest fraction of objects. Dances, music, stories, and more left no trace. The Paleolithic art that re-

mains is enough to confirm that humans are prone to such creative endeavors. It implies that this vivifying elaboration and expression are derived from an elemental need, a hunger that is satisfied only with the essential nutrient of art making. Fulfilling who and what we are, it is the imagined that highlights the real. Utility is not enough; it is what ants do. But why humans? Why did earlier hominids not do this in such a major way?

THE SURGE OF ART IN THE LATE PALEOLITHIC

Homo erectus and *Homo neanderthalensis* were not so different from humans: they built lean-to shelters, stoked their campfires, laced together warm clothing, and probably plotted hunting strategies, and maybe even gossiped. The record even suggests a little art in their lives: for example, the inclusion of a beautiful fossil embedded in the center of a flint hand ax. There was likely more art in their lives than was preserved in the archaeological record. But comparisons are clearly a matter of degree, and when the artifacts of humans are compared with those of other members of our genus, we find some major differences.

The appearance of visual art, soon after humans began to appear in the fossil record, seems nothing short of an outburst, as Julian Huxley emphasized in the opening epigraph of this chapter. If we are correct in pointing to art making as an offshoot of play that serves to activate creativity, then we would expect other things to accompany the emergence of art making in the archaeological record—things like a greater complexity in social cooperation, communication, exchange of goods, including

This woolly rhino is drawn with an attempt at foreshortened angles, yet the inexperience of the artist shows. We are lucky to be able to make a species identification; without its nose-horn it could have been identified as any number of animals. Lascaux, Fr.

Playing with two heads and one body. Delightful horse and ibex engraved on the walls of Pair-non-Pair, Fr. It appears that the ibex was added, along with a cloven hoof, after the horse had been engraved. This image is often mistakenly redrawn as a foreshortened horse.

Instead of a single body and two heads, here we have multiple bodies and a single head. This artful design is from much a later time in India, at Ajunta Cave.

rapid diffusion of information, inventions, and discoveries. And we might see a quantitative sign of these changes reflected in growing population numbers, as expressed in more campsites of slightly larger size and density. Indeed, more complex and more specialized tools, more effective weaponry, evidence of more sophisticated clothing, and expansion into areas previously uninhabited do accompany the late Paleolithic outburst of human art making.

The emergence of art making was evidently part of extensive changes in human evolution, involving, among other things, some major brain reorganization. But why did it not happen in these other species of *Homo?* Bear in mind that these other hominids were unlikely to have experienced any raw, day-to-day evolutionary incompleteness. In their way, they were quite successful. Humans just upped the ante with regard to imagination and flexibility. This departure in human evolution was likely due to the alignment of some unusual circumstances. Perhaps it was the combination of an already innovative African hominid and an unusual climate and biotic opportunities during the last Interstadial, roughly 30,000–100,000 years ago. This was a time when the climate was generally more equable than the present in many ways, yet immensely

more unstable. There must have been repeated abrupt swings from scarcity to richness in diversity and density of large-mammal species. Humans were confronted with jerky cycles of extraordinary opportunities and difficult challenges—where a thoughtful and creative hominid excelled.

But our minds boggle when we try to glimpse the evolution of this creative intellect—using that ability to contemplate the origins of itself. That is another form of art.

Scholarship, Science, and Art as Human Play

Good science consists largely of play disguised as work.

E. O. Wilson, *Consilience*

It should be clear by now that my sense of art making's playful essence is so broad as to be connected to virtually all creative endeavors. Many other modes of creativity might come to mind before the practice of science, but science (or, as Wilson noted, good science) is provoked by an innate attraction to the pleasures of wondering and understanding. People vary a lot in how much pleasure they get out of this kind of venture, even professionally trained scientists. In fact, training may have little to do with it. B. F. Skinner puzzled over this in his commentary on science: "It is a bold thing to say that we know how to train a man to be a scientist. Scientific thinking is the most complex and probably the most subtle of all human activities" (1956, 222). A background of rich youthful play and art in its broader definition seems to be a critical feature of most creative and outstanding scholars and scientists (Brown 1998).

Creativity is something more than just doing things differently or unconstrained novelty. It is about beautiful alternatives within apt constraints. In science, for example, the active players embrace contextually fitting principles because of their elegance, even though these principles are often rather amorphously understood and

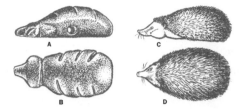

A–B, This miniature Paleolithic carving (ornament?) from Petersfels, Ger., seems to be a hedgehog (*Erinaceus europa*), a creative way to handle a difficult subject. **C–D** are my drawings of a hedgehog.

Human evolution has made us more childlike in many ways, particularly with regard to play and art. One could argue that some of Leonardo da Vinci's immense talent was due to his retaining an adolescent-like enthusiasm for so many things. And, indeed, so many of his designs were subjects of interest to a young boy. His notebooks abound with creatively new devices of violence: fortifications, siege breakers, weaponry, etc. Here are three ingenious ideas: multiple-barreled gun, bow-shield, and mortars that shot exploding shells. After a sketch in Leonardo's notebooks.

difficult to inculcate. Mostly those new ideas are evaluated on their originality and excellence of insights by the consilient interlinkage of their explanatory power, but always within the constraints of reason. Likewise, even in child's play, games operate with rules, chaos becomes ordered within broad boundaries, and when these are circum-

vented the play world often collapses. Real creativity flourishes within apt constraints; it is not totally wild and incoherent. The same has always been true of poignant visual art, music, poetry, and so on. And this paradoxical kind of freedom is laced all through the best of human enterprises.

It seems that various aptitudes for art and rational thinking within the constraints of reason usually develop very readily in children, though they are unfathomably complex if one tries to dissect the processes. How can we preserve and nurture these aptitudes? Perhaps the answer is, by a lot of early unharnessed play, exploring the constraints of freedom. In *Emile* Jean-Jacques Rousseau said: "May I set forth at this point the most important and the most useful rule in all education? It is not to save time but to waste it. Nature wants children to be children before they are men. If we deliberately depart from this order we shall get premature fruits which are neither ripe nor well flavored and which soon decay. We shall have youthful sages and grown up children" (1993, 23). Judging from their art, that seems to have been the Paleolithic standard of youthful fun.

Not Art for Art's Sake . . .

Our limbic rewards evolved to adaptively adjust our activities, making some things feel good and others not so good. Reynolds (1973) showed that creative play is so internally driven that rewards, beyond general support, did not increase it and sometimes even subverted the creative process. It is like trying to formulate how to talk a healthy person into eating pie made from good peaches, fresh out of the oven, and topped with ice cream. Most art making, like singing or drawing, also needs no external reward. The patterns and forms of Paleolithic art reassure us that art behavior in the late Pleistocene was also driven by internal rewards and was not viewed as labor or as the creation of symbols for particular purposes, as the twentieth-century

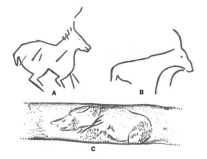

Just remember, even a beginning drawer with a simple piece of charcoal or a sharp rock could make a few lines and—poof!—create an animal. It must have been a real high in the Pleistocene, long before videos, movies, magazines, and photographs set us awash in a sea of images. Even a very young person could do it on any public space—as much as one wanted, it wasn't illegal. **A**, Kleins Schulerloch, Ger. **B**, Kastlhänghöhle, Ger. **C**, La Vache, Fr.

academics have seen it. Paleolithic art was done by people who had episodes of free time, occasional plenty, and the social context that encouraged play. Further, I suspect much of it was done at a time in life when creative play provided the most fun. So calling it "art for art's sake" may not be quite accurate. And though fun was the organic driver for art, it has deeper evolutionary agendas. In that role it is much more than a cluster of symbols for secondary meanings or some epiphenomenon of being human. Rather, Paleolithic art is that first clear spoor of advancing creativity in the human line—as Dissanayake said, "not art for art's sake, but art for life's sake" (1992, 12).

Kids doodling on the walls, playing in their secret camp, talking big of bears and sexual goodies . . . picture it. They are carefully tutored by the older-kid tradition inside the freedom of long unschooled days, playing at the calisthenics of logic and imagination. Once such a boy, I can nearly speak their minds, squat in the same cave dampness, and see the moving shadows beneath the ghostly white-hand negatives. What an incredible yarn an old club-member could spin for them — my own mix of science and art. Too far beyond their need-to-know, they would not believe the alchemy of hormones swelling their glands and minds, waves of ionic depolarization the physics of their thoughts, their brain halves sparking binary bits, radiowave hiss of an expanding universe, giant planets pinpricks of light in the evening sky, worlds like, but unlike, our own, cooled molten balls from the gasses that firmed our own firmament, shifting crusty continents underfoot, mother evolution — mammoths from tiny ancestors, us leaning against lovely limestone rocks ancient seafloor skeletons, flowers a trick on insect pollinators, fruit the bait for seed dispersers, our lunch salmon's round-trip across blue waters beyond dimension. Wild talk. A strange and beautiful game the clan has made, playing at tales of science and art . . . perhaps the ultimate sport.

8

Bands to Tribes

The End of the Pleistocene and the
Extinguishing of Paleolithic Art

The everlasting freedom of Paleolithic art is an embarrassment to Prehistorians.   M. Lorblanchet, *From Man to Animal and Sign in Paleolithic Art*

Lifeways and Art Making

When the Pleistocene ended, so did Paleolithic art;
post-Pleistocene art is unmistakably different. What
circumstances would have been so powerful as to keep
Paleolithic artistic unity intact for so long, and what
forces led to the global extirpation of this artistic tradition? What does this artistic transition suggest
about art making, and are there insights into human
nature and human responses to radically changed contexts that we can draw from this? There is a story here

Throughout this book I have emphasized that many of the images from Paleolithic art were done in a distinctive, representational, straightforward style, even though often by an inexperienced hand. And now it is time to try to make some sense of that pattern. A thick-bodied bison from La Marche, Fr., epitomizes the figurative style—note the double hump characteristic of steppe bison.

Elaborate Maori carving from historic times, showing abstract patterning. If you look carefully, you can see a man and woman.

that may change forever the way you look at human history, but let me begin with a brief aside that affords a topsy-turvy insight into the Paleolithic even though most of its events took place less than a thousand years ago. It is a story about hunting dependency lost, regained, and lost again.

THE LONG WHITE CLOUD OVER ABSTRACTION AND REALISM

During the late Paleolithic, Mongoloid peoples of eastern Asia were large-mammal hunters. At the end of the Pleistocene, like many other peoples, they diversified into socially complex pastoral and agrarian societies. Some became seagoing sailors, and by one thousand years ago the Polynesian branch had colonized islands across vast stretches of the tropical Pacific.

Polynesian men were astounding sailors and fishermen and Polynesian women were remarkable artisans and agriculturists, keeping diverse domestic plants and animals. Polynesians would beach their boats on a new island and in a few generations have it tamed to their order. Their cultures were sophisticated, with complex religions and social practices, and their visual arts were abstract and highly elaborate. They commanded large, beautifully decorated, outrigger canoes, and they sported magnificent stylized tattoos and created intricate feather and tapa cloth ceremonial robes. Alas, as colonized islands filled with people, conflict and war became recurrent—a strong motivator to search for new islands.

Whether by systematically following the millions of migrating birds winging down the central Pacific flyway from the Northern Hemisphere or perhaps by less deliberate voyaging, Polynesian explorers beached their sea ca-

noes on the shores of New Zealand. They were the first humans to set foot on this great pair of islands, which lie in a cool sea under an ever-present long white cloud. Pioneer Polynesians found these islands unlike any they had previously known. The cool climate could not support the colonists' tropical agriculture, and they had either left their stocks of pigs and chickens behind or eaten them on the way. The Polynesians did bring dogs, but none of their other livestock and very little of their array of domestic plants were successfully introduced to New Zealand. Even fishing required new approaches in New Zealand's cold waters. The pioneers must have indeed felt they had landed in a new world.

Not only were the Polynesian colonists the first people to set foot on those beaches, but they and their dogs were the first terrestrial mammalian predators to inhabit New Zealand in at least 65 million years. If they arrived hungry and empty-handed, they didn't stay that way long. The Polynesian agriculturists and fishermen quickly reverted to a more Pleistocene-like lifeway, with hunting as their mainstay. But Paleolithic hunting was never so easy. Almost predator free, the shores of New Zealand hosted many of the fur seal and albatross rookeries of the Southern Hemisphere. Sea birds and seals appeared seasonally in the millions, and since they were unfamiliar with human predation (with an evolved, dodo-like, insular lack of caution), it is likely the colonists had to do little more than walk up and club them.

With this apparently inexhaustible bounty, New Zealanders largely abandoned farming and fishing and became prosperous hunters. Their oldest archaeological sites contain evidence of coastal species as the main dietary

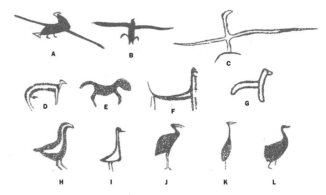

A comparison of two Maori art styles. A, The three birds are rock engravings of moas (South Canterbury). Because moas were hunted to extinction 500–600 years ago, we know these bird images date from the time when Polynesians began to exploit New Zealand. Until the island's large birds and rich coastal mammal populations were depleted, the Polynesian colonists had a hunting economy. Art from this period tends to be more naturalistic and representative. B, The Hei Tiki, a stylized ornament of mystical significance, is from a much later time. Such ornaments were worn by many people at the time of European contact, but by then Maoris were village farmers and fishermen.

Some early Maori art. Three subjects often reoccur; one is the giant eagle species, now extinct. This enormous raptor was the only serious predator on the island. Another common image is domestic dogs, which were brought to New Zealand by Polynesian colonizers. Moas are the third favorite image. Some moas were larger than ostriches. Eagles: A and C, South Canterbury; B, Weka Pass. Dogs: D, North Otago; E, Waipapa; F, South Canterbury; G, Weka Pass. H–L, Moas from North Otago.

item, but heavy use of these easy pickings appears to have greatly reduced the coastal bounty within a few generations. As human numbers expanded, the New Zealanders began to hunt farther afield, exploring the dense inland forests on trails made by moas, the enormous, flightless birds endemic to New Zealand (Anderson 1983).

There were no native land mammals, but eleven species of moas occupied New Zealand's large-herbivore niches. Moas were mainly shrub browsers, and some of them were so large as to dwarf an ostrich—or a man. Polynesian hunters carried their heavy loads of meat back to coastal villages, where beaches became white with bone refuse (British colonists would later ship many of these phosphate-rich bone deposits back to fertilize the fields of England). But not all the meat was taken back to the beaches to be eaten. Inland, under rock shelter overhangs and in cave entrances, protected from the frequent island drizzle, hunters roasted moa drumsticks as big as venison hams. Occasionally, on the stone walls of these inland camps, the hunters drew rather simple images, mostly of moas, dogs, and giant eagles (Trotter and McCulloch 1989).

Some of these artworks survive (the meat of this little story), and most are rather straightforward, representational works, remarkably unlike the visual art that generations of Polynesians had made in the Cook Islands, the islands from which the New Zealand pioneers probably set

sail. The moa hunters produced art with little evident imagery of gods and little elaborate stylization. Notably, there is no midden evidence of cannibalism from this period, no remnants of weapons of war, and no mass burials from war's aftermath. The moa hunters' art appears more individually improvisational, more casual—in short, more akin to the spirit of Paleolithic imagery.

As happened previously on other islands, human numbers increased. Moas and other species of flightless birds became extinct from overhunting, and eventually, the Maoris returned to sea protein sources and fired the native forests, increasingly relying on cultivated foodstuffs, especially a finger-sized potato-like plant. They also returned to warfare and began hunting one another, escalating the odds with some of the most extreme cannibalism practices known. European explorers described their music as stirring elaborations of war chants, and their visual arts, from tattoos to carvings, as stunningly stylized and intricately abstracted with patterns rivaling those found elsewhere in Polynesia. Meanwhile, lichen-flecked remnants of more representational images made by moa hunters awaited discovery and recognition.

Thus, our tale of double reversal: Paleolithic Asian hunters first adapted to fishing and agriculture-based

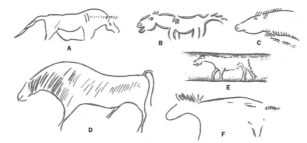

Paleolithic artists' drawings record behavior observed in wild horses: head is out-stretched and tails held in threatening postures. Most of these were not done by accomplished drawers, but one can still catch the essence. **A**, Cheval, Fr. **B**, La Madeleine, Fr. **C**, Marsoulas, Fr. **D**, Lluera, Sp. **E**, Schwiezersbild, Ger. **F**, Tito Bustillo, Sp.

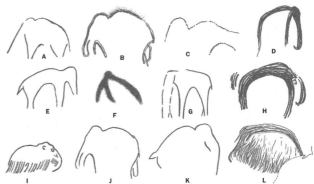

A collage of mammoths from Paleolithic art. These are all done simply, with just a few lines that attempted to capture mammoth contours. Nothing about these suggests that they were part of some religious ceremonial art. Like many other illustrations in this book, the makers of these images were clearly developing their drawing skills. How many mammoths does one make before one becomes technically proficient—hundreds, thousands? And what happens to all those early images? It is obvious from a sample like this that Paleolithic art contains lots of "early works" by Pleistocene artists, as well as the masterful works of accomplished artists. **A**, Pair-non-Pair, Fr. **B** and **J**, Bernous, Fr. **C**, Oulen, Fr. **D** and **H**, La Baume Latrone, Fr. **E** and **G**, Jovelle, Fr. **F**, Cougnac, Fr. **I**, Gargas, Fr. **K**, Croze à Gontran, Fr. **L**, Gönnersdorf, Ger.

economies with higher-density cultures in which visual art was abstract and stylized. Much later, when New Zealand colonizers were engaged in large-animal hunting and living at lower densities, their visual art also changed, becoming more representational and figurative. Finally, as hunting lifeways vanished once again, and Maori villages grew to tribal dimensions and increased their reliance on domesticated food sources, Maori art became more stylized and abstract. Thus the hypothesis: that there may be profound relationships between a culture's lifeway and its art. At least in the situations I am discussing, the state of mind and preoccupations of its members are often reflected in the culture's art-making norms. Ample evidence suggests this interaction was not peculiar to Polynesians, and Paleolithic art is, of course, part of that evidence.

WHAT WAS SO DIFFERENT ABOUT THE CONTEXT IN WHICH PALEOLITHIC ART WAS MADE?

Like the first New Zealand pioneers, Paleolithic peoples lived at a demographic scale that was exceedingly limited both in the size of human groups and in the density of those groups. As I emphasized in earlier chapters, the technology and resources available to Paleolithic bands meant cooperation was essential. In such a lifeway there would not have been more than the occasional property tensions and likely relatively little violent discord within bands, be-

tween sexes, and even among bands. Survival depended on exquisite attention to one's natural surroundings, and Paleolithic individuals and groups were probably less preoccupied with strategic and organizational concerns regarding future stores, future status, future alliances, and future hostilities than were later, tribal peoples.

In this chapter we will explore ways that visual art dramatically reflects and records individual experience when framed in contexts of Paleolithic scale, as compared to tribal contexts. Of course, such contextual shifts involve both ecological and sociocultural dimensions. I don't mean to imply some biological imperialism here. We always live in a human-made world of language, craft, knowledge, and so on. Experience is always culturally shaped, but never exclusively so. Life occurs in earthly contexts subject to particular ecological possibilities and constraints, and in this chapter we will try to imagine how threshold changes, from Paleolithic to tribal scale, seem to have shifted claims on human attention that are, ultimately, entwined with art making.

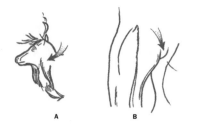

As hunters who dismembered animals, Paleolithic artists noticed trivial anatom-
ical details, details beyond what was necessary to draw an identifiable subject.
Here are but two examples: **A**, Reindeer neck muscle, the *brachiocephalis*, from
La Mouthe, Fr. **B**, Mammoth skin fold of elbow, olecranon process, Chabot, Fr.

The wealth of representational detail in Paleolithic art records a frame of mind
aligned toward the study of the natural world. Because of thick facial pelage used
mainly to absorb the frontal blows of an opponent (Guthrie 1966), bison and
musk oxen have a unique orbit that extends out away from the face. These special rings around bison eyes were noticed and recorded by the people who engraved these plaquettes at La Marche, Fr. (*left*). My x-ray reconstruction of bison
(*right*). Arrow points to protruding bison orbit.

Remember that within the variations of Paleolithic art,
we met a host of animals portrayed in a rather realistic
figurative manner, including bison, horses, mammoths,
bears, ibex, salmon, human faces, and voluptuous ladies.
Paleolithic images are characterized by a combination of
spontaneous ease and a wealth of observed detail, and this
is true, in relative degree, of work by beginners and accomplished artists alike. The art of later tribal and village
people is generally quite different. It would be almost
hopeless, for example, to try to use classic Polynesian,
West African, Northwest Coast Indian, or Zulu art to reconstruct the appearance of the respective local wildlife.
What is at the root of these differences? Let's approach this
problem in terms of three interrelated questions:

► What forces contributed to the long continuity, the sta-
 sis, of large-mammal hunting lifeways during the late
 Pleistocene?

► What happened around 10,000–12,000 years ago that
 provoked such widespread and transformative changes
 in the way people lived?

► Why were those changes reflected so dramatically in
 the art?

The Paleolithic Platform of Human Nature

In chapter after chapter I have outlined aspects of our natural history as social hunters of large mammals—pair-
bonding and the inclusion of fathers in parental love and

care of a rather small number of children, the eroticization
of sex in human life, living cooperatively in small hunting
bands—and how these characteristics were thoroughly
linked to the evolution of intelligent, creative, and empathetic consciousness. In that lifeway our ancestors pros-
pered, but that niche had its ecological limits, despite all
its flexibility. Archaeological sites spanning some 30,000
years of the Eurasian late Pleistocene testify to a core similarity, including living in small bands, relying on wild resources, and using a fairly similar array of simple tools.
There is no evidence of transformative technical change
on the scale of domestic animals (even dogs), no permanent or fortified residences, no sophisticated watercraft,
and no organized warfare throughout that incredibly long
time. Yet our reconstruction of that period suggests fully
human lives, with associated intellectual and artistic capacity and much else we associate with modern people.
Why is it that for 30,000 years we see no agriculture, urban
life, written language, pottery, refined metals, cloth, or
any other of the dynamic panoply of innovations that
shaped the lives of most of our Holocene ancestors?

There is so much natural order underlying Paleolithic art that we can safely complete many of the unfinished drawings because they are largely representational images from the natural world. The incomplete image at top right is from Chauvet, Fr. It would be inconsistent to complete this as an exotic shamanistic image because the rest of Paleolithic art is a very clear prompter as to how the drawing should be completed as a representational image (my drawing below). The neckline, two long ears or antler spikes, and hump are from a giant deer, the shelk.

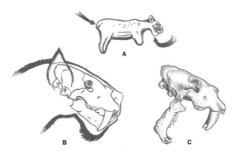

A, This little carving from Isturitz, Fr., is a puzzle. It could be a lynx or a scimitar-toothed cat (*Homotherium*). Paleontological material shows that the latter species was present during the Pleistocene, but none have been found in the late Pleistocene. **B**, Note its short tail, lump jaw, posteriorly set ears, and rather heavy-set body contours. If it is a scimitar-toothed cat, one might say it had only a "walk-on" part on the Pleistocene stage. **C**, The long, thin, sharp, and serrated-edged canines were probably used in a killing neck-bite, slicing carotids and jugulars; whereas other large felines, like lions, use a stranglehold.

Was the continuity of Paleolithic art simply due to a lack of creativity? I don't think so. Everything we know and can deduce about human life during the Paleolithic suggests that a very high level of imagination and intelligence was essential to sustain life generation after generation. Surely, the surviving traces of Paleolithic art are evidence of creative vision. All we have inferred about the challenges of their lifeway as hunters of large mammals reinforces the sense that intelligent innovation and high individual achievement, as well as family bonding and group cooperation, were essential dimensions of our Paleolithic nature. Remember that life was no idyll; the big guns of necessity and constraint were constantly lined up along the edges of Paleolithic life.

A DIFFICULT EDEN

Prior to 10,000 or so years ago, the Pleistocene environment itself may have been the most critical factor constraining human lifeways to large-mammal hunting and its diverse supplements. Archaeological evidence suggests that Paleolithic people never regularly obtained sufficient resources to sustain individual bands of large size or any but the thinnest regional density of bands. The Eurasian Pleistocene climate was comparatively demanding, both during the cold and dry extremes of the last Glacial maximum (around 10,000–25,000 years ago) and in the unpre-

dictable irregularity of the preceding Interstadial (around 25,000–50,000 years ago). Climatic constraints therefore placed a low ceiling on human density and, to a great degree, restricted geographic expansion.

These climatic strictures were not limited to Eurasia. The Glacial maximum and preceding Interstadial were felt throughout the globe; indeed, the rarity of human fossils makes studying archaeological issues during this time difficult. Either cold or aridity or both were extreme. These climatic parameters meant that such potential food sources as edible plants, fish, and migratory birds had sharply seasonal, or episodic, availability. Likewise, the seasonally sparse rangelands meant that the dominant large-mammal species were not only elusively mobile but also nomadically unpredictable. In sum, the carrying capacity of Eurasian late Pleistocene landscapes was quite low for most mammals, including humans.

THE IMPORTANCE OF DEMOGRAPHICS

We might imagine that, in the Pleistocene context, village life was a strategy no group dared attempt on a consistent basis, because an increase to much over forty people would have meant trouble—social trouble, biological trouble,

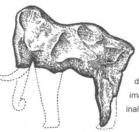

Most Paleolithic art pieces are unique. At their best, they show close attention to the details of large mammals. Broken or incomplete images allow us to roughly reconstruct the original. Partial adult mammoth from Pavlov, Czech.

Family bond in Paleolithic art? Someone carved a man and woman from the dental cementum on the base of two horse incisors (just the size of your little finger). Mas d'Azil, Fr.

every brand of trouble. Absent a more generous climate and Holocene technological innovations to harvest that bounty, late Pleistocene humans were subject to many of the same forces regulating other wild hunters—forces analogous to those that keep a wolf pack small—and we simply don't find packs of forty wolves or, for that matter, prides of forty lions or clans of forty hyenas.

The foraging of such a larger group would have exhausted local resources too quickly, necessitating more frequent moves. The small scale of Pleistocene archaeological sites and abundant ethnographic analogs make these parameters clear. If ephemeral good times did allow occasional population increases, most likely a band would simply have separated into two bands. During severely difficult conditions, some bands may have failed, probably being replaced during later, prosperous peaks that supported opportunities for band cleavages. There was likely a size range that functioned best: at one extreme, individuals, or even nuclear families alone, were too vulnerable, and somewhere around forty—certainly by fifty—people, things likely became too inflexible and ecologically strained. Our distance makes it tempting to blur the Paleolithic into a steady-state kind of low-level prosperity, but I am sure this apparent smoothness is merely statistical. The "on-the-ground" experience was no doubt composed of peaks of exhilarating success and well-being, ease and daring, as well as troughs of near-unimaginable effort, loss, and suffering.

NOBLE PHILOSOPHIES AND FLY-BLOWN CAMPS

In earlier chapters we utilized both Paleolithic art and modern and historical analogs to conclude that within the Paleolithic band, there were basically two adult vocations: two overlapping, but distinct, mainstream ways to live an adult life, each with its respective focus on skills and responsibilities. Women's and men's lives were differentially focused with respect to parenting, physical and social skills, modes of risk taking, kinds of responsibility, resource acquisition, and areas of knowledge. Of course, experimentation, inquiry, and creativity were equally essential. The Holocene extension of attention in other directions, for example, to the development of cereal hybrids, pottery, smelted metals, boats, gardens, or hounds, apparently required more freedom to renegotiate these demanding bimodal generalist job descriptions. Our challenge in this chapter will be to construct the most credible scenario of what made the Holocene changes possible.

I want neither to glorify nor to disparage Paleolithic lifeways. It is essential to appreciate both the enormous depth of time and the implacable sternness with which many practices we rightly claim as definitively moral and good were contextually enforced in Paleolithic life. It was, perhaps, the only life possible for peoples along the edges of those desiccated African savannas and on the windblown steppes and in the sheltered valleys of Eurasia, and it was a life close to that for which evolution had tailored us. Nevertheless, we can appreciate the appealing power of Holocene possibilities. If there is any question that peoples of that time experienced Holocene innovations as improvements, one has only to look at the rapidity with which those innovations spread. For example, the first indisputable signs of dog domestication occur at around 13,000 in the Middle East, and by 11,000 their barks could be heard on the coast of Tierra del Fuego. Dogs were likely a revolutionary aid in finding game, holding it at bay, and

This Paleolithic point- or shaft-straightener, from Grotta del Caviglione, It., was made from a horse metacarpal. This is an unusual piece, done where no reindeer antlers or mammoth ivory were available. It was a good substitute for such a forceful wrench. These slender cannon bones have a thick cortex, and the distal spongy bone is quite dense, making it unlikely to break. These people were experienced with the empirical aspects of bone, probably much more so than modern biologists.

The risk reduction brought about by domestication and civilization has not come without costs. The experiences of wolves and terriers are very different, with regard to both fullness of life and risk. If you had to be one or the other, which would you prefer?

tracking down wounded game—magnifying hunting success perhaps several times over the Pleistocene norm.

While late Pleistocene life may, today, appear as noble, we must also realize that its grace was strictly proscribed. Shepard (1973), Meeker (1980), Schmookler (1995), and other scholars, fascinated by the contrasts between large-mammal hunters and tribalists, have tended to overglorify hunting cultures but still miss the most poignant and revealing interactions at the heart of the post-Pleistocene changes in the scale and power of human life. In a modern mix of Rousseauian tradition and landscape ethics many writers have focused on the light ecological footprint of Paleolithic life. That light touch was, however, not a matter of choice. Nor should we imagine their lives as neat and tidy. Archaeological coprolites suggest that toilet practices were taken care of near at hand. And what we have reconstructed of Pleistocene campsites reveals a mess of fly-blown debris, but again, not too big a mess. There simply wasn't much garbage, and they moved often.

They likely practiced little in the way of game conservation management, if recent subsistence hunter-gatherers are any analog (e.g., Anderson 1997; Espinoza et al. 1997; Steadman 1997). These hunters are known to have killed well beyond what they could consume, when that was possible—the same way most other carnivores do. Of course, such possibilities were not common. It would have been these stringently limited possibilities, more than conscious restraint, that kept Paleolithic hunters on track

ecologically. They were part of an interdependent ecological system all right, but one that could well have done without them, except for a few mice, ravens, and jays that were addicted to their meager refuse. There is every reason to believe these people were at heart like us, but not exactly. It was a very different time and context. As a metaphor—the stars we see today were not exactly in the same constellations, and the earth did not even turn around the same Pole Star.

The Holocene Crease Line in Human Experience

PATHS OF SATURN AND JUPITER—AND CULTURAL CHANGE ON EARTH

Archaeological sites record a demographic breakout from band-sized groups to larger villages at the start of the Holocene. Indeed, prehistorians speak in terms of revolutions, of creative explosions in human cultures. These changes at the end of the last Glacial were too rapid and too widespread to have been a matter of genetic shifts. Likewise, various technical revolutions that supported increased human populations were far too diverse to be accounted for by simple models of cultural diffusion. The rapidity of changes on a global scale points to extraterrestrial forces.

The demographic and technical transformations with which we are now concerned began at the onset of the Holocene, an episode researchers have called the "Cli-

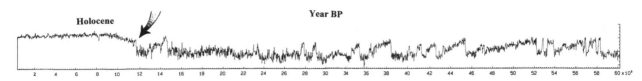

Year BP

Holocene

Climate changed 12,000 years ago, but more than mean change it was the change in variation itself that was the most dramatic. These are proxy data on global climate from cores taken from the Greenland ice sheet (Schackleton 1995). Vertical scale represents average annual temperature.

Because of the ubiquitous grassland habitat, saiga antelope (*Saiga tatarica*) were distributed from England to Alaska during much of the late Pleistocene. They would have been familiar to Paleolithic Eurasians. At moderate speeds, saigas use an unusual gait, the pace (*left*), in which limbs on the same side move together, very unlike a trot. At much faster speeds, saigas of course gallop (*right*).

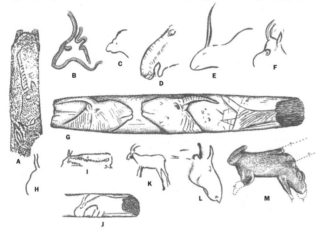

Probable images of saiga antelope in Paleolithic art: **A** and **H**, Altxerri, Sp. **B**, Rouffignac, Fr. **C**, Réseau Clastres, Fr. (more likely an ibex). **D**, Gönnersdorf, Ger. **E**, La Colombière, Fr. **F**, Les Combarelles, Fr. **G**, La Vache, Fr. **I**, Bize, Fr. **J**, Peyrat, Fr. **K**, Trois Frères, Fr. **L**, Abri de la Souquette, Fr. **M**, Enlène, Fr.

matic Optimum" (Kutzbach and Street-Perot 1985). This was the greatest consistent change in Earth's climate that had occurred throughout the entire span of our species, that is, during the last 100,000 years or so of human existence. This extraordinary climatic change is attributed to the largest planets in our solar system, Jupiter and Saturn,

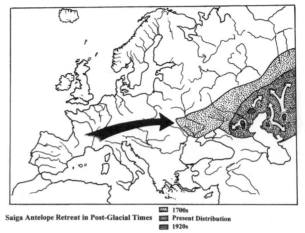

Saiga Antelope Retreat in Post-Glacial Times
▨ 1700s
▨ Present Distribution
▤ 1920s

Map of Europe showing retreat of saiga antelope from Spain and England since the last Glacial. Saiga antelope are now found only in midlatitude Asia but were once very widespread even in the far north. (After Altuna and Apellaniz 1976.) Along with horses and bison, saigas did not become extinct but simply underwent a dramatic retreat in their distribution centers, following the retreating grasslands.

being aligned in such a way that not only was Earth's orbit changed, but the very Sun itself was pulled well off center. Put simply, the orbit of Earth was brought closer to the Sun, causing Earth to receive more of the Sun's energy and producing the warmth of an Interglacial. Upper atmospheric "greenhouse" gasses became more dense, and less solar energy was reflected back into black space. Changed ocean currents recast continental climates, producing cloudier skies with more moisture, moderating aridity, and reducing temperature extremes across the entire Mammoth Steppe (Guthrie 2001a). The human species had always lived with some version of Glacial climates, which, for humans at least, had created a demanding and unpredictably variable environment over most of the globe (see Soffer and Gamble 1990; Vrba et al. 1995).

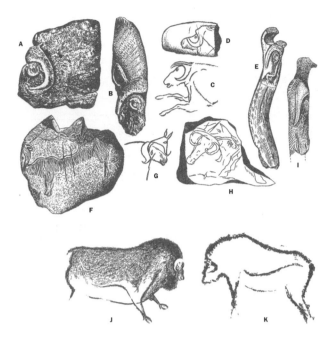

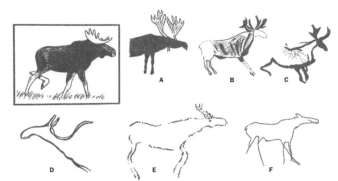

Images of moose (*Alces*) are rare in Paleolithic art because they were not really steppe animals. As we have already seen, most Paleolithic art is about species of the Mammoth Steppe. Moose are common today throughout the boreal forest, but they were pushed south during the last glaciation. Images of moose are found in Paleolithic art only in the most southern parts of Europe: Italy and the Pyrenees and south into Spain: **A–B**, Minateda, Sp. **c**, Altamira, Sp. **D** and **F**, Gargas, Fr. **E**, Val Camonica, It.

Musk oxen fossils and art images far to the south of their present distribution highlight the kind of climate and habitat that sometimes existed during the European late Pleistocene. **A**, Laugerie-Haute, Fr. **B**, Kesslerloch, Switz. **c**, La Mouthe, Fr. **D–E**, Arudy, Fr. **F**, La Colombière, Fr. **G**, Lascaux, Fr. **H**, Limeuil, Fr. **I**, Courbet, Fr. **J–K**, Chauvet, Fr.

About 12,000 years ago a true Interglacial, the Holocene, began.

Core samples from deep-sea sediments and the Greenland Ice Cap record major changes about 10,000–12,000 years ago. These mark the onset of the Holocene, which continues to the present (GRIP 1993; Stuiver and Grootes 2000). The present Holocene Interglacial is unlike the previous Interglacial, which peaked at around 125,000 years ago, in that our present Interglacial is much less variable by far (Tzedakis, Bennett, and Magri 1994). Again, let me stress that these consistent and equable climatic conditions were novel to human experience. The rapid end of Pleistocene conditions in continental Europe is documented by classic French paleontological, sedimentological, and palynological studies (e.g., Delpeche 1975; Laville 1975; Paquereau 1976; Leroi-Gourhan 1977; Woillard 1978). European prehistorians working with faunal assemblages (e.g., Uerpmann 1989) speak of changes occurring in a span of nearer a hundred years than a thousand.

One does not need to be an environmental determinist to appreciate that, in this case, there were dramatic correlations between climate and cultural change (White 1985).

The cold and dry Mammoth Steppe was rapidly replaced in Europe by more humid mixed forests, and large-mammal faunas shifted from more nomadic herds to favor territorial woodland species. David (1973) has argued that human cultural shifts occurred as a product of such megafaunal changes, particularly the collapse of large migrating game populations. Perhaps this is true, but the enormity of climatic and vegetation shifts likely had many dimensions which significantly prompted cultural change more globally.

THE GOLDEN AGE OF THE CLIMATIC OPTIMUM

Holocene conditions brought about a stunning increase in Earth's biomass, increasing the total mass of living organisms. It has been estimated that the terrestrial carbon in circulation more than doubled over preceding Ice Age concentrations (Adams et al. 1990). Holocene climates and attendant floral and faunal changes produced a new organic wealth, which, for the first time in human experience, could be transformed into a dependable harvest of

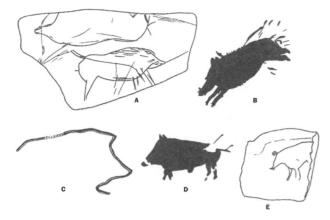

Wild pigs are mainly forest animals, mast-eaters, so during the last glaciation the steppes confined their distribution to the south. Though wild pigs are one of the dominant large mammals in Europe today, they do not figure importantly in Paleolithic art, but there are a few: **A**, Parpalló, Sp. **B**, El Civil, Sp. **C**, Quintanal, Sp. **D**, Cañada Remigia, Sp. **E**, Romanelli, It.

Well astride this critical period, we see that 15,000–16,000 years ago there are few archaeological sites, while at 7000–8000 years ago the world is thick with sites and most are extensive. I use these dates because there seems to have been an increase in resource diversity and human density associated with an ameliorating climate in the latest Paleolithic, identified culturally with the latest Magdalenians (say, at 14,000 years ago). However, this increase was orders of magnitude lower than the surge in population in the early Holocene (say, at 8000 years ago).

From Bands to Tribes

MORE SPECIALIZED CREATIVITY
AMONG LARGER GROUPS

Imagine a group of tribes living within reach of one another. If all choose the way of peace, then all may live in peace. But what if all but one choose peace, and that one is ambitious for expansion and conquest?

A. B. Schmookler, *Parable of the Tribes*

surplus foods. Early Holocene fossils show an increase in such potential human foodstuffs as nuts, annual cereals and legumes, woodland large mammals, whales, and fish, and much of that surplus was storable. Storability made a huge difference.

If ever there was a "Golden Age" in prehistory it was surely this period of the early Holocene. Paleoecologists have remarked on its rich, unweathered, and uneroded post-Glacial soils, plants at maximum productivity, and weather most suitable for human prosperity (e.g., Sahlins 1974; Roberts 1998). Such conditions would have promoted significant increases in human survival and net reproduction. Indeed, archaeological sites show just such a rapid increase in human numbers (Cobb 1959; Cohen 1977, 1985). Increasing density in turn drove colonization. The archaeological record eloquently testifies to the rapid post-Glacial spread of people into and across the high-latitude Arctic, down through Alaska, and onward through the Americas. Holocene organic abundance underwrote surplus-producing innovations in hunting and fishing, including fishnets, skin boats, fishhooks and gorges, dip nets, toggle-harpoons, basket traps, whale drag-floats, adzes, dogs, ceramic cooking pots, and the bow and arrow.

The logic goes like this—the jump into Holocene innovation and change *demanded a critical mass of people*. We accounted for the first step toward that change by the unusually favorable and less variable Holocene climate. The increasing scale of tribal life, supported by stored surpluses, meant that more specialization in creative focus was possible; and, of course, each technical change tended, in turn, to sustain further population growth.

Holocene specialization was also possible in art making. Artists in later tribal settings needed to address wholly new creations, new layers of complex tribal realities. Their images and forms became increasingly stylized and reflected their greater preoccupation with tribal concerns and local myth and magic. In sum, the more specialized art makers of the tribal world had both reason and occasion to express and elaborate on these new aspects of experience attendant with living at higher densities.

Though often artistically powerful and creative, tribal art makers are usually constrained by their intense in-

Throughout the evolution of our species we have lived in intimate small groups. That sphere of sociality affected the balance sheet of our evolutionary strategies—who we are.

An example of one kind of signature in the development of crafted traditions in tribal art. Tlingit hat design with calligraphic effect of using a wedge-shaped, flat brush. With this instrument, one can make smooth and parallel-edged ogives as the brush rotates. These same patterns are then incorporated into Northwest Coast Indian carving and weaving. But the aesthetic seems derived from the brush-and-ink work, in a highly developed art form.

volvement with group identity (Groenfeldt 1985). Received artistic norms are close to the bone. For example, each tribe may have its own ceramic patterns, dress decorations, basket designs, totem styles, etc. They may even consider these, not as art or even decoration, but as essential components of a proper pot, dress, hairstyle, or blanket. People studying such traditions say that these patterns carry symbolic meaning and that their shared visual reading gives emphasis to group cohesion and order. A distant analogy for us might be the way some people feel about team-sport, religious, or nation-state emblems: St. Louis Cardinal, Maple Leaf, Fleur-de-lis, Star of David, or Stars and Stripes.

THE PLEISTOCENE SCALE OF HUMAN SOCIALITY

Most of us would find it difficult to imagine living one's entire life with only thirty or so people—most of whom would have been related by blood or marriage. Although there may have been occasional visits with neighboring groups and likely seasonal rendezvous with other bands, Paleolithic life would generally have been lived in one's small band. Such a combination of intimacy and isolation may be nigh unimaginable, but most of the human past has been lived at such a scale; indeed, this intimate social scale is probably close to the evolutionary norm to which we were fitted. Judging from social patterns among other apes and the archaeological sites of related hominids, some version of a small human band extends several million years into our deepest past.

When we consider how profoundly persistent our evolutionary adaptations to that scale of sociality are, we can then realize that the larger tribal groups that arose in the Holocene constituted a major qualitative shift. Indeed, there were many *threshold effects* associated with this increase from Pleistocene numbers and scale. Various sorts of thresholds occur in many behaviors. For example, at different densities many antelope species shift social behaviors from individual to class hierarchies (from pecking order to territoriality).

At least since Herodotus, the scale of human social organization has been a subject of great interest and speculation. The ideas of Service (1962), who introduced the *band-versus-tribe* dichotomy, have been important in anthropological thinking. Flannery (1972) refined this categorization even more: *bands, tribes, chiefdoms, and nation-states*. Other authors have speculated that the members of bands and of tribes have different psyches (e.g., Shepard 1973; McNeil 1976; Dunbar 1996; Wrangham and Peterson 1996). But since I would like to focus on the late Paleolithic and the early Holocene, and maintain our viewpoint of natural history and evolutionary biology, let me simply say that, whatever the myriad dynamics and events of the past 10,000 years, I contend that the essential outlines of human nature were critically shaped by Pleistocene norms, and I include human sociality in that, quite aware that our sociality is an amalgam of biology and culture.

THE HUMAN SCALE OF DENSITY: NEPOTISM AND RECIPROCITY

What are some of the dynamics of animal sociality? Why not just go it alone? Tree squirrels, foxes, spiders, and even

Chinese Shang architecture, clothing, weaponry, furniture, etc., are replete with motifs done in a style similar to that of Northwest Coast Indian art. One can see remnants of how this aesthetic, too, arose from a brush-and-ink tradition.

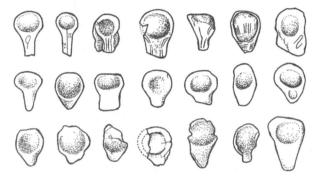

When it was dark, most Paleolithic people probably crawled beneath the soft fur blankets, but some lit the darkness with lamps. It would be almost critical to be able to make light: children can get sick at night, and there were many adult health and comfort issues that had to be attended to at night. Imagine a small group sitting around a 1-candlepower lamp. These are some Paleolithic lamps, consisting of a hollowed stone that contained some burnable oil and a wick. All are from French sites. *Top row:* Bois du Roc, Lascaux, Gabillou, Vallée de la Couze, Laugerie-Basse, Grand Moulin, Gabillou. *Middle row:* Houleau, La Mouthe, Solvieux, Jaurias, Chaire-à-Calvin, two from La Faurélie 11. *Lower row:* Saint Mathieu-de-Tréviers, La Garenne, Rond du Barry, Saut-du-Perron, Scillels, La Faurélie 11, Solvieux.

Humans were not the only ones with stable family bonds in the late Pleistocene. Other species passed down culture between generations, they shared family and mate loyalty, traditions, etc. **A**, Woolly rhinos, like these pictured here from Rouffignac, Fr., were apparently social and had close-knit family groups, as do African white rhinos today. **B**, Something similar is true of ibex, like these from Lascaux, Fr. **C**, Horses had harems, where mares were close and were protected by a single male and sometimes his male offspring (Limeuil, Fr.). **D**, Mammoths (Rouffignac, Fr.) were apparently like today's elephants, which travel in matriarchal herds, with lifelong affiliation and deep cultural connections, both socially and with their landscape.

A collage of lions from Chauvet, Fr. The lions' forms and coat patterns were recorded in detail. Lions are social creatures, and Paleolithic artists often portrayed them in small prides, not just as individuals. There is no need to envision these images as springing from a dream or hallucinatory world. They are subjects chosen from the experienced world of the drawers' real lives, animals they undoubtedly saw as beautiful and some they probably feared 30,000 years ago.

one species of great apes generally live alone. The obvious answer would be that in some contexts there can be important adaptive advantages to living more socially, but how then to mediate problems that arise from the direct competition inherent in such togetherness? Biologists are familiar with the underlying evolutionary perspective behind this question. In fact, there is a subfield of ethology that deals with this specific issue. Researchers have identified two main roots for the evolution of these social negotiations. The kind of sociality we observe within family-based groups, such as wolves, hyenas, lions, coyotes, elephants, and many other mammals, is primarily structured around *nepotistic* relationships. Members benefit genetically by cooperating, because family members are various versions of one's own genome or, in the case of spouses, those with whom we mix our genes. An individual potentially increases his or her own genetic fitness by working for the common good of the extended family, even though that individual may never even get to breed. Sterile worker-bees are an extreme form of this social force based on genetic relations.

The other main biological mode of sociality encompasses the advantages in cooperating with those who lie outside the family circle, and thus who share far fewer genes. Ethologists refer to this second mode as *reciprocity*, because these interchanges and associations are distinguished by exchanges of individual favors with some accounting. Technically, such social forms can be practiced in groups of larger size (often among subsets of coalitions or friends) where genetic relationships may be relatively dilute. In fact, the rituals of reciprocity often use gestural and other behavioral elements pirated from family (nepotistic) contexts. Grooming is an example.

African impala live in rather large herds that include animals that are not closely related, yet they groom one another. Impala have specialized lower canines and incisors that form a sort of comb which is used for tick removal, but there are places on their bodies that they cannot reach alone, particularly the head area. Independent of degree of kinship, each impala gains in such an exchange of mutual grooming. When these grooming bouts are timed, the exchanges clock out approximately equal. You scratch my back, I'll scratch yours, sort of.

When we look at the social interactions of chimps, it is clear that although things are quite complex, both modes of sociality may be in play at any one time, with varying emphasis. An especially prime food item, such as a piece of meat, is normally shared, though often reluctantly. What is particularly interesting is that sharing creates obligations that can be, and usually are, called on later. Unlike the impala's reciprocity, which is immediately repaid, chimps remember their favors and debts for a long time. Moreover, chimps' favors can be repaid in other currencies: grooming or sexual access can be exchanged for a food debt. Even in a large group, this accounting is remarkably accurate; individual chimps keep close tabs—commanding to memory complex networks of obligations (De Waal and Lanting 1997). Some other primate species that live in large groups also practice long-term accounting alongside their nepotistic obligations.

Where is this discussion taking us? As uncomfortable as it was for many people in the late 1970s to confront the idea of sociobiology, it is clear that aspects of social behavior are shaped by evolutionary patterns. Even though our social propensities may have originated from multiple sources and are quite flexible across a variety of circum-

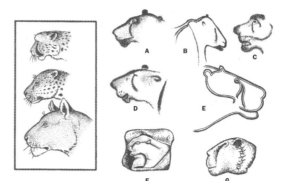

Over and over, if you look at the details of Paleolithic art, you see traces of the process of people becoming good observers. We can use their observations to say something about species that lived tens of thousands of years ago. For example, many Paleolithic images of lions show black eye stripes. Several cat species today have these eye stripes, especially cheetahs, and even leopards have a small one, but living lions do not have them. **A–E**, Chauvet, Fr. **F**, Abri Durif à Enval, Fr. **G**, Vogelherd, Ger. *Box, top to bottom:* extant cheetah, leopard, lion.

stances, they have roots in the deep past. Family-based relationships are the taproot and thus a deeper part of our evolutionary soul, a part of our unconscious nature. The thick tangles of reciprocity are also part of our evolutionary heritage, but these are more consciously counted.

Though the Pleistocene seems to have honed capacities that enabled later peoples to live in settings enormously different in character and scale, the Paleolithic platform was distinctly smaller. When tribal-sized groups first arose amid Holocene abundance, I think that some threshold was crossed, and what may appear to us as quite small numerical differences very likely led to significant alterations within families and groups and among groups.

THRESHOLDS AND EXPONENTIAL CHANGES WITH SCALE

A moment's exercise with numbers underscores some relevant dynamics in changes of social scale. In a group of 30 people one's relationships to others can be represented numerically as 29 ($n - 1$); however, in addition to our personal interactions, we are also aware, in small groups at least, of interactions among members, and that is represented as $n \times n - 1$, or 870. Even if we imagine being born into a Paleolithic family-based group, such a dense net of awareness would have required considerable attention.

Compare that number of relationships to those within a group of 200 individuals. Being intimately aware of each individual's relationships with one another would result in a formidable 200 × 199 = 39,800 relational arrows. Of course, we should additionally consider that the nature of relationships is dynamic, each changing with time and carrying generations-deep accretions of personal history. The point is that relational connections grow exponentially, and this exponential expansion means that the brink of unwieldiness is reached soon after a group grows to include 30 to 40 individuals. There is a threshold at which the trellis of relations collapses or, more accurately, must shift to a different mode. While we live in a world of innumerable acquaintances, meeting new people all the time, that older context in which our social capacities evolved is still reflected in the fact that the people we know well probably still number under 30.

The benefits of pursuing possibilities in the new Holocene context were enormous, and yet life at higher densities was fraught with new kinds of tensions, trouble, and danger. Complexly arranged reciprocity, new abstractions of authority, new customs to shape intra- and intertribal relations, and much else had to be reconfigured with this threshold change in social scale. One persistent difficulty arose from the existence of the new abundance: who controlled the stored surpluses and the means to produce them. In the Pleistocene context, profound conflicts of interest would have been rare, so a simpler arithmetic of reciprocity and custom was adequate. The new social scale and attendant greater diversity, specialization, and divergence of interest required something new—a tribal calculus.

Storable Surplus

How do we best encapsulate the advantages that allowed or necessitated the change from Pleistocene living to the tribal way ubiquitous in the post-Pleistocene? Scholars

Holocene Eskimo hunting tally piece(?), Point Barrow, Alaska: enumerating twelve whale flukes and whaleboat, plus hunters and kayak with five caribou.

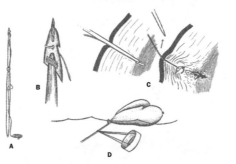

Technological revolutions can change density and geographic colonization. A radically new Holocene harpoon system was the key change in the Thule Eskimo whale-hunting revolution. **A**, Throwing harpoon with slightly flexible joints. **B**, Detachable toggle-harpoon head. **c**, Upon entering a young whale, the barb caught and rotated the point, so that it fixed itself parallel to the whale's skin. **D**, An attached line connected to a sealskin float and a submersed water drag. Pulling this drag, the swimming whale became exhausted and could be killed with lances or spears. The revolutionary toggle-harpoon combined with a drag transformed Eskimo marine-mammal hunting. It produced an enormous storable resource of fatty blubber (rendered into oil) and frozen rich meat.

have captured that answer in just two words: *storable surplus*. A band shared surplus with band members and with neighbor bands. This sharing tended to be practiced more with close relatives than with distant ones. Lee (1979) discussed foraging and farming in terms of differences in *sharing versus saving*, noting this was one reason Bushman found the transition to Bantu-style farming awkward—sharing went against key Bantu traditions of keeping one's bounty to one's self, even when that meant keeping milk goats or crop seed-stocks away from the cooking fires of relatives.

1 + 1 = 3: THE CRITICAL ROLE OF STORABLE SURPLUS

Animal populations are held in check by some seasonal bottleneck, usually in the form of limited resources. Storing surpluses from the fat time of the year for the lean time is a way of widening that bottleneck, but the trouble comes in finding, acquiring, and defending easily stored food. McNeil (1976) and Testart (1988) have championed the idea that profound changes occur in a human society when significant surplus resources are available and there is a focus on the storage of that surplus. The synergistic effects of accumulating surplus food are reinforced by biological links between food, fertility, and fecundity. It is a simple equation: surpluses allow stores, and stores mean greater availability of food during the leanest times of the year. The right kind of food, during that critical bottleneck, accelerates growth and fecundity, which in turn promote early sexual maturity, early pregnancy, early weaning, and rapid recovery of fat to resume ovulation, and thus a shortened time between births. The steady calories of stored food surpluses tend to support health, postpone

menopause, and facilitate more energy-demanding work. While each of these is likely to increase reproduction and overall survivorship, these individual effects compound in their interaction, and the natural outcome is marked population growth.

Foods for storage should, ideally, both be rich in nutrients and calories and keep well for a long period. But it is difficult to meet both of these ideals. For locally diverse reasons, it tends to be much easier to find storable energy (calories) than nutrients. In cool climates, animal fat is high in energy and can be stored; indeed, many marine-mammal hunters do store fat in the form of oil from seals and whales. Interior Alaskan Athabascans and coastal Indians of the Pacific Northwest store dried salmon—which are saturated with fat as an adaptation to their long upstream migrations. Domestic livestock, especially sheep and pigs, were bred for their ability to accumulate body

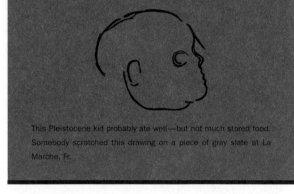
fat—storable surpluses on the hoof. Storable milk curds and yogurt are high in milk sugars and milk fats. At lower latitudes, seeds can be collected or cultivated in quantity; acorns, maize, wheat, rice, millet, and legumes supply concentrated storable starches. Both nuts and annual cereal grains have evolved to overwinter in a dried state and are not defended against herbivory by toxins, because their tasty starches and hard coats were part of a seed-dispersal strategy, an adaptation allowing a few seeds to escape being masticated and to pass through the gut of large mammals.

Once we appreciate the role of stored surpluses, it is clear we cannot distinguish band from tribal lifeways simply by a reliance on wild versus domestic foods (Testart 1988). The extensive fish stores of Northwest Coast Indians made their cultures more akin, in many ways, to those of agricultural tribalists. Likewise, coastal Eskimos who lived in large villages that were organized for whaling also kept extensive food stores and experienced the full benefits and detriments of tribal village life (Burch 1980; Sheehan 1985). Interestingly, the visual arts of these groups also disclose tribal concerns and tribal identifications. A regard for such classification heterogeneity (as reviewed by Gardner 1991) helps us understand that Paleolithic lifeways were not just a matter of eating wild. It is noteworthy that there is no evidence of storage pits or other storage facilities until after the last Glacial maximum (Soffer 2000), that is, the latest Paleolithic, the sweep into the Holocene.

Some social anthropologists have voiced objections to McNeil's and Testart's ideas about the critical role of surplus, primarily on the basis that human cultural patterns are unrelated to environmental circumstance and, also, that surplus is a matter of degree. But simple assertions that cultural patterns are unconstrained or unaffected by environmental context are untenable, and certainly surplus and storage are a matter of degree. Human stores of some sort are nearly universal; the crux occurs when importance *centers* on degree. These issues are all ones of degree—calories/nutrients, large/small groups, stasis/change, genetic/nongenetic components, wealth/poverty, sharing/storing, reason/revelation. And, of course, so is representational and abstract visual art. But, as we have noted, changes along gradients are not equally incremental in effect: quantitative gradients do often produce disjunct qualitative changes—dramatic threshold effects.

BAND STASIS AND TRIBAL GROWTH

Growth in the Pleistocene was risky, but it was risky *not* to grow in the Holocene. Once begun, tribal lifeways

Murder or capital punishment? Arrow-riddled Holocene African from Witzieshoek, R.S.A. Similar images are found in Paleolithic art. But unlike in African art, Paleolithic ones never accompany battle scenes.

With the post-Paleolithic tribal revolution, this changed. Each of the discoveries and inventions of village life encouraged normative solutions that concentrated focus and increased the dependence on regularity. The domestication of animals and plants was one result of the period's security, even as it contributed ever more security. Archaeological and climatic evidence are clear about this shift. Statistically, at least, life became organized around a regular and hospitable climate—almost always the salmon or eels arrived, the corn got enough rain, the forage for livestock was lush, and the dogs found moose. Less frequent and less disruptive climatic/ecological changes and the deployment of new methods to harvest the earth's bounty helped promote a focus on predictable population growth and expansionary expectations. When bad luck did arrive, it may have seemed very strange and unreasonable, a matter of who or what to blame.

swamped those of everyone else. Throughout the Holocene, the Pleistocene-scale lifeways of hunter-gatherer bands were obliterated in all but the most unproductive corners of the earth. By pervasive power and sheer force, the new technologies of hunting and fishing and, later, domestic plants and animals spread rapidly. This new Holocene context was first about growth and then about competitive growth. Expansion in numbers of people, in technical power, and in organization became centrally important as small groups were gobbled up by larger ones. Such expansion now seems a universal part of history, and expected, but this was not always so. Paleolithic folks lived with much uncertainty, but because these uncertainties could be mitigated only very slightly, the human adaptive themes of flexibility and creativity were crucially important.

Holocene Changes in Individual Experience

THE LAST OF THE MAMMOTH TIMES

What was it like to live in the Paleolithic? Paleolithic opportunism had to be honed by close observation and practical reasoning. Flexibility and cooperation in efforts to secure food and shelter must have centered on a core of objective assessment that had to pervade all strategies and backup strategies and the people's core psyche. No one solution was guaranteed; no pat answer or ploy could be relied upon. One had to closely monitor changing realities: avoiding illness from food spoilage and infections, daily use of dangerously sharp flint tools and weapons, exposure to the vagaries of more extreme climates, severe consequences of the wrong choice in clothing or its poor

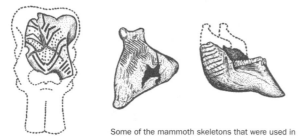

Some of the mammoth skeletons that were used in house construction at Mezin, Ukraine, had abstract patterns painted on them. It is thought that these bones were not only visual art images but musical percussion instruments. They make wonderful resonating soundboards when beaten with a bony or ivory tool. Some even show marks from such beating. Skull fragment, scapula, and mandible

workmanship, scant backups in many aspects of life, forced mobility from local resource depletion, rigorous commitment to child care and education, enormous self-reliance as well as regard for others, few storable surpluses, irregular successes and failures, and frequent life-or-death decision making.

These tight feedback loops must have kept one belly-close to objective reality and attentive to all manner of empirical observations—full attention, full rationality, and full creativity had to describe life in the Paleolithic band. It is that edge which engraved the art, and it shows clearly. Drawing in that representational and figurative style was both a product of and an exercise in careful observation, reason, and memory.

MOVING INTO THE KRAAL

Paleolithic hunters were not the savages early writers imagined, driven only by gnawing urges of belly and libido, but their lifeway certainly left them exposed to the consequences of actions and events, with more immediate rewards for success and penalties for failure. I doubt that fear originated with agriculture and pastoralism; it was Paleolithic fears that prompted people to invent or accept new domestic solutions.

The distinctive feature to recognize in our long Paleolithic heritage is neither an absence of fear nor domination by fear but that life within the band and between bands was supported by contextual limits on scale and density that shaped long-standing human values. Individ-

The Ice Age Band's Evolutionary Legacy of Small-Group Intimacy Today Though the circumstances of our lives are much changed, the Paleolithic legacy of a small band remains part of our marrow. Certainly, that long tenure remains in an inner need for the kind of intimacy and thoughtful empathy possible in a small group—and much more that makes us human. For example, Ornish (1998) has reviewed the research showing positive linkages between human intimacy and health (immune function, stress resistance, rate of aging, and longevity). Our Paleolithic legacy sometimes interacts with modern circumstances rather inappropriately, however. Earlier, I discussed such a mismatch in the Pleistocene intensity of our hunger for fat and today's more sedentary life.

Evolution did not prepare us for life in groups far larger than band size, and many of our current mental- and physical-health problems (loneliness, depression, even some kinds of criminal behavior, and certainly occasional acts of inhumanity to our fellows) may be linked to both individual and cultural disregard for the demands posed by this new setting. Grasping for something missing, we often substitute pets; pets seem to be assuming an increasing role as surrogate people. Perhaps we depreciate some aspects of being a Pleistocene organism in modernity because we really believe that Holocene power will provide sufficiency, security, and unlimited possibilities.

ual and group well-being were both fairly transparent and generally in alignment. A group debate about whether or not to move camp is very different from a tribal deliberation about how much land will be planted and by whom. In the Paleolithic band the debate on what was true and right was likely directed more at natural systems, the non-human earth.

Larger, more permanent concentrations of people, made possible by secure stores, allowed new, tribal realities to emerge, new ways of perceiving the world, and, with all that, a wealth of advantages (Harris 1978). A more diverse social life and broader exchange networks of trade within

What Paleolithic art is not. These stylized patterns and subject matter are not found in Paleolithic art: **A**, Scythian red deer. **B** and **G**, Pueblo pot and Kachina doll. **C**, three Tassili Neolithic rock images of camps and mothers with children. **D**, Zebu bull in rock art from India. **E**, Celtic coin from Le Loubiére. **F**, Sonoran Desert, Caso, California. **H**, Aztec maize goddess. **I**, Hopewell U.S.A. clay figurine of mother nursing. **J**, Humanoid figure from southwestern U.S.A. **K**, stylized Peugeot lion emblem. **L**, Tassili mother nursing.

and outside the tribe became possible. Job specializations contributed to a broader base of aggregate knowledge. I imagine life in a village was more entertaining. For many, if not most, it brought greater economic wealth and greater physical comfort. But life in the tribes came at some cost.

In tribal society, most individuals learn to conform, learn not to stand out, so as to be privileged to compete within the protection and good graces of the tribe (Morris and Levitas 1987). The larger tribal scale is associated with a more abstract social power, power that by necessity is overtly and unequally distributed according to strength, resources, and usually birth. This abstract and social intensification at the larger scale of village life seems to have been associated with a dilution of intimate ties, loss of sexual parity, and other social inequalities (Cashdan 1980). Parental engagement with children was reduced while the advantages of cheating were increased. There was an inherent shift toward greater personal and family acquisitions, including both wealth and power, and abuses of authority were more likely. Individuals and even entire classes lost the ability to minutely observe and interpret the processes of the natural world. One of the ironies is that despite the comforting security of stored food, higher tribal density was accompanied by increases in nutritional deficiencies, the kinds and spread of contagious diseases, and the likelihood of raiders from beyond the horizon. I digress along these lines for a moment because it will help us to understand the changes in the art.

DIMINISHED BODIES AND DIETARY INSUFFICIENCIES

Most Holocene Eurasians were smaller than their Pleistocene counterparts. While stored foods may have more dependably provided day-to-day calories, they did not necessarily constitute a nutritionally superior or even balanced diet. More individuals were sustained by the new energy-rich stored starches, but nutrient quality declined, probably because the higher density meant a dilution of the more limited nutrients. This Holocene decline in nutrition is evident in the archaeological record in the form of small stature (Bogin 1999). Growth ceased well short of full genetic potential. Holocene patterns of reduced development may also reflect the drain of chronic contagious diseases and parasites (Bogin 1999).

DISEASES

Paleolithic peoples were apparently free of many contagious diseases characteristic of later, larger populations, including measles, smallpox, typhus, cholera, influenza, and even the common cold (McNeil 1976, 1980). These diseases require a certain density of hosts. Furthermore, virtually all of our most virulent contagious diseases are

Neolithic domestication allowed for genetic alteration of cereals, forbs, and a variety of animals. These not only provided power and transportation, they expanded the Pleistocene bottleneck of resource availability or access (in this case a chariot engine). *Left,* wild horse; *right,* domestic one.

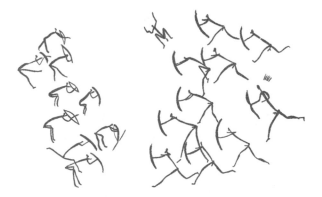

Tribal competition means one's welfare is greatly affected by the neighbors. Population increases cause villages to compete; the consequences are usually raids and war, especially if one has stored surpluses. Bushman painting from Orange Free State. I suggest that the "big men" on the right are portrayed as very masculine with erect penises, while those on the right are shown more neutered, unmasculine (the enemy).

now understood to have developed as mutant cross-specifics from domesticated animals: smallpox from cowpox, measles from canine distemper, influenza from similar diseases in swine, and so on. Runny noses and pock-marked faces are thus rather recent in the human past. The extremely low densities, cool climate, and high mobility of Eurasian Paleolithic peoples probably also meant low parasite loads. The almost universally heavy parasite loads of tribal peoples result from lack of adequate sanitation at higher densities and a more sedentary life.

It is important to note here that the increased mortality among tribes from contagious diseases and poor nutrition fell disproportionately on the very young. I observed in 1980 that children in rural Malawi were not given their adult names until age five; more than half of the infants did not reach their fifth birthday. Such tribal mortality patterns have traditionally been a strong incentive to maximize fecundity and thus inadvertently reduce parental investment in each individual child.

WARFARE

A Paleolithic band had to need neighbors. Bonds were created and maintained by sharing goods and exchanging brides with neighboring bands, who were still "we." A tribe inevitably is more self-contained than a band. A village is large enough that one normally chooses mates locally. Kids don't flow outward as they come of age; the group just gets bigger. Because of that, a village's relations with neighboring groups were different: neighbors were viewed as potential competitors more than near relatives. Dynamics of scale made the abstraction necessary and it was easier for "them" to become the enemy. Separateness and specialization led to greater differences among the lifeways of neighboring tribe: art styles, manners, accents, and tastes. Another repercussion directly involved stored surpluses. A tribe's wealth took great effort to amass in the fields, but much less if it could be pillaged.

It is not that covetousness, envy, and homicide weren't part of the Paleolithic world, but we may be mistaken when we think warfare is an inherent part of our early human nature. War does seem to be recurrent among cultures living at tribal (and greater) densities, but persistent group violence could simply not have been a characteristic of Paleolithic life. This does not mean that confrontation or even violence between bands never occurred. Aspects of our behavior and that of our nearest relatives, chimps, are a clue to the deep roots of such occasional group violence (Wrangham and Peterson 1996). But it would not normally have made sense for a bandsman to risk his own and his family's lives to sow seeds of enmity by murderous disregard of a band of neighboring relatives, especially if all that was won was a different horizon to hunt, likely no better than the one he already had.

More than economic forces are involved here. Empathy, the emotion that underwrites our mutual regard, can falter as scale grows—"we" can more easily disintegrate into "us and them." And them-ness can easily cross into being less-than-human. The de-individualizing of neighbors invites a "mob effect" of disregarding one's principles and values and subscribing to the superorganism's prejudices. Today, we can see the risks of too much emphasis on old tribal identity—Palestinian and Jew, Zulu and Xhosa, despite the origin of these people from the same stocks, Semitic and Bantu respectively.

Holocene warriors with weapons and shields, Neolithic rock art, Helanshan, China. Foraging from one's neighbors' stored surpluses can be more efficient than trying to grow one's own wheat.

A war party from Holocene Bushmanland, Chikupu, R.S.A. There are a lot of war themes in most tribal prehistoric art, but not from the Paleolithic.

A Crow Indian shield, made from heavy hide to catch or deflect arrows and lances. Note bison decoration not too different from Paleolithic art; see some in Cosquer Cave for comparison. Note how the tail is raised, feces dribbling, penis with a large erection. A touch of testosterone never hurts in this kind of art.

Other things, like polygamy, were often a logical consequence of the steep gradient in tribal social status. A tribe produced, so to speak, a surplus of young expendable males for intertribal pillaging and slave or wife capturing. For them, raids or attempts at the destruction of others were worth considerable risk. As densities increased, it was virtually guaranteed that some other groups would attempt to attack you, and first-strike attacks are usually a more winning strategy than counterattacks. So the tribal world invented a new role for young men, that of warriors, enlisting vibrant youthful testosterone and ardor in organized, authorized missions to win valor by killing people defined as the enemy.

This shortcut to stored bounty by raiding the wealth of others became a universal tribal phenomenon: warring conflicts constitute most of recorded and mythic Holocene history. But Paleolithic art shows no drawings of group conflict, and there is virtually no indication from late Paleolithic skeletons of murderous violence. There is one Magdalenian skeleton from Le Veyrier, France, whose skull is marked with what appears to be a blow. A poorly preserved skull from Boil-Blu, France, likely of Aurignacian age, has a small flint embedded in the temporal bone. However, there are no Paleolithic "after-the-battle" mass burials of warrior-aged males, which are common among later tribal groups.

Is it possible that what we have learned so thoroughly from history—the inescapability of war—is not the whole truth? Is it possible that warfare is not an inherent part of our entire past? That is what I propose. And I reiterate the enormous difference between hunting and warfare. To propose that risky and violent group hunting activities played a central role in our evolutionary past is not synonymous with seeing warfare as part of our adaptive history.

This distinction should be utterly clear to readers who have come this far, but our thinking tends to be tangled with deep beliefs. Ample evidence suggests a Paleolithic past in which lethal weapons were a matter of keenest importance to everyone, a part of the bloody violence which sustained human pleasure, human life, and human values. But these weapons were not designed to be used against people. The human capacity for violence between groups is well proven; however, I maintain there is little evidence that those capacities were cultivated or regularly exercised in the late Paleolithic. This is a remarkable distinction, and it deserves our attention.

Democratic Empiricism, Kids, and Authority

Every time a savage tracks his game he employs a minuteness of observation, and an accuracy of inductive and deductive reasoning which, applied to other matters, would assure some reputation as a man of science. . . . The intellectual labor of a "good hunter or warrior" considerably exceeds that of an ordinary Englishman.

Thomas H. Huxley, *Lay Sermons, Addresses, and Reviews*

We have discussed ways that hunting and tracking require a keen alertness to clues about an animal's movements

The Missing Shields in Paleolithic Art

Wars and battles must have been a fascinating subject for tribal people because we find war scenes in most post-Paleolithic art. Not only are battle scenes missing from Paleolithic art, but something else is missing too—there are no images portraying shields! Unlike a spear, a shield is a specialized tool for a particular use. Its sole purpose is to defensively deflect *human* attack. It can parry javelins, clubs, pikes, swords, maces, flails, slings, spears, darts, arrows, and so on. A shield is not a hunting tool. It is expressly about human-human group violence—the first "antimissile defense system."

Warriors universally seized upon the logic of such a deflector of projectiles and created many forms of shields. Given the prevalence of testosterone themes in Paleolithic art, we can be assured that if they had had shields, these would likely have been portrayed. But there are none. Why? The most parsimonious explanation is that this absence in the art reflects their actual absence in Paleolithic life. If lethal violence was mostly an individual matter, mainly among band

Wherever tribes fight with flying projectiles, people have invented shields. Shields are about warfare or the threat of war. No warrior is well dressed without one, but it is nothing but an encumbrance in hunting. There is no record in Paleolithic art of shields. Prehistoric, Rio Grande rock art, American Southwest.

members and perhaps rare at that, a shield would have been useless or too burdensome to carry when so seldom used.

The lack of images of shields or combat scenes in Paleolithic art, combined with the absence of fortified sites, which are so common in later cultures, is eloquent evidence that formalized intergroup violence was likely rare during the Pleistocene. This inference is reinforced by the imagery on preserved Paleolithic weapons, discussed in chapter 5. There are lots of scenes of hunting violence, and masculine erotic themes, but none of human-human violence—these Paleolithic tools were weapons of hunters, not of warriors.

and intentions and a flexible questioning of one's assumptions and analyses. Those metaphors of a hunting lifeway were used to highlight how it constantly calls upon reason and very egalitarian debate. Memory, experience, and creative intuition all contribute, and each situation opens a slightly new chapter. A tracker constantly tests hypotheses and is rewarded with success or left empty-handed with refutation. Wrong ideas often become clearly falsifiable from the data underfoot. It is a process that is both profoundly empirical and storied. Again and again, the emergent story and data interact while compelling incentives keep everyone's attention "on track" in a cooperative effort to get it right. One might say that the pivotal attribute of this integrative, investigative pursuit is its democratic recentering structure. *Its practitioners must report their methods as well as their results.* Certainly at heart, if not in detail, these

experiences, and the outlook and practices they foster, are similar to ones we know in the lives of scientists and scholars.

In tracking, neither magic nor appeals to omniscient authority are possible. What counts is finding spoor and interpreting its truths. Each person's sight and insight can contribute, so tracking is inherently egalitarian (Liebenberg 1990a). When dead-ended, it is time to backtrack, to refind the trail, to reconsider one's premises and logic, and to learn from the process. This aspect of tracking is a metaphor for most other endeavors in a hunting lifeway.

Ethnobotanists have found that hunter-gatherers' knowledge of indigenous floras is usually remarkably detailed and articulated, and there is more involved in this than nutrition and digestibility. All plants have evolved defenses against animal herbivory. Each group of plants tends to have specific kinds of toxins, and these can be

A bison from La Vache, Fr., with tracks. Tracks must have been keenly important to Paleolithic hunters. For a hunter, tracks are almost as informative as seeing the real animal, and since Paleolithic hunters used projectiles that resulted, at best, in fairly slow deaths, they had to track down virtually all game.

Paleolithic trackers had to be adept; they had to see the tracking process as an empirical enterprise, relying on the trustworthiness of an objective reality similar to how we approach much of science, automobile repair, child rearing, etc., today. Bovine hooves: **A**, Lascaux, Fr. **B–C**, Mas d'Azil, Fr. **D**, Marsoulas, Fr.

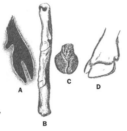

very potent. If you simply start eating wild plants at random (tubers, mushrooms, green leaves, or blossoms), you will soon be quite ill or dead. "Naturalness" should not be equated with wholesomeness. Among many hundreds of wild plant species one must ascertain identity, be alert to time of year, stage of plant development, and details of preparation in order to avoid toxins or render them harmless. Some of this information is so esoteric it is difficult to imagine how it was ever gained. Yet detailed lore regarding plants' usefulness as medicines, dyes, fishing and hunting poisons, preservatives, and so on is found among many hunter-gatherers (e.g., Heinz 1978).

How does one learn these things? Profound empiricism, trial and error, tradition and investigation, imagination, and cultivated memory are all involved. As with hunting and tracking, there is every incentive to stay alert to many details and to their possible causes and effects. This was true for children as well as for women and men. The effective apprenticeship of children was crucial—constant quizzes, show-and-tell, questions, and arguments.

In Paleolithic society the enormous complexity of the practical education required to function well as an adult meant that adult relatives had to do much of the educating. It could not be left to nonrelatives (i.e., to the youths' peers) as it is in a tribal society. Engraving from La Marche, Fr.

PARENT REARING OR PEER REARING?

It is no wonder that every man can carve when the fathers take as active and persuasive a part as they do in the teaching of their children. On King Island, in particular, no boy grows up without being surrounded by talk and actions of carving when men gather in the kazgi during the winter between hunting excursions. The Eskimo carvers believe that a boy cannot become proficient unless he begins very young, practices the same things over and over for years, and handles countless pieces of ivory.

Dorthy Jean Ray, *Artists of Tundra and Sea*

Let's return to the subject of children, for as we have seen, children are central to this story. Growing up in a band seems to have been fundamentally different from growing up in a tribal village (e.g., Barry, Child, and Bacon 1959; Rohner 1975). Cross-cultural studies of hunter-gatherers have shown that the higher the contextual risk in child rearing, the greater the focus and attentiveness of parenting (Chamberlain 2000). A child in a nuclear-family-centered small band played with peers but had to be raised by parents. In a tribe, children played with and were effectively raised by peers and older kids (Draper and Cashdan 1988). The larger scale of tribal life also meant that a child's awareness was explicitly focused on tribal power and identity, tribal obedience, tribal rank, and tribal responsibility. In contrast, a budding Paleolithic adolescent did not merely need to learn to handle the equivalent of the family farm or car dealership, but much of the well-being of the known human world rested on his and her emerging capacities.

Metaphorically, one could contrast the two childhood experiences by saying that one lived among a complexly interacting complement of plants and animals, resonant with diverse powers and meaning. The other lived among corn and weeds, sheep and varmints, and even these were merely backdrops; the key stories were no longer found among these "backdrops" but in the much more interesting goings-on within the tribe. This shift in focus is evident in the visual arts.

Konner concluded that agricultural and pastoral societies "bring much more work and drudgery into the lives of children than do hunter-gatherers. Thus, the lenient modern educational philosophy might be viewed as in some respects restoring the hunter-gatherer playful-learning pattern" (1982, 247). In part this is true because young tribal children can contribute directly to the group's economy, much more so than children of hunter-gatherers (Draper 1976). In chapter 7 I showed how we might expect that creativity prospers when children are raised with a greater emphasis on individualized parental attention, self-reliance, and individual incentives in a more flexible milieu. If we understand anything about the development of creativity at all (and we don't know much), these early freedoms seem critical. The fecund imaginations and individual ingenuity that show through in Paleolithic art forcefully point to an upbringing that encouraged creativity.

Experiences quite early in human life may not be totally overcome by compensating experiences later. Certainly, we can observe the significance of quality rearing in other species, such as chimps. Jane Goodall has said that this is one of the most important insights that she has gained during her career: "Over 30 years, I have had the opportunity to watch infants grow up, those with supportive affectionate mothers grew up to be confident, high ranking and assertive. Those mothers that were rejecting and nervous tended to produce offspring that were jumpy and that had difficulty in entering into calm relaxed relationships. Humans can hide the effects of the small traumas of early life, but you can see them clearly in the chimp" (1992, 38). Quality parenting or lack of it makes a difference. Among many tribes, goals of expansion consumed men and women, which meant that kids often received

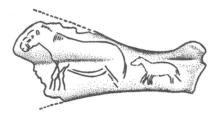

Being a mom is serious business. Foals are cared for over a period of a couple of years before they go out into the world. By then they are culturally schooled by good example as to what constitutes appropriate food, the best mates, social discipline and protocol, fearful situations, escape technique, and good nurturing skills. Mare and foal, Mas d'Azil, Fr.

minimal parenting. Tribal traditions of dispersing children to more distant relatives or assigning kids to rear one another (especially boys) undoubtedly had excitements and riches, but these situations also had the potential to disintegrate into undisciplined, rule-by-bare-knuckle, authoritarian modes, which kids would ultimately carry into adulthood.

Among many tribal groups individual children receive less attention, and a small, malformed, or less hardy child is often discriminated against. When parents have fewer children, with wider age gaps between them, it is easier to pleasantly attend to each child's needs. For example, several decades ago Bushman children were widely spaced, and weaning transitions were gradual and begun late. More recently, many Bushman women have children almost every year, and Lee (1994) observed that small children of pregnant mothers are now miserable compared with such children earlier. Both mothers and children seem to be showing the stresses of shorter birth spacing, in which the average is less than 12 months nursing and carrying, compared to the former traditions of 35–50 months. Self-reliance is molded by a secure situation in the first years of life, the years through age five being the most critical. Short birth spacing makes this more difficult.

Among hunter-gatherers, wild resources posed so many contingencies that every child had to be carefully tutored toward success as a resourceful and responsible adult member (Draper 1976). Among such groups production of resources does not exceed consumption until eighteen or so years of age (Kaplan 1996). Yet this gradual development in day-to-day successes of providing from wild resources seems to have created self-confidence in their ability to cooperatively procure and prepare food and to understand the natural order about them. This style of child rearing seems to promote an outlook that is deeply empirical, reasonable, and tolerant.

Connections between art and the supernatural seem to have been exaggerated and more common at higher Holocene densities. What are the criteria we can use to make those judgments from the fossil art itself?

Separating Natural Realities from Supernatural Ones in Prehistoric Art

The representations of animals by prehistoric man are utterly and awfully serious; not the least concession to vulgarity is allowed; though at times movement is attempted, the images are of hieratic profundity, full of religious force and thus can clearly be classified as Sacred Art, the first in the history of humanity.

M. T. Garcia Guinea, *Altamira and Other Cantabrian Caves*

Without any written or oral records from an extinct culture, how are we to determine, as Garcia Guinea did in the above quotation, whether or not its art served some mystical or magical symbolic purpose? What are the parts that are diagnostic of their uses in supernatural contexts? I would suggest that art made with those motives in mind exhibits several common features:

➤ Most symbolic "tribal art" has a studied replication about it. Special mystical symbols have a hierarchy of value, and the most important ones are *repeated over and over,* and not just the subjects but the forms themselves—the visual equivalent of a liturgy.

➤ Because of the conservative nature of religious art there should be *little diversity in subject matter.* These specifically identified forms, which theoreticians label as mystically symbolic because of their special character, should numerically constitute most of the quan-

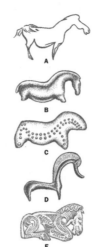

Paleolithic drawings and engravings of large-mammal images were somewhat constrained by representational accuracy, but small three-dimensional carved forms required a degree of generalization. **A,** Very straightforward representational horse, Ardales, Sp. **B,** Horse with some degree of abstraction, Vogelherd, Ger. **C,** Abstract animal sculpture from Sungir, Rus., so abstract its identity is unclear (found in a grave site). **D,** Small bronze, Villanovan (ca. seventh century B.C.). **E,** Scythian horse (3000 B.P.). These latter two types of stylization do not occur in Paleolithic large-mammal imagery or are extremely rare.

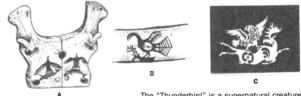

In addition to anthropomorphs, Holocene Bushman rock art also illustrates mythical creatures, such as these (various localities, South Africa). Portrayals of such creatures are quite rare in Paleolithic art.

The "Thunderbird" is a supernatural creature common in North American mythologies and art. Here are three Holocene representations of it attacking whales, caribou, and moose. **A,** Whaling harpoon rest with polar bears, Cape Prince of Wales, Alaska. **B,** Pipestem scrimshaw, Norton Sound, Alaska. **C,** Bronze Age leather panel, Siberia.

tity of the art for it to all be classified as mystically symbolic art.

➤ The more symbolic the art becomes, the more it loses its natural character. Parts are stressed for symbolic recognition and dramatization so that the essence of the subject matter may be there but the art begins to deviate considerably from the representational. In essence, it becomes *more stylized.*

Holocene age tribal arts often contain all kinds of enigmatic creatures: **A**, The Nadubi spirit, from Kakadu, Northern Territory. **B**, The mystical "Lightning Man," from Ingaladdi, Victoria River, Northern Territory, Austrl.

> - The more symbolic art becomes, the more likely the stylizations will be expressed in *certain limited poses;* such a development can be seen in Christian art and in the depictions of deities in Egyptian and Polynesian art.
> - The more symbolic the content of art, the more likely the stylizations will take on *geometric, nonrepresentational form.* In current conceptions we might call this a switch from complex right-brain imagery to left-brain notation.
> - The more symbolic the content of art, the more likely it is to *exclude poor draftsmanship.* When it becomes more symbolic, art is often taken over by a few specialists and one seldom sees poor draftsmanship, or art is reduced to easily produced patterns that can be mastered by all.
> - The more symbolic the characters in the art, the higher the proportion of characters that are enigmatic to observers from a quite different culture. If the art is highly symbolic, it is likely that there will be a high proportion of repeated cryptic metaphors in the form of *enigmatic images,* such as "anthropomorphs."

The more mystically laden or symbolic the imagery of distant cultures, the more alien we would expect it to appear. Bushman and Aboriginal art have many enigmatic scenes and individual figures that are difficult to interpret simply on the basis of familiarity with their environment. Scholars like Lewis-Williams (1981, 1983) and Vinnicombe (1976) have made great progress in explaining

Representation and Symbols Once an image becomes truly symbolic and stands for a very different entity or concept than it portrays literally, something almost mystical happens to that image in the human brain. Even the most objective symbols, like numbers, can acquire auspicious or inauspicious qualities. Word symbols are particularly susceptible to this conflationary phenomenon. For example, it does not help to explain that a blasphemous or obscene word is only an arbitrary sound-mix label, not the thing itself.

It works the same with visual symbols. The images of a swastika, national flags, certain graffiti, trademarks, and clothing styles take on meaning way beyond their inherent substance. This is so much a part of modern life that it is hard to think objectively of its larger implications. But this expansion of meaning seldom happens with figurative art. Its intent is the expression of the real, the vivifying union of felt experience or insight with the material stuff of charcoal, stone, and other media. In contrast, the repeated stylized imagery of symbolic art stiffens, sets up like concrete, soon tending toward the conflated iconographic—the ark of the covenant or the cross.

them with the help of the ethnography of existing Bushman and Aboriginals. I would reiterate, however, that similarly enigmatic forms such as strange anthropomorphs make up a modestly small fraction of Paleolithic art.

At the end of the Pleistocene when tribal organizations emerged, they often took the supernatural and elaborated it into something else, becoming organized religions, institutions that dominated everyday life. As Block (1977) and Brown (1991) propose, it was in the interest of hereditarily stratified tribal society to convert knowledge into ideology, history into mythology, biography into hagiography, and realistic imagery into iconography.

We could thus hypothesize that at tribal densities human inclinations toward the supernatural tend to change

A few natural contours of Combarelles Cave, Fr., brought to mind some animate image. This has been casually referred to as an anthropomorphic bison or a shaman, but it is more likely(?) to be a rudimentary attempt at drawing a bison, suggested by the natural cave contours; note beard and neck mane.

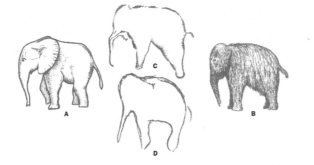

Paleolithic art is remarkably reliable. For example, several investigators, seeing the apparent lack of hair on images of young proboscideans portrayed in Paleolithic art, contended that these must be elephants. But when you can compare the Paleolithic images in question with the contours of living elephants and of mammoth mummies, the identity of the Paleolithic imagery is obvious. A, Elephant young. B, Woolly mammoth young. C, El Castillo, Sp. D, Arcy-sur-Cure, Fr. (reversed for comparison).

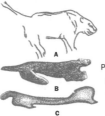

Paleolithic images of large mammals are seldom highly abstract. There are exceptions, as in these two sculpted Paleolithic images. Compare them with the lion engraving from La Marche. From top to bottom, increasing abstraction of lions: A, La Marche, Fr. B, Pavlov, Czech. C, Bezymiannaya, Rus. The latter's species identity is not totally clear; it could be a horse.

state and become fully institutionalized into formal religion—the business side of the mystical. If so, religion as we know it seems to have been a Holocene product. This change in scale of spiritual power was likely accompanied by a more prominent role for the supernatural to meet a suite of critical needs. Indeed, using the above criteria, this shift is visible in much of tribal art. Ideology is laced into tribal images and vice versa—images mean more, or at least take on meanings far removed from the portrayal itself.

The question is, If the supernatural had permeated Paleolithic art to the same degree that it did the art of most later tribal peoples, could we expect it to have taken on the repeated abstract-design qualities outlined in the above list? That is, could bands with such an elaborate religion also have this tribal kind of art?

The answer to that question seems to be yes; it is the process of using images more strictly as symbols that seems to produce the repetitious abstract features listed above, and the clearest expression of this phenomenon is best developed when these symbols refer to supernatural identities. If that conclusion is even approximately correct, it allows us to see Paleolithic art in a sharper image—for their art did *not* resemble the pattern in the above list.

The implications of this are that while the supernatural was undoubtedly important in their lives wherever it met their needs, there is no indication of ideological constraints on freedom and flexibility in their art. There are no inculcated or liturgical programmatic elements such as we associate with later tribes or even with the world's dominant modern religions (which were derived originally from tribal roots). Paleolithic spiritual life, though perhaps not so organized and powerful, could well have been more locally integrated with the sweetness and tragedy life brought. In that setting one might even picture the supernatural to be more clearly a fix rather than a cause. In a small band, everyone was known intimately, authority was contingent, and opinions and probabilities would have loomed larger than revelations and certainties. In the last chapter I stressed the necessarily close-linked feedback in the Paleolithic between theory and empirical experience as providing focus and limits to their lives. This likely extended to supernatural realities—their tether for embellishment inherently short-reined by the constraints of a Paleolithic lifeway.

More Historical Analogs: From Figurative to Abstract Art Traditions

The lifeways of more recent hunter-gatherers do not provide simple analogs to the Paleolithic, yet, as with my story about moa hunters, some other groups have undergone artistic and lifeway changes that are, to some degree, analogous to the Paleolithic-Holocene shifts we are discussing. Two of these are particularly relevant: the visual art of African Bushman and Australian Aboriginals.

While both historic Bushman and Aboriginals did hunt large mammals, they actually relied on a diverse array of resources, including plants, invertebrates, reptiles, fish, birds, and small mammals; and unlike Paleolithic peoples, both these later groups used hunting dogs. Thus, although Bushman and Aboriginals were hunters, they were not dependent on large mammals in the same way that Eurasian Paleolithic peoples were. The archaeological record, however, suggests that earlier Australian and Bushman groups may have been more dependent on large mammals, and also that they formerly lived in social contexts closer to those of Paleolithic bands. If my view of transformative changes in the scale of lifeways is correct, we would expect the older art of these peoples to be more like Paleolithic art. Is that the case?

AUSTRALIAN ABORIGINALS

Chaloupka (1984) has studied Aboriginal art in northern Australia in great detail and has proposed a chronology of stages based, among other things, on which styles of rock art are consistently superimposed upon other styles. Chaloupka identified the oldest art as the Naturalistic, or Pre-Estuarine, Phase, and this chronology is supported by the fact that the Naturalistic Phase includes images of now-extinct large mammals (thylacines and devils). Art of this Naturalistic Phase consists of less-abstract representations of large mammals (predominantly kangaroos, walleroos, and wallabies), hand stencils, and images of people done in "dynamic style," engaged in regular sorts of activities, many of which I would call "testosterone events."

Chaloupka argues that this early Australian art is different from the art of later periods (the Estuarine Phase) in that the animals are more realistically portrayed. Later art goes through a succession of changes, becoming more ab-

Two extremes of Australian Aboriginal art. To the left are kangaroos done in a highly representational style, technically very accomplished. Wilton, New South Wales. On the right is the highly mystical art of the Caterpillar Clan at Emily Gap, Northern Territory. I had to swim the pond that naturally preserved access to this latter site to obtain a photo of this caterpillar image.

stract, more "progressively stylized." He proposes: "The conceptual change from naturalism to schematisation of the previous styles. . . . reflects a change in the artist's psychological environment. This change was accompanied by transformation of a once semi-arid region, with abundant large mammals, into a wet lowland by the invasion of the rise in sea level at the beginning of the Holocene. This 120m rise created an estuarian environment with rich but diverse resources of fish, marine invertebrates, aquatic birds, etc., which still prevails in much of Arnhem Land" (1984, 41).

Thus, in this instance we have some confirmation of my hypothesis concerning lifeways, demographic scale, and visual art. Earlier Aboriginals in northern Australia, Arnhem Land, living at quite low densities (Haskovec 1993) were a closer analog to Paleolithic peoples than late Holocene Aboriginals in those same areas. Human densities increased during and after sea-rise, likely due to richer wild resources as well as new immigration and new tools. We know also that language diversified into complex subgroups. Images from the later Estuarian Phase show more enigmatic and symbolic art, and notably images from this latter period include, for the first time, scenes of battles showing large groups of armed men.

By the time of white contact, native Australians were no longer truly dependent on large mammals; they mainly subsisted on "bush-tucker," which included wild plants, insects, birds, and reptiles. Much of their art was highly abstract and symbolic, with significant mystical content. Again, simply subsisting on wild resources does

Just prior to their extinction, Drakensberg Bushman captured horses and in many ways adopted traits of other cultures: raiding, weapons, dress, etc. After all, hunter-gatherers must be flexible and opportunistic. *Left,* at Giant's Castle, R.S.A., we see paintings of probably the first European expedition. They even observed and remembered the one white foot on the horse. *Right,* Mpongweni, R.S.A. Before long some Bushman had their own horses.

Not all Pleistocene art is Eurasian. For example, this quadruped image on a stone was excavated from Apollo II Cave in Namibia. Associated charcoal dates are between nineteen and thirty thousand years ago. Thus, this African art is as old as the images found in Eurasian art.

not constitute the lifeway I am projecting as Paleolithic in character. As Ucko and Rosenfeld noted of Aboriginals at the time of European contact: "In terms of religious and metaphysical thought the Australian Aboriginal system is one of the most complex known among any people (including pastoralists and agriculturists) living today. . . . To know that a people live by hunting and gathering does not, therefore, enable one to generalize about many features of their culture" (1967, 150–151).

AFRICAN BUSHMAN

Though also not simply analogous to the Eurasian Paleolithic, the lifeways of Bushmen, as known from the past few centuries, are certainly closer analogs than, for example, their nearest tribal relatives, the Khoi/Hottentot grazer pastoralists. There seems to be a distinct difference in rock art between Bushman and the Hottentots who displaced them in large areas (Rudner and Rudner 1970; Van Rijssen 1984). The subject matter and style of Bushman art are recognizably realistic, whereas art of the Hottentot herders includes more abstract signs of dots and circles (Van Rijssen 1984). While there is considerable argument over many details of South African rock art meaning and authorship, this characterization seems to be well documented.

Bushman were not large-mammal-dependent spear-hunters like Paleolithic peoples. Bushman life would have been very different without dogs, bows, poison arrows, and richly diverse Holocene plant resources. Also, prior to

European contact and study, Bushman had undergone well over a thousand years of cultural contact and exchange with Bantu and Hottentots; aspects of religion, technology, and art were diffused among the various cultures. Bushman musical instruments, for example, became basically pan-Bantu. More recent Bushman rock-shelter paintings seem to contain symbolic and mystical images; older art, including the many thousands of images found hammer-peened into stones in open-air sites, featured more directly representational images of animals, particularly the hunted large mammals—with virtually no images that have been explicitly identified as mystically symbolic or somehow associated with shamanic art. Yet their images are replete with an extraordinary freedom.

Freedom of Art in Tribes and Bands

The strength of specialized tribal craftwork, agronomy, and animal husbandry is that, relative to Paleolithic lifeways, they can be encoded, must be encoded, into a set program. In a tribal system, what one has to master is the craft, the received and refined prescription of successful recipes. We know from the historical records and prehistoric artifacts that in its simple form or even in its complex forms, this program is repeated and repeated, often without reference to the earth, often until the land is milked of every nutrient or the trees are all cut. The tribe then moves to a more fertile region and the program is reinstituted. There is creativity among job specialties, and new developments are quickly institutionalized and spread. It is a life that must include much rhythm and repetition—and

Two sides of the same rock, Pleistocene faces from La Marche, Fr.

Throughout much of the region where Paleolithic art is preserved, it changed dramatically in the closing millennia of the last glaciation, but particularly in the east. The main tendency was for the visual art to become more abstract, stylized, schematic, and less representative. Rhythmic, repetitive patterns became more dominant. **A**, Pont d'Ambon, Fr. **B**, Pekarna, Czech. Both dating from the latest Pleistocene.

Sometimes the shape of the sketchbook page forces a modification of the image: **A**, Ibex, Mas d'Azil, Fr. **B**, Red deer, El Castillo, Sp. This factor was not limited to the Pleistocene but is seen throughout history: **c**, Red deer, Pre-Samartian, Volga River, fifth century.

from these emerge other repetitions, as we see in much of tribal art, for example, when the geometric stylized art from woven fabrics is applied to pottery decoration.

While accumulation of livestock or grain stores fell short of full environmental control, these steadying practices made the few uncontrollables loom much larger by contrast. Once the crops are seeded and the season of weed hoeing begins, success or failure is mainly dependent on the whims of parasites, disease, weather, and other forces more or less beyond one's control, and why they come and at which time is not only uncontrollable but unknowable. Only the unknowables can intervene on your behalf. Some kinds of worship and doctrine became a form of attempting to influence control in these areas. Doctrine began to dominate critical observation and reason as a guiding force. The successes of the tribal program freed the upper classes from daily labor, and the stores removed them from the Paleolithic vicissitudes of life. Tribal life allowed the upper classes to expand their mythology and the rhythms of their art. Tribal life was rich but perhaps in ways not so multicolored.

As the tribal ruling classes and their shamans became further removed from working with natural processes, their images of what was real began to take on bigger-than-life forms, super-natural in both senses of the word. Old stories were retold with more mystery and power than the originals. The feats of ancestors were inflated way beyond their accomplishments when alive. Other worlds grew in importance. We can reconstruct Paleolithic life as far from idyllic, and there were probably adequate chal-

The Potential of Visual Art to Disrupt Tribal Order Visual art can have a potent influence on established cultural order. Art's ability to embody and to emphasize experience, to make more real, means that visual images can work against an established social order as well as express the "right" set of meanings. Perhaps this is what underlies some religious proscriptions against visual art. A very familiar example comes from the Middle East. In a mass exodus, followers of the Egyptian sect of Akhenaton fled into the desert to avoid religious persecution. According to their tradition, they were given ten moral commandments by their tribes' own god, Yahweh. The second on the list was much later translated into King James English as "Thou shalt not make unto thee any graven image, or any likeness of anything that is in the heaven above, or that is in the earth beneath, or that is in the water under the earth" (Exodus 20:4). This revelation was intended to destroy not just idols but all representative art. And various sects of Judeo-Christian and Islamic religions have long heeded that second decree.

Perhaps, too, figurative images may have had a much more active effect on viewers in some past contexts, a haunting presence far beyond their simple forms. This does seem to be a common theme in ethnography involving idols, charms, amulets, talismans, voodoo dolls, and such. Maybe this concentrated potency is part of what kept so many individual tribal artists producing traditional and often abstract patterns. However that may be, the freedom we see in Paleolithic art does not exhibit any such iconographic inhibitions.

lenges between oneself and the earth that eclipsed making trouble with gods and neighbors. The tribalists' more certain control over aspects of the natural outer world may be the hinge factor which turned people more toward greater attention to the psychic spheres, with its benefits and detriments. Perhaps the switch in the art is indicative of those changes—the switch from the band's outer world of realistic natural subjects and large-mammal-centered imagery to an art of complex tribal abstractions of human images and human products, an inner world.

CREATIVITY AND ART: SOME CAVEATS

Art . . . constantly adventures, raids the inarticulate, and puzzles even its makers. Art is not a soothing and cohesive instrument (as ritual and craft are), but a way of exploring the open plasticity inherent in individual and social life.

Donald Brook, "Comments on Art"

I don't intend to propose some exclusionary dichotomy of band versus tribal art, for there are frequent occasions when tribal societies erupt irreverently outside their iconographic norms with wonderful flashes of originality and humor. It is these surprises among Mayan art, such as a ceramic form of two little plump dogs dancing arm in arm, that confer greatness upon those pieces amid the more repetitious forms. Wonderfully creative images can be found among most tribal art. It is as though the human creative spirit is difficult to bridle in spite of the best efforts of tribal normative strictures. In defiance of the official harnessing of art for symbolic secondary purposes, originality in art seems to keep effervescing along the flow of human endeavor.

Another way to get at a prime difference between Paleolithic and most tribal art is to understand that we can date archaeological finds of ceramics and woven fabric from Mesoamerica, Egypt, China, the Near East, and most other tribalist art by the changes in subject matter, motif, shape, and other aspects of style. This is not unlike changes in modern fashions. A number of investigators have tried to establish a chronological calendar of Paleolithic art fashion, but they have not been very successful (Clottes 2000). Paleolithic art is too free.

EVERLASTING FREEDOM

The essential message of this chapter is that to survive and prosper, Paleolithic peoples needed to construct a lifeway

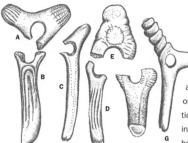

Remember, the Paleolithic theme that I am outlining describes patterns in imagery, but a pattern is not a law, only a skew. There are exceptions to the themes I am proposing. For example, some osseous holed straighteners do not have figurative imagery. A few have more abstract designs: **A–B**, Mas d'Azil, Fr. **C** and **G**, Le Placard, Fr. **D**, Isturitz, Fr. **E**, Gourdan, Fr. **F**, Laugerie-Basse, Fr.

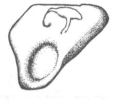

Holocene cobble engraved at Bushman Fountain, R.S.A. Note how serendipity played a role when an artist used the little indentation that caught rainwater and pecked a flamingo leaning forward to drink from the little pond.

that allowed them to be deeply empirical, rational, flexible, and imaginative—and these qualities are indeed reflected in Paleolithic art. That observation is particularly striking when compared to what happened at the end of the Pleistocene. Though freely and often quickly executed, Paleolithic works of art reveal the artists' absorption in observed details about their living subjects, quite different from works arising from traditions of visually codified and highly symbolic images. The diversity of images, the lack of set repetition, and the numerous sketchy, incomplete pieces by novices allow a backdoor view into the minds of Paleolithic artists. These illustrate again and again points of developmental maturation in the complex look-draw-look-draw process of art making, which paralleled their "empirical-rational-creative" freedoms in life.

One might say that a tribal artist tends to be more occupied with meaning and chooses to work with common subjects and recurrent themes or motifs that carry a load of meaning that is shared and understood by members of the group. That is probably what gives the recognizable stamp of refined and repeated continuity to much tribal art. As outsiders we may be struck by the beauty, the vigor of design, and the visual power of such work even when we don't know the insiders' story, the context of belief and

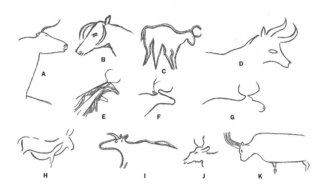

Most endeavors in the late Paleolithic, whether clothing construction, tanning, tracking, fishing, camp chores, child rearing, or whatever, required much learning to reach a reasonable facility. Drawing also required learning, but it differed from many other activities in one important way. It left fossils of this learning process. These aurochs images are evidence of the self-correcting aspects of practice and empirical thought. **A**, Niaux, Fr. **B**, La Loja, Sp. **C**, La Clotide, Sp. **D**, Gabillou, Fr. **E**, Sant Gregori, Sp. **F–G**, Cosquer, Fr. **H**, Pair-non-Pair, Fr. **I**, Niaux, Fr. **J**, Las Chimeneas, Sp. **K**, Niscemi, It.

Not only do the rudimentary Paleolithic sketches show few overtones of mystico-religious purpose and meaning, but most more accomplished pieces also lack overt symbolic overtones, such as this beautiful bull and cow pair, done in bas-relief, from Bourdeilles, Fr. One must have a solid empirical connection, a base of deep observation, not merely a knowledge of what aurochs symbolize or stand for, to make images with this clarity of representational realization.

practice. Occasionally, we can tune in to those meanings thanks to the work of ethnographers, historians, or an eloquent guide, and we gain a new dimension of appreciation. But this does not mean that all art is made from such a context. Art doesn't have to carry such a freight of identified belief. Paleolithic art certainly appears to me to be less "meaning-full," less belief bound, and more a matter of individual perception and experiment. Let me repeat this chapter's opening quote by Lorblanchet: "The everlasting freedom of Paleolithic art is an embarrassment to Prehistorians." Might I suggest a reason for this embarrassment? It is because prehistorians have been looking among Paleolithic images for stamps characteristic of tribal art, which simply are not there. All they find is everlasting freedom, the freedom the Pleistocene took with it when it left.

Throughout this book I have used natural history to examine Paleolithic art and to review a range of ideas about the human experience, using this old art as an informant, presuming throughout that close attention to earthly processes may enlighten us about our nature. Where do we go from here? If our experiences with art are not off-limits to the lamp of natural history, perhaps the spiritual is not either. So, again with Paleolithic art as our concrete focus, let's see how natural history might inform our understanding of the spiritual.

9

Throwing the Bones

Paleolithic Art and the Evolution
of the Supernatural

The predisposition to religious belief is the most complex and powerful force in
the human mind and in all probability is an ineradicable part of human nature.

E. O. Wilson, *On Human Nature*

A discussion about the natural history of art would be
incomplete without treating the possibility of a natural history of the supernatural—but it goes beyond
that. Let me hypothesize that there are areas of aesthetics (such as art), the spiritual (the supernatural),
and much of science (including natural history) that
are more interconnected than we are accustomed to
thinking. If that is correct, and we can comprehend
that connection, it offers an opportunity to under-

Belief in the supernatural is so ubiquitous among humans that we can, with considerable certainty, say it was around the hearths in the Paleolithic. Boys from La Marche, Fr.

A, The famous painting from the cave of Trois Frères, Fr., appears to represent a dancer in ceremonial or mystical disguise. **B,** There is a remarkably similar image from much later prehistoric Bushman art at Afvallingskop, R.S.A. The Paleolithic male figure is clearly human except for the mask and tail. One could say something similar for the male portrayed in Bushman rock art. Note, as an aside, in **B** the line running at right angles to the Bushman's penis. This is a bony insert, used by prehistoric tribes in South Africa and found in excavated burials. **C–D,** Images from historic times made by Sioux, from the American Plains.

stand Paleolithic art better, and maybe ourselves as well. Therefore, I do three things in this chapter. First, I look at the nature of human belief in a supernatural. Second, I try to account for our attraction to a supernatural in evolutionary terms in order to winnow out a little order in human prehistory and history. In the end, I explore some tangible examples of how art has combined with the supernatural throughout our natural history, examples that intimately relate to prehistoric art.

This way of dealing with the supernatural will be very off-putting to some people, but here I must speak in the broadest terms. By "supernatural" I refer to that heterogeneous arena of special arrangements with the universe, things like fate, luck, karma, grace, transcendence, sorcery, magic, and holiness. I include the divine, sanctified, providential, sacred, prophetic, clairvoyant, blessed, mesmeric, ectoplasmic, and so on. What the items in this heterogeneous list have in common is that they normally enlist supernatural forces. That is, they are not things typically searched for by astronomical telescopes, dealt with in chemistry and physics labs, or examined in biological field studies or by neurophysiologists, cognitive psychologists, and so forth; thus, they are often referred to as alternative realities.

Alternative Realities

I'll start by making the leap of faith that the people who made this old art were involved with the supernatural. I can safely do that because belief in a supernatural falls among the list of human universals for all cultures (Brown 1991) and so is perhaps a natural part of our predisposition (Boyer 1994). Although no Paleolithic images fall unequivocally into the category of the supernatural, there are a few that may, like the well-known "Sorcerer" from Trois Frères Cave in France. If this piece and perhaps some others do represent an early belief in the supernatural, their presence opens several lines of reasoning. We can ask why traces of the supernatural experience are not nearly as frequent in Paleolithic art as they are among later tribal peoples. Perhaps more important, their presence in Paleolithic art allows us to ask whether a universal inclination toward the mystical implies that it has been a part of our nature for a very long time—and, if so, where it would have come from. Ultimately, it forces us to wonder whether the Paleolithic supernatural was somehow an antagonist to reason or whether reason and the grace of revelation have something in common as part of the human experience that we have failed to emphasize.

Take a mundane subject like the study of bones, for example. Bones contain much forensic information. Paleontologists can reconstruct a lot about the appearance of extinct species by studying their bones. Using the same reliance on reason, orthopedic surgeons can deduce from x-rays the degree and nature of, say, osteoporotic disease.

We can follow the rationale of these processes. But this reliance on explicable reason is not the same process that "seers" of many cultures employ in their examination of the scatter of tossed bones as a way to divine the future. Sometimes scapulae are thrown into the fire to let the pattern of their cracking reveal new, nonrational truths. Likewise, relicts, often bone fragments of deified leaders, biblical figures, religious martyrs, or otherwise sanctified personages, are used for their magical power to consecrate holy places. For example, bones attributed to the three Magi, Melchior, Balthazar, and Caspar, are housed in the cathedral at Cologne, just a bicycle ride away from Bonn, where my family and I are living as I start this chapter. These different uses of old bones make rough but perhaps poignant metaphors about our humanness, our alternative ways of approaching reality. Reason and revelation: the differences between these approaches are obvious you might say, but in this chapter I am mainly after some of their connected parts, parts still connected today as well as in the Paleolithic.

The hypothesis that the two ways of knowing, reason and revelation, are parts of a whole is derived from the fact that evolution has influenced all of our perceptions, though sometimes in an imbalanced way, and therefore, even our sensitivities and values about aesthetics and the supernatural should also have been shaped by evolution. Evolution has affected how we experience events, and in that reality, portions of biology, art, and the religious experience are not so disparate. Moreover, the perceived does not necessarily equal some objective "actual," and that insight is the key to the ideas we are going to examine.

Evolution does not select for an animal's ability to record the complete reality, only some particular version or segment, for example, insect ultraviolet visual ranges, bat sonar night images, and snake infrared sensitivity. These species-specific distortions in perception are, to them, more relevant, more advantageous, than some unedited whole-spectrum view. This distortion amounts to more than adaptively economic selectivity. It actively blinds organisms to other whole ranges of access—the Consig-

Fear-inspiring figures play an important role in enforcing ethical behavior in most human groups. Prehistoric, but rather recent, rock art from Tamgali, Kazakhstan.

liere's lies of omission. Has it done that for us? Of course. But this idea entails more than physical senses and even includes how ideas are processed. For example, we easily succumb to the narrowness of parochialism, from the level of the neighborhood to nationalism, we are unable to comprehend geological time and galactic space, we find the complexity of our own unconscious homeostatic processes impenetrable, and most of us cannot accept death, especially our own, and on and on. The inherent distortions of the arts, in a way, are almost a metaphor here—making objective reality more subjectively real—similar to how, in this book, I use the Consigliere metaphors as a kind of distortion to try to make the tangle-knotted details of evolution more understandable. Remember the Oscar Wilde quotation "The final revolution is that Lying, the telling of beautiful untrue things, is the proper aim of Art" (1970, 992).

But evolution lies not only by omission but by commission as well. For example, I have talked about exaggerated body modeling with fat depots and fake jaw contours from beards, but there is more blatant evolutionary lying by mimicry of eyespots on insect wings and by the fake eyes and snout on the tail end of some worms and snakes that make it look like the head end. There are even fake fangs (Guthrie 1971a) and false horns (Guthrie and Petocz 1970) on some large mammals. The *whole truth* is often not selectively the most advantageous. Evolution "fills in" the vertebrate retinal blind spot (yours too) using nearby images, erasing the black hole made by the base of the optic nerve. What about our wide view out across the humanscape? Evolution has really pulled off a good one there. For evolution's purposes, the supernatural often becomes a better metaphor than the gritty details of the natural.

It is unlikely that all Paleolithic disguises were for purposes of hunting, though clear depictions of disguises in ceremony and dancing are rare indeed. I suspect that Paleolithic dancers, like the dancers shown in this later Holocene Bushman art from Medanke Cave and Cathedral Peak, R.S.A., also expressed delight and wonder in other species as well as their symbolic spiritual connections.

As I said, all human groups, wherever they occur, on the remotest isolated islands, out on the Arctic pack ice, in the densest jungles—whatever the climate or resources—have in common the experience of and reference to the supernatural. So it is virtually certain that the people who made Paleolithic art shared that behavior with us.

In fact, it has become traditional to assume that these Pleistocene people were so drenched in the supernatural that it was the only theme of their art. The evidence is otherwise, and up to this point in the book I have explored those other, more natural themes. By emphasizing aspects of Paleolithic natural history I did not mean to discount the idea that Paleolithic people believed in the supernatural. How much of a role did the supernatural play in their lives? We may never know, because the actual evidence is meager. More on that later, but measurement is not my main concern here. Rather, my concern lies more in the direction of where this supernatural bent came from and how it arose in the Pleistocene—how is its natural history relevant to Paleolithic art?

It is traditional to say that the supernatural is what must be resorted to when we cannot explain things by natural processes. That is probably true, but the supernatural, both institutionalized and not, is much more. The supernatural (again, using the word here in its broadest sense) is a powerful psychic force in maintaining emotional health and physical well-being and is something, I would argue, that is unparalleled in the rest of human behavior. Behavior centering on the supernatural has life consequences that are too important for natural selection to have ignored. These supernatural forces include the balm for a troubled mind where immediate or perceived truth is too unacceptable, the unguent for unendurable physical pain, and the familiarity of traditional rites in the face of uncertainty and the unfamiliar. It is particularly important in the case of illness. Supernatural forces are also the ultimate comfort against the grinding reality of our inherent loneliness, age-related disabilities, and much more. The supernatural has enormous power. It is important in supporting authority by maintaining the hierarchies within groups, just as it is the main ingredient in cooperation or conflicts between groups.

Life is fragile, and down deep some emotional perils of the Pleistocene have not changed much; the roar of traffic is not as frightening as that of lions, but the finality of death from both causes is identical. Pain is still painful. Grief is just as sorrowful. Worry and loneliness do not change state wherever they occur. That is a hard reality. And not only is life's frailty much the same since the Paleolithic, but our remedies have not really changed much either. The key medication is that inner core of confidence in the supernatural aegis (Aegis, remember, was the name of the god Zeus's shield) that allows humans to see themselves as more special than they actually are in the natural scheme of things. Even though aspects of the supernatural may not play a conscious or even significant role in everyday life, they do emerge in some form. And these images of the supernatural and their symbols do get into art.

The supernatural is often entangled with the arts: music, singing, dance, the graphic arts, architecture, dress, theater, stories, and the sagas of myth and legend. Though art and the supernatural are officially different sectors of our lives, they are systemically related. Like the supernatural, art intends to abstract out a more meaningful reality from the dither and noise of the daily grind among the natural—to construct super-nature, a step beyond what we find growing wild, to make reality more real than real.

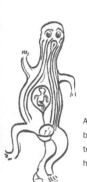

All life is risky, and more so at the crossroads of change, puberty, mating, and especially birth. We can use some extra protection beyond that available naturally. Holocene x-ray motherhood, Victoria River, Austrl.

David Robert's powerful artworks of North African ruins from 1824 still convey much more of the impact of their grandeur than any of today's color photos.

In a few pages I will go into the details of how we might identify this category of supernatural image in Paleolithic art, or for that matter in any prehistoric art of vanished cultures. But first I want to pursue the hypothesis that the universal tendency to incorporate the supernatural into one's thinking is part of an adaptive process—and this accounts for why it emerged and still emerges in the human experience. I think to appreciate those particular images in the art, to even identify them, we have to acknowledge the nature of powerful biological forces behind the supernatural.

We really didn't need to know that we share over 98% of our genes with chimps to recognize our affinity with other primate species—all products of evolution's dictates in a bed of chaos, fragile sacks of protoplasm, giant colonies of sister cells, weavings of synapses, fathered by lust, bathed in a billion parasites, immoral and moral, yammering in different tongues, bonding to others, all finite and mortal. That is real. It is objective reality, and for the time being, it is true to the best we can discern. Yet, another voice says, that may be, but it is not all, there is another reality, an alternative reality, some meaning above and beyond nature. We have no evidence from their behavior that chimps, or any animal other than ourselves, share any such perception—at least in its well-developed state.

That sense of an alternative reality, outside reason, seems to pervade all human groups, and maybe all individuals, in varying degrees. There is this inclination to jump beyond the dictates of logical cause-effect reasoning, expecting some force beyond the palpable. In its more dilute strength this tendency takes the form of bucking the odds in gambling or being reluctant to wear a shirt you were wearing the last time you had a miserable experience. There is a part of us that demands some additional forces beyond logic, forces weighing in for our side, our team, our group. Are they out there, beyond the natural realities of frigid black outer space, the incredible span of light-years between us and pinprick galaxies, in among the fine rumble of Brownian movement's blind chance, staving off senility and damp decomposing graves, something armed against the natural vicissitudes of calamity, something to counter stories of the selfish gene?

It is not a new insight that this proneness to believe in an alternative, nonrational reality is a part of our makeup, a genetic program within us, like nurturance and lust, but it is an idea that is not often expressed. Many might be offended by my dichotomizing the rational and the nonrational. But here I am using "nonrational" in a more explicit sense: I am not saying that a given route to a belief may not have followed a rational path—just that it is not then subjected to analysis through the venue common to secular matters. Religious congregations are not gathered to hear recent data on tests about the efficacy of different prayer postures, like a business or scientific meeting, rather they are there to reiterate the goodness and power of their common faith. What I want to emphasize is that rational and nonrational are not totally exclusive, but we must first see them as two different modes.

Evaluating the Adaptive Nature
of Alternative Realities

Nor must we overlook the probability of the constant inculcation in a belief in God on the minds of children producing so strong and perhaps an inherited effect on their brains not yet fully developed, that it would be as difficult for them to throw off their belief in God, as for a monkey to throw off its instinctive fear and hatred of a snake.

Charles Darwin, *The Origin of Species*

Earlier in this book, we evaluated whether or not a character had an evolutionary adaptive component by subjecting it to several criteria, and among these were the following. (1) To be able to separate a character from an epiphenomenon it must be improbably complex. (2) There must be some heritability to its variations. (3) There must be obvious potential selective forces, that is to say, reproductive advantages, that would favor those genes underlying its expression. And (4) we can often appreciate these fitness benefits best by looking at how they are not without costs; that is, the character may exist at considerable biological expense. So how does the character of emotions and behavior relating to the supernatural among humans hold up to this scrutiny?

1. The human attraction to the supernatural certainly involves a constellation of improbably complex psychic characteristics. Its predisposition is unusually tenacious. I already alluded to the cross-cultural ubiquity of human behaviors that employ the "supernatural." This often involves special emotional states that have few counterparts in the rest of human experience: being in the spirit, trance states, speaking-in-tongues, visions, mystic states, a sense of blessedness and certitude that comes from "standing in the light." These may possibly all be related to the same core emotion. Similar widespread core emotions, like lust, jealousy, envy, romantic love, seem to be annealed in the evolutionary foundry. The supernatural, as a character, bears all the earmarks of an evolved trait in that respect.

2. But these aspects of a spiritual sense and its accompanying behavior may all be cultural artifacts. How can we assess whether any of this has an underlying biology? We know that the predilection toward soliciting the supernat-

The snake is another figure that is found repeatedly in much of Holocene tribal art. This is the "Rainbow Serpent" from Victoria River, Austrl.

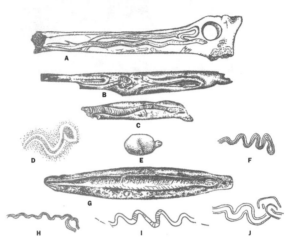

Reptiles are rather rare in Paleolithic art, and those found are not markedly stylized. **A**, Montgaudier, Fr. **B**, Lespugue, Fr. **C**, Gourdan, Fr. **D**, **F**, **H**, and **J**, Rouffignac, Fr. **E**, Saint-Cirq, Fr. **G**, Lortet, Fr. **I**, Eino, Sp. **E** is probably a tortoise; the rest are serpents.

ural is individually variable, but is it heritable? If "religiosity" (that is the testers' unfortunate shorthand term for this tendency toward preoccupation with the spiritual) has a genetic component, we would expect it to show up in studies of personality differences. Loehlin and Nichols (1976) studied 850 high-school monozygotic and dizygotic twins and found the genetic contribution toward variations in religiosity to be around 20%. Waller et al. (1990) also found a positive genetic contribution to religiosity. One of the many human properties measured in the Minnesota Twin Study of identical (monozygotic) twins reared apart in different families from birth (Bouchard et al. 1990) was religiosity, and they found a moderately high heritability of 0.49. Which is to say, about half of the observed variability of scores on a standard test of personal inclination toward religiosity could be attributed to genetic variation and about half came from environmental influences. A few of Bouchard's critics, in several

In this recent tribal Eskimo art, Nulukhtulogumut, the spirit reindeer, and its *inua* are linked by a line connecting their throats. Images that are enigmatic to an outsider are not the norm in Paleolithic art.

Later Holocene tribal art about going to war, Bourke, Austrl. The first religions were probably monotheistic, a special god for our own group, a protector, perhaps a bigger-than-life ancestor, who looked out for our group, our tribe—some superparent on our side.

X-ray view of three caribou (American wild reindeer) skewered by an arrow, from recent Eskimo art. Bering Sea, Alaska.

studies since, have disputed the exact range of this figure, but even critics in the technical literature arrive at figures substantially higher than zero. This supports other cross-cultural observations that there seems to be an inherent part of our personalities which predisposes us toward an alternative, supernatural reality, and like virtually everything else, it varies from individual to individual.

3. But what are the evolutionary "fitness" benefits? I don't really pretend to know the common stickum that combines diverse complex uses of the supernatural. Yet it is plain even to me that throughout human history we have not ventured into the world of the supernatural on an even front but along many related tributaries, each to resolve fundamental human concerns:

➤ Goblins, devils, and demons are probably the most rudimentary supernatural tools used to maintain power and order.

➤ Legends, sagas, and myths, campfire tales of "just-so" stories about external reality, are a primary medium of oral traditions: why the raven is black, and why hail must be the rainbow's eggs. These kinds of stories form the basic cultural folklore of every society. They help erase the ideological vacuum of our *sapiens* want—our need to understand.

➤ The same is true for understanding our internal reality; we have used supernatural constructions to account for the workings of our own psyches: love, hatred, gentleness, madness, rage, evil and goodness, dreams, hypnotic states, trance, and the mind's more deviant turns of extreme cruelty and mental illness.

➤ Our need for or uncertainties about leadership have perhaps led to ancestor worship: parents, superparents, chiefs, heroic chiefs, long-dead great chiefs, idealized forefathers, and deities, in something like that developmental progression (Wilson 1978; Alexander 1979; Cook 1980). Ulcers and stress insomnia are almost unknown among ten-year-olds; they snooze under the blanket of parental protection. In adult life, superparents and deities provide an enormous cushion of guardian security.

➤ One has only to be desperately sick or have loved ones who are suffering when natural forces offer no healing to witness the balm afforded by the supernatural.

➤ Supernatural ingredients harnessed into group identity, validating and blessing it, add up to the best weapon of defense or offense: God Bless America, *Gott mit uns.*

4. Counterbalancing the great benefits of employing the supernatural are its costs. For starters, its rituals and development often require considerable time, resources, and energy. Its greatest cost is in its occasional major distor-

tions of objective reality, which can produce debilitating stresses of hexes, curses, and guilt. Most organized religions are "exclusive" by definition, us and them, and that exclusivity has often been used as the main program underlying class discrimination and group conflict. Name the warring hot spots on the globe, and religion is, unfortunately, always a key player: Israel, Northern Ireland, Tibet, Afghanistan, the Balkans, and so on.

As with most evolutionary things, we are caught in the vise of balanced selection. That squeeze of course is the counterbalancing force that holds back greater selection for supernatural ways of thinking—they cannot expand infinitely. One's spiritual side has the potential to get you into trouble, decreasing your fitness—the solace against disease and anguish can become derailed to unreasonable cures. There are many despots, demagogues, and prophets out there bartering for your soul, deluded by wild, convoluted malignancies—at their extreme, sacrificing baby daughters to Baal, drinking poison Kool-Aid in Jonestown, Sitting Bull's Ghost Dance cult, on down an unimaginably long list of genocides in the name of holiness. Reason normally allows humans to avoid these, but not always.

Despite its risks and costs, the empirical evidence shows that uses of the supernatural sector of reality are not a biological waste of time. Studies that seek to identify the constellation of lifestyles that promote good health (physically, emotionally, and socially), as seen in longer life spans, reproductive health, strong immune systems, reduced recovery time from accidents, lower rates of suicide, reduced drug addiction, low crime rates, and so forth, seldom fail to cite the necessity of a balanced spiritual life (e.g., Ornish 1998).

Although we could add more to the list, these examples are sufficient to remind us that the supernatural is a powerful force on many fronts—too potent a heritable behavior for evolution to have left as one of life's frills.

But as with other evolutionary concerns, the proximate is difficult to tease apart from the ultimate. We are not normally drawn to the supernatural by some rational calculus concerning the above lists. The Consigliere has installed directive emotions as intermediaries, just as there are for dining or reproducing. Human experience with the supernatural involves what is often referred to as "sensing the presence of the spirit," and I will return to these intermediaries later.

OUR SPIRITUAL FIX

Let us explore the possibility that our bent toward the pursuit of the supernatural comes from our very nature. I have repeatedly emphasized that to occupy the human-style Pleistocene niche, our human ancestors needed a whole constellation of items that enabled them to function in that lifestyle: language, cooperation, refined child care, and many others. Among those were the three skills of being able to (1) objectively observe empirical evidence, (2) reason logically, often dispassionately, and (3) creatively come up with perceptive new ideas. In this chapter I will use the terms "rationality" or "reason" as shorthand to refer to this entire complex. But to occupy our niche we may have needed something more: special treatment by the universe for ourselves, our family, our group, the confidence that something out there was on our side more than the other person's or group's.

The adaptive aspects of our attraction to the supernatural are not easy to see. Our immense malleability, derived from the opportunistic features of our evolutionary niche, inadvertently obscures our basic biological nature. It is not immediately obvious that we trail long evolutionary strings behind us: the purpose behind our sweaty hands is not so apparent when we make a tense telephone call as it was when we wielded tree limb, pike, or digging stick with a better grip. Although the Consigliere's work may be both wonderfully amazing and at the same time a little sloppy, not quite optimum, the human program does function well. If they could speak, the extinct woolly beasts in Paleolithic art would testify to that, for they must have felt the power behind our evolution—weaponry, knowledge, creativity, and, above all, the strength we, as bands and individuals, gathered from the supernatural forces who accompanied us.

THE PLEISTOCENE MIRROR PROBLEM

Our intellectual edge that allowed us to observe objectively, reason logically, and use imagination came with some mental perils. This clarity of complex awareness and comprehension had the potential to lead us into places of mind we should not trespass, should not worry about. Though good enough for most purposes, imaginative reason may overexpose us to both real and imagined worry, tragedy, isolation, and pain, and we malfunction. Rational literalness can sometimes be too destabilizing, unsettling, or unhealthy. The Consigliere's evolutionary handiwork was laid bare as dangerously illogical—playing looked like a waste of time, the good of sharing seemed unreasonable, sexual fidelity too restrictive, aging too unfair, death too final, and life was heading nowhere. Old evolutionary shortcuts came home to roost when this new organism turned its reason to the mirror. The risks of this potential problem were unavoidable, but there were ways in which they could be ameliorated if not completely fixed.

NATURAL FIXES AND EVOLUTIONARY ACCESSORIES

My evolutionary metaphors of a Don and Consigliere fall short here. A Consigliere's simple solution to the Don's assignment usually works, but it often creates other problems or repercussions. And for that there is a Fixer. The Sicilian analog's namesake in real life is the negotiator whom parties approach to solve conflicts, sweeten the pot, or add the caveat clauses. She fixes the solution so it works better, and then fixes the parts of the fix that dysfunction.

Evolution likewise zigzags along, not so much by total reorganization but by add-on fixes or patches. Some have called this process tinkering. These kinds of little add-on fixes can accumulate and turn organisms into something

By age thirty-five one was an elder in the Pleistocene. **A**, Here is a wise old Paleolithic guy who was responsible for the male side of wisdom and who must have spent much time telling stories to the young. **B**, My redrawing. La Marche. Fr.

quite different from their ancestors. Whales came from terrestrial animals but became amazingly adept at marine life. But they did so by an enormous string of add-ons that allowed them to make the best of air-breathing and still be deep divers. The existence of add-ons allows us to work out the evolutionary history of many organisms because each species retains all kinds of hints of their past underneath the tacked-on additions. For example, our worm-segmented past is still there in our stuttering of vertebrae, ribs, and the segmental branches of our neural wiring.

To use the crude analogy of a car engine: just look under the hood and see all the added complexity of fixes to compensate for the limitations of the Benz and Daimler's 1885–1886 simple design by using the added assets of a battery, alternator, water cooling device, fuel injection, air and gas filters, oil pump, computer, and so forth (every year more is crammed into the engine compartment). The gasoline engine has taken many different directions, and with each comes a plethora of different modifications. By using other processes, evolution normally works though analogous add-on enhancements in response to the pressures of new demands on older systems that do not meet current competitive standards. But in evolution the choices available are often limited.

Archaeologists have nicknamed this little Paleo-lithic hooded image "the bust." It comes from Balzi Rossi, It., and is perhaps part of a pendant (judging from the other artifacts at that site). We think in metaphors, and whoever she was meant to represent would make a good metaphor for all the "fixing" that needed to be done in her time and the 25,000 years since.

Mystical rain animal? This is a common design from rather recent but prehistoric Bushman groups in South Africa.

The problem is that selection has to work on existing variations. Even when there are suitable variations available to be selected (perhaps most of the time none are), these variants are not usually along some conceivably optimum pathway but more often are just handy quick duct-tape solutions. Genetics textbooks use the extreme example of the sickle-cell antidote to malaria. One homozygote easily succumbs to malaria; the other is debilitated by sickle-cell anemia. The heterozygote is resistant to both. But to achieve the heterozygote condition, every generation many lethal or sublethal homozygotes must be produced. As a result, this adaptive system is costly and wasteful in individual tragedies, but it did allow people to live in areas with untreatable malaria, at least if they had enough kids to compensate for the higher mortality. The genetic variations for this antimalaria fix were apparently easily available; more sophisticated and efficient antimalaria defenses were not. Conclusion: some fixes are far from ideal.

THE FIXER'S SOLUTION TO THE MIRROR PROBLEM

Now this is where I am going: the Fixer's tacked-on solution for the perils of the rational system. Remember, the rational system can be reflected back on our own nature, often discovering unacceptable images—images that tell us things we don't want to know. But those kinds of reflections can be edited. Our editor, or repair substance, seems to have been spirituality—the emollient of the supernatural. With that, the engine of the rational brain not only works but runs even better, most of the time. The fix was to isolate a few of the processes of reason which dealt with

meaning and purpose and to make those sectors accept meaning by grace, authority by revelation, and an alternative cast to reality outside the natural world. We all use this in different ways and degrees, nobody is exempt, it is part of being human.

Why did we need this fix in the first place? Evolution of the ability to reason creatively was a little like other biological fixes; at the outset its advantages outweighed its "side effects." The ability to reason started as a complex biological system to approximate truth, not meaning. But meaning has a truth too. Once humans' amazing ability to exploit complex reason continued to expand, this analytical awareness began to short-circuit. A rational mind could better comprehend and be overwhelmed by the meaning of death, illness, isolation, and loss and better imagine eternity. What variations were available to cement the patch? There were undoubtedly few. The most direct was to simply "screen out the offending red blood cells," that is, to have sectors of our experience where we screen out the relevant natural world and our troubled reasoning about it—parts that will, or are likely to, trigger severe emotional conflict.

Or we can make substitutions. For that fix we leaned on the evolutionary handmaiden of reason, the creativity that had evolved as a necessary adjunct. In those sectors where reason weighed too heavily, humans seem genetically predisposed to creatively insert alternative realities—often, the revelations of the supernatural. For that, we tapped the emotional predispositions already handy in the primate brain to make the nonrational credible—a deference that yielded reason to *authority* in exchange for peace of mind, group unity, and ethical cohesion.

Now, recall from chapter 7 that art making may be a part of the backdoor route toward developing creativity, part of a fix for managing the expansion of old ape uninspired literal reason. It was not art for art's sake. Here, likewise, it was not the supernatural for its own sake. The supernatural seems also to be a Consigliere fix for the expanded potential for human literal reason and imagination—just treating a different sector from art. And now here they all are: art, the spiritual, and reason, all meeting at the same intersection. Ironically, the same natural perceptive creativity that forced the need for the supernatural was waiting on the other side to create the artistic flourish that embroidered its fabric and made beautiful its rituals.

This cobbled-up combination of bone forensics and throwing the bones is far from being fool-proof, because both systems, of reason and of revelation, use evolution's Mallmart-economical versions. For example, for human reason to function and be flexible, it must rely on many precious years and many costly mistakes in the acquisition of some semblance of wisdom. Installing this system into a savanna ape was an elegant feat, but it came with a few design failures that could have been easily solved by the genetic inheritance of acquired knowledge or access to infallible sources of all-knowing swami revelations, but apparently evolution could not find either, at least any affordable ones. But a patch worked, more or less: the appearance of infallible grace was almost as good as the real thing, and like art, in some ways it may be better.

African Bushman have a dance-trance tradition that they apparently shared to some degree with early Bantu neighbors. In trance, Bushman often bleed from the nose. And nosebleeds in the art often seem to represent a trance condition when shamans are in "out-of-body" states, imagining they are other species. But this does not mean that all animals portrayed as bleeding from the nose in prehistoric Bushman art are shamans in trances. Rather, it is clear that many of the Bushman images are portraying lung hits, as we have seen in Paleolithic and other art among hunting societies. You need to be aware that nosebleeds occur for different reasons.

So while it is our specialty, humans are not totally creatures of rationality and reason, but in a curious way we can use reason to understand the adaptive nature of our non-rational processes. And that is what I am trying to do in these last pages. That is, we can use a double mirror to look behind us and apply reason to the very supernatural substance designed as the default mode around that literal reason. And for that, the joint interactions of natural history, the supernatural, and art allow us the right-of-entry, for despite its name, the supernatural has a natural history.

The Bumpy Road to Finding Order and Truth in All This Stuff about Art and the Supernatural

Then Miss Watson took me in a closet and prayed, but nothing came of it. She told me to pray everyday, and whatever I asked for I would get. But I tried it. Once I got a fish-line, but no hooks. It warn't any good to me without hooks. I tried for the hooks three or four times, but somehow I couldn't make it work. By and by, one day, I asked Miss Watson to try for me, but she said I was a fool. She never told me why, and I couldn't make it out no way.

Mark Twain, *Adventures of Huckleberry Finn*

To find the order in the preceding ideas about the supernatural and art I must remind you of our present context. Two current philosophies have dominated Western thought throughout the last century: modernism and postmodernism. Through these paradigms somehow the idea of alternative realities got mixed up with the idea of maybe no realities. And it is this relativism of no reality that interferes with looking to Paleolithic art for some substance.

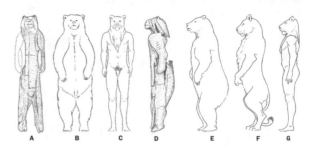

It is not always easy to identify Paleolithic images specifically made for mystical purposes. For example, this small carved image (front view in **A** and side view in **D**) from Hohlenstein-Stadel, Ger., has been described as a "lion-man" shaman, meant to represent a person with a lion head or mask (**C** and **G**). My drawings (**B** and **E**) show how this could just as likely have been an attempt to represent a bear standing on two legs (familiar to people as the circus "dancing-bear" posture). It is a common posture used by wild bears to look around. Lions seldom use this upright posture (**F**).

MODERNIST AND POSTMODERNIST EXTREMES AND THEIR APPROACHES TO PALEOLITHIC ART

The modernists matched the progressive air of technology with that same view of art. The innovative movements of oils done *en plein air,* impressionistic freedoms, and dramatic abstractions were revolutionary and awesome at their outset. Indeed, innovative change is our forte and has an inherent appeal. And so it became a mystical assumption that art should embody the new, that some form of striking novelty itself was art's highest value and deepest meaning. That approach meant that the early representational nature of Paleolithic art was a stage long past, passé. But with time this modernist position of ever-upward and ever-new began to show strain: white canvases with single red lines, and strings of pebbles on museum floors. How to relieve this strain? Postmodernists chose to adjust the modernist ideology by arguing that art value is not necessarily progressive, not time related, but constructed locally, each culture with its own treasures, each time with its own gems. Postmodernism grew out of cultural determinism—the axiom that you and I are products of our times, in an infinitely flexible milieu, our philosophies, tastes, and beliefs products of our particular biases. It was an appealing substitute.

Indeed, much of the thrust of postmodernism has significant substance: literal facts do not automatically convert on their own into universal truth and order; indi-

Carved bone necklace from Labastide, Fr., with images of bison and/or ibex.

Natural history is richly depicted in Paleolithic art. **A–B**, These "anthropomorphs" are actually the flightless giant auk, a seabird that became extinct in the Atlantic within historic times, but was widespread in the Mediterranean during late Paleolithic times, as shown in these two images from Cosquer, Fr. **c**, My illustration of this species.

vidual people make the always flawed translation. Postmodernism and deconstructivist ideas (which have dominated the humanities and social sciences for the last three decades) have added much depth to historical perspectives and assessments in our own time. But their fundamentalist axiom of relativity can become too extreme when taken literally. We are not only reflections of our times. We are more than victims of our social circumstance, reality is more than the version shouted the loudest by the most powerful, there is timeless beauty, and there is some order among the chaos—a few universals behind jumble. Paleolithic art, both its aesthetics and its content, should not be set adrift in a postmodern sea of relativism.

Every shred of evidence, and the archaeological record is part of that, argues for the truth in there being an objective reality outside our beings, which was there long before we were and will be there after we cease being—as individuals and as a species. True, science can never contend that its truths are unchangeable, final versions, nor that its approximations of truth are more than that, but the first step in finding order seems to arise from the observation that reasonable truth is out there, difficult though it may be for this ape to fathom. One can deny that, only by totally resorting to some other principle of revealed truth, not reason.

Though each of us can bring our own individual sensibilities to Paleolithic art, as we might to a contemporary art exhibit, the outstanding unknowns about Paleolithic

art not only are about the artists' aesthetic experiences and the individual meanings or purposes of the art to them, or to us, but also include the real grit and texture of objective reality, parts of which we can tease from this old art. Real people from the Ice Age made those drawings, and we can know something about the subjects they chose and reconstruct fragments about who these people were. And because of that, it has the potential to be enlightening far beyond simple stories of magic.

The more partisan unbridled extremes of both modernism and postmodernism still affect how we see Paleolithic art, but the distortions of those ideologies are on the decline. In that regard we are returning to some of the fundamentals of what appears to be our Paleolithic past, where creativity and excellence were important within traditions that gave life its vital quality—a quality we can indeed glimpse in Paleolithic art. But the power and truths of these freedoms lie in the fact that they were cued from real earth. In this pursuit of truth it helps that, whatever we are, we are, first of all, organisms with a long trail of involvement with our natural surroundings.

MOVING BEYOND POSTMODERNISM, STILL LOOKING FOR TRUTH, ORIGINS, AND ESSENTIALS IN PALEOLITHIC ART

As for "truth, origins, and essentials" beyond the "metanarratives," the naturalist has a peculiar advantage—by attending to species who have no words and no text other than context and yet among whom there is an unspoken consensus about the contingency of life and real substructures. A million species constantly make "assumptions" in their body language, indicating a common ground and the validity of their responses. A thousand million pairs of eyes, antennas, and other sense organs are fixed on something beyond themselves that sustains their being, in a relationship that works. To argue that because we interpose talk or pictures between us and this shared immanence, and that it therefore is meaningless, contradicts the testimony of life itself. The non-human realm tests reality every hour.

Paul Shepard, "Virtual Hunting Reality in the Forests of Simulacra"

Certainly, Paleolithic artists and hunters were akin to other animals, and that forms our baseline of truth, but, arising from that, it is the unique human natural history which is key to this story. Elbowing their way up through

Even in the rudimentary images, there is a strong texture of reality in Paleolithic artworks. Nowhere is this more striking than among the horse images. If some look strange, that is because they are not all horses. European asses, *Equus hydruntinus*, appear in the art and in our fossil collections. Note the differences: horses on the left, asses on the right (my visual summary below). **A** and **C**, Saint-Cirq, Fr. **B**, La Griega, Sp. **D**, Polesini, It. Note the "ewe" neck, concave throat, long ears, and hairless dock of the tail of the ass.

Images of a horse and an ass on the same stone. Gourdan, Fr.

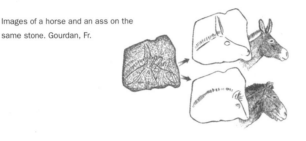

Pleistocene wild ass fossil bones as well as images from Paleolithic art show that this species was widespread: **A–B**, Trois Frères, Fr. **C** and **E–F**, Levanzo, It. **D**, Bernifal, Fr. **G**, Cosquer, Fr. **H**, Bara-Bahau, Fr.

the Pleistocene, it was the reasoned and objective reality and imagination these early peoples carried in their quivers and gathering bags, more powerful than any atlatl or digging stick, that set them apart from other animals. As an integral part of that, they carried the supernatural in that same container. It was part of their adaptation; it kept them confident, unified, healthy, and whole; it was a part of them, and is now inherited by us. But in these modern times, if not around those Paleolithic campfires, reason was sometimes turned on the supernatural just as reason can be used to understand why animals migrate or how to best raise children. The motivations to migrate or to love children do not totally arise from reason; indeed, most aspects of these behaviors lie in a separate sphere from the experience of reason. But they can be examined and refined by reason. So here we are trying to make some reason out of Paleolithic, and perhaps our own spirituality and its art.

In matters of reason there may be few categories where natural history fails to contribute some insights. We used to assume that things of the human heart were exempt: jealousy, love, mourning, depression, spirituality, and others. But these too are more richly vibrant when seen in the context of their natural history (Wright 1994; Brockman 1995). It is a sobering fact that the basic emotional states of our consciousness take place in formats of biochemistry, and even things as earthy as plant toxins can tweak those around (Pollan 2001). Reason is not only something out there which can inform us about the surface of the moon but has insights about football violence and behaviors among the gangs in the back alleys or company at the dinner table. Your loneliness, depression, state of grace, and euphoria are not exempt from evolutionary insights, nor are your daydreams or even your tastes in art. Even the supernatural may be subject to the insights of natural history.

There are disagreeable truths inherent in our being foremost an animal, subject to evolutionary forces as are all other organisms. Evolution may concoct sterling creations, but it also miscopies, mutates malignantly, aborts, and makes people who are dullards or congenitally evil. Evolution does not guarantee goodness, nor does it guarantee happiness, and certainly not equality. And yet, most

This drawing was likely the representation of a specific Paleolithic individual. What stories and insights this person could tell us. La Marche, Fr.

A, This figure engraved on the cave wall at Les Combarelles, Fr., was interpreted by some authors (e.g., Henri Breuil) as a mammoth-man shaman or something of the sort. B, Others (e.g., Archambeau) reproduced it as a mammoth-like biped. C, More recently, Barrière (1997) has carefully studied this image, and from his redrafting one can more properly imagine it as a rudimentary human, as are many other images from that same cave (a few presented elsewhere in this book).

of what we have that is good can only have come from that same evolutionary route. We can step back and see ourselves as a product of this australopithecine past and account for some of our plight and pleasures by this mode of reason. The answers are not always clear or pleasing, but no other narrative meshes as well with the facts. We are left with the unavoidable—that what we think of as good is not always true and what is true we may not always consider good. Though evolution is not about goodness, neither has it left goodness alone. And in the present context this gets entangled with a discussion of art, especially ideas and interpretations about Paleolithic art. These inherent tensions between art and goodness are perhaps what make value and art such a difficult subject.

Next, we'll look at several areas of human behavior, using them as examples of how art, the supernatural, and natural history become intertwined in our evolution and behavior.

The Natural History of the Supernatural and Its Art: Some Specific Examples

Art and aesthetics deal in personal values, in judgments, from deep reaches of the brain whose logic is often inaccessible. Likewise, those elements of our lives that deal with the supernatural, making up an ancient core of self, seem to come from similar deep-brain sources. And our natural history is often knee-deep in the midst of this. To examine these interconnections I present five examples in the following subsections: breeding taboos, our strengths and handicaps in numericity, a special wariness (our dark demons), the mystery of death, and our irrepressible virtue.

ANTI-INCEST BEHAVIOR: OVERLAPPING BIOLOGY, THE SUPERNATURAL, AND ART

Every mammalian group has behaviors that discourage inbreeding. Instead of keeping genealogies, many mammalian species avoid sex with any animal that is recognized as a relative by its similar smell. Incest is a controversial nature-nurture topic, but I want to argue that we have a genetic bent toward anti-incest preferences and behaviors that are adaptive—an emotion felt by virtually all people growing up in genetic families. We are describing an emotion (for which there is no word) more than a social behavior. Of course, most systems have some failure rate—incest does occur, because innate behaviors direct rather than dictate (chimps also have an occasional anti-incest failure). Every human society has rules pertaining to incest—again, one of the universals (Brown 1991; Shepher 1983; van den Berghe 1983) of human cultures. Outbreeding advantage is a proper metaphor of how the supernatural can incorporate the common biological wisdom (Ember 1975) into incest taboos.

The developmental trigger of this recognition of individuals as subject to anti-incest emotions seems to be twofold (Erickson 1999). One occurs in childhood toward other members of the stable nuclear family; the second takes place in adulthood, from family bonding with children. This is consistent with the observation that parents

These little images are repeated over and over in the Holocene rock art of the American Southwest. They are stylized clan symbols of tribal people. Many tribal groups use such sacred kinship markers and identities as an aid to outbreeding. *Left to right:* Gray Flute, Mole, Snake, Spider, Antelope, Blackbird, Eagle, Sunflower, Rabbit, Coyote.

who relinquish their offspring at birth feel no incest aversions toward their children upon becoming reacquainted (Greenberg and Littlewood 1995). Also, sexual abuse is rare among stepfathers who were involved in the early care of their wives' young; whereas it is comparatively high among stepfathers who did not participate in caring for young children in their families (Parker and Parker 1986). If external sanctions on incest emotions were governed only by politics and economics (van den Berghe 1980), then we would expect stepparents to behave the same way as genetic parents. In fact, one of the important mortality factors for very young children is stepfathers (Daly and Wilson 1996): homicide rates are about 50 times that of genetic fathers.

How do people in other societies explain these incest taboo feelings? Most explain it as religiously forbidden and punishable, even enforced with the penalty of death. The institutionalization of these taboos sometimes takes the form of membership in totems or moieties that are labels for genetic dissimilarity, and as we know, totem images often play a large role in visual art. I live in Alaska, where totem-pole motifs are common; they were once a household's graphic stack of matrilineal ancestry (often including images that reference a story only family members are allowed to know). In a way, aesthetic images of clan signs and totems are a shortcut to the complex education of tribal members about the genealogically important requirement for outbreeding, which is difficult both to understand and to explain. When genealogy is linked with some easily understood mystical force that employs a visible clan art symbol, the whole process is given both

clarity and clout. In many ways this is a metaphor for how the supernatural is employed to support many of our natural predispositions. And it shows how art making mixed with the supernatural can easily buttress innate behavioral predispositions. Paleolithic peoples must have heeded the inner discouragement of incest, but their art shows no hint of clan symbols that we see from later art; choosing one's spouse from the neighbor band probably sufficed.

SHORTCUT NUMERICITY, AVOIDING TYPE II ERRORS, AND ART

Aspects of Paleolithic life would have made great demands on intuitive mathematics—a sense of scale and memory for particulars. Our legacy from that past is that humans worldwide have a wonderfully complex sensitivity to the various elements of value, equity and indebtedness, and basic economics. But the ability to make formal quantifications seems to have come rather late in the human experience. Nowhere is this more true than in statistics. If math abstracts pure and certain ideals, then statistics deals with the sector of experience that can be expressed only in degrees of uncertainty. It is still not popular in schools because of this messy uncertainty. Nevertheless, basic statistics is a wonderful tool that supplements the stochastic power of reason. The general population needs elementary statistics much more than calculus because, unlike revelation, reason always deals with degrees of uncertainty. Handling uncertainty was what Paleolithic life was all about, so one would think that evolution would have installed statistical quantification as basic brain hardware. But it didn't. However, our bodies, our gut feelings, are set up with a powerful, yet simple, shortcut approach to evaluating small samples, and we preferentially avoid risking certain kinds of statistical errors more than others. It is

For a Paleolithic person it mattered little whether a reindeer herd had 153 individuals or 151. For a tribal pastoralist it is very important. Successful pastoralists have to know a lot about range management, that is, how many animals you can let forage on a given amount of land. How much vegetation is needed for each animal? How many of one's flock must one kill each autumn to overwinter an optimum number? Paleolithic people did not have to worry about such exact math. They did, however, need to have a refined intuitive sense of many things, like game populations and their movements, that greatly affected their own welfare, mobility, and choice of camps. La Marie, Fr.

an interesting story that affects us all and particularly involves judgments about the supernatural. It also explains why risk assessments are experienced more as art than reason.

Statisticians have established, backed by theory and many empirical tests, that one needs a substantial sample size for many kinds of logical evaluations. Yet humans, and all other animals, place high value on first impressions—a sample size of one. In everyday life we seldom use an approach involving adequate samples for our evaluations: food preferences, befriending or rejecting new acquaintances or potential mates, tips on the stock market, buying automobiles, and tastes of all sorts. For obvious reasons it is an axiom in proper statistical protocol that "you cannot legitimately test a hypothesis on the same data that first suggested that hypothesis" (Moore and McCabe 1993, 477). This is what underlies the classic statistician's listing of sample size as $n - 1$. Despite that obvious advice, we still rely heavily on those first impressions. Art tastes are almost instantaneous (people's faces, clothing, auto designs, etc.). The truth of art is a singular event. First impressions underlie all fads and styles, and advertisements press firmly on that part of our brain.

One can see why the metaphorical Consigliere took this shortcut route in constructing the circuitry of our judgments, because there are many things to which one should pay attention in a sample size of one, forget the

minus. Nausea biologically activates a lingering repulsion aimed at the last food item because it isn't worth the risk of trying a potentially dangerous toxin several times in a row just to be assured that it was the flu you had and not the aged salmon. But the shortcut judgment goes beyond potentially dangerous things and uses this system for most of our experiences—it avoids the complicated calculations as to whether our ideas have proper statistical credentials. Statistics, like the ideas behind evolution, has an abstruse side; though the steps of the logic are simple, its emergent truths are counterintuitive in everyday judgments: if a shaman predicts rain and it rains, bingo. In real life, decisions are hard to make and sample size usually consists of small unique events, so despite its limitations, this faulty statistical procedure does have an adaptive side in the whole balance of errors and correct judgments. But these are not symmetric.

In statistics a Type I error is concluding that a hypothesis is false when it is, in fact, true; a Type II error is concluding that a hypothesis is true when it is, in fact, false. One problem in medicine is the difficulty of designing a good test of a cure's efficacy. That is why there are so many "alternative" drugs on the market. For example, the hypothesis "Siberian ginseng helps prevent cancer" is very difficult to manipulate statistically. The power of the test is normally greater, more precise, if one tests a *null* hypothesis, the negative expression. Therefore, strange as it may seem, it is easier to design experiments to test a hypothesis proposing that "Siberian ginseng does not help prevent cancer." It would be a Type I error if we could not support this null hypothesis and it was, in fact, true (ginseng indeed did not prevent cancer). It would be a Type II error if we refused to reject this hypothesis and it was, in fact, false (ginseng turned out to be one of the best cancer prevention medications).

Statisticians argue that it is more difficult to determine the risks of making a Type II error (Kachigan 1991). The reasons are complex but one factor is that the consequences of error differ for the two types. Making the error

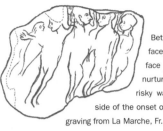

Between babyhood and senility humans face major "at-risk" ages. Young women face difficult times in the birth and early nurture of their first child. Males behave in risky ways during the few years on either side of the onset of reproductive maturity. Plaquette engraving from La Marche, Fr.

A spiny mystical worm-man, surrounded by walrus and seals, decorates the bottom of a bentwood bowl. Late Holocene Nulukhtulogumut, Eskimo.

of taking an ineffective (but perhaps dangerous) medication and making the error of never taking an effective one are far from being similar kinds of mistakes. In certain categories of behavior, evolution has organized our brains to try and avoid Type II errors. Indeed, avoiding Type II errors often pays off. That is at the core of the placebo advantage.

Both the risks (penalties) and the benefits of Type I and Type II errors are usually asymmetric. Gamblers know the obvious truth that a Type II error—missing out on a winning ticket—stands between them and immense good fortune. However, we are all familiar with the expense of gambling (making a Type I error), even though a dollar lost is not as psychologically "valuable" as the dollar won. Consider the philosopher Pascal's dilemma: if spending an eternity in paradise is based on whether you believe in God or not, many people favor the odds of trying hard to believe in that revelation. If you did not make the effort to believe, and on the Day of Judgment you are found guilty of disbelief, this would be a Type II error (erroneously accepting the null hypothesis that there is no God). Trying to avoid Type II errors involving the supernatural encourages enthusiasm, good health, honesty, and noble purpose and creates beauty where little is produced from literal reason. This approach is not without potential problems, but it may be what saves people from the apparent lack of meaning experienced by many who see this as "only the reasoned approach of materialistic science." Outward displays of Type II avoidance are responsible for much of the art that announces your decisions to others: wearing crosses, putting red dots on foreheads, wearing "proper" hairstyles, clothes, or tattoos, listening to the "right" kinds of music, and so on—and above all, choosing the right kinds of subjects for your art or art for which you show admiration.

A TOUCH OF ADAPTIVE PARANOIA AND ART

There is something in our soul that keeps looking back over our shoulders, a touch of generalized wariness. The human joke of "I'm not paranoid, everyone really is out to get me," is close to the truth for a wild fox, hare, or impala and maybe holds a little truth for us too. If we still lived with real Paleolithic wilderness around us, the adaptiveness of a little paranoia would be more obvious. My life is far from the Pleistocene, but from my door stoop I look out at the edge of wild forests stretching almost unbroken to the Bering Sea, and from there to the Urals. It gives one a different sense of wild space. Living around the wild mammals and unforgiving landscapes which occupy this vast region, one can mildly empathize with an underlying paranoia. Fellow species here do not live in terror exactly; it is more like chronic wariness. A strolling Dall sheep grazes, focusing on the next best bite, until all of a sudden it jerks its head up and intently scans the surrounding skyline with what seems to be an alert anxiety; in humans we would call it fear. For Dall sheep this fear is adaptive, because wolf packs, grizzlies, and of course human hunters will show up on the horizon someday. It never pays to meditate on grass for long.

Adult large mammals in the wild do not have to learn to fear people; they have to learn *not* to fear people. As a general rule—*one can predict that large herbivores living where there is at least one significant large predator species fear other large mammals unless conditioned otherwise.* One can

Adaptive paranoia(?), La Marche, Fr.

Sorcery art? From later tribal people,
Flinders group, Queensland, Austrl.

see adaptive fearfulness by looking at the special case of its exception among island large animals. On islands with no predators, populations become dodo-dumb, as they developmentally and genetically reduce or totally lose their capacity for paranoia. In Alaska we have island foxes that are unnervingly tame—often sticking a nose in your tent. But, normally, generalized fear is a ubiquitous mind device shaped by evolutionary pasts, suspecting threats where they are not now present.

MacLean (1969) argued that there is also a touch of innate paranoia in humans. Our Pleistocene experience saw to that. Throughout our evolution it has not paid to be overconfident, and as a result we experience a whole range of innate phobia behaviors. A little bit of vertigo keeps the kids from playing along the cliff edge; the same is true for not toying with snakes and spiders and being concerned about big things that lurk under the water—our paranoia has some biological direction. Again, looking at this from the other angle makes that clearer. Being hit by an automobile does nor register as the nightmare risk it really is—even though it is much more violent and gory and far more likely than a snakebite. Though snakes are common in rural Venda, in South Africa, there is something that rural people here (where I am on sabbatical as I write this section) are more afraid of than snakes—it is spooks. *Spook* is the Afrikaans term that everybody here knows well.

The fear of strangers that develops around five months of age may be explained as the start of an adaptive alert. There are things to be afraid of as infants begin to gain capacity to move away from mother and father. The timing of this fear onset has a heritability (Alexander 1977). Even in older children and adolescents there is a significant heritability to fearfulness (Stevenson, Batten, and Cherner

1992). We seem to have specialized neurons devoted to a touch of fear; clinical paranoia seems to be a neuro-hormonal phenomenon, a pathological exaggeration of the normal brain module, and it can be greatly ameliorated by physical intervention in the brain or by chemical medications.

It is possible that the more abstract evil forces we have incorporated into our ideology throughout human history are products of that adaptive fear, and we also easily recognize their antitheses, the superparental protectors to defend us from those unknowable evils. Our fear of evil forces must at least tinge the strange images pictured in bold lines under the rock overhangs above the Dordogne, on the Drakensberg cliffs, and on the stone surfaces at Kakadu. And these fears can be exploited:

But the wise old men, who are supposed to know everything, have a cunning little way of telling awful tales about debbil-debbils, so as to get the best things for themselves. For ages upon ages, the old men have told the young men and lubras that they must not eat fat turkeys, or the tail of the kangaroo, or indeed, any of the best things that they find when hunting. If they do, a terrible thing will happen, for a big Hunting debbil-debbil will come with a rush, and, in a moment, make them very old and weak. "Look at us!" cry the old rascals. "We eat these things, and behold, we are weak old men, with no strength to fight an enemy!" (Gunn 1990, 159)

If a person is very experienced and clever, one does not have to just use physical strength, or the threat of physical strength, to both maintain dominance and keep order. The strength and speed of the young surpass the abilities of older people, yet the young seldom control the group. How are elders able to do this? They do it by their accu-

La Marche, Fr. When a senile male lion is challenged by more virile contenders, he usually loses his pride. A Paleolithic man did not necessarily lose his status or his marriage partner as he aged; he could marshal supernatural power to bolster his accumulated wisdom.

Why Children Must Not Cry

When grandfather wished
That we should not cry,
He sang us the song
Of the beast of prey:

Leave off making noise,
For the beast will hear
If ye raise your voice.

The beast, when he hears
A little child cry,
He follows the sound,
He comes to the hut.

Approaching, he comes,
He stealthily walks.
He springs, taking aim,
And catches the child.

He takes it away,
He swallows it down.
He, altogether,
Kills children who cry.

Excerpt from a Bushman song (Markowitz 1956)

mulated experience and wisdom. Elders traditionally held onto their rights mainly through supernatural powers—the threat of mystical powers beyond one's own strength. This tactic is not used just by men. In many cultures older women not only participate but often hold senior positions of wisdom and reverence. Additionally, younger women find supernatural powers especially useful in raising children. In modern times we have forgotten that in most societies mothers have only to say that the Muri, Devil, Bogeyman, Goblin, Witch, Troll, or whatever will "get you," as an easy form of child control.

Anyone who has raised children knows about goblins, for they are still around—despite my most comforting and emphatic denials. Always fond of the dark, they particularly like to lie squeezed in under children's beds. Also, by definition, they are never present when an adult, especially an elder, is about. It is that talent of imagination running amuck again. These fantasy fears in childhood are not easily abandoned, as testified by the popularity of horror movies and the frequent threats in the tabloids that satanic cults are flourishing in suburbia. The threat of goblins, sharks, bears, snakes, and spiders meshes well with our programmed biological fears and always overrides the statistics of risks from automobile accidents or recreational drugs.

Like all things that preoccupy the mind of the artist, these supernatural forces can become part of the art. But how would you recognize an image of a goblin in prehistoric art? What form could we expect one to take? Supernatural badness, how does that appear? The evidence is that their forms embody the more fearful images from real nature. In their simpler incarnations these evil keepers-of-

order take on the characteristics kids learn to fear from the beginning, things like big sharp teeth, sharp horns, or scaly skin, glowering stare, and of course gigantic proportions. Our devils are not small, soft, and cuddly. More often than not, these anatomies are welded onto the human form, animal savagery combined with human cunning—what a ferocious combination. Those of you who were a child or the parent of a child in the last forty or so years know Maurice Sendak's children's book *Where the Wild Things Are* (1963). These kinds of strange figures dominate the rock art of many tribes.

Among human bands with their extended kinship base, where control is on a family scale, the supernatural levers appear to have taken more ephemeral forms, elastically modified in story and song. In Paleolithic art there are few images that make one think of demons, or at least

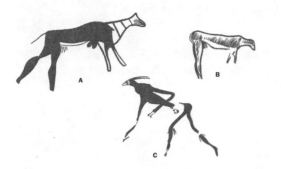

These figures in more recent Bushman art do appear to be mystical anthropomorphs: **A**, Vaalbank, R.S.A. **B**, Tsisab Ravine, Namibia. **C**, Kambe, R.S.A.

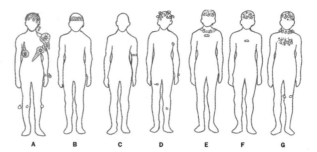

Illustration on schematic body outlines of the location of osseous tools and ornamentations found in seven Paleolithic burials in southern Europe: **A**, Grotta delle Arene Candide, It. **B–C**, Grotte des Enfants, Fr. **D**, Grotta Paglicci, It. **E–G**, Barma Grande, It. (Remember, leather, fur, and fiber are not preserved.)

Perforated teeth are often used as ornaments in Paleolithic art, like this Magdalenian necklace. Teeth, in addition to being the hardest and most durable of animal tissues, are beautiful. Their striking appearance, with white glossy enamel, conveys carnivore ferocity, power, and risk. All primates except humans fight with their teeth. Our ancestors once did so and perhaps shadows of those older synaptic organizations still linger. Whatever the cause, humans around the world have adorned themselves with teeth, especially carnivore canines.

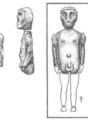

As far as I could determine, the only image of a person ever found in a Paleolithic grave was a small doll-like man with movable arms, hands, and legs. Brno, Czech. The two images on the right are my reconstruction.

that we might safely label as intentional, not just the product of lack of artistic skill or knowledge of anatomy. None are consistently repeated. If there are demons, they seem not to be recurring icons used to rivet ethical codes. That is reasonable because in a small family-based band moral codes could be enforced by benign family pressure, though a few may have kept general order as in the Bushman song above.

PALEOLITHIC ART AND BURIALS

In this book I have emphasized a common human genetic program centered on many things critical to Paleolithic people's lives, but I don't want to overlook trying to stay alive. The deep desire to stay alive is one of the most powerful evolutionary directives. In short, those who lived brief lives left few offspring. And so, continuing to live has created the lust beyond all other lusts. Evolution saw to it that the loss of one's life and the loss of those dearest to oneself are the most emotionally threatening forces we

know. Few other things cause such trauma as the onset of a potentially deadly disease or a death in the family. Our adeptness at death denial is shown by the fact that despite the certainty of our deaths and those of family members in the comparatively near future, deathbed time is emotionally devastating. Few things attract the supernatural more than dying or the threat of dying. We can assume it was so in the Paleolithic as well—and there are some traces of evidence.

The presence of deliberate burials in the Paleolithic has sometimes been taken as evidence of some kind of metaphysical belief. In fact, Neanderthal burials are used as an argument that, over a hundred thousand years ago, this species too had a spiritual, mystical orientation. *Sépulture,* the French word for "grave" or "tomb," carries with it religious overtones—and in most cases this is probably correct, but it may not always be so. Again, we must be cautious about not seeing everything through magic-colored glasses. Covering a dead body with dirt had several practical features. It better protected the remains from carnivore-scavenger consumption. Leaving the remains of the dead out in the open invited dangerous carnivores, and one certainly would not want to encourage their eating of flesh with a human scent, and hence overcoming their fear of humans. Also, removing the dead from sight is an important psychological move, allowing people to get on with their lives without the visual reminder of the trauma which produced the mangled and rotting deceased.

Elephants have a behavior that is as close to post-mortem burial as one can see in other species. The close-knit matriarchal herd hangs around a dead member for several days, and they often attempt to cover the body with dirt and brush. One can observe the blatant discomfort and grief among the survivors, the uncertainty and puzzlement of what to do next, in the sagging muscles, the groans, and lack of eating. Later, when passing by the death site, elephants sometimes gently caress and smell the bones. All of this speaks to emotions not so different from our own. After the death of a comrade or family member, one must go on literally and figuratively, so disposing of the body out of sight is one of the more practical metaphors. But for humans it is something more.

The difference between a living body and one lying lifeless is so incomprehensible it is difficult not to give it metaphysical qualities. Life is of such unimaginable molecular, cellular, tissue, and organ complexity that its functions are mostly out of range of human understanding and resolving power—life and death are not a clear dichotomy. We appear to die suddenly, but biologically it is by degree. Even psychologically, death has no clear boundaries: memories of the deceased persist in our minds beyond the cessation of respiration and reproduction, beyond their physical death. In my head, I have phantom phone talks with my mother despite her no longer being there to hear them.

Looking at excavated Paleolithic skeletons gives some hint of the emotions that must have accompanied that individual's death. Occasionally objects that could have belonged to the deceased are interred in the same grave: jew-

Cannon Bone at Namutoni

Saw a cannon bone today, lying near that same waterhole.
Bleached fragment of a life I once saw, in black and white.
Zebra stallion standing there trembling, facing the night.
Feverish, yet not in shock, bravery in his eyes, a long drink
to quench the fiery fever and to cool the mind's last day.
Mid-tibia shattered, uninsured, unwarrantied, unrepairable.
No tearing bloody marks of a lion's or hyena's near miss
this, a social break, a kick from his own kind, victor stallion.
About what? Was it about females, status, love and power?
Is that what evolution is made of, these high-risk stakes?
He had sought the waterhole, hobbled on three good legs.
A bracing swig to face the inevitable terrible night.
White metatarsal on cracked mud, a metaphor of all our ends?

elry, clothing, weapons, or tools. Sometimes an antler or horn was included with the corpse. This may have been a widespread practice, for we find antlers and horns in graves from different regions and at widely divergent times in prehistory (see reviews in May 1986; Binant 1991b). Why the recurring habit of antler inclusion across these very different cultures? Were antlers something people associated with elegance and power, or more complexly did the bones of other animals symbolize a sort of cyclicity about life and death? We can only wonder.

What is certain is that occasionally Paleolithic people were buried; again, how often that happened we don't know. Of those who were buried, at least a few were pre-

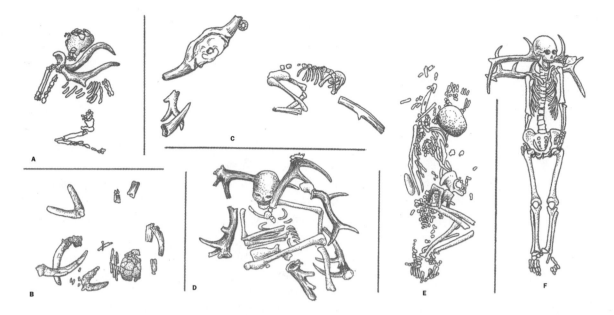

Some curious burials with accompanying horns and antlers from large mammals: **A**, Cervid antler accompanying the Skuhl burial, Middle East (middle Paleolithic). **B**, Ibex horn cores from Teshik-Tash, Uzbekistan (infant skeleton). **C**, Reindeer antlers and bison horns with the skeleton from Saint-Germain-la-Rivière, Fr. **D**, Red deer antlers with Mesolithic burial, Hoëdle, Denmark. **E**, Small antlers with Cueva de los Canes burial, late Paleolithic. **F**, Red deer antlers with Mesolithic burial, Bogehakken, Denmark.

served and a few of these have been found and excavated. The small decorated items included in those few graves have become part of our collection of Paleolithic art.

THE SUPERNATURAL, ART, AND VIRTUE: THE CONSIGLIERE'S GIFTS

Throughout this book I have tried to explore the link between the evolution of art, how it connects to our origins within the human niche, and our particular brand of individual and social behavior. This route has been a little bit gory at times, muddy, pornographic, and frequently male dominated. But this circuitous evolutionary connection can also combine natural history, art, and goodness.

This chapter has followed the others in referring to the patterning of human behavior and trying to fit it into some reasonable order. The argument is credible that the Con-

sigliere installed a self-rewarding predisposition toward belief and faith in the supernatural for important practical reasons. In the right context these predispositions contain adaptive elements of the good life. For, just as we experience pleasurable directives with the first whiff of a tasty hot dish, we also experience the pleasure of turning toward the good life through the satisfactions of behaving virtuously. The "good life" is shorthand for reaching our evolutionary social target by being rewarded aesthetically with innate emotional pleasures as well as the practical benefits of cooperation, friendship, and love, which we have talked so much about.

I realize that it is hard to accept the evidence of an evolutionary model that portrays most of our behavior as ultimately being a product of our taking better care of our own genes (or genes identical to ours among related people). While that is how evolution works (Dawkins 1976), it is not as simple as it sounds. "Selfish" genes can produce a good heart. Many biologists these days are delving into the unwritten rules (morals we can call them) of animal social behavior by using mathematical game theory for clues to the optimal behavioral strategy (see Ridley 1996 for a popular review). Their conclusions so far about human morality suggest that the complexities of human interaction and confrontation are not simple models of

The person who engraved this face and the person to whom it belonged were undoubtedly virtuous people, a behavior installed by evolution, but even so, all Paleolithic folks had to look over their shoulders now and then. Marsoulas, Fr.

reciprocity, nor are they tit-for-tat or even just some Machiavellian behavioral manipulations. Rather, among a mix of diverse social "strategies," the winning game strategy of humans confronted by these different unpredictable social interactions generally falls to the ones who behave virtuously, and indeed that does describe our actual accustomed norm. Why?

It seems that evolution has just taken the simple way out. Again we'll invoke the Consigliere and his "just get it done" approach. In the same way that snowshoe hares turn white with the coming of the twelve daylight hours of autumnal equinox, no matter whether it has snowed or not, so humans generally behave virtuously. On the computer game boards and in practice, culture after culture use versions of this strategy. The Consigliere's first commandment seems to be "Behave well toward others, as you would wish others to behave toward you or your near relatives." This is true even if others behave badly in return. And if in the next encounter they still behave badly, you still behave well. If they continue to behave badly, even after seeing your long-term good intentions, you must make appropriate adjustments (for we cannot in the long run tolerate consistent cheaters and freeloaders in our system). On the other hand, if they "ask forgiveness" and behave virtuously, then you return to your original position, which presumes reasonable behavior and decency.

This empathetic driver is the Consigliere's simple and inexpensive shortcut. As an overall pattern there are clear costs, but other strategies turn out to be even more costly; that is, they are less successful in genetic terms. We are a caring and virtuous species. Presumptions of decency are so standard that contrary instances stand out as glaring exceptions—they make the rounds of gossip, the newspa-

pers, the police blotters, and once in a while end in the grave.

Beneath all this virtuousness, there lies a metaphoric contract—a genetic pact—made within that Pleistocene hunting band. To operate in their socioecological niche, our ancestral band members had to cooperate more than compete; otherwise, they were all doomed to failure. So they took care of one another, not out of some theoretical principle of benevolence, but because natural selection had provided an aesthetic for virtue. The Consigliere, if you will, had implanted the emotion of empathy. The evolutionary mechanism, of course, was that more selfless individuals who exhibited thoughtful, empathetic behavior were genetically favored, deferred to as leaders, taken better care of in times of illness, loved more as children, befriended in adulthood, and married if possible. In the end they stood a better chance of leaving more quality young. Indeed, despite our modern change of state, that still holds today. True selfishness is rewarded only in extreme occasions of almost complete anonymity, and among humans a life of complete anonymity is already lost.

In culture after culture, the supernatural has always waded right in at this juncture. Whatever form the supernatural takes, it gets involved with morals, backing the selfless—that is, when not being leveled against the heathen opponent. As with the case of incest taboos, institutionalized religion adds backbone to the natural inclination to do the right thing. Other than its occasional lapses, such as pogroms against infidel neighbors (every group's history tells its members about the goodness of fighting their neighbors' evils), the spiritual is about being good. Religious services are mutual ceremonies to remind people to be virtuous to one another, to savor this virtue, and to depart in its grace.

But the devil is in the details; as in most instances, evolution has been two-sided here as well. Tolerance of distant groups does not come easily. Even within one's own group the intensity of many kinds of selection is "frequency dependent"—the selective value of friendship,

So we end this book, with dizzying exposure to many images, mostly those of large mammals, like these quick engravings of a lion and horse from La Marche, Fr. It is a scratchy record full of noise and static, but it still plays on our phonograph. On their own, some details, like the tufted lion tail, seem trivial, but together, as pieces of a puzzle, they compose a remarkable record of perceptive people growing up in distant times—folks much like ourselves. Their art focused on a narrow sweep of their surroundings, that part for which evolution had provided juice and direction. Out of that I have tried to make some order.

trust, and honesty is highest where qualities are not completely pervasive. That is, at the population and personal level there are some evolutionary advantages to the demonic streak, cheating at goodness, so long as these are infrequent or minor infractions. We saw this frequency-dependent balance in the selection for deviation from exclusive mate fidelity. So there is an emotionally loaded tension between these two natures of light and darkness. The two compose a large part of the arts.

It has often been said that art can be an important vehicle to transmit aspects of moral goodness, from epic tribal legends to children's stories. Perhaps American cinema dominates world entertainment because its financially winning and satisfying formula is to avoid a bad ending (in Ingmar Bergman fashion) but rather to have heroes and heroines wander through a storyline of danger, tragedy, mayhem, or sadness and still have a good, if not happy, ending. We want video, theater, novels, music, and portraits to assist us in parlaying our natural expectation of the way things should work out in this battle of light and dark. All this may be at the root of why we tried to impose noble purpose onto Paleolithic art: mother goddesses, adolescent education, hunting and fertility magic, or religious rites (we'll even accept uncivilized shamanism as close enough). And if we are disappointed because the actual images in Paleolithic art do not rise to these expec-

tations, that may explain why there has been such half-hearted effort to make order out of all those thousands of images or to sing their wonderful praises.

For most people, the irregular scatter of graffitiesque images in among a few fine works does not presage a good ending for the story of Paleolithic art. However, it can be said that resident in the preserved fraction of this art, including the blood, sex, and kids' handiwork, is an edge, not of an adult pat belief with clear meaning to elucidate, but the vital edge of growing—youthful risk and fun. This testy vitality showing through the crude scratches and crayon lines, as much as the persuasive beauty of Lascaux, is our Paleolithic legacy.

That is the good ending to the story of this book: the Paleolithic graffiti edge needn't be read as portending the development of a coarse and brutal savage but instead portrays a step along the normal route to a compassionate and virtuous everyday person.

AN EVOLUTIONARY SEER'S FINAL LOOK AT PALEOLITHIC ARTIFACTS

That pimpled kid in the shadows, caught red-handed in the firelight flicker with a lamp held in one hand and ocher crayon in the other, was on a collegial foray cementing the bonds of friendship. Later in life he would find pleasure in bonding with a spouse and becoming a dedicated parent as well as a contributing, virtuous member of his group. These evolved social behaviors are at the core of our biological niche that describes our species. And despite each of our many lapses and foibles, we still consider it a failure if we do not follow that ancient prescription of virtue, whose spirit we all feel, if not comprehend. As I write this page, I just got off the phone with a friend who is taking the ashes of his son to a wilderness river where the two of them once had good times collecting mammoth bones. There is no one among us who could deny both the beauty and the reasonableness of that spiritual journey.

La Marche, Fr.

The inclusive grace of this view lets us leave behind dogmatic religions and frightening shamanistic practices in favor of a bigger story. All life is kin here on earth. Not only are we a truly human family, but we share our origins with the gray crane and the monarch butterfly. It is a marvelous and powerful grace to be a spiritual human animal among other animals, standing on this blue-green ball, dinosaur and mammoth bones underfoot, hurdling at light-speed through black space, our planet's moon softening our nights—so normal and yet so incredible. Even more unimaginable is that we retain messages encoded from Pleistocene times, when steppes formed the skyline and cheeks felt the cool wind from continental ice.

Paleolithic art is a silent touch from distant ancestors, their marks a reminder of our own vitality and mortality, a prompter to savor our present in this ancient arena of life. Despite our sometimes muddy and bloody way of arriving, we are sisters and brothers in time and space. Like the gravedigger, those of us who are grave digger-uppers are often aware that we too do not have forever—that our now-vivid times will also pass, like those halcyon days around the campfires with skewered shelk roasts and extravagant sunsets. A seer throws the old ivory carvings, kneels, and reads them thoughtfully: "They say, 'Wake up, you are on; we have had our time and this is yours.'" She smiles and—I thought she was mocking, but perhaps not—goes on to say that the truly good message from Paleolithic art is "that one would be wise to play: play physically, play mentally, and, above all, play artfully."

Riding Green Planet in Black Ether near Rim of Galaxy 793491-Zebra

Our sign and mark began to show on Earth,
a minor planet near one galaxy's outer rim.
Lightly at first, shallow steps at Laetoli,
tracks in the white smoke of rift's breath.
A scatter of chert spalls where no frost fell.
Lightly, it takes a good tracker, we move on.

Herders cleaned the abri of gray flaked flints,
pitched the thick bones — more room for sheep.
Old hearths uncovered, stone engravings
stacked as fence cobbles to kraal the flock.
Ignorant of the spoor lying there in hand.
Lacking the strivings of hunter's quest.

Crinkled molar here, smear of rusty ocher there.
Healed collarbone from anger long forgotten.
Bone of healed cripple, mark of someone's care.
Busty Taliswoman, could spoor of passion linger?
Bog-pickled heads, like dried Neolithic muti.
The scent of our back trail getting stronger.

Kids back to camp yelling, they found a cave.
Ahh! we see it, new questions torchlight the dark.
The light of colored figures playing on the wall.
Cave spoor sealed since time long forgotten,
edges sharp and vivid, crisp as they were lain,
beneath the paths of human history overhead.

See all the magic spoor of us in other times,
these tracks of ancient mind and quick crayon.
Marks straight from glowing synapse, telling—
What? Of the life we once knew and were. Lions
in the haze, stag bugles, vapor of aurochs blood,
Full curves, wild passion, and . . . imagination.

Appendix One

Paleolithic Handprint Analysis

ARNY BLANCHARD

Missing data were filled using regression relationships. The mean palm width for the Ice Age data was used to fill missing palm width measurements. All other missing measurements were filled using the regression relationships of hand measurements taken from Alaskan people between palm width and the other variables. I also tried thumb width but it was obvious that the regression relationships based on thumb width were overestimating the measurements for other variables. This was based on my comparisons of the estimated measurements with the available measurements at similar thumb widths in the Ice Age data.

The Paleolithic data were classified according to sex using discriminant analysis. Forward stepwise multiple discriminant functions determined from the measurements of Fairbanks people were used to calculate the Mahalanobis distances used for classification for the Ice Age handprints. These distances are calculated from each group multivariate mean, called the centroid. For each case, the group centroid with the smallest distance to the multivariate mean for a case is considered to be the centroid for that case, and thus, the case belongs to that group. I used Statistica to estimate discriminant function and to calculate the distances and used Excel to find the smaller distances and count how many males and females there were.

I was concerned about the high correlations of the data used in the discriminant analysis and decided to verify the output using logistic regression. I used palm width as the independent variable and determined the regression relationship between the sex of Fairbanks people and their palm widths. Then, I used this relationship to categorize the Ice Age handprints. Statistica was used to determine the logistic regression equation.

Age for each case was estimated using the regression of Fairbanks people's age in months to total hand length (Tlength3). I first used forward stepwise multiple regression to determine which variables might be useful for predicting age in months. The two variables called Tlength were selected. Since most variables were highly correlated, I had decided that only one variable would be used. I determined the regression relationship between age in months and Tlength3 for the Fairbanks sample and used that relationship to estimate the age in months of the handprints from the Ice Age data. Statistica was used to determine the regression equation.

These analyses are based on assumptions that are both statistical and biological. First, the discriminant analysis assumes multivariate normality. Second, the linear regression performed assumes that the errors are independent and normally distributed with constant variance. Third, these analyses are based on the assumption that the growth relationships of the Fairbanks sample are similar to those Ice Age people making the handprints.

Results

The categorization of the Ice Age data using the discriminant function from the Fairbanks data suggested that most of the handprints were of males. The discriminant analysis of the Fairbanks data resulted in a model with six variables: Thumb width, Tlength3, Palm width, Hand breadth, Index width, Middle width, Middle length (Wilks' Lambda: 0.679 approx. $F = 80.77$, $p < 0.0000$). Of the 201 cases in the Paleolithic data, 162 were classified as male and 39 female or quite young males.

The estimation of the age in months of the person making the handprints suggested that most were children under eighteen years of age. The regression relationship between age in months and Tlength3 for the Fairbanks data is Age $= -127 + 1.696$ Tlength3 ($F = 1213$, $p < 0.00001$, $R^2 = 0.66$). Applying this to the Ice Age data, most age estimates based on Tlength3 were under eighteen years of age.

Thanks, Arny!

Appendix Two

An Intuitive Way to Look at the Hand
Biometrics Using Bivariate Plots

R. DALE GUTHRIE

Prior to undertaking a formal biometric study of hand
proportions I found myself studying the differences in
the hands of my family and friends. As this preoccupation grew, I also began looking at hands of acquaintances and strangers. I extended this impressionistic
study of "hand watching" by pouring over hundreds
of photocopies of students' hands and eventually was
able to regularly predict the sex of photocopied hands
(nineteen out of twenty times) when hand images
were those of people over age twelve. Under that age, it
was difficult. This impressionistic proficiency encouraged me to pursue a more analytical approach. And as
I showed in chapter 3, the use of a suite of thirteen different hand width and length measurements was
quite successful in discriminating age and sex.

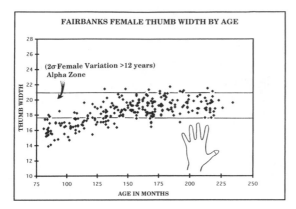

Fig. A1. Fairbanks school sample of female thumb width plotted by age. Hand growth, using thumb width as an example, all but ceases at around age twelve. The cluster of thumb widths between 17.5 and 21 mm thus includes most sexually mature females. That range, referred to here as the alpha zone, includes the mean with 2 standard deviations on either side (2σ).

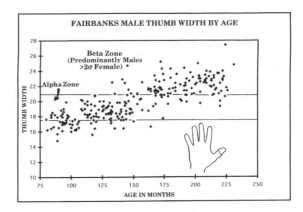

Fig. A2. Fairbanks school sample of male thumb width plotted by age. Unlike females, hand growth in males does not cease around twelve but continues until seventeen to eighteen years of age. The male hand width measurements normally rise above the alpha zone, outside the normal range of females at 2σ, into a region I refer to as the beta zone.

Though multivariate and discriminate analysis can perform excellent abstract quantitative sorting, the logic is rather recondite for visually oriented thinking. Therefore, while my statistician was working the multivariate manipulations, I pursued other, more visually focused approaches, to help me comprehend the various factors underlying the multivariate composites. It is these I want to discuss in this appendix. Though not as elegantly discriminating, I found these simpler two-dimensional manipulations useful for visualizing what underlies the complex computer logic and stochastic patterns.

Thanks to desktop computers and Excel software I could easily see dozens of bivariate scatterplots and percentage polygon graphs. Like different brush strokes, each new plot—sex specific, age specific, and Paleolithic-modern comparisons—was quite informative. They confirmed what my intuition and other data had already predicted—that hand widths were best for sexing. But in a simple bivariate plot, age and sex tended to confound one another. Handprints of children under twelve were relatively easy to age but almost impossible to sex, so I focused on finding a way to age and sex the handprints of people over age twelve using the six width measurements: four

fingers, thumb, and palm. The Excel plots provided just the clues I needed to penetrate this problem.

The solution is based on baseline sample evidence of sex-specific growth patterns: female hands tend to stop growing at around twelve years of age, whereas boys' hands keep growing until around seventeen to eighteen. Scatterplots for age against width measurements were thus quite different for girls' and boys' hands. Size/age plots for females show a marked flattening earlier than males (fig. A1—an example showing thumb width in millimeters). In contrast (fig. A2), the regression trendline of males continues upward toward nineteen. All the other hand width measurements of females show a similar flat regression trendline after age twelve, with a mean R^2 of 0.05 ± 0.16—in comparison to robust male trendlines after age twelve, with a mean R^2 of 0.25 ± 0.03. Trendlines of female widths depart from those of males at an average point of 93 ± 13.3 months for the six different width measurements, or about eight years of age plus or minus a year.

This hand width pattern is summarized in figure A3. At an average age of 167 ± 9.20 months (about fourteen years), the male running mean (trendline) crosses the upper postpuberty female 2.0σ mark (the boundary at two

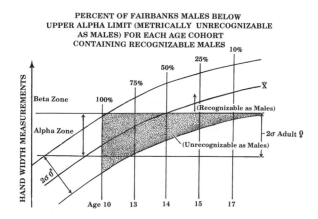

Fig. A3. The arcing mean with its accompanying 2σ variation represents the population of Fairbanks males growing through time. While most hands in the beta zone belong to males, so also do a percentage of the hands beneath the alpha zone, which would go unrecognized as males if only this one measurement is used. For example, 50% of the fourteen-year-old boys have hand width measurements that fall below the beta zone.

standard deviations from the postpuberty female mean). That is, an average fourteen-year-old boy would have hands larger than 95% of all mature females. Further along the point scatter in the male hand width charts, growth stabilizes at eighteen years of age, overlapping only 5% with the point scatter of girls (where the 2σ boundaries of each sex converge). In other words, at eighteen years there is no significant overlap in hand width measurements between males and females. So, while it is difficult using simple width *bivariate* plots to positively identify a female in this scatter, we can work backward and identify what she is not. And that becomes our key— females always overlap with males, but males do not always overlap significantly with females.

Geometry of the Aggregate of Handprint Measurements

My Fairbanks baseline sample of postpuberty female hand measurements has a cluster (at 2σ above and below its mean) that I call the *alpha zone*. Beyond the upper margin

of the alpha zone the dots are mainly males, and I refer to this latter area as the *beta zone* (fig. A3). Of course, the hand measurements for a number of males from a mixed-age population including young males will fall below the beta zone. Nevertheless, we now have a means of identifying, statistically, a large fraction of the hand images of Paleolithic males.

This same symmetrical exclusion principle allows us to say something about very young age classes. Below the lower margins of the alpha zone we can say that individual dots likely belong to children, male and female, younger than twelve. Of course, dots below this alpha zone undercount numbers of young in the sample because hand sizes of many individuals younger than twelve (particularly males) do scatter up into the alpha zone.

Again, this approach is not as robust in its ability to predict age and sex of an individual Paleolithic handprint as is our more complete multivariate analysis. What it does do is help us visualize the general patterns. With all this in mind then, let's turn to the Paleolithic measurements. Since we do not know the ages of the Paleolithic hands, these cannot be plotted along the *x* axis like the modern Fairbanks sample in figures A4A and A4B. But we can project the numbers of each hand width measurement on the *y* axis and look at the relative numbers in relation to which fall into the alpha zone, beta zone, and below the alpha zone. That is, we can look at the overall geometry of the sums.

What follows in figures A4C–A4K is a theoretical black shadow on the *y* axis of a projected plot of different age/sex groups. For example, if equal numbers of individuals of each age and sex left their prints in caves, the width distributions would appear as in figure A4C. The mean and heaviest loading would be in the lower part of the alpha zone. Each of the successive plots shows what we might expect if hand size is not a random representation; each plot shows a characteristic distribution signature. I continue with theoretical plots: adult females would cluster in the alpha zone, adult males would cluster in the beta

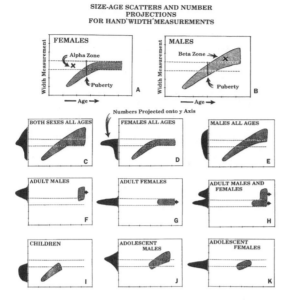

Fig. A4. **A** and **B** stylize the different growth patterns of males and females with regard to the hand width measurements. These can be projected on the *y* axis as a shadow that is diagnostically different for different age and sex combinations (**c–k**). For example, if all the hands in Paleolithic art had belonged to adult females, the shadow distribution would fall almost entirely within the alpha zone, as shown in **G**. These characteristic patterns give us one way of assessing the aggregate population assemblage in the following six graphs of width measurements of Paleolithic hands.

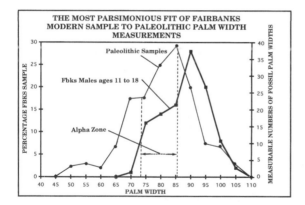

Fig. A5. The thin line shows Paleolithic palm widths plotted against numbers (*right*). The mode falls at the juncture of the alpha and beta zones, but the variation is high. This polygon best fits the shadow on the *y* axis from fig. A4**J**. Taking population blocks in equal numbers in every age and both sexes, the most parsimonious fit with the Fairbanks sample is a polygon (*thick line*) generated by all males aged eleven to eighteen (percentage numbers shown at left). The shape of the fit is good but not precise, so the actual age-sex distribution of Paleolithic hand ownership would likely have included some younger people and Paleolithic females.

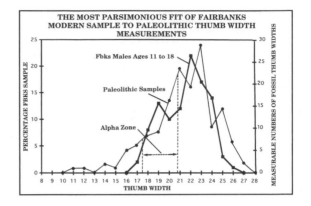

Fig. A6. Same as fig. A5 except using thumb width. Paleolithic curves and most parsimonious fit from Fairbanks school sample of males aged eleven to eighteen are good. Note that the mean and mode fall clearly into the beta zone. Thumb width is one of the best statistical informants of sexual identity.

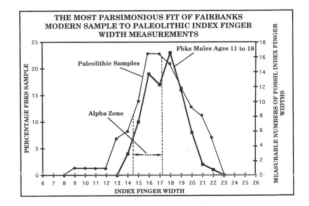

Fig. A7. Same as fig. A5 except using index-finger width.

zone, and if both adult males and females are plotted, then the projection would be bimodal, and so on.

Next, we can look at the actual Paleolithic pattern for each hand width measurement (figs. A5–A10; I rotate these shadow plots 90° for convenience so that width is on the *x* axis). Remember that many handprints are incomplete, so any one measurement will not describe exactly the same sample as any other. I have used only width measurements here because in my baseline Fairbanks sample the most robust predictors of sex were the widths of palm, thumb, index finger, ring finger, and little finger. The resultant pattern among all six measurements is clear: the

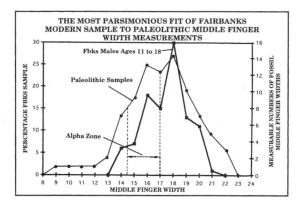

Fig. A8. Same as fig. A5 except using middle-finger width.

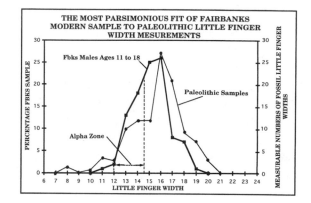

Fig. A10. Same as fig. A5 except using little-finger width.

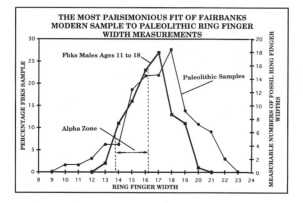

Fig. A9. Same as fig. A5 except using ring-finger width.

mean and mode fall at or above the alpha zone into the beta zone, which allows us to delineate males.

Does the geometry of these polygon graph shapes allow us to say anything about the numbers of young males who are hidden in the alpha zone itself? We can first look at this theoretically. Theory would suggest that at trendline intercept (eight years of age) 100% of the males fall below the beta zone—at the intercept point of the male mean (trendline) with the lower margin of the beta zone. About age fourteen, 50% of the male scatter occupies the alpha and 50% the beta zone. At maturity (age eighteen), under 5% of males lie within the alpha zone and over 95% in the beta zone. So for each of the male age cohorts under eighteen that show up in the beta zone, there would be large numbers of individuals that would scatter within the alpha zone (fig. A10).

Taking simple blocks of sex and age cohorts from the Fairbanks sample, how can we best re-create the unknown age-sex Paleolithic pyramidal polygon, its shape and mean? What is the most parsimonious fit? Remember, any large block of children beneath the age of twelve will drag the mean well below the beta zone. So indeed would large blocks of females in the post-twelve age categories. Males must predominate to get the curve beyond the alpha zone range. In fact it turns out that the most parsimonious fit to these Paleolithic polygons of age is an aggregate block from my Fairbanks samples (equal numbers for each age-group) of males eleven to eighteen years of age. These are shown in figures A5–A10. This sorting is the best-of-fit in terms of peak positions (means) and so are the variances, spreading almost symmetrically up and down the scale. Most important, the variance of the male eleven to eighteen age fills the volume of the alpha zone (Note A4J).

When large numbers of females are added to this attempt at parsimony, they fall on top of the young male variants (smaller cohorts of those in the lower beta zone) in the alpha zone and produce a high peak within that zone. If the Paleolithic sample was mainly hands of older mature males, the apex peak would fall to the far right of the alpha zone. Instead, the sharp peak is found in the low end of the identifiably male zone. All this implies that most of the unknown occupants of the volume of the alpha zone in the Paleolithic sample are accounted for by young male variants—interpolated from known quantities of Paleolithic male age-groups in the beta zone. The superimposition of these two curves (the Paleolithic number summary and the modern Fairbanks percentage distributions from ages eleven through eighteen) shows that very small numbers from other age-sex categories need to be added to exactly match the two curves.

The skew toward adolescent males shows that there is an age and sex bias as to who went back into caves in the Paleolithic and left their handprints. Other age-sex combinations would yield quite differently shaped polygons (see figs. A4C–A4K). Some cave-use theories have envisioned male initiation rites, but if only older males and pubertal boys (fourteen to sixteen) left their marks on cave walls, the variances would not penetrate sufficiently down-scale into the alpha zone and lower. If only young boys aged ten to fourteen were going back into caves, a significant number of variants would fall into the male-only zone, yet the pyramidal peak itself would not reach into the beta zone. This attempt at parsimony does not at all mean that no females went back into caves, nor that none left their handprints on the cave walls, just that, statistically, young males predominated.

Pattern of Individual Handprint Measurements

There is another way of approaching this question of identifying which hand images were those of males and especially the ages of those males. What follows depends on your focused visual imagination, so grab your hot herb tea and take this slowly. I tried to sex each Paleolithic hand image by printing out the six hand width measurements. Any hand that contained a measurement that fell within the beta zone I highlighted as a hit (recall there were not many females in the beta zone—only around 5% of adult women). In some hands all the potential measurements

were highlighted—statistically, these hands can be identified as belonging to Paleolithic males. Remember that due to their poor quality and incompleteness, all six width measurements were not available for many hands. Paleolithic hands with at least one hit among the possible measurements available constituted 70% (141 of the 201 hands) of the sample. Of the 141 with at least one hit, only 30% had all potential measurements as hits (1 out of 1, 2 out of 2, etc.). What does this mean? Are those with one hit among, say, three measurable widths in an incomplete hand image to be identified as males or not?

I went back to the Fairbanks sample for help. One can see from a plot (figs. A11–A12) that for each of the six critical width measurements of young males of known age, the percentage of male individuals with "hits" rises from 10% about age nine to ten to around 50% at age 14 on through to about 90% at age eighteen. Likewise, figure A13 shows percentages in the population that scored one to six hits per hand (the value 6 represents the percentage of cases in which all are hits); this is a different way of plotting the data from figure A12. One can again see that individuals who have all potential measurements as hits do not exist before age twelve and constitute only 25% at age thirteen, rising to 50% at age fourteen, 75% at age fifteen, and then on to over 90% at age eighteen. So younger males generally do not have a full complement of hits for all their potential measurements.

Thus, we can reasonably conclude that if, as an aggregate, the hands in Paleolithic art exhibited hits in all potential width measurements, they would likely belong to males eighteen years old and older. However, if most had less than all potential width measurements as hits, they would likely, as an aggregate, belong to young males. One can see (fig. A14) that indeed the latter scenario was the case, implying that most of the hand owners were adolescents, centered in the zone between twelve and seventeen years of age.

In this large sample, 70% of the Paleolithic hands have at least one hit. Do all those with one hit belong to males? We might be more stringent and require something like

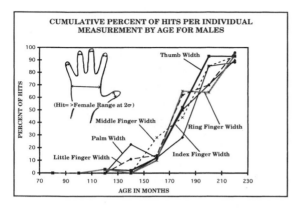

CUMULATIVE PERCENT OF HITS PER INDIVIDUAL MEASUREMENT BY AGE FOR MALES

Thumb Width

(Hit= >Female Range at 2σ)

Middle Finger Width

Palm Width

Little Finger Width

Ring Finger Width

Index Finger Width

PERCENT OF HITS

AGE IN MONTHS

Fig. A11. The cumulative percentage of hits for each of the hand width measurements from the baseline Fairbanks school sample according to age. "Hits" are defined here as the sizes that would place males in the beta zone, that is, above the statistical range of mature females. All six measurements rise in about the same pattern; very few males are still in the beta zone (overlap with females) by age seventeen to eighteen.

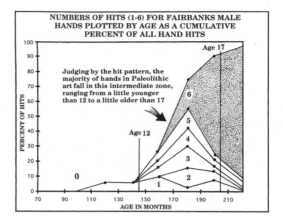

NUMBERS OF HITS (1-6) FOR FAIRBANKS MALE HANDS PLOTTED BY AGE AS A CUMULATIVE PERCENT OF ALL HAND HITS

Age 17

Judging by the hit pattern, the majority of hands in Paleolithic art fall in this intermediate zone, ranging from a little younger than 12 to a little older than 17

Age 12

PERCENT OF HITS

AGE IN MONTHS

Fig. A13. This graph plots information from fig. A12 but uses a cumulative scale with each contribution broken down by categories. A hit is defined in fig. A11. Though this distribution is based on the modern Fairbanks sample, we can use it to evaluate our earlier polygon graphs, figs. A5–A10, of the Paleolithic data. Most of the hands in Paleolithic art show some hits but as an aggregate do not fall largely into the extremes of either only one hit or six hits per hand. That is, most cluster between ages twelve and seventeen.

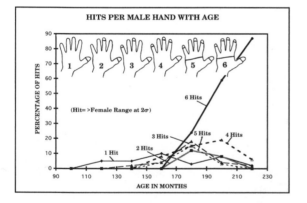

HITS PER MALE HAND WITH AGE

1 2 3 4 5 6

6 Hits

(Hit= >Female Range at 2σ)

3 Hits   5 Hits   4 Hits

1 Hit   2 Hits

PERCENTAGE OF HITS

AGE IN MONTHS

Fig. A12. This graph plots the numbers of hits (see fig. A11 for definition) *per hand* according to age for the modern Fairbanks sample. Examples are shown stylistically in the scatter of hands at the top. One hit would be a handprint that had one of the available measurements falling in the beta zone (I use the thumb here for an example). Two hits could be any combination of two potential measurements (I show here the thumb and middle finger), and so on. The number of hits per hand begins to rise precipitously at about age thirteen. At age fifteen, the numbers in the five-hits-or-less categories begin to decline, being displaced by the rapid rise of all six measurements being hits.

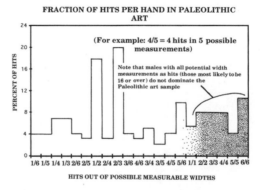

FRACTION OF HITS PER HAND IN PALEOLITHIC ART

(For example: 4/5 = 4 hits in 5 possible measurements)

Note that males with all potential width measurements as hits (those most likely to be 16 or over) do not dominate the Paleolithic art sample

PERCENT OF HITS

1/6 1/5 1/4 1/3 2/6 2/5 1/2 2/4 2/3 3/6 4/6 3/5 3/4 4/5 5/6 1/1 2/2 3/3 4/4 5/5 6/6

HITS OUT OF POSSIBLE MEASURABLE WIDTHS

Fig. A14. Columnar spread of the Paleolithic hands with hits (defined in fig. A11), for which we can assume most are males. This portrays the number of hits out of the possible measurements available. Many handprints were incomplete, and so fewer than six clear, dependable measurements could be taken. My stippling highlights those hands that had 100% of the potential measurements as hits (i.e., 1 out of 1, 2 out of 2, on up through 6 out of 6). These would be males in their late teens or adults. Note how this stippled area, while fairly large, does not dominate the volume of the spread, especially when we can see from fig. A13 that a significant number of those within the stipple were younger than seventeen. So while male identities are the most common in our Paleolithic hand sample, older men seem not to have been the predominant part of the assemblage.

two hits out of five potential measurements (or 40%). This would reduce the directly identifiable male fraction from 70% to 64%. Of the remaining 36% of the hands not meeting this standard of male identity, 20% fall below the lower limit of the alpha zone, meaning that they are likely hands of young children. This leaves only 16% of the total polygon volume in the alpha zone (remember that most of this 16% is shared by age-groups of children scattering up from below and young-aged male groups). If, as suggested by the sizes, most of the 64% identifiable males are teenagers, males included in that 64% had age-group cohort members who would have had no hits and hence would have scattered into the alpha zone. We can clearly see this phenomenon in the Fairbanks known-age-sex data set, where 60% of the twelve- to fourteen-year-old males, 20% of the fourteen- to sixteen-year-old males, and even 10% of the sixteen- to eighteen-year-old males fall in the alpha zone.

As stated in the text, we can also conclude from this second approach that individuals of most ages and both sexes left handprints in Paleolithic caves, but handprints of young people predominate and specifically handprints of teenaged males.

Some Words of Thanks

My wife, Mary Lee Morris Guthrie, helped me write this book. Its subjects generated thousands of hours of discussion, humor, and arguments over the years. Our kids were dragged into museums and caves: they grew up with the book in talks over the supper table, arguments during jogs, poems posted on the cupboard door, and trial balloons launched over long-distance drives. Family conversations formed the very anvil of these pages. My wife is a professional artist, an experienced outdoorswoman and she is interested in ideas. Though she has not agreed with everything in the book, and indeed was often unreceptive to my blurted-out flashes of insight, she made me think more critically than I would have otherwise. And for such a controversial study, her challenges were probably one of the best gifts.

During the time I wrote this book I taught in the Biology and Wildlife Department with a joint research appointment at the Institute of Arctic Biology and a joint title in the Anthropology Department and Museum, University of Alaska in Fairbanks. The Institute members were favorably tolerant of this part of my work, even though it fell toward the outer edge of their official interests. They kindly allowed me time to devote to these studies, and critical time to visit sites in Europe, Africa, and Australia. Indirectly, this was underwritten by the kind people of Alaska. Thank you! Most writing was tucked in among my normal research as a mammalian paleobiologist. Time was found over decades, in the corners of summer breaks, between-semester vacations, in three glorious sabbaticals, in between labs and lectures, and most recently, in the more spacious state as emeritus. It was a pleasure to do this work, to get back to it after days or weeks away. No one could have had a hobby more engrossing.

I am particularly grateful for the Alexander von Humbolt Foundation Senior Scientist Award and the hospitality of Wighart von Koenigswald at the University of Bonn, Germany, which allowed me a crucial and unique nine months to devote time to illustrating and editing this book. Final assembling and wrap-up were done while I was a visiting senior fellow for two terms at Corpus Christi College, Cambridge, England, and I want to thank the college and especially Paul Mellars for this invitation.

My Alaskan colleagues who take anal temperatures of chickadees, map rutting pits of moose, core lakes for pollen, and age fish scales, may have thought my interests in old drawings of painted hands and carved vulva somewhat strange, but they were consistently helpful, and discussions with them were always stimulating. In particular, colleagues Dave Klein, Fred Dean, Fred West, Ron Smith, Paul Matheus, Joan Braddock, Brian and Martin M. Barnes, Chase Hensel, and Phyllis Morrow helped with details, and many served as trial "readers" for early drafts of different chapters or of the whole book. Statistician Arny Blanchard helped with the hand study. My friend Bill Paton—orthopedic surgeon, hunter, and outdoorsman— read the entire manuscript several times and had many good suggestions. Thanks to Erik Granqvist, friend of many years and co-imaginer of the Paleolithic.

I cannot thank senior editor Christine Henry enough. Her steady pleasantness and confidence encouraged me during setbacks. She seemed to share delight in advances like a family member. Copyediting, as an art form, was supplied by Pam Bruton. The striking design and layout of the book is not mine, but came from the creative hand of

Jill Shimabukuro. I thank fate for linking me up with these three: may all writers be so lucky.

Many people have provided valuable assistance, information, discussions, insight, or hospitality over the years while I visited foreign museums, field research areas, caves, and so on. In no particular order some of them are: (*in France*) Jean Clottes, Jean-Philippe Rigaud, Bruno Guy, Michel-Alain Garcia, Jean-Michel Geneste, Bernard Jodelet, Maryléne Patou, Philippe Fosse, François Rouzaud, Valérie Feruglio, Silvana Condemi, Denis Vailou, Jean-Daniel Larribau, Henri Delporte, and Dominique Baffier. *In Finland:* Björn Kurtén, Mikael Fortelieus, and Eirik Granqvist. *In Switzerland:* Hans-Georg Bandi. *In Spain:* Emilia Calleja Peredo and Nuria Garcia. *In Italy:* Immanuel Anati and Margherita Mussi. *In the United Kingdom:* Antony and Una Sutcliff, Ann Sieveking, Adrian Lister, and Paul Mellars. *In Poland:* Henrik Kubiak. *In Russia:* Andrei Sher, Zoya Abromova, Gerady Baryshnikov, and N. K. Vereshchagin. *In Southern Africa:* Jeramie Anderson, Norman Owen-Smith, Johan DuToit, Petri Viljon, and J. D. Lewis-Williams. *In Australia:* Alex Baynes, Richard Kimber, and Rod Wells. *In New Zealand:* Atholl Anderson. *In Germany:* Hans-Peter Uerpmann, Wighart von Koenisgwald, Joachim Hahn, Hans Müller-Beck, Gerhard Bosinski, Nicholas Conard, Martin Street, and Elaine Turner. *In the Netherlands:* Thijs von Kolfschoten, Dick Mol, Jon Vos, and Wil Roebroeks. *In the U.S.A.:* Valerius Geist, George Frison, Larry Agenbroad, Olga Soffer, Margaret Conkey, Richard Scott, Roger Powers, Fred Hadleigh West, Jean Auel, Paul Martin, Dave Webb, and John Hoffecker. Owen, my son and hunting partner, helped with the hand study and organization of the book. Owen and my daughters Mareca and Tamia were a vital part of many discussions which underlie the book's contents.

The Fairbanks kids at Pearl Creek Elementary, Ryan Junior High, and West Valley High Schools lent me their hands to digitize, as did students and faculty at the university in Fairbanks. Our work together was especially fun.

References

Abramova, Z. A. 1995. *L'art paléolithique d'Europe orientale et de Sibérie.* Jérôme Millon, Grenoble.

Absolon, K. 1949. The diluvial anthropomorphic statuettes and drawings, especially the so-called Venus statuettes discovered in Moravia. *Artibus Asiae* 12: 201–220.

Adams, C. J. 1990. *The sexual politics of meat.* Continuum Publishing Co., New York.

Adams, D. B. 1983. Why are there so few women warriors? *Behavioral Science Research* 18: 196–212.

Adams, J. M., H. Faure, L. Faure-Denard, J. M. McGlade, and F. I. Woodward. 1990. Increases in terrestrial carbon storage from last glacial maximum to present. *Nature* 348: 711–714.

Adovasio, J. M., O. Soffer, D. C. Hyland, B. Klíma, and J. Svoboda. 1999. Textil kosíkárstvi a site v gravettienu Moravy. *Archeologické Rozhledy* 51: 58–94.

Agenbroad, L. D. 1990. The mammoth population of Hot Springs Site and associated megafauna. In *Megafauna and man,* ed. L. D. Agenbroad, J. I. Mead, and L. W. Nelson, 32–41. University of Arizona Press, Flagstaff.

Aiello, L. C., and P. Wheeler. 1995. The expensive tissue hypothesis: The brain and digestive system in human and primate evolution. *Current Anthropology* 36: 119–221.

Airvaux, J. 2001. *L'art préhistorique de Poitou-Charante.* La Maison des Roches, Editeur, Paris.

Alcock, J. 1979. *Animal behavior: An evolutionary approach.* Sinauer Associates, Sunderland, Mass.

———. 1993. *Animal behavior.* 5th ed. Sinauer, Sunderland, Mass.

Aldis, O. 1975. *Play fighting.* Academic Press, New York.

Alexander, R. D. 1977. Natural selection and analysis of human sociality. In *The changing scenes in natural sciences, 1926–1976,* 283–337. Academy of Natural Sciences Publications 12. Philadelphia.

———. 1979. *Darwinism and human affairs.* University of Washington Press, Seattle.

Alland, A. 1977. *The artistic animal: An inquiry into the biological rules of art.* Doubleday-Anchor, New York.

Allen, L. S., and R. A. Gorski. 1986. Sexual dimorphism of the human anterior commissure. *Anatomical Record* 214: 3A.

Allman, J. M. 1999. *Evolving brains.* Scientific American Library, New York.

Altuna, J. 1979. La faune des ongulés du Tardiglaciaire en pays Basque et dans le reste de la région cantabrique. In *La fin des temps glaciaires en Europe,* 85–96. CNRS Colloques Internationaux 271. CNRS, Paris.

———. 1983. On the relationship between archaeo-faunas and parietal art in the caves of the Cantabrian region. *British Archaeological Reports Series* 163: 227–238.

———. 1996. *L'art des cavernes en pays Basque.* Editions du Seuil, Paris.

Altuna, J., and J. M. Apellaniz. 1976. *Las figuras rupestres paleoliticas de la cueva de Altxerri (Guipuzcoa).* Sociedad de Ciencias Aranzadi 28, Munibe, San Sebastián.

Alvard, M. S. 2001. Mutualistic hunting. In *Meat-eating and human evolution,* ed. B. C. Stanford and H. T. Bunn, 261–278. Oxford University Press, Oxford.

Alvarez, F. 1990. Horns and fighting in male Spanish ibex, *Capra pyrenaica. Jour. Mamm.* 71: 608–616.

Anati, E. 1989. *Les origines de l'art et la formation de l'espirit humain.* Albin Michel, Paris.

Anderson, A. 1997. Prehistoric Polynesian impact on New Zealand environment. In *Historical ecology of the Pacific Islands,* ed. P. V. Kirch and T. C. Hunt, 271–283. Yale University Press, New Haven.

Anderson, A. J. 1983. *When all the moa ovens grew cold.* Otago Heritage Books, Otago.

Anderson, R. L. 1979. *The art of primitive societies.* Prentice-Hall, New York.

Andrew, R. J. 1978. Increased persistence of attention produced by testosterone, and its implications for the study of sexual behavior. In *Biological determinants of sexual behavior,* ed. J. B. Hutchinson, 255–275. Wiley, Chichester, England.

Ann, M., and D. Myers-Imel. 1995. *Goddesses in world mythology.* Oxford University Press, Oxford.

Anthoney, T. R. 1968. The ontogeny of greeting, grooming, and sexual motor patterns in captive baboons. *Behavior* 31: 358–372.

Anzenberger, G. 1992. Monogamous social systems and paternity in primates. In *Paternity in primates: Genetic tests and theories,* ed. R. D. Martin, A. F. Dixon, and E. J. Wicklings, 203–224. S. Karger Publishing, New York.

Apellaniz, J. M. 1984. L'auteur des grands taureaux de Lascaux et ses successeurs. *L'Anthropologie* 88: 539–561.

Appavoo, D. M., S. Kubow, and H. V. Kuhnlein. 1991. Lipid composition of indigenous foods. *Journal of Food Composition and Analysis* 4: 107–119.

Ardrey, R. 1966. *The territorial imperative.* Atheneum, New York.

Armelagos, G. J., D. P. van Gerven, D. L. Martin, and R. Huss-Ashmore. 1984. Effects of nutritional change on skeleton biology of Northeastern African (Sudanese Nubian) populations. In *From hunters to farmers,* ed. J. D. Clark and S. A. Brandt, 132–151. Cambridge University Press, Cambridge.

Arndt, S., and M. Newcomer. 1986. Breakage patterns on prehistoric bone points: An experimental study. In *Studies in the Upper Paleolithic of Britain and northwest Europe,* ed. D. A. Roe, 165–180. British Archaeological Reports, International Series, 246. BAR, Oxford.

Atkins, R. C. 1992. *Dr. Atkins' new diet revolution.* Avon Books, New York.

Bachofen, J. J. 1967. *Myth, religion, and mother right.* Trans. R. Manheim. Princeton University Press, Princeton.

Bachu, A. 1993. *Fertility of American women: June 1992.* U.S. Bureau of the Census Current Population Reports Series P-20, no. 470. Government Printing Office, Washington, D.C.

Bader, O. M. 1978. *The Sungir Upper Paleolithic site.* Nauka, Moscow.

———. 1984. *Paleolitaicheskie pogrebenia i paleoanthropologicheskie nakodik na Sungire* (Paleolithic burials at Sungir), 6–13. Ed. A. A. Zubov and V. M. Kharitonov. Nauka, Moscow.

Baffier, D. 1984. Les caractères sexuels secondaires des mammifères dans l'art pariétal paléolithique franco-cantabrique. In Bandi et al. 1984, 143–154.E

Bagatell, C. J., and W. J. Bremner. 1996a. Androgens and behavior in men and women. *Endocrinologist* 7: 97–10.

Bahn, P. 1980. Crib-biting: Tethered horses in the Paleolithic. *World Archaeology* 12: 212–217.

———. 1983. Late Pleistocene economics of the French Pyrenees. In *Hunter-gatherer economics in prehistory,* ed. G. Bailey, 168–186. Cambridge University Press, Cambridge.

Bahn, P., and J. Vertut. 1988. *Images of the Ice Age.* Facts on File, Oxford.

———. 1997. *Journey through the Ice Age.* Wiedenfeld and Nicholson, London.

Baker, R., and M. A. Bellis. 1995. *Human sperm competition: Copulation, masturbation and infidelity.* Chapman and Hall, London.

Balbín-Behrmann, R. de, and J. J. Alcolea-González. 1999. Vie quotidienne et vie religieuse: Les sanctuaires dans l'art paléolithique. *L'Anthropologie* 103: 23–49.

Baldwin, D. 1993. *Male sexual health.* Hippocrine Books, New York.

Baldwin, J. D., and J. I. Baldwin. 1974. Exploration and social play in squirrel monkeys. *Amer. Zool.* 14: 303–315.

Ballet, O., A. Bocquet, R. Bouchez, J. M. D. Coey, and A. Cornu. 1979. Etude technique de poudres colorées de Lascaux. In *Lascaux inconnu,* ed. A. Leroi-Gourhan and J. Allain, 171–174. Editions du CNRS, Paris.

Bancroft, J. 1984. Hormones and human sexual behavior. *Journal of Sex and Marital Therapy* 10: 3–27.

Bancroft, J., and F. C. W. Wu. 1983. Changes in erectile responsiveness during androgen replacement therapy. *Archiv. Sexual Behav.* 12: 59–66.

Bandi, H.-G. 1984. Contribution de la zoologie et de l'ethologie à l'interprétation de l'art des peuples chasseurs préhistoriques. *L'Anthropologie* (Paris) 88: 563–571.

Bandi, H.-G., W. Huber, M.-R. Sauter, and B. Sitter. 1984. *La contribution de la zoologie et de l'ethologie à l'interprétation de l'art des peuples chasseurs préhistoriques.* Editions Universitaires, Fribourg, Switzerland.

Bandi, H.-G., and G. Maringer. 1955. *L'art préhistorique.* Picard, Paris.

Bannikov, A. G. 1959. Habitat characteristics and some biological features of Przewalsky's horse. In *Proceedings of the first international symposium on the Przewalski horse* (in Russian), 13–30. Prague. British Library, Wetherby, Translation RTS 7272.

Baring, A., and J. Cashford. 1991. *Myth of the goddess.* Arkana, New York.

Barrière, C. 1976. *L'art pariétal de la Grotte de Gargas.* British Archaeological Reports, Supplementary Series, 14. BAR, Oxford.

———. 1997. *L'art pariétal des grotes des Combarelles.* Paleo-Horo Serie. ISSN Collection PALEO: 1145–3370.

Barry, H., I. L. Child, and M. K. Bacon. 1959. Relation of child training to subsistence economy. *American Anthropologist* 61: 51–63.

Bate, D. M. A. 1950. The "Licorn" of Lascaux: Is it *Pantholops? Archaeol. Newsletter* 2: 182–184.

Beach, F. A. 1957. Characteristics of masculine "sex drive." In *Nebraska Symposium on Motivation, 1956,* ed. M. R. Jones, 1–32. University of Nebraska Press, Lincoln.

Becker, J. B., S. M. Breedlove, and D. Crews, eds. 1992. *Behavioral endocrinology.* MIT Press, Cambridge.

Bednarik, R. G. 1986. Parietal finger markings in Europe and Australia. *Rock Art Research* 3: 30–61.

———. 1994. About rock art vandalism and graffiti. *International Newsletter on Rock Art* 8: 22–23.

———. 1995. First Paleolithic rock art found in Germany. *International Newsletter on Rock Art* 11: 3–4.

Bégouën, H., and H. V. Vallois. 1927. Les empreintes de pieds préhistoriques. In *Institut International d'Anthropologie* (Amsterdam) 111ᵉ session: 323–338.

Bégouën, M. 1925. *Les bisons d'Argile.* Picard, Paris.

Bégouën, R. L., J. Clottes, J.-P. Giraud, and F. Rouzaud. 1982. Plaquette gravée d'Enlène, Montesquieu-Avantès (Ariège). *Bulletin de la Société Préhistorique Française* 79: 103–109.

Behrensmeyer, A. K., and L. F. Laporte. 1981. Footprints of a Pleistocene hominid in northern Kenya. *Nature* 289: 167–169.

Behrmann, B., J. J. Alcolea-González, and M. Santonja Gómez. 1996. Siega Verde: Un art rupestre paléolithique à l'air libre dans la vallée du Duro. *L'art préhistorique* 209: 98–105.

Bekoff, M. 1974. Social play in coyotes, wolves, and dogs. *Bioscience* 24: 225–230.

Bekoff, M., and J. A. Beyers, eds. 1998. *Animal play.* Cambridge University Press, Cambridge.

Bemelmans, L. 1939. *Madeline.* Puffin Books, New York.

Berenbaum, S. A., and M. Hines. 1989. Hormonal influences on sex-typed toy preferences. Paper presented at the Biennial Meeting of the Society for Research in Child Development, Mar. 7–10, 1989, Kansas City, Mo.

Bernstein, I. S., T. P. Gordon, and R. M. Rose. 1974. Behavioral and environmental events influencing primate testosterone levels. *Journal of Human Evolution* 3: 517–525.

Bersheid, E. 1981. *An overview of the psychological effects of physical attractiveness.* Psychological Aspects of Facial Form. Center for Human Growth and Development, University of Michigan, Ann Arbor.

Berthold, P., W. Wiltschko, H. Miltenberger, and W. Querner. 1990. Genetic transmission of migratory behavior into a non-migrating population. *Experientia* 46: 107–108.

Betzig, L. 1988. Mating and parenting in Darwinian perspective. In *Human reproductive behaviour: A Darwinian perspective,* ed. L. Betzig, M. Borgerhoff Mulder, and P. Turke, 3–20. Cambridge University Press, Cambridge.

———, ed. 1997. *Human nature, a critical reader.* Oxford University Press, Oxford.

Beyers, J. A. 1977. Terrain preferences in the play of Siberian ibex kids (*Capra ibex sibirica*). *Zeitschrift Tierpsychol.* 44: 199–209.

———. 1984. Play in ungulates. In *Play in animals and humans,* ed. P. K. Smith, 43–69. Basil Blackwell, Oxford.

———. 1998. Biological effects of locomotor play: Getting into shape or something more specific? InBeckoff and Beyers 1998, 205–220.

Biesele, M. 1993. *Women like meat.* Witwatersrand University Press, Johannesburg, R.S.A.

Binant, P. 1991a. *Archeologie aujourd'hui: Les sepultures du Paléolithique.* Edition Errance, Paris.

———. 1991b. *La prehistoire de la mort.* Editions Errance, Paris.

Birch, E. S., Jr. 1974. Eskimo warfare in northwest Alaska. *Anthropological Papers of the University of Alaska* 16: 1–14.

Birdsell, J. B. 1968. Some predictions based on the Pleistocene equilibrium systems among recent hunter-gatherers. In Lee and DeVore 1968, 229–273. Birkhead, T. R., L. Atkin, and A. P. Møller. 1987. Copulation behavior in birds. *Behavior* 101: 101–138.

Bischoff, J. L., N. Soler, J. Maroto, and R. Juliá. 1989. Abrupt Mousterian/Aurignacian boundary at c. 40 ka BP: Accelerator ¹⁴C dates from L'Arbreda Cave (Catalunya, Spain). Journal of Arch. Sci. 16: 563–576.

Bjorklund, D. F., and A. D. Pellegrini. 2002. *The origins of human nature: Evolutionary developmental psychology.* American Psychological Association, Washington, D.C.

Blake, V. 1927. *The art and craft of drawing.* Oxford University Press, Oxford.

Block, M. 1977. The past and present in the present. *Man* 12: 278–292.

Blurton-Jones, N. G. 1967. An ethological study of some aspects of social behavior of children in nursery schools. In *Primate ethology,* ed. D. Morris, 96–118. Aldine Publishing Co., Chicago.

———. 1987. Bushman birth spacing: Direct tests of some simple predictions. *Ethol. Sociobiol.* 8: 183–203.

Blurton-Jones, N. G., and M. J. Konner. 1976. !Kung knowledge of animal behavior. In *Kalahari hunter-gatherers,* ed. R. B. Lee and I. DeVore, 35–63. Harvard University Press, Cambridge.

Blurton-Jones, N. G., and R. M. Sibley. 1978. Testing adaptiveness of culturally determined behavior. In *Human behavior and adaptation,* ed. N. G. Blurton-Jones and V. Reynolds, 26–89. Taylor and Francis, London.

Bogin, B. 1999. *Patterns of human growth.* Cambridge University Press, Cambridge.

Bongaarts, J., and R. G. Potter. 1983. *Fertility, biology, and behavior: An analysis of the proximate determinates.* Academic Press, New York.

Bonner, J. T. 1988. *The evolution of culture in animals.* Princeton University Press, Princeton.

Boone, J. L., III. 1986. Parental investment and elite family structure in preindustrial states: A case study of late medieval–early modern Portuguese genealogies. *American Anthropologist* 88: 859–878.

Boorstin, D. J. 1992. *The creators.* Vintage Press, New York.

Borgerhoff Mulder, M. 1988a. Reproductive consequences of sex-biased inheritance. In *Comparative socioecology of animals and man,* ed. R. Foley and V. Standon, 405–427. Basil Blackwell, London.

———. 1988b. Reproductive success in three Kipsigis cohorts. In *Reproductive success,* ed. T. H. Clutton-Brock, 419–435. University of Chicago Press, Chicago.

Bosinski, G. 1981. *Gönnersdorf: Eiszeitjager am Mittelrhein.* Landesmuseum, Koblenz.

———. 1990. *Homo sapiens: L'histoire des chasseurs du Paléolithique supérieur en Europe (40,000–10,000 avant J.-C.).* Editions Errance, Paris.

Bouchard, T. J., D. T. Lykken, M. McGue, N. L. Segal, and A. Tellegen. 1990. Sources of human psychological differences: The Minnesota study of twins reared apart. *Science* 250: 223–227.

Bouckaert, A., and B. Boulanger. 1997. Marriage distance between birthplaces and age differences between mates. *Hum. Biol.* 69: 241–251.

Boyd, R., and J. R. Silk. 1996. *How humans evolved.* Norton, New York.

Boyer, P. 1994. *The naturalness of religious ideas: A cognitive theory of religion.* University of California Press, Berkeley.

Brassaï. 1966. *Picasso and company.* Trans. Francis Price. Doubleday, Garden City, N.Y.

Breuil, H. 1952. *Quatre cents siècles d'art parietal.* Max Fourny, Paris.

——— (with the collaboration of M. T. de St.-Péreuse). 1969. Comments. In Pales and de St.-Péreuse 1969, 123–127.

Brickman, J. 1978. Erotica: Sex differences in stimulus preferences and fantasy content. Ph.D. thesis, University of Manitoba.

Brockman, J. 1995. *The third culture.* Simon and Schuster, New York.

Broglio, A. 1995. Les sépultures Epigravettiennes de la Venete (Abri Tagliente et Abri Villavruna). In Otte 1995, 847–870.

Brook, D. 1977. Comments on art, behavior, and anthropologists by Denis Hutton. *Current Anthropology* 19: 394–395.

Broude, G., and S. Greene. 1976. Cross-cultural codes on twenty sexual attitudes and practices. *Ethnology* 15: 409–429.

Brown, D. E. 1991. *Human universals.* McGraw-Hill, New York.

Brown, J. K. 1970. A note on the division of labor by sex. *American Anthropologist* 72: 1073–1078.

Brown, R. D., ed. 1983. Antler development in the Cervidae. Texas A&M University, Kingsville.

Brown, S. 1998. Play as an organizing principle: Clinical evidence and personal observations. In Bekoff and Beyers 1998, 243–259.

Bubenik, A. B. 1998. Moose behavior. In *Ecology and management of the North American moose,* 173–222. Smithsonian Institution Press, Washington, D.C.

Bubenik, G. A., and A. B. Bubenik, eds. 1990. *Horns, pronghorns, and antlers.* Springer-Verlag, New York.

Bunn, H. T. 1999. Comments addressing cooking and human origins by Wrangham et al. *Current Anthropology* 40: 579–580.

Bunn, H. T., and J. A. Ezo. 1993. Hunting and scavenging by Plio-Pleistocene hominids: Nutritional constraints, archaeological patterns, and behavioral implications. *Journal of Arch. Sci.* 20: 365–398.

Bunn, H. T., and E. M. Kroll. 1986. Systemic butchery by Plio/Pleistocene hominids at Olduvai Gorge, Tanzania. *Current Anthropology* 27: 431–452.

Burch, E. 1980. Traditional Eskimo societies in northwest Alaska. In *Alaska native culture and history,* ed. Y. Kotani and W. Workman, 253–304. Senri Ethnological Studies 4. National Museum of Ethnology, Osaka.

Burghardt, G. M. 1998. The evolutionary origins of play revisited: Lessons from turtles. In Beckoff and Beyers 1998, 1–26.

Buss, D. M. 1988a. The evolution of human intersexual competition: Tactics of mate attraction. *Journal of Personality and Social Psychology* 54: 628–661.

———. 1988b. From vigilance to violence: Mate guarding tactics. *Ethol. and Sociobiol.* 9: 291–317.

———. 1989. Sex differences in human mate preferences: Evolutionary hypotheses tested in 37 cultures. *Behavior and Brain Science* 12: 1–49.

———. 1992. Mate preference mechanisms: Consequences for partner choice and intrasexual competition. In *The adapted mind,* ed. J. H. Barkow, L. Cosmides, and J. Tooby, 249–266. Oxford University Press, New York.

———. 1994. *The evolution of desire: Strategies of human mating.* Basic Books, New York.

———. 1997. Sex differences in human mate preferences: Evolutionary hypotheses tested in 37 cultures. In Betzig 1997, 175–190.

Cabrera Valdes, V., and J. L. Bischoff. 1989. Accelerator ^{14}C dates for early Upper Paleolithic (Basal Aurignacian) at El Castillo Cave (Spain). *Journal of Arch. Sci.* 16: 577–584.

Camps, G. 1984. La défécation dans l'art paléolithique. In Bandi et al. 1984, 251.

Capitan, L. 1911. Les empreintes de mains humaines dans la grotte de Gargas. *Bulletin Archéologique,* pp. 87–88.

Capitan, L., and Abbé J. Bouyssonie. 1924. *Un atelier d'art préhistorique Limeuil: Son gisment á gravures sur pierres de l'âge du renne.* Masson, Paris.

Carbonell Roura, E. C. 1999. Comments addressing cooking and human origins by Wrangham et al. *Current Anthropology* 40: 580–581.

Cardale de Schrimpff, M. 1989. The snake and the fabulous beast: Themes from the pottery of the Ilama culture. In *Animals into art,* ed. H. Morphy, 75–106. Unwin Hyman, Boston.

Caro, T. M. 1987. Indirect costs of play: Cheetah cubs reduce maternal hunting success. *Animal Behavior* 35: 295–297.

Carpenter, E. 1973. *Eskimo realities.* Holt, Rinehart, and Winston, New York.

Cartailhac, E. 1906. Les mains. *Bulletin de la Société Anthropologique du Midi de la France* 37: 141.

Cartmill, M. 1993. *A view to death in the morning.* Harvard University Press, Cambridge.

Cashdan, E. A. 1980. Egalitarianism among hunters and gatherers. *American Anthropologist* 82: 116–120.

Casteret, N. 1934. Les mains fantômes. *Revue de Comminges* 44: 110–116.

Cavalli-Sforza, L. L., and W. Bodmer. 1971. *The genetics of human populations.* Freeman and Co., New York.

Cavalli-Sforza, L. L., and F. Cavalli-Sforza. 1995. *The great human diasporas: The history of diversity and evolution.* Addison Wesley, Harlow, England.

Cavalli-Sforza, L. L., P. Menozzi, and A. Piazza. 1994. *The history and geography of human genetics.* Princeton University Press, Princeton.

Chaline, J. 1979. Les modifications de paysages et de climats de la fin des Temps glaciaires en France (domaine boréal) révélées par les migrations de rongeurs. In *La fin des Temps glaciaires en Europe,* CNRS Colloques Internationaux 271. CNRS, Paris.

Chaloupka, G. 1983. Kakadu rock art: Its cultural, historic and prehistoric significance. In *The rock art sites of Kakadu National Park: Some preliminary research findings for their conservation and management,* ed. G. Gilespie, 3–33. Australian National Parks and Wildf. Serv. Special Publication 10. Canberra.

———. 1984. *From Paleoart to casual paintings.* Northern Territory Museum of the Arts and Sciences. Monograph Series 1. Darwin, Northern Territory, Australia.

Chamberlain, A. 2000. Minor concerns: A demographic perspective on children in past societies. In Derevenski 2000, 206–212.

Chamberlain, W. 1976. *Wilt.* Warner Books, New York.

Childe, V. G. 1951. *Social organization.* Watts, London.

Chodorow, N. 1978. The reproduction of mothering: Psycho-analysis and sociology of gender. University of California Press, Berkeley.

Churchill, S., V. Formicola, T. Holiday, B. Holt, and B. Schumann. 2000. In *Hunters of the Golden Age,* ed. W. Roebroeks, M. Mussi, J. Svoboda, and K. Fennema, 31–58. University of Leiden, Netherlands.

Clottes, J. 1985. Conservation des traces et des empreintes. *Histoire et Archéologie* 90 (Jan.).

———. 1989. The identification of human and animal figures in Paleolithic art. In *Animals into art,* ed. H. Morphy, 38–50. Unwin Hyman, Boston.

———. 1997a. New laboratory techniques and their impact on Paleolithic art. In *Beyond art: Pleistocene image and symbol,* ed. M. W. Conkey, O. Soffer, D. Stratmann, and N. G. Jablonski, 37–52. Memoirs of the California Academy of Sciences 3. San Francisco.

———. 1997b. Art of the light and art of the depths. In *Beyond art: Pleistocene image and symbol,* ed. M. W. Conkey, O. Soffer, D. Stratmann, and N. G. Jablonski, 203–216. Memoirs of the California Academy of Sciences 3. San Francisco.

———. 2000. Art between 30,000 and 20,000 B.P. In *Hunters of the Golden Age,* ed. W. Roebroeks, M. Mussi, J. Svoboda, and K. Fennema, 87–104. University of Leiden, Netherlands.

———. 2003. *Chauvet Cave: The art of earliest times.* University of Utah Press, Salt Lake City.

Clottes, J., J. Courtin, and H. Valladas. 1992. A well-dated Paleolithic cave: Cosquer Cave at Marseille. *Rock Art Research* 9: 122–129.

Clottes, J., M. Garner, and G. Maury. 1994. Magdalenian bison in the caves of the Ariège. *Rock Art Research* 11: 58–70.

Clottes, J., and D. Lewis-Williams. 1996. *Les chamanes de la préhistoire: Transe et magie dans les grottes ornées.* Editions du Seuil, Paris.

Clutton-Brock, T. H., and G. A. Parker. 1995. Sexual coercion in animal societies. *Animal Behavior* 49: 1345–1365.

Cobb, E. 1959. The ecology of imagination in childhood. *Daedalus* 88: 537–548.

Cohen, C. 2003. *La femme des origenes.* Herscher, Paris.

Cohen, D. 1987. *The development of play.* New York University Press, New York.

Cohen, M. N. 1977. *The food crisis in prehistory: Overpopulation and the origins of agriculture.* Yale University Press, New Haven.

———. 1985. Prehistoric hunter-gatherers: The meaning of social complexity. In *Prehistoric hunter-gatherers,* ed. T. D. Price and J. A. Brown, 99–119. Academic Press, New York.

Colinvaux, P. A. 1979. *Why are big animals rare?* Princeton University Press, Princeton.

Collins, D. 1986. *Paleolithic Europe.* Clayhanger, Tiverton, England.

Conkey, M. W. 1980. The identification of prehistoric hunter-gatherer aggregation sites: The case of Altamira. *Current Anthropology* 21: 609–630.

———. 1983. On the origins of Paleolithic art: A review and some critical thoughts. In *People and wildlife in northern North America,* 201–227. British Archaeological Reports, International Series, 164. BAR, Oxford.

———. 1991. Contests of action, contexts of power: Material culture and gender in the Magdalenian. In *Engendering archaeology: women in prehistory,* ed. J. M. Gero and M. W. Conkey, 57–92. Basil Blackwell, Oxford.

Cook, J. H. 1980. *The evolution of human consciousness.* Clarendon Press, Oxford.

Coope, G. R. 1977. Fossil coleopteran assemblages as sensitive indicators of climatic changes during the Devensian (Last) Cold Stage. *Philosophical Transactions of the Royal Society of London* (B) 280: 313–340.

Cooper, S. M. 1991. Optimal hunting group size: The need for lions to defend their kills against loss to spotted hyenas. *Afr. Jour. Ecology* 29: 130–136.

Coren, S. 1993. *The left-hand syndrome: The causes and consequences of left-handedness.* Vintage, New York.

Costin, C. 1996. Exploring the relationship between gender and craft in complex societies: Methodological and theoretical issues of gender attribution. In *Gender and archaeology: Essays in research and practice,* ed. R. P. Wright, 111–142. University of Pennsylvania Press, Philadelphia.

Couraud, C., and A. Laming-Emperaire. 1984. Les colorants. In *Lascaux inconnu,* ed. A. Leroi-Gourhan et J. Allain, 153–170. Editions du CNRS, Paris.

Crader, D. C. 1983. Recent single-carcass bone scatters and the problem of "butchery" sites in the archaeological record. *British Archaeological Reports Series* 163: 107–142.

Csikszentmihalyi, M. 1975. *Beyond boredom and anxiety: The experience of play in work and games.* Jossey-Basse, San Francisco.

Daly, M., and M. Wilson. 1983. *Sex, evolution, and behavior.* Willard Grant Press, Boston.

———. 1988. *Homicide.* Aldine De Gruyter, New York.

———. 1996. Violence against stepchildren. *Current Directions in Psychological Science* 5: 77–81.

———. 1997. Cinderella revisited. In Betzig 1997, 194–208.

Dansky, J. L. 1982. Play and creativity in young children. In *The many faces of play,* ed. K. Blanchard, 69–79. Association for the Anthropological Study of Play, vol. 9. Human Kinetics Publishers, Champaign, Ill.

Dansky, T., and I. W. Silverman. 1973. Effects of play on associative fluency of preschool aged children. *Develop. Psych.* 9: 38–44.

Darwin, C. 1859. *On the origin of species by means of natural selection.* Murray, London.

David, N. 1973. On Upper Paleolithic society, ecology, and technological change. In *The explanation of culture change,* ed. C. Renfrew, 87–123. Duckworth, London.

Davidson, I. 1986. Freedom of information: Aspects of art and society in Western Europe during the last Ice Age. In *Animals into Art,* ed. H. Morphy, 440–456. Unwin Hyman, Boston.

———. 1997. The power of pictures. In *Beyond art: Pleistocene image and symbol,* ed. M. W. Conkey, O. Soffer, D. Stratmann, and N. G. Jablonski, 125–160. Memoirs of the California Academy of Sciences 23. San Francisco.

da Vinci, L. 1996. *An edited reproduction of Leonardo da Vinci's notebooks.* Barnes and Noble Books under arrangement with Orbis Publishing Ltd., Novara, Italy.

Davis, E. G. 1976. *The first sex.* Penguin Books, Middlesex, England.

Dawe, B. 1997. Tiny arrowheads: Toys in the toolkit. *Plains Anthropologist* 42: 303–318.

Dawkins, R. 1976. *The selfish gene.* Oxford University Press, Oxford.

DeLamater, J. 1981. The social control of sexuality. In *Annual review of sociology,* ed. A. Inkeles et al., 263–290. Annual Reviews, Menlo Park, Calif.

Delluc, B., and G. Delluc. 1991. *L'art pariétal archaïque en Aquitaine.* Editions du CNRS, Paris.

Delpech, F. 1975. Les faunes du Paléolithique supérieur dans le sud-ouest de la France. Doctoral thesis, University of Bordeaux.

Delporte, H. 1979. *L'image de la femme dans l'art préhistorique.* Picard, Paris.

———. 1984. L'art mobilier et ses rapports avec la faune paléolithique. In Bandi et al. 1984, 111–154.E

———. 1990. *L'image des animaux dans l'art préhistorique.* Picard, Paris.

———. 1993. *L'image de la femme dans l'art préhistorique.* Rev. ed. Picard, Paris.

Dench, G. 1994. *The frog, the prince, and the problem of men.* Neanderthal Books, London.

Denton, K. 1991. Comments: P. M. Gardner's "Foragers' pursuit of individual autonomy." *Current Anthropology* 32: 561.

Deonna, W. 1914. Les masques quaternaires. *L'anthropologie* 25: 107–113.

Derevenski, J. S., ed. 2000. *Children and material culture.* Routledge, London.

D'Errico, F., and P. Villa. 1997. Holes and grooves: The contribution of microscopic analysis and taphonomy to the problem of art origins. *Journal of Human Evolution* 11: 1–31.

Devlin, B., M. Daniels, and K. Roeder. 1997. The heritability of IQ. *Nature* 338: 468–471.

De Waal, F. 1998. *Chimpanzee politics: Power and sex among apes.* Johns Hopkins University Press, Baltimore.

De Waal, F., and F. Lanting. 1997. *Bonobo the forgotten ape.* University of California Press, Berkeley.

Diana, L. 1985. *The prostitute and her clients.* Charles Thomas, Springfield, Ill.

Dissanayake, E. 1992. Homo aestheticus: *Where art comes from and why.* Free Press, New York.

Dittman, R. W. 1992. Body positions and movement pattern in female patients with congenital adrenal hyperplasia. *Hormones and Behavior* 26: 441–456.

Dolhinow, P. J., and N. H. Bishop. 1970. The development of motor skills and social relationships among primates through play. In *Minnesota symposium on child psychology,* ed. J. P. Hill, 180–198. University of Minnesota Press, Minneapolis.

Donaldson, A. S. 1993. The rape crisis behind bars. *New York Times,* Dec. 29, 1993.

Donner, J. J. 1975. Pollen composition of the Abri Pataud sediments. In *Excavation of the Abri Pataud,* ed. H. L. Movius Jr., 160–173. American School of Prehistoric Research Bulletin 30. Peabody Museum, Harvard University, Cambridge.

Draper, P. 1976. Social and economic constraints on child life. In *Kalahari hunter-gatherers: Studies of !Kung San and their neighbors,* ed. R. B. Lee and I. DeVore, 179–247. Harvard University Press, Cambridge.

Draper, P., and E. Cashdan. 1988. Technological change and child behavior among the !Kung. *Ethnology* 27: 339–365.

Dubourg, C. 1994. Les expressions de la saisonnalité dans les arts paléolithiques: Les arts sur support lithique du Bassin d'Aquitaine. *Bulletin de la Société Préhistorique de l'Ariège* 49: 145–189.

Duday, H., and M. Garcia. 1983. Les empreintes de l'homme préhistorique: La grotte du Pech-Merle à Caberets (Lot). *Bulletin de la Société Préhistorique Française* 8: 205–215.

———. 1985. L'homme et la caverne. *Histoire et Archéologie* 90: 35–39.

———. 1990. L'ichnologie ou la mémoire des roches. In *La mémoire,* vol. 11, *Le concept de mémoire,* ed. N. Navialoff, R. Jaffard, and P. Brenot, 55–66. Hartman, Paris.

Duhard, J.-P. 1989. La gestuelle du membre supérieur dans les figurations féminines sculptées paléolithiques. *Rock Art Research* 6: 105–117.

———. 1993. *Réalisme de l'image féminine Paléolithique.* Editions du CNRS, Paris.

Dumond, F. V., and T. C. Hutchinson. 1967. Squirrel monkey reproduction: The fatted male phenomenon and seasonal spermatogenesis. Science 1958: 1067–1107.

Dunbar, R. I. M. 1995. Neocortex size as a constraint on group size in primates. *Journal of Human Evolution* 20: 469–493.

———. 1996. *Grooming, gossip, and the evolution of language.* Harvard University Press, Cambridge.

———. 1998. The social-brain hypothesis. *Evol. Anthrop.* 6: 178–190.

Durant, W. [1970] 1991. *The story of philosophy.* Reprint, Pocketbooks, New York.

Eades, M. R., and M. D. Eades. 1996. *Protein power.* Bantam, New York.

Eastman, A. 1986. The season or the symbol: The evidence of swallows in the Paleolithic of Western Europe. Abstract of paper presented at ICAZ (International Council for Archaeozoology), Aug. 25–30, 1986, Bordeaux.

Edwards, B. 1979. *Drawing on the right side of the brain.* J. P. Tarcher, Los Angeles.

Edwards, D. A. 1951. Differences in distribution of subcutaneous fat with sex and maturity. *Clinical Sci.* 10: 305–315.

Ehrenberg, M. 1989. *Woman in prehistory.* British Museum, London.

Ehrhardt, A. A., and S. W. Baker. 1974. Fetal androgens, human DNA differentiation, and behavior sex differences. In *Sex differences in behavior,* ed. R. C. Fridman, R. M. Richart, and R. L. Van de Wilde, 33–51. Wiley and Sons, New York.

Eibl-Eibesfeldt, I. 1970. *Ethology, the biology of behavior.* Holt, Rinehart, and Winston, New York.

———. 1989a. The biological foundation of aesthetics. In *Beauty and the brain: Biological aspects of aesthetics,* ed. I. Rentschler, B. Herzberger, and D. Epstein, 29–68. Birkhauser, Basel.

———. 1989b. *Human ethology.* Aldine de Gruyter, Hawthorn, N. Y.

Ellis, B. J., and D. Symons. 1990. Sex differences in sexual fantasy: An evolutionary psychological approach. *Jour. Sex Res.* 27: 527–555.

———. 1997. Sex differences in sexual fantasy: An evolutionary psychological approach. In Betzig 1997, 194–208.

Ellis, M. J., and G. J. L. Scholtz. 1978. *Activity and play of children.* Prentice-Hall, New York.

Ember, M. 1975. On the origin and extension of the incest taboo. *Behavioral Science Research* 10: 249–281.

Erickson, M. T. 1999. Incest avoidance and familial bonding. *Journal of Anthropological Research* 45: 267–291.

Espinoza, E. O., B. C. Yates, M.-J. Mann, A. R. Crane, K. W. Goodard, J. P. LeMay, K. W. Speckman, and M. A. Webb. 1997. Taphonomic indicators used to infer wasteful subsistence hunting in northeast Alaska. In *Anthropologia,* 25–26: 103–136. CNRS, Konstanz, Switzerland.

Espmark, Y. 1964. Rutting behavior of reindeer (*Rangifer tarandus* L.). *Anim. Behav.* 12: 159–163.

Estioko-Griffin, A., and P. Bion Griffin. 1981. Women the hunter: The Agta. In *Woman the gatherer,* ed. F. Dahlberg, 113–130. Yale University Press, New Haven.

Ewer, R. F. W. 1968. *Ethology of mammals.* Plenum Press, New York.

———. 1973. *The carnivores.* Cornell University Press, Ithaca.

Eysenck, H. J. 1976. *Sex and personality.* Open Books, London.

Fagen, R. 1981. *Animal play behavior.* Oxford University Press, New York.

———. 1984. Play and behavioral flexibility. In *Play in animals and humans,* ed. P. K. Smith, 159–173. Basil Blackwell, London.

Fisher, E. 1979. *Woman's creation.* McGraw-Hill, New York.

Fitzpatrick, P. 1984. *Jock of the Bushfeld.* A. D. Donker, Parklands, R.S.A.

Flannery, K. 1972. The cultural evolution of civilizations. *Annual Review of Ecology and Systematics* 3: 399–426.

Flerov, K. K. 1952. *Fauna of the USSR.* Vol. 1, no. 2, *Musk deer and deer.* Academy of Sciences of the USSR, Institute of Zoology, Moscow. Fluehr-Lobben, C. 1979. Marxist reappraisal of the matriarchate. *Current Anthropology* 20: 341–359.

Foley, D. 1962. *Toys through the ages.* Troubador Press, New York.

Foley, R. 1987. *Another unique species: Patterns of human evolutionary ecology.* Longman, Harlow, England.

———. 2001. The evolutionary consequences of increased carnivory in hominids. In Stanford and Bunn 2001, 305–331.

Follingstad, D. R., and C. D. Kimbrell. 1986. Sex fantasies revisited: An expansion and further clarification of variables affecting sex fantasy production. *Archiv. Sex Behav.* 15: 475–486.

Formicola, V. 2000. Aging and genetics of obesity. In *Abstract Issue of the American Journal of Physical Anthropology Annual Meeting,* Sept. 30, p. 151.

Fossey, D. 1976. The behavior of the mountain gorilla. Ph.D. thesis, Cambridge University, Cambridge.

Frank, H., and M. G. Frank. 1987. The University of Michigan canine information-processing project. In *Man and Wolf,* ed. E. K. Frank, 143–167. W. Junk Publishers, Boston.

Franzmann, A. W., and P. D. Arneson. 1976. Marrow fat in Alaskan moose femurs in relation to mortality factors. *Journal of Wildlife Management* 40: 353–359.

Frayer, D. W. 1980. Sexual dimorphism and cultural evolution in the late Pleistocene of Europe. *Journal of Human Evolution* 9: 399–415.

Freeman, D. 1983. *Margaret Mead and Samoa: The making and unmaking of an anthropological myth.* Harvard University Press, Cambridge.

———. 1999. *The fateful hoaxing of Margaret Mead.* Westview Press, Oxford.

Freeman, L. G., J. González Echegaray, F. Bernaldo de Quiros, and J. Ogden. 1987. *Altamira revisited and other essays on early art.* Instituto de Investigaciones Prehistoricas, Santander, Spain.

Frisch, R. E. 1976. Fatness of girls from menarche to age 18 years, with a tomogram. *Hum. Biol.* 48: 353–359.

———. 1988. Fatness and fertility. *Scientific American* 258: 88–95.

Frisch, R. E., and J. W. McArthur. 1974. Menstrual cycles: Fatness as a determinant of minimum weight necessary for the maintenance or onset. *Science* 53: 384–390.

Frison, G. C. 1978. *Prehistoric hunters of the High Plains.* Academic Press, New York.

Fuentes, A. 1999. Re-evaluating primate monogamy. *Journal of Physical Anthropology* 100: 890–907.

Gagnon, J. H., and W. Simon. 1973. Scripts and the coordination of sexual conduct. In *Nebraska symposium on motivation,* ed. J. K. Cole and R. Dienstbier, 27–59. University of Nebraska Press, Lincoln.

Gallagher, W. 1994. How we become what we are. *Atlantic Monthly* 274: 38–61.

Gamble, C. 1982. Interaction and alliance in Paleolithic society. *Man* 17: 92–107.

———. 1986. *The Paleolithic settlement of Europe.* Cambridge University Press, Cambridge.

———. 1987. Man the shoveler. In *The Pleistocene Old World,* ed. O. Soffer, 81–99. Plenum Press, New York.

Garcia, M. 2003. Prints and traces of humans and animals. In Clottes 2003, 34–43.

Garcia, M., S. Cours, and H. Duday. 1987. Les Chalcolithiques de la grotte de Foissac en Aveyron. *Objects et Mondes (Revue du Musée de l'Homme)* 25: 3–12.

Garcia, M., and H. Duday. 1993. Les emprintes de mains dans l'argile des grottes ornees. In *La main dans la préhistoire,* 56–59. *Dossiers d'Archéologie* 178. Paris.

Garcia Guinea, M. T. 1979. *Altamira and other Cantabrian caves.* Silex, Madrid.

Gardner, H. 1980. *Artful scribbles: the significance of children's drawing.* Basic Books, New York.

———. 1982. *Art, mind, and brain.* Basic Books, New York.

Gardner, P. M. 1991. Foragers' pursuit of individual autonomy. *Current Anthropology* 32: 543–572.

Garn, S. M. 1954. Fat patterning and fat intercorrelations in the adult male. *Human Biology* 26: 59–69.

Geist, V. 1966. The evolution of horn-like organs. *Behavior* 27: 177–214.

———. 1978. *Life strategies, human evolution, and environmental design.* Springer, New York.

Gero, J. M. 1991. Genderlithics: Women's role in stone tool production. In *Engendering Archaeology: Women in prehistory,* ed. J. M. Gero and M. W. Conkey, 163–193. Basil Blackwell, Oxford.

Gimbutas, M. 1982. *The goddesses and gods of Old Europe.* University of California Press, Berkeley.

Gittelman, J. L. 1989. The comparative approach in ethology: Aims and limitations. *Perspectives in Ethology* 8: 55–77.

Gold, P. E. 1987. Sweet memories. *American Scientist* 75: 151–155.

Goldberg, S. 1996. The erosion of the social sciences. In *Dumbing Down,* ed. K. Washburn and J. F. Thornton, 97–113. W. W. Norton, New York.

González Echegaray, J. 1974. *Pinturas y grababos de Las Chimeneas (Pueute Viesgo, Santander).* Monografías de Arte Rupestre, Arte Paleolítico 2. Instituto de Prehistoria y Arqueología, Barcelona.

González Morales, M. R. 1991. From hunter-gatherers to food producers in northern Spain: Smooth adaptive shifts or revolutionary change in the Mesolithic? In *Perspectives on the Past: Theoretical basis in Mediterranean hunter-gatherer research,* ed. G. A. Clark, 204–216. University of Pennsylvania Press, Philadelphia.

———. 1997. When the beasts go marchin' out! The end of the Pleistocene art in Cantabrian Spain. In *Beyond art: Pleistocene image and symbol,* ed. M. W. Conkey, O. Soffer, D. Stratmann, and N. G. Jablonski, 189–199. Memoirs of the California Academy of Sciences 23. San Francisco.

Goodale, J. C. 1971. *Tiwi wives: A study of the women of Melville Island, north Australia.* University of Washington Press, Seattle.

Goodall, J. 1986. *The chimpanzees of Gombe.* Harvard University Press, Cambridge.

———. 1992. Quotation from "Apes and humans." *National Geographic* 181: 38.

Gordon, B. 1990. World *Rangifer* communal hunting. In *Hunters of the recent past,* ed. L. B. Davis and B. O. K. Reeves, 277–296. Unwin Hyman, London.

Goss, R. J., ed. 1983. *Deer antlers: Regeneration, function, and evolution.* Academic Press, New York.

Gottlieb, J. F. 1985. Sex and handedness differences in the use of autoerotic fantasy and imagery: A proposed explanation. *International Journal of Neuroscience* 26: 259–268.

Gowaseb, M. 1992. Reversing marriage conventions: Bushmen women ask for the man's hand. *New Era,* Apr. 1, p. 27.

Greenacre, P. 1959. Play in relation to creative imagination. *Psychoanalytic Study of the Child* 14: 61–80.

Greenberg, M., and R. Littlewood. 1995. Post-adoption incest and phenotypic matching: Experience, personal meanings and biosocial implications. *British Journal of Med. Psychol.* 68: 29–44.

Grimm, L. 2000. Apprentice flintknapping: Relating material culture and social practice in the Upper Paleolithic. In Derevenski 2000, 53–71.

GRIP. 1993. Climate instability during the last interglacial period recorded in the GRIP ice core. *Nature* 364: 203–207.

Groenen, M. 1987. Les representations des mains negatives dans les grottes de Gargas et de Tibran. Thesis Faculte de Philosophie et Lettres. Universite Libre de Bruxelles.

Groenfeldt, D. 1985. The interpretation of prehistoric rock art. *Rock Art Research* 2: 20–31.

Groos, K. 1898. *The play of animals.* Trans. Elizabeth L. Baldwin. Appleton, New York.

———. 1901. *The play of man.* Trans. Elizabeth L. Baldwin. Appleton, New York.

Grötzinger, W. 1970. *Kinder Kritzeln, Zeichnen, Maln: Die Früformen kindlichen Gestaltens.* Prestel-Verlag, Munich.

Guerin, C., and M. Faure. 1984. Les hommes du Paléolithique européen ont-ils chassé le rhinoceros? In *La faune et l'homme préhistorique,* ed. F. Poplin, 29–36. Memoires de la Société Préhistorique Française 19. Paris.

Gunn, Jeannie. 1990. *We of the never-never; The little black princess.* Angus and Robertson, North Ryde.

Guthrie, R. D. 1966. Pelage of fossil bison: a new osteological index. *Jour. Mamm.* 47: 735–737.

———. 1967. The ethnical relationship between humans and other organisms. *Perspectives in Biology and Medicine* 11(1): 52–62.

———. 1968. Paleoecology of the large mammal community in interior Alaska. *American Midland Naturalist* 79: 346–363.

———. 1971a. Evolution of the cervid labial spot. *Jour. Mamm.* 52: 209–212.

———. 1971b. A new theory of the evolution of mammalian rump patches. *Behavior* 38: 132–145.

———. 1976. *Body hot spots: The anatomy of human social organs and behavior.* Van Nostrand: New York.

———. 1983. Osseous projectile points: biological considerations affecting raw material selection and design among Paleolithic and Paleoindian peoples. *British Archaeological Reports Series* 163: 273–294.

———. 1984a. Alaskan megabucks, megabulls, and megarams: The issue of Pleistocene giagantism. In *Contributions in Quaternary Vertebrate Paleontology,* ed. H. H. Genoways and M. R. Dawson, 483–500. Carnegie Museum of Natural History Special Publications 8. Pittsburgh.

———. 1984b. Ethological observations from Paleolithic art. In Bandi et al. 1984.

———. 1990. *Frozen fauna of the Mammoth Steppe: The story of Blue Babe.* University of Chicago Press, Chicago.

———. 1996. The Mammoth Steppe and the origin of Mongoloids and their dispersal. In *Prehistoric Mongoloid dispersals,* ed. T. Akazawa and E. J. E. Szathmáry, 172–186. Oxford University Press, Oxford.

———. 1997. Fossil fat: A forensic key to understanding life in the late Paleolithic of northern Eurasia. In *L'alimentation des hommes du Paleolithique,* 93–126. Etudes et Recherches Archéologiques de l'Université Liège 83. Belgium.

———. 2000. Paleolithic art as a resource in artiodactyl paleoecology. In *Antelopes, deer, and relatives,* ed. E. Vrba and G. Schaller, 96–127. Yale University Press, New Haven.

———. 2001a. Origin and causes of the Mammoth Steppe: A story of cloud cover, woolly mammal tooth pits, buckles, and inside-out Beringia. *Quaternary Science Reviews* 20: 549–574.

———. 2001b. Paleobehavior in Alaskan Pleistocene horses: Social structure, maturation dates, uses of the landscape, and mortality patterns. In *People and wildlife in northern North America,* 32–49. British Archaeological Reports, International Series, 944. London.

———. 2002. Paleolithic atlatl weights and their decoration: How function affects fancy. *Arctic Anthropology* 2: 137–154.

Guthrie, R. D., and J. V. Matthews, Jr. 1971. The Cape Deceit fauna: Early Pleistocene mammalian assemblage from the Alaskan Arctic. *Quarternary Research* 1: 474–510.

Guthrie, R. D., and R. Petocz. 1970. Weapon automimicry among mammals. *American Naturalist* 104: 585–588.

Guthrie, R. D., A. V. Sher, and C. R. Harington. 2001. New radiocarbon dates on saiga antelopes (*Saiga tatarica*) from Alaska, Canada, and Siberia: Their paleontological significance. In *People and wildlife in northern North America,* 50–57. British Archaeological Reports, International Series, 944. London.

Guthrie, R. D., and T. van Kolfschoten. 2000. Neither warm nor moist, nor cold and arid: The ecology of the Mid Upper Paleolithic. In *Hunters of the Golden Age,* ed. W. Roebroeks, M. Mussi, J. Svoboda, and K. Fennema, 13–20. University of Leiden, Netherlands.

Guthrie, R. D., and W. von Koenigswald. 1997. Puncture wounds in Pleistocene bison skulls: A case of archaeology or paleontology. In *Spuren der Jagd—Die Jagd nach Spuren,* ed. I. Campen, J. Hahn, and M. Uerpmann, 415–424. Tübingen Monographien zur Urgeschichte 11. Mo Vince Verlag, Tübingen.

Guthrie, S. 1993. *Faces in the clouds.* Oxford University Press, Oxford.

Gvozdover, M. D. 1989. The typology of female figurines of the Kostenki Paleolithic culture. *Soviet Anthrop. and Arch.* 27: 32–94.

———. 1995. *Art of the mammoth hunters: The finds from Avdeevo.* Oxbow Monograph 49. Oxford University Press, Oxford.

Hadingham, E. 1979. *Secrets of the Ice Age: The world of the cave artists.* Walker and Co., New York.

Hahn, J. 1976. Das Gravettien in Westlichen Mitteleuropa. In *Perigordien et Gravettien en Europe,* ed. B. Klíma, 68–85. Colloque 15, IXe Congrés de l'Union Internationale des Sciences Préhistorique et Protohistoriques. Paris.

———. 1986. *Kraft and Aggression: Die Botschaft der Eiszeit Kunst im Aurignacien Süddeutschlands?* Verlag Archaeologica Venatoria 7. Tübingen.

Halverson, J. 1987. Art for art's sake in the Paleolithic. *Current Anthropology* 28: 63–89.

Hamilton, T. M. 1982. *Native American Bows.* Missouri Archaeological Society Special Publications 5. Columbia, Mo.

Hancar, F. 1940. Zum Problem der Venus Statuetten im eurasiatischen Jung-Palaeolithicum. *Prähistorische Zeitschrift* 18: 30–31.

Harcourt, R. 1991. Survivorship costs of play in the South American fur seal. *Animal Behavior* 42: 509–541.

Harris, A. S., and L. Nochlin. 1977. *Women artists, 1550–1950.* Alfred A. Knopf, New York.

Harris, D. R. 1978. Settling down: An evolutionary model for the transformation of mobile bands into sedentary communities. In *The evolution of social systems,* ed. J. Friedman and M. Rowlands, 401–417. University of Pittsburgh Press, Pittsburgh.

Harris, M. 1989. *Our kind: Where we are going.* Harper and Row, New York.

Harrison, G. A., J. M. Tanner, D. R. Pilbeam, and P. T. Baker. 1988. *Human biology.* Princeton University Press, Princeton.

Hart, B. J. 1995. Analyzing breed and gender differences in behavior. In *The domestic dog,* ed. J. Serpell, 65–80. Cambridge University Press, Cambridge.

Haskovec, I. P. 1993. Rock art, languages and archaeology of the Top End of Australia. In *Rock art studies,* ed. M. Lorblanchet and P. Bahn, 195–210. Oxbow Monographs 35. Oxford University Press, Oxford.

Hass, A. 1979. *Teenage sexuality.* Macmillan, New York.

Hass, M. 1954. *The unwritten laws of Albania.* Cambridge University Press, Cambridge.

Hawcroft, J., and R. Dennell. 2000. Neanderthal cognitive life history and its implications for material culture. In Derevenski 2000, 89–99.

Hawkes, K. 1991. Showing off: Tests of an hypothesis about men's foraging goals. *Ethology and Sociobiology* 12: 2954.

———. 2001. Is meat the hunter's property? In Stanford and Bunn 2001, 219–236.

Hayden, B. 1981a. Research and development in the Stone Age: Technological transitions among hunters-gatherers. *Current Anthropology* 22: 519–548.

———. 1981b. Subsistence and ecological adaptation of modern hunter-gatherers. In *Omnivorous primates,* ed. R. S. O. Harding and G. Teleki, 344–431. Columbia University Press, New York.

———. 1993. The cultural capacities of Neanderthals: A review and re-evaluation. *Journal of Human Evolution* 24: 113–146.

Hayden, B., B. Chisholm, and H. P. Schwartz. 1987. Fish and foraging. In *The Pleistocene of the Old World,* ed. O. Soffer, 89–123. Plenum Press, New York.

Heinz, H. J. 1978. The Bushman's store of scientific knowledge. In *The Bushmen,* ed. P. V. Tobias, 148–161. Human and Rosseau, Cape Town, R.S.A.

Heinz, H. J., and M. Lee. 1978. Namkwa: *Life among the Bushmen.* Jonathan Cape, London.

Hemingway, E. 1935. *The green hills of Africa.* Charles Scribner's and Sons, New York.

———. 1939. *Death in the afternoon.* Random House, London.

Hess, E. H. 1975. *The tell-tale eye: How your eyes reveal hidden thoughts and emotions.* Van Nostrand Reinhold, New York.

Hessellund, H. 1976. Masturbation and sexual fantasies in married couples. *Archives of Sexual Behavior* 5: 133–147.

Hewlett, B. S. 1988. Sexual selection and paternal investment among the Aka Pygmies. In *Human reproductive behaviour: A Darwinian perspective,* ed. L. Betzig, M. Borgerhoff Mulder, and P. Turke, 89–102. Cambridge University Press, Cambridge.

Hickle, W., and B. Hickle. 1984. Similarity and prehistoric non-representational petroglyphs from South-West Africa to young children's art. In Bandi et al. 1984, 423–432.

Hier, D. B., and W. F. Crowley. 1982. Spatial ability in androgen-deficient men. *New England Journal of Medicine* 306: 1202–1205.

Higley, J. D., P. T. Mehlman, R. E. Poland, D. M. Taub, J. Vickers, S. J. Soumi, and M. Linnoila. 1996. CSF testosterone and 5-HIAA correlate with different types of aggressive behaviors. *Biol. Psychiatry* 40: 1067–1082.

Hill, K. 1988. Macronutrient modifications of optimal foraging theory: An approach using indifference curves applied to some modern foragers. *Human Ecology* 16: 157–197.

Hill, K., and K. Hawkes. 1983. Neotropical hunting among the Ache of eastern Paraguay. In *Adaptive responses of Native Amazonians,* ed. R. B. Hames and W. T. Vickers, 139–188. Academic Press, New York.

Hill, K., and A. M. Hurtado. 1989. Hunter-gatherers of the New World. *American Scientist* 77: 436–533.

Hill, K., and H. Kaplan. 1988. Tradeoffs in male and female reproductive strategies among the Ache. In *Human Reproductive Behaviour: A Darwinian perspective,* ed. L. Betzig, M. Borgerhoff Mulder, and P. Turke, 277–305. Cambridge University Press, Cambridge.

Hladik, C. M., et al. 1993. *Tropical forests, people, and food: Biocultural interactions and applications to development.* Man and the Biosphere 13. Pantheon, Pearl River, N.Y.

Hölldobler, B., and E. O. Wilson. 1994. *Journey to the ants.* Harvard University Press, Cambridge.

Holt, B. S., and S. Churchill. 2000. Aging and genetics of obesity. In *Abstract Issue of the American Journal of Physical Anthropology Annual Meeting,* Sept. 30, p. 182.

Honor, H., and J. Fleming. 1982. *A world history of art.* Macmillan, New York.

Howell, N. 1979. *Demography of the Dobe !Kung.* Academic Press, New York.

Hrdy, S. B. 1981. *The sex that never evolved.* Harvard University Press, Cambridge.

——. 1999. *Mother nature: A history of mothers, infants, and natural selection.* Pantheon Books, New York.

Hudson, L., and B. Jacot. 1991. *The way men think.* Yale University Press, New Haven.

Huizinga, J. 1938. *Homo ludens.* Harper and Row, New York.

Humphreys, A. P., and P. K. Smith. 1984. Rough and tumble play in preschool and playground. In *Play in animals and humans,* ed. P. K. Smith, 241–266. Blackwell, London.

Huxley, T. H. 1907. Mr. Darwin's critics. Reprinted in *Collected Essays,* vol. 2, *Darwinia Essays.* Macmillan Press, London.

——. 1971. *Lay sermons, addresses, and reviews.* Appleton Press, New York.

Irons, W. 1979. Cultural and biological success. In *Evolutionary biology and human social behavior,* ed. N. Chagnon and W. Irons, 79–123. Duxbury, North Scituate, Mass.

——. 1983. Human female reproductive strategies. In *Social behavior of female vertebrates,* ed. S. K. Wasser, 169–213. Academic Press, New York.

Irving, L., K. Schmidt-Nielsen, and N. S. B. Abrahamsen. 1957. On the melting points of animal fats in cold climates. *Physiol. Zool.* 30: 93–105.

Isbell, L. A., and T. P. Young. 1996. The evolution of bipedalism in hominids and reduced group size in chimpanzees: Alternative responses to decreasing resource availability. *Journal of Human Evolution* 30: 389–397.

Iwawaki, S., and G. Wilson. 1983. Sex fantasies in Japan. *Personality and Individual Differences* 4: 543545.

Jaquish, C. E., S. Coady, R. R. Fabsitz, M. G. Larson, L. A. Cupples, R. H. Myers, and D. Levy. 2000. Aging and genetics of obesity. In *Abstract Issue of the American Journal of Physical Anthropology Annual Meeting,* Sept. 30, p. 88.

Jochim, M. 1983. Paleolithic cave art in perspective. In *Hunter-gatherer economy in prehistory,* ed. G. Baily, 212–219. Cambridge University Press, Cambridge.

——. 1987. Late Pleistocene refugia in Europe. In *The Pleistocene of the Old World,* ed. O. Soffer, 317–331. Plenum Press, New York.

Jones, D. 1996. *Physical attractiveness and the theory of sexual selection.* Museum of Anthropology, Ann Arbor.

Julien, M. 1982. *Les harpoons Magdalenians.* XVIIᵉ supplément à Gallia-Préhistoire. Editions du C.N.R.S., Paris.

Kachigan, S. A. 1991. *Multivariate statistical analysis.* Radius Press, New York.

Kaplan, H. 1996. A theory of fertility and parental investment in traditional and modern human societies. *Yearbook of Physical Anthropology* 39: 91–135.

Keeley, L. H., and N. Toth. 1981. Micro-wear polish on early stone tools from Koobi Fora, Kenya. *Nature* 293: 464–465.

Kehoe, T. F. 1996. The case for the ethnographic approach to understanding Paleolithic art. *Spuren der Jagd—die Jagd nach Spuren,* ed. I. Campen, J. Hahn, and M. Uerpmann, 193–202. Tübingen Monographien zur Urgeschichte 11. Mo Vince Verlag, Tübingen.

Kellog, R. 1955. *What children scribble and why.* Self-published, San Francisco. (Cited by Morris 1962.)

——. 1970. *Analyzing children's art.* Mayfield Publishing Co., Palo Alto, Calif.

Kemper, T. D. 1990. *Social structure and testosterone: Explorations of the Socio-bio-social chain.* Rutgers University Press, New Brunswick, N.J.

Kenrick, D. T., and R. C. Keefe. 1992. Age preferences in mates reflect sex differences in reproductive strategies. *Behav. and Brain Sci.* 15: 75–133.

Kensinger, K. M. 1989. Hunting and male domination in Cashinahua society. In *Farmers as hunters,* ed. S. Kent, 18–26. Cambridge University Press, Cambridge.

Kimbel, W. H., R. C. Walter, D. C. Johansen, K. Reed, J. L. Aronson, Z. Assefa, C. W. Marean, G. G. Eck, R. Bobe, E. Hovers, Y. Rak, C. Vondra, T. Yemane, D. York, Y. Chen, N. M. Evensen, and P. E. Smith. 1996. Late Pliocene *Homo* and Oldowan tools from the Hadar Formation, *Ethopia. Journal of Human Evolution* 31: 549–561.

Kimura, D. 1999. *Sex and cognition.* MIT Press, Cambridge.

Kingdon, J. 1979. *East African Mammals.* Vol. 3B. University of Chicago Press, Chicago.

Kinsey, A., W. B. Pomroy, and C. E. Martin. 1948. *Sexual behavior in the human male.* W. B. Saunders, Philadelphia.

Kinsey, A., W. B. Pomroy, C. E. Martin, and P. H. Gebhard. 1953. *Sexual behavior in the human female.* W. B. Saunders, Philadelphia.

Kirk, R. L. 1986. Aboriginal man adapting. Oxford University Press, Oxford.

Klein, D. R., M. Melgaard, and S. G. Fancy. 1987. Factors determining leg length in *Rangifer tarandus. Journal of Mammology* 68: 642–655.

Klein, R. G. 1989. *The human career.* University of Chicago Press, Chicago.

——. 1999. *The human career: Human biological and cultural origins.* University of Chicago Press, Chicago.

Klein, R. G., and K. Scott. 1991. Glacial/Interglacial size variation in fossil spotted hyenas (*Crocuta crocuta*) from Britain. *Quaternary Research* 32: 88–95.

Klíma, B. 1990. *Loci mamutu z Predmostí.* Academia, Prague.

Knoth, R., K. Boyd, and B. Singer. 1988. Empirical tests of sexual selection theory: Predictions of sex differences in onset, intensity, and time course of sexual arousal. *Journal of Sex Research* 24: 73–80.

Koford, C. B. 1963. Group relations in an island colony of rhesus monkeys. *Science* 141: 356–357.

Kohts, N. 1935. *Infant ape and human child.* Scientific Memoirs of the Museum Darwinianum, Moscow. (Cited by Morris 1962.)

Konner, M. 1982. *The tangled wing.* Heinemann, London.

Kowalski, J. K., and S. K. Kowalski. 1979. *Upper Paleolithic and Mesolithic in Europe: Taxonomy and prehistory.* Polska Akademia Nauk, Warsaw.

Kowalski, K. 1967. The Pleistocene extinction of mammals in Europe. In *Pleistocene extinctions: Search for a cause,* ed. P. Martin and H. E. Wright, 343–363. Yale University Press, New Haven.

Krebs, J. R., and N. B. Davies. 1992. *An introduction to behavioral ecology.* Blackwell, London.

Kurtén, B. 1968. *Pleistocene mammals of Europe.* Weidenfield and Nicholson, London.

——. 1976. *The cave bear story.* Columbia University Press, New York.

——. 1985. The Pleistocene lions of Beringia. *Annals Zoologica Fennica* 22: 117–121.

Kutzbach, J., and F. A. Street-Perot. 1985. Milankovich forcing of fluctuations in the level of tropical lakes from 18 to 0 kyr BP. *Nature* 317: 130–134.

Laming-Emperaire, A. 1962. *La signification de l'art rupestre paléolithic.* Picard, Paris.

Lansival, R. 1990. *Les "Venus" du Paléolithic supérieur.* Mémoires de Préhistoire Liègeoise 14. A.S.B.L., Belgium.

Larson, D. E., ed. 1996. *Mayo Clinic family health book.* William Morrow and Co., New York.

Laughlin, W. S. 1961. Acquisition of anatomical knowledge by ancient man. In *Social life of early man,* ed. S. L. Wasburn, 112–153. Aldine Publishing Co., Chicago.

——. 1968. An integrating behavior system and its evolutionary importance. In Lee and DeVore 1968, 304–320.

Laville, H. 1975. *Climatologie et chronologie du Paléolithique en Périgord: Etudes sedimentologique de dépots en grottes et sous abris.* Université de Provence, Etudes Quaternaires, Memoire 4. Marseilles.

Lazenby, A., and P. McCormack 1985. Salmon and malnutrition on the Northwest Coast. *Current Anthropology* 26: 379–384.

Leach, M. 1997. *The great apes.* Blandford, London.

Lee, P. C. 1994. Social structure and evolution. In *Behavior and Evolution,* ed. P. J. B. Slater and T. R. Haliday, 266–303. Cambridge University Press, Cambridge.

Lee, R. B. 1968. What hunters do for a living, or how to make out on scarce resources. In Lee and Devore 1968, 30–48.

——. 1978. Ecology of a contemporary San people. In *The Bushmen,* ed. P. V. Tobias, 94–114. Human and Rousseau, Cape Town, R.S.A.

——. 1979. *The !Kung San: Men, women, and work in a foraging society.* Cambridge University Press, Cambridge.

Lee, R. B., and I. Devore, eds. 1968. *Man the hunter.* Aldine Publishing Co., Chicago.

Lent, P. 1964. Calving and related social behavior of the barren-ground caribou. Ph.d. thesis, University of Alberta, Edmonton.

Lerner, G. 1986. *The creation of patriarchy.* Oxford University Press, Oxford.

Leroi-Gourhan, André. 1964. *Les religions de la préhistoire (Paléolithique).* P.U.F., Paris.

——. 1965. *Préhistoire de l'art occidental.* Mazenod, Paris.

——. 1967. Les mains de Gargas. *Bulletin de la Société Préhistorique Française* 44: 107–122.

——. 1982a. The archaeology of Lascaux Cave. *Scientific American* 246: 104–113.

———. 1982b. *The dawn of European art.* Cambridge University Press, Cambridge.

———. 1983. Une tête de sagaie à armature de lamelles de silex à Pincevent (Sein-et-Marne). *Bulletin de la Société Préhistorique Française* 80: 154–156.

Leroi-Gourhan, A., J. Allain, L. Balout, C. Basier, R. Bouchez, J. Bouchud, C. Couraud, B. Delluc, D. Delluc, J. Evin, M. Girard, A. Laming-Emperaire, M. Sarradet, F. Schweingruber, Y. Taborin, D. Vialou, and J. Vouvé. 1979. *Lascaux inconnu.* XIIᵉ supplément à Gallia-Préhistoire. Editions du CNRS, Paris.

Leroi-Gourhan, Arl. 1977. Les climats, les plantes et les hommes (Quaternaire Supérieur d'Europe occidentale). *Studia Geologica Polonica* 52: 249–261.

Levy, J. S. 1979. Play behavior and its decline during development in rhesus monkeys. Ph.D. thesis, Cambridge University, Cambridge.

Lewis-Williams, J. D. 1981. *Believing and seeing: Symbolic meanings in southern San rock paintings.* Academic Press, New York.

———. 1983. *The rock art of southern Africa.* Cambridge University Press, Cambridge.

———. 1997. Harnessing the brain: Visions and shamanism in Upper Paleolithic western Europe. In *Beyond art: Pleistocene image and symbol,* ed. M. W. Conkey, O. Soffer, D. Stratmann, and N. G. Jablonski, 321–342. Memoirs of the California Academy of Sciences 3. San Francisco.

———. 2002. *The mind in the cave.* Thames and Hudson, London.

Lewis-Williams, J. D., and T. Dowson. 1989. *Images of power: Understanding Bushman rock art.* Southern Book Publishers, Johannesburg, R.S.A.

Leyhausen, P. 1973. On the function of the relative hierarchy of moods (as exemplified by the phylogenetic and ontogenetic development of prey-catching in carnivores. In *Motivation of human and animal behavior: An ethological view,* ed. K. Lorenz and P. Leyhausen, 144–291. Van Nostrand, New York. (Reprinted and translated from a 1965 article in *Zeitschrift für Tierpsychologie.*)

Liebenberg, L. 1990a. *The art of tracking: The origin of science.* David Philip Publishers, Cape Town, R.S.A.

———. 1990b. *A field guide to the animal tracks of southern Africa.* David Philip Publishers, Cape Town, R.S.A.

Lieberman, J. N. 1965. Playfulness and divergent thinking: An investigation of their relationship at the kindergarten level. *Journal of Genetic Psychology* 107: 219–224.

Lillehammer, G. 1989. A child is born: The child's world in an archaeological perspective. *Norw. Arch. Rev.* 22: 89–105.

———. 2000. The world of children. In Derevenski 2000, 17–26.

Loehlin, J. C., and R. C. Nichols. 1976. *Heredity, environment, and personality.* University of Texas, Austin.

Lorblanchet, M. 1980. Peindre sur les parois des grottes. *Revivre la Préhistoire,* pp. 33–39. Dossier de l'Arch. 46.

———. 1986. From man to animal and sign in Paleolithic art. In *Animals into art,* ed. H. Morphy, 110–143. Unwin Hyman, Boston.

———. 1991. Hands-on artistry of the cave painter. *Archaeology,* Nov./Dec., pp. 26–31.

———. 2001. *La grotte ornée de Pergouset.* Editions de la Maison des Sciences de l'Homme. Paris.

Lorenz, K. 1952. *King Solomon's ring.* Penguin Books, New York.

———. 1966. *On aggression.* 1935. Harcourt Brace and World, New York.

Lovejoy, C. O. 1981. The origins of man. *Science* 211: 341–350.

———. 1993. Modeling human origins: Are we sexy because we are smart, or smart because we are sexy? In *The origin and evolution of humans and humanness,* ed. D. T. Rasmussen, 1–126. Jones and Bartlett Publishers, Sudsbury, Mass.

Low, B. S. 2000. *Why sex matters.* Princeton University Press, Princeton.

Loy, J. 1970. Behavioral responses of free-ranging rhesus monkeys to food shortage. *American Journal of Physical Anthropology* 33: 236–271.

Lunn, D. 1987. Foot asymmetry and cognitive ability in young children. M.S. thesis, Department of Psychology, University of Western Ontario, London, Canada.

Luquet, G. 1910. Sur les caractères des figures humaines dan l'art paléolithique. *L'Anthropologie* 21: 409–423.

Lye, W. F. 1975. *Andrew Smith's journal of his expedition into the interior of South Africa, 1834–1836.* A. A. Balkema, Cape Town.

Lynch, C. B. 1988. Response to divergent selection for nesting behavior in *Mus musculus. Genetics* 96: 757–765.

Macintosh, N. W. G. 1977. Beswick Creek Cave two decades later: A reappraisal. In *Form in indigenous art,* ed. P. J. Ucko, 191–197. Duckworth, London.

MacLean, P. O. 1969. The paranoid streak in man. In *Beyond reductionism,* ed. A. Koestler and J. R. Smythies, 258–278. Hutchinson and Co., London.

Macrae, A. D. F. 1995. *W. B. Yeats: A literary life*. Saint Martin's Press, New York.

Markowitz, A. 1956. *The uplifted tongue: Stories, myths and fables of South African Bushmen told in their manner*. Central News Agency, R.S.A.

Marks, S. 1976. *Large mammals and a brave people: Hunters in Zambia*. University of Washington Press, Seattle.

Marshack, A. 1972. *The roots of civilization*. McGraw-Hill, New York.

——. 1985. Theoretical concepts that lead to new analytic methods, modes of inquiry and classes of data. *Rock Art Research* 2: 95–111.

——. 1989. Evolution of the human capacity: The symbolic evidence. *Yearbook of Physical Anthropology* 32: 1–34.

Marshall, L. 1976. Sharing, talking, and giving: Relief of social tensions among the !Kung. In *Kalahari hunter-gatherers,* ed. R. B. Lee and I. DeVore, 89–120. Harvard University Press, Cambridge.

Martin, N. G., L. J. Eaves, and H. J. Eysenck. 1977. Genetical, environmental and personality factors influencing the age of first sexual intercourse in twins. *Jour. Biol. Sci.* 9: 91–97.

Martin, P., and P. Bateson. 1984. The time and energy costs of play behavior in the cat. *Zeitschrift für Tierpsychologie* 64: 298–312.

Masson, J. M. 1999. *The emperor's embrace: Reflections on animal families and fatherhood*. Pocket Books, New York.

Masson, J. M., and S. McCarthy. 1995. *When elephants weep*. Delcorte Press, New York.

Masters, W. H., and V. E. Johnson. 1966. *The human sexual response*. Little, Brown, and Co., Boston.

Matthews, K. A., C. D. Batson, J. Horn, and R. H. Roseman. 1981. Principles in his nature which interest him in the fortune of others. . . . The heritability of empathic concern for others. *Journal of Personality* 49: 237–247.

May, F. 1986. *Les sépultures préhistoriques*. Editions du CNRS, Paris.

McCaul, K. D., B. A. Gladue, and M. Joppa. 1992. Winning, losing, mood and testosterone. *Hormones and Behavior* 26: 486–504.

McCoid, C. H., and L. D. McDermott. 1996. Toward decolonizing gender. *Archaeology Annual Editions* 97/98: 70–76.

McGue, M., and D. T. Lykken. 1992. Genetic influences on risk of divorce. *Psychol. Sci.* 3: 368–373.

McNeil, W. H. 1976. *Plagues and peoples*. Anchor Press/Doubleday, Garden City, N.Y.

——. 1980. *The human condition: An ecological and historical view*. Princeton University Press, Princeton.

——. 1989. *Ecological imperialism and biological expansion of Europe, 900–1900*. Cambridge University Press, Cambridge.

Mead, M. 1955. *Male and female*. Mentor Books, New York.

Meeker, J. W. 1980. *The comedy of survival: In search of an environmental ethic*. International College, Los Angeles.

Meikle, A. W., T. D. Bishop, J. D. Stringham, and W. D. West. 1987. Quantitating genetic and nongenetic factors that determine plasma sex steroid variation in normal male twins. *Metabolism* 35: 1090–1095.

Mellars, P. 1985. The ecological basis of social complexity in the Upper Paleolithic of southwestern France. In *Prehistoric hunter-gatherers,* ed. T. D. Price and J. A. Brown, 271–297. Academic Press, New York.

——. 1996. *The Neanderthal legacy, an archaeological perspective from Western Europe*. Princeton University Press, New Jersey.

——. 1998. The Upper Paleolithic revolution. In *Prehistoric Europe,* ed. B. Cunliffe, 42–78. Oxford University Press, Oxford.

Merbs, C. F. 1983. *Patterns of activity induced pathology in a Canadian Inuit population*. Mercury Series 119. Canadian National Museum of Man, Ottawa.

Merriwether, J. B., and M. Millgate. 1968. *Lion in the garden: Interviews with William Faulkner*. Random House, New York.

Meskell, L. 1995. Goddesses, Gimbutas and "New Age" archaeology. *Antiquity* 69: 74–86.

Michael, J. A. 1983. *Art and adolescence*. Teachers College Press, Columbia University, New York.

Miller, M. N., and J. A. Beyers. 1998. Sparring as play in young pronghorn antelope. In Beckoff and Beyers 1998, 141–160.

Milton, K. 1999. A hypothesis to explain the role of meat-eating in human evolution. *Evolutionary Anthropology* 8: 11–21.

Mitani, J. C., and D. P. Watts. 1999. Demographic influences on hunting behavior in chimpanzees. *American Journal of Physical Anthropology* 109: 439–454.

Mitchell, G. 1979. *Behavioral sex differences in non-human primates*. Van Nostrand Reinhold, New York.

Moir, A., and D. Jessel. 1991. *Brain sex: The real difference between men and women*. Dell Publishing, New York.

Møller, A. P. 1987. Advantages and disadvantages of coloniality in the swallow. *Animal Behavior* 35: 819–832.

Molleson, T. 1996. The importance of porridge. In *Nature and Culture,* ed. M. Otte, 2: 481–484. E.U.R.A.L. 8. Colloque de Liège. Liège, Belgium.

Moore, D. S., and G. P. McCabe. 1993. *Introduction to the practice of statistics.* 2d ed. W. H. Freeman and Co., New York.

Morris, D. 1962. *The biology of art.* Alfred Knopf, New York.

——. 1967. *The naked ape: A zoologist's study of the human animal.* McGraw-Hill, New York.

——. 1969. *The human zoo.* McGraw-Hill, New York.

——. 1976. *Manwatching.* Harry N. Abrams, New York.

——. 1986. *Dogwatching.* Grafton, London

——. 1987. *Bodywatching.* Grafton, London.

——. 1990. *Animalwatching.* Arrow Books, London.

——. 1994. *The human animal.* Crown Publishers, New York.

——. 1997. *The human sexes: A natural history of man and woman.* Crown Publishers, New York.

Morris, J., and B. Levitas. 1987. *South African tribal life today.* College Press, Cape Town, R.S.A.

Movius, H. L. 1950. A wooden spear of third interglacial age from lower Saxony. *Southwestern Journal of Anthropology* 6: 139–142.

Murdock, G. P., and C. Provost. 1973. Factors in the division of labor by sex: A cross-cultural analysis. *Ethnology* 12: 203–225.

Murdock, I. 1977. *The fire and the sun: Why Plato banished the artists.* Oxford University Press, Oxford.

Murie, O. J. 1954. *A field guide to animal tracks.* Houghton Mifflin, Boston.

Mussel, K. 1984. *Fantasy and reconciliation: Contemporary formulas of women's romance fiction.* Greenwood Press, Westport, Conn.

Mussi, M. 1995. Rituels funeraires dans les sépultures Gravettienes des grottes de Gramaldi et de la Grotte Delle Arene Candide, un mise au point. In Otte 1995, 1: 833–842.

Mussi, M., J. Cinq-Mars, and P. Bolduc. 2000. Echoes from the Mammoth Steppe: The case of the Balzi Rossi. In *Hunters of the Golden Age,* ed. W. Roebroeks, M. Mussi, J. Svoboda, and K. Fennema. University of Leiden, Netherlands.

Muybridge, E. 1887. *Animal locomotion: An electro-photographic investigation of consecutive phases of animal movement.* (Excerpted photos are published in *The Male and Female Figure in Motion* [Dover Publications, New York, 1957].)

Myrberget, S., and H. J. Skar. 1976. Fat and caloric content of willow grouse in autumn and winter. *Norwegian Journal of Zoology* 24: 41–45.

NASA. 1978. *Anthropomorphic source book.* Vol. 2, *A handbook of anthropometric data.* National Aeronautics and Space Administration Reference Publication 1024. Scientific and Technical Information Office, Washington, D.C.

Neel, J. C. 1992. The thrifty genotype revisited. *Serono Syposium* 47: 281–293.

Neiland, K. A. 1970. Weight of dried marrow as indicator of fat in caribou femurs. *Journal of Wildf. Management* 34: 904–907.

Nelson, R. 1992. The way of the hunter (interview with Jonathan White). *Sun Magazine* (Chapel Hill, N.C.), issue 198, pp. 3–9.

Nesse, R. M. 1984. An evolutionary perspective on psychiatry. *Comp. Psychiatry* 25: 575–580.

Netboy, A. 1968. *The Atlantic salmon: A vanishing species.* Blackwell, London.

Nobmann, E. 1993. *Nutrient value of Alaskan native foods.* U.S. Department of Health and Human Services Publication. Native Health Service, Anchorage, Alaska.

Noe-Nygaard, N. 1974. Mesolithic hunting in Denmark illustrated by bone injuries caused by human weapons. *Jour. Arch. Sci.* 1: 217–278.

——. 1995. *Ecological, sedimentary, and geochemical evolution of the late-glacial to postlacial Åmose lacustrine basin, Denmark.* Scandinavian University Press, Copenhagen.

Noiret, P. 1990. *Le décor des bâtons percés paléolithiques.* 2 vols. Mémoires de Préhistoire Liégeoise. Liége, Belgium.

Nougier, L.-R. 1966. *L'art préhistorique.* Presses Universitaires de France, Paris.

——. 1984. *Premiers éveils de l-homme: Art, magie, sexualité, dans la préhistoire.* Editions Lieu Commun, Paris.

Oakley, K. P., P. Andrews, L. H. Keeley, J. D. Clark. 1977. A reappraisal of the Clacton spear point. *Proceedings of the Prehist. Society* 43: 1–12.

Olins B. 1992. Des preuves des sens ludiques dans l'art au Pléistocène Supérieur. *L'Anthropologie* 96: 219–244.

Ornish, D. 1998. *Love and survival: The scientific basis for the healing power of intimacy.* Harper Collins, New York.

Ornitz, E. M. 1983. Normal and pathological maturation of vestibular function in the normal child. In *Development of auditory and vestibular systems,* ed. R. Romand, 499–536. Academic Press, New York.

Ortega y Gasset, J. 1972. *Meditations on hunting.* Charles Scribner's Sons, New York.

Otte, M. 1990. The northwestern European plain around 18,000 B.P. In Soffer and Gamble 1990, 54–68.

———, ed. 1995. *Nature et culture.* Vol. 1. E.U.R.A.L. 8. Colloque de Liège. Liège, Belgium.

Overfield, T. 1985. *Biological variation in health and illness: Race, age, and sex differences.* Addison-Wesley, New York.

Pales, L. 1954. Les empreintes de pieds humains de la Tana della Basura (Toirano). *Revue d'Etudes Ligures* 1: 1–12.

——— (with the collaboration of M. T. de St.-Péreuse and M. Garcia). 1976. Les empreintes de pieds humains dans les cavernes. *Archives de l'Institut de Paléontologie Humaine, Paris,* 36: 1–166.

Pales, L., and M. T. de St.-Péreuse. 1969. *Les gravures de La Marche.* Vol. 1, *Félins et ours.* Publication de l'Institut de Préhistoire de l'Université de Bordeaux, Mémoire 7. Bordeaux.

———. 1976. *Les gravures de La Marche.* Vol. 2, *Les humains.* Editions Orphys, Paris.

———. 1981. *Les gravures de La Marche.* Vol. 3, *Equidés et bovidés.* Editions Orphys, Paris.

———. 1989. *Les gravures de La Marche.* Vol. 4, *Cervidés, eléphants et divers.* Editions Orphys, Paris.

Paquereau, M. M. 1976. La vegetation au Pleistocene Supérieur et au Début de l'Holocene dans le Sud-Ouest. Pp. 525–530. In La Préhistoire Francaise. H. de Lumley (ed.) C.N.R.S., Paris.

Parker, H., and S. Parker 1986. Father-daughter sexual abuse: An emerging perspective. *Amer. Jour. Orthopsych.* 56: 531–549.

Parker, R., and G. Pollack. 1981. *Old mistresses: Woman's art and ideology.* Pantheon Books, New York.

Parkington, J., and A. Manhire. 1997. Processions of groups: Human figures, ritual occasions, and social categories in the rock paintings of the Western Cape. In *Beyond art: Pleistocene image and symbol,* ed. M. W. Conkey, O. Soffer, D. Stratmann, and N. G. Jablonski, 301–320. Memoirs of the California Academy of Sciences 3. San Francisco.

Partridge, T. C., B. A. Wood, and P. B. deMenocal. 1995. The influence of global climatic change and regional uplift on large-mammal evolution in East and Southern Africa. In Vrba et al. 1995, 331–354.

Peckham, M. 1973. *Man's rage for chaos: Biology, behavior, and the arts.* Clinton Books, New York.

Perrins, C. M. 1965. Population fluctuations and clutch size in the great tit, *Parus major. Journal of Animal Ecology* 34: 601–647.

Pettitt, P. 2000. Chronology of the Mid Upper Paleolithic: The radiocarbon evidence. In *Hunters of the Golden Age,* ed. W. Roebroeks, M. Mussi, J. Svoboda, and K. Fennema, 21–30. University of Leiden, Netherlands.

Pfeiffer, J. E. 1982. *The creative explosion.* Harper and Row, New York.

Piaget, J. 1964. *Play, dreams, and imitation in childhood.* W. W. Norton, New York.

Pianka, E. R., and W. S. Parker. 1975. Age-specific reproductive tactics. *American Naturalist* 109: 453–454.

Pidoplichko, I. G. 1956. *Materials on the study of the fossil fauna of the Ukraine* (in Russian). No. 2. Izd. Academy of Sciences, Kiev, Ukranian SSR.

Pinker, S. 1997. *How the mind works.* Penguin Press, New York.

Pollan, M. 2001. *The botany of desire.* Random House, New York.

Pond, C. M. 1978. Morphological aspects and the ecological and mechanical consequences of fat deposition in wild vertebrates. *Ann. Rev. Ecol. and Syst.* 9: 519–570.

———. 1998. *Fats of life.* Cambridge University Press, Cambridge.

Poplin, F. 1979. Le destin de la grande faune européene à la fin des Temps glaciaires: Le changement de nature et l'appel de la domestication. In *La fin des Temps glaciaires en Europe,* 77–84. Colloques Internationaux de CNRS 271. Editions CNRS, Paris.

Popova, N. K, N. N. Voitenko, A. V. Kuklikov, and D. F. Avgustinovich. 1991. Evidence for the involvement of central serotonin as a mechanism of domestication in silver foxes. *Pharm. Biochem. Behav.* 40: 751–756.

Posner, M. I., and M. E. Raichel. 1994. *Images of mind.* Scientific American Library, New York.

Powers, W. R. 1990. The peoples of eastern Beringia. In *Prehistoric Mongoloid Dispersals,* 53–74. Special Issue 7. University Museum, University of Tokyo.

Pradel, L. 1975. Les mains incomplètes. *Quartär.* 26: 161.

Pruitt, W. O. 1960a. Behavior of the barren-ground caribou. *Biological Papers of the University of Alaska* 3.

———. 1960b. Snow as a factor in the winter ecology of the barren-ground caribou (*Rangifer arcticus*). *Arctic* 12: 159–179.

———. 1966. The function of the brow-tine in caribou antlers. *Arctic* 19: 111–113.

Pruitt, W. O., and H. Pepper. 1986. "Pepper's patches" on *Rangifer* pelage. *Rangifer,* Special Issue 1: 227–334.

Przbyla, D. P. J., D. Byrne, and K. Kelley. 1983. The role of imagery in sexual behavior. In *Imagery: Current theory, research, and application,* ed. A. Shiek, 290–233. Wiley, New York.

Puisségur, J.-J. 1979. Indications fournie par les mollusques dans les climats du Würm récent et du Tardiglaciaire en Bourgogne et en Alsace. In *La fin des Temps glaciaires en Europe,* 113–126. Colloques Internationaux de CNRS 271. Editions CNRS, Paris

Rasmussen, K. 1930. *Intellectual culture of the Iglulik Eskimos: Report on the fifth Thule Expedition, 1921–1924.* Glydendals Forlagstrykheri, Copenhagen.

Ray, D. J. 1981a. *Aleut and Eskimo Art.* C. Hurst and Co., London.

———. 1981b. *Artists of tundra and sea.* University of Washington Press, Seattle.

Reed, D., and M. S. Weinberg. 1984. Premarital coitus: Developing and established sexual scripts. *Social Psychology Quarterly* 47: 129–138.

Regnault, F. 1873. *Fouilles dans la grotte de Gargas.* Comptes Rendus Congrés Scientifique de France, Pau.

Reinisch, J. M., M. Ziemba-Davis, and St. A. Sanders. 1991. Hormonal contributions to sexual dimorphic behavioral development in humans. *Psychoneuroendocrinology* 16: 213–278.

Rensch, B. 1965. Über ästhetische Faktoren im Erleben höherer Tiere. *Naturwiss. und Medizin* 9: 43–57.

Reuning, H. 1988. Testing Bushmen in the central Kalahari. In *Human abilities in cultural context,* ed. S. H. Irving and J. W. Berry, 89–101. Cambridge University Press, Cambridge.

Reynolds, R. P. 1973. The operant training of creativity in childhood. Ph.D. diss., University of Illinois, Urbana.

Rice, P. C. 1981. Prehistoric Venuses: Symbols of motherhood or womanhood? *Journal of Anthropological Research* 37: 402–414.

Richard, N. 1993. De l'art ludique à l'art magique: Interpretations de l'art parietal au XIXe siècle. *Bulletin de la Société Préhistorique Française* 90: 60–68.

Ridley, M. 1993. *The red queen: Sex and the evolution of human nature.* Viking, London.

———. 1996. *The origins of virtue: Human instincts and the evolution of cooperation.* Penguin Press, New York.

———. 2003. *Nature via Nurture.* Harper Collins, New York.

Rigaud, J.-P. 2000. Human adaptation to the climatic deterioration of the last Pleniglacial in southwestern France. In *Hunters of the Golden Age,* ed. W. Roebroeks, M. Mussi, J. Svoboda, and K. Fennema, 325–336. University of Leiden, Netherlands.

Rigaud, J.-P., and J. F. Simek. 1990. The last Pleniglacial in the South of France (24,000–14,000). In Soffer and Gamble 1990, 69–86.

Roberts, D. F. 1978. *Climate and human variability.* Cummings Printing Co., Menlo Park, Calif.

Roberts, N. 1998. *The Holocene.* Blackwell, Oxford.

Rodgers, G. B., D. K. Tinsworth, C. Polen, S. Cassidy, C. M. Trainor, S. R. Heh, and M. F. Donaldson. 1994. *Bicycle use and hazard patterns in the United States.* U.S. Consumer Product Safety Commission. Washington, D.C.

Roebroeks, W. 2000. A marginal matter: The human occupation of northwestern Europe, 30,000 to 20,000 B.P. In *Hunters of the golden age,* ed. W. Roebroeks, M. Mussi, J. Svoboda, and K. Fennema, 299–313. University of Leiden, Netherlands.

Rohner, R. P. 1975. *They love, they love me not: A world wide study of the effects of parental acceptance and rejection.* HRAF Press, New Haven.

Rousseau, J.-J. 1993. *Emile.* Repr., Everyman's Library, New York.

Roveland, B. 2000. Footprints in the clay: Upper Paleolithic children in ritual and secular contexts. In Derevenski 2000, 29–38.

Rudnai, J. A. 1973. *Social life of the lion.* Medical and Technical Publishers, Lancaster, England.

Rudner, J., and I. Rudner. 1970. *The hunter and his art: A survey of rock art in southern Africa.* A. A. Balkema, Cape Town, R.S.A.

Ruff, C. B., and E. Trinkaus. 2000. Aging and genetics of obesity. In *Abstract Issue of the American Journal of Physical Anthropology Annual Meeting,* Sept. 30, p. 246.

Rushton, J. P., D. W. Fulker, M. C. Neale, D. K. B. Nias, and H. J. Eysenck. 1986. Altruism and aggression: The heritability of individual differences. *Journal of Personality and Social Psychology* 50: 1192–1198.

Rushton, P. R. 1997. *Race, evolution, and behavior: A life history perspective*. Transactional Publishers, London.

Ruspoli, M. 1987. *The cave of Lascaux: The final photographic record*. Thames and Hudson, London.

Russell, P. M. 1989. Plaques as Paleolithic slates: An experiment to reproduce them. *Rock Art Research* 6: 68–69.

Sahlins, M. 1974. *Stone age economics*. Tavistock, London.

Sahly, A. 1963. Nouvelles découvertes dans la grotte de Gargas. *Bulletin Soc. Préhist. Ariège* 18: 65–74.

———. 1969. Le problèm des mains mutilés dans l'art préhistorique. Thèse de doctorat ès lettres, University of Toulouse.

Salzano, F. M., J. V. Neel, and D. Maybury-Lewis. 1967. Further studies on the Xavante Indians. 1. Demographic data on two additional villages: Genetic structure of the tribe. *American Journal of Human Genetics* 19: 463–489.

Schackleton, N. J. 1995. New data on the evolution of Pliocene climatic variability. In Vrba et al. 1995, 242–248.

Schaller, G. B. 1972. *The Serengeti lion*. University of Chicago Press, Chicago.

———. 1977. *Mountain monarchs*. University of Chicago Press, Chicago.

Schmookler, A. B. 1995. *The parable of the tribes*. State University of New York, Albany.

Schneider, B. 1990. The last Pleniglacial in the Paris Basin (22,500–17,000). In Soffer and Gamble 1990, 41–53.

Schultz, A. H. 1969. *The life of primates*. Universe Books, New York.

Scott, G. R. 1991. Dental anthropology. In *Encyclopedia of Human Biology*, 789–804. Academic Press, New York.

Sendak, M. 1963. *Where the wild things are*. Harper and Row, New York.

Service, E. R. 1962. *Primitive social organization: An evolutionary perspective*. Random House, New York.

Sharp, H. S. 1988. Dry meat and gender: The absence of Chipewyan ritual for the regulation of hunting and animal numbers. In *Hunters and Gatherers*, ed. T. Ingold, D. Riches, and J. Woodburn, 2: 80–94. Berg, New York.

Shea, J. C. 1979. Social behavior of wintering caribou in northwestern Alaska. M.S., University of Alaska, Fairbanks.

Sheehan, G. 1985. Whaling as an organizing focus in northwestern Alaskan Eskimo society. In *Prehistoric hunter-gatherers: The emergence of cultural complexity,* ed. T. Price and J. Brown, 123–154. Academic Press, New York.

Sheel, D., and C. Packer. 1991. Group hunting behavior of lions: A search for cooperation. *Animal Behavior* 41: 679–709.

Shepard, P. 1966. *Traces of an omnivore*. Island Press, Washington, D.C.

———. 1973. *The tender carnivore and the sacred game*. Scribners, New York.

———. 1995. Virtual hunting reality in the forests of Simulacra. In *Reinventing nature: Responses to postmodern deconstruction,* ed. M. Soulé and G. Lease, 17–30. Island Press, Washington D. C.

Shepher, J. 1983. *Incest: A biosocial view*. Academic Press, New York.

Sherwin, B. B., M. M. Gelfand, and W. Bender. 1985. Androgen enhances sexual motivation in females: A prospective crossover study of sex steroid administration in the surgical menopause. *Psychosomatic Medicine* 47: 339–351.

Sieveking, A. 1979. *The cave artists*. Thames and Hudson, London.

———. 1986. Comment on Marshack's paper. *Rock Art Research* 63: 66–67.

———. 1991. Engraved art of the Magdalenian. *Ann. Rev. Arch.* 12: 24–29.

Silber, S. J. 1981. *The male from infancy to old age*. Granada, London.

Silberbauer, G. B. 1963. Marriage and the girl's puberty ceremony of the G/WI Bushmen. *Africa* 33: 1–64.

———. 1980. Hunter/gatherers of the Kalahari. In *Omnivorous primates,* ed. R. S. O. Harding and G. Teleki, 455–498. Columbia University Press, New York.

———. 1981. *Hunter and habitat in the central Kalahari Desert*. Cambridge University Press, Cambridge.

Singh, D. 1993. Body shape and woman's attractiveness: The critical role of waist-to-hip ratio. *Human Nature* 4: 297–321.

———. 1994. Is thin really beautiful and good? Relationship between waist-to-hip ratio (WHR) and female attractiveness. *Personality and Individual Differences* 16: 123–132.

Sini, W. A. 1989. Growth rates and sexual dimorphism in evolutionary perspective. In *Analysis of prehistoric diets,* ed. R. I. Gilbert and J. H. Mielke, 191–226. Academic Press, New York.

Skinner, B. F. 1956. A case history of the scientific method. *American Psychologist* 11: 221–233.

Slatkin, W. 1990. *Women artists in history*. Prentice-Hall, New York.

Smith, N. S. 1970. Appraisal of condition estimation methods for East African ungulates. *East African Wildlife Journal* 8: 123–129.

———. 1989. *A psychology of Ice Age art.* Stanford University Press, Stanford.

Smithers, R. H. W. 1983. *Mammals of the South African region.* University of Pretoria, Pretoria, R.S.A.

Snow, C. P. 1993. *The two cultures.* 1959. Repr., Cambridge University Press. Cambridge.

Snyder, R. G., L. W. Schneider, C. L. Owings, H. M. Reynolds, D. H. Golomb, and M. A. Schork. 1977. *Anthropometry of infants, children, and youths to age 18 for product safety design.* Highway Safety Research Institute, University of Michigan, Ann Arbor. PB-270 227. U.S. Department of Commerce, National Technical Information Service, Washington, D.C.

Soffer, O. 1987. The Upper Paleolithic connubia, refugia, and the archaeological record from Eastern Europe. In *The Pleistocene of the Old World,* ed. O. Soffer, 332–347. Plenum Press, New York.

———. 2000. Gravettian technologies in social contexts. In *Hunters of the Golden Age,* ed. W. Roebroeks, M. Mussi, J. Svoboda, and K. Fennema, 59–77. University of Leiden, Netherlands.

Soffer, O., and C. Gamble. 1990. *The world before 18,000 B.P.* Vol. 1. Academic Press, New York.

Sollas, W. J. 1914. Crô Magnon Man. *Nature* 93: 240.

Sonneville-Bordes, D. de, and P. Laurent. 1983. Le phoque à la fin des Temps glaciaires. In *La faune et l'homme préhistorique,* ed. F. Poplin, 69–80. Memoires de la Société Préhistorique Française 16. Paris.

Spencer, B., and F. S. Gillen. 1968. *The natives of Central Australia.* Repr., Dover Publications, Sydney.

Speth, J. D. 1991. Protein selection and avoidance strategies of contemporary and ancestral foragers: Unresolved issues. *Philosophical Transactions of the Royal Society of London* 334: 265–270.

Speth, J. D., and E. Tchernov. 2001. Neandertal hunting and meat-processing in the Near East: Evidence from Kebara Cave (Israel). In Stanford and Bunn 2001, 52–72.

Spiess, A. E. 1979. *Reindeer and caribou hunters: An archaeological study.* Academic Press, New York.

Stanford, C. B. 1999. *The hunting apes, meat eating, and the origins of human behavior.* Princeton University Press, Princeton.

———. 2001. A comparison of social meat-foraging by chimpanzees and human foragers. In Stanford and Bunn 2001, 122–140.

Stanford, C. B., and H. T. Bunn, eds. 2001. *Meat-eating and human evolution.* Oxford University Press, Oxford.

Stanford, C. B., J. Wallis, E. Mpongo, and J. Goodall. 1994. Hunting decisions in wild chimpanzees. *Behavior* 131: 1–18.

Steadman, D. W. 1997. Extinction of Polynesian birds: Reciprocal impacts of birds and people. In *Historical ecology of the Pacific Islands,* ed. P. V. Kirch and T. C. Hunt, 51–79. Yale University Press, New Haven.

Stephens, D. W., and J. R. Krebs. 1986. *Foraging theory.* Princeton University Press, Princeton.

Stevenson, J., N. Batten, and M. Cherner. 1992. Fear and fearfulness in children and adolescents: A genetic analysis of twin data. *Journal of Child Psychology and Psychiatry* 33: 977–985.

Steward, U. H. 1968. Causal factors and processes in the evolution of pre-farming societies. In Lee and DeVore 1968, 321–334.

Stoller, R. J. 1985. *Observing the erotic imagination.* Yale University Press, New Haven.

Strand, F. 1983. *Physiology: A regulatory system approach.* 2d ed. Macmillan, New York.

Straus, L. G. 1990. The last Glacial maximum in Cantabrian Spain: The Solutrean. In Soffer and Gamble 1990, 89–105.

Strum, S. 1987. *Almost humans.* Random House, New York

Stuiver, M., and P. M. Grootes. 2000. GIPS2 oxygen isotope rations. *Quaternary Research* 53: 277–284.

Sutcliffe, A. J. 1969. Adaptations of spotted hyenas to living in the British Isles. *Bull. Mamm. Society of the British Isles* 31: 1–4.

———. 1970. Spotted hyena: Crusher, gnawer, digester and collector of bones. *Nature* 227: 1110–1113.

Sutton-Smith, B. 1967. The role of play in cognitive development. *Young Children* 22: 361–370.

Svensson, S. 1993. Leksaker och spel. *Nordisk kultur* 24: 97–103.

Symons, D. 1978. *Play and aggression: A study of rhesus monkeys.* Columbia University Press, New York.

———. 1979. *The evolution of human sexuality.* Oxford University Press, New York.

Symons, D., C. Salmon, and B. J. Ellis. 1997. Unobtrusive measures of human sexuality. In Betzig 1997, 209–212.

Szalay, F. S., and R. K. Costello. 1991. Evolution of permanent estrus displays in hominids. *Journal of Human Evolution* 20: 439–464.

Szombathy, J. 1925. Die diluvialen Menschenrest aus der Fürst-Johanns-Höhle bei Lautsch im Mähren. *Die Eiszeit* 2: 1–34.

Taborin, Y. 2000. Gravettian body ornaments in Western and Central Europe. In *Hunters of the Golden Age,* ed. W. Roebroeks, M. Mussi, J. Svoboda, and K. Fennema, 135–142. University of Leiden, Netherlands.

Taçon, P. S. C. 1987. Internal-external: A re-evaluating of the "x-ray" concept in Western Arhnem Land rock art. *Rock Art Research* 4: 36–50.

Taylor, L. 1986. Seeing the "inside": Kunwinjku paintings and the symbol of the divided body. In *Animals into art,* ed. H. Morphy, 371–389. Unwin Hyman, Boston.

Taylor, T. 1996. *The prehistory of sex: Four million years of human sexual culture.* Bantam, London.

Teilhard de Chardin, P. 1958. *El fenómeno humano.* Cited in Garcia Guinea 1979.

Testart, A. 1988. Some major problems in the social anthropology of hunter gatherers. *Current Anthropology* 29: 1–31.

Thackeray, J. F. 1983. Disguises, animal behavior and concepts of control in relation to rock art of southern Africa. *South Afr. Archaeol. Soc. (Goodwin Series)* 4: 38–43.

Thieme, H., and S. Veil. 1997. Neue Untersuchungen zum eemzeitlichen Elefanten-Jagdplaz Lehringen, Ldkr Verde. *Die Kunde,* n.s., 36: 11–58.

Thomas, E. M. 1988. *The harmless people.* Africansouth, Cape Town, R.S.A.

———. 1993. *The hidden life of dogs.* Houghton Mifflin, Boston.

Thornhill, R., and N. W. Thornhill. 1983. Human rape: An evolutionary analysis. *Ethol. and Sociobiol.* 4: 137–183.

Tiefer, L. 1987. Social constructionism and the study of human sexuality. *Review of Personality and Social Psychology* 7: 70–94.

Tiger, L. 1992. *The pursuit of pleasure.* Little, Brown, Boston.

Tiger, L., and R. Fox. 1971. *The imperial animal.* Holt, Rinehart, and Winston, New York.

Tindale, N. B. 1928. Native rock shelters at Oenpelli Diemen Gulf, North Australia. *South Australian Nature* 9: 35–36.

Tooby, J., and L. Cosmides. 1992. The psychological foundations of culture. In *The adapted mind,* ed. J. H. Barkow, L. Cosmides, and John Tooby, 19–136. Oxford University Press, New York.

Tooby, J., and I. DeVore. 1987. The reconstruction of hominid evolution through strategic modeling. In *The evolution of human behavior: Primate models,* ed. W. G. Kinzey, 76–104. SUNY Press, New York.

Torrance, E. P. 1964. Education and creativity. In *Creativity: Progress and potential,* ed. C. W. Taylor, 26–86. McGraw Hill, New York.

Torroni, A., H.-J. Bandelt, L. D'Urbano, P. Lahermo, P. Moral, D. Sellitto, C. Rengo, P. Forester, M.-L. Savontaus, B. Bonné-Tamir, and R. Scozzari. 1998. MtDNA analysis reveals a major late Paleolithic expansion from southwestern to northeastern Europe. *American Journal of Human Genetics* 62: 1137–1152.

Tower, R. B., and J. L. Singer. 1980. Imagination, interest and joy in early childhood. In *Children's humor,* ed. P. E. McGhee and A. J. Chapman, 89–107. Wiley, Chichester.

Treswell, A. S., and J. D. L. Hansen. 1976. Medical research among the !Kung. In *Studies of the !Kung,* ed. R. B. Lee and I. DeVore, 156–194. Harvard University Press, Cambridge.

Trivers, R. L. 1972. Parental investment and sexual selection. In *Sexual selection and the descent of man,* ed. B. Campbell, 136–179. Heinemann, London.

———. 1985. *Social evolution.* Benjamin-Cummings, Menlo Park, Calif.

Trotter, M., and B. McCulloch. 1981. *Prehistoric rock art of New Zealand.* Longman Paul, Auckland.

———. 1989. *Unearthing New Zealand.* GP Books, Wellington.

Turnbull, C. M. 1968. Discussions. In Lee and DeVore 1968, 341.

Tutin, C. E. G. 1979. Mating and reproductive strategies in a community of wild chimpanzees. *Behav. Ecol. and Sociobiol.* 6: 29–38.

Twain, M. 2001. *Adventures of Tom Sawyer.* Repr., Classics Collection, Grand Haven, Mich.

———. 2002. *Adventures of Huckleberry Finn.* Repr., Classics Collection, Grand Haven, Mich.

Tzedakis, P. C., K. D. Bennett, and D. Magri. 1994. Climate and the pollen record. *Nature* 370: 513.

Ucko, P. J. 1962. The interpretation of prehistoric anthropomorphic figurines. *Journal of the Royal Anthropological Institute of Great Britain and Ireland* 92: 38–54.

———. 1968. *Anthropomorphic figurines.* Andrew Szmidla, London.

Ucko, P. J., and A. Rosenfeld. 1967. *Paleolithic cave art.* World University Library, London.

Uerpmann, H.-P. 1989. Animal exploitation and the phasing of the Paleolithic to the Neolithic. In *The walking larder,* ed. J. Clutton-Brock, 91–96. Unwin Hyman, London.

Ullrich, H. 1996. Reconstruction of close biological relationship in Paleolithic burials. In *Nature and culture,* vol. 2, ed. M. Otte, 763–794. E.U.R.A.L. 8. University of Liège.

Urdy, J. R., and J. O. G. Billy. 1987. Initiation of coitus in early adolescence. *American Sociol. Review* 52: 841–855.

Urdy, J. R., J. O. G. Billy, N. M. Morris, T. R. Groff, and M. H. Raj. 1985. Serum androgenic hormones motivate sexual behavior in adolescent boys. *Fertility and Sterility* 43: 90–94.

Urdy, J. R., and B. K. Ekland. 1984. Benefits of being attractive: Differential payoffs for men and women. *Psychological Reports* 54: 47–56.

Urdy, J. R., L. M. Talbert, and N. M. Morris. 1986. Biosocial foundations of adolescent female sexuality. *Demography* 23: 217–228.

Vague, J., and R. Fenasse. 1965. Comparative anatomy of adipose tissue. In *1965 Handbook of Physiology,* ed. A. E. Renold and G. F. Cahill, 25–36. American Physiological Society, Washington D. C.

Vailou, D. 1991. *La préhistoire.* Editions Gallimard, Paris.

Vallois, H. V. 1962. Les empreintes de pieds humains des grottes préhistoriques du midi de la France. *Paleobiologica* 4: 84.

Van Andel, T. H., and P. C. Tzedakis. 1996. Paleolithic landscapes of Europe and environs, 150,000–25,000 years ago: An overview. *BioSci.* 41: 78–88.

van den Berghe, P. L. 1980. Incest and exogamy: A sociobiological consideration. *Ethology and Sociobiology* 1: 151–162.

———. 1983. Human inbreeding avoidance: Culture in nature. *Behavioral and Brain Sciences* 6: 91–123.

Van der Brink, H., and P. Barruel. 1967. *Guide to Mammals of Europe.* Houghton Mifflin, Boston.

Vandiver, P., O. Soffer, B. Klima, and J. Svoboda. 1990. Venuses and wolverines: The origins of ceramic technology ca 26,000. In *The changing roles of ceramics in society,* ed. W. D. Kingery, 13–81. American Ceramic Society, Westerville, Ohio.

Vangen, O. S., and G. Klemetsdal. 1988. Genetic studies of Finnish and Norwegian test results in two breeds of hunting dog. Paper presented at Sixth World Conference on Animal Production, Helsinki, paper 425.

van Noten, F. 1982. Comments on Lewis-Williams' article "Southern San Rock Art." *Current Anthropology* 23: 444.

Van Rijssen, W. J. J. 1984. Southwestern Cape rock art: Who painted what? *South African Archaeological Bulletin* 39: 1 25–129.

Verbrugge, A. R. 1969. *Le symbole de la main dans la préhistoire.* Self-published.

Vinnicombe, P. 1976. *People of the eland.* Natal University Press, Pietermaritzburg.

Visser, J., and D. S. Chapman. 1979. *Snakes and snake bites.* Centaur Publishers, Johannesburg, R.S.A.

Vrba, E. 1995. On the connections between paleoclimate and evolution. In Vrba et al. 1995, 24–48.

Vrba, E., G. H. Denton, T. C. Partridge, and L. H. Burckel. 1995. *Paleoclimate and evolution.* Yale University Press, New Haven.

Walker, A. 1984. Extinctions in hominid evolution. In *Extinctions,* ed. M. E. Nitecki, 119–152. University of Chicago Press, Chicago.

Waller, N. G., B. A. Kojetin, T. J. Bouchard Jr., D. T. Lykken, and A. Tellegin. 1990. Genetic and environmental influences on religious interests, attitudes, and values: A study of twins reared apart and together. *Psychol. Sci.* 1: 138–142.

Walsh, G. L. 1988. *Australia's greatest art.* E. J. Brill and Robert Brown and Associates (Australia), Sydney.

Wannenburgh, A. 1979. *The Bushmen.* New Holland, Cape Town, R.S.A.

Washburn, S. L., and C. S. Lancaster. 1968. The evolution of hunting. In Lee and DeVore 1968, 293–303.

Wasser, S. K., and D. P. Barash. 1983. Reproduction suppression among female mammals: Implications for biomedicine and sexual selection theory. *Quat. Rev. Biol.* 58: 513–538.

Watchman, A. 1997. Paleolithic marks: Archaeometric perspectives. In *Beyond art: Pleistocene image and symbol,* ed. M. W. Conkey, O. Soffer, D. Stratmann, and N. G. Jablonski, 19–36. Memoirs of the California Academy of Sciences 3. San Francisco.

Watson, L. 2001. *Jacobson's organ and the remarkable nature of smell.* New York: Penguin Books.

Watson, P. J., and M. C. Kennedy. 1991. Development of horticulture in the eastern woodlands of North America: Women's role. In *Engendering archaeology: Women in prehistory,* ed. J. M. Gero and M. W. Conkey, 255–275. Basil Blackwell, Oxford.

Weissen-Szumlanska, H. 1937. *Des mains projetées sur les parois des grottes préhistoriques.* No. 1. Centre Préhistorique Français 12. Toulouse-Foix.

Welté, A.-C. 1986. An approach to the theme of confronted animals in French Paleolithic art. In *Animals into art,* ed. H. Morphy, 215–235. Unwin Hyman, Boston.

West, D. L. 1997. *Hunting strategies in central Europe during the last Glacial.* British Archaeological Reports, Oxford.

White, R. 1985. *Upper Paleolithic land-use in the Périgord: A topographic approach to subsistence and settlement.* British Archaeological Reports, Oxford.

———. 1989. Toward a conceptual understanding of the earliest body ornaments. In *The emergence of modern humans,* ed. E. Trinkhaus, 211–231. Cambridge University Press, Cambridge.

White, R. M. 1982. *Comparative anthropometry of the foot.* Technical Report TR-83/010. U.S. Army Natick Research and Development Laboratories, Natick, Mass.

Whitehead, K. 1972. *Deer of the world.* Constable, London.

Wickler, W., and U. Seibt. 1983. Monogamy: An ambiguous concept. In *Mate choice,* ed. P. Patterson, 33. Cambridge University Press, Cambridge.

Wilcox, A. R. 1982. Animal disguises used by hunters. *Digging Stick* 12: 8.

———. 1985. Animal disguises used by hunters. *Digging Stick* 15: 8.

Wilde, O. 1970. The decay of lying. In *The complete works of Oscar Wilde,* ed. Vyvyan Holland. Collins, London.

Williams, B. J. 1968. The Birhor of India and some comments on band organization. In Lee and DeVore 1968, 126–131.

Williams, G. C. 1991. The dawn of Darwinian medicine. *Quart. Rev. Biol.* 66: 1–24.

———. 1992. Natural selection, domains, levels, and challenges. *Evolution* 11: 398–411.

Williams, J. D., and D. E. Harmel. 1984. Selection for antler points and body weight in white-tailed deer. *Proceedings of the Annual Conference of the Southeast Association of Fish and Wildlife Agencies* 38: 43–50.

Williams, J. D., A. W. F. Kreuger, and D. E. Harmel. 1994. Heritabilities for antler characteristics and body weight in yearling white-tailed deer. *Heredity* 73: 78–83.

Willis, M. B. 1995. Genetic aspects of dog behavior with particular reference to working ability. In *The Domestic Dog,* ed. J. Serpell, 51–64. Cambridge University Press, Cambridge.

Wilson, E. O. 1978. *On human nature.* Harvard University Press, Cambridge.

———. 1994. *Naturalist.* Time Warner, New York.

———. 1998. *Consilience: The unity of knowledge.* Alfred F. Knopf, New York.

Wilson, J. Q., and R. J. Herrenstein. 1985. *Crime and human nature.* Simon and Schuster, New York.

Wilson, M., and M. Daly 1992. The man who mistook his wife for chattel. In *The adapted mind,* ed. J. H. Barkow, L. Cosmides, and J. Tooby, 289–325. Oxford University Press, New York.

Wilson, S. C., and D. G. Kleiman. 1974. Eliciting play: A comparative study. *Amer. Zool.* 14: 34–370.

Winget, C., M. Kramer, and R. Whitman. 1972. Dreams and demography. *Canadian Psychiatric Association Journal* 17: 203–208.

Wingfield, J. C., C. S. Whaling, and P. Marler. 1994. Communication in vertebrate aggression and reproduction: The role of hormones. In *The physiology of reproduction,* ed. E. Knobil and J. D. Neil, 303–342. Raven Press, New York.

Woillard, G. 1978. Grande Pile peat bog: A continuous pollen record for the last 140,000 years. *Quaternary Research* 9: 1–21.

Wooden, W., and J. Parker. 1982. *Men behind bars: Sexual exploitation of sexual aggressions.* AMS Press, New York.

Woodhouse, H. C. 1978. *Pride of South Africa: Rock art.* Purnell, Cape Town, R.S.A.

———. 1984. Hunting disguises: Why ostriches? *South African Archaeol. Bull.* 39: 138.

Wrangham, R. W., W. C. McGrew, F. B. M. de Waal, and P. G. Heltne. 1994. *Chimpanzee cultures.* Harvard University Press, Cambridge.

Wrangham, R. W., and D. Peterson. 1996. *Demonic males.* Houghton Mifflin, New York.

Wright, R. 1994. *The moral animal.* Vintage Books, New York.

Zilhão, P. J. 1996. L'art rupestre paléolithique de plein air: Vallée du Côa (Portugal). *L'Art Préhistorique* 209: 106–117.

Index

Abramova, Z. A., 9, 142
Abri Cellier, 143, 191, 359
Abri du Poisson, 174, 268, 298, 359
Abri Durif à Enval, 414
Abri Faustin, 354
Abri Fongal, 12
Abri Jolviet, 356
Abri Moran, 356
Abri Pataud, 55, 356, 359
Absolon, K., 204, 366
Abzac, 138
Adams, C. J., 179, 235, 235
Adams, J. M., 410
Adaptation criteria, 15
Addura, 26, 117, 162, 256, 308, 347, 375, 393
Adovasio, J., 200
Afontova Gora, 27
Agenbroad, L. D., 44
Aiello, L. C., 230
Airvaux, J., 32, 90
Alcock, J., 312, 381
Aldéne, 47, 88, 93
Aldis, O., 383
Alexander, R. D., 13, 441, 453
Alland, A., 385, 391

Allen, L. S., 167
Allman, J. M., 156, 165, 218, 235, 254
Altamira, xi, xii, 13, 28, 71, 72, 92, 102, 104, 105, 110, 119, 136, 225, 238, 240, 272, 282, 346, 357, 367, 368, 374, 385, 388, 394, 410
Altuna, J., 11, 20, 265, 409
Altxerri, ix, xi, 3, 11, 26, 35, 80, 85, 86, 87, 120, 134, 145, 409
Alvard, M. S., 232
Alvarez, F., 86
Andernach, 222, 364, 367
Anderson, A. J., 403, 408
Anderson, R. L., 392
Andrew, R. J., 171
Angles-sur-l'Anglin, 37, 38, 59, 60, 108, 131, 135, 207, 305, 324, 353
Ann, M., 368
Anthoney, T. R., 69
Anzenberger, G., 251, 318
Apellaniz, J. M., 36, 108, 409
Appavoo, D. M., 245
Appetite for risk, 185–90
Arcy-sur-Cure, 56, 62, 329, 428
Ardales, 13, 28, 214, 426
Ardrey, R., 233
Arene Candide (Grotta delle Arene Candide), 455
Arndt, S., 291
Arneson, P. D., 332
Art in motion, 99–101
Art ludique, 7
Art magique, 7
Art pour le art, 7
Artistic licenses, 104
Arudy, 27, 80, 108, 155, 191, 225, 282, 284, 290, 380, 410
Atkins, R. C., 245
Atlantic current, 19
Atlatl weights, 285–93
Atlatls, 285–93

Aurignacian, 25
Australopithecus, 211–15
Avdeevo, 116, 135, 142, 145, 207, 332, 353, 355, 362

Bacon, M. K., 424
Bader, O. M., 282
Bahn, P., 36, 52, 108, 114, 268, 283, 294, 296, 364, 366
Baker, S. W., 168, 181
Balcayre, 25
Baldwin, D., 168, 324
Ballet, O., 32
Balbín-Behrmann, R. de, 41
Balzi Rossi, 364, 381, 444
Bancroft, J., 329
Band art, 401–30
Band size, 157
Bandi, H.-G., viii, 11
Bannikov, A. G., 77
Bara-Bahau, 190, 240, 251, 284, 293, 448
Barash, D. P., 338
Barbed points, 297, 298
Barma Grande, 204, 455
Barrière, C., 118 , 124, 125
Barruel, P., 299
Barry, H., 424
Baseline sample. *See* Hand baseline sample
Batausserie, 190
Bate, D. M. A., 106
Bateson, P., 379
Baume Latrone, 56, 93, 96, 115, 404
Baume Noire (and Abri Sud de la Baume Noir), viii, 155
Bayol, 132
Beach, F. A., 170
Bédeilhac, 28, 46, 59, 80, 106, 182, 207, 241, 281, 290, 295, 329, 357, 381
Bednarik, R. G., 33, 198, 199
Bégouën, M., 126
Bégouën, R. L., 363

Climatic variability, 22

Clottes, J., 9, 10, 28, 29, 32, 37, 45, 59, 125, 128, 198, 199, 432

Clutton-Brock, T. H., 179

Cobrantes, 36, 182

Cohen, C., 366

Cohen, D., 393

Colinvaux, P. A., 370

Collins, D., 264

Commarque, 191, 324, 329, 354, 381

Comparative approach, 11–13

Compargue, 174

Conkey, M. W., 11, 25, 163

Consigliere, 248, 278, 437, 442–43, 445, 458

Cook, J. H., 261, 441

Coope, G. R., 20

Cooper, S. M., 20, 176

Corvalinas, 75

Cosmides, L., 14

Cosquer, 12, 13, 26, 28, 66, 86, 87, 141, 143, 145, 147, 182, 199, 238, 284, 299, 318, 360, 433, 447, 448

Costello, R. K., 313, 370

Costin, C., 163

Coto del Ramat, 87

Cougnac, 26, 49, 57, 111, 115, 182, 272, 353

Couraud, C., 32

Courbet, 54, 286, 341, 381, 410

Cours, S., 129,

Covalanas, 60, 273

Crader, D. C., 266

Cricket, 191

Crô-du-Chamier, 106

Crowley, W. F., 168

Csikszentmihalyi, M., 388

Cualventi, 36

Cuava de Navarro, 272, 274

Cueto de la Mina, 145, 183, 358, 391

Cueva de Hoz (La Hoz), 26, 136

Cueva de la Peña, 349

Cueva de Valle, 232

Cullalvera (La Cullalvera), 361

Daly, M., 159, 165, 259, 312, 316, 450

Darwin, C., 79, 394, 440

David, N., 410

Davidson, I., 32, 40

Davies, N. B., 14

Dawe, B., 137, 300

Dawkins, R., 457

De Waal, F., 308, 414

Deep cave art, 37–38

Della Mura, 13

Delluc, B., 410, 241

Delluc, G., 410, 241

Delpech, F., 20

Delporte, H., 120, 204, 237, 265, 332, 333, 366

Dench, G., 170

Dennell, R., 23

Deonna, W., 111

Derava, 55

D'Errico, F., 23

Detective work, 15

Deux Avens, 136

Deux Ouvertures, 329

DeVore, I., 235

Disfigured horns and antlers, 109–10

Disguise, 278–80, 300

Dissanayake, E., 389, 390, 391, 399

Dittman, R. W., 170

Dobranitcheva (Dobranitchevka), 369

Dolhinow, P. J., 393

Dolni Věstonice, 4, 80, 88, 142, 155, 171, 204, 207, 332, 340, 341, 342, 350, 351, 355, 359, 366, 376, 381, 386

Domestication, 407–10, 420

Doña Trinidad, 272

Donaldson, A. S., 174

Donner, J. J., 10

Double-entendre, 300, 327, 355

Draper, P., 424, 425

Dubourg, C., 11

Duday, H., 125, 126, 127

Duhard, J.-P., 318, 339–40, 342, 349, 363

Dunbar, R. I. M., 219, 235, 256, 412

Durant, W., 238

Duruthy, 147, 204, 299, 326

Eades, M. D., 245

Eades, M. R., 245

Eastman, A., 8

Eaves, L. J., 321

Eboulis, 38

Ehrenberg, M., 370

Ehrhardt, A. A., 168, 181

Eibl-Eibesfeldt, I., 314, 321, 391

Eino, 440

Ekain, 35, 52, 86, 104, 112, 135, 155, 298

Ekland, B. K., 319

El Castillo, 2, 12, 28, 72, 87, 106, 108, 232, 272, 276, 284, 298, 329, 359, 395, 428

El Civil, 411

El Linar, 284

El Niño, 97

El Patatal, 36

El Pendo, 11, 13, 27, 181, 183, 191, 298, 354, 391

El Pindal, 59, 272, 273, 281, 298, 361

El Quintanal, 272

El Ramu, 210

El Rascano, 298

Ellis, B. J., 329, 330

Ellis, M. J., 393

Elseevichi, 27, 332

Ember, M., 449

Emitta, 240

Enlène, 9, 27, 48, 92, 140, 191, 198, 201, 204, 207, 241, 289, 295, 298, 329, 352, 363, 409

Penises, 141, 152, 167, 172, 178, 183, 198, 311, 324, 346, 353, 356

Pepper, H., 84

Pergouset, 9, 91, 136, 143, 146, 174, 284, 329, 379

Perrins, C. M., 15

Petersfels, 6, 341, 362, 367, 398

Peterson, D., 174, 175, 179, 183, 227, 229, 243, 246, 253, 321, 370, 412, 421

Petocz, R., 437

Pettitt, P., 20

Peyrat, 409

Pfeiffer, J. E., 36, 39

Philandering, 320–21

Philos, reproductive potential, 315–20

Piaget, J., 136, 385

Piazza, A., 90, 120

Picasso, P., 134

Pidoplichko, I. G., 265

Pileta (La Pileta), 2, 11, 87, 182, 221, 240, 272, 329, 349, 357, 368, 378

Pilismarol, 363

Pin Hole Cave, 346

Pinker, S., 262

Placard Type image, 360

Planchard (Grotte du Planchard), 359

Plant images, 21

Play, 378–91

Point straighteners. *See* Shaft/point straighteners

Polesini, 72, 104, 120, 221, 293, 307, 356, 448

Pollan, M., 448

Pollen cores, 19

Polvorin, 293

Polynesians, 401–4

Pond, C. M., 332, 333, 336–40

Pont d'Ambon, 431

Poplin, F., 20

Popova, N. K., 173

Porquerizo, 272

Portel (Le Portel), xi, 67, 71, 75, 103, 115, 131, 135, 136, 167, 174, 224, 273, 284, 346, 359, 368, 385, 394

Postmodernism, 164, 446–48

Potter, R. G., 322, 350

Pradel, L., 117, 118, 127

Pradiéres, 272

Prado del Navarro, 13, 59

Predation, 211–27

Predmosti, 116, 358

Pre-human art, 374

Preorbital gland, 64

Propensity to obesity, 347–60

Propensity to play, 380–81

Provost, C., 162–65, 202

Pruitt, W. O., 16, 17, 65, 84

Puisségur, J.-J., 20

Puy de Lacan, 10, 53, 109

Quagga, 80–83

Quality-plus children, 117, 253, 305, 357

Rasmussen, K., 219, 261

Ray, D. J., 183

Raymonden, 6, 11, 222, 391

Rébieres, 171

Reindeer cow antlers, 14–17

Reinisch, J. M., 168, 179

Reliability of art, 55–56

Religiosity, 440

Rensch, B., 143

Representational art, 44–45

Réseau Clastres, 128, 359, 409

Réseau-de-Font-Serene, 4

Reynolds, R. P., 398

Rice, P. C., 319

Richard, N., 7

Ridley, M., 223, 229, 230, 235, 250, 256, 258, 457

Rigaud, J.-P., 28, 29

Risk-averse, 156

Roberts, D. F., 411

Roberts, N., 119

Roc-aux-Sorciers, 174

Roc de Birol, vii

Roc-de-Marcamps, 375, 381, 383

Roc de Sers, 9, 65, 111, 161, 281, 349

Rochereil, 45, 71, 174, 348, 354, 356, 359, 374

Roc-la-Tour, 104, 146, 161, 238, 284

Roebroeks, W., 280

Romanelli, 359, 378, 411

Romito, 66

Rond du Barry, 341, 413

Rorschach test, 135–40

Rose, R. M., 171

Rosenfeld, A., 10, 40, 430

Roucadour, 25, 26, 353

Rouffignac, xi, 7, 13, 28, 35, 56, 59, 60, 63, 73, 75, 96, 104, 108, 143, 161, 171, 190, 266, 273, 378, 381, 383, 409, 413, 440

Rousseau, J.-J., 398

Roussot, A., 28

Rudnai, J. A., 368

Rudner, I., 430

Rudner, J., 430

Ruff, C. B., 344

Rupestral art, 40

Rushton, P. R., 160, 178

Ruspoli, M., 192

Rytirska, 340

Sagvardzhile, 204

Sahlins, M., 411

Sahly, A., 26, 117, 120, 127

Saint-Cirq, 91, 95, 182, 284, 329, 354, 378, 440, 448

Saint Germaine-la-Riviére, 204

Saint Gregori, 433

Saint Martin, 55, 273

Saint Mathieu-de-Tréviers, 413

Saint-Andree-d'Allas, 28

Saint-Eulalie, 95